AUSTRIA

W. Buss/Michelin

"Land of mountains, land on the river,
Land of fields, land of cathedrals,
Land of hammers, rich in outlook!
You are the native home of great sons,
A people uniquely gifted for the beautiful,
Much applauded Austria."
Austrian National Anthem
(Translation of original text by
Paula von Preradović)

Editorial Director   Cynthia Clayton Ochterbeck

THE GREEN GUIDE AUSTRIA

Editor   Alison Coupe
Principal Writer   Andrea Schulte-Peevers
Contributing Writer   Gordon Lethbridge
Production Manager   Natasha G. George
Cartography   Alain Baldet, Andre Prevault,
                                Peter Wrenn
Photo Editor   Yoshimi Kanazawa
Proofreader   Emmelie Haarhoff
Layout & Design   Therese Schnieder
Cover Design   Laurent Muller, Ute Weber

Contact Us: The Green Guide
                                Michelin Maps and Guides
                                One Parkway South
                                Greenville, SC 29615
                                USA
                                www.michelintravel.com
                                michelin.guides@us.michelin.com

                                Michelin Maps and Guides
                                Hannay House
                                39 Clarendon Road
                                Watford, Herts WD17 1JA
                                UK
                                ☎ (01923) 205 240
                                www.ViaMichelin.com
                                travelpubsales@uk.michelin.com

Special Sales: For information regarding bulk sales,
                                customized editions and premium sales,
                                please contact our Customer Service
                                Departments:
                                USA   1-800-432-6277
                                UK   (01923) 205 240
                                Canada 1-800-361-8236

Note to the Reader

One Team…
A Commitment to Quality

There's just one reason our team is dedicated to producing quality travel publications—you, our reader.

Throughout our guides we offer **practical information**, **touring tips** and **suggestions** for finding the best places for a break.

Michelin driving tours help you hit the highlights and quickly absorb the best of the region. Our descriptive **walking tours** make you your own guide, armed with directions, maps and expert information.

We scout out the attractions, classify them with **star ratings**, and describe in detail what you will find when you visit them.

Michelin maps featured throughout the guide offer vibrant, detailed and easy-to-follow outlines of everything from close-up museum plans to international maps.

Places to stay and eat are always a big part of travel, so we research **hotels and restaurants** that we think convey the essence of the destination and arrange them by geographic area and price. We walk you through the best shopping districts and point you towards the host of entertainment and recreation possibilities available.

We **test**, **retest**, **check and recheck** to make sure that our guidebooks are truly just that: a personalized guide to help you make the most of your visit. And if you still want a speaking guide, we list local tour guides who will lead you on all the boat, bus, guided, historical, culinary, and other tours you shouldn't miss.

In short, we remove the guesswork involved with travel. After all, we want you to enjoy exploring with Michelin as much as we do.

The Michelin Green Guide Team

PLANNING YOUR TRIP

INTRODUCTION TO AUSTRIA

©Masahiro Sato/Photononstop/Tips Images

CONTENTS

DISCOVERING AUSTRIA

HOW TO USE THIS GUIDE

PLANNING YOUR TRIP

The blue-tabbed PLANNING YOUR TRIP section at the front of the guide gives you **ideas for your trip** and **practical information** to help you organize it. You'll find tours, a host of activites in the great outdoors, a calendar of events, information on shopping, sightseeing, kids' activities and more.

INTRODUCTION

The orange-tabbed INTRODUCTION section explores **Nature** and the alps. The **History** section spans the Habsburg Empire through today. The **Art and Culture** section covers architecture, art, literature, language, traditions and folklore, while the **Country Today** delves into modern Austria.

DISCOVERING

The green-tabbed DISCOVERING section features Austria's Principal Sights, arranged alphabetically and by region,

Sidebars

Throughout the guide you will find peach-colored text boxes (like this one), with lively anecdotes, detailed history and background information.

featuring the most interesting local **Sights**, **Walking Tours**, nearby **Excursions**, and detailed **Driving Tours**.

🗒 Contact information, ✆ admission charges, 🕒 hours of operation, and a host of other **visitor information** is given wherever possible. Admission prices shown are normally for a single adult.

STAR RATINGS★★★

Michelin has given star ratings for more than 100 years. If you're pressed for time, we recommend you visit the ★★★, or ★★ sights first:

★★★ Highly recommended
★★   Recommended
★   Interesting

Address Books - Where to Stay, Eat and more...

WHERE TO STAY

We've made a selection of hotels and arranged them within the cities by price category to fit all budgets (👝 *see the Legend on the cover flap for an explanation of the price categories*). For the most part, we've selected accommodations based on their unique regional quality, their regional feel, as it were. So, unless the individual hotel embodies local ambience, it's rare that we include chain properties, which typically have their own imprint.
👝 *See the back of the guide for an index of where hotels featured throughout the guide can be found.*

WHERE TO EAT

We thought you'd like to know the popular eating spots in Austria. So, we selected restaurants that capture the regional experience—those that have a unique regional flavor (👝 *see the Legend on the cover flap for an explanation of the price categories*). We're not rating the quality of the food per se; as we did with the hotels, we selected restaurants for many towns and villages, categorized by price to appeal to all wallets.
👝 *See the back of the guide for an index of where restaurants featured throughout the guide can be found.*

MAPS

😊 Regional **Driving Tours** map and **Places to Stay** map.
😊 Austria map with the **Principal Sights** highlighted.
😊 Maps for major **cities** and **villages**.
😊 **Local tour** maps.

All maps in this guide are oriented north, unless otherwise indicated by a directional arrow. The term "Local Map" refers to a map within the chapter or Tourism Region. A complete list of the maps found in the guide appears at the back of this book, as well as a comprehensive index and list of where restaurants and accommodations are to be found.
👍 *See the map Legend at the back of the guide for an explanation of map symbols.*

ORIENT PANELS

Vital statistics are given for each principal sight in the DISCOVERING section:

🛈 **Information:** Tourist Office/Sight contact details.
▶ **Orient Yourself:** Geographic location of the sight with reference to surrounding boroughs, towns, and roads.
🅿 **Parking:** Where to park.
😊 **Don't Miss:** Unmissable things to do.
🕘 **Organizing Your Time:** Tips on organizing your stay; what to see first, how long to spend, crowd avoidance, market days and more.
Kids **Especially for Kids:** Sights of particular interest to children.
👍 **Also See:** Nearby PRINCIPAL SIGHTS featured elsewhere in the guide.

SYMBOLS

Spa	Spa Facilities	👣	Tours
Kids	Interesting for Children	🅿	On-site Parking
👍	Also See	▶	Directions
🛈	Tourist Information	✕	On-site eating Facilities
🕘	Hours of Operation	⌇	Swimming Pool
🕗	Periods of Closure	⛺	Camping Facilities
🔒	Closed to the Public	🏖	Beaches
💰	Entry Fees	☕	Breakfast Included
🚫	Credit Cards not Accepted	😊	A Bit of Advice
♿	Wheelchair Accessible	😊	Warning

Contact - Addresses, phone numbers, opening hours and prices published in this guide are accurate at the time of press. We welcome corrections and suggestions that may assist us in preparing the next edition. Please send your comments to:

UK
Michelin Maps and Guides
Hannay House
39 Clarendon Road
Watford, Herts WD17 1JA
travelpubsales@uk.michelin.com
www.michelin.co.uk

USA
Michelin Maps and Guides
Editorial Department
P.O. Box 19001
Greenville, SC 29602-9001
michelin.guides@us.michelin.com
www.michelintravel.com

MAIN LOCAL MAPS PRINTED IN THIS GUIDE

Vorarlberg - Tyrol: 550km - 342 miles - 4 days, including 1 day in Innsbruck.

Hohe Tauern - Salzkammergut: 750km - 466 miles 6 days, including 1 day in Salzburg.

Austrian Baroque: 1 150km - 715 miles - 8 days, including 1 day in Salzburg and 2 days in Vienna (Wien).

Styria - Carinthia: 1 200km - 747 miles - 8 days, including 1 day in Graz.

Vienna (Wien) and surrounding area: 300km - 186 miles 4 days, including 2 days in Vienna (Wien).

Driving tours

Grossglockner-Hochalpenstrasse, Heiligenblut
© Österreich Werbung / W. Weinhaeupl

MICHELIN DRIVING TOURS

Regional Drives

ⓒ*See Driving Tours Map*

+ **Vorarlberg – Tirol**
+ **Hohe Tauern – Salzkammergut**
+ **Austrian Baroque**
+ **Styria – Carinthia**
+ **Vienna (Wien)**

Local Drives

ⓒ*Use the A–Z Discovering section:*

+ **Aflenzer Seebergstrasse**
+ **Arlberg Pass**
+ **Brandner Valley**
+ **The Flexen Pass**
+ **Dachstein**
+ **Donautal**
+ **Eisenerzer Alpen**
+ **Felbertauernstrasse**
+ **Fernpassstrasse**
+ **Gailbergsattel Straße**
+ **Gasteiner Tal**

+ **Gerlos-Alpenstrasse**
+ **Grossglockner Hochalpenstrasse**
+ **Hochtannenbergstraße**
+ **Innsbruck**
+ **Oberes Inntal**
+ **Kaisergebirge**
+ **Karwendelgebirge**
+ **Kauerntal**
+ **Kleinwalsertal**
+ **Linz**
+ **Montafon**
+ **Pack- und Stubalpenstraße**
+ **Saalachtal**
+ **Salzachtal**
+ **Salzatal**
+ **Salzkammergut**
+ **Schneeberg**
+ **Seefelder Sattel Straßen**
+ **Silvretta-Hochalpenstrasse**
+ **Steierische Weinstrasse**
+ **Stubchtal**
+ **Stubaital**
+ **Wienerwald**
+ **Östliches Weinviertel**
+ **Wien (Vienna)**
+ **Zillertal**

WHEN AND WHERE TO GO

When to Go

Austria, two-thirds of which is covered by mountains, is justlifiably popular for its ski resorts in **winter**, with slopes suitable for everyone from beginners to experts. The fun in the snow kicks off in the Arlbergpass region around Lech and St. Anton in the far western corner of the country. This transitions seamlessly into the Tirol, the most popular area, whose profile was raised considerably by the Winter Olympic Games held in Innsbruck in 1964 and 1976. The Salzburg region is also well developed for skiing, with major resorts such as the Sportwelt Amadé. Styria offers a variety of opportunities in the ski resorts of the Dachstein-Tauern and Schladming areas.

In **spring** it is still possible to ski at higher altitudes, with longer days being a welcome bonus. The season is also enlivened by carnival processions. **Summer** is the time to enjoy Austria's mountain scenery to the full and to make the most of its rich cultural scene. Welcoming Carinthia, with its warm-water lakes, attracts swimmers, water-skiing enthusiasts, and anglers. Colder, but more romantic, are the picturesque lakes of the Salzkammergut. Mountaineers will be drawn by the glaciers of the Ötztal or the Hohe Tauern, or the slopes of the Karwendel, the Kaisergebirge, the Dachstein, or the Gesäuse.
Fall, with the sun shining and a nip in the air, sheds a particularly beautiful light on the old stone buildings in the

towns. This is a good season to discover the wealth of Austria's museums. The wooded valleys of Styria and Carinthia are a pleasure to explore on foot. A journey through the vineyards of the Burgenland or Lower Austria, or along the Danube beneath the Wachau, is unforgettable at this time of year, which is also marked in Vienna by the reopening of the theatrical and musical seasons (September 1 and October respectively).

Where to Go

WALKING TOURS

Austria has a well developed network of marked trails in the valleys and high in the mountains. One way to enjoy the mountains without decending each night to the valley is to hike hut-to-hut. Mountain inns or huts can be found in the Kaisergebirge, the Karwendal, Stubai Alps, Hohe Tauern and Dachstein ranges as well as many other areas

CYCLING TOURS

Surprisingly, considering the mountains Austria has a well developed network of cyle paths. Some of the major ones are the Danube Cycle Path, The Salzkammergut Cycle Path and Tauern Cycle Path from Krimml to Salzburg.

FOOD AND WINE TRAILS

Eastern Austria produces some fine wines and there is a Wine Road to follow in Styria. In the west of Austria there is a Cheese Road in the Bregenzerwald (*see entry*).

SHORT BREAKS

Innsbruck, Salzburg and Vienna are all great cities for a short break and can be visited around themes such as Music, The Hapsburgs or architecture.

KNOW BEFORE YOU GO

Useful Websites

www.austria.info
The official website maintained by the Austrian National Tourist Office is an excellent pre-trip planning tool with information about the regions, eating and drinking, accommodation, history, famous people, and other topics.

www.austria.org
Excellent general website maintained by the Austrian Press and Information Service of the Austrian Embassy in Washington, DC. It includes travel information as well as a link to Facts & Figures.

www.austria.gv.at.
This Austrian federal government website is a portal to the country's political landscape with links to all ministries. Learn about Austrian current affairs and policy stance on such issues as security, bioethics, and data protection.

www.tiscover.com
Another useful vacation planner, this site has detailed information on all provinces and allows you to book hotels, packages, and cars. It also has a route planner and details about road closures, current traffic, weather reports, and other useful data.

www.lawine.at
Go here for up-to-date information about snow conditions, avalanche warnings, and other snow-related information (in German only).

http://austria-forum.org
This encyclopedia-style database has 14 000 entries on history, culture, geography, politics, and other topics; a music archive that allows you to download and listen to original works;

as well as image, video, and photo libraries. Mainly in English.

Tourist Offices

The Austrian National Tourist Office (ANTO) offers information on a whole range of special deals for tourists and other practical details of interest to vacationers in Austria.

AUSTRIAN NATIONAL TOURIST OFFICES

Australia and New Zealand
1st Floor, 36 Carrington Street,
Sydney, NSW 2000
☏02 9299 3621.

Ireland
Merrion Hall, Strand Road,
Sandymount,
PO Box 2506, Dublin
☏01 283 0488

UK and Ireland
9011 Richmond Bldgs,
London W1D 3HF
☏UK: 0845 1011 818
☏Ireland: 189 0930 118
http://uk.myswitzerland.com

USA and Canada
PO Box 1142,
New York, NY 10018-1142
☏USA: 212-944-6880
☏Canada: 416-967-3381

TOURIST OFFICES OF THE AUSTRIAN PROVINCES

Burgenland
Burgenland-Tourismus,
Schloss Esterházy,
A-7000 Eisenstadt
☏0 26 82/6 33 84 22
Fax 0 26 82/6 33 84 20
www.burgenland.info

Carinthia
Kärnten Information,
Casinoplatz 1, A-9220 Velden
☏0 463/52 10 00
Fax 0 42 74/5 21 00 50
www.kaernten.at.

Lower Austria
Niederösterreich Information,
Im Palais Niederösterreich,
Herrengasse 13,
A-1014 Wien
☏01/53 61 00
Fax 01/53 61 01 98 5
www.niederoesterreich.at.

Salzburg (province)
SalzburgerLand Tourismus GmbH,
Wiener Bundesstraße 23,
A-5300 Hallwang bei Salzburg
☏06 62/6 68 80
Fax 06 62/66 88 66
www.salzburgerland.com.

Styria
Steirische Tourismus GmbH,
St.-Peter-Hauptstraße 243,
A-8042 Graz,
☏03 16/4 00 30,
Fax 03 16/40 03 10
www.steiermark.com

Tirol
Tirol Info,
Maria-Theresien-Straße 55,
A-6010 Innsbruck
☏05 12/72 72
Fax 05 12/7 27 27
www.tirol.at

Upper Austria
Oberösterreich Tourismus
Information,
Freistädter Straße 119,
A-4041 Linz
☏05 12/7 27 20
www.oberoesterreich.at

Vienna
Wiener Tourismusband,
Obere Augartenstraße 38,
A-1020 Wien
☏01/2 45 55
Fax 01/24 55 56 66
www.wien.info

Vorarlberg
Vorarlberg Tourismus,
Bahnhofstraße 14,
A-6901 Bregenz
☏0 55 74/42 52 50
Fax 0 55 74/42 52 55
www.vorarlberg-tourism.at

LOCAL TOURIST INFORMATION CENTRES

These are indicated by the symbol ▯ on the town plans in this guide. Addresses and telephone numbers are given in the Admission times and charges section. Further addresses and details can be obtained from the national or regional tourist offices.

International Visitors

FOREIGN EMBASSIES IN AUSTRIA

Australia   **Embassy**
12 Talbot Street
Forrest, Canberra ACT 2603
(Postal address: PO Box 3375,
Manuka, ACT 2603)
☎02 6295 1533
www.austria.org.au

Ireland   **Embassy**
15 Ailesbury Court
93 Ailesbury Road
Dublin 4
☎01 269 4577

UK   **Embassy**
18 Belgrave Mews West,
London SW1X 8HU
☎(020) 73 44 32 50
www.aussenministerium.at/london

USA   **Embassy**
3524 International Court NW,
Washington DC 20008
☎202-895-6700
www.austria.org

AUSTRIAN EMBASSIES ABROAD

Australia   **Embassy**
Mattiellistraße 2–4,
A-1040 Wien,
☎01/50 67 40
www.australian-embassy.at

Ireland   **Embassy**
Rotenturmstraße 16-18, 5th Fl,
A-1010 Wien
☎01/7 15 42 46

UK   **Embassy**
Jauresgasse 12,
A-1030 Wien,
☎01/71 61 30
www.britishembassy.at

USA   **Embassy**
Boltzmanngasse 16,
A-1090 Wien
☎01/31 33 90
www.usembassy.at

ENTRY REQUIREMENTS

Most citizens of the European Union only need their national identity card or **passport** to enter Austria. Citizens of Australia, Canada, New Zealand, the USA, and Israel need a valid passport but no visa for tourist stays up to 3 months. Citizens from most other countries need to apply for a visa at the **Austrian Embassy** in their home country. Austria is part of the Schengen Agreement for holders of visas to other Schengen countries.

CUSTOMS REGULATIONS

EU citizens may import (duty free) 800 cigarettes or 200 cigars or 1kg/2.2lb tobacco, 10l/2.6 US gal spirits, 90l/23.7 US gal wine (max. 60l/15.8 US gal sparkling wine), 110l/29 US gal beer. **Non-EU citizens** may import (duty free) 200 cigarettes or 50 cigars or 250g/8.8oz tobacco; 2l/0.5gal wine and 1l/.2 US gal liquor; 50g/1.7oz perfume and 0.25l/8.4fl oz eau de toilette; and additional items up to €175 in value per traveler. Contact your country's customs office for duty-free restrictions and other regulations about what you may bring back home. UK Revenue & Customs, for instance, produces a helpful guide downloadable for free at *www.hmrc. gov.uk* (link to Travel Information). The US Customs & Border Protection has a similar publication called *Know Before You Go* available at *www.cbp. gov/xp/cgov/travel/vacation/kbyg*.

Health

Citizen of the EU should obtain a European Health Insurance Card (EHIC) from their local health authority, which entitles them to receive low-cost or free emergency health care while in Austria. It does not cover emergency repatriation. You can apply for a card at www.ehic.org.uk or pick up a leaflet at your local post office. Non-EU residents should check that their private health insurance policy covers them for travel abroad, and if necessary take out supplementary medical insurance with specific overseas coverage. All prescription drugs should be clearly labeled, and it is recommended that you carry a copy of the prescription with you.

Accessibility

Regional tourist offices provide information about traveling in Austria as a disabled person. Some have put together handy guides of which the following are available online: Tirol Without Barriers (www.easyaccess.tirol.at), Upper Austria's Ferien ohne Handicap (www.oberoesterreich.at/nohandicap, in German only) and Vienna for Visitors with Disabilities (http://info.wien.at, link to 'Specials'). For barrier-free farm holidays, consult Urlaub am Bauernhof (www.farmholidays.com). Austrian rail, the Österreichische Bundesbahnen (ÖBB), operates a hotline (☎05/17 17) offering trip-planning assistance for the mobility-impaired. Many of the sights described in this guide are accessible to people with special needs. Those marked with the symbol ♿ offer access for wheelchairs. However, it is always best to phone ahead for details.

GETTING THERE AND GETTING AROUND

By Plane

Airlines providing scheduled flights to Austria include: **Austrian Airlines** (www.aua.com), **Aer Lingus** (www.aerlingus.ie), **British Airways** (www.ba.com), **British Midland** (www.flybmi.com), **easyJet** (www.easyjet.com), **Germanwings** (www.germanwings.com), **Jet2.com** (www.jet2.com), **Lauda Air** (www.laudaair.com), **Lufthansa** (www.lufthansa.com), **Niki** (www.flyniki.com), **Ryanair** (www.ryanair.com) and **thomsonfly** (www.thomsonfly.com).

Most flights land at Vienna, although there are an increasing number of services to Graz, Klagenfurt, Linz, Salzburg, and Innsbruck.

From North America the only direct flights are operated by **Austrian Airlines** and **Delta** (www.delta.com). Your options widen if you fly to another major European hub, such as London or Frankfurt, and catch a connecting flight there.

By Train

Austria is well served by rail from destinations throughout Europe. Coming from the UK, the easiest way is to catch the **Eurostar** (www.eurostar.com) from London-St Pancras International to Paris Nord, change to Paris Est and there board the one direct daily train bound for Salzburg and Vienna-Westbahnhof. The trip takes about 15hr 30min and 19hr 30min, respectively.

A good source for tickets and information is **Rail Europe** (www.raileurope.co.uk). The website maintained by **Österreichische Bundesbahnen** (Austrian rail; www.oebb.at) has comprehensive timetable information and other details as well.

Steam engines and tourist trains

Steam engines and tourist trains operate in many regions year round, but predominantly during the summer season. These offer a pleasant and relaxing way of discovering some of Austria's most beautiful natural regions. Further information is available from Erlebnis Bahn & Schiff Österreich (www.erlebnis-bahn-schiff.at).

By Coach/Bus

ÖBB Postbus (☎+43 (1) 711 01 (from abroad) 0810-222333 (in Austria). www.postbus.at) operates an extensive network across all of Austria including some of the more remote areas. Prices are similar to those charged for rail travel.

By Car 🚗

Austria is linked to its neighboring countries by fast and well-maintained highways. Coming from the UK, you can be just about anywhere Austria in about 10 to 12 hours, depending on where you arrive on the Continent. Besides the Eurotunnel linking Folkestone with Coquelles near Calais (France), there is ferry service from Dover to Calais, from Hull and Rosyth (near Edinburgh) to Zeebrugge (Belgium), from Harwich to Hook van Holland (Netherlands) and from Newcastle to Amsterdam. Michelin offers a free and handy online route planning service at www.viamichelin.com, which calculates distance, time and gasoline use.

Motorail train services, where you load your car (and yourself) onto a train, operate between Vienna and Villach (372km/231mi), Vienna and Salzburg (317km/197mi), Vienna and Innsbruck (572km/355mi), Vienna and Feldkirch (731km/454mi), Graz and Feldkirch (607km/377mi) and Villach and Feldkirch (466km/290mi) and Vienna and Lienz (476km/296mi). An hourly motorail shuttle also runs

through the **Tauern tunnel** (Böckstein-Mallnitz, 8km/5mi).
For further details, including fares, contact Österreichische Bundesbahnen (Austrian rail; 05/17 17, www.oebb.at).

DOCUMENTS

It is necessary to have a valid driving license (preferably an international drivers' license), and third party insurance cover is compulsory. Carrying the International Green Card from insurance companies may be helpful.

ROAD REGULATIONS

🚗 Traffic in Austria drives on the right and the minimum driving age is 18.

🚗 Driving with the lights on at all times is now compulsory, as is the wearing of seat belts at all times, and the carrying of a first aid kit, an emergency triangle, and a warning vest.

🚗 Children under the age of 12 and less than 1.5m/4ft 11in tall must travel in appropriate and approved booster seats.

🚗 The blood alcohol limit is 0.5ml/g.

🚗 The use of cell (mobile) telephones inside a moving vehicle is only permitted if you have a hands-free set.

🚗 Motorcyclists must wear a helmet.

Speed Limits

Unless signposted otherwise, speed limits are 130kph/80mph on autobahns/highways, 100kph/62mph on country roads, and 50kph/31mph in built-up areas. Private cars towing a load in excess of 750kg/1 650lb must not exceed 100kph/62mph on autobahns/highways, 80kph/50mph on country roads and 50kph/31mph in built-up areas.

BREAKDOWN SERVICE

This is provided (charge for non-members) by two Austrian automobile clubs:

🚗 **ÖAMTC** Österreichischer Automobil-, Motorrad- und Touring Club,

Schubertring 1-3, A-1010 Wien, ☎01/71 19 90, *www.oeamtc.at*, breakdown number ☎120.

🚗 **ARBÖ** Auto-, Motor- und Rad-fah-rer-bund Österreich, Mariahilfer Straße 180, A-1150 Wien, ☎01/89 12 10, *www.arboe.at*, breakdown number ☎123.

ROAD TOLLS (MAUTGEBÜHREN)

Tolls are levied on autobahns, dual carriageways and urban highways in Austria. Drivers must buy a toll disc (vignette, or "Mautpickerl") and display it behind their windshield. Vignettes are available for 10 days (€7.70), 2 months (€22.20), and one year (€73.80; valid Dec 31–Jan 1). Vignettes can be bought from Austrian motoring associations (ARBÖ, ÖAMTC), larger petrol stations, post offices and tobacconists' and at the border crossing points.

Vehicles weighing more than 3.5 tons must be equipped with a so-called GO-Box, a small electronic device that registers the kilometers you've driven every time you pass by a toll gantry and deducts the appropriate amount from the pre-paid credit stored in the GO-Box. Boxes are available for €5 from gas stations mostly located along autobahns. Charges start at €0.16 per kilometer. For full details, consult *www.go-maut.at* and *www.oesag.at*.

Additional Tolls

These are levied on certain stretches of road not covered by the vignette:

♦ **Arlberg-Schnellstraße** (information line ☎0 54 46/20 66 67; car toll €8.50);
♦ **Brenner-Autobahn** (☎05 12/52 01 20; total stretch €8; *www.autobrennero.it*);
♦ **Dachsteinstraße** (☎0 36 87/8 18 33; €8);
♦ **Felbertauernstraße** (☎0 48 52/6 33 30; €10; *www.felbertauernstrasse.at*);
♦ **Gerlos Alpenstraße** (☎0 65 64/72 61; €7; *www.gerlosstrasse.at*)
♦ **Grossglockner-Hochalpen-straße** (☎0 65 46/6 50; €26; *www.grossglockner.at*);
♦ **Karawankentunnel** (☎0 42 53/26 60; €6.50);
♦ **Maltatal-Hochalmstraße** (☎0 47 33/2 20 15; €15.50);
♦ **Nockalmstraße** (☎0 47 36/2 65; €13; *www.nockalmstrasse.at*);
♦ **Pyhrn-Autobahn** (☎03 16/6 07 30; total stretch €12);
♦ **Silvretta-Hochalpenstraße** (☎0 55 58/8 31 50; €10.90);
♦ **Tauernautobahn** (☎06 62/62 05 11; total stretch €9.50);
♦ **Timmelsjoch-Hochalpenstraße** (☎05 12/58 19 70; €13; *www.timmelsjoch-hochalpenstraße.at*);
♦ **Villacher Alpenstraße** (☎0 6 62/8 73 67 30; €13; *www.villacher-alpenstrasse.at*).

For some of these tollroads, monthly or annual passes are available.

Winter Pass and Tollroad Closures

Pass	Linking
Bielerhöhe	Partenen – Galtür
Furkajoch	Laterns – Damüls
Grossglockner-Hochalpenstraße	Ferleiten – Heiligenblut
Hahntennjoch	Boden – Imst
Sölker Pass	Gröbming – Murau
Timmelsjoch	Obergurgl – St. Leon-hard im Passeier Tal

Tollroad	Toll point
Breitlahner Schlegeis-Stausee	Ginzling/Mayrhofen
Maltatal-Hochalmstraße	Fallerhütte – Kölnbreinsperre
Silvretta-Hochalpenstraße	Galtür – Partenen
Sölden-Rettenbachstraße	Ötztaler Gletscher
Timmelsjochstraße	Gurgl

Name of pass	Altitude (meters)	Route	Michelin map 730 fold no	★ = road barred; 🚫 = not recommended
Seefelder Sattel (1)	1 180	Innsbruck – Mittenwald	16	★
Rottenmanner Tauern	1 265	Oberes Murtal – Ennstal	22	🚫
Aflenzer Seeberg	1 254	Mariazell – Aflenz	23	🚫
Präbichl	1 227	Ennstal – Leoben	23	🚫
Bielerhöhe	2 036	Silvrettastraße	28	★
Hochtannbergpass	1 679	Reutte – Dornbirn	28	🚫
Timmelsjoch (2)	2 474	Ötztal – Italy	29	★
Gerlospass (3)	1 507	Zell am Ziller – Zell am See	29	★
Hochtor	2 505	Grossglockner – Hochalpenstraße	31	★
Kartitsch-Sattel	1 529	Kötschach – Sillian	32	🚫
Radstädter Tauernpass (4)	1 739	Radstadt – St. Michael im Lungau	32	🚫
Katschberg (5)	1 641	St. Michael im Lungau – Spittal an der Drau	33	🚫
Turracher Höhe	1 793	Murtal – Carinthian lakes	34	🚫
Loibltunnel	1 067	Klagenfurt – Slovenia	35	🚫
Gaberl-Sattel (5)	1 551	Direct link: Oberes Murtal – Graz	36	★★

(1) Easy access to Seefeld when heading from Mittenwald to Innsbruck.
(2) Access for caravans less than 3.4m/ 11ft high along the Ötztal as far as Untergurgl.
(3) Easy access to the Gerlos pass and to Gerlos heading east-west.
(4) We recommend taking the A 10 motorway
(5) Inaccessible in winter; not recommended in summer.

ROUTE PLANNING

The **Michelin map 730** (scale 1:400 000) covers the entire country and gives details of likely road closures in winter. For online route planning, go to *www.viamichelin.com*. The hikers' maps published by Freytag and Berndt are useful for more detailed exploration.

TRAFFIC REPORTS

These are given on the hour, after the news bulletin, on radio station Ö3. Information on traffic and road conditions is also available on the ÖAMTC's recorded message service ☎*01/1 75 20*.

CAR RENTAL

Car-rental firms:
- **Avis**: ☎08 00/08 00 87 57 (toll-free), *www.avis.at*
- **Europcar**: ☎01/8 66 16 33, *www.europcar.co.at*
- **Hertz**: ☎01/7 95 32, *www.hertz.com*
- **Sixt**: ☎0 08 00/11 11 74 98 (toll-free), *www.sixt.at*

DRIVING IN WINTER

In snowy conditions winter tires should be fitted, or chains if conditions are particularly severe. The ÖAMTC and ARBÖ have snow chain rental outlets in every Austrian province.

Winter closures – In winter the passes and tollroads listed in the charts above are closed.

CARAVANS

Some mountain roads have gradients steeper than 20% (1 in 5), as well as very narrow stretches. Steep gradients are indicated on **Michelin map 730**, which also gives dates of likely road closures in winter. Certain stretches of road, such as the approach roads to the Tauerntunnel, may be unsuitable for caravans because of heavy traffic. The table above indicates the most difficult stretches on the various access routes across the Alps (east to west).

WHERE TO STAY AND EAT

Where to Stay

HOTELS

Hotel and Restaurant recommendations are located in the Address Books throughout the Discovering Austria section of this guide. For coin ranges and for a description of the symbols used in the Address Books, see the Legend on the cover flap."

FARM HOLIDAYS

These are popular in the Tirol in particular, and they can often be combined with some sort of course (embroidery, sculpture, horseback riding, etc.). Themed holiday accommodation on offer includes organic farms and healthy farm holidays. Details available from the Austrian National Tourist Office or from the Austrian farm holiday association Urlaub am Bauernhof in Österreich (Gabelsberger Straße 19, A-5020 Salzburg, ☎06 62/88 02 02, Fax 06 62/88 02 023, *www.farmholidays.com*).

CAMPING AND CARAVANING

Autria has about 500 campsites, many of which are open year round. For lists of campsites contact the following Austrian associations: Camping- und Caravaningclub Austria (CCA), *Maria-hilfer Straße 180, A-1150 Wien,* ☎*01/89 12 12 22, www.campsite.at/cca*; and Österreichischer Campingclub (ÖCC), *Schubertring 1–3, A-1010 Wien,* ☎*01/7 13 61 51, www.campingclub.at*. Another excellent online resource with a searchable campsite database (in English) is Camping in Austria at *www.camping.at*.

YOUTH HOSTELS

Austria has about 100 youth hostels affiliated with Hostelling International. Staying here requires an HI membership card from your home country. Non-members need to buy a Gästekarte (guest card) for €3.50 per night from any hostel. For addresses check with the Austrian youth hostel association (Österreichischer Jugendherbergsverband, *Schottenring 28, A-1010 Wien,* ☎*01/5 33 53 53, www.oejhv.at*).

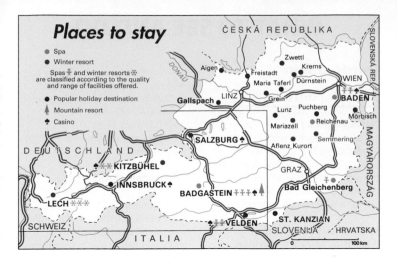

"SCHLANK & SCHÖN IN ÖSTERREICH"

Health, beauty treatments, stress management and relaxation are the goals of the "Schlank & Schön" ("Slim and Beautiful") organization. The catalog is available from the Austrian National Tourist Office or directly from "Schlank & Schön in Österreich" *(Ossiacher-See-Süduferstraße 59-61, A-9523 Landskron/Villach, ☎0 42 72/36 20 40, www.schlankundschoen.at).*

MAP OF PLACES TO STAY

The map of places to stay above shows the principal Austrian vacation resorts (spas, winter sports, and mountain resorts).

Where to Eat

Specific restaurants in major cities are mentioned in the **Address Books** within the *Discovering Austria* section. Restaurants tend to be rather formal places with crisp table linen and attentive service. For a more casual atmosphere, head to a Gasthof or a Gasthaus, which are traditional inns with a homely, authentic ambience. In wine regions, the place to go for atmosphere is a Heurige, an earthy wine tavern where food is usually pre-sented buffet-style. Austria's famous Kaffeehäuser (cafés) also serve hot meals, while places called Café-Konditorei are best for sampling Austria's delicious cakes and pastries. Celebrated staples here include Sachertorte, a chocolate cake filled with apricot-jam, and Linzer Torte, an almond pastry with red currant jam.

Traditional Austrian cuisine is hearty fare, with dishes usually revolving around some cut of meat, potatoes, boiled vegetables and gravy. A full meal consists of three courses, often starting with a clear, flavor-packed soup. The best known main course is the Wiener Schnitzel, a thin slice of breaded veal panfried to a crispy, golden tan and served with a slice of lemon. Other classic dishes commonly found on menus are Zwiebelrostbraten (roast beef slices doused in fried onion slices); and Backhendl (fried breaded chicken).

Austrians truly excel when it comes to desserts. Temptations include Apfelstrudel (apple strudel), filled with apples and raisins, sprinkled with powdered sugar, served hot or cold; and Palatschinken, a pancake filled with apricot jam or curd cheese.

Wine and beer are the most common beverages of choice. Many Austrians like to finish their meals with a Schnaps, a potent spirit usually flavored with fruit.

WHAT TO SEE AND DO

Outdoor Fun

THE GREAT OUTDOORS

National parks

Austria's six national parks let you appreciate nature at its unspoiled best: rare flora and fauna, magnificent scenery, trails off beaten track and other charms await. For an overview, see www.nationalparksaustria.at.

Nationalpark Hohe Tauern (Carinthia, Salzburg province, Tirol)

The park authorities offer excursions, slide shows and other events such as "children's days" or Alpine hikes (www.hohetauern.at).

◆ Regionalverband Nationalpark Hohe Tauern, A-5722 Niedernsill
☏ 0 65 48/84 170
◆ Nationalparkverwaltung Kärnten, A-9843 Grosskirchheim
☏ 0 48 25/61 61 14
◆ Nationalparkverwaltung Tirol, A-9971 Matrei in Osttirol
☏ 0 48 75/51 610

Nationalpark Neusiedler See-Seewinkel (Burgenland)

This is the only nature reserve of the steppes in central Europe. It offers guided excursions, tours in horse-drawn carts, on horse-back or by bicycle. A must for keen bird watchers.

◆ Nationalpark Informationszentrum, A-7142 Illmitz
☏ 0 21 75/3 44 20
www.nationalpark-neusiedlersee-seewinkel.at

Nationalpark Nockberge (Carinthia)

This national park lies between the Lieser Valley and the Turracher Höhe range and is characterized by its gently undulating hills of crystalline rock ("Nocken").

◆ Nationalparkverwaltung, A-9565 Ebene Reichenau 22
☏ 0 42 75/66 50
www.nationalparknockberge.at

Nationalpark Kalkalpen (Upper Austria)

This park in the Pyhrn-Eisenwurzen region extends as far as the High Alps. It runs a varied program for walkers of all levels of experience and fitness.

◆ Nationalparkverwaltung, A-4591 Molln
☏ 07584 3651
www.kalkalpen.at

Nationalpark Thayatal (Lower Austria)

This cross-border park is managed in cooperation with the Czech Republic. The Thaya Valley cuts deeply into the ancient rock of the mountains, forming a breach.

◆ Nationalparkverwaltung, A-2082 Hardegg
☏ 029 49/7 00 50
www.np-thayatal.at

Nationalpark Donau-Auen (Lower Austria)

This park stretches from just east of Vienna to the Slovakian border and is home to a tremendous variety of flora and fauna, earning it the nickname of "Central Europe's rainforest." Its unique features can be discovered on foot or by boat.

Nationalpark Hohe Tauern

© NPHT Tirol/D.Mahler

◆ Nationalparkverwaltung, Schloss Orth, A-2304 Orth an der Donau, ☎0 22 12/34 50 www.donauauen.at

Nationalpark Gesäuse

Rocky cliffs, shaggy meadows, thick forest and the gushing Enns River characterize the country's youngest national park in Styria in central Austria. Its boasts 50 types of wild orchid and serves as the breeding ground of 60 bird species.

◆ Nationalparkverwaltung, A-8911 Admont ☎0 36 13/2 11 60 20 www.nationalpark.co.at

Nature parks

The 40 Austrian nature parks are also conservation areas and cluster mostly in eastern Austria, especially Styria, Lower Austria and Burgenland. For details contact **Verband der Naturparke Österreichs** (*Alberstraße 10, A-8010 Graz, ☎03 16/31 88 48 99, www.naturparke.at).*

BIRD WATCHING

◆ **Burgenland**: Neusiedler See; Seewinkel/Lange Lacke; veterinary care centre for storks and other birdlife at Parndorf (A-7111).
◆ **Carinthia**: Eagle observation point from the castle ruins at Landskron; bird reserve on Grossedlinger Lake (near Wolfsberg); Völkermarkter reservoir.
◆ **Lower Austria**: Danube, March and Thaya river plains; Thaya Valley near Hardegg.
◆ **Salzburg (province)**: Pinzgau (between the Gastein and Habach valleys); Zeller See (south shore of the lake).
◆ **Styria**: Mur reservoir (southern Styria).
◆ **Upper Austria**: Danube plain in the Linz Valley; Schmiding bird reserve.

ANGLING

On the whole, two fishing permits are required: One valid for the whole province, and the other a local, private one from the owner of the stretch of water. For details, contact **Verband der Österreichischen Arbeiter-Fischerei-Vereine** *(A-1080 Wien, Lenaugasse 14, ☎01/4 03 21 76, www.fischerei.or.at).*

WATER SPORTS AND BOATING

Austria boasts no fewer than 1 000 lakes, including 200 in Carinthia alone and several with drinking-quality water. For information on water temperature: ☎01/15 28 (recorded message May–Oct) or ☎01/89 12 17 (ARBÖ information service).
From mid May to the end of September, there are regular passenger boat or ferry services on some of the larger lakes, such as the Achensee, the Attersee, Lake Constance, the Hallstätter See, the Ossiacher See, the Traunsee, the Wörthersee, and the Wolfgangsee. In almost all cases, it is possible to row, sail, surf, water ski, or quite simply swim in Austria's lakes. Further information on these possibilities is provided by the tourist offices of the lakeside communities.

Boat trips on the Danube

From early April to the end of October, a number of companies offer boat trips on the Danube, including:

◆ **DDSG Blue Danube Schiffahrt** Friedrichstraße 7, A-1010 Wien, ☎01/5 88 80, www.ddsg-blue-danube.at
◆ **Donauschiffahrt Ardagger** A-3321 Ardagger 155, ☎0 74 79/6 46 40, www.tiscover.com/donau schiffahrt
◆ **Donauschiffahrt Wurm & Köck** Untere Donaulände 1, A-4020 Linz, ☎07 32/78 36 07, www.donau schiffahrt.at

RAFTING & CANOEING

Rafting is permitted from May to October, but is not allowed in the Hohe Tauern National Park. Rivers on which it is possible to go rafting are:

◆ in **Carinthia**, the Gail, Gurk, Isel, Lieser and Möll;

- in **Lower Austria**, the Enns, March, Salza and Thaya;
- in the province of **Salzburg**, the Enns, Lammer, Mur, Saalach and Salzach;
- in **Styria**, the Enns and Salza;
- in the **Tirol**, the Gerolsbach, Inn, Isel, Ötztaler and Tiroler Ache, Sanna and Ziller;
- in **Upper Austria**, the Enns, Steyr and Traun.

The website of the Austrian National Tourist Office has links to numerous outfitters.Altenatively contact the regional tourist offices or the Austrian canoe association, **Österreichischer Kanuverband** (Giesereistraße 8, A-5280 Braunau, ☎0 77 22/8 16 00, www.okv.at).

HANG-GLIDING AND PARAGLIDING

Venues for hang-gliding and paragliding include:

- **Carinthia** – Bad Kleinkirchheim, Katschberg, Seeboden;
- **Salzburg** – Dorfgastein, Golling-Werfenweng, Mattsee, Salzburg;
- **Styria** – Graz, Gröbming, Ramsau am Dachstein;
- **Tirol** – Galtür, Hall, Kössen, Lienz, Neustift im Stubaital, Niederau, Seefeld;
- **Upper Austria** – Hinterstoder, Leonstein, Linz, Spital am Pyhrn, Weyregg;
- **Vorarlberg** – limited to certain summits and following prescribed routes only.

For further details, contact **Österreichischer Aero-Club** (Prinz-Eugen-Straße 12, A-1040 Wien, ☎01/5 05 10 28; www.aeroclub.at).

GOLF

The popularity of golf in Austria has steadily increased in recent years and the country now boasts 128 golf courses in all provinces. For details, contact the Austrian golfing association **Österreichischer Golf-Verband** (Prinz-Eugen-Straße 12, A-1040 Wien, ☎01/5 05 32 45, www.golf.at).

CYCLING & MOUNTAIN BIKING

Austria has over 10 000km/6 200mi of cycle paths to offer sightseers on two wheels. One of the most popular is the **Donauradweg**, a cycle path following the Danube from Passau to Hainburg (305km/190mi). The Austrian National Tourist Office publishes a brochure called *Radtouren in Österreich* with detailed route descriptions and lodging information about select long-distance cycle routes. it can be ordered from **Radtouren in Österreich** (c/o Oberösterreich Tourismus Information, Freistädter Straße 119, A-4041 Linz, ☎0732/22 10 22). Or check the organization's website at www.radtouren.at.

Mountain bikers are well taken care of as well in Austria with some 17 000km/10 625mi of well-marked routes throughout the Alpine regions. For further details, contact **Mountainbike Holidays** (Glemmerstraße 21, A-5751 Maishofen, ☎0 65 42/8 04 80 22; www.bike-holidays.com).

Cycles can be transported by rail, or hired from some 50 Austrian railway stations. Check with the tourist office for details or consult the website of Austrian Rail (**ÖBB**, www.oebb.at), which has a section called *Bahn & Bike* (in German only).

HIKING

With a network of about 50 000km/31 100mi of waymarked trails, Austria is a hiker's paradise. Ten long-distance trails *(Weitwanderwege)* make it possible to explore the entire country on foot, if such is your wish. Three long-distance European long-distance trails also cut across Austria. Many villages who promote nature tourism have formed an association called **Österreichische Wanderdörfer** (Austrian hiking villages, *Unterwoll-aniger Straße 53, A-9500 Villach, ☎0 42 42/25 75 31, www.wanderdoerfer.at).

This association publishes a quarterly newsletter as well as an annual catalog (both free) with route descriptions and lodging and dining recommen-

SalzburgerLand Tourismus GmbH

Hiking in the mountain

dations. It is also available from the Austrian National Tourist Office.

WALKING IN THE MOUNTAINS

Austria boasts about 680 mountain peaks over 3 000m/10 000ft and 528 carefully managed mountain huts, offering mountain enthusiasts a wide variety of possibilities for walking and climbing routes of every imaginable degree of difficulty. Many of these are managed by the **Österreichischer Alpenverein** *(Wilhelm-Greil-Straße 15, A-6010 Innsbruck, ☎0512/5 95 47 17; www.alpenverein.at).*
For safety reasons, it is essential to plan the route of any mountain excursions very carefully in advance, to ensure that you have the right equipment and to match the route to your level of fitness.

Mountain safety

The mountains, while spectacular to behold, conceal very real dangers, which can catch both inexperienced and experienced hikers alike una-wares. Avalanches, rock-falls, sudden weather changes, heavy mists, unsta-ble terrain, the icy water of mountain streams and lakes, loss of orientation, mistaken judgement of distances—all these represent potential danger to mountaineers, skiers, and hikers. Mists and storms are difficult to anticipate and can manifest themselves unex-pectedly even in high summer. At high

altitudes, the snow cover remains into early July and snow banks often make north-facing slopes impassable. Never to set off alone or without having communicated your planned route and estimated time of return to a third party.

Lightning

In rocky countryside the arrival of lightning is often heralded by an electrostatic charge in the air (and one's hair). During storms you should not seek shelter on narrow ridges, or under overhanging rocks, just inside the entrance to caves or in clefts in the rock. You should also avoid standing under isolated trees or near metal objects (such as fences). Crampons and ice-axes should not be carried on your person. If possible, you should put at least 15m/49ft between your-self and any outcrop (such as a tree or a rock) and remain in a crouched posi-tion with your knees well drawn up to your chest and any exposed areas of skin (such as your hands) not touching any rock. During storms, the car is an excellent refuge, as it acts as a Faraday cage (electrostatic screen).

MOUNTAIN CLIMBING

Mountain guides and climbing schools are to be found in the following areas:
* **Carinthia**: Ferlach, Gmünd, Grosskirchheim, Heiligenblut,

Kolbnitz, Kötschach-Mauthen, Spittal an der Drau, Villach;
- **Lower Austria**: Gloggnitz, Puchberg am Schneeberg;
- **Salzburg**: Filzmoos, Kaprun, Maria Alm, Mauterndorf, Neukirchen, Salzburg;
- **Styria**: Bad Aussee, Graz, Ramsau am Dachstein, Schladming;
- **Tirol**: Ehrwald, Ellmau, Fulpmes, Galtür, Going, Innsbruck, Kufstein, Landeck, Lanersbach, Mayrhofen, Nauders, Obergurgl, St. Anton, St. Johann, Sölden;
- **Upper Austria**: Ebensee, Gosau am Dachstein, Grünau im Almtal, Gschwandt, Hallstatt, Hinterstoder, Linz, Mondsee, Spital am Pyhrn, Windischgarsten;
- **Vorarlberg**: Bartholomäberg, Brand, Lech, Mittelberg, Vandans.

Further information is available from **Verband Alpiner Vereine Österreichs** (Bäckerstraße 16, A-1010 Wien, ☎01/5 12 54 88, www.vavoe.at), an umbrella organization for a dozen Alpine hiking organizations, including the Österreichischer Alpenverein (◐ see Walking in the Mountains).

WINTER SPORTS

Austria has numerous famous ski areas equipped with excellent infrastructures; useful websites are listed throughout this book, or contact the regional or local tourist offices for details.

Year-round skiing is possible at the following resorts:
- in **Carinthia**, Mölltaler Gletscher;
- in **Salzburg**, Kaprun/Kitzsteinhorn;
- in **Styria**, Ramsau/Dachstein;
- in the **Tirol**, Hintertux/Tuxer Gletscher, Kaunertal, Stubaier Gletscher, Ötztal/Rettenbach-und Tiefenbachferner, Pitztal/Mittelbergferner.

For the most current snow and weather reports, as well as avalanche warnings, visit www.lawine.at.
All the resorts shown in the table opposite have ski schools.

Spas

Austria has a wide selection of spa resorts equipped for the most varied treatment. In the skiing season many of these spa resorts (such as Badgastein) keep their thermal baths open.

Sulphur springs
These are used mainly to remedy ailments of the joints, muscles, the nervous system and skin troubles at resorts such as Baden whose thermal beach draws many Viennese and, in the Salzkammergut, at Bad Ischl and Bad Goisern.

Salt springs
Waters impregnated with sodium chloride (salt) from natural springs or "mother-waters," the residues of the refining of industrial salt, are exploited alongside the salt mines themselves. They are used in douches and baths and are good for gynecological and infantile diseases, and for inhaling, when they clear the bronchial tubes. To this group may be added the bicarbonate-bearing waters, like those of Bad Gleichenberg in Styria, which are also recommended for drinking to treat the stomach, intestines, and kidneys.

Iodized springs
These are invaluable for curing metabolic and circulatory disorders, and for vision and glandular troubles. They are particularly well represented by Bad Hall in Upper Austria. In addition to the true mineral springs, some hot springs, such as those at Badgastein, also have radioactive properties. The Austrian National Tourist Office has a list of establishments offering various treatments (spa, thermal baths, Kneipp, etc.). Regional tourist offices can provide specialized lists of spa resorts in their area.

Further details can also be obtained from the **Österreichischer Heilbäder- und Kurorteverband** (Josefsplatz 6, A-1010 Wien, ☎01/512 19 04, Fax 01/512 86 39).

WINTER SPORTS RESORTS(1)	Michlein map 730 fold #	Altitude above sea-level of the resort in meters	Cable-cars	Chair-lifts and ski tows	total length in km of ski slopes	distance (in km) covered by cross-country ski runs	Skating rink	Indoor swimming pool	Horse-drawn sleigh rides	Summer Skiing
Aflenz-Kurort St	23	765 - 1 180		8	20	18	x	1		
Altenmarkt/Zauchensee S	20	856-2 130	3	24	150	150		5		
Badgastein/Sportgastein S	33	1 083-2 686	6	25	175	31	x	10		
Berwang T	16	1 336-1 740		14	40	15	x	4		
Brand V	27	1 050-1 920		9	30	36	x	6		
Brixen im Thale/Westendorf T	18	800-1 827	1	12	32	18		1		
Dorfgastein S	33	835-2 033	3	19	80	20		1		
Ehrwald T	16	1 000-3 000	3	18	25	50	x	7		
Ellmau T	18	820-1 550	1	12	35	10	x	2		
Filzmoos S	20	1 057-1 645	1	15	32	34		6		
Flachau/Flachauwinkl S	20	925-1 980	7	45	60	150	x	6		
Fulpmes/Schlick 2000 T	30	960-2 260	2	7	20	15	x	8		
Galtür T	28	1 584-2 297		11	40	45	x	2		
Gargellen V	27	1 430-2 300	4	9	33			3		
Gaschurn/Partenen V	27	1 000-2 370		27	100	30	x	6		
Gerlos T	31	1 250-2 300	2	26	70	25		9		
Gosau O	20	766-1 800	3	35	65	45		2		
Großarl S	34	920-2 033	3	21	80	15		4		
Heiligenblut K	32	1301-2 902	1	11	55	14	x	5		
Hermagor/Sonnenalpe/ Naßfeld K	33	600-2 004	4	22	101	100	x	3		
Hofgastein (Bad) S	33	870-2 300	3	21	175	37	x	10		
Innsbruck/Igls T	30	575-2 256	5	7	25	25	x	15		
Ischgl T	28	1 377-2 872	5	36	200	48	x	11		
Kaprun S	32	800-3 029	5	22	50	15	x	10	x	🛷
Kaunertal T	29	1273-3 160		8	25	15	x	2		🛷
Kirchberg in Tirol T	18	860-1 995	1	17	44	30	x	7	x	
Kitzbühel T	18	800-2 000	4	24	158	48	x	12	x	
Kleinarl S	33	1 014-1 980		11	120	20		2	x	
Kleinkirchheim (Bad) K	34	1 100-2 055	3	29	85	16		16	x	
Kleinwalsertal/Hirschegg Mittelberg Riezlern V	15	1 088-2 080	2	33	80	44	x	30	x	
Kössen T	18	600-1 700	1	10	25	83		1	x	
Kühtai T	29	2 020-2 520		10	40	15		3		
Lech/Oberlech V	28	1 450-2 444	5	29	110	19	x	15	x	
Lermoos T	16	1 004-2 250		19	29	61	x	10	x	
Leutasch T	16	1 130-1 605		4	9	150	x	8	x	
Lienz T	32	673-2 250	1	11	55	23	x	3		
Lofer S	19	639-1 747	2	12	30	50	x	6	x	

WINTER SPORTS RESORTS(1)	Michlein map 730 fold #	Altitude above sea-level of the resort in meters	Cable-cars	Chair-lifts and ski tows	total length in km of ski slopes	distance (in km) covered by cross-country ski runs	Skating rink	Indoor swimming pool	Horse-drawn sleigh rides	Summer Skiing
Mallnitz K	33	1 200-2 650	1	11	36	28	x	1	x	
Maria Alm S	19	800-2 000	2	33	70	30		8	x	
Mariazell St.	23	785-1 267	1	6	11	70	x	1	x	
Matrei in Osttirol T	32	1 100-2 400		6	29	29	x	2	x	
Mayrhofen T	31	630-2 250	3	20	90	10		13	x	
Mitterndorf (Bad) St.	21	812-1 965		21	25	95	x	1	x	
Mühlbach am Hochkönig S	20	853-1 826	1	22	160	12	x	2	x	
Nauders T	28	1 400-2 750	1	15	65	40	x	6	x	
Neukirchen am Grossvenediger S	31	856-2 150	2	13	30	35	x	3	x	
Neustift/Hochstubai T	30	1 000-3 250	4	26	68	124	x	17	x	☞
Obergurgl/Hochgurgl T	29	1 930-3 080	1	21	110	17	x	14		
Obertauern S	33	1 740-2 335	1	25	120	17		10	x	
Partenen V	28	1 100-2 370	5	27	100	30	x	6	x	
Radstadt S	20	856-1 677		10	17	150	x	3	x	
Ramsau am Dachstein St	21	1 100-2 700	1	20	40	155		5	x	☞
Rauris S	32	950-2 200	1	9	25	43		4	x	
Saalbach-Hinterglemm S	19	1 003-2 100	9	50	180	10	x	20	x	
Saalfelden S	19	744-1 550		5	14	80	x	2	x	
St. Anton am Arlberg/St. Christoph T	28	1 304-2 810	4	37	260	19	x	8	x	
St. Gallenkirch/Gortipohl V	27	900-2 370	4	24	100	30		3		
St. Jakob in Defereggen T	31	1 389-2 520	1	8	35	26	x	2	x	
St. Johann im Pongau/Alpendorf S	20	650-1 850	2	26	19	25	x	5	x	
St. Johann in Tirol T	19	663-1 700	2	16	60	114	x	6	x	
St. Michael im Lungau S	34	1 075-2 360		11	60	65	x	7	x	
Schladming St	21	750-1 894	1	23	25	10	x	1	x	
Schruns/Tschagguns V	27	700-2 380	3	10	40	13	x	5	x	
Seefeld in Tirol T	16	1 200-2 100	3	18	25	170	x	32	x	
Semmering N	24	1 000-1 339		5	12	18	x	6	x	
Serfaus T	28	1 427-2 700	2	17	80	42	x	14	x	
Sölden/Hochsölden T	29	1 377-3 250	3	30	101	6	x	6		
Tauplitz/Tauplitzalm St	21	900-2 000		18	25	80		2	x	
Turrach/Turracherhöhe K/St	34	1 763-2 200		11	30	25	x	3	x	
Tuxertal/Lanersbach T	30	1 300-3 250	4	29	126	23	x	11	x	☞
Wagrain S	20	900-2 014	6	42	150	35	x	3	x	
Werfenweng S	20	1 000-1 836		12	25	38		2	x	
Wildschönau T	18	828-1 903	2	25	42	30		4	x	
Zell am See S	19	758-1 969	6	27	70	40	x	15	x	
Zürs V	28	1 720-2 450	5	29	110	4		3		

(1) The letter following the name of the resort denotes the Land in which it is situated: B Burgenland, N Niederösterreich, S Salzburg, T Tirol, K Kärnten, O Oberösterreich, St. Steiermark, V Vorarlberg

Activities for Children

In this guide, sights of particular interest to children are indicated with a KIDS symbol Kids. Some attractions may offer discount fees for children. Across the alps there are a group of independently managed Kinder Hotels *(Postfach 10, A-9580 Villach/ Drobollach, ☎04254/44 11. www. kinderhotels.com)* specifically catering for families with young children. Activities and services are all child or family oriented.

Calendar of Events

Below is a selection of Austria's most popular events. Most take place annually, although precise dates may vary slightly. ♿For details, contact the local or regional tourist offices. For additional events, see the Address Book sections under Graz, Innsbruck, Klagenfurt, Linz, Salzburg, St. Pölten and Wien/Vienna.

TRADITIONAL FOLK FESTIVALS

JANUARY

Jan 6: **Bad Gastein** — *Perchtenlauf:* Carnival procession (every 4 years, next time 2010)

FEBRUARY

Imst — *Bubenfasnacht:* Carnival procession (every 4 years, next time 2010)
Imst — *Schleicherlaufen:* carnival procession (every 4 years)
Telfs — *Schleicherlaufen:* Carnival procession (every 4 years, next time 2009)

MAY & JUNE

1st May weekend: **Zell im Zillertal** — *Gauderfest:* Centuries-old beer festival with folk music and other events, ☎*0 52 82/22 81, www.gauderfest.at*

Whit Monday: **Freistritz an der Gail** (west of Villach) — *Gailtaler Kufenstechen:* A joust using a barrel as target, followed by dancing
Corpus Christi (2nd Thu after Whitsun): **Bischofshofen** — Procession with floral poles *(Prangstangen)*
Corpus Christi: **Brixental in Tirol** — Procession on horseback
Corpus Christi: **Gmunden** — Procession
Corpus Christi: **Deutschlandsberg** — Procession and carpet of flowers
Corpus Christi: **Hallstatt, Traunkirchen** — Processions on the lake
June 24: **Zederhaus** — *Prangstangentragen:* Flower-decorated poles up to 8m/26ft long are carried to the church in a procession and left there until Assumption Day (Aug 15)

AUGUST

early Aug: **Krakaudorf** Murau (15 August) — "Samson" processions

SEPTEMBER–DECEMBER

late Sept, early Oct: **Burgenland and Lower Austria** — Wine harvest: processions, wine fountains, fireworks
late Nov–Christmas: **Nationwide** — Advent and Christmas markets
Dec 5: **Bad Mitterndorf** — *Nikolospiel:* Street festival in honor of St. Nicholas
Dec 27–Jan 15: **Thaur** (northeast of Innsbruck) — Christmas nativity scenes are on display in people's houses, some of which are open to the public

FESTIVALS

MARCH–APRIL

Graz — Diagonale: Austrian film festival
Salzburg — Easter Festival

MAY–SEPTEMBER

Apr–May: **Krems und Wachau** — Danube festival, with a wide range of theater, dance, music, arts, etc., ☎ *0 22 36/21 2 12, www.donaufestival.at*

May–Jun: **Vienna** — Vienna Festival

May–Sept: **Millstatt** — International Music Festival

Jun–Jul: **Innsbruck** — Tanzsommer: Summer dance festival

Jun–Aug: **Wiesen** — Open-air festivals (reggae, alternative rock, jazz, rock, reggae-Afro-Latin), ☎ *0 26 26/81 64 80, www.wiesen.at*

Jul–Aug: **Ossiach/Villach** — Carinthian Summer Festival

Jul–Aug: **Klagenfurt** — Musikforum Viktring

Jul–Aug: **Innsbruck** — Festival of ancient music, Schloss Ambras concerts

Jul-Aug: **Petronell** — Art Carnuntum: world theater festival, ☎ *0 21 63/ 34 00, www.artcarnuntum.at*

Jul–Aug: **Vienna** — Musikalischer KlangBogen

mid-Jul–late Aug: **Mörbisch** — Operetta festival (by Neusiedler See)

late Jul–end Aug: **Bregenz** — Lakeside festival

late Jul–end Aug: **Salzburg** — Salzburg Festival

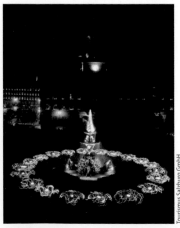

Torchlight dance at the Festival opening, Salzburg

Tourismus Salzburg GmbH

SEPTEMBER

Linz — Festival Ars Electronica

St. Anton am Arlberg — Film festival ("mountains, people, adventure"), ☎ *0 54 46/22 690*

1st week: **Mondsee** — Mondsee festival of chamber music and literature, ☎ *0 62 32/35 44*

2nd week: **Eisenstadt** — International Haydn Festival in Schloss Esterházy, ☎ *0 26 82/6 18 66*

Sept–Oct: **Linz** — International Bruckner Festival

Sept–Oct: **St. Pölten** — Musica Sacra

OCTOBER

Graz and its surroundings — Steirischer Herbst: Styrian autumn festival

PASSION PLAYS

late May: **Erl** (northeast of Kufstein) — Every 6 years (next time 2014)

May-Oct: **Thiersee** — Every 6 years (next time 2011)

Shopping

LOCAL CRAFTS

Those looking for good quality souvenirs in memory of their holiday should visit the **Heimatwerk**, an official outlet for the work of local artisans. Burgenland – China (Stoob), basketweaving (Piringsdorf and Weiden am See), jade jewelry and serpentine marble (Bernstein).

- **Carinthia** – Kärntner Heimatwerk, *Herrengasse 2, A-9020 Klagenfurt,* ☎ *04 63/55 5 75. www.kaerntner heimatwerk.at.* Costumes, ceramics, carved wooden boxes; wrought iron (Friesach).
- **Salzburg** – Salzburger Heimatwerk, *Residenzplatz 9, A-5010 Salzburg,* ☎ *06 62/84 41 10. www. sbg.heimatwerk.at.* Pewter, china, regional costumes.
- **Styria** – Steirisches Heimatwerk, *Paulustorgasse 4, A-8010 Graz,* ☎ *03 16/82 71 06.* Printed linens, jewelry

(Bad Aussee), carved wooden masks (Mitterndorf), painted pottery (Gams), *Loden* cloth (Ramsau and Mandling).

◆ **Tirol** – Tiroler Heimatwerk, *Meraner Straße 2–4, A-6020 Innsbruck, ☎0 51 25/58 23 20. www.tiroler.heimatweg.at.* Wooden Christmas cribs, table-cloths and embroidered fabrics, wrought-iron; majolica (Schwaz), cut and engraved glassware (Kufstein and Kramsach).

◆ **Upper Austria** – Oberösterrei-chisches Heimatwerk, *Landstraße 31, A-4020 Linz, ☎07 32/78 45 62. http://ooe.heimatwerk.at.* Painted glassware and painted wooden boxes: handwoven linen (Haslach); leatherwork, candles (Braunau); wrought iron, steel-engravings (Steyr); china (Gmunden); headdresses and silver jewelry (Bad Ischl).

◆ **Vienna** – Petit point, Augarten porcelain, embroidered blouses. Viennese bronze and enamel.

◆ **Vorarlberg** – Vorarlberger Heimatwerk, *Montfortstraße 4, A-6900 Bregenz, ☎0 55 74/4 23 25.* Wooden articles, painted glass-ware, hand weaving; embroidery (Schwarzenberg and Lustenau); candles (Schruns).

MARKETS

Markets and fairs are a traditional part of Austrian life. During the summer there are countless street markets in the charming surroundings of villages squares. Local Tourist Offices will have information on local markets and local or regional newspapers will often publish the dates.
The Naschmarkt near the Karlsplatz in Vienna is the largest street market in Austria.

Books

The Austrians: A Thousand Year Odyssey by Gordon Brook-Shephard
A Brief Survey of Austrian History by Richard Rickett

Contemporary Austria and the Legacy of the Third Reich by Robert Knight
Chronicle and Works (volume 2) *Haydn at Esterházy 1776–1790* by H.C. Robbins Landon
Fin de Siècle Vienna by Carl E. Schorske
Mountain Walking in Austria by Cecil Davies
Music and Musicians in Vienna by Richard Rickett
The Fall of the House of Habsburg by Edward Crankshaw
The Habsburg Monarchy 1618–1815 by Charles Ingrao
The Habsburg Monarchy 1765–1918 by Robin Oakey
Vienna, the Image of a Culture in Decline by Edward Crankshaw

LITERATURE

Aichinger, Ilse: *Die größere Hoffnung*
Bachmann, Ingeborg: *Malina, Die gestundete Zeit*
Frischmuth, Barbara: *Die Schrift des Freundes*
Bernhard, Thomas: *Das Kalkwerk (The Limeworks), Die Berühmten (The Famous), Holzfällen (Woodcut-ters), Heldenplatz (Heroes' Square)*
Freud, Sigmund: *Die Traumdeutung (The Interpretation of Dreams), Das Unbehagen in der Kultur (Civiliza-tion and its Discontents)*
Handke, Peter: *Die Angst des Tormanns beim Elfmeter (The Goal-ie's Anxiety at the Penalty Kick), Die linkshändige Frau (The Left-Handed Woman), Publikumsbeschimpfung (Offending the Audience), Wun-schloses Unglück (A Sorrow Beyond Dreams)*
Hofmannsthal, Hugo von: *Jeder-mann (Everyman), Das Salzburger Grosse Welttheater, Der Rosenkava-lier* **(libretto)**, *Chandos-Brief* **(essay)**, *Cristinas Heimreise (Christi-na's Journey Home), Der Turm (The Tower)*
Rilke, Rainer Maria: *Sonette an Orpheus (Sonnets to Orpheus), Duineser Elegien (Duino Elegies)*
Roth, Joseph: *Radetzkymarsch (Radetzky March), Kapuzinergruft (The Capuchin Tomb)*

Schnitzler, Arthur: *Liebelei (Playing with Love), Reigen (Merry-Go-Round), Leutnant Gustl (None But the Brave), Der Weg ins Freie (The Road to the Open)*

Stifter, Adalbert: *Der Nachsommer (Indian Summer), Bunte Steine (Colorful Stones)*

Zweig, Stefan: *Schachnovelle, Sternstunden der Menschheit (The Tide of Fortune), Ungeduld des Herzen (Beware Pity)*

Films

Café Electric: *(1929)*
A silent movie starring Marlene Dietrich slumming it in Café Electric with her boyfriend who is not all he seems. Filmed in Vienna.

Der Kleine Straßensänger, (An Orphan Boy of Vienna): *(1936)*
A touching story of an orphan and a street singer who gets the boy accepted by the Vienna Boys Choir.

The Third Man: *(1949)*
A classic film set in Vienna just after World War II.

Sissi... Forever My Love: *(1962)*
Starring Romy Schnieder as Sissi this film charts the romantic hurdles faced by the young Emperor Franz Josef and his beloved Sissi.

The Sound of Music: *(1965)*
A novice nun transforms the children of widower Baron von Trapp into a singing group while falling in love with him. Filmed in Salzburg.

The Counterfeiters: *(2008)*
Won Best Foreign Language Film at the 2008 Oscars. Tells the story of the counterfeiting operation set up by the Nazis in 1936 and the story of the Jew spared because of his counterfeiting skills.

Quantum of Solace: *(2008)*
James Bond movie where some scenes were shot on location in Bregenz.

BASIC INFORMATION

Business Hours

Most shops are open Mon–Fri 9am–6pm, Thu and Fri some are open till 9pm, and Sat 9am–1pm (to 6pm in Vienna and other bigger cities). Shops in tourist areas often remain open longer (Mon–Fri until 9pm, Sat until 6pm, in some stations and airports daily until 11pm).

Communications

The international dialing code for Austria is 43, so to call from abroad dial +43, then the local code (minus the first zero), then the correspondent's number.

To call abroad from Austria, dial 00, then the appropriate international dialing code (Australia: 61, Canada: 1, Eire: 353, New Zealand: 64, UK: 44, USA: 1), then the local code (minus the first zero, if applicable), then the correspondent's number.

Telephone cards (*Telefon-Wertkarte*) for pay phones are on sale at post offices, Tabaktrafiken and hotels. Austria has excellent cell phone coverage. Buying an Austrian SIM card is the cheapest way to use a cell phone.

Electricity

Voltage in Austria is 220V and the standard European 2-pin plug is used for electrical appliances. An adaptor may be required.

Emergencies

- ✚ Fire: 122
- ✚ Police: 133
- ✚ Ambulance: 144
- ✚ Breakdown service: 120 or 123

Mail/Post

Post offices (where currency can also be changed) are generally open Mon–Fri 8am–noon and 2pm–6pm. Cash-desks close at 5pm. A small number of post offices open on Sat 8am–noon. In major cities, one or two post offices may keep longer hours or even stay open 24hr, including at weekends. Stamps are also sold at *Tabaktrafiken* (tobacconists). Letters addressed to a destination in Austria should indicate the international abbreviation "A" in front of the post code.

Sending a postcard or letter up to 20g costs 55¢ to an address within Austria or Europe and €1.25 to anywhere else.

Money

Austria uses the euro (€) as its currency. One Euro is divided into 100 cents. Euros come in seven notes (five, 10, 20, 50, 100, 200 and 500 euros) and eight coins (one and two euro coins and one, two, five, 10, 20 and 50 cent coins).

Traveler's checks and foreign currency can be changed into Euros at banks, bureaux de change, and in some travel agencies and hotels. Major credit cards such as Visa and MasterCard are generally accepted throughout Austria, although you should always check before making your purchases.

Banks are generally open 8am–12.30pm and 1.30pm–3pm on Mon, Tue, Wed and Fri, and 8am–12.30pm and 1.30pm–5.30pm on Thu.

Public Holidays

January 1 (New Year), January 6 (Epiphany), Easter Monday, May 1 (Labor Day), Ascension Day, Whit Monday, Corpus Christi, August 15 (Assumption of the Virgin Mary), October 26 (Austrian National Holiday), November 1 (All Saints' Day), December 8 (Immaculate Conception), December 25 and 26 (Christmas).

Reduced Rates

The following cities and regions offer special discount tickets covering a range of leisure and cultural activities, as well as transport: Innsbruck, Carinthia, Linz, Salzburg, Salzburg region and Vienna.

ÖBB Vorteilscard

If you're planning extensive rail travel within Austria, this rail card (€99.90) may save you a bundle. For the period of one year, it entitles the holder to reductions of 45% (50% for tickets bought online or from vending machines) on standard fares within the ÖBB network and most private lines. For trips outside Austria, the discount is 25%. Holders also qualify for cheaper rates in sleeper cars, free bicycle transportation and assorted other benefits. The card is also available for people under 26 (€19.90) and seniors (€26.90). It is sold at Austrian railway stations and travel agencies with ticket sales facilities and some mainline stations abroad. For further details call ☎05/17 17 or check *www.oebb.at*.

Smoking

Smoking in cafés and restaurants will be banned in Austria from January 1, 2009.

Time

Austria is on Central European Time (GMT +1hr). Clocks move forward one hour on the last Sunday of March and move back the last Sunday of October.

Tipping

Tipping is customary in Austria, especially in restaurants, cafes and bars where you should tip about 10% or round up the bill. Taxi drivers, hairdressers, room cleaning staff, bellhops and other service personnel also appreciate a small tip.

Menu Reader

Backhendl	Fried chicken in breadcrumbs
Baunzerl	White bread roll
Buchteln	Sweet dumplings cooked in milk and sugar
Blunzen	Black pudding
Erdäpfel	Potato
Faschiertes	Mince, meat balls
Fisolen	Green beans
Frittaten	Pancakes cut into strips and put in soups
Gansljunges	Dish made out of goose giblets
Geselchtes	Salted or smoked meats
Golatschen	Small, usually square, filled pastry
G'spritzter	Wine mixed with soda water
G'spritzter Obi	Apple juice mixed with soda water
Häuptlsalat	Lettuce
Hasenjunges	Jointed hare
Heuriger	Young wine (less than a year old) or the inn where you get it from
Hupfauf	Tirolean dessert
Indian gefüllt	Stuffed baby turkey
Jungfernbraten	Roast loin of pork with caraway seeds
Kaiserfleisch	Cured pork spare ribs
Kaiserschmarren	Dessert made with eggs and raisins
Karfiol	Cauliflower
Kohlsprossen	Brussels sprouts
Kracherl	Fruit-flavoured soft drink
Kren, Apfelkren	Horseradish, horseradish sauce with apples
Kukuruz	Sweetcorn
Marillen	Apricots
Nockerln	Dumplings
Obi	Apple juice
Palatschinken	Thin pancake filled with apricot jam or chocolate sauce
Paradeiser	Tomatoes
Powidl	Plum jam
Quargel	A type of cheese
Ribisel	Blackcurrants
Risibisi	Rice and peas
Schill	Perch
Schlagobers	Whipped cream
Schmankerl	Hot sweet pudding
Schöberl	Little biscuits (similar to croutons), put in soups
Schwämme, Schwammerln	Mushrooms
Seidel Lichtes	Small lager
Steirisches Schöpsernes	Styrian mutton dish
Strudel	Thin pastry roll with various fillings
Tafelspitz	Boiled beef and vegetable stew
Topfen	Type of cream cheese (Quark)

CONVERSION TABLES

Weights and Measures

1 kilogram (kg)	**2.2 pounds (lb)**	**2.2 pounds**	*To convert*
6.35 kilograms	14 pounds	1 stone (st)	*kilograms*
0.45 kilograms	16 ounces (oz)	16 ounces	*to pounds,*
1 metric ton (tn)	**1.1 tons**	**1.1 tons**	*multiply by 2.2*
1 litre (l)	**2.11 pints (pt)**	**1.76 pints**	*To convert litres*
3.79 litres	1 gallon (gal)	0.83 gallon	*to gallons, multiply*
4.55 litres	1.20 gallon	1 gallon	*by 0.26 (US)*
			or 0.22 (UK)
1 hectare (ha)	**2.47 acres**	**2.47 acres**	*To convert*
1 sq. kilometre	**0.38 sq. miles**	**0.38 sq. miles**	*hectares to*
(km²)	**(sq.mi.)**		*acres, multiply*
			by 2.4
1 centimetre (cm)	**0.39 inches (in)**	**0.39 inches**	*To convert metres*
1 metre (m)	**3.28 feet (ft) or 39.37 inches**		*to feet, multiply*
	or 1.09 yards (yd)		*by 3.28; for*
			kilometres to miles,
1 kilometre (km)	**0.62 miles (mi)**	**0.62 miles**	*multiply by 0.6*

Clothing

Women				Men			
	35	4	2½		40	7½	7
	36	5	3½		41	8½	8
	37	6	4½		42	9½	9
Shoes	38	7	5½	**Shoes**	43	10½	10
	39	8	6½		44	11½	11
	40	9	7½		45	12½	12
	41	10	8½		46	13½	13
	36	6	8		46	36	36
	38	8	10		48	38	38
Dresses	40	10	12	**Suits**	50	40	40
& suits	42	12	14		52	42	42
	44	14	16		54	44	44
	46	16	18		56	46	48
	36	06	30		37	14½	14½
	38	08	32		38	15	15
Blouses &	40	10	34	**Shirts**	39	15½	15½
sweaters	42	12	36		40	15¾	15¾
	44	14	38		41	16	16
	46	16	40		42	16½	16½

Sizes often vary depending on the designer. These equivalents are given for guidance only.

Speed

KPH	10	30	50	70	80	90	100	110	120	130
MPH	6	19	31	43	50	56	62	68	75	81

Temperature

Celsius (°C)	0°	5°	10°	15°	20°	25°	30°	40°	60°	80°	100°
Fahrenheit (°F)	32°	41°	50°	59°	68°	77°	86°	104°	140°	176°	212°

To convert Celsius into Fahrenheit, multiply °C by 9, divide by 5, and add 32.
To convert Fahrenheit into Celsius, subtract 32 from °F, multiply by 5, and divide by 9.
NB: Conversion factors on this page are approximate.

Hundertwasserhaus, Vienna
©Masahiro Sato/Photononstop/Tips Images

NATURE

Topography

At the heart of the Alps, Austria covers an area of 84 000sq km/32 432.5sq mi, stretching for 580km/360.4mi from Switzerland to Hungary. For a distance of 2 600km/1 615.5mi it shares a border with Germany, the Czech and Slovak republics, Hungary, Slovenia, Italy, Switzerland, and Liechtenstein.

The River Danube, which acts as a catchment for virtually all the rivers of Austria, flows west-east for 360km/223.7mi across the Danube plateau, a vast upland region abutting the Bohemian mountains to the north and encompassing the mountainous Wachau region. This is the historical heart of Austria. Two-thirds of the country is covered by the Alpine chain. To the east, Austria runs into the Puszta, or Hungarian plain.

ALPINE COUNTRY

The Austrian Alps are divided from north to south into three chains: The Northern Limestone Alps, the High or Central Alps, and the Southern Limestone Alps, separated from each other by the valleys of the Inn, the Salzach and the Enns in the north; and the Drava and the Mur in the south.

The Northern Limestone Alps

These overflow into Bavaria and extend—west to east—into the massifs of Rätikon, Lechtal, Karwendel, Kaisergebirge, Steinernes Meer, Tennengebirge, Dachstein, the Alps of Ennstal, Eisenerz, Hochschwab and Schneeberg. The highest point is the Parseierspitze at 3 038m/9 967ft.

Transverse valleys

The Northern Limestone Alps are divided into distinct massifs by transverse valleys, along which the Lech, Ache (the Alz in Bavaria), Saalach and Enns rivers flow toward the Danube plateau. As a result, it's not particularly difficult for drivers to cross or go around these massifs.

Karst plateaux

East of the Ache, the Dachstein, the Hochschwab and the Raxalpe rise sharply to more than 2 000m/6 500ft. Due to the porous nature of the limestone, these mountains are like stony deserts, scored here and there with narrow furrows. Here, the flow of the water is almost entirely subterranean, which has resulted in the formation of numerous caves, including the famous ones in the Dachstein.

Long river valleys

The Northern Limestone Alps are bounded to the south by a deep cleft, separating them from the High Alps. This cleft is divided into valleys, each with its own river, the Inn, the Salzach and the Enns. This major break in the landscape makes it possible to drive along the chain for its entire length.

The High or Central Alps

The High Alps, mostly of crystalline rock, appear as a succession of ridges topped by glaciers, comprising (west to east): The Ötztal Alps, the Hohe Tauern and the Niedere Tauern. For more than 250km/155mi the crestline rarely drops below 3 000m/9 842.5ft. The Brenner pass, the medieval route to Venice, links the valleys of the Inn and the Adige. The Grossglockner Hochalpenstraße and the Felbertauern tunnel make it possible to cross the imposing massif of the Hohe Tauern. To the south of the High Alps, the furrows of the Drava, Mur and Mürz rivers form the natural link between Vienna and northern Italy.

The Southern Limestone Alps

The Carnic Alps and the Karawanken are Austrian on their northern slopes only. Under the terms of the St-Germain-en-

Laye Peace Treaty in 1919, the southern part of the Tirol was ceded to Italy and the Julian Alps to then to Yugoslavia.

ALPINE GLACIERS

About 10 000 years ago, immensely thick Alpine glaciers advanced northward, extending over the Bavarian plateau almost as far as modern Munich.

The glaciers substantially remodeled the relief of the Alpine valleys. They scooped out natural amphitheaters known as cirques (like the one closing off the Brandnertal), scoured valleys into a U-shaped section (like the steep-sided Saalach Valley north of Saalfelden), and created hanging valleys (such as the one above the Achensee). These funnel-shaped basins with their steep cliffs often feature spectacular waterfalls.

Glaciers tended not to follow the existing continuous slope of a valley but to carve out a series of well-defined steps (as evident in the Karawanken), creating natural sites for modern hydroelectric plants. The reservoirs often lie amid breathtaking mountain scenery, as in the case of the impressive Glockner-Kaprun installation.

Carrying along a mass of rocky debris, which when deposited is known as a moraine, the glaciers added an extra, complex layer to the landscape of the pre-alpine plateau. The semi-circular moraines created natural dams behind which water accumulated to form the lakes of the Bavarian plateau and of the northern Salzkammergut.

MOUNTAIN CLIMATES

In contrast to weather in the valleys, the mountain climate varies considerably according to altitude, geography, or exposure to sunshine.

Winds

In the late morning warm, expanded air creeps up from the valley and causes cloud formations around the summits. Due to this weather phenomenon, viewpoints atop the mountains are best visited early to mid-morning. Around 5pm, the cold mountain breezes sweep back down into the valley, creating a sudden plunge in temperature.

The Föhn

This warm fall wind is most strongly felt north of the Alps, in the Alpine valleys of the Rhine, the Inn (especially in the Ötztal) and the Salzach. It is caused by the passage of a deep depression along the north slope of the Alps. Having shed its moisture on the Italian slope of the range, where storms and rain are frequent, the air drawn in by the depression spills over the crestline. Warmed by compression as it loses altitude, it is transformed into a dry, warm wind that creates wonderfully clear skies.

In the mountains, everyone is on the alert. Torrents are in spate, avalanches rumble, and the risk of fire is great. Locals live in such a state of nervous exhaustion that, for example, examinations are sometimes suspended in Innsbruck schools. The Föhn is even said to be submitted as a mitigating circumstance in criminal trials.

Flora

In mountain areas the pattern of vegetation is not only influenced by soil type and climate, but also strongly linked to altitude and aspect. Tree species in particular tend to succeed one another in clearly defined vertical stages, though this staging is much modified by human influences as well as by the orientation of the particular slope. Northern, i.e. south-facing, sunny slopes offer the best growing conditions and have therefore been the most subject to deforestation. Southern, i.e. north-facing, slopes by contrast have tended to keep their trees, which flourish in the prevailing wetter and more shady conditions. This pattern is seen at its best in valleys running east–west.

In most parts of the Alps, farming is practiced up to about 1 500m/5 000ft. Above here is a belt of conifer forest that gives way to alpine pastures at around 2 200m/7 000ft. Above 3 000m/10 000ft bare rock prevails, only occasionally relieved by mosses and lichens.

Edelweiss
Leontopodium alpinum
July to September

Stemless Trumpet Gentian
Gentiana acaulis
May to August

Alpine Sea Holly
Eryngium alpinum
July and August

Martagon Lily
Lilium martagon
June to August

Orange Lily
Lilium bulbiferum
June and July

Alpenrose
Rhododendron ferrugineum
July and August

M. Janvier/ MICHELIN

43

TREES

The following conifers dominate the Alpine forests:

Spruce (Fichte)
This is the typical tree of north-facing slopes. It has a pointed outline, drooping branches, reddish bark, and sharp needles.

Larch (Lärche)
The only European conifer to lose its needles in winter, the larch is prevalent on south-facing slopes. Its delicate light-green foliage casts a relatively light shade, allowing grass and herbs to grow underneath. The small cones are carried upright on the twigs.

Austrian pine (Schwarzkiefer)
The medium-high Austrian pine has a dense crown, dark green foliage and a pale and darkly fissured bark. Its needles grow in pairs. It is undemanding in terms of soil and climate and frequently used in reclamation work in difficult conditions (e.g. on thin limestone soils).

M. Janvier/ MICHELIN

Austrian Pine

Stone pine (Zirbel)
This pine has upward-curving branches that make it look like a candelabrum. It grows right up to the tree line, often twisted into fantastic shapes by the wind. Its bluish-green needles grow in clusters of five. The dense wood of this pine is much appreciated by woodcarvers and makers of rustic furniture.

ALPINE FLORA

The name "Alpine" is normally used to describe plants growing above the tree line. Because of the short growing season (June to August), they tend to flower early and be resistant to drought (woolly leaf surfaces, thick leaves for water storage). Flowering plants found in the Austrian Alps include the Alpine Rose, Gentian, Primrose, Globe Flower and Cyclamen, Martagon Lily, Alpine Aster, Carline Thistle, and, on the edges of the snow-fields, Soldanellae. Rocky areas are home to Edelweiss, Saxifraga, Alpine Poppy, and Glacier Crowfoot.

Fauna

Austria has a rich and varied animal life. The shores of the Neusiedler See are a paradise for 250 species of waterfowl and waders (*see illustration under entry*), including kingfishers, river terns, spoonbills and herons. Storks are also regular visitors here. On the lakes of the Salzkammergut and Upper Austria, swans add a fairy-tale element to the scene.

The Danube is home to 60 of the 80 species of fish to be found in Austria, including eels, perch, and catfish.

Various kinds of deer, wild boar, badgers and foxes make their home in Austria's forests, while the fields and woodlands are a playground for rabbits and hares.

ALPINE FAUNA

Visitors never fail to succumb to the charms of Austria's cutest Alpine resident, the grey-brown **marmot**. Unfortunately, being of a somewhat shy disposition, it only rarely grants lucky ramblers a public audience (*see MALTATAL, Excursion: Nationalpark Nockberge*). The **blue hare** is another cautious creature.

Herds of nimble **chamois** are to be seen principally in the Limestone Alps. **Alpine ibex**, equally agile and also very strong, live above the tree line. Red deer are common throughout Austria.

Typical Alpine bird life includes the snow-partridge, the Alpine jackdaw, the griffon vulture and the capercaillie. On the whole, and especially during the mating season, these birds are more likely to be heard than seen. King of them all, however, is surely the **golden eagle**, a truly majestic bird with a wingspan of 2m/6.5ft, which sadly rather seldom makes an appearance.

HISTORY

Time Line

The main events since the rise of the Habsburgs.

THE HABSBURGS

1273–1291 — **Rudolf I**, founder of the Habsburg dynasty, is elected by the German princes to succeed the Babenbergs, defeats Ottokar and divides Austria and Styria between his sons.

1335 — Carinthia and Carniola are annexed to the Habsburg territory.

1358–65 — Reign of **Rudolf IV**. The Tirol is annexed to Austria (1363).

1440–93 — **Friedrich III**, Duke of Styria, inaugurates a policy of political succession and intermarriage which raises the Habsburgs to the highest rank in the west. His son, Maximilian, is the first to benefit from this.

EXPANSION OF THE HABSBURG EMPIRE

1493–1519 — By his marriage to the daughter of Charles the Bold, **Maximilian I**, Emperor of the Holy Roman Empire, gains possession of most of the Burgundian states. He marries his eldest son, Philip the Handsome, to the Infanta of Spain. Their son, Charles V, inherits the all of their possessions.

1519–56 — Reign of **Emperor Charles V**. Vienna is besieged by the Turks (1529).

1556 — Abdication of Charles V and partition of the Empire. Charles' brother, Ferdinand I, becomes Emperor and head of the Austrian branch of the House of Habsburg. He founds the Austrian Monarchy and also reigns over Bohemia and Hungary. Charles' son, Philip II, is given Spain and Portugal, Sicily, Naples and northern Italy, the Low Countries and Burgundy.

1618–48 — Thirty Years' War begins as a religious conflict and ends up as a Europe-wide power struggle.

CONSOLIDATION OF THE AUSTRIAN EMPIRE

1657–1705 — Reign of Leopold I. Vienna is again besieged by the Turks (1683). The Hungarian monarchy falls to the Habsburgs (1687).

18C — Throughout this century, Austrian policy is overshadowed by three great problems: The Succession to the Empire; the territorial threat from the Turks, the Piedmontese and the French; and the unified administration of very different countries.

1713 — To ensure his daughter's succession to the imperial crown in the absence of male heirs, Charles VI sacrifices territorial rights to the great European countries and promulgates the Pragmatic Sanction. When the king dies, Maria Theresia has to defy its signatories in order to keep her empire. War of the Austrian Succession (1740–48). Seven Years War (1756–63).

1740–90 — Reign of **Maria Theresia** (1740–65). With the help of able ministers, she becomes popular for her financial and administrative reforms. Reign of **Joseph II** (1765–90) who, in the authoritarian manner of enlightened despotism, continues the reorganization begun by his mother.

1781 — Abolition of serfdom.

Akademie der Bildenden Kuenste, Vienna/akg-images

Maria Theresia

1786 — Secularization: Dissolution of 738 houses of contemplative orders under Joseph II.

1792–1835 — Reign of **Franz II**. In 1805 Austria receives the territory of the archbishops of Salzburg as compensation for the losses of territory suffered under the Treaty of Pressburg. Franz II renounces the title of Holy Roman Emperor and adopts that of **Franz I**, Emperor of Austria in 1806.

1809 — Austrian policy, particularly foreign policy, is directed by Chancellor **Metternich** who seeks revenge against France. Andreas Hofer leads the Tirolean rebellion against the Franco-Bavarian alliance.

TROUBLE AND DOWNFALL OF THE MONARCHY

1814–15 — **Congress of Vienna** redraws the map of Europe. Austria recovers Lombardy and Venetia, lost in wars with France, and takes a leading position in the Germanic Confederation, of which Metternich is the mastermind.

1848–49 — March Revolution in Vienna. Fall of Metternich, Hungarian rebellion is suppressed with the help of Russia.

1848–1916 — Reign of **Franz Joseph**.

1866 — War between Austria and Prussia. Austria is defeated, gives up on intervening in German politics and looks toward the Balkans.

1867 — Creation of the dual Austro-Hungarian monarchy, with common foreign, defence and economic policies.

1914 — Outbreak of World War I (1914–18), triggered by the assassination of Crown Prince Franz Ferdinand at Sarajevo in Bosnia and Austria's subsequent attack on Serbia.

1916–18 — Reign of **Karl I**. Collapse of the Austro-Hungarian monarchy after defeat in the First World War.

THE REPUBLIC

1919 — The Treaty of St. Germain-en-Laye re-draws national border, ceding South Tirol to Italy. Following a plebiscite (1920) southern Carinthia remains in Austria and is not be ceded to then-Yugoslavia. Women are given the vote.

1920 — Federal constitution passes.

1933 — Chancellor **Engelbert Dollfuß** inaugurates an authoritarian regime, hostile both to the Social Democrats and to the Nazis.

1934 — Social Democratic Party banned. Suppression of Nazi putsch. Assassination of Dollfuß. His successor seeks to avoid war with Germany at all costs.

1938 — Hitler annexes Austria to the German Reich. Austrians approve the annexation (**Anschluß**) in a referendum.

1939–45 — World War II.

1943 — In the Moscow Declaration the four Allied Nations undertake to restore Austria's independence after the war and restore the frontiers of January 1, 1938.

1945 — The Russians occupy Vienna on April 11. On April 27, a new government forms, led by Karl Renner. Austria and Vienna are divided into four occupied zones.

1949–66 — Coalition government formed by the "People's Party" (ÖVP) and the Social Democrats (SPÖ).

May 15, 1955 — Following the **Staatsvertrag** treaty, occupying troops withdraw from Austria.

Oct 26, 1955 — Austria declares its neutrality.

1956 — Austria is accepted onto the Council of Europe.

1970–83 — Social Democrats form a government under Chancellor Bruno Kreisky, for the first time with an absolute majority in Parliament.

1983–2000 — Government is once again a coalition of the SPÖ and ÖVP.

1989 — Austria applies for membership in the European Union. Death of Zita of Bourbon-Parma, last Empress of Austria and Queen of Hungary, in exile since 1919.

Jan 1, 1995 — Austria joins the **European Union**.

1998 — Austria is admitted to the European Monetary Union.

2000-7 — Coalition government formed by the ÖVP and the right-wing Austrian Freedom Party (FPÖ, later BZÖ). EU briefly imposes sanctions in protest.

2003 — FPÖ posts huge losses during elections but remains in a coalition government with the ÖVP

2003 — The Danube floods and Austrian ex-body builder-turned-actor, Arnold Schwarzenegger, is elected governor of California.

2004 — Heinz Fischer is sworn in as Austria's new president. Pope John Paul II beatifies the last Habsburg emperor, Karl I.

2005 — Devastating floods as the Danube bursts its banks.

2006 — Social Democrats (SPÖ) narrowly defeat the conservative People's Party (ÖVP). The two agree on a coalition.

2007 — After the last election, again a great coalition between ÖVP and SPÖ, headed by Chancellor Dr. Alfred Gusenbauer (SPÖ), was established.

2008 — Together with Switzerland, Austria hosted the European Championship in soccer.

THE EASTERN MARCH

Celtic tribes had established settlements throughout Austria for about 500 years by the time the Romans arrived in the Danube Valley around 15 BC.

In the 4C, tribal migrations brought on the decline of the Roman Empire, resulting in a political vaccuum until the territory fell to Frankish ruler Charlemagne (747–814). He established a province called Ostmark or Ostarrîchi, the forerunner to "Österreich." The Magyars conquered the land in 907 but lost it to Otto the Great in 955. In 976, Otto, now Holy Roman Emperor, granted the Ostmark to Leopold von Babenberg.

THE HOUSE OF BABENBERG (976–1246)

The Babenbergs ruled first as margraves, then as dukes since 1156, giving them greater independence from imperial power. They chose as residences Pöchlarn, Melk, Tulln, the Leopoldsberg and finally Vienna and founded the abbeys of Kremsmünster, St. Florian, Melk, Göttweig and Klosterneuburg.

The last of the Babenbergs, Frederick II, was killed in 1246 fighting the Magyars.

BOHEMIAN INTERVENTION (1246–1278)

Frederick died childless, so Ottokar of Bohemia laid claim to the possessions of the Babenbergs, even marrying Frederick's sister. When Ottokar refused to swear allegiance to Rudolf of Habsburg, who had beaten him in the election for king of the Holy Roman Empire, war ensued. Ottokar was killed at Marchfeld and Rudolf granted the duchies of Austria and Styria to his two sons, thereby laying the corner stone of the House of Habsburg rule.

The Imperial Crown

Austria Est Imperare Orbi Universo—"Austria shall rule the world"—was the proud motto of the **Habsburg** dynasty *(see Genealogical Tree)*. And for a while, it looked as though it would be so.

In the 16C, a clever marriage policy vastly enlarged Austria's territory: Maximilian I acquired the Franche-Comté and the Low Countries by marrying Mary of Burgundy, daughter of Charles the Bold. Maximilian's grandson, **Charles V**, ended up as the most powerful sovereign in Europe, being Holy Roman Emperor, King of Spain, possessor of Naples, Sicily and Sardinia and of territories in the two Americas. Upon his abdication in 1556, the Habsburg territory fell to his brother Ferdinand I.

MARIA THERESIA "THE GREAT" (1740–80)

When Charles VI died without a male heir, the crown went to his daughter

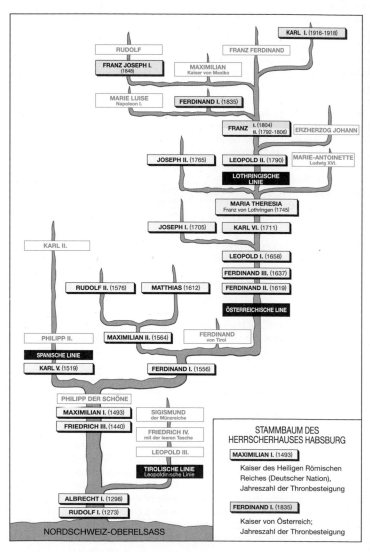

KARL I. (1916-1918)

RUDOLF — FRANZ FERDINAND

FRANZ JOSEPH I. (1848) — MAXIMILIAN Kaiser von Mexiko

MARIE LUISE Napoleon I. — FERDINAND I. (1835)

FRANZ I. (1804) II. (1792-1806) — ERZHERZOG JOHANN

JOSEPH II. (1765) — LEOPOLD II. (1790) — MARIE-ANTOINETTE Ludwig XVI.

LOTHRINGISCHE LINIE

MARIA THERESIA Franz von Lothringen (1745)

JOSEPH I. (1705) — KARL VI. (1711)

KARL II. — LEOPOLD I. (1658)

FERDINAND III. (1637)

RUDOLF II. (1576) — MATTHIAS (1612) — FERDINAND II. (1619)

ÖSTERREICHISCHE LINE

PHILIPP II. — MAXIMILIAN II. (1564) — FERDINAND von Tirol

SPANISCHE LINIE

KARL V. (1519) — FERDINAND I. (1556)

PHILIPP DER SCHÖNE

MAXIMILIAN I. (1493) — SIGISMUND der Münzreiche

FRIEDRICH III. (1440) — FRIEDRICH IV. mit der leeren Tasche

LEOPOLD III.

TIROLISCHE LINIE Leopoldinische Linie

ALBRECHT I. (1298)

RUDOLF I. (1273)

NORDSCHWEIZ-OBERELSASS

STAMMBAUM DES HERRSCHERHAUSES HABSBURG

MAXIMILIAN I. (1493)
Kaiser des Heiligen Römischen Reiches (Deutscher Nation), Jahreszahl der Thronbesteigung

FERDINAND I. (1835)
Kaiser von Österreich; Jahreszahl der Thronbesteigung

IMPERIAL AUSTRIA

Territories united or associated with the Austrian Empire in the course of history

Present-day Austria

Maria Theresia. An intelligent, shrewd and determined woman, she "stood her man" against the Prussians in the War of the Austrian Succession (1740–48) and the Seven Years' War (1756–63), winning the respect from other rulers and the affection of her people. An "enlightened despot," she lived unostentatiously and introduced a number of popular reforms. She and her husband, Holy Roman Emperor Francis I, had 16 children.

THE STRUGGLE WITH FRANCE (1792–1815)

For the 23 years during which France was at war with the rest of Europe, Austria was, together with England, her most determined opponent.

The accession of Napoleon to the Imperial French throne in 1804 dealt a heavy blow to the Habsburg monarchy. Napoleon I opened his reign with the victories of Ulm and Austerlitz (1805) and forced Franz II to sue for peace and renounce the crown of the Holy Roman Empire.

In 1809 the defeat of the French on the battlefields of Essling and Aspern and the successful Tirolean rebellion led by **Andreas Hofer** brought new hope to the Austrians. Eventually, though, the humiliating **Treaty of Vienna** forced Austria to relinquish Carniola, Carinthia, Trieste, Rijeka (or Fiume) and Galicia.

In 1810 Napoleon married Marie-Louise, daughter of the vanquished emperor. Metternich, however, refused to accept defeat and threw all of Austria's forces against Napoleon. In 1814, Austrian troops marched into Paris. The **Congress of Vienna** renewed the power of the Habsburgs.

THE CENTURY OF FRANZ JOSEPH

Franz Joseph's astonishing 68-year reign (1848–1916) ranks as a particular milestone in Austrian history, largely due to the monarch's personality and policies. Although he had to overcome enormous political and personal difficulties (including the suicide of his only son, Rudolf, and the assassination of his wife, Elisabeth), his reign is widely regarded as a success.

The Republic of Austria

Since adopting a federal constitution in 1920, the Republic of Austria has been a Federal State consisting of nine autonomous provinces.

THE AUSTRIAN PROVINCES (BUNDESLÄNDER)

Every five or six years, each province (*Land*) elects a **Provincial Diet** with a number of members ranging from 36 and 56 depending on the province's population. Only the Diet of Vienna has 100 members. The diet elects the members of the **Provincial Government** (*Landtag*), which is the administrative organ of the *Land*.

Burgenland

3 965sq km/1 531sq mi – population 281 500 – capital: Eisenstadt
Predominantly agricultural, this German-speaking province on the border of Hungary has been the republic's easternmost province since 1921. A touristic highlight is the **Neusiedler See** (☝see entry) on the edge of the Central European steppes.

Carinthia (Kärnten)

9 533sq km/3 681sq mi – population 561 157 – capital: Klagenfurt
This lake-studded southern province has the only considerable national minority in Austria (4% of its residents are of Slovenian descent). In a 1920 referendum, the southern districts voted in favor of staying with Austria vs becoming part of Yugoslavia.

Lower Austria (Niederösterreich)

19 174sq km/7 403sq mi – population 1 599 413 – capital: St. Pölten
Considered the country's historical cradle, this is Austria's largest and most prosperous province. It has extensive agriculture, is rich in oil and other natural resources and boasts a thriving industry, mainly concentrated around Vienna.

Upper Austria (Oberösterreich)

11 980sq km/4 625.5sq mi – population 1 409 518 – capital: Linz
This region between the Salzkammergut and Bohemia is highly developed agriculturally and industrially. Tourism is of great importance in the lake district of the Salzkammergut.

Salzburg

7 154sq km/2 762sq mi – population 150 378 – capital: Salzburg
The former domain of the prince-archbishops of Salzburg did not become part of Austria until 1805. Its economy was based on salt. The Salzburg Festival, ritzy spas and modern ski resorts lure scores of visitors every year.

Styria (Steiermark)

16 388sq km/6 327sq mi – population 1 197 500 – capital: Graz
The "green province" of Austria (half its surface is covered by forest) is one of the oldest industrial regions in Europe, with important timber and steel industries, stock-breeding and mining.

Tirol (Tirol)

12 648sq km/4 883sq mi – population 638 300 – capital:
The Tirol is a world-famous destination that generates more tourist euros than any other Austrian province. Although about 35% of its area is given over to agriculture, industry also plays an important role. Southern Tirol was ceded to Italy in 1919, separating eastern Tirol from the rest of the province.

Vorarlberg

2 601sq km/1 004sq mi – population 367 048 – capital: Bregenz
The smallest Austrian province has a thriving textile and tourism industry and is a major producer of hydroelectric power.

Vienna (Wien)

415sq km/160sq mi – population 1 680 47
The services and ministries of the Federal Government and of the *Land* of Vienna are headquartered in the capital.

FEDERAL ORGANIZATION

The **Federal Assembly** *(Bundestag)* consists of the members of the National Council and of the Federal Council, who share the legislative power.

The **National Council** *(Nationalrat)* has 183 members elected by a nationwide popular vote for four years. The minimum voting age is 18. It is convoked or dissolved by the Federal President.

The **Federal Council** *(Bundesrat)* is formed by 63 representatives elected by the provincial diets. Its role is to safeguard the rights of the provinces in the administrative and legislative fields *vis-à-vis* the Federation. On the federal level, it has the right to propose laws and its approval is necessary for international agreements and treaties.

The **Federal President** *(Bundespräsident)* is elected for six years and holds executive power together with the Federal Government. The president represents Austria abroad, appoints the chancellor and senior civil servants, and promulgates the laws.

The **Federal Government** *(Bundesregierung)* is made up of a chancellor, a vice-chancellor, ministers and secretaries of state, appointed by the Federal President on advice of the chancellor.

ART AND CULTURE

Art and Architecture

ART AND ARCHITECTURAL TERMS USED IN THIS GUIDE

Apse: Semicircular vaulted space terminating the east end of a church

Baldaquin: Altar canopy supported on columns

Barrel vault: Simple, half-cylindrical vault

Bas-relief: Sculpture in which the figures project only slightly from the background

Capital: Molded or carved top of a column supporting the entablature

Cartouche: Ornamental panel with inscription or coat of arms (Baroque)

Chapter-house: Building attached to religious house used for meetings of monks or clergy

Chiaroscuro: Treatment of areas of light and dark in a work of art

Cupola: Small dome

Curtain wall: Stretch of castle wall between two towers

Entablature: Projecting upper part of building supporting the roof

Flamboyant: Final phase of French Gothic style (15C) with flame-like forms

Fresco: Watercolor wall painting on plaster

Grisaille: Monochrome painting in shades of gray

Hall-church: Germanic church in which aisles are of the same height as the nave

Lantern: Windowed turret on top of a dome

Lintel: Horizontal beam over a door or window

Narthex: Rectangular vestibule between the porch and nave of a church

Oriel: Bay window corbelled out from an upper floor level

Ossuary: Place where the bones of the dead are stored

Pendentive: Triangular section of vaulting rising from the angle of two walls to support a dome

Peristyle: Colonnade around a building

Pilaster: Shallow rectangular column projecting from a wall

Predella: Altar platform divided into panels

Putto/i: Painted or sculpted cherub

Quadripartite vaulting: Vault divided into four quarters or cells

Reredos: Screen to the rear of an altar

Reticulated: Patterned like a net

Rib: Projecting band separating the cells of a vault

Saddleback roof: Roof with a ridge between two gables, suggesting a saddle shape

Sgraffito: Decoration made by scratching through a layer of plaster or glaze to reveal the color of the surface beneath

Shingle: Wooden tile

Stucco or stuccowork: Decorative plasterwork

Transept: Wing or arm of a church at right angles to the nave

Triptych: Set of three panels or pictures, often folding and used as an altarpiece

Trompe-l'œil: Use of techniques such as perspective, or the combination of sculptures and painted figures, to deceive the viewer into seeing three dimensions where there are only two

Tympanum: Space between the lintel and arch of a doorway

Volute: Spiral scroll on an Ionic capital

Over the centuries Austria has been a meeting place for varied cultures. Its artistic achievement has often reflected these external influences which provided some of its best sources of inspiration. At certain periods, however, a style developed which matched the nation's aspirations, particularly in the 18C, under the enlightened rule of the Habsburgs, when Austrian Baroque blossomed so

ABC of Architecture

Ambulatory: an extension of the aisles around the chancel; in pilgrimage churches, it allowed the faithful to file past the relics

High altar

Axial chapel: in churches not dedicated to Our Lady, this is frequently the Lady Chapel

Chancel: in most churches orientated east (towards Jerusalem)

Side aisle (can be double)

Apse (interior)/ **chevet** (exterior): far (usually east) end of chancel

Porch

Nave

Narthex: vestibule at the church entrance (usually west end), separated from the nave by a wall, screen or railing

Radiating or apsidal chapels

Transept chapel

Bay: transverse section of the nave between two pillars

Side chapel

Transept crossing

Transept arm

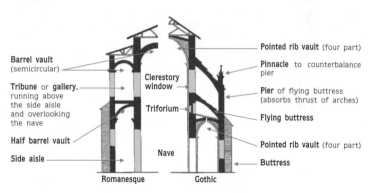

Barrel vault (semicircular)

Tribune or **gallery,** running above the side aisle and overlooking the nave

Half barrel vault

Side aisle

Clerestory window

Triforium

Nave

Romanesque

Gothic

Pointed rib vault (four part)

Pinnacle to counterbalance pier

Pier of flying buttress (absorbs thrust of arches)

Flying buttress

Pointed rib vault (four part)

Buttress

Riesentor (west door) of Stephansdom, Vienna (1230-40)

Tympanum: space enclosed by the arch above a door or window, delimited by the archivolt and the extrados

Mandorla: almond-shaped glory around the head or body of a holy figure (such as Christ or Our Lady)

Capital: top of a pillar or column, linking the shaft with the entablature above

Shaft: body of a pillar or column

Architraves: arch mouldings making up the archivolt

Archivolt: ornamental band of mouldings around the outside (extrados) of an arch

Frieze: decorative carved band below the cornice

Pillar: load-bearing element supporting the structure above an opening in the wall

M. Guillou/MICHELIN

Chancel of Wilhering Abbey Church (1734-48)

Altarpiece: shrine-like structure above the altar, usually framing a painting; can also refer to the painting itself

Squinch: section of wall, often decorated, bridging the gap between a square plan structure and a circular or polygonal superstructure

Cornice: structural moulding running round projecting sections of wall, just below ceiling level

Canopy or baldaquin projecting above the pulpit

Chancel organ: small organ in the chancel or by the wall closing it off from the nave; often as a counterpart to the pulpit opposite

High altar: at the far (east) end of the body of the church

Pulpit: elevated platform for the preacher, usually beneath a canopy or sounding board and reached up a flight of steps

Rocaille cartouches: medallion-shaped ornaments with a coat of arms or other motif, framed in elaborate scroll-like ornamentation featuring shell motifs, characteristic of the Rococo

Tabernacle: ornamental box set in the middle of the altar in which the vessels containing the Blessed Sacrament are kept in Roman Catholic churches

M. Guillou/MICHELIN

Melk Abbey Church (1702-36)

Flaming urns: a common decorative element during the Baroque period

Lantern: opening to let in light above a dome

Finial

Onion dome crowning a tower

Dome

Cornice: structural moulding running round projecting sections of wall, just below roof level

Bull's-eye window or oculus (round or oval)

Blind window: with no actual opening

Balustrade: low protective wall composed of shaped balusters divided at intervals by pedestals

Curved fronton

Pilaster: flat engaged pillar, that is, projecting only slightly from the wall behind it

Corniced pediment

Twin columns

Doorway and window group, concave in profile

Oberes Belvedere, Vienna (1722)

Mansard roof: with a double slope, the lower of which is steeper

Pier: segment of wall between two windows at the same level

Piano nobile: principal storey in a house, usually the first floor; houses formal reception and dining rooms

Attic storey: built above the wall cornice as a crowning feature of the façade

Socle: lowest storey which offers the possibility of compensating for uneven ground

Axis: row of tall windows along the building's façade

Burg Rappottenstein (12C-16C)

Palace or **manor house:** stands in the inner bailey close to the keep and contains living, sleeping and banqueting rooms, as well as the storage cellars

Inner bailey

Inner castle wall

Clock tower

Fortified tower: set into and projecting from the curtain wall, enables defenders to cover outside of wall with their fire

Keep: main stronghold of the castle, in the form of a massive tower which served as a refuge and a lookout, in the most secure part of the castle compound

MAIN CASTLE

Waste opening

Castle outbuilding: with stables, storehouses and servants' quarters

Outer castle wall

Battlements: defensive parapet with openings from which guns can be fired

Machicolations: openings through which boiling oil and tar could be poured onto attackers

Gatehouse flanked by two towers and defended by a drawbridge on the outside and a portcullis on the inside

Lucarne: small, ornate dormer window in the roof

Cowl: roofing tile which lets air through at the end of a ventilation shaft

Acroterion: pedestal bearing a statue or ornament at the peak of a pediment

Modillion: small bracket or console supporting a cornice

Entablature: in Classical architecture, horizontal structure consisting of architrave (below), frieze and cornice (above)

Portico: colonnaded porch marking the main entrance to a building

Mascaron: ornamental sculpted face, either human or part-human, usually caricatured

Pilaster: engaged pillar with a capital and base

M. Guillou/MICHELIN

vigorously that previous achievements paled in comparison.

The Roman occupation has left traces at Carnuntum (Petronell), in the Danube Valley, downstream from Vienna, which was then called Vindobona, in Enns (Lauriacum) where St. Florian was martyred and especially in Carinthia, at Teurnia (near Spittal) and Magdalensberg overlooking St. Veit an der Glan, but also in the Tirol at Aguntum (near Lienz).

ROMANESQUE

From the 12C onward, church building flourished in Austria as in all Christian Europe. The main centers of the Romanesque style were the Episcopal seats of Salzburg, Passau, and Brixen. The style was also promoted by the foundation of many Benedictine, Cistercian and Augustinian convents and monasteries, such as those at Melk, Göttweig, Klosterneuburg, Zwettl, Seckau and Heiligenkreuz. The best preserved buildings from this period are the cathedrals of and Seckau, but the cloisters at Millstatt and the great door of the Stephansdom in Vienna are all outstanding Romanesque examples.

Mural paintings developed most extensively in the Archbishopric of Salzburg The interior of Gurk cathedral and the frescoes at Lambach Abbey are especially noteworth in this context.

Stephansdom, Vienna

GOTHIC

In the 14C and 15C the Gothic style arrived in Austria. Most Gothic churches are of the **hall church** *(Hallenkirche)* type with nave and aisles of equal height, as in Vienna in the Augustinerkirche, the Minoritenkirche, and the church of Maria am Gestade. The most characteristic Gothic building in Austria, though, is the Stephansdom in Vienna, begun in 1304 by architects who were in touch with their contemporaries in Regensburg and Strasbourg.

Until the 16C there was a preference for sectional vaulting where decorative ribs form a pattern of groined or star vaulting in which richness of design contrasts boldly with the bare walls. This **Late Gothic** *(Spätgotik)* developed into a style of long straight lines—the exact opposite of the ornamental opulence of the Flamboyant Gothic to be seen in France at this period.

Paired naves were the fashion in the Alps, especially in the Tirol: Two naves at Feldkirch, four at Schwaz.

The great Gothic altarpieces, which were a synthesis of architecture, sculpture and painting have, for the most part, sadly suffered extensive damage over the centuries. Two are of exceptional quality: Kefermarkt, which was restored at the instigation of the writer Adalbert Stifter, and especially St. Wolfgang, painted and carved in 1481 by a Tirolese, **Michael Pacher**, the greatest Late Gothic artist. A few 15C secular buildings have been preserved as well, such as the Kornmesserhaus at Bruck an der Mur and the Goldenes Dachl at Innsbruck. The decorative elements adorning their façades, though, herald the Renaissance.

THE RENAISSANCE

Although Austria did not close itself off to new ideas, the Gothic tradition continued to dominate in the 16C. Even the Innsbruck tomb of Emperor Maximilian I (1493–1519), which is regarded as a typical product of the German Renaissance, is still clearly influenced by such famous Gothic tombs as the ones of the dukes of Burgundy in Dijon. Although comparatively rare, there are some fine examples of the Renaissance in Austria, such as the arcaded courtyards at Schloss Schallaburg near Melk, at Schloss Porcia in Spittal an der Drau and at the Landhaus in Graz. Another major exception is Salzburg, which the prince-archbishops essentially dreamed of making into a second Rome.

BAROQUE (17C–18C)

The revolution in the arts originating in Italy at the end of the 16C derives its name from the Portuguese word *"barroco"* meaning something irregularly shaped (originally used of pearls). The Baroque affected all aspects of the arts—architecture, painting, sculpture—as well as literature and music.

In Austria, the style stimulated the richest artistic period since the Gothic. There are various reasons why this new direction in art found such fertile ground in Austria. In essence a religious art, it accorded perfectly with the mood of mystical rejoicing following the Council of Trent. It enjoyed the favor of the Habsburgs, ardent supporters of the Counter Reformation, and benefited from the euphoria after the defeat of the Turks at the gates of Vienna in 1683. At the time, the entire country was seized by a passion for building—at last the danger that had overshadowed the lives of generations of Austrians was no more. Another factor in the triumph of the Baroque style was the Austrian love for dramatic effects, elegance, color and *joie de vivre*.

The churches, monasteries and palaces of the Baroque can only be understood fully in relation to the new liturgical and festive music that emerged ever more strongly after 1600, in which a dominant melodic line supplanted the older and more complex vocal polyphony. The pomp and circumstance of the new liturgies (in the wake of the Council of Trent, 1545–63) were backed by the rich and powerful sounds of ever more sophisticated church organs.

Austrian Baroque architecture

Austrian Baroque needs to be seen as an essentially home-grown phenomenon, the expression of an authentically Austrian sensibility, and not as an import. With its irregular outlines, abundance of forms and richness of ornament, the Baroque is above all a style of movement. Its dynamism results from color (the use of both bright and delicate colors, the contrast of black, white and gilt), line (curves and undulations), the exuberant treatment of features like pediments, cornices, balustrades, statues and a delight in unexpected effects of angle and perspective.

The great Baroque abbeys

St. Florian, Melk, Altenburg, Kremsmünster, Göttweig… these great abbeys are manifestations of Austrian Baroque at its peak, surpassing in their magnificence any secular buildings of the period. Often prominently sited, these "monuments of militant Catholicism" (Nikolaus Pevsner) draw together bold terraces, elegant entrance pavilions, inner and outer courtyards and main wings of imposing dimensions into harmonious compositions of unparalleled splendor. The scale and lavishness of ornamentation of these vast structures give rise to a certain duality of feeling; places of worship, they are also temples dedicated to art, to which the Baroque assigned a key role in celebrating divine creation.

Churches

All over Austria stand graceful onion-domed churches, their elegant exteriors concealing the delights awaiting within. It is only once inside the church door that the Baroque, that love of exuberant decoration capable of transforming the most modest of structures, bursts into full and glorious voice.

Many such churches actually evolved from Gothic (Rattenberg, Mariazell)—or even Romanesque (Rein, Stams)—buildings and were only remodeled in the 17C and 18C. A supreme example of Baroque religious architecture in Austria is the unique Dreifaltigkeitskirche (Holy Trinity Church) at Stadl-Paura, every aspect of which symbolizes the Trinity.

Secular buildings

Their façades alive with color and movement, palace and town house alike became stage sets for the urban theater. In the 17C, sumptuous residences took shape on the edge of towns like Graz (Schloss Eggenberg) and Salzburg (Schloss Hellbrunn) as well as Vienna (Belvedere).

Great Baroque architects

Numerous famous Italian architects such as Domenico dell'Allio and the Carlones left their mark on Austria's Baroque buildings. But contributing in equal if not greater measure were a number of local masters, many of whom had received their architectural training in Italy or at least undertaken a study tour of the country.

Among them was **Johann Bernhard Fischer von Erlach** (1656–1723), who created a monumental, national style based on his own interpretation of foreign (particularly Italian) influences. The Dreifaltigkeitskirche at Salzburg is one of the prototypes of this style. Many of the most beautiful buildings in Vienna bear the stamp of his genius: The Nationalbibliothek, the Palais Schwarzenberg, and the winter palace belonging to Prince Eugene. Most of these buildings were completed after his death by his son, Joseph Emmanuel (1693–1742), who also built the indoor riding school (Winterreitschule) in the Hofburg.

Johann Lukas von Hildebrandt (1668–1745) settled in Vienna after a period of study in Italy and worked with Fischer von Erlach. In Vienna he designed the two palaces at the Belvedere, the Peterskirche with its oval cupola, the Piaristenkirche and the Palais Kinsky, and in Salzburg Schloss Mirabell. His considerable body of work had a significant influence on the artists of his generation.

The Tirolean architect **Jakob Prandtauer** (1660–1726) had a masterly touch in relating massive structures to their landscape setting. Thus, while his church interiors are conventional, or even somewhat heavy, his staircase at St. Florian and the two pavilions and great bastion at Melk are achievements of a very high order. The abbey at Melk, a jewel of Austrian Baroque, was completed by Prandtauer's son-in-law, **Josef Munggenast** (1680–1741), who later went on to work at Dürnstein, Altenburg and Geras. Prandtauer did not limit his

talents to religious architecture, however. He was also responsible for several gorgeous secular buildings, including Schloss Hohenbrunn.

Baroque painting and sculpture

Baroque architecture is unimaginable without its natural complements of painting and sculpture. Together with delicate stuccowork decorations, they breathe joyful life into the spaces created by the architect. Church walls disappear beneath elaborate altarpieces, myriad saints and angels fill the ceilings and an army of statues puts to flight their Gothic predecessors. Palaces and abbeys are endowed with huge stairways, while cheerfully colored and stuccoed façades lend a theatrical air to both village street and town square.

Great painters and sculptors devoted their talent to the decoration of palaces and churches. Among them were **Johann Michael Rottmayr**, Fischer von Erlach's preferred collaborator and the precursor of a specifically Austrian pictorial style; **Balthasar Permoser** whose famous marble of the Apotheosis of Prince Eugene graces the museum of Baroque art in Vienna; **Daniel Gran** who executed the painting of the Nationalbibliothek in Vienna; **Paul Troger**, master of Austrian ceiling frescoes; **Martin Johann Schmidt** ("Kremser Schmidt") whose altarpieces are to be found all over Lower Austria; **Bartolomäus Altomonte** who decorated the splendid library at Admont, and his uncle **Martin Altomonte** whose airy frescoes and altar paintings grace Wilhering. It is however with **Franz Anton Maulbertsch** that Austrian painting of this period attains its peak. **Georg Raphael Donner**, sometimes referred to flatteringly as the "Austrian Michelangelo," is best known for the fine fountain in the Neuer Markt in Vienna.

ROCOCO

Inspired by the French rocaille, this style reached its highest form of development in Bavaria. It carries the decorative refinements of the Baroque to their limit, giving them priority over architecture: Painting in *trompe-l'œil*, marble, stucco, bronze and wood are used in lavish profusion by artists who allowed their imaginations free rein. The stuccoists combined garlands, medallions, vegetation and shell work. Often two art forms would overlap: A painted figure passes indistinguishably into sculpture, with the head perhaps in *trompe-l'œil* and the body in relief, without the transition between the two being apparent.

The burning passion of the Baroque gives way to a delight in sophisticated effects, monumentality to delicacy and playfulness. Baldaquins, sham draperies, superimposed galleries, niches overladen with gilding and painted in pastel shades add to the prevailing impression of being in a theater rather than a church. The interior of the church at **Wilhering** near Linz is the most accomplished example of a religious Rococo building, while in the east of the country Rococo is found again at **Schloss Schönbrunn**.

19C

Neoclassicism

After the excesses of Rococo came the triumph of Neoclassicism, inspired by Greece and Rome, a comparatively cold style characterized by the columns and pediments of Classical antiquity. This tendency, which had little in common with the Austrian and even less with the Viennese character, was favored mostly by German rulers, including Ludwig I of Bavaria who transformed Munich. Vienna saw the construction of several buildings of great sobriety like the Technische Hochschule, the Schottenstift and the Münze (Mint). The equestrian statue of Joseph II in the Hofburg by **Franz Anton Zauner** is a typical example of Neoclassical sculpture.

Biedermeier (early 19C)

Biedermeier is the name given to the style which dominated the "Vormärz" (Pre-March), the period between the Congress of Vienna in 1814 and the insurrections of March 1848, the "Year of Revolutions." It is an essentially middle-class style, reflecting the prosperity and settled way of life of this increasingly important section of society.

Comfortable furniture

The cozy interiors inhabited by the rising Vienna bourgeoisie were furnished with simple yet elegant pieces, frequently fashioned in pleasingly light-colored woods, their design reflecting new ideas of function and comfort. Eventually, though, the discretion and modesty of this utterly unpretentious style fell out of fashion. Incidentally, the term "Biedermeier" was only coined around 1900 and is a rather unflattering combination of *"bieder"* (meaning solid or worthy) and "Meyer" (the most common German surname). The Kaiserliches Hofmobiliendepot (national furniture collection) in Vienna has an important

M. Hertlein/ MICHELIN

Schloss Schönbrunn seen from the gardens

©Österreich Werbung/Wiesenhofer

Biedermeier chair, Kaiserliches Hofmobilienmuseum, Vienna

collection of Biedermeier furniture and other objects.

Realistic painting

Austrian painting, and Viennese painting in particular, developed in a remarkable way during this period. **Georg Ferdinand Waldmüller** showed himself to be a master of light and color in his rendering of landscape, while **Friedrich Gauermann** captured the atmosphere of the age with great accuracy and left many fine drawings of outstanding quality. The art of watercolor was popular during this period. **Rudolf von Alt** was the greatest master in this medium, becoming honorary president of the Vienna Secession at an advanced age.

Historicism (late 19C)

Between 1840 and 1880, on Emperor Franz Joseph's orders, Vienna's encircling fortifications were pulled down and work begun on the great processional way known as the Ringstraße, or "Ring." The buildings along the new boulevard were designed according to the dictates of **Historicism**, an eclectic movement in fashion at the time and drawing on a great variety of past styles for inspiration: Florentine Renaissance (e.g. Museum für angewandte Kunst (MAK) by Heinrich von Ferstel), Greek Classical (Parlament by Theophil Hansen), Flemish

Gothic (Rathaus by Friedrich Schmidt), and French Gothic (Votivkirche, also by Heinrich von Ferstel).

Having triumphed in the capital, Historicism went on to leave its mark elsewhere. Toward the end of the 19C, however, opposition to this uncreative and backward-looking style began to grow in Vienna, culminating in open revolt by a number of artists who joined forces to found the famous Vienna Secession movement in 1897.

Late-19C painting and sculpture

Sculpture flourished during this period, not least because of the abundance of public commissions. These included the martial statues of Prince Eugene and Archduke Karl (by **Anton Fernkorn**) in Vienna's Heldenplatz and the moving monument to Andreas Hofer (by Natter) on the Bergisel in Innsbruck.

The late 19C was a turning point for Austrian painting. The great tradition of Realism continued in the work of such landscape painters as **Emil Jakob Schindler**. However, the highly original talent of artists including **Anton Romako** increasingly addressed more serious subject matters, such as decline, decay and death.

JUGENDSTIL (EARLY 20C)

In the final years of the 19C, a new artistic movement known as the Jugendstil swept through all the German-speaking countries, with its epicenter in Munich. It took its name from the widely read magazine *Jugend* (Youth), published between 1896 and 1940, which contained illustrations by artists.

In Vienna, the movement was headed by two exceptionally talented figures, the painter **Gustav Klimt** and the architect **Otto Wagner**. Its influence was felt in the provinces, too, albeit in a more subdued form, and there are good examples of Jugendstil buildings in such places as Wels or Graz.

Jugendstil drawing and painting are characterized by flat surfaces, curvilinear forms, and floral decoration. The movement was paralleled by **Art Nouveau** in France, Modern Style in Britain, and Stile Liberty in Italy.

The Secession by J.M. Olbrich, Building

The Secession

On May 25, 1897 a small group of friends, led by Gustav Klimt, founded the **Association of Austrian Artists**, the **Vienna Secession**. The following year, the architect Joseph Maria Olbrich built an exhibition hall—the Secession—in the Karlsplatz. Completed in only six months, this building remains one of the purest expressions of Jugendstil aspirations, even though contemporaries nicknamed it the "Golden Cabbage" because of its dome of gilded laurel leaves. Its façade proclaims the slogan "Der Zeit ihre Kunst—der Kunst ihre Freiheit" (To each age its art, to art its liberty). Olbrich's Secession building was home to numerous exhibitions of contemporary, progressive art, many of them international in scope. It became a focus of opposition to the values represented by Historicism, academic art and the tendency toward pastiche that had characterized artistic life in Vienna during construction of the Ringstraße. For the artists of the Secession art was above all a matter of personal expression, requiring sincerity and a quest for truth as well as a rejection of prevailing social and aesthetic conventions.

Gustav Klimt (1862–1918)

Painter and interior designer Gustav Klimt was a leading exponent of the Jugendstil, and in many ways the typical Secession artist; his elegant and subtle works are world renowned.

Early in his career he put his academic training behind him and abandoned all attempts at naturalism in favor of rich and subtle decorative effects carried out on a two-dimensional surface free of the constraints of perspective. His sinuous line, his original use of color (especially greens and gold), his stylized foliage, his cult of the sensual and the delicacy of his female portraits provoked a revolution in Viennese artistic circles. Symbolism was an additional influence in the work of this major figure, the forerunner of what was later known as "**Viennese Expressionism**," represented by painters like Egon Schiele and Oskar Kokoschka.

Detail of Beethoven frieze (1902) by Gustav Klimt, Secession, Vienna

Otto Wagner (1841–1918)

Wagner was the dominant architectural figure of the Jugendstil period. Born in Biedermeier times and educated in the most classical tradition, he rose to become professor at the Academy of Fine Arts and imperial architectural adviser for the city of Vienna. For more than 20 years his career was one of conventional success; he designed a number of buildings in neo-Renaissance style along the Ring for example. But in 1899 Wagner broke decisively with his past and joined the Secession. He had already outlined his uncompromisingly contemporary views in his *Modern Architecture* (1895), still a standard reference text. Wagner favored the use of glass and steel, a rational approach to spatial design and the omission of superfluous ornament. His finest works include the pavilions for the Karlsplatz underground railway station (1894) in Vienna, the Postsparkasse (1906) near the Ring and the Steinhof Church (1907).

Wiener Werkstätten (Vienna Workshops)

The Wiener Werkstätten were founded in 1903 by the banker Fritz Waerndorfer, the architect Josef Hoffmann and the artist **Kolo Moser**, one of the most gifted members of the Secession movement. They were intended to make good art accessible to all and to put both artist and craftsman on a firm professional footing. A wide range of products was made adopting Jugendstil tenets, from household utensils, furniture and wallpaper to fashion garments and jewelry. Though expensive, these products were much in demand among the wealthier

strata of society. Beauty of form and the use of high quality materials ranked as more important than functionality. Financial woes led to the workshops' closure in 1932. Together with Klimt's paintings, the output of the Wiener Werkstätten marks the high point of Austrian Jugendstil and enjoys enduring acclaim.

Josef Hoffmann (1870–1956)

This highly versatile figure was one of Otto Wagner's most talented students. Hoffmann designed not only buildings but also their interiors, including furniture and fittings. He was strongly influenced by the work of Scottish architect and designer Charles Rennie Mackintosh, founder of the Glasgow School of Art Nouveau. Hoffmann co-founded the Wiener Werkstätten in 1903 and worked closely with them until 1931. One of the results of this fruitful collaboration is the magnificent **Palais Stoclet** in Brussels. As well as designing material for private clients, Hoffmann also received numerous commissions from the Vienna city council, for whom he produced several housing complexes, including Klosehof. He also designed the interior of the Fledermaus revue theater (1909).

Adolf Loos (1870–1933)

Educated by the Benedictine monks of Melk, this innovative architect called himself a stonemason, though he was considered by Le Corbusier to be the forerunner of architectural Modernism. An admirer of the sober Classicism of Palladio, Loos made a violent attack on the Historicist architecture of Vienna's Ring in 1898, in the pages of the Secessionist journal *Ver Sacrum*. He was soon to break with the architects of the Secession, however, accusing them of "gratuitous ornamentalism." Following a period of residence in the USA (1893–96), and influenced by the Chicago School, he built a number of villas, housing blocks and cafés in Vienna, adopting the principles of a purely functional architectural style. In addition, he designed sculpture and furniture. His work reached maturity in the Goldman and Salatsch store (1909) and in his controversial Michaeler Platz building

Museum für angewandte Kunst, Wien - G. Zugmann

Tea service by Josef Hoffmann, Österreichisches Museum für Angewandte Kunst, Vienna

(1908) which attracted bitter criticism because of its total lack of ornament. Loos has gone down in history as one of the high priests of 20C functionalism. His ideas were taken up and developed by architects the world over. He was a particularly strong influence on artists of the International style.

Music

♪ *see WIEN: "Vienna, Capital of Music"*

MIDDLE AGES

9C — Musical culture flourished in the monasteries where Gregorian chant was sung. The earliest examples of written music in Austria are the Lamentations from the abbey at St. Florian and the Codex Millenarius Minor from Kremsmünster.

12C and 13C — The Germanic troubadours, known as the **Minnesänger**, celebrated the joys and sorrows of "courtly love" at the court of the Babenbergs in Vienna as well as at St. Veit an der Glan in Carinthia, drawing their inspiration from the Volkslied (folk song), an authentic expression of popular feeling. The most famous were Reinmar von Hagenau and his pupil, Walther von der Vogelweide, Hermann von Salzburg, and Neidhart von Reuenthal.

14C and 15C — The burgher-class **Meistersinger** (Mastersingers), organized into guilds, continued the aristocratic *Minnesang* tradition, setting strict rules and testing their skills in competitions.

RENAISSANCE

This was the age of polyphony, pioneered in Austria by the Tirolean Oskar von Wolkenstein, who worked at the court at Salzburg. Later it developed throughout the Empire in the work of several musicians belonging to the Franco-Flemish School.

THE 17C

1619 — The accession to the Imperial throne of Archduke Ferdinand of Styria marked the beginning of the supremacy of Italian music in Austria, notably in opera and oratorio. A long line of Italian masters directed the music of the Court Chapel, the last of them being none other than Mozart's great rival, **Antonio Salieri** (1750–1825).

GLUCK AND OPERA REFORM

Vienna was the setting for the reform of opera, thanks to the German composer, Gluck.

1714–1787 — **Christoph Willibald Gluck** considered opera as an indivisible work of art, both musical and dramatic; he sought, above all, natural effects, truth, simplicity, and a faithful expression of feeling.

1754 — Gluck is named Kapellmeister of the Opera at the Imperial Court of Maria Theresia.

1774 — Two of his operas inagurate in Paris: *Iphigenia in Aulis* and *Orpheus and Euridice*.

THE VIENNESE CLASSICS

This was the age of Haydn, Mozart, Beethoven and Schubert, all Viennese by birth or adoption. Their primarily instrumental work dominated the musical world for almost a century and made Vienna its uncontested capital.

1732–1809 — **Joseph Haydn**
A conductor and composer attached to the service of Prince Esterházy at Eisenstadt for 30 years, Haydn was the creator of the string quartet and laid down the laws of the classical symphony.

1756–91 — Wolfgang Amadeus Mozart

Mozart brought every form of musical expression to perfection, owing to his exceptional fluency in composition and constantly renewed inspiration. His dramatic genius produced great operas of enduring appeal: *The Marriage of Figaro, Don Giovanni, Così fan Tutte* and *The Magic Flute* (see SALZBURG for details of Mozart's life and work).

1770–1827 — Ludwig van Beethoven

Heir to Haydn and Mozart, Beethoven had a Romantic conception of music. He was much affected by the ideas of the French Revolution and felt himself to be the bearer of a message for humankind.

1805 — First performance of Beethoven's only opera, *Fidelio,* at the Theater an der Wien.

1824 — The Ninth or Choral Symphony concluding with the *Ode to Joy* (fourth movement) with words by Friedrich Schiller. In 1972, this Ode to Joy was adopted as the European anthem.

ROMANTICISM

1797–1828 — Franz Schubert

Blessed with a great sensibility, Schubert was an outstanding improviser, who rediscovered in the Lieder the old popular themes of the Middle Ages. His Lieder, of which he wrote more than 600, even more than his symphonies, masses, impromptus and compositions of chamber music, made him the leading lyrical composer of the 19C.

THE VIENNESE WALTZ AND OPERETTA

1820 — In Vienna, a musical genre, the **waltz**, which had its origins in popular triple-time dance, was triumphant. Adopted first in the inns and then in the theaters on the outskirts of the city, the waltz scored such success that it appeared at the Imperial Court.

Two men, **Joseph Lanner** (1801–43) and **Johann Strauss** (1804–49), helped to give this musical form such a prominent place that the most popular waltz is now known worldwide as the "Viennese Waltz." The Strauss sons, Joseph and Johann, carried the waltz to a high degree of technical perfection, taking it farther and farther from its origins to make it a symphonic form.

With the performance at the Carltheater in 1858 of Offenbach's *Die Verlobung bei der Laterne*, Vienna's enthusiasm for **operetta** knew no bounds. Encouraged by Offenbach, **Johann Strauss the Younger** (1825–99) enjoyed equal success with his *Fledermaus* and *Zigeunerbaron* (Gipsy Baron). Other great operetta composers were **Franz von Suppé** (1819–95), **Franz Lehár** (1870–1948, *The Merry Widow, The Land of Smiles*), **Ralph Benatzky** (1884–1957, *White Horse Inn*), and **Robert Stolz** (1880–1975, *Spring in the Prater*).

SYMPHONIC RENEWAL

1824–1896 — Anton Bruckner ranks among the most significant composers of church music, producing nine great symphonies, numerous mass settings and the *Te Deum*. He spent many years as organist of St. Florian and at Linz Cathedral before his appointment as professor at the Vienna Conservatory.

1833–97 — Of German origin but settled in Vienna, **Johannes Brahms** composed a large body of work of a lyrical nature, inestimable in its impact (1868, *A German Requiem*).

1842 — Founding of the Vienna Philharmonic Orchestra playing under the guidance of illustrious conductors (Richard Strauss, Wilhelm Furtwängler) chosen by the players themselves.

1860–1903 — **Hugo Wolf**, a tormented spirit who eventually became insane, composed fine Lieder in his lucid periods, based for the most part on the poems of Goethe, Mörike and Eichendorff.

1860–1911 — **Gustav Mahler**, a disciple of Bruckner, was the last of the great Romantic composers. He composed many Lieder as well as his nine symphonies. He helped to set in motion the revolutionary changes in music at the turn of the century.

20C

From 1903 onward the "New Viennese School," led by Schönberg, was a major influence in the evolution of modern music, as seen in the work of composers such as Ernst Krenek and Pierre Boulez.

1864–1949 — The German composer/conductor **Richard Strauss** carried on the Classical/Romantic Austrian tradition, composing symphonic poems and operas. He was one of the founders of the Salzburg Festival.

1874–1951 — **Arnold Schönberg**, whose early works clearly reflect the influence of Wagner and Mahler, revolutionized music by rejecting the tonal system which had prevailed for 300 years. Together with his followers **Anton von Webern** (1883–1945) and **Alban Berg** (1885–1935) he introduced a new method of atonal composition, based on the concept of series. This is known as "dodecaphony," or in its more advanced form, as "serial composition." His change of style did not meet instant approval with the public, however—the première of his first chamber symphony provoked a riot!

Having pursued his study of atonality in Berlin, Schönberg was exiled from Germany under the Nazis and settled in the United States, where he finally adopted US citizenship.

1894–1981 — The conductor **Karl Böhm** helped to stage two operas composed by his friend Richard Strauss. His fame rests on his seminal interpretations of the works of the great German composers.

1908–89 — The conductor **Herbert von Karajan** brought classical music to a wide audience by his mastery of audio-visual techniques. For many years he presided over the destinies of the Salzburg Festival as well as directing both the Vienna Philharmonic and the Berlin Philharmonic orchestras.

1947 — Salzburg première of the opera *Danton's Death* by **Gottfried von Einem** (b. 1918).

1958 — *"Die Reihe"* ensemble founded by **Friedrich Cerha** (b. 1926) and Kurt Schwertsik (b. 1935)

1994 — American-born, Vienna-resident **Nancy van de Vate**, one of the most heavily recorded living composers of orchestral music, is granted dual citizenship by Austria.

1996 — Death of **Gottfried von Einem** who had for a long time played an important part in Austrian cultural life.

21C

2006 — Austria celebrates Mozart's 250th birthday with a series of events and concerts throughout the country.

People

FAMOUS AUSTRIANS OF THE 19C AND 20C

Franz **GRILLPARZER** (1791–1872): Poet and dramatist (historical plays).

Adalbert **STIFTER** (1805–68): Novelist and short story writer *(Indian Summer)*.

Gregor Johann **MENDEL** (1822–84) Biologist specializing in heredity.

Marie von **EBNER-ESCHENBACH** (1830–1916): Author, editor of short stories.

Bertha von **SUTTNER** (1843–1914) Novelist *(Lay Down Your Arms!)* and prominent pacifist, winner of the Nobel Peace Prize in 1905.

Sigmund **FREUD** (1856–1939): Founder of psychoanalysis.

Arthur **SCHNITZLER** (1862–1931) Writer. His novella, *Leutnant Gustl*, introduced interior monologue to German literature as a new mode of expression.

Daniel **SWAROVSKI** (1862–1956): Jeweler and glass-cutter who patented an electric cutting machine that facilitated the production of lead crystal jewelry.

Karl **LANDSTEINER** (1868–1943): Pathologist and winner of the Nobel Prize for Medicine in 1930 for his discovery of human blood types.

Hugo von **HOFMANNSTHAL** (1874–1929): Poet and dramatist *(Everyman)*, wrote the libretti of a number of Richard Strauss' operas including *Rosenkavalier*.

Rainer Maria **RILKE** (1875–1926): One of the great poets of the 20C.

Karl **KRAUS** (1874–1936): Journalist, writer *(The Last Days of Mankind)*.

Lise **MEITNER** (1878–1968): Physicist.

Robert **MUSIL** (1880–1942): Novelist and short story writer *(The Man without Qualities)*.

Stefan **ZWEIG** (1881–1942): Novelist *(Amok, Schachnovelle)* and biographer *(Marie Antoinette)*.

Erich von **STROHEIM** (1885–1957): Film-maker and actor *(La Grande Illusion; Sunset Boulevard)*.

Georg Wilhelm **PABST** (1885–1967): Film-maker *(The Trial, 1947)*.

Karl von **FRISCH** (1886–1982): Behaviorist, Nobel Prize for Medicine in 1973.

Fritz **LANG** (1890–1976): Film producer *(Metropolis, 1926; "M," 1931)*.

Josef von **STERNBERG** (1894–1969): Film producer, discovered Marlene Dietrich *(The Blue Angel, 1930)*.

Friedrich August **HAYEK** (1899–1992): Winner of the 1974 Nobel Prize for Economics; basic principles of economic science.

Ödön von **HORVÁTH** (1901–38): Writer *(Tales from the Vienna Woods, Jugend ohne Gott)*.

Konrad **LORENZ** (1903–89): Behaviorist, Nobel Prize for Medicine in 1973.

Herbert von **KARAJAN** (1908–89): Conductor, founder of the Salzburg Festival (1967).

Kurt **WALDHEIM** (1918–2007): Secretary-General of the UNO (1972–81), Austrian President (1986–92).

Ingeborg **BACHMANN** (1926–73): Poet (novel, *Malina*)

Alfred **HRDLICKA** (b. 1928): Sculptor and draughtsman.

Friedensreich **HUNDERTWASSER** (1928–2000): Painter and architect.

Thomas **BERNHARD** (1931–89): Controversial novelist and dramatist.

Peter **HANDKE** (b. 1942): Producer, novelist and film scriptwriter with Wim Wenders.

Dietrich **MATESCHITZ** (b. 1944); Entrepreneur and owner of energy drink Red Bull and the Formula 1 racing team of the same name.

Elfriede **JELINEK** (b. 1946): Playwright and novelist who won Nobel prize for literature in 2004.

André **HELLER** (b. 1947): Multimedia artist, founder of Roncalli Circus among other things.

Niki **LAUDA** (b. 1949): Formula 1 racing driver, three times world champion; founder of LAUDA AIR airline company (1979).

THE COUNTRY TODAY

The Economy

Austria has a population of 8.3 million people, about a fourth of whom live in Vienna and its suburbs. Only four other cities have more than 100 000 inhabitants: Graz, Linz, Salzburg, and Innsbruck. Austria has a population density of 98 people per sq km—one of the lowest in Europe (France: 114sq km/295sq mi, Germany: 230sq km/596sq mi). Almost 98% of Austrians speak German as their first language, and there are six recognized ethnic minorities: Slovenians, Croatians, Hungarians, Czechs, Slovaks, and Romany-Sinti gypsies. Around 74% of the population is Roman Catholic; only 4.7% are Protestant, only slightly more than Muslims at 4.2%.

Austria has been a member of the European Union (EU) since January 1995. It has been implementing the Schengen Agreement since 1998 and joined the European Monetary Union in 1999. The Euro has been circulating as the official currency since January 2002. In 2007, Austria's gross domestic product (GDP) was €245 billion.

AGRICULTURE AND FORESTRY

Although vast areas of mountainous land in Austria are not suitable for cultivation, **agriculture** is an important sector of the Austrian economy, providing for almost 100% of national food requirements. About 189 000 people, or around 5% of the country's workforce, are employed in agriculture and forestry. In 2003, there were still 190 400 farm and forestry businesses, although the majority—115 000—were smaller than 20ha/49.4 acres. Only 7 400 were larger than 100ha/247 acres.

Forests represent one of Austria's richest natural resources. Consisting mostly of coniferous trees, they cover about 47% of the country's total surface area—a statistic surpassed within Europe only by Sweden and Finland. In 2006, 19.1 million cu m/674 cu ft of timber were felled. Agriculture and forestry represent less than 3% of gross domestic product. Agriculture and forestry represent about 2% of Austria's gross domestic product.

NATURAL RESOURCES AND INDUSTRY

The break-up of the Austro-Hungarian Empire in 1919 cut Austria off from its traditional markets and some of its raw material sources. The situation was exacerbated by the fact that in the 19C Austrian industry had been focused purely on meeting the needs of its own huge empire instead of gearing up to compete in international markets.

These days, however, Austria is one of the wealthiest countries in the EU (measured by gross domestic product) and ranks as a highly developed industrial power with a significant services industry sector.

ENERGY SOURCES

As a mountainous country laced by numerous rivers, Austria is a major producer of **hydroelectric power**. Most of its domestic energy requirements are met by the output from some 1 300 power stations. Those along the Danube alone generate a quarter of the state electricity production.

Oil is a natural resource that has been developed since 1937. It still plays a role in the Austrian economy, with production holding more or less steady at just below 1 million tons per year. Most oil fields cluster northeast of Vienna, in the Vienna Basin, which accounts for 95% of the country's oil production. The single largest field is in Matzen. The remaining 5% come from fields in Upper Austria, near Salzburg.

The oil is refined at Schwechat near Vienna, which has a capacity of just below ten million tons. In addition to domestic oil, it also processes Imported crude oil. This travels to Schwechat via the Adria-Wien-Pipeline (AWP), which runs from Trieste/Italy to Vienna and is a branch off the huge Transalpine Ölleitung (TAL; Trieste to Ingolstadt/Germany).

Natural gas from Austria's oilfields is highly prized by the country's industrial concerns. Production hovers around 2 billion cu m/70 billion cu ft annually. To meet national demand, though, an additional 6 billion cu m/212 billion cu ft has to be imported each year, mainly from Russia.

MINING AND HEAVY INDUSTRY

Austria is a country with a long tradition in mining and heavy industry. In the Tirol especially, gold, silver and copper were mined intensively up to the 17C. Salt mining and the mining of non-ferrous minerals are still carried out today. In fact, Austria is among the world's most important producers of **magnesite**, a mineral used in fireproofing blast furnaces and smelting ovens and also in construction work.

Of key importance to **heavy industry** in Austria is production in the metallurgical basin in Styria, home of the well-known Erzberg (Iron Mountain). The biggest opencast mine in Europe, it ships about 6 000 tons of iron ore daily to the blast furnaces of Donawitz, which produce steel sections, and to those of Linz, which produce sheet metal.

SALT MINING

Salt mining is now only of minor importance. Nonetheless, since prehistoric times the precious mineral has played such a part in the civilization of the eastern Alps that it's hard to overlook the various enterprises still operating in the Salzburg area. Moreover, the salt waters of numerous spa resorts such as Bad Aussee, Bad Ischl and Hall in Tirol continue to be prized in the treatment of a variety of illnesses. Place names often include the prefix *Salz* or *Hall*—synonymous terms meaning salt or salt works. Touring a salt mine is a memorable experience. Tour guides are often former miners who stick faithfully to their traditional vocabulary—the greeting *"Glück auf!"* (Hope you come up again!) is still heard. Many also wear their dress uniform and regale you with tales about the underground world.

Melting mountains

Except in the natural springs *(Solequellen)* of Bad Reichenhall/Germany, the mineral deposits in the Salzburg region consist of a mixture, called *Haselgebirge*, of salt, clay and gypsum. The miners begin by making a pit in the bed, which they flood and keep supplied regularly with fresh water. This water dissolves the rock on the spot and so, being saturated with salt (27%), sinks to the bottom of the basin, from which it can be pumped, while impurities are left behind. Modern methods of extraction involve the drilling of boreholes and the dissolving of the deposit by the injection of hot water. The brine *(Sole)* is brought to the surface and pumped into the vats of the salt factories *(Sudhütten)*, for the production of domestic or industrial salt.

The first pipelines

By the 17C much of the forest around the salt mines had been burnt up as fuel in the furnaces. This, coupled with the remoteness of many of the mines, led to attempts by the authorities to relocate the centers of salt production closer to the markets. This involved the construction of impressive lengths of pipeline made of timber,

SALT-MINING IN THE SALZBURG REGION

● Natural saline springs

⚒ Working salt-mine open to visitors

Bad Ischl Saline spa

▬ ▬ "Soleleitung": in service

- - - "Soleleitung": out of service

lead or cast iron, to bring the brine down from the mountains to the lowlands. The longest of these **Soleleitungen** ran 79km/49mi from Bad Reichenhall to Rosenheim in Bavaria and was in use from 1810 to 1958.

Pumping stations (Brunnhäuser) kept up a constant flow of brine, over hill and dale. To prevent too sudden a drop, the aqueducts included long mountainside sections, as in the water-conduits (bisses) of the Swiss Valais. The footpaths (Soleleitungswege) paralleling them made splendid corniche routes. The mine road from Hallstatt to Bad Ischl, for instance, dramatically clings to the mountainside above the lake of Hallstatt.

When the salt had been refined, it was shipped by river—on the Inn below Hall in Tirol and the Lower Traun—or in carts. Many salt roads (Salzstraßen) in Austria, one of the best known being the Ellbögener Straße (see INNSBRUCK: Tour of the Mittelgebirge), recall memories of this traffic, so fruitful for the country's economy and the public treasury.

OTHER MAJOR ECONOMIC ACTIVITIES

Austria's most important and internationally competitive industry sectors are the machine building and steel industries, chemicals and textiles and engine and automobile parts manufacture, most of it for export. Austria also has international standing in the production of electronic components such as microchips and integrated circuits (it produces components for Airbus and high-speed trains). In general, Austrian industry is strongly export-oriented. About two-thirds of its foreign trade is conducted with fellow European Union countries. The most important customer is Germany, which accounts for fully one-third of exports.

Food production, especially the luxury food sector, contributes about 3.5% of GDP and principally caters to domestic consumption. The largest proportion of gross domestic product, around 68%, is generated by the services industry.

TOURISM

Austria is a tourist destination par excellence, offering magnificent scenery, major historical monuments, a wide range of leisure opportunities year-round, and an outstanding tourist infrastructure. Tourism is extremely important to the Austrian economy both in terms of job creation and as a source of revenue. In 2007, it generated about €24 billion, contributing 10% to the GDP. The number of foreign visitors was 31.12 million, the majority of whom were German and Dutch. Traditionally, the Tirol attracts most visitors from home and abroad, followed by Salzburg and Carinthia.

Traditions and Customs

RELIGIOUS BELIEFS

Austria is a country steeped in tradition. Old customs are kept very much alive, particularly in rural communities. A deeply rooted religious faith has left its mark on town and countryside alike.

Roofed crosses (Wiesenkreuze), set up at the roadside or in the middle of a field, are thus very much a feature of Austria's rural landscape and particularly prevalent in the Tirol. A common sight in Carinthia is a post (Bildstock) with a little roof protecting a faceted pole decorated with paintings of Biblical scenes. Crucifixes are commonly displayed inside Austrian homes, in a part of the house called the Herrgottswinkel (God's corner). These are especially prevalent in the Tirol where you'll find them in virtually every house, including guesthouses and inns.

Religious figures are also a common subject for the paintings to be found on many an Austrian façade (Lüftlmalerei): St. Florian features particularly prominently in these in his role as protector against fire. Another popular figure is St. George, the dragon slayer. You may also come across churches containing an enormous painting of St. Christopher (e.g. in Imst). These arose in response to the popular belief that looking at the image of this saint would protect the viewer from a violent death for another day. The figure of St. John of Nepomuk is often to be found adorning bridges and fountains, of which he is the patron saint (having been martyred by being thrown off a bridge in Prague).

A CUSTOM FOR ALL SEASONS

See Calendar of Events.

The year begins with processions of masked "Perchten" accompanying St. Nicholas through the villages during the "bitter nights" leading up to Epiphany on January 6. The costumed figures representing good and evil spirits can be beautiful or ugly—the latter are usually clad with shaggy fur and wearing scary horned masks—and are supposed to banish the cold and dark of winter and bring fertility and blessings for the coming year. The feast of the Epiphany itself brings Christmas celebrations to a close by commemorating the journey of the Three Kings guided by the Star of Bethlehem. Festivities involve children's carol singing and processions (*Sternsingen* and *Dreikönigsritte*). In some places, locals parade around sporting giant head-dresses decorated with bells (*Glöcklerläufe*).

Carnival time, or **Fasching** (*Fasnacht* in western Austria), is ushered in as early as January in Vienna with the start of the ball season. Elsewhere, Fasching is celebrated with traditional carnival parades, to which a colorful note is added by the masks handed down from generation to generation. Some of the most famous of these parades include those in the Tirol, at Imst (*Imster Schemen*) and Telfs (*Schleicherlaufen*); the Bad Aussee carnival with its original and colorful *Trommelweiber* and *Flinserln*; and the *Fetzenfasching* in Ebensee.

Palm Sunday is marked by the blessing of the "palm branches"—generally willow catkins or box. This is closely followed by May Day celebrations (May 1), complete with maypole (*Maibaum*), climbing competitions (*Maibaumkraxeln*) and dancing. The feast of Corpus Christi sees more processions, which vary according to the particular traditions of the region: Carrying 8–10m/25–30ft wooden poles

wound around with garlands of fresh flowers (*Prangstangen*) in Bischofshofen and Zederhaus (June 24); laying down a carpet of flowers (*Blumenteppich*) in Deutschlandsberg; processions on horseback, as in Brixental in Tirol, or on water, as in Traunkirchen and Hallstatt. In August, Murau and Krakaudorf (Styria) are the scene of *Samsonumzüge:* parades involving a giant 5m/16ft figure of Samson carried by one man—this show of strength was believed in the 17C and 18C to protect the religious procession. In August and September many communities celebrate the consecration of their local church (*Kirtag*) with a fair. Fall is the time for the Harvest Festival (*Erntedankfest*) season. This is also when the livestock is brought down from the mountain pastures to its winter quarters.

The feast of St. Hubert is celebrated on November 3 (church services, parades on horseback, etc.), while St. Leonard (patron saint of livestock) is honored on November 6. A few days later, the feast of St. Martin, with torchlit processions, brightens up a dark winter night. The periods of Advent and Christmas make December full of events, from the feast of St. Nicholas (December 6), with the *Nikolospiel* parade in Bad Mitterndorf, through to the Nativity scenes displayed in public sites and inside people's homes (e.g. Thaur in the Tirol).

TRADITIONAL COSTUMES

Although traditional local costumes are rarely worn as a daily outfit any more, they occasionally make an appearance at religious and local festivals.

The velvet corsages of the women of Bad Ischl, the embroidered silk blouses of those from the Wachau, the colorful, ribbon-laced bodices of the Montafon, the finely pleated costumes of the Bregenzerwald and the lace aprons of the Burgenland are all evidence of a rich tradition of local folklore. Men wear leather or *Loden* wool breeches (tight at the knee) or shorts (which are less restrictive for the brisk movements of Tirolean dancing), wide braces with a decorated chest panel, and short, collarless jackets. The shape of the hat indicates the region its wearer comes from.

House built around a square courtyard
in the Mühlviertel (Upper Austria)

Traditional Austrian houses

House in the Bregenzerwald
(Vorarlberg)

Tyrolean country chalet

Rural estate in Lower Austria

M. Guillou/MICHELIN

The traditional **dirndl** (pleated skirt, pastel colored apron, full white blouse with short puffed sleeves and a buttoned or laced bodice) and the *Steirer Anzug* ("Alpine dinner jacket," consisting of grey or brown *Loden* breeches embroidered in green, white socks and a long, flared coat with green embroidery and gilt buttons) are not that common a sight these days. However, they are the original inspiration behind the so-called "traditional Austrian look," which combines modern styles with traditional decorative features and natural materials such as linen, cotton, felt and heavy, water-resistant sheep's wool *(Loden)*.

RURAL SCENERY

Fences woven from laths were once the most common style delimiting fields in the Salzburg, Tennengau and Pinzgau regions, but they are increasingly rare. Still, it is not unusual to see farmers piling hay at harvest time onto special drying racks made of metal wire or wooden stakes, to keep it off the damp ground while it is drying.

In the Carinthian Alps, grains are grown on the sunny slopes up to a height of 1 500m/4 500ft, but the harvest often has to be gathered early to avoid frost. The sheaves are spread out on wooden dryers with horizontal struts, sometimes covered, so the grain is able to ripen.

URBAN SETTLEMENT

In Styria, Carinthia and the Danubian countryside the most interesting examples of urban development usually sprouted around the main road. When a town was first developed, the old road was widened to form a sort of esplanade, known as the **Anger**. When all the land on each side of the *Anger* was built over, the resulting form was known as a **Strassenplatz** (street-square). These street-squares, shaped like spindles or regular oblong rectangles, form the heart of the town, approached by the once fortified gateways. The square, which is often called Hauptplatz, is usually dotted with fountains and columns, such as the **Pestsäule** (Plague Column) set up to commemorate the end of a plague.

Food and Drink

Austrian cooking draws from the culinary traditions of the different peoples that once formed the old Empire: German, Italian, Hungarian, Serb and Czech.

Austrian cooking

Soup is served first, followed by the main dish, almost always consisting of meat, fried in breadcrumbs or boiled, accompanied by salad and stewed fruit (such as bilberries: *Preiselbeeren*). Dumplings *(Knödel)* made of liver or flour may be served instead of vegetables. Middle Eastern influences can be detected in the liberal use of spices in many Austrian dishes.

Meat

The most famous dish *(Wiener Schnitzel)* is thin fillet of veal, dusted with egg and breadcrumbs and fried in butter; it's often served with potato salad. Goulash is a highly-flavored stew of Hungarian origin, spiced with red pepper or paprika and garnished with tomatoes, onions and potatoes. In Graz and Styria, duck or chicken, fried in egg and breadcrumbs, is delicious. Game of all kinds is widely available in season.

Dessert

Austrians are famous for the variety of their desserts. The most famous cake, the *Sachertorte*, invented by Prince Metternich's chef, has a subtle and delicate flavor. It is a large, rich chocolate cake covered with chocolate icing above a thin layer of apricot jam; the original recipe remains a secret (but everyone offers a version of it). Other favorites include a jam tart *(Linzertorte)*, consisting of pastry made with almonds, filled with apricot or raspberry jam and covered with a pastry lattice; a turnover *(Strudel)* filled with apples, cherries or cream cheese and currants; plum or apricot fritters; and a sweet soufflé *(Salzburger Nockerl)*.

Austrian Wine

Vineyards cover about 48 500ha/120 000 acres in Lower Austria, in the Weinviertel, on the slopes near Vienna, and in the Burgenland and Styria. White wine (81%) is much more popular than red. Annual

© Österreich Werbung / Bartl

Sachertorte

production is of the order of 2.8 million hectoliters/62 million gallons, of which more than a third is exported.

White wines

Well-known Austrian white vintages include Grüner Veltliner, Müller-Thurgau and Welschriesling. Most vintages yield pleasant table wines which are often light and slightly sparkling. New wine, made that year, is drunk in the typical wine taverns called *Heurige* or *Buschenschenken*. The district of Wachau in the Danube Valley produces wines with a delicate bouquet (Spitz, Dürnstein, Weissenkirchen, Krems, Langenlois). Grinzing, the most famous of Vienna's suburban wine villages, makes a pleasant sparkling wine.

Red wines

The red wines, especially the Blauer Portugieser and the Blaufränkischer, are of high quality. In Lower Austria, the best-known wines are those from Bad Vöslau, south of Vienna, from Retz (the Retz wine is known as *Spezi*—not to be confused with the popular cola- and orange-mix drink of the same name!), from Haugsdorf and from Matzen, in the Weinviertel. In the Burgenland the wines of Pöttelsdorf, Oggau and particularly Rust, and in Styria those of Leibnitz, have a great reputation.

Wine Regions

Austria is divided into four official wine regions: The Weinland Österreich (Lower Austria and the Burgenland); Steirerland (Styria); Vienna; and Bergland (Upper Austria, Salzburg, Carinthia, Tirol, Vorarlberg). Weinland Österreich alone accounts for 91.8% of total production while the Bergland, by contrast, only contributes a tiny 0.04%.

The regions are further subdivided into 19 wine-growing areas, of which the Weinviertel, the Neusiedlersee and the Neusiedlersee-Hügelland are the most important, accounting for 32%, 17% and 8% of output, respectively.

For full details, consult www.wines fromaustria.com.

The best way to get acquainted with Austrian wine is by exploring the country's wine routes. The most famous of these is the Lower Austria Wine Route, an 830km/518mi-long ribbon meandering through the wonderful countryside of the Carnuntum, Weinviertel, Wachau, Thermenregion, Donauland, Kamptal, Traisental and Kremstal growing areas. A section of this route is described in some detail under Östliches Weinviertel. Styria has eight wine routes, including the delightful Schilcher Trail, Sausal Trail and South Styrian Route, described under Steirische Weinstraße. (🔎 *see STEIRISCHE WEINSTRASSE*).

Cross-country skiing near Lech
© Österreich Werbung / Mallaun

STIFT ADMONT★

STEIERMARK

ALT 641M/2 103FT

The Benedictine Abbey of Admont was founded in the 11C by St. Hemma of Gurk (*see GURK*) and Archbishop Gebhard of Salzburg. The abbey buildings were completely rebuilt after a fire in 1865 that fortunately spared the magnificent library and its precious collection of manuscripts and books.

- **Information:** Rathaus, A-8911. ☎0 36 13/2 31 20. www.stiftadmont.at.
- ▶ **Orient Yourself:** Admont is in northern Styria, at the western entrance of the Gesäuse Valley.
- **Don't Miss:** The Stiftsbibliothek with its seven ceiling frescoes.
- **Also See:** EISENSTADT, EISENERZER ALPEN.

Visit

Stiftsbibliothek (Abbey Library)★★

Apr–Oct, daily 10am–1pm, 2pm–5pm; Mar–Nov, daily 10am–5pm. €9.
☎0 36 13/2 31 26 01.
The exuberant Late Baroque library, completed in 1776, stretches for 70m/229.6ft and is the world's largest abbey library. Selections from its collection of more than 200 000 volumes are shown on a rotating basis. The seven **ceiling frescoes** by Bartolomeo Altomonte (1702–83) depict allegorical scenes of theology and the arts and sciences, while the bookcases contain valuable medieval illuminated manuscripts, early printed books, and other prized treasures.

Museums

The **Museum of Fine Arts** displays a fine selection of paintings, sculptures, textiles, and other objects from the Middle Ages through the Baroque period, including a portable altar dating from 1375. Particularly remarkable are the ceremonial vestments and paraments, all products of the Admont School of Embroidery that flourished in the 17C. Upstairs are works by contemporary Austrian artists, part of a continuously growing collection. Another attraction in Admont is the **Natural History Museum**, which is famous for its huge insect collection of some 252 000 specimens.

Admont Abbey Library

Trumler/ÖSTERREICH WERBUNG

AFLENZER SEEBERGSTRASSE★

STEIERMARK

This 1 253m/4 111ft mountain pass road links the industrialized Mürz valley with the pilgrimage town of Mariazell and offers sweeping views of the Hochschwab massif along the way.

▶ **Orient Yourself:** The road runs north out of Bruck an der Mur to Mariazell.
- **Don't Miss:** The traditional wooden houses on the road from Aflenz to Au.
- **Organizing Your Time:** Allow at least two hours.
- **Also See:** BRUCK AN DER MUR, MARIAZELL.

Driving Tour

Aflenzer Seebergstraße Tour

61km/38mi

Bruck an der Mur★
See BRUCK AN DER MUR.

▶ *Start out from Bruck an der Mur northward on the road to Vienna.*

Leaving Kapfenberg, the road meanders through the narrow Thörlbach Valley to Thörl.

Thörl
This little settlement, lying in a rocky cleft, began as a fortification barring the entrance to the Aflenz basin. Exactly in line with the valley, the ruins of the stronghold of Schachenstein stand on their steep-sided spur. The castle was built in 1464 and was the summer residence of the Abbot of St. Lambrecht. Beside the road, to the south, an oratory shelters a Calvary dating from 1530.
On the mountainside there is an 18C building through which the road once passed, a semicircular tower and a chapel dedicated to St. Barbara.
The village is also a good starting point for hikes in the Hochschwab massif.

Aflenz-Kurort

Aflenz is a popular, medium-altitude climatic health resort in a quiet location. In winter the chair-lift to the Bürgeralm delivers skiers to the sunny Schönleiten plateau, while in summer it serves the mountaineers aiming for the Hochschwab massif. The Late Gothic **church**, which is squat and rustic, boasts a fortified tower and a remarkable south door that has a design of little columns and string-courses superimposed on multilobed archwork. Inside, the most striking features of the pillar-free interior are the rib vaulting and the statues of the 12 Apostles. The altars date from the second half of the 18C, while the wooden cross to the left of the choir is Romanesque (1135).
From Aflenz to Au the **road**★ runs along the last foothills of the Hochschwab passing by many houses with wooden galleries that are typical of the area.
The final climb begins at **Seewiesen**, whose 14C Gothic church stands on a small hill. To the west the Seetal is headed by the great blocks of the Hochschwab massif, including the Aflenzer Staritzen and the Mitteralm.

Brandhof
This hunting lodge was created by Archduke Johann. It was here where he secretly got married to Anna Plochl, the daughter of the local postmaster, on February 18, 1829 (*see BAD AUSSEE*). The climb to Mariazell offers fine views of the famous pilgrimage church in its wonderful setting.

Mariazell★ *See MARIAZELL.*

STIFT ALTENBURG★★
NIEDERÖSTERREICH

Founded in 1144, this Benedictine abbey was repeatedly assaulted and all but ruined when a handful of monks set out to reconstruct it in 1645. The result is a masterpiece of the Baroque, boasting one of the finest abbey libraries in Austria and numerous frescoes by the masterful Paul Troger.

- **Information:** ☎0 29 82/34 51. www.stift-altenburg.at.
- ▶ **Orient Yourself:** Stift Altenburg is about 86km/53.4mi northwest of Vienna.
- **Parking:** Parking places are readily available.
- **Don't Miss:** The library, the crypt, and the church.
- **Organizing Your Time:** Allow an hour for the tour another for the church.
- **Also See:** SCHLOSS ROSENBURG, EGGENBURG, STIFT ZWETTLE.

Visit

Stiftskirche (Abbey church)

The undisputed star features of this beautifully proportioned church are Paul Troger's stunning **ceiling frescoes** depicting the struggle between good and evil. Troger also painted the *Assumption* above the high altar and several pictures on the side altars. The **stuccowork** is from the workshop of Franz Joseph Holzinger of St. Florian. Also note the **organ** of 1773, elegantly encased in delicately gilded woodwork.

Originally a Gothic church, Altenburg Abbey was gently transferred into Baroque style between 1730 and 1733.

R. Chéret/MICHELIN

Detail of the rescoes in the "Krypta", Altenburg Abbey

Stiftsgebäude (Abbey buildings)

Guided tour (1hr) Easter Day–Oct, daily 10am–5pm. ☎€9. ☎0 29 82/34 51.

This is one of the liveliest and most complete groupings of Baroque buildings in the country.

Library

The vestibule, with a dome fresco by Johann Jakob Zeiler, is a mere overture to the magnificence of the church-like library, a collaboration of master architects, painters, and sculptors. Paul Troger painted the ceiling frescoes on the theme of Human and Divine Wisdom. It is at Altenburg more than anywhere else that one can appreciate the Baroque concept of the library, which keeps 10 000 books, as the temple of the spirit and enlightenment.

"Krypta"

This vast, luminous space has no equal among the abbeys of Austria. Its frescoes, painted by several of Troger's pupils, deal lightly with death, mixing the macabre with floral motifs.

Sala terrena

Painted with exuberant frescoes, these four rooms are the epitome of Baroque extravagance while also evoking the charm and humor typical of the style. The themes of the first three rooms are water, the source of life and of purity, and the four seasons. The fourth, or "Chinese," room is a timeless vision of the Far East.

ARLBERGGEBIET★★
VORARLBERG UND TIROL

Wedged between the Upper Rhine and the Inn corridor, the mountainous region of the Arlberg was for a long time a formidable obstacle to communications. Nowadays, the road to the Arlberg Pass, a 10km/6.2mi long railway tunnel and the 14km/8.7mi long Arlberg road tunnel link the Vorarlberg and the Tirol.

▶ **Orient Yourself:** West of Innsbruck.
▣ **Parking:** Parking is plentiful and, outside of the resorts, free.
◷ **Organizing Your Time:** Allow one day for each of the tours described.
⏃ **Also See:** LECH, ZÜRS, MONTAFON, SILVRETTASTRASSE, ST. ANTON AM ARLBERG.

A Bit of History

Cradle of Alpine skiing

The Arlberg region is one of the prime skiing destinations in the Austrian Alps with a pedigree going back to 1901, when the country's first ski club was formed here. Twenty years later, local boy **Hannes Schneider** (1890–1955), who some consider the 'father of modern skiing,' founded Austria's first ski school in St. Anton. Together with British skiing pioneer **Sir Arnold Lunn** (1888–1974), Schneider also organized the first **Arlberg-Kandahar Cup** in 1928, a series of famous downhill and slalom races that continues to this day.

Sight

Biosphären Park Großes Walsertal

Kirchberg 24, A-6733 Fontanella. ☎05 55/ 4 51 50. www.walsertal.at.

The six village communities in this alpine valley are included in the biosphere reserve which received UNESCO recognition in November 2000. Hiking the 250km/155.3mi of mountain paths takes you to summer alps where cheese is still made in the traditional way. Traditional farming and forestry management ensure that the great diversity of plant and animal life are not threatened. Follow the educational trails or take a guided walk to learn more of the way of life in the valley

Driving Tours

1 Arlberg Pass Tour★
68km/42.3mi

Bludenz

This town at the meeting point of five valleys (Walgau, Brandnertal, Montafon, Klostertal, and Großwalsertal) centers

---

Why Kandahar?

The first downhill race on skis was organized at Montana in Switzerland on January 6, 1911 by Sir Arnold Lunn, who promoted competitive Alpine skiing.

The race was sponsored by Lord Roberts of Kandahar (1832–1914), a British Field Marshal who took his title from the name of a town in Afghanistan which was captured by the Indian army during a military campaign. His name was then adopted for the Kandahar skiing club, founded by Lunn (⏃*see above*) in 1924. The Arlberg-Kandahar Ski Cup, an international skiing event held at Arlberg since 1928 and still contested today, takes its exotic name from this club.

Skiers who are named five times among the first three in the downhill, slalom or combined event are awarded the Kandahar diamond. Karl Schranz of Austria has gained this honor twice in his career.

The Brotherhood of St. Christoph

Crossing the Arlberg pass used to be a major hurdle for travelers. Many risked, or even lost, their lives due to storms, severe cold or the hazards of the route. For this reason, Heinrich the Foundling from Kempten had an emergency shelter and chapel built just below the pass in 1386. Heinrich founded the brotherhood for the upkeep of the hospice, its charitable works to be funded by donations. Even royalty joined the association and its patrons came from as far afield as Prague, Magdeburg and Strasbourg. The Reformation heralded the decline of the brotherhood and it was finally disbanded under Emperor Joseph II. However, it was reinstated by the Tirolean bishopric in 1961 and now has more than 11 000 members globally, whose donations go toward helping those in need all over the world.

on a handsome old town and is an ideal base for local excursions.

▶ *An alternative to the Arlberg tunnel road is the old road via Innerbraz, Dalaas, Wald and Klösterle. It is slower and quieter but will treat you to plenty of delightful mountain views.*

On leaving Bludenz, the craggy outcrop of the Roggelskopf (2 284m/7 494ft) comes into view. After Dalaas, a nice fresh panorama opens out with the steep wooded slopes of the Batzigg (1 833m/6 014ft) backed by the Rohnspitze peak (2 455m/8 055ft).
At **Langen** is the monumental entrance to the **Arlberg tunnel road**, which ends at St. Anton 14km/8.7mi later.

Stuben

From this tiny, peaceful village, skiers can travel directly to the St. Anton ski slopes. Three chair-lifts give access to the **Albonagrat**★ ridge and there's excellent off-piste skiing as well.

St. Christoph am Arlberg

The Brotherhood of St. Christoph has maintained a hospice here since 1386. Travelers can still find shelter in a hospice-hotel and visit the Brotherhood Chapel nearby.

St. Anton am Arlberg

See ST. ANTON AM ARLBERG.

Address Book

For coin ranges, see cover flap.

WHERE TO STAY

BLUDENZ

◯◯◯**Schlosshotel Dörflinger**
– *Schlossplatz 5.* ☎*0 55 52/6 30 16.*
www.schlosshotel.cc. 42 rooms.
Restaurant◯◯◯*.* The hotel's position gives great views across the town and the mountains beyond. The rooms are classic yet modern.

Stanzertal

After St. Anton, the road traverses the bucolic **Stanzertal**, also known as the Valley of the Rosanna, carving its way between the Lechtal Alps to the north and the Hoher Riffler range to the south. After passing through such attractive resorts as **St. Jakob**, **Pettneu**, **Schnann** and **Flirsch**, the valley narrows and the road runs between forested slopes. Shortly after **Strengen**, the last resort in the Stanzertal, the amazing **Trisannabrücke**★, a steel-construction railway bridge across the River Trisanna, comes into view. A masterpiece of engineering, it was completed in 1884 and is 86m/282ft high and 120m/393.7ft long.

Landeck

Landeck, where the Arlberg road meets the Inn Valley, lies at the foot of an imposing **castle** (13C–18C), now a local history museum. The nearby **Liebfrauenkirche** is the only Late Gothic

M. Hertlein/ MICHELIN

The galleries of the Flexen pass road seen from Stuben

church in the northern Tirol and has an impressive winged altarpiece representing the Adoration of the Magi.

② Flexen Pass Tour ★

17km/10.5mi

▶ *The road is open year-round from the turn-off as far as Lech. The stretch farther north, between Lech and Warth, is often closed by snow in winter.*

The scenic and winding Flexen pass road branches off the Arlberg pass road east of Stuben and runs over the Flexen pass (1 773m/5 816ft) into the Lech Valley and to the ski resorts of Zürs and Lech.

Zürs

⚘*See ZÜRS.*

After two tunnels just before Lech the valley narrows into a breathtaking rocky ravine only a few meters wide.

Lech

⚘*See LECH.*

After Lech, the road runs halfway up the valley through a less rugged landscape. Softly undulating Alpine meadows alternate with steep rocky cliffs, dotted with majestic spruce trees. At the entrance

to Warth, the imposing Biberkopf peak (2 599m/8 527ft) comes into view.

Warth

This small resort is less frenetic than Lech and Zürs and offers great hiking in summer and the full range of snow sports in winter.

▶ *From Warth you can choose between either continuing to Lake Constance through the Bregenzerwald region (⚘see BREGENZERWALD) or crossing the upper Lech Valley (⚘see OBERES LECHTAL) toward Reutte and the border with Germany.*

③ Brandner Valley Tour

15km/9.3mi along narrow roads plus a 2hr round trip walk.

On leaving Bludenz, the well-built road toward Brand offers an overview of the town before climbing through a forest. Past Bürserberg the view opens out along the Brandner Valley toward the Schesaplana summit (2 965m/9 728ft). Beyond here, the valley gets increasingly narrow. Through a gorge to the left there is a **view** ★ of the Zimba peak (2 643m/8 671ft), the "mini-Matterhorn" of the Arlberg region. The route

---

Hut-to-Hut

In summer the mountains are popular with hikers enjoying the hut-to-hut experience. The term hut (or *hütte*) is a bit of a misnomer as they are more akin to mountain inns. These are spread across the high alpine pastures, passes and slopes of the mountain regions.

Refreshments are served at these mountain huts and many of them will also offer hostel style accommodation. Many hikers will plan their route around the huts stopping for a drink, a snack or lunch and maybe dinner and a bed for the night.

In all of Austria there are 528 huts many of which are operated by the **Österreichischer Alpenverein** (*Wilhelm-Greil-Str. 15; A-6010 Innsbruck; ☎05 12/5 95 47 7; www.alpenverein.at*). There are also many independent, family run huts.

Generally the food is good but basic and because of the difficulty in supplying the huts the choice will be limited. Dairy products will feature in those huts where the owner has a few cows or goats being pastured during the summer.

Maps of where the huts are can be picked up in most local tourist offices and are also marked on the hiking maps. If planning to stay overnight booking is recommended. Members of any alpine club affiliated to Österreichischer Alpenverein will get a discount on the overnight rates.

down into the Brand basin reveals the resort's picturesque **setting**★ to full advantage.

Brand

This village, founded by immigrants from the Valais region, is a popular year-round resort. The road out of the village climbs to the foot of the **cirque**★★, a great natural amphitheater closing off the valley. The road ends after the Schattenlagant refuge.

▶ *Leave the car at the lower cable-car station.*

Lünersee★★

2hr round trip, including 10min by cable-car. ©*Operates end May–mid-Oct, daily 8am–12.30pm, 1pm–5pm on the hour.* ☞€*8.70 round trip.* ☏*0 55 56/ 74 44 40.*

The **Lünerseebahn cable-car** delivers you to the lake shore next to the Douglasshütte chalet. Set in a ring of jagged rocky crests, the Lünersee (1 970m/6 463ft), in its original state, was the largest natural mountain lake of the eastern Alps. In 1958 the water level was raised 27m/88.6ft by a dam, creating a vast reservoir feeding the Lünersee and Rodund power stations more than 1 000m/3 281ft below.

4 Montafon Valley Tour★

⚫ *See MONTAFON.*

5 Silvretta Alpine Road Tour★★

⚫ *See SILVRETTASTRASSE.*

SCHLOSS-MUSEUM ARTSTETTEN★★

NIEDERÖSTERREICH

Artstetten is most famous for being the final residence of Archduke Franz Ferdinand and his family before their assassination at Sarajevo in 1914. He and his wife are buried beneath the church. A fortified residence since the 13C, the castle was repeatedly attacked and ravaged by fire. Most of what you see today is from the 17C and 18C, although the complex did not get its distinctive onion-domed silhouette until 1912. In 1823 it became the property of the Imperial family and it still belongs to its descendants today.

- 🛈 **Information:** ☏0 72 13/83 02 30. www.schloss-artstten.at.
- ▶ **Orient Yourself:** 18km/11.2mi west of Melk.
- 🅿 **Parking:** Available at the castle.
- 🅐 **Don't Miss:** Erzherzog-Franz-Ferdinand Museum.
- ◑ **Organizing Your Time:** Allow at least an hour.
- ⚫ **Also See:** STIFT MELK, SCHLOSS SCHALLABURG.

A Bit of History

Archduke Franz Ferdinand

In the service of the Empire

Franz Ferdinand was born in 1863 in Graz as the son of Archduke Karl Ludwig and the nephew of Emperor Franz Josef I. Since in his youth there seemed to be no prospect of his ever succeeding to the throne, he decided to embark on a military career. After five years of train-

ing, he commanded a regiment of hussars in Hungary and was instrumental in building up Austria's navy, which earned him a promotion to the rank of admiral. The archduke was an accomplished horseman, an excellent shot, a patron of the arts, and an avid traveler. With the death of his father in 1896, he became crown prince and heir to the throne. In June 1900, against family objections, he married **Sophie Chotek**, a woman five years younger than him, who, although a countess herself, was not regarded as

© Österreich Werbung / Ramstorfer

Schuloss Artstetten

a suitable match for a future monarch. Together they had three children.

Assassination at Sarajevo

On Sunday June 28, 1914, the arch-duke and his wife were on an official visit to Bosnia, which had recently been annexed by the Empire. The political situation was rather tense, but nobody had an inkling that a group of young Bosnian anarchists was preparing to assassinate the archduke. As the Austrian motorcade drove through the crowds in Sarajevo, one of the conspirators threw a grenade at the archduke's car. It rolled off the folded-back hood and exploded underneath the following vehicle, injuring a number of attendants and onlookers. The procession fled the scene quickly, reaching the town hall for the official reception with-out further incident. After the speeches were over, Franz Ferdinand insisted on visiting the wounded attendants in a local hospital, against the advice of local officials who felt they could not ensure his safety. Unfamiliar with the changed route, the archduke's driver took a wrong turn. When he tried to back up, another of the seven conspirators, Gavrilo Princip, seemingly coming out of nowhere, fired two shots at almost point-blank range, killing both the archduke and his wife. Princip was quickly apprehended and sentenced to 20 years in prison, where he died of tuberculosis in 1918. The assassination was to be one of the direct causes for the outbreak of World War I. Austria-Hungary suffered 1 567 000 losses in World War I.

Erzherzog-Franz-Ferdinand Museum★★

🕐 *Apr–Oct, daily 9am–5.30pm.* 🎫*€7.* ☎*0 74 13/8 00 60.*

An exhibit inside the recently renovated castle, called "For Heart and Crown," chronicles the life and times of Franz Ferdinand and his family. Displays include personal effects, photos, furniture, weapons and other objects once belonging to the Imperial family and associated with events leading to the assassination and outbreak of war in 1914.

BAD AUSSEE ✝

STEIERMARK

POPULATION 5 037

Bad Aussee is the capital of the Styrian Salzkammergut, a region deeply steeped in tradition. It sits at the confluence of two upper branches of the Traun and is surrounded by rugged mountains, including the Dachstein and the Totes Gebirge. The town provides access to two lovely lakes, the Altausseer See and the Grundlsee, and offers an exceptional choice of walks and excursions. Bad Aussee makes both industrial and medical use of the sodium-sulphate waters harvested from the mines of Altaussee.

- **Information:** Koloman-Wallisch-Platz, A-8990. ☎0 36 22/5 23 23. www.ausseerland.at or www.badaussee.at.
- ▶ **Orient Yourself:** Bad Aussee claims to be at the geographical center of Austria in the southeastern Salzkammergut.
- **Parking:** Difficult in summer close to the lakes.
- **Don't Miss:** A visit to the salt mines at Altaussee.
- **Organizing Your Time:** Two days are needed to cover all the excursions.
- **Also See:** DACHSTEIN (Dachstein Riesenhöhle (giant ice caves), HALLSTATT.

A Bit of History

The people's prince

If Bad Ischl owed its fortune to Emperor Franz Joseph, the great man of Bad Aussee was **Archduke Johann**. The prince's controversial romance with Anna Plochl, the daughter of the local postmaster, and their nearly clandestine marriage at Brandhof in 1829 filled the romantic chronicles of the period, confirming the popularity of the "Prince of Styria." Not surprisingly, in Bad Aussee you will find the prince's statue in the municipal gardens (Kurpark), the medallion of the couple on the bridge over the Grundlseer Traun (Erzherzog-Johann-Brücke), and souvenirs of the Plochl family preserved in the former post office (Alte Pferdepost) at Meranplatz 37.

Sights

Chlumeckyplatz

This central square, with a fountain and a plague column, is a pleasant place for a stroll. Also here is the Kammerhof, an impressive Gothic mansion with Renaissance embellishments that was

Address Book

⏚For coin ranges, see cover flap.

WHERE TO STAY

BAD AUSSEE

◒◒◒◒**Erzherzog Johann –** *Kurhausplatz 62.* ☎*0 36 22/5 25 07. www.erzherzogjohann.at. Closed Nov 15–30. 62 rooms.* [Spa] *. Restaurant*◒◒◒. In the center of the town this hotel achieves a warm feeling by its use of natural materials and stylish design. A wellness spa offers health and beauty treatments.

ALTAUSSEE

◒◒◒◒**Seevilla** *– Fischerndorf 61.* ☎*0 36 22/7 13 02. www.seevilla.at. 53 rooms.* [Spa] *. Restaurant* ◒◒◒. Situated directly on the shore of Altaussee with impressive views all around make this hotel something special. All rooms are all stylishly decorated with ultra-modern ensuite bathrooms. A large summer terrace overlooks the lake where Brahms composed two of his works. The wellness spa features an indoor pool with a panoramic views the surrounding alpine scenery.

once the office of the salt mine regulators. Note the marble doorway and window surrounds, the cartouches with cable mouldings, and the coat of arms featuring the Imperial eagle above the main entrance. It now houses the local museum, the **Kammerhofmuseum** (◷*Palm Sun–Jun 14 & Oct, Tue 4pm–6pm, Fri & Sun 10am–noon;* ◉*€3.50;* ☎*0 36 22/5 37 25 13*) with displays on local history and former salt production.

Excursions

Grundlsee★

5km/3mi to the Grundlsee resort; 10km/6.2mi to the Gössl fork. Leave Bad Aussee by the Grundlseer Straße.
At Seeklause (a landing-stage at the head of the lake) there is a **view**★★ over the large Grundlsee, overlooked on the left by the Backenstein promontory. The road skirts the foot of this after passing through the resort of **Grundlsee** from where you get an open view across to the snow-capped summits of the Totes Gebirge.

Drive along beside the lake to visit the hamlet of Gössl, from where a 20min walk will bring you to the rugged beauty of the **Toplitzsee**. The views from the lake can be seen only by taking the **motorboat excursion** (*⬤◄guided tour of 3 lakes (3hr) May 10–Oct 8, daily 10.30am, 11.45am, 1.35pm, 2.45pm & 4.25pm*). Beyond the final isthmus lies the little **Kammersee**, hemmed in by the walls of the Totes Gebirge.

Altausseer See★

5km/3mi to the north.
The road ends at the climatic resort of **Altaussee**, from where you can walk round the lake *(max 2hr)* or descend into the nearby salt mines (**Salzwelten Altaussee** (*⬤◄guided tour (1hr 20min) May–end Oct, daily 10am–4pm on the hour; Apr 16–30 & Oct, daily 10am, noon & 2pm; Nov–Easter, Thu 2.30pm;* ◉*€10.90;* ☎*0 61 34/84 00*). On guided tours through the show-mine you can see the chambers where the Nazis stored looted art during World War II, a salt chapel, and an underground lake with a sound and light show.

Loser Panoramastraße★

13km/8mi – about 1hr. Leave Altaussee to the north and follow the "Loser Panoramastraße" signs: toll point after 3.4km/2mi.
This delightful scenic road climbs to an altitude of 1 600m/5 250ft. From the mountain restaurant (Bergrestaurant) parking lot there is an extensive view over the Altaussee Lake, the sheer "Weiße Wände" ("White Walls") cliffs and, in the distance, the Dachstein range and the Hunerkogel. The parking lot is the starting point for a number of marked trails.

BADEN ♨♨

Baden is a well equipped, modern spa resort with a historic pedigree. Its heyday was in the early 19C when Emperor Franz I spent his summers here from 1814 through 1834, attracting such luminaries as Beethoven and Napoleon in his wake. Baden is beautifully located amid vineyards and meadows, and is noted for its charming villas and elegant Biedermeier architecture. It also hosts the well-known Baden Operetta Festival every summer *(http://operettaheaven.com)*.

- **Information:** Brusattiplatz 3, A-2500. ℡0 22 52/2 26 00. www.baden.at.
- ▶ **Orient Yourself:** The town lies on the eastern edge of the Vienna Woods along the Schwechat River, about 25km/15.5mi south of Vienna.
- **Parking:** Parking (*fee*) is available at the Römertherme and at the Parkdeck Zentrum Süd, right by the town's shopping district.
- **Don't Miss:** Kurpark and Römertherme.
- **Organizing Your Time:** Take a stroll around town, then spend a relaxing afternoon at a thermal bath.
- **Especially for Kids:** The Thermalstrandbad has a playground and special pools for little ones.
- **Also See:** WIENER NEUSTADT, EISENSTADT.

A Bit of History

Spa resort
It was the Romans who first enjoyed the healing properties of Baden's hot-water springs. Nowadays, the spa's 14 sulfurous springs yield more than 4 million l/880 000gal per day, reaching a natural temperature of up to 36°C/97°F. The mineral waters are particularly effective in treating rheumatic ailments.

Famous visitors
Musicians were particularly fond of this idyllic town. **Wolfgang Amadeus Mozart** wrote his "Ave Verum" here and **Franz Schubert** came as well. **Ludwig van Beethoven** visited Baden hoping to cure his deafness. Great waltz and operetta composers, including **Strauss**, Lanner, Millöcker and Zeller, also visited.

Sights

Kurpark★
This park sprawls from near the center of town as far as the Vienna woods. At its edge looms the beautifully restored **Casino**, the oldest gambling hall in Austria and one of the most magnificent. Nearby, the Jugendstil **Sommerarena** (1906), with its movable glass roof, provides a charming backdrop for the operetta festival. Free afternoon concerts take place at the **music pavilion**.

Dreifaltigkeitssäule and Rathaus

M. Hertlein/MICHELIN

Spa town architecture★

In the first half of the 19C, numerous thermal establishments were built in Baden in the Neoclassical style. The **Josefsbad**, a domed, yellow building, now serves as a coffee house; the **Frauenbad** (in Frauengasse), with its pillared portico, is an art gallery; the **Franzensbad** is a glassmaking workshop; and the **Leopoldsbad** (on Brusattiplatz) houses the tourist office.

Spas   `Kids`

Baden's two main public pools complexes are the summer-only **Thermalstrandbad** (www.baden.at/pages/tour ismus/strandbad.shtml), an art deco outdoor playground with a huge, sandy beach and modern additions, and the top-class indoor **Römertherme** (www.roemertherme.at), the largest fully air-conditioned spa in Europe with a freely suspended glass roof.

Hauptplatz

Baden's central square is dominated by the impressive, columned **Rathaus** (town hall), constructed in 1815. In front is the ornate baroque **Dreifaltigkeitssäule** (Trinity Column).

Beethovenhaus

Rathausgasse 10. 🕐*Tue–Fri 10am–noon, 4pm–6pm, Sat, Sun & public holidays 9am–11am & 4pm–6pm.* 🕐*Closed Jan 1, Dec 24, 25, 31.* ✎€2.50. ☎0 22 52/ 86 80 05 90.

The great composer wrote part of the *Missa Solemnis* and completed his *Ninth Symphony* while staying here between 1821 and 1823. You can see his bedroom and living room as well as a small exhibit on his life and work.

Doblhoff Park

The main attraction here is the **Rosarium★**, a redolent display of 20 000 roses of 600 different varieties. In June, the Badener Rosentage attract flower-lovers galore.

BRAUNAU

OBERÖSTERREICH

POPULATION 17 300

ALT 352M/1 155FT

Braunau has had a civic charter since 1260, it flourished through the salt trade in the 15C, but only became part of Austria in 1779. A bridge over the River Inn connects the town with Simbach in Bavaria, Germany. Although (in)famous as the birthplace of Adolf Hitler, Braunau is really more noteworthy for its pretty town center and the numerous Gothic houses that miraculously survived the great fire of 1874.

- 🄸 **Information:** Stadtpl. 2, A-5280. ☎0 77 22/6 26 44. www.tourismus-braunau.at.
- ▶ **Orient Yourself:** Braunau is in the Innviertel right on the border with Germany about 60km/37.2mi north of Salzburg and 90km/56mi west of Linz.
- 🄿 **Parking:** Look for fee-based parking lots along Ringstraße.
- 🄲 **Also See:** STIFT MELK, SCHLOSS SCHALLABURG.

Sights

Altstadt

The focal feature is the **Stadtplatz**, an elongated square framed by houses from various architectural periods. Also see the **Glockengießerhaus** (Johann-Fischer-Gasse 18), built in 1385, retaining its original bell-foundry workshop

Stadtpfarrkirche St. Stephan

Dominating Braunau's skyline is the landmark steeple of the town's parish church. The Late Gothic church, an ebony-yellowish brick building, has three naves and is filled with treasures, most notably the late 15C **Bäckeraltar** (Bakers' Altar), donated by the bakers' guild.

BREGENZ★★

VORARLBERG
POPULATION 29 120
ALT 398M/1 306FT

Bregenz is the administrative capital of the Vorarlberg and scenically located on the shore of Lake Constance (Bodensee to German speakers), at the point where the mountains spill down to the "Swabian Sea." The lakeside draws active travelers with its wide variety of water sports and splendid views. Music lovers flood the town during the Bregenz Festival in summer.

- 🅸 **Information:** Bahnhofstr. 14, A-6900. ☎0 55 74/4 95 90. www.bregenz.ws.
- ▶ **Orient Yourself:** Bregenz is on the eastern shore of Lake Constance at the foot of the Pfänder mountain.
- 🅿 **Parking:** With 2 300 spots, Bregenz has public parking aplenty. An automated guide system directs you to the nearest garage or lot with open spaces.
- 👁 **Don't Miss:** A walk around the Oberstadt; a trip up the Pfänder Mountain.
- 🕐 **Organizing Your Time:** Spend the day in town, then head up the mountain late in the day for sunset views.
- 🖐 **Also See:** BREGENZERWALD, DORNBIRN.

Sights

Lower Town *(Innenstadt)*

Lake Shore (ABY)

The main shopping streets (pedestrian zone) cluster at the foot of the former fortified city (Oberstadt or Altstadt) of the counts of Bregenz and Montfort. In the Middle Ages, the lake waters still lapped against the base of the little **Seekapelle** (lakeside chapel – **BY**). Insulated from road traffic by the railway, the shady quays and flowerbeds of the lake shore stretch from the **Seeanlagen** (**AY**) to the passenger port. A walk along the landscaped harbor breakwater is particularly pleasant and offers fabulous **views**★ (**BY**) extending to Upper Swabia with the island of Lindau in the foreground. Farther west is the **Festspielhaus** (**AY**), a complex of buildings designed specifically for the Bregenz Festival *(www.bregenzfestspiele.com)*, which hosts cultural events year-round and is the prime venue during the festival. The most spectacular performances, though, are held on the **Seebühne** (**AY**), a floating stage jutting out into the lake outside the festival hall. In 2008 the floating stage features in a scene in the James Bond film, *Quantum of Solace.*

Address Book

🖐 *For coin ranges, see cover flap.*

WHERE TO STAY

🍶🍶🍶🍶 **Weißes Kreuz** – *Römerstr. 5.* ☎*0 55 74/4 98 80. 44 rooms.* A short walk from the lake shore, this 100-year-old hotel has combined exposed beams with modern innovations.

WHERE TO EAT

🍶🍶🍶🍶 **Neubeck** – *Anton Schneider St. 5.* ☎*05574/43609. www.neubeck. at. Closed Sun–Mon, public holidays.* Eat in the elegant dining-room or the Mediterranean Wintergarden. French and Asian cuisine are specialties.

WHERE TO SHOP

Wolford – *Wolfordstraße 1–2. Open Mon–Thu 9am–19.30pm, Fri 9am–9pm, Sat 9am–5pm (boutique, outlet shop, restaurant). www.wolford.com.* Famous for fashionable and high-quality legwear and lingerie, Wolford offers products and items from well-known partners at its two shops.

BREGENZ			Bahnhofstr.		AY	Maurachgasse		BY	12
			Kaiserstr.		BY	5	Mehrerauer Str.	AY	15
Am Steinenbach	BY	14	Kirchstr.		BYZ	6	Rathausstr.	BY	16
Amtsstorstr.	BZ	2	Kornmarktstr.		BY	8	Thalbachgasse	BZ	17
Anton-Schneider-Str.	BY	3	Leutbühel		BY	9			

Vorarlberger Landesmuseum★ (BY)

🕐 *Jun 21–Aug, daily 10am–8pm; early Sept–early Oct, Tue–Sun 10am–6pm, Thu until 8pm.* ⊜€6. ☎0 55 74/4 60 50. www.vlm.at.

The collections are particularly well displayed in the prehistory and Roman departments on the first floor. The second floor presents folkloric costumes and musical instruments, including a fancily carved portable organ from the early 16C. The third floor focuses on religious art scavenged from the richest churches in the province, including an early 16C crucifix from the former abbey church at Mehrerau. On the same floor are works of mythological or religious inspiration and portraits *(Duke of Wellington)* by **Angelika Kauffmann** (1741–1807), considered a native of the Vorarlberg because of her connection with the Bregenzerwald. She lived in Rome, Venice and England, where she was a founding member of the Royal Academy in 1768 and a follower of Reynolds.

On nearby Karl-Tizian-Platz and close to the shores of Bodensee is the 1997 **Kunsthaus Bregenz★ (BY)**, an unapologetically modernist structure by Swiss master architect Peter Zumthor. Behind

Bregenz

the striking façade of etched glass are changing contemporary art exhibits.

Upper Town *(Oberstadt)* and Church Quarter

With its quiet squares and lanes, this charming quarter makes for a peaceful contrast to the bustling lake shore. It can be reached by car via the Kirchstraße, the Thalbachgasse, and the Amtsstorstraße. If you're walking, stroll up from the central intersection of the Leutbühel by the paved ramp of the Maurachgasse as far as the Martinstor, an old fortified gateway.

Altes Rathaus

The 17C, half-timbered Old Town Hall was built in 1662 and remained the seat of the municipal authorities until the 19C. A relief shows the Celtic goddess of agriculture, Epona, on horseback holding a horn of plenty.

Martinsturm (BY)

🕐 *May–Oct, daily 9am–6pm.* ⊕*1€.* ☏*0 55 74/4 66 32.*

A Bregenz landmark, this 13C tower only got its huge onion dome (one of the largest in Austria) around 1600. The chapel in the tower base contains a massive Late Gothic altar canopy and fairly well preserved 14C frescoes. Upstairs is a small military museum through whose windows you can enjoy **glimpses**⋆ of the remains of the wall, the old town,

the lake and belfries of Lindau and, in the distance, the Appenzell Alps.

Pfarrkirche St. Gallus (BZ)

This streamside single-nave Baroque church is decorated in the restrained ecclesiastical style typical of the Vorarlberg churches, which contrasts with the more opulent style of the Tirolean and Bavarian churches of the same period. The walnut stalls were made about 1740 for the nearby abbey of Mehrerau and are decorated with effigies of saints.

Excursion

Pfänder★★

Summer mists make it advisable to do this excursion either in the early morning or in the evening before sunset. Leave Bregenz on **1** *(👣see map) and take the lakeside road to Lindau.*

To drive up the Pfänder, turn right toward the village of **Lochau**. Past the church in Lochau turn right onto the steep and twisting by-road, which reaches a parking lot (fee) after about 6km/3.7mi. From here, you can get out and take the 15min walk to the Pfänder summit (1 064m/3 491ft).

If you continue driving for another half a mile or so, you reach a plateau with the Pfänder mountain refuge (🅿*fee-based parking available*). From opposite the mountain hut a small trail leads to the Pfänder summit in a matter of minutes. An alternate way to get up the mountain is by taking the modern **Pfänderbahn cable-car** (🕐 *daily 8am–7pm every 30min;* 🕐 *2nd & 3rd weeks in Nov;* ⊗ *€10.40 round trip;* ☎ *0 55 74/ 42 16 00; www.pfaenderbahn.at*).

The breathtaking **panorama**★ from the plateau takes in—from left to right— the Allgäu Alps, the snow-covered Schesaplana, the great furrow of the Rhine and the Altmann, and the Säntis on the Swiss side. Paragliders contribute to the scenery as well.

North of the plateau is the **Alpenwildpark** game reserve where a 30min circuit introduces you to Alpine fauna such as moufflons, ibex, marmots and red deer, housed in generous enclosures. The circuit also takes you past the eagle observation point where there are **bird of prey flight displays** twice a day in summer (*Displays (40min)* 🕐*May–Sept, daily 11am, 2.30pm;* ⊗*€4.80;* ☎*06 64/9 05 30 40*).

BREGENZERWALD★★

VORARLBERG

Its German name implies that the Bregenzerwald is a dense forest. However, it is in fact a wonderfully diverse natural playground with landscapes ranging from softly rolling hills to majestic Alpine peaks. The unspoiled countryside, the traditional wooden houses and villages, and a local population that still cherishes their ancient customs, make the Bregenzerwald a popular destination.

- 🛈 **Information:** Gerbe 1135, A-6863 Egg. ☎0 55 12/23 65. www.bregenzerwald.at.
- ▶ **Orient Yourself:** The Bregenzerwald is located between Bregenz on Lake Constance and the Arlberg range.
- ⊙ **Don't Miss:** Rappenlochschlucht.
- [Kids] **Especially for Kids:** Inatura in Dornbirn.

Driving Tour

Hochtannenbergstraße

65km/40.4mi

▶ *The road between Warth and Schröcken may be closed for several days at a time between November and March because of risk of avalanches.*

This route crosses the **Hochtannberg pass** (1 675m/5 495ft), which is closed occasionally, and follows the twisting Bregenzerach River. The crossing of the Bödele pass lends a mountainous character to the final leg of the trip and gives magnificent views of the Rhine Valley. Between Warth and Nesslegg the road runs through the Hochtannberg pastureland.

Nesslegg★

From the viewpoint by the Hotel Widderstein, you'll have a fine overview of the cirque closing the upper valley of the Bregenzerach. From left to right you can see the Mohnenfluh, the Braunarlspitz and its snowfields, the Hochberg, the Schadonapass gap, and the Hochkünzelspitze.

From Nesslegg, the road plunges down through forest, offering occasional glimpses of the village of **Schröcken**. Downstream from the splendidly engineered Hochtannberg bridge appears the hamlet of **Unterboden**, a typical Valaisian settlement. Between Schoppernau and the resort of **Mellau**, the varied form of the Kanisfluh is revealed; its north face is formed of particularly steep cliffs. The road continues through a succession of idyllic landscapes. Farther on, wide valleys with their fruit-growing enterprises are graced by the villages of **Bezau** and Schwarzenberg.

Damüls Uga, Bregenzerwald

Schwarzenberg

This sleepy village is centered on a pretty **square**★ flanked by flower-festooned houses (e.g. Gasthof Hirschen). The parish church features several works by the famous artist, **Angelika Kauffmann** (1741–1807), including the medallions representing the Apostles and Jesus' disciples, and the picture on the high altar. Look for the artist's bust on the north wall of the nave. More of her works can be seen in the Vorarlberger Landesmuseum in Bregenz and the Heimatmuseum in Schwarzenberg.

Crossing the Bödele ridge gives clear **views**★ to the east of the open basin of the Bregenzerwald and the Allgäu Alps marking the German border. On the Rhine slope, after a long run through forest, the **panorama**★ opens out near **Ammenegg** extending, in clear weather, to Lake Constance and the Appenzell Alps.

Dornbirn Kids

The largest town in Vorarlberg, Dornbirn has few tourist-worthy sights. An exception is the child-friendly **Inatura** *(Jahngasse 9;* ◔ *daily 10am–6pm;* ◈ *€9.50, children 6–15 €4.80;* ☏ *0 55 72/2 32 35; www.inatura.at)*, a modern and edutaining journey into the natural history of the Vorarlberg. Experiences include a visit to an underwater cinema and a virtual trip back into prehistoric times.

▶ *Leave Dornbirn on the road toward Ebnit/Gütle. After about 3.5km/2.2mi you reach the parking lot for the Rappenlochschlucht* 🅿.

Rolls-Royce-Museum

Gütle 11a. ◔ *Apr–Oct, Tue–Sun 10am–6pm; Nov–Mar, Tue–Sun 10am–5pm.* ◈ *€8.* ☏ *0 55 72/5 26 52. www.rolls-royce-museum.at.*

A 19C textile factory houses the world's largest collection of Rolls Royces with more than 1 000 vehicles, including those once used by the Queen Mother, King George V, Prince Ali Khan, and Spanish dictator General Francisco Franco. A reconstruction of F. H. Royce's garage gives an insight into his work more than a hundred years ago.

Rappenlochschlucht★

▶ *Allow about 1hr 30min for the walk as far as the road to Ebnit.*

◔ *Mid-Apr–late Oct.* ☏ *0 55 72/ 2 21 88. www.rappenlochschlucht.at.* ◉ *Free guided walks Jul–mid-Sept, Thu 10.30am, meeting at the Gasthof Gütle parking lot* 🅿.

About a 20min walk along wooden walkways above the turbulent waters of the Dornbirner Ache brings you to the mighty rocky cliffs of the 72m/236ft Rappenloch gorge.

Beyond here, a path along the Staufensee reservoir and power station leads to the Alploch gorge, which is still impressive with its waterfall if less breathtaking than the Rappenloch. It takes about 20min as far as the Ebnit road. From here, retrace your steps to the parking lot.

KäseStraße Bregenzerwald

Strictly speaking, the *KäseStraße* (Cheese Road) in Bregenzerwald is not a set route from one sight to another, rather it is an association of farms producers, dairies, guesthouses, and inns and restaurants that either produce, sell, or serve local cheeses. What you visit is your choice depending on your interests. Hikers, cyclists and motorists can each choose their own routes on this 70km/43.5mi route. There are mountain huts where cheese is made in the traditional way that are only accessible on foot.

Old sawmills are included as they provided the wood used to produce the cheese-making tools and the moulds. Numerous restaurants serve typical cheese dishes including fried cheese and cheese dumplings.

All members of the association are signposted with, and display the letter "K" (for *Käsestraße*). To find out more, contact ☎0 55 12/ 2 36 50. or visit *www.kaesestrasse.at.*

BRUCK AN DER MUR★

STEIERMARK
POPULATION 15 090
ALT 481M/1 578FT

Bruck is lorded over by the romantically ruined fortress of Landskron. It's a busy, industrial town whose main sights orbit Koloman-Wallisch-Platz, the main square.

- ℹ **Information:** Koloman-Wallisch-Platz 26, A-860. ☎0 38 62/5 18 11. www.bruckmur.at.
- ▶ **Orient Yourself:** Bruck an der Mur lies at the confluence of the Mur and Mürz rivers in northern Styria, about 50km/31mi north of Graz.
- 🅿 **Parking:** Alongside the Mürz on Wienerstraße.
- 😊 **Don't Miss:** Eiserner Brunnen.
- 🚲 **Also See:** LEOBEN.

A Bit of History

Bruck an der Mur flourishd during the 14C and 15C due to its trade with Venice. The town became famous for the wrought-ironwork of its blacksmiths especially local master craftsman, Hans Prasser, which can be seen in several places in the town.

Sights

Eiserner Brunnen★★ (A)

The ornate fountain (1626) by local artisan Hans Prasser is considered a superb example of Styrian wrought-ironwork.

Old Houses

Bruck still has several 15C and 16C houses with arcaded courtyards, most notably the **Rathaus** (A R – town hall) and the **Flössmeisterhaus** *(no. 5)* (B B). The nicest historic building, though, is the **Kornmesserhaus** ★ (B), named for its builder, the wealthy merchant Pankraz Kornmess.

Pfarrkirche (A)

This Gothic parish church counts among its highlights a wrought-iron **sacristy door**, believed to come from the Kornmesserhaus, and a fine late 18C **altar of the Holy Cross** in the north side chapel.

| Flößmeisterthaus | B | B | Rathaus | A | R |

DACHSTEIN★★

SALZBURG, STEIERMARK UND OBERÖSTERREICH

The Dachstein massif (highest point 2 995m/9 826ft) forms a superb backdrop to several Alpine lakes. The range is also honeycombed by labyrinthine cave systems formed millions of years ago.

🛈 **Information:** Kirchengasse 4, A-4822 Bad Goisern. ☎0 61 35/83 29. www.inneres-salzkammergut.at.
▸ **Orient Yourself:** The Dachstein massif forms the southern border of the Salzkammergut region.
🅿 **Parking:** Plenty of parking at the cable-car stations.
🅐 **Don't Miss:** Cable-car ride to Krippenstein, Giant Ice Caves, Hunerkogel.
🕓 **Organizing Your Time:** Allow a day each for the North Face and the South Face; more if you plan to do any hiking.
🖕 **Also See:** SCHLADMINGER TAUERN, SALZKAMMERGUT.

Driving Tour

Dachstein Circuit

Tour★★ *218km/135.5mi*

(*See Salzkammergut Map Tour* **4**)

Bad Ischl⚕ 🖕*See BAD ISCHL.*

▸ *Head south from Bad Ischl along the little river Kaltenbach and via Bad Goisern to Steeg and along the western shore of Hallstätter See to Hallstatt.*

Hallstatt★★ 🖕*See HALLSTATT.*

▸ *For the last part of the way, continue through the tunnel to Obertraun.*

Ascent of the Krippenstein★★

🕐 *Cable-car operates May–mid-Oct & Christmas–Easter, daily 8.40am–5pm every 15min. Summer ☞€13.90 round trip; winter €30.10 ski pass. ☎0 61 34/84 00. From Hallstatt, 4km/2.5mi in the direction of Obertraun; then bear right 2km/1.2mi beyond the end of the lake.*

The cable-car drops off visitors to the caves at the **Schönbergalpe** *(alt 1 345m/4 413ft)* station, before continuing to the upper station.

Enjoy sweeping **views**★★ of the Dachstein plateau from the chapel *(alt 2 109m/6 919ft)*. To get a **bird's-eye view**★★ of the lake at Hallstatt, follow the marked path at the beginning of the Krippenstein road to the Pioneers' Cross (Pionierkreuz, *allow an extra 30min*).

Dachstein-Rieseneishöhle★

2hr 30min walk from Obertraun or a ride on the Krippensteinbahn cable-car to Schönbergalpe followed by 15min walk. 🚡*Warm clothing is advisable.* 🌬*Guided tour (1hr) May–mid-Oct, daily 9.20am–4pm, early Jun–Aug, daily 9.20am–4.30pm.* ☞ € 9.80. ☎0 61 34/84 00.

The spectacular Giant Ice Cave, whose ice draperies, icicles and other formations are illuminated by colored lights, can only be seen guided tour. It is one of Europe's largest subterranean ice caves.

Mammuthöhle

30min there and back on foot from Schönbergalpe station. 1km/.6mi walk through the cave. 🌬*Guided tour (1hr) mid-May–Oct, daily 9.20am–2.30pm.* ☞€9.80. ☎0 61 34/84 00.

These limestone caves were carved by a subterranean river and are not as impressive as the Giant Ice Cave, but a tour is still worth it for the excellent sound and light show.

▶ *Return and turn left at Gosaumühle.*

After passing under the saltwater aqueduct *(Soleleitung)* the road enters a valley carved by the Gosaubach creek.

▶ *Turn toward the Gosauseen lakes and park at the end of the road.*

Gosauseen★★★

👁*See GOSAUSEEN.*

▶ *Backtrack north to Gosau; turn left onto the Gschütt pass road.*

Abtenau

This resort in the Lammertal at the foot of the Kogel is a popular departure point for hikes. The drive to St. Wolfgang along the **Postalmstraße** *(toll payable)* is especially scenic. The Postalm is the largest area of Alpine meadows in Austria, and Europe's second-largest high-lying plateau.

▶ *Return east; turn right to Annaberg along the "Salzburg Dolomites" road.Take the road NE out of Eben im Pongau to Filzmoos.*

Filzmoos★

Towering above the village is the distinctive outline of the **Bischofsmütze** (Bishop's Mitre, *alt 2 454m/8 051ft*). In summer, Filzmoos is a great base for walks in the surrounding mountains. A climb to the **Gerzkopf**★★ summit *(1 729m/5 673ft, 4hr round trip walk from Schattbach)* is particularly recommended.

Rossbrand★★

After taking the Papagenobahn cable-car, follow the easy ridge trail west to the summit *(2hr round trip)*. The great **panorama**★★ takes in 150 peaks, mainly of the Dachstein range, the Schladminger Tauern, the Ankogel range, the Hohe Tauern and the Hochkönig.

▶ *Carry on toward Ramsau. After 12km/7.4mi, turn left and then take a small toll road to the right up to the foot of the Hunerkogel.*

Hunerkogel★★★

Alt 1 700m/5 576ft.

🕐*Cable-car operates Jun–end Apr, daily 8.30am–4.50pm. ☞€20.40 round trip. ☎0 36 87/8 12 41, allow at least 1hr round trip.*

From the end of the toll road, the Hunerkogel (2 700m/8 858ft) can be seen looming like some impregnable fortress. The ascent of the sheer rock face by the **Dachstein-Südwand-bahn** cable-car (also known as the Gletscherbahn Ramsau) is spectacular. The new Sky-Walk platform at the top offers breathtaking views of the craggy peaks.

Ramsau am Dachstein★
Alt 1 150m/3 773ft.
Ramsau is a hiker's delight, even in winter when 70km/43.5mi of groomed trails make walking easy. The **cross-country skiing** ★★★ is excellent here, with over 150km/93.2mi of tracks. The nearby Dachstein glacier also offers cross-country ski tracks at an altitude of 2 700m/8 858ft.

▶ *The road follows the Enns valley to Trautenfels.*

Schloss Trautenfels
Apr 8–Oct, daily 9am–5pm. €6.
0 36 82/2 22 33.
With origins in the 13C, this is a lovely Baroque country palace with richly decorated rooms, including stuccowork and valuable frescoes by Carpoforo Tencalla. The collection of antlers is impressive.

▶ *At the Trautenfels crossroads, turn left on road no. 145.*

Pürgg
Art lovers should go up to the bluff-top **Johanneskapelle**, a small chapel endowed with some terrific **Romanesque frescoes** depicting the Annunciation, the Birth of Christ, a fabulous fight between cats and mice, the Wise and Foolish Virgins and other scenes.

Bad Mitterndorf⚜

This place is known both as a spa and a winter sports resort.

Bad Aussee⚜ *See BAD AUSSEE.*

Grundlsee★ and Toplitzsee★
See BAD AUSSEE: Excursions.

▶ *Return to Bad Ischl via the Pötschenhöhe pass (alt 992m/ 3 255ft) and road no. 145.*

DONAUTAL★★
DANUBE VALLEY – OBERÖSTERREICH AND NIEDERÖSTERREICH

The Danube is the longest river in Central Europe (2 826km/1 756mi) and the second longest in Europe. It flows through or skirts 10 states, and four capital cities have been built on its banks, bearing witness to its importance.

🛈 **Information:** Lindengasse 9, A-4040. ☎73 22 21 022. www.oberoesterreich. at/donau.ooe (for Upper Ausria section); Schlossgasse 3, A-3620 Spitz an der Donau. ☎0 27 13/3 00 60 60. www.donau.com (for Lower Austria section)

▶ **Orient Yourself:** The Danube is Austrian for 360km/223.7mi from Achleiten, near the German border, to Hainburg, near Bratislava.

😊 **Don't Miss:** Wachau with Melk Abbey, Artstetten Castle & Museum, Krems und Stein, Vienna.

🕐 **Organizing Your Time:** Allow five days to complete the length of the Austrian Danube.

👁 **Also See:** PASSAU, LINZ, DURNSTEIN, MELK, KREMS UND STEIN, WIEN.

A Bit of History

The Austrian section of the Danube is entirely navigable and has always been a vital artery for the country's economy. As such, its banks are graced with time-worn fortified castles, gracious Renaissance palaces, and beautiful churches and abbeys that will captivate most visitors. These buildings tell the long and varied history of the river that composers and writers have praised in word and music. Although its waters may not always be the color evoked in the famous Strauss-waltz-song *The Blue Danube* from 1867, this stream still meanders through plenty of idyllic scenery.

Driving Tours

1 From Passau to Linz
86km/53.4mi

From Passau (in Germany) to Aschach, the route runs along the south bank of the river. From the north bank rise the granite heights of the Mühlviertel.

Passau★★

The well-preserved old town of Passau occupies a tongue of land between the Danube and the Inn, its cobbled streets clustered around the cathedral of St. Stephan. Overlooking the "town of three rivers" (the Danube, Inn and Ilz converge here) from their hilltop perches are the formidable Oberhaus fortress to the north and the Baroque pilgrimage church of Mariahilf to the south. From either vantage point, you'll have highly photogenic views of the town.
For a more detailed description see The Green Guide Germany.

▶ *Leave Passau by crossing the Inn and heading toward Linz.*

The wide and majestic river parallels the road, carving through wooded, rocky slopes. At Obernzell, it spills out into the reservoir of the Jochenstein dam, a magnificent lake. The **Jochenstein power station** generates 850 million kWh annually. From Engelhartszell to Wesenufer the valley narrows. The cliff-top road offers some fine views, with various castles occasionally coming into view in the distance. A little after **Wesenufer**, a pretty village with flowered balconies, the road leaves the riverbank and climbs through a wooded gorge to the picturesque Aschach Valley. Beyond here, it crosses the Danube below another one of five Donau power stations, the **Aschach-Kraftwerk**, one of the largest power stations of its kind in Europe.

▶ *Beyond Ottensheim and its dam, the road follows the river to Linz.*

2 From Linz to Grein
72km/45mi

Linz★ *See LINZ.*

Below Linz, the valley opens out into a wide, fertile basin where wheat, sugarbeet, and fruit trees flourish. To the north lie the slopes and forested ridges of the Mühlviertel and farther on, the Waldviertel.

▶ *Leave Linz to the southeast via St.-Peterstraße toward Grein.*

The road continues through the industrial zone of Linz and crosses the Danube at the Steyregg bridge beyond which it cuts across a plateau to return to the Danube plain at St. Georgen.

▶ *Take the turn toward the camp (Lager) at Mauthausen.*

Mauthausen ॐ *See MAUTHAUSEN.*

From Mauthausen to Dornach the road crosses a vast cultivated plain that gradually changes to a wooded landscape.

▶ *Near Saxen turn right toward Burg Clam.*

Burg Clam★
Guided tour (45min) May–end Oct, daily 10am–5.30pm. ॐ€8. ☎0 72 69/7 21 70. www.burgclam.com.
Dominated by its central tower, the castle rises romantically from its leafy surroundings. The rock on which it

stands has been fortified since 1149. The residential part of the castle revolves around the charmingly irregular arcaded Renaissance **courtyard**★. Inside, highlights include an unusually complete **pharmacy** from 1603, fine Vienna and Meissen porcelain, and some rare Louis XVI armchairs.

▶ *Return to the Danube road.*

Below Dornach the road hugs the north bank of the river whose waters are hemmed in by rocky, wooded slopes. The approach to Grein is particularly pretty.

Grein
This charming summer resort town is dominated by the hills of the Mühlviertel. Turreted houses frame the pretty Stadtplatz (town square), while the parish church contains an 18C high altar with an altarpiece by Bartolomäus Altomonte. Grein is justifiably proud of its little **Rokoko-Theater** (*guided tour (20min) Apr–end Oct, daily 9am, 11am, 1.30pm and 4pm;* ॐ€2.50; ☎0 72 68/ 70 55) in the town hall. Made entirely of wood, it dates back to the end of the 18C and is still in use every summer.

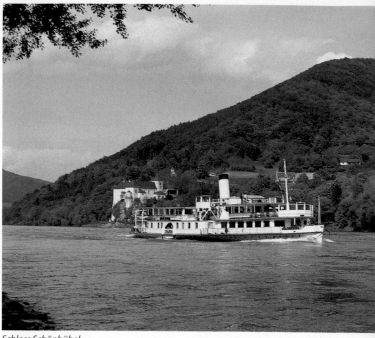

Schloss Schönbühel

Greinburg Castle

Still under the ownership of the House of Saxe-Coburg-Gotha, is a four-winged structure wrapped around a romantic fountain-studded Renaissance **courtyard**★ with three tiers of arcades. Inside, the **Schifffahrtsmuseum** (🕐*Jun–end Sept, Tue–Sun 10am–6pm; May & Oct, Tue–Sun 10am–noon & 1pm–5pm;* 💶*€2.20;* ☎*0 72 68/70 07)* is a local navigation museum with models of bridges, landing-stages and locks as well as works of art evoking life on the great river in this part of Austria.

③ From Grein to Krems
95km/59mi

Between Grein and Krems stretches the most picturesque section of the Danube Valley in Austria. It is hollowed out of the granite of the Waldviertel, which forms the last foothills of the Bohemian massif.

Grein ♿*Description under* ②.

From Grein to Ybbs, the **Strudengau**★, wedged between high wooded cliffs that are often shrouded in mist, provides a heroic and romantic setting. The castle ruins of Burg Struden and Burg Sarmingstein are particularly eye-catching. The river embraces willow-covered islands, then expands into a splendid lake formed by the Ybbs-Persenbeug dam.

Persenbeug

The last Austrian emperor, Karl I, was born in this rocky castle in 1887. The valley surrounding Persenbeug features in the legendary Middle High German epic poem, the *Nibelungenlied (The Song of the Nibelungs)*. It was here, in the **Nibelungengau**, that Gunther and Hagen undertook their rides through the forest and where they gathered their knights to go to Attila's court at the invitation of Kriemhild, who had married the King of the Huns to avenge the murder of her first husband, Siegfried.

In a splendid **site**★ on a hillock to the left is the 1660 pilgrimage church of **Maria Taferl**, with its splendid façade and dome by Jakob Prandtauer.

© Österreich Werbung/Jezierzanski

Artstetten Castle and Museum★★ 👍 *See SCHLOSS-MUSEUM ARTSTETTEN.*

▶ *Take the bridge over the Danube to Melk.*

Melk Abbey★★★ 👍 *See MELK.*

The 35km/21.7mi stretch of the Danube between Melk and Krems is known as the **Wachau**★★. It's a picturesque and fertile region famous for its apricots (locally known as *Marillen*) and dotted with delightful villages, good restaurants using local specialties, clifftop fortresses, and onion-domed churches.

Schönbühel

From the main road, **Schloss Schönbühel** can be spotted on the south bank, its rocky promontory setting and onion-domed tower creating a charming picture.

▶ *Take the road on the north bank toward Krems.*

Burgruine Aggstein★

Its exceptional **site**★, some 300m/984ft above the Danube, and its colossal size, made this 12C fortress one of Austria's finest strongholds in its heyday. The ruined towers and defensive walls are still an impressive sight today. A steep path *(2hr round trip walk)* leads from Aggstein hamlet up to the castle gate. At the top you'll be treated to superb views.

At **Willendorf** a 25 000-year-old limestone statue, known as the **Venus of Willendorf**★, was found in 1906. It is now kept in Vienna at the Naturhistorisches Museum *(👍 see WIEN).*

Spitz★

Placid Spitz lies half-hidden behind a curtain of fruit trees below a terraced vineyard. Spitz has fine old town houses, especially along Schlossgasse, which leads to the 17C castle. The Gothic **Pfarrkirche** *(🕐Apr–Sept, daily 8am–7pm; Oct–Mar, daily 8am–5pm; ☎0 27 13/22 31)* has an unusual chancel out of line with the nave. The organ loft is adorned with statues of Christ and the 12 Apostles (c. 1420). The altar-

piece (1799) by Kremser Schmidt over
the Baroque altar shows the martyrdom
of St. Maurice.

Weissenkirchen

This wine-growing village has an imposing, Gothic, fortified church lording it
above a pretty town with cobbled path-
ways and fine old houses.

Wachaumuseum

◷_Apr–Oct, Tue–Sun 10am–5pm._ ◉€5.
☏_0 27 15/22 68._
The museum is housed in the Teisen-
hoferhof, a 16C fortified farm with an
arcaded courtyard and a richly decorated covered gallery. Inside are works
by Wachau painters (from the turn of
the 20C).

Dürnstein★ _♨See DÜRNSTEIN._

4 From Krems to Vienna
_83km/51.5mi_

Krems und Stein★★
♨See KREMS und STEIN.

▸ _Cross the Danube on the great steel_
bridge at Stein, west of Krems.

A little after Mautern on the right,
crowning a wooded hill, stands the
impressive Benedictine abbey called
Stift Göttweig. It has a grand Imperial
staircase adorned with a ceiling fresco
by Paul Troger, and a wonderfully exuberant Baroque church.

Tulln _♨See TULLN._

At Greifenstein, with its privately owned
castle near the Vienna Woods, the valley
narrows, and the road squeezes through
a passage between the river and high
wooded hills.

Klosterneuburg★
♨See KLOSTERNEUBURG.

The road then enters the suburbs
of Vienna.

Vienna★★★ _♨See WIEN._

4 From Vienna to Hainburg
_84km/52mi_

The route follows the south bank of
the river through a wide valley.

▸ _Leave Vienna on the B 9 for_
Schwechat, famous for its
breweries and giant oil refinery.

Petronell-Carnuntum
♨See PETRONELL-CARNUNTUM.

The range of hills between Bad Deutsch-
Altenburg and Hainburg are the Little
Carpathians, the last outrunners of the
mountains encircling the Hungarian
plain.

Hainburg

Hainburg had an important strategic
role in the Middle Ages on the highway
linking Vienna and Bratislava. The town
close to the Slovakian border still retains
its ring of walls and fortified gateways
from the 13C. Above the town are the
remains of its 11C castle.

DÜRNSTEIN ★

NIEDERÖSTERREICH
POPULATION 1 000
ALT 209M/686FT

Dürnstein, considered the "pearl" of the Wachau region, lies above a scenic bend of the Danube and boasts a bevy of beautiful old houses. Girded by ancient walls, it is crowned by a ruined fortress where Richard I (the Lionheart) was once held prisoner.

- **Information:** Rathaus, A-3601, ☎0 27 11/2 19. www.duernstein.at.
- ▶ **Orient Yourself:** The town is in the heart of the Wachau, about 90km/56mi west of Vienna.
- **Don't Miss:** Monastery church of Stift Dürnstein.
- **Organizing Your Time:** Budget one or two hours.
- **Also See:** KREMS, SCHLOSS GRAFENEGG, STIFT MELK, SCHLOSS-MUSEUM ARTSTETTEN.

A Bit of History

Richard the Lionheart

Shortly after being crowned King of England in 1189, Richard I (1157–99), better known as Richard the Lionheart, set out to lead the ill-fated 3rd Crusade to liberate Jerusalem from Sultan Saladin. Diplomacy was not his forte, and he clashed with the Austrian Duke, Leopold V, during the conquest of Acre in 1191. Returning from the crusade, he was taken prisoner at an inn near Vienna and held for several months at the fortress in Dürnstein. Here, according to legend, he was tracked down by his faithful minstrel, Blondel. Blondel could not rescue his master, however, who was tranferred to Emperor Heinrich VI and held prisoner for almost a year at Trifels Castle (Germany) before being granted his liberty for an enormous ransom in 1194.

Sights

Stift Dürnstein

🕐 Apr–end Oct, Mon–Sat 9am–6pm, Sun 10am–6pm. ⊚€2.60. ☎0 27 11/3 75. www.stiftduernstein.at (German only).
The former Augustine canons' monastery was founded in the 15C and got its Baroque look in the 18C courtesy of master architect Josef Munggenast. A splendid gate leads into the courtyard surrounded by old monastic buildings, but the most striking element is the church's landmark blue and white **tower**★. The church interior is adorned with restrained stuccowork and curved wooden balconies, while the side chapels house paintings by Kremser Schmidt.

Castle Ruins

45min round trip walk.
The trail to the castle ruins (*Burgruine*) begins at the ramparts east of the town and is worth the climb for the remarkable **view** of Dürnstein and the valley.

Dürnstein

© Österreich Werbung / Diejun

SCHLOSS EGGENBERG★★

STEIERMARK

This delightful Baroque palace is the largest in Styria. It was begun in 1825 at the behest of Johann Ulrich von Eggenberg, who required a suitably representative building after his promotion to governor of Inner Austria the same year. The palace is surrounded by a lovely park that's perfect for taking a stroll.

- **Information:** http://cms.graztourismus.at.
- ▶ **Orient Yourself:** 3.5km/2.2mi west of Graz
- **Don't Miss:** Planetensaal, Alte Galerie, Strettweg Votive Chariot, Planetengarten.
- **Organizing Your Time:** Start with a tour of the state rooms, then check out some of the museums and finish up with a wander round the gardens.
- **Also See:** GRAZ, MURTAL.

A Bit of History

Architectural theme

The castle was owned by the Eggenburg family from 1460 and was enlarged in 1623 by Johann Ulrich who had become Ferdinand II's first minister and wanted a residence that would match his status. The Italian architect **Pietro de Pomis** conceived an elaborately detailed allegory of the universe, teeming with images and symbols of the cosmos and the four elements. The four towers stand for the four cardinal points of the compass and there are 365 windows; one for every day of the year. There's also a suite of 24 state rooms symbolizing every hour of the day, which in turn are illuminated by 52 windows, one for every week of the year.

Visit

From the landscaped grounds where deer and peacock roam free you enter the impressive galleried courtyard.

State Apartments (Prunkräume)★★★

2nd floor. ✎Guided tour (45min) Easter–Oct, Tue–Sun 10am–6pm; Nov–Mar until 5pm; tours on the hour except 1pm. €7 (admission free Oct 26). ☎ 03 16/58 32 64. www.museum-joan neum.steiermark.at.
The palace jewel is the **Planet Hall**★★★ (Planetensaal), a sizeable festival hall festooned with elaborate frescoes of the planets, the signs of the Zodiac and the four elements painted by the Styrian artist Hans Adam Weissenkirchner. The hall gives way to a ring of 24 equally lavish staterooms, decorated in a hodgepodge of themes ranging from classical mythology to oriental fables and Biblical scenes. There are also three rooms with Chinese and Japanese décor, a style very much en vogue at the time.

Museums

State room tickets also include admission to the palace's three collections from the Landesmuseum Joanneum, Austria's oldest public museum headquartered in Graz.

Alte Galerie★★

Moved here from Graz several years ago, the spectacular Old Gallery presents paintings and sculptures from the 13C to the Baroque in 22 rooms, innovatively presented by theme rather than chronology. Star pieces worth keeping an eye out for include a stained- glass *Admont Madonna* from 1320, a *Martyrdom of St. Thomas à Becket* by Michael Pacher from 1470–80, and a large Mariazell altarpiece from 1518–22. There are also important works by Jan Bruegel the Elder, Pieter Brueghel the Younger, Lucas Cranach the Elder, and German Baroque artists such as Johann Michael Rottmayr, Josef Stammel, and Paul Troger.

R. Chérer/MICHELIN

Schloss Eggenberg

Ur- und Frühgeschichtliche Sammlung

The Pre- and Early History Collection presents archeological findings from the Stone Age through the early Middle Ages, including the world-famous 2 700-year-old impressively ornamented bronze **Strettweg Votive Chariot**★★, a moving work from the Hallstatt period. It was found in a burial mound near Judenburg in Styria. The chariot is surrounded by soldiers and hunters on horseback and on foot, and the sculptor has captured them performing the swirling movements of a ritual dance.

Münzensammlung

The coin cabinet had its origin in the private collection of Archduke Johann and is the second largest of its kind in Austria. It includes 17C coins stamped with the profile of Johann Ulrich von Eggenberg himself.

Planetengarten★★

Just like the main palace, the design of the newly restored Planet Garden is a romantic allegory of the universe. Along the northern edge of the palace grounds, it poetically reflects the seven then-known planets through plants, trees and flowers.

EGGENBURG★

NIEDERÖSTERREICH
POPULATION 3 658
ALT 325M/1 066FT

The town of Eggenburg features some beautiful medieval and Renaissance architecture and can still boast a historic town center, a town wall preserved almost in its entirety, and three medieval gate towers: The Holturm, the Wahrsagerturm, and the Kanzlerturm.

- **Information:** Krahuletzplatz 1, A-3730. ☎0 29 84/34 00. www.eggenburg.at.
- ▶ **Orient Yourself:** Eggenburg lies between the Waldviertel and the Weinviertel regions.
- **Don't Miss:** Österreichisches Motorradmuseum and the Krahuletz-Museum.
- **Organizing Your Time:** Visit the town before moving on to the museums.
- **Especially for Kids:** Krahuetz-Museum.
- **Also See:** GRAZ.

Sights

Fully preserved walls enclose the center of this town.

Hauptplatz

Eggenburg's main square is lined by charming old houses, including the **Gemaltes Haus** with a sgraffito façade sporting images from the Old Testament. Other outstanding features are the **pillory** (Pranger), the Adlerbrunnen (Eagle Fountain), the Mariensäule (Mary column), and the Trinity plague column.

Krahuletz-Museum★

Apr–Dec, Mon–Fri 9am–5pm, Sat–Sun 10am–5pm. €6; €1.50 children (admission free Oct 26). ☎0 29 84/34 00. www.krahuletzmuseum.at.

This collection of minerals, fossils, and archeological finds is of international standing and was assembled by local geology professor, Johann Krahuletz in the 19C. Cleverly presented, and very hands-on, the informative displays include a **landscape model★** showing the transformation from the "Eggenburg-on-Sea" of 20 million years ago via the primeval Danube of 11 million years ago through the present. Upstairs, exhibits focus on regional cultural history and include an impressive collection of watches and clocks.

There is a geology-themed walking trail outside where you search for fossils—e.g. shells, shark's teeth, and snails—in what was once the Eggenberg Sea.

Österreichisches Motorradmuseum★

Mon–Fri 8am–4pm. Sat, Sun & public hols 10am–5pm. Dec 21–Jan 5. €6; children €3. ☎0 29 84/21 51. www.motorradmuseum.at.

Established in 1980, this was the first museum of its kind. It is still Austria's largest motorcycle collection and boasts around 320 motorcycles, mopeds, scooters, and every other conceivable motorized two-wheeled vehicle in mint condition from every phase of motorcycling history. It is all displayed in a historical factory and is a must for motorbike enthusiasts. Look out for the three-seater Böhmerland 600 from 1929, the longest motorcycle that ever went into production.

Excursions

Stoitzendorf
4km/2.5mi east of Eggenburg on B 303. Follow the signs for "Kellergasse."
Stoitzendorf's **Kellergasse** is an unspoiled example of the roads to be found in Austrian wine-growing areas just outside the villages. It's lined with small, mostly single-story "Presshäuser," where the grapes are pressed. Here in the western wine-growing area, these buildings are embedded in the soft loam soil.

Pulkau
8km/5mi northwest of Eggenburg
Pulkau is a large wine-producing township near the Czech border. It has a **parish church** with traces of early 14C frescoes and the **Heilig-Blut-Kirche** with a 16C altarpiece carved and painted by artists of the Danube School.

Retz
Retz is in northcentral Austria, right on the border with the Czech Republic, about 78km/48.5mi northwest of Vienna.
Retz (population 4 370), near the Thaya Valley, is an important wine-growing and farming center in a hilly region of the Bohemian Forest. The old town still has its medieval ramparts and defensive towers. Its emblem is a windmill, built in 1772 and still operational.

Hauptplatz★
Retz's rectangular main square is anchored by a column to the Holy Trinity and surrounded by several architecturally remarkable buildings. Most notable are the crenelated **Verderberhaus** on the north side and the **Sgraffitohaus**, opposite. The latter is a handsome building with a carved doorway and a façade covered with inscribed maxims. Also here is the ochre-colored **Rathaus**

Pillory, Eggenburg

R. Chéret/MICHELIN

(town hall, with tourism information), which was converted from a Gothic church in the 16C.
Local wines can be sampled during a tour of the **Retzer Erlebniskeller** (*Meet outside the Rathaus; guided tours (1hr 30min) May–Oct, daily 10.30am, 2pm, 4pm; €7; 0 29 42/27 00*). At 21km/13mi long and 30m/98.4ft deep, this is Austria's largest historic wine cellar and was used to store the entire regions wine stock. The wine cellar actually passes under the Hauptplatz.

"Ausg'steckt Is"

In the "Presshaus," the grapes are pressed and the must is then stored in barrels for fermentation in the tunnel-like cellar in back. The Presshaus, however, is not only used for pressing the grapes but also as a wine tavern. Whenever you see a pine or fir branch displayed above the door, this indicates that the vintner is pouring his own wines, alongside such hearty homemade snacks as "Blunzn" (blood sausage), Geselchtes (smoked pork) and Speck (streaky bacon). In fine weather, the nicest seats are in the shade of the walnut trees along Kellergasse.

EISENERZER ALPEN

STEIERMARK

The Eisenerz Alps cradle the astonishing Erzberg on which the industrial power of the former Austrian Empire was built. They join up in the northwest with the limestone Ennstal Alps, whose impressive walls line the Gesäuse Gorge, which became Austria's newest national park in 2003.

- **Information:** Freiheitsplatz 7, A-8790. ☎0 38 48/37 00. www.eisenerz.at.
- ▶ **Orient Yourself:** This mountain range is in upper Styria between the Ennstal and Murtal valleys, which are linked by the Präbichl pass.
- **Don't Miss:** Erzberg and Gesäuse Gorge.
- ⏱ **Organizing Your Time:** Allow a whole day for Erzberg.
- **Kids Especially for Kids:** Erzbergbahn and Erzberg.
- **Also See:** LIENZ.

Sight

Erzberg★★ Kids
Guided 90min tour of exhibition mine May–end Oct, daily 10am–3pm. Trip on the Hauly truck (1hr) P14. Tours of the mine €14. Joint ticket for mine and truck €24. ☎0 38 48/32 00. www.abenteuer-erzberg.at.

A tour of the Erzberg is a highlight of any visit to Styria. The mine can be explored in two ways. Descend into the bowels of the earth on the same train that once transported miners until below-ground mining ceased in 1986. An 800m/2 624ft section of this subterranean labyrinth is now a **Schaubergwerk** (exhibition mine), where you learn all about how the ore was extracted and experience an audiovisual simulation of a blasting. Another unforgettable experience is the trip on the **Hauly**, an 860hp truck with a viewing platform that takes you above ground through many of the 42 slopes, from which there is a fine **view**★ of the town, the landscape, and the blue lake which has formed at the foot of the mountain.

Driving Tours

1 Gesäuse Gorge Tour
44km/27.3mi

Liezen★ See LIENZ.

The 16km/10mi-long **Gesäuse gorge** takes its name from the noise made by the waters of the Enns rushing over their rocky bed. Between Liezen and Admont the road winds along the Enns Valley.

▶ From the touring route, follow the signposts on the left for Frauenberg.

Frauenberg
This pilgrimage church, in Italianate Baroque style, has lavish stucco decoration matching the richly gilded altars and pulpit. The terrace offers a fine **view**★ of Admont and various mountains.

Admont★ See ADMONT.

The best **view of the Gesäuse**★★ comes after Admont (*B 146 at kilometer 93.2, by the bus stop and the turn-off for the village of Weng*), when the magnificent rock faces of the Hochtor unfold before you. There's another fabulous view of this mountain from the Haindlkarbrücke, a bridge over a small tributary of the Enns.

Gstatterboden
This is a popular gateway to the Gesäuse and the starting point for climbing tours.

Hieflau★
The village has a wooded setting where the valley widens.

② The Styrian Iron Road Tour *50km/31mi*

Hieflau★

From Hieflau to Eisenerz the Erzbach Valley has beautiful, winding gorges and offers fine panoramas of the Tamischbachturm (tower). When reaching the basin of Eisenerz, with a view of the **Erzberg**★★, make a small detour to the Leopoldsteiner See.

Leopoldsteiner See★★

This small lake with its deep green waters lies in one of the finest settings in Styria, below the rock cliffs of the Seemauer in the Hochschwab range.

Eisenerz ⓘ*See Excursion.*

Past Eisenerz, the road crosses the **Präbichl Pass** *(alt 1 232m/4 042ft)*. To the northwest the rocky summit of the Pfaffenstein dominates.

Polster★★

About 1hr 30min round trip from the Präbichl, including 30min by **chair-lift** *and 30min on foot.* ⓞ*Chair-lift operates daily 9am–5pm (9am–4pm in winter).* ⓞ*Easter–end May, Nov.* ⓢ*€7.50 two-way trip.* ☎*0 38 49/6 06 00.*
From the summit *(alt 1 910m/6 266ft)*, there is an excellent **view** of the Erzberg, standing out in all its red-brown mass against the green Alpine pastures.

Vordernberg

Informationszentrum der Steirischen Eisenstraße – ♿ⓞ*May–Oct, Mon–Sat 10am–4pm; Nov–Apr, Mon–Sat 9am–noon.* ☎*0 38 49/8 32.*

This market town has several fascinating **monuments** and **museums of technical interest** associated with iron-working.

Ask at the information center about the 🅺🅸🅳🆂 **Erzbergbahn**★★, a railway running from Vordernberg over the Präbichl to Eisenerz, going both around and through the Erzberg. Originally it was built as a cog railway in 1891 and operated with steam hauled trains. In 1978 the line was closed and it is now operated privately by volunteers and enthusiasts.

Leoben ⓘ*See LEOBEN.*

Excursion

Eisenerz

Eisenerz is in northern Styria, about 25km/ 15.5mi north of Leoben.

Eisenerz is an old mining town at the foot of the mighty stepped pyramid of the Erzberg (Ore Mountain). Its silhouette is oddly impressive, especially in late afternoon light. Since 712, more than 230 million tons of ore have been extracted from this mountain, which is the largest opencast ore mine in central

Leopoldsteiner See

© Österreich Werbung / Jezierzanski

Europe. The town istelf is not without charm and is noted for its many historic and pompous buildings, especially around Bergmannplatz.

St. Oswald★
Easter–end Nov, daily 8am–7pm.
0 38 48/22 67.
This Gothic church is the largest fortified house of worship in Styria. It got its fortress-like ramparts in 1532 in order to keep marauding Turkish troops at bay. The tympanum above the north porch has an *Expulsion from the Garden of Eden* showing Adam as a miner. Also worth seeing is the old organ loft. The church is reached by the "Church Stairs" which start at the Bergmannsplatz in the center of town.

Stadtmuseum
Kammerhof, Schulstraße 1. May–Oct, Tue–Fri 9am–noon, 2pm–5pm, Sat 10am–noon, 2pm–5pm; Nov–Apr, Tue–Fri 9am–noon. €3.90. 0 38 48/36 15.
This museum vividly presents the art and culture of those associated with the world of mining, as well as the techniques of mining ore.

Schichturm
This Renaissance style "shift tower" was built in 1582 above the town. The bell was used to call the miners to work. Later the tower was used as a fire watch because of the view over the town. Today it is privately owned. The walk up is worth it for the fine views over the town and of the Erzberg. There is also a nature trail close by.

Leoben

Leoben is about 20km/12.4mi west of Bruck an der Mur, on the Mur River in central Austria.
Leoben has been the center of the Styrian metalworking industry since the Middle Ages thanks to its proximity to the Erzberg with its vast iron ore deposits. The city's industrial suburbs form a striking contrast to its medieval center and the Alpine surroundings.

Old town
The **Hauptplatz** is lined with gracious façades, such as the red 17C **Hacklhaus** with its sculpted decoration. West of here is the **Stadtpfarrkirche St. Xaver** (*daily 8am–7pm; 0 38 42/4 32 36)*, an early Baroque church once part of a Jesuit College. The interior preserves the original **furnishings**★ of 1670, including the richly gilded main altar with its twisted columns framing a painting of St. Francis Xavier by Heinrich Schönfeld.

MuseumsCenter & Kunsthalle★
Kirchgasse 6 & 8. MuseumsCenter. Year-round Tue–Sun 9am–6pm. €5.50. Kunsthalle daily 9am–6pm. fee varies. 0 38 42/4 06 24 08.
In 2004, the sweeping collections of Leoben's local history museum were dusted off, rearranged and presented in a modern, appealing fashion using clever lighting techniques and multimedia technology. Seven themed sections spotlight Leoben's industrial heritage as well as major historical milestones such as the signing of the peace treaty between Napoleon and Emperor Franz II in 1797. It's all housed in a former Jesuit monastery. A modern, purpose-built annex, the **Kunsthalle Leoben**, often presents large-scale, high-caliber temporary exhibits, usually with an ethnological bent.

Stiftskirche Göss
By appointment only.
0 38 42/ 2 21 48.
In the southern suburb of Göss, this **church** counts an early Romanesque **crypt**, unusual twisted pillars resting on star-shaped bases and a richly carved **south porch**★ among its outstanding features. It is surrounded by a former Benedictine convent whose buildings now house the **Gösser brewery**, which is open for tours and also contains a small museum.

EISENSTADT★

BURGENLAND
POPULATION 12 190
ALT 181M/594FT

The administrative capital of the Burgenland, Eisenstadt has a mild climate allowing grapes, peaches, apricots, and almonds to flourish. it is an important market in the region for wine and has a delightful old town. Its main draw card, though, is the legacy of composer Joseph Haydn, who lived here on and off for around 30 years.

- **Information:** Schloss Esterházy, A-7000. ☎0 26 82/6 33 84 15. www.eisenstadt-tourism.at.
- ▶ **Orient Yourself:** About 60km/37.3mi south of Vienna on the south slopes of the Leithagebirge.
- P **Parking:** There are fee-based parking garages at Esterházyplatz, the Rathaus, and Hotel Burgenland.
- **Don't Miss:** Schloss Esterházy, Haydnsaal.
- **Also See:** NEUSIEDLER SEE, BURG FORCHTENSTEIN, WIENER NEUSTADT.

A Bit of History

Haydn's town
The composer, **Joseph Haydn** (1732–1809), was in the employ of Prince Miklós József Esterházy for nearly 30 years, living sometimes at Eisenstadt, sometimes at the Esterháza palace in Hungary. Haydn had been appointed assistant conductor in 1761 and promoted to musical director in 1766. With an orchestra and theater at his disposal, Haydn achieved growing fame.
For Haydn's birthplace at Rohrau see PETRONELL-CARNUNTUM: Excursions.

Sights

Schloss Esterházy★ (A)
Jan–mid-Mar & mid-Nov–Dec, Mon–Thu 9am–5pm, Fri until 3pm; mid-Mar–mid-Nov, Mon–Sun 8.30am–6pm. €6.50. ☎0 26 82/7 19 30 00. www. haydn-zentrum.at.
Eisenstadt was one of the favorite residences of the noble Esterházy clan, the Magyar family that contributed largely to the establishment of the Habsburg rule in Hungary. The original 17C Baroque palace, by Italian architect Carlo Martino Carlone, was built on the site of a medieval fortress and a century later received some Neoclassical touches courtesy of Charles de Moreau. It now houses local administrative offices, but some rooms can be seen by guided tour.

Esterházy Exhibit & Haydnsaal
The highlight of any palace tour is the **Haydnsaal**★, a magnificent hall resplendent with stucco, *grisailles* of Hungarian kings and frescoes with scenes from Greek mythology. In the 18C the marble floor was replaced with parquet for better acoustics, which you'll get to enjoy during a short concert. It was here that Haydn conducted the court orchestra almost nightly. Other rooms recall the importance of the Esterházy family.

Haydn-Haus (A)
21 Haydn-Gasse. *Apr–mid-Nov, daily 9am–5pm.* €4 (admission free Oct 26). ☎ 0 26 82/6 26 52 29. www.haydn-zentrum.at.
The modest Baroque house was bought by Haydn in 1776. Inside are period rooms, a hammer piano, and an organ table (18C), as well as early prints of his compositions.

Kalvarienberg and Haydnkirche ★ (A)
Easter–Oct, daily 9am–noon, 1pm–5pm. €3. ☎0 26 82/6 26 38. www.haydn kirche.at.

Haydn was buried in the Haydnkirche (also known as Bergkirche), after some vicissitudes—his skull was removed and only reunited with the body in 1954. The church is by an artificial hill known as the Kalvarienberg where 24 **Stations of the Cross**★, made of 260 wooden and 60 stone figures, portray the story of the Passion with dramatic intensity and Baroque flair.

Rathaus (B R)

The 17C Renaissance town hall features a highly original façade with three oriel windows, scrolled gables and a round-arched doorway with diamond-cut stonework.

Domkirche (B)

This Late Gothic hall-church from the 15C and 16C is dedicated to St. Martin, patron saint of the Burgenland. A charming pulpit and the choir, complete with organ, remain of the original Late Baroque interior decoration. Note the beautiful relief of the Mount of Olives, dating from before 1500.

Östereichisches Jüdisches Museum★ (A M¹)

Unterberggasse 6. *May–Oct, Tue–Sun 10am–5pm; Nov–Apr, Mon–Thu 9am–4pm, Fri 9am–1pm.* *0 26 82/6 51 45. www.ojm.at.*
When Emperor Leopold I expelled the Jews from Vienna in 1671, many sought

"Court Jews"

Medieval statutes forbade Christians to handle interest on loans, which is why, in the 17C and 18C some Jews came to play a crucial role in financial dealings. The Habsburg rulers appointed "court Jews," who enjoyed freedom of trade. Among them was Samuel Oppenheimer, a banker from Speyer, Germany, who financed Prince Eugen of Savoy's campaigns against the Turks. Another was his son-in-law Samson Wertheimer, who worked for Leopold I, Joseph I and Karl VI. Such privileges remained reserved for a chosen few, and many other members of the Jewish community continued to be oppressed.

refuge in Eisenstadt where a thriving Jewish community sprang up in the Unterberg district. In a former private home, this museum has displays on Jewish holidays as well as an impressive synagogue, which once was private. The Jewish cemetery is nearby at the end of Wertheimergasse.

Landesmuseum (A M²)

Museumsgasse 5. &. ◐*Tue–Sat 9am– 5pm. Sun and hols 10am–5pm.* ◑*Jan 1, Dec 25, 26.* ◉€3 (admission free Oct 26). ☏0 26 82/6 26 52.

The regional museum is devoted to the ethnological and cultural history of the region and includes a section on the ethnic minorities that live in the Burgenland.

EISRIESENWELT★

SALZBURG

With over 40km/24.8mi of subterranean passages, the 'world of the ice giants' is the largest accessible ice cave system in the world. An 800m/2 625ft-long show cave reveals ice formations shaped into fans, curtains, cathedrals and other fantastical features in icy air—even in summer.

- **Information:** ☏06 62/84 26 90 14. www.eisriesenwelt.at.
- ▶ **Orient Yourself:** The entrance to the caves is at 1 641m/5 384ft on the western cliffs of the Hochkogel about 6km/3.7mi northwest of Werfen.
- P **Parking:** There is a parking lot at about 1 000m/3 281ft elevation on the mountain road.
- ◐ **Organizing Your Time:** Allow at least three hours for the trip up and through the caves.
- ◔ **Also See:** DACHSTEIN, Dachstein-Rieseneishöhle.

Tour of the Caves

◐◐*Caves can only be seen by guided tour (1hr 15min) Jul–Aug, daily 9am–4.30pm; May, Jun, Sept–Oct 26, daily 9am–3.30pm.* ◉€8. *Eisriesenwelt-Linie – Bus operates May–Oct and Jul–Aug, daily 9am– 4.30pm, hourly or every 15min if busy.* €8.50 two-way trip. ☏0 64 68/52 93.

As the average temperature in the caves is around 0°C in summer, warm clothing is advisable and good ▣ hiking shoes will serve better when climbing the

many steps in the caves. To protect this nature monument, visited by around 2 500 people a day during the opening period, photography is not allowed. Getting to the cave entrance requires a moderate level of fitness, but you'll be spoiled with terrific views all the way.

1. From Werfen, the mountain road climbs steeply for 5km/3mi to the P parking lot at 1 000m/3 281ft. It can be traveled in your own car or by shuttle bus (journey time: 5min) leaving from the Werden

train station and from the bottom of the Eisriesenweltstraße near the village.

2. From the parking lot, it's a 20min walk to the Wimmer Hütte (hut).

3. At Wimmer Hütte, catch the **cable-car** (◯*operates Jul–Aug, daily 9am–6pm; May, Jun, Sept–Oct 26, daily 9am–5pm; ⊜€9 round trip; ✆06 62/84 26 90 14)* to the "Dr.-Oedl-Haus" mountain inn (1 575m/5 167ft).

4. From the inn, it's another 20min walk to the cave entrance.

Guided tour of the caves
About 1hr 15min.

By the light of acetylene and magnesium lamps, visitors enter the ice world of the caves, climbing up to the Posselt-Halle gallery (named after the first explorer to discover the caves in 1879). The "Hrymr Hall," with its Hrymr Mountain, and "Niflheimr" with Frigg's Veil, are both examples of fantastic ice architecture

What's in a name…

The origin of many of the names of the galleries in the Eisriesenwelt subterranean complex is Old Norse mythology, as featured in the Old Icelandic saga "Edda": **Ốïinn** is the father of the gods; **Frigg** is his wife and at the same time goddess of fertility; **Hrymr** is an ice giant; **Ásgarẙr** is the home of the Æsir gods, who are at war with the Vanir; and **Niflheimr** is the world of shadows in the frozen north that existed before this world was created.

The Alexander-von-Mörk-Dom, however, is named after its discoverer, who also is buried there.

enhanced by clever lighting. At the back of the "Ốïinn Gallery" is a throne-like ice formation called Ásgarẙr. Another highlight is the "Cathedral."

ENNS★

OBERÖSTERREICH
POPULATION 10 890
ALT 281M/922FT

Enns is among the oldest towns in Austria founded as a Roman camp in the 2C AD. It was here that St. Florian, the patron saint of Upper Austria, suffered martyrdom under Diocletian at the beginning of the 4C. Much of the town's 12C fortifications, including the ramparts, moats, and six watchtowers, have survived.

🛈 **Information:** Linzerstraße 1, A-4470. ✆0 72 23/83 26 10. www.enns.or.at.
▶ **Orient Yourself:** Enns is at the confluence of the Danube and the River Enns.
🅿 **Parking:** Look for parking in lots and garages along or near Stadtgasse.
😊 **Don't Miss:** Pfarrkirche St. Marien.
🕐 **Organizing Your Time:** Start in the Hauptplatz.
🖐 **Also See:** LINZ, ST FLORIAN.

Sights

Hauptplatz
Enns' pretty medieval old core revolves around the Hauptplatz, the central square, punctuated by the landmark **Stadtturm** (Z). Soaring 60m/197ft high, the tower is adorned with the Imperial eagle and the Habsburg coat

of arms. Climb the 156 steps to the gallery to enjoy a marvelous **view**★. Hauptplatz is also orbited by many attractive Gothic burgher houses with Renaissance arcaded courtyards. The former town hall at No. 19 contains the **Museum Lauriacum (Z M)** (www.museum-lauriacum.at) with Roman-era archeological exhibits.

Bräuergasse	Z	4	Linzerstr.	Z	8	Vilma-Eckl-Pl.	Y 16
Dragonerstr.	Z	5	Pfarrgasse	Z	13	Westbahnstr.	Y 18
Forstbergstr.	Z	7	Steyrerstr.	Z	15	Zeltwegstr.	Z 20

Stadtmuseum Lauriacum	Z	M

Pfarrkirche St. Marien★ (Z)

Mon–Sat 7am–7pm (5pm Oct–Apr), Sun 8am–7pm (5pm Oct–Apr). Guided tours possible as part of a tour of the town or by appointment. ☎0 72 23/8 28 55.
This is one of the oldest Mendicant Order churches in Austria, built by the Minorites in 1276–7. It's an austere, two-nave church whose ornamentation is limited to beautifully carved keystones; modern 20C glass windows are extraordinarily colorful. Three Gothic arches lead into the **Wallseerkapelle**, a chapel named for a former local ruling family. A remarkable painting from 1625 depicts the *Lorcher Bishops*, a view of the town featuring local religious dignitaries. Also note the 13C seated Madonna. The Gothic cloister has a peaceful ambience.

Basilika St. Laurenz (Y)

daily 8am–7pm. Guided tour (1hr) mid-Apr–mid-Oct, daily 4pm. Parts of the church may be visited unaccompanied. Telephone in advance for guided tours. €3. ☎0 72 23/8 74 12.
The basilica occupies a site on the edge of the ancient Roman camp. Roman stones were used in the construction of the 13C tower, the oldest extant part of the church, which is attached to a 14C choir. Between the nave and chancel, archeological excavations have revealed vestiges of walls from earlier buildings on this site: A Gallo-Roman temple (180), the first Christian church (bishop's see, 370) and early Carolingian church buildings (740). Decorative highlights include a Late Gothic tabernacle and Pietà, as well as Austria's two largest oil paintings from the 18C

Address Book

For coin ranges, see cover flap.

WHERE TO STAY

Lauriacum – *Wiener Str. 5.* ☎0 72 23/8 27 77. www.lauriacum. at. 31 rooms. A family-run hotel in the center of town. All the rooms are individual in style with modern ensuite facilities.

FELBERTAUERNSTRASSE ★

SALZBURG AND TIROL

The Felbertauern road has made a considerable difference to the lives of residents in the eastern Alps. Its core is a 5.3/3.3mi long tunnel that has connected eastern Tirol with Innsbruck in northern Tirol since opening in 1967. The panoramic road carves through the peaceful Alpine countryside of the Hohe Tauern National Park (www.hohetauern.at).

- 🛈 **Information:** Albin-Egger-Straße 17, Lienz. ☎0 48 52/6 33 30. www.felbertauernstrasse.at.
- ▶ **Orient Yourself:** This scenic road runs from Lienz to Mittersill in the Pinzgau.
- 🅿 **Parking:** Numerous stops along the route with parking and picnic facilities.
- 😊 **Don't Miss:** Walk to Innergeschlöss.
- 🕐 **Organizing Your Time:** Budget half a day for the Innergschlöss hike, a full day for the Drei-Seen-Tour.
- 🖢 **Also See:** GROSSGLOCKNER HOCHALPENSTRASSE.

Driving Tours

Combining the Großglockner Hochalpenstraße *(summer only)* and the Felbertauern road into a circular tour gives you magnificent views of the Grossvenediger snows. The Grossvenediger summit was first conquered by 26 men in September 1841.

1 Lienz to the Felberntauer Tunnel

41km/25.4mi

Lienz 🖢*See LIENZ.*

- ▶ *From Lienz follow the road up the long, wooded valley of the Isel.*

Matrei in Osttirol ★

🖢*See MATREI IN OSTTIROL.*

Past Matrei is Schloss Weissenstein, a former outpost of the Salzburg archbishops.
The road now continues through the **Tauern Valley**★★, passing through the Prosschegg gorge to reach an open valley overlooked by the hanging glacier of the Kristallkopf.
It is possible at this point to continue north directly via the Felbertauern tunnel (🖢 *see Tour 2*) or to make a detour to explore the Grossvenediger massif (🖢*see Excursion*).

2 Felbertauern Tunnel to Mittersill *16km/10mi*

On the north face of the Tauern the road emerges from the tunnel into the upper Amertal, a rugged and more or less deserted high-altitude valley.

- ▶ *9km/5.6mi after the exit from the tunnel turn left toward Hintersee. After 500m/547yd, 🚶park the car on the right to visit the Schößwend gorge.*

Detour Walk to Schösswendklamm ★ 🚶

15min round trip walk.
Cross the road to the path leading down to the Felberbach and across the river. Following the river bank, the trail offers good **views**★ of the sculptured rock faces carved by the crystal-clear water and beautiful waterfalls.

- ▶ *Drive on for 3km/1.8mi to the end of the road.*

Hintersee ★

This mountain lake surrounded by spruce forest lies in the upper Felber Valley below a magnificent high mountain range, from which a number of waterfalls tumble from great heights. To the south lies the Tauernkogel massif *(alt 2 989m/9 806ft)*. Several information panels explain the geology of the area. It is possible to walk around the lake.

▶ *Turn back to B 108.*

This stretch of road leads through Alpine meadows to the resort of **Mittersill** from where roads lead off to the Thurn *(north)* and Gerloß *(west)* passes.

Walking Excursions

Grossvenediger Massif★★

Take a small mountain road to the left of the road leading to the Felbertauerntunnel (toll), and follow it along the valley floor to the Matreier Tauernhaus (alt 1 512m/4 961ft), a mountain hotel. Allow at least 2hr there and back for a brief visit, or—better—a whole day to include some sightseeing on foot.

Walk to Innergschlöss★★

4hr round trip hike or head up in a horse-drawn carriage or on a little train. It takes 45min to get to Aussergschlöss (alt 1 695m/5 561ft). The romantic scenery surrounding the chalet almost pales beside the sight of the majestic Großvenediger *(alt 3 674m/12 054ft)* with its cowl of glaciers. The fairly easy trail continues to Innergschlöss.

Drei-Seen-Tour★★

From Matreier Tauernhaus, walk along the road direction Venedigerhaus, then climb a steep grassy slope from the former valley station of the Venedigerblick chair-lift to the former mountain station at 1 982m/6 503ft. From here, follow the Panoramaweg to the Tauernbach creek and then the creek itself across a meadow to St. Pöltner Hütte mountain lodge at 2 481m/8 140ft, then along gravelly and rocky trail sections. From the lodge continue along a narrow, rocky path to the St.Pöltner Ostweg past the Grauer See (Grey Lake), Schwarzer See (Black Lake) and Grüner See (Green Lake), then along the Messeling Creek across meadows and back to the mountain station of the chair-lift and down the slope to the valley station.

If you're fit enough, continue on to the Messelingkogel *(alt 2 694m/8 839ft – 45min round trip)* where you can enjoy a unique **panorama**★★★ over the three lakes, the Großglockner (in the distance), the Tauerntal Valley and the huge glaciers of the Großvenediger.

Hike to the Zirbelkreuz★

1hr 45min, 600m/1 969ft difference in altitude down the mountain.
From the former mountain station of the Venedigerbahn chair-lift, the trail leads along the mountainside and finally climbs up to a bridge and then to the cross.

▶ *After exploring the Großvenediger Massif, drive back to the main road.*

Hintersee

© Österreich Werbung / Mallaun

FELDKIRCH★★

VORARLBERG
POPULATION 32 140
ALT 459M/1 506FT

Feldkirch is the gateway to Austria for travelers coming from the west. Right on the busy road to the Arlberg pass, the little fortified town nestles at the foot of Schattenburg Castle and has preserved the symmetry of its medieval layout and the old-world charm of arcaded squares.

- **Information:** Herrengasse 12. ☎0 55 22/7 34 67. www.feldkirch.at.
- ▶ **Orient Yourself:** Feldkirch is on the Liechtenstein/Switzerland border.
- **Parking:** Several parking lots and garages are near the old town. An automated parking guide system directs you to the nearest one with available spaces.
- **Don't Miss:** Basilika Rankweil and the Old Rampart Walk.
- **Organizing Your Time:** Start in Marktplatz.
- **Also See:** ARLBERGGEBIET.

Sights

Marktplatz

The heart of Feldkirch's old town, this long, arcaded square has retained the charm and tranquillity of a bygone age. Wherever you look, an inn with a colorful façade, an onion-domed corner tower, or a Gothic oriel window catch the eye. To the south the view is bounded by the plain belfry and façade of the Johanniskirche. This is the former church of the monastery of the Hospitallers of St. John of Jerusalem, who were entrusted with the protection of the Arlberg Pass (*see ARLBERGGEBIET: Driving Tour*).

Domkirche St. Nikolaus

⊙*Daily 8am–7pm. ☎0 55 22/ 7 22 32.*
The twin-nave Late Gothic cathedral was first mentioned in documents in 1287, but had to be rebuilt after a fire. It sports delicate net vaulting and beautiful, if modern, stained-glass windows (1959–1961) by the local artist, Martin Häusle, depicting some of the saints. Included, high above the altar, is a red-robed St. Nicholas, patron saint of the church. Over the right side altar is a **Descent from the Cross**★ painted in 1521 by Wolf Huber, a native of Feldkirch and a leading artist of the Danube School. The pulpit boasts a splendid wrought-iron canopy that was originally a Gothic tabernacle.

Schattenburg

Heimatmuseum – ⊙*Jan–Mar, Mon–Fri 1.30pm–4pm, Sat–Sun 11m–4pm; Apr–Oct, Mon–Fri 9am–noon, 1.30pm–6pm, Sat–Sun 9am–6pm.* ☜ € 3. ☎0 55 22/7 19 82. *Reachable by car via a new access road and Burggasse and on foot via the Schlosssteig stairs.*
The Schattenburg has a pedigree going back to 1200 and is one of the best-preserved castles in Austria with great views over the town and surrounds. Originally the seat of the counts of Monfort, it has walls up to 4m/13.1ft thick and lovely frescoes in the chapel. Some of the Gothic wood-panelled rooms contain the Heimatmuseum, a museum displaying local religious art, Gothic furnishings, arms, armor, coins and other medieval bits and pieces.

Excursion

Basilika Rankweil

19km/11.8mi round trip. Leave Feldkirch on the road to Bregenz.
The hilltop pilgrimage church, dedicated to the Virgin Mary, overlooks the idyllic Austrian Rhine Valley and its orchards. A church has stood here since the 7C. After a fire in the 15C, it was rebuilt as a fortified Gothic church. In 1986 it was raised to the status of basilica minor.
The **Gnadenkapelle**, or Chapel of Miracles, houses the church's treasured

Late Gothic Madonna, attributed to the Swabian School. Above the main altar hangs the so-called "miracle-working" silver cross.

From the **old rampart walk**★ (Wehrgang) on the Liebfrauenberg you get a marvelous view of the upper Rhine valley, the Swiss and Vorarberg Alps and Lichtenstein.

To return to Feldkirch, follow the valley floor to Satteins, bear right at the entrance to Satteins and join the B 1.

FERNPASSSTRASSE★

TIROL

The picturesque road across the Fernpass has been an important Alpine crossing since Roman times when it was part of the Via Claudia Augusta. A vital trade route connecting Augsburg and Venice in the Middle Ages, it now primarily a tourist link between the resorts of the Bavarian Alps and Innsbruck.

- **Information:** Maria-Theresien-Str. 55. Innsbruck. ☎05 12/72 72. www.tirol.at.
- ▶ **Orient Yourself:** Links Oberes Lechtal with Inntal in western Austria.
- **Parking:** Several places along the route including at the pass itself.
- **Don't Miss:** Zugspitze Summit.
- **Organizing Your Time:** Allow a whole day if ascending the Zugspitze.
- **Also See:** OBERES LECHTAL.

Driving Tour

Telfs to Reutte *64km/39.7mi*

From **Telfs** (*see SEEFELDER SATTELSTRASSEN*) to Holzleiten the road traverses the gentle slopes of the Mieming plateau, from which the well defined crests of the Miemingergebirge rise up. Near Obermieming, views of the Inn Valley open out to the left against the snow-capped peaks of the Samnaungruppe, which is shared by Austria and Switzerland.

Driving down toward **Nassereith** from the **Holzleitner Sattel** *(alt 1 126m/3 694ft)*, there is a series of delightful **views**★ of countryside dotted with villages against a mountain backdrop. Several tunnels later, the road reaches Fernstein with "Schloss Fernsteinsee" hotel on the left. To the right of the road,

Address Book

🪙For coin ranges, see cover flap.

WHERE TO STAY

EHRWALD

🍴🍴🛏🛏**Alpen Residence** – *Florentin Wehner-Weg 37*. ☎*0 56 73/22 55 55. www.alpenresidence.at. 45 rooms.* A family-run hotel, enlarged in 2008, at 914m/3 000ft just five minutes walk from the town. It has a spa, beauty center and restaurant.

REUTTE

🍴🛏🛏**Zum Mohren** – *Untermarkt 26.* ☎*0 56 72/6 23 45. www.hotel-mohren.at. 54 rooms.* Here you will find traditional Tirolean hospitality in a modern setting. A well-being center is particularly nice after a day in the mountains on foot or on skis.

below the 🅿parking lot, lies the idyllic **Fernsteinsee**★.

Fernpass

Alt 1 209m/3 967ft. The pass breaches a crest between Fernstein and Biberwier. The road corkscrews up the south slope through rugged, isolated gorges and cirques. About 1km/.6mi beyond the pass itself, stop at the "Zugspitzblick" restaurant to take in the stunning **panorama**★ of the Zugspitze, the distinctive Sonnenspitze peak and other striking summits. Below lies the **Blindsee**★, a long and picturesque lake.

The Blindsee is an ideal spot for a swim or lakeside walk. Access is on the way down from the Fernpass, from the left of the road (before the information point).

▶ *Follow the road along the north slope of the Fernpass toward Biberwier.*

At the Biberwier junction, look for **Weissensee** lake on the right. The road from Biberwier to Lermoos, skirting the Lermoos-Ehrwald basin, offers fine **views**★★ of the Wetterstein and the Mieminger range.

Ehrwald★

Despite the numerous lovely hikes, most people come here for the **Tiroler Zugspitzbahn** cable-car ride to the top of Germany's highest mountain.

Ascent to the Zugspitze★★★

Allow about 2hr, including 10min for the cable-car ride. Operates Whitsun–Oct, Christmas–1st week after Easter, daily 8.40am–4.40pm every 20min. Journey time: 10min. 🎫€*33 two-way trip.* ☎*0 56 73/23 09. www.zugspitzbahn.at.* A 4.5km/2.8mi-long road runs from Ehrwald to Obermoos and the valley station of the Tiroler Zugspitzbahn cable-car.

View of the Mieminger range

M. Hertlein/MICHELIN

Zugspitze summit★★★
The cable-car drops you off on the western peak of the Zugspitze summit *(alt 2 964m/9 724ft)*, and a breathtaking panorama taking in four countries and countless peaks, many soaring above 3000m/10 000ft. Information boards help you identify the craggy summits of the Hohe Tauern, the Tirolean High Alps, the Dachstein and many others.
Also up here is the multimedia exhibit called **Faszination Zugspitze**★ that traces the history of the mountain from its first ascent in 1820 to the present. Sadly, the glacier is melting away, though covered by special tarpaulins to protect it from the sun. A 3D film that lets you experience a virtual flight over the peaks.
In winter there is access to numerous first-class **ski runs**, including the great *Gattlerabfahrt* of nearly 23km/14.8mi back to Ehrwald *(guide recommended)*.

Lermoos★★
The best place to admire the Northern Limestone Alps, dominated by the Zugspitze and the Sonnenspitze summit.

▶ *To cross from the Loisach basin into that of the Lech, follow the valley named Zwischentoren ("between gates").*

Ehrenberger Klause
From the 16C to the 18C, Ehrenberg Fortress was key in defending the Tirol. Before reaching Reutte, it is worth taking a short detour to the Plansee *(about 20km/12.4mi round trip)*.

Plansee★
The road runs through a forest, then skirts the lake shore for a 6km/3.7mi stretch. At the northeast tip the view stretches southwest through the small strait separating the Plansee from the Heiterwanger See, as far as the Thaneller peak (2 341m/7 680ft). Nice walks or a sheduled boat trip allow for a relaxing time in great natural surroundings.

▶ *From here you can continue to Linderhof and Oberammergau in Germany via the Ammersattel pass.*

Reutte ⚭ *See OBERES LECHTAL.*

BURG FORCHTENSTEIN★
BURGENLAND

The fortress of Forchtenstein overlooks charming scenery from its bluff-top site in the Rosaliengebirge foothills. It is dominated by its massive 50m/164ft keep, which is the oldest surviving part of the original construction.

🛈 **Information:** Hauptstraße 54, Forchtenstein. ☎0 26 26/6 31 25.
▶ **Orient Yourself:** The castle is 23km/14.3mi southeast of Wiener Neustadt, access is via Mattersburg.
🅿 **Parking:** At the fortress.
⊛ **Don't Miss:** Treasury.
🕓 **Organizing Your Time:** Allow 2 hours.
Kids **Especially for Kids:** A variety of child-oriented guided tours are available.
⚭ **Also See:** WIENER NEUSTADT, EISENSTADT, NEUSIEDLER SEE.

A Bit of History

The fortress was built at the beginning of the 14C by the counts of Mattersdorf. The Esterházy family, owners of Forchtenstein since 1622, added the ring of bastions to stave off marauding Turkish tropps. After the family moved to Schloss Esterházy in Eisenstadt in the early 18C, Forchtenstein became a treasury, arsenal and archive. It is still owned by the Esterházys.
Forchenstein village, which developped around the fortress, has some 2 800 inhabitants and is proud of its pilgrimage church (1347) and chapel.

The legend of Rosalia

Legend has it while Giletus, the first lord of Forchtenstein was away on the battlefield, his wife Rosalia ruled the fortress with an iron fist. After learning of his wife's misdoings, Giletus decided to describe the incident to her as if he was talking about some stranger, even asking her opinion on what would be appropriate punishment. Rosalia foolishly recommended imprisonment in the fortress dungeon! And so she ended her days, her restless spirit allegedly haunting the fortress until Giletus had the Rosalienkapelle built to appease it.

Visit

Guided tour (1hr 15min) on the hour; Apr–Oct, daily 10am–6pm. €8. 0 26 26/8 12 12. www.esterhazy.at/de/burg-forchtenstein (Greman only).

A tour of the castle takes in one of Europe's largest private family collections with about 20 000 items. Highlights include the **treasury** (art and precious objects, clocks and automata, silverware, chinoiseries, porcelain and library); the **picture gallery** (family portraits and battle scenes); and the **arsenal** (arms and armor, trophies from the wars against the French and the Prussians, and the "Turkish booty" from the field campaigns of Prince Paul Esterházy (1652–1713). The cistern in the courtyard (142m/465ft deep) was dug by Turkish POWs.

Follow the road further uphill from the fortress for 4km/2.5mi to reach the **Rosalienkapelle** (1670), a chapel dedicated to Rosalia, curer of plagues, from where there is a good **view**★ as far as Eisenstadt and the Neusiedler See.

FREISTADT★

OBERÖSTERREICH
POPULATION 7 460
ALT 560M/1 837FT

Freistadt is a former stronghold on the ancient salt route to Bohemia. Its extensive, largely intact, fortifications include a double town wall, towers and gateways. With its pretty main square, web of spidery lanes and picturesque houses, Freistadt makes for an idyllic visit.

- **Information:** Hauptplatz 12, A-4240, 0 79 42/7 57 00. www.freistadt.at.
- ▶ **Orient Yourself:** Freistadt is in the lower Mühlviertel, about 30km/18.6mi northeast of Linz.
- **Parking:** Parking in the historic center is short-term only. Long-term parking is available in lots along Linzerstraße.
- **Don't Miss:** Hauptplatz.
- **Also See:** LINZ, KEFERMARKT.

Sights

Hauptplatz★

This rectangular main square is framed by beautiful old pastel-painted houses adorned with delicate stucco; many are fronted by porches or arcades. In the center of the wide square (6 500sq m/ 7 774sq yd) is a carved fountain dedicated to the Virgin Mary, while on the west side looms the **Rathaus** (R) in a wonderfully pure Italian Renaissance style. Waagstraße, behind the town hall, is lined by exceptionally beautiful buildings, many sporting oriels and sgraffito façades.

quaint and picturesque alley with flower-decked balconies and passages.

Stadtpfarrkirche

The parish church's elegant Baroque tower, just south of the Hauptplatz, is another characteristic feature of Frei-stadt's skyline. The church itself is Gothic and

Schloss

North of the Hauptplatz is Freistadt's 14C castle with its robust tower that forms part of the fortifications. Inside, the **Schlossmuseum** examines various aspects and phases of regional history. It is reached via **Schlossgasse**, a

has a triple-aisled nave crowned with a ribbed vaulted ceilings. Also note the **organ case**, beautifully adorned with statues.

Again, a few steps south of the Stadtpfarrkiche, is Dechantenhof, another impressive building in Baroque style.

FRIESACH★

KÄRNTEN
POPULATION 5 3270
ALT 637M/2 090FT

Carinthia's oldest town is greatly appealing with its three ruined castles, six churches and well-preserved fortifications. It belonged to the archbishopric of Salzburg from 960 to 1803 and was a key staging point along the Vienna-Venice trade route.

- **Information:** Hauptplatz 1, A-9360. ☎0 42 68/43 00; www.friesach.at.
- ▶ **Orient Yourself:** Friesach is some 40km/25mi north of Klagenfurt near the border with Styria on the Metnitz River.
- **Don't Miss:** Town fortifications, Die Spur des Einhorns.
- ⏱ **Organizing Your Time:** Budget two or three hours.
- **Especially for Kids:** Die Spur des Einhorns.
- **Also See:** GURK, ST. VEIT AN DER GLAN.

Sights

Town fortifications★

The fortifications, including the only water-filled town moat in the German-speaking world, encircle the town center with an 820m/896.7yd-long for-

tified wall. Only three of the original 11 defense towers remain.

Stadtbrunnen★

This Renaissance fountain anchors the Hauptplatz, surrounded by beautiful old houses. Reliefs with scenes from ancient

Greek mythology adorn the basin, which is crowned by a small bronze group depicting Poseidon, the Greek god of the sea.

Dominikanerkloster & Kirche

Friesach monastery, dating from 1217, was the first foundation of the Dominican Order in a German-speaking country. Its three-nave church is the largest in Carinthia and rather simple in keeping with the rules of the Mendicant order. There is a splendid winged altar, ornate epitaphs and two precious Early Gothic treasures: a sandstone Madonna and a huge wooden crucifix.

Petersberg

For the best view over the town, head to this small hilltop **church** in the northern old town. Nearby, the 28m/92ft-high 12C keep is all that remains of Petersberg castle, the former residence of the Salzburg archbishops. It now houses

the **Stadtmuseum** (⊙*May 10–Sept 28, Tue–Sun 11am–5pm;* ≈€3 *(admission free May 1 and Oct 26);* ☎*0 42 68/26 00)*, which relates the history of Friesach and the region. ⊛Be warned: There are 127 steeps to climb within the keep. Summer open-air theater productions are staged in the former castle courtyard *(Friesacher Burghofspiele infoline* ☎*42 68/25 1 51)*.

Die Spur des Einhorns   Kids
⊙*May–Oct, daily 10am–5pm.*≈€5.50. ☎*0 42 68/43 00.*
For a memorable break from the church-square-castle sightseeing circuit, visit this multi-dimensional art, sound, and light installation in the former granary. The fascinating experience takes you on a virtual journey through medieval mythology. There are interactive encounters with a magic forest, King Arthur's sword Excalibur, a terracotta army of crusaders and a giant wheel of fortune in the moat.

GAILBERGSATTEL STRASSE
KÄRNTEN

This road runs between Oberdrauburg and Kötschach linking the upper valleys of the Drava (Drau) and the Gail and crossing the pass at 982m/3 222ft.

🛈 **Information:** 9653 Liesing 29. ☎0 47 16/242 12. www.lesachtal.com.
▶ **Orient Yourself:** South of Lienz and close to the Italian border.
⊛ **Don't Miss:** Luggau Water Mills.
🕓 **Organizing Your Time:** Budget a day for an easy tour.
⌛ **Also See:** LIENZ.

Driving Tour

Oberdrauburg to the Lesach Valley *67km/41.6mi*

The most attractive part of the route is the stretch of road climbing the north slope in a series of hairpin bends through larch forest.

Laas
The Late Gothic **Filialkirche St. Andreas** sports doorways and windows framed in local red sandstone and delicate ribbed **vaulting**★★. It is a masterpiece by Bartimä Firtaler.

Kötschach
The small market community of **Kötschach-Mauthen**, set between the Gailtaler and Karnische Alps, is a popular medium-altitude (710m/2 329ft), mountain-air health resort. The **Pfarrkirche Unsere Liebe Frau** (also known as the "cathedral of the Gailtal") was consecrated in 1485 and completely rebuilt by Bartlmä Firtaler in the early 16C; it embodies the final, exuberantly decorative stage of the Gothic style and has stunning **traceried rib vaulting**★. The fresco on the north chancel wall depicts the Death and Assumption of the Virgin

Mary. The "miraculous" statue enclosed in the high altar is a black Madonna.

Lesachtal★
The road follows this charming valley along the Gail, climbing from 900m/2 953ft to 1 200m/3 937ft. Off the beaten track, it has remained largely unspoiled.

St. Lorenzen
This quiet village is dominated by the Late Gothic parish church of St. Laurentius, which boasts some remarkable frescoes. It is set amidst lovely painted farmhouses with shallow gable roofs.

Maria Luggau
The church, also by Bartlmä Firtaler, was consecrated in 1536. The Baroque tower dates from 1736. The object of veneration is a Late Gothic miraculous image of Our Lady of Sorrows. The statue of the Pietà stands on a valuable tabernacle shrine from the late 18C.

A short steep path leads to the picturesque **Luggau water mills**. These five

Church vaulting, Kötschach

timber constructions are over 200 years and all that remains of 100 mills once operating in the Lesach Valley.

Kartitscher Sattel
This pass is the highest point along the road (1 530m/5 020ft), which has a 13% gradient in some parts.

GASTEINER TAL ❄❄ ❄
SALZBURG

The Gasteiner Tal, a long, wide river valley, is one of the most attractive vacation destinations in Austria. It encompasses three main resorts: Dorfgastein (830m/2 723ft), Bad Hofgastein (860m/2 822ft) and Bad Gastein (1 000m/3 281ft). The latter developed into a leading spa resort as early as the 15C. With its exceptional setting amid medium- and high-altitude mountains, the valley has much to offer both skiers in winter and hikers in summer.

- 🚹 **Information:** Tauernplatz 1, 5630 Bad Hofgastein. ☎0 64 32/3 39 30. www.gastein.com
- ▶ **Orient Yourself:** A 40km/24.8mi-long valley in the Hohe Tauern National Park.
- 🅿 **Parking:** Plenty of places along the route.
- 😊 **Don't Miss:** Climbing the Stubnerkogel peak in summer and skiing the Kreuzkogel in winter.
- 🕐 **Organizing Your Time:** Budget at least a couple of days to fully appreciate the magnificent scenery.
- 👣 **Also See:** KAPRUNERTAL.

A Skiing Paradise

Much younger than spa tourism in Gasteiner Tal, but just as attractive, are the valley's winter sports facilities. Skiers and snowboarders can enjoy four ski areas which are suitable for beginners as well as experts: Stubnerkogel-Angertal-Schlossalm, Dorfgastein-Großarl, Sportgastein, and Graukogel. These winter

sports meccas offer some 200km/124mi
pistes from late November until the end
of April. If snow conditions are not perfect, extensive snow-making makes up
for this. And, of course, the après-ski-
scene is very vibrant as well.

Cross-country skiers have 90km/56mi
of track at their disposal, covering the
whole valley floor from Dorfgastein as
far as Sportgastein.

Thermal cures

In the 19C Bad Gastein evolved into one
of the ritziest spa towns of the age, visited by emperors and politicians, famous
artists and writers alike. It is now a thor-
oughly modern health resort and home
of a balneological research institute.
The thermal water forms from rain
water seeping into the Graukogel and
Hüttenkogel massifs, which heats up
underground and then emerges from
17 thermal springs with a daily output of 5 million liters (1.32 million US
gal) and an average temperature of
44.3°C/111.7°F.
The healing effect of Gastein's thermal
water is not so much due to its temperature, however, but to its radon

content. This radioactive noble gas
can be administered through bathing
or inhalation. While in the body, radon
gives off helium nuclei that energize the
body and regenerate damaged cells. In
conjunction with the mild mountain climate, the naturally enriched water helps
prevent or soothe rheumatism, respiratory diseases, circulatory problems and
other ailments.
Visitors can "take the cure" at numerous
hotels, health centers or public pools.
Alternatively, spend a session in the
Heilstollen (www.gasteiner-heilstollen.
com), a tunnel in which the temperature
is 37.5–41.5°C/99.5–106.7°F.

Driving Tour

From Lend to the Tauerntunnel

*41km/25.5mi including excursion
to Sportgastein*

After leaving Lend at the northern
entrance to Gasteiner Tal, the road
makes its way over the Klamm pass.
Take the tunnel to avoid the often steep
old road along the floor of the gorge.
Beyond the tunnel, the Gasteiner Tal
soon widens out.

Dorfgastein★
Alt 830m/2 723ft.
This pretty village on the valley floor
fringed by lush forests perkily shows off
its idyllic setting below Sun–drenched
Alpine meadows. In winter, there are
extensive ski slopes nearby, with a
connection to the Großarl ski slopes,
overlooked by the Fulseck summit
(55km/34.2mi of slopes). The drop in
altitude is over 1 100m/3 609ft, and
there are good opportunities for off-
piste skiing as well.

▷ *On B 167 Gasteiner Bundesstraße,
Bad Hofgastein will be reached
within less than 15 min. The B 167
connects all villages in Gasteiner
Tal, exept Sportgastein, and ends
at the Tauerntunnel.*

Stubnerkogel above Bad Gastein via the Anger Valley.

Pfarrkirche

The parish church is a testimony to Bad Hofgastein's heyday as regional capital when this was the mother church of the valley. The imposing Late Gothic nave has handsome stellar and ribbed vaulting. The church exterior and the niches flanking the main doorway are adorned with elaborate epitaphs of wealthy local gold- and silver-mine owners.

Schlossalm★

Alt 2 050m/6 726ft. Cable-car, followed by chair-lift. ◷*Operates Jun–mid-Oct, Dec–mid-Apr, daily 8am–4pm on the hour.* ◈*€13.80 two-way trip.* ☎*0 64 32/64 55.*
Come here for a good **panorama**★ of the ski slopes and the summits of the Stubnerkogel, Ankogel range, Graukogel and Gamskarkogel. From the second terrace of the restaurant, the view stretches as far as the Dachstein.

Bad Gastein‡‡‡

Alt 1 013m/3 323ft. ▯ *Bad Gastein, Kaiser-Franz-Josef-Str. 27, A-5640* ☎*0 64 34/2 53 10.*
Bad Gastein ranks among the most glitteringly beautiful spas and winter sports resorts in Austria. It is located amid spectacular mountain **scenery**★, flanked by the Stubnerkogel and the Graukogel, and boasts palatial hotels and elegant boutiques. The roaring Gasteiner Ache creates a waterfall right in town. The east bank of the river is paralleled by the **Kaiser-Wilhelm-Promenade**★, which gives lovely views of the town and surroundings.
Bad Gastein has numerous top-notch leisure facilities, including a skating rink, fitness centers, a nine-hole and an 18-hole golf course, tennis courts, and a casino. The **Felsentherme Gastein** is a thermal swimming pool built against the actual rock face.

Bad Hofgastein‡‡

Alt 860m/2 821.5ft. Bad Hofgastein Spa & Tourist Office, ☎*0 64 32/71 10. www. badhofgastein.com*
Bad Hofgastein lies in the broadest, sunniest stretch of the valley. This smart and lively health resort has numerous hotels offering the same spa facilities as Bad Gastein. Furthermore, the resort boasts modern, beautifully laid out spa gardens and the **Alpentherme** thermal pool and sauna complex. Winter brings excellent cross-country skiing in the valley and downhill in the Schlossalm massif. Slopes are linked with those on the

Local ski slopes include fine runs down the Stubnerkogel and the Graukogel.

Stubnerkogel★★
Alt 2 246m/7 369ft.
Allow 1hr round trip. Ascent is in a chair-lift in two stages. ⏱*Operates Jun–mid-Oct, Dec–end Apr, daily 8.30am–4pm on the hour.* ☞€*13.80 two-way trip.* ☎*0 64 32/64 55.*

The **panorama**★★ encompasses the Graukogel, the Ankogel glacier massif, the Kreuzkogel and the Anger Valley with the glaciers of the Hohe Tauern in the background, as well as the lower reaches of the Gasteiner Tal.

Tauerntunnel
Regular train service between Mallnitz and Böckstein: Mallnitz May 28–Sept, hourly 6.10am–11.10pm; Oct 2–Jun 9, hourly 6.10am–9.10pm; Böckstein May 28–Sept, hourly 5.40am–10.40pm; Oct 2–Jun 9, hourly 6.40am–9.40pm. Journey time: 12min. Phone for prices. ☎*0 47 84/6 00.*

The 8.37km/5.2mi double-track railway tunnel runs through the Tauern ridge between Böckstein in Salzburg and Mallnitz in Kärnten. Until the opening of the Felbertauern road tunnel this was the only way through the eastern Alps into the Tauern region. Even now, some motorists prefer loading their vehicle onto the train as opposed to driving through the road tunnel.

Excursions

Sportgastein★★

Toll road, free to ski pass holders.
From Bad Gastein, the road reaches Sportgastein, a broad high-altitude plateau set against a majestic back-drop of rocky peaks and glaciers after 6km/3.7mi. Infrastructure is minimal as of yet, consisting essentially of a large parking lot and a guesthouse.
The altitude guarantees excellent snow cover, much to the delight of cross-country (7km/4.3mi of tracks) and downhill skiers alike. A modern cable-car leads up to the Kreuzkogel summit, from where some exhilarating downhill runs drop more than 1 100m/3 609ft.

Kreuzkogel★★★
Ascent by cable-car in two stages.
Views★★ are impressive from the mountain station, but it's well worth taking the 15min walk up to the summit, marked by a cross, to fully soak up the spectacular **panorama**★★★. Wear mountain boots, as the snow can be quite deep in places.

▶ *Travel back down to Böckstein. It is possible to carry on into Carinthia through the Tauerntunnel.*

Exploring on Foot

With its varied terrain suited to walkers of all abilities, the Gasteiner Tal is one of the best places in Austria for hiking. Walks are especially pretty along the **Kaiserin-Elisabeth-Promenade**, from Bad Gastein to Böckstein, and along the **Gasteiner Hohenweg**, which follows the mountain slope from Bad Gastein to Bad Hofgastein.
☞*Be sure to pick up a detailed map and plan your route carefully.*

Zitterauer Tisch und Bockhartsee★★★
Allow a full day, including 4hr 30min walking time. Enquire at the tourist office about bus timetables between Sportgastein and Bad Gastein for your afternoon return.

Take the cable-car up to the top of the Stubnerkogel. Turn right at the mountain station and follow the route marked with red and white flashes and red arrows. In just under 1hr the mountain path reaches the Zitterauer Tisch (2 461m/8 074ft). There is a terrific **view**★★★ of the entire Gasteiner Tal, especially the upper reaches of the val-ley. To the northeast, the view stretches as far as the Dachstein.
The path plunges down to pastures, before weaving through a bleak and craggy landscape. After another hour, you'll reach the Miesbichlscharte *(alt 2 238m/7 342.5ft)*.
On the way down to the Unterer Bock-hartsee there are good views of the glaciers and waterfalls of the Schareck massif as well as of the Hocharn and the Ankogel. From the lakeshore climb up to

the hut and then down to Sportgastein. Take the bus back to Bad Gastein.

Graukogel★★

2hr 30min round trip walk. Difference in altitude of about 500m/1 640ft. This walk is recommended for good walkers wearing sturdy shoes. ⊙Chair-lift operates mid Dec–end Mar, daily 8.30am–4pm on the hour. Closed in poor weather. ⊛€13.80 round trip. ☎0 64 34/6455.

Take the two chair-lifts up to Tonis Almgasthof *(alt 1 982m/6 502.6ft)*. A path leads from behind the guesthouse up to the Hüttenkogel summit *(alt 2 231m/7 320ft)* from where you'll have an incredible **panorama**★★ of the Hohe Tauern range, and the spectacular Reedsee lake.

Next, follow the path along the ridge (extra care is needed in some of the steeper places) to the **Graukogel** summit for an even broader **view**★★ as far as the Dachstein. The Palfnersee can be seen glistening immediately below.

Walk to the Palfnersee★

1hr 45min round trip

This is an easy walk through some beautiful countryside. Take the two chair-lifts up the Graukogel, walk past the hut and continue straight on. The mountain trail gives you a good **view**★ of Schareck, Hoher Sonnblick and Hocharn before climbing up to the Palfnersee *(alt 2 100m/6 890ft)*. From here, you could carry on to the **Palfner Pass**★ *(alt 2 321m/7 615ft)* for even better views *(allow an extra hour round trip)*.

STIFT GERAS★

NIEDERÖSTERREICH

The Premonstratensian abbey of Geras, set in a quiet spot far from the main tourist centers, enjoys considerable renown in Lower Austria. It is surrounded by the Naturpark Geras, a **nature reserve** where fallow deer, roe deer, wild boar and other animals roam within large enclosures.

- 🖫 **Information:** Hauptstraße 16, A-2093. ☎0 29 12/70 50. www.stift-geras.at.
- ▶ **Orient Yourself:** Geras is in the eastern Waldviertel, not far from the Czech border.
- ☺ **Don't Miss:** Marmorsaal (Marble Hall).
- 🕓 **Organizing Your Time:** Allow an hour for the Abbey tour.
- 👁 **Also See:** ALTENBURG.

Visit

Stift *(Abbey)*

Guided tour (1hr) May–Oct, Tue–Sun 10am, 2pm, 3.30pm. ⊛€7.50. ☎0 29 12/34 52 89. www.stiftgeras.at.

This Premonstratensian monastery was founded in 1153 but was redesigned and enlarged in Baroque style by Joseph Munggenast in the 18C. The highlight of the guided tour is the solemn and refined **Marmorsaal**★ (Marble Hall), the former summer refectory, reached via a beautiful staircase with a statue of Pallas Athene, the Greek goddess of wisdom. The hall's magnificent **ceiling fresco**★ by Paul Troger depicts the mira-

cle of the loaves and fishes. Troger is also responsible for the paintings hanging above the two fireplaces, including the *Wedding Feast at Cana*.

Stiftskirche

The colorful abbey church is Romanesque in origin but was completely redone in exuberant Baroque style following a fire in 1730. It has wonderfully delicate stuccowork and sensitive frescoes depicting the life of the Virgin painted by Franz Zoller, a pupil of Paul Troger. Also note the main door, which is decorated with statues of St. Norbert and St. Augustine, two major figures of the Premonstratensian Order.

Naturpark Geras

⏰ *Sun before Easter–Oct, Tue–Sun 9am–6pm.* ♿ *€2.60.* ☎ *06 64/5 52 65 53. www.naturparkgeras.at*

Roe and fallow deer and boar roam in large enclosures in this nature reserve. There are plenty of waterfowl and woodland birds in this nature reserve that surrounds the abbey.

Excursion

Pernegg

12km/7.4mi southwest of Geras.

Set in peaceful, unspoiled countryside, Pernegg was founded in 1153 as a Premonstratensian convent but became affiliated with Geras Abbey following the death of the last nun in 1585. Since 1995 it has been used as a center for religious seminars and fasting retreats. Its church blends Late Gothic, Renaissance and Baroque elements and features a modern high altar decorated with a 16C Crucifixion.

GERLOS-ALPENSTRASSE★

TIROL UND SALZBURG

The Alpine road zigzagging over the Gerlos pass connects the Tirol with Salzburg and offers panoramic views of the Salzach valley and the Zillertal Alps. It also skirts the spectacular Krimmler Wasserfälle, the highest waterfalls in Europe.

- **Information:** ☎ 0 65 64/72 61. www.gerlosstrasse.at.
- ▶ **Orient Yourself:** The road links the Zillertal valley with the Oberpinzgau basin.
- **P Parking:** At viewpoints along the route and at Krimml Wasserfälle.
- **Don't Miss:** Krimmler Wasserfälle.
- **Organizing Your Time:** Allow plenty of time to negotiate this curvy mountain road. The hike up and down the Krimml falls takes at least 3hr.
- **Especially for Kids:** Wasserwunderwelt at Krimml Falls.
- **Also See:** ZILLERTAL.

Driving Tour

Zell am Ziller to Krimml

38km/23.6mi

- ▶ *The road is steep and narrow in places. Between the Gerlos pass and Krimml, a toll is charged.*

Zell am Ziller ♿ *See ZILLERTAL.*

On leaving Zell am Ziller the road climbs quickly in hairpin bends up the Hainzenberg slope. Soon the pilgrimage chapel of **Maria Rast** (1748), with its distinctive red onion domes, comes into view. After Hainzenberg the road enters the Gerlos Valley.

Gerlos

At an altitude of 1 250m/4 101ft, this village offers excellent downhill and cross-country skiing in winter and hiking and climbing in summer. Water sports enthusiasts head to the attractive **Durlassbodensee**.

After the toll point the road reaches the rugged moorland landscape of the Gerlos plateau. There are several parking lots here for enjoying superb **views**★★ of the Krimml falls. The walk to the falls starts in the parking lot further downhill, just before the toll booths to the Gerlach pass road.

Krimmler Wasserfälle★★★

The waterfalls can be visited from mid-Apr–Oct or at your own risk in winter.

€2. ℡0 65 64/72 12. www.wasserfaelle-
krimml.at.

The Krimmler Ache, which flows from
the glacier of that name at more than
3 000m/9842.5ft above sea level, cas-
cades in three stages down the forested cliff sides of the Salzachtalkessel.
The falls, the highest in Europe, drop
380m/1 246.7ft in total and are a magnificent sight, especially in the midday
sun when the spray glitters in every
color of the rainbow.

Before climbing the 4km/2.5mi path up
the falls, be sure to take in the viewpoint
at the foot of the lowest fall where the
water thunders onto a rocky barrier. The
broad path zigzags beneath a canopy of
trees to the Schettkanzel at the top of
the falls at 1 465m/4 806.4ft. Just above
the middle falls, you can fortify yourself
at the Schönangerl mountain inn before
the final, steep climb.

At the entrance to the falls is the
Kids **Wasserwunderwelt**★ (Water Won-
derland; ◷Apr–Oct, daily 9.30am–5pm),
an interactive theme park with 3D and

Krimml falls

multimedia exhibits about the falls,
playful toys such as a water-powered
swing, and a look at the falls through a
telescope. Just beyond here is a national
park information center.

GMUNDEN★

OBERÖSTERREICH
POPULATION 15 075
ALT 420M/1 378FT

Gmunden is a popular lakeside summer resort that experienced its first heyday
in the 19C when it became the darling of artists, poets and politicians. These days
it is known for its fine ceramics as well as its busy beaches, lake cruises and the
Esplanade, an elegant promenade along the northern shore of Lake Traunsee.

- **Information:** Am Graben 2, A-4810. ℡0 76 12/6 43 05. www.gmunden.at.
- ▶ **Orient Yourself:** Gmunden is on the northern shore of Traunsee lake in
  the Salzkammergut.
- **Parking:** There is a parking lot (fee) in Seilergasse.
- **Don't Miss:** A stroll along the Esplanade.
- **Organizing Your Time:** Allow a day to include excursions.
- **Also See:** BAD ISCHL.

Sights

Historic Center

The Renaissance **town hall** on Rathausplatz, the main square, has a ceramic
glockenspiel that chimes out several
times daily. North of here, the town's
medieval warren of lanes is punctuated

by the **Stadtpfarrkirche** with a precious
high altar by Thomas Schwanthaler
depicting the *Adoration of the Magi*.
In the former salt administration building east of the town hall, the **Kammerhofmuseum** (◷mid-Apr–Oct, daily
9am–6pm; Nov–Dec, Tue–Sun 10am–
5pm; ◷Dec 24; €6; ℡0 76 12/79 44

© Österreich Werbung/Jezierzanski

Schloss Ort, Gmunden

20) has exhibits on local history and a selection of local ceramics. Considerably more memorable is the quirky **Klo & So Sanitärmuseum** (⊙*same hours as Kammerhofmuseum;* ⊗*€4.20;* ☎*0 76 12/9 44 25)* at Traungasse 4, which has a bizarre collection of toilet bowls, chamber pots, sinks and bidets, including one used by Empress Elisabeth.

Seeschloss Ort★

On a little island accessed by a wooden bridge, this landmark palace (www.schlossort.gmunden.at) wraps around a triangular arcaded courtyard with elaborate sgraffito decoration and a Late Gothic exterior staircase. Weddings take place here regularly (except 2008).

Excursions

Schloss Scharnstein★

30km/18.6mi round trip.
Leave Gmunden to the east on B 120.
This Renaissance castle perches above the Alm River and houses two unusual museums and a reptile collection.
The 21 rooms of the **Österreichisches Kriminalmuseum** (Austrian Crime Museum; ⊙*May–Oct 15, Tue–Sun 9am–5pm;* ⊗*€5;* ☎*0 76 15/25 50)* traces the fight against crime from the Middle Ages to today. Displays include devices of tor-

ture and execution that are not for the faint of heart, let alone children.
Fans of contemporary Austrian history will likely enjoy the **Zeitgeschichte Museum Scharnstein**, which chronicles all 20C milestones, including the Third Reich years.
Down in the cellar is the extraordinary **Reptilienzoo – Haus der Gifte** (Reptile Zoo, House of Poison: ⊙*May–mid-Oct, Tue–Sun 9am–5pm, Nov–Apr, Sun and public holidays 1pm–4pm.* ⊗*€5.* ☎*0 76 15/77 65; www.hausdergifte.at.tf)* with poisonous snakes, reptiles, scorpions, giant spiders, and natural poisons.

Vöcklabruck

With a population of 12 000, Vöcklabruck bestrides the old main road halfway between Salzburg and Linz and has a pedigree going back to the 12C. Today, the place is still a busy market town and educational center for the surrounding countryside. It also benefits from its proximity to the famous Salzkammergut (🕭 *see SALZKAMMERGUT)* tourist area and the nearby Attersee and Traunsee lakes.

Stadtplatz

As is frequently the case in Austria, the town square is simply a widening of the main road. Most buildings are decorated with Baroque façades but are in fact much older, including no. 14, which has an arcaded courtyard very much in the style of the Italian Renaissance. The square is bookended by two towers. One of them, the **Unterer Stadtturm** (Lower Tower), features the coats of arms of the various possessions of Burgundy as well as those of the Habsburgs. This is a visual reminder of the marriage of **Emperor Maximilian I**, who owned a house in town, to Mary of Burgundy.

Dörflkirche St. Ägidius

Leave the town via the Unterer Stadtturm and cross the river; the church is just over the bridge on the right. If the door is closed, ring at the presbytery. ☎0 76 72/7 26 08. This elegant building is the successor to a much earlier church, first consecrated in

1143. It was built in 1688 by the architect **Carlo Antonio Carlone** and decorated by Giovanni Battista Carlone. Its Baroque splendor was restored in 1980.

GOSAUSEEN★★★
OBERÖSTERREICH

The Gosau lakes lie amid the craggy peaks of the Dachstein range and are a fantastic destination for nature lovers.

- 🚩 **Information:** Naturschutzgebiet Gosausee, Gosau, A-4824. ☎0 61 36/82 95.
- ▸ **Orient Yourself:** The lakes are some 15km/9.3mi northwest of Hallstadt.
- 👁 **Also See:** HALLSTADT, DACHSTEIN

Sights

Vorderer Gosausee★★★
Alt 933m/3 061ft.
About 5km/3mi past the village of Gosau, this lake affords unforgettable **views**★★ of the Hoher Dachstein range. The setting is especially magical early or late in the day for the dramatic interplay of light and shadow between valley and glaciers. It takes about an hour to walk around the lake. For even better views, take the **Gosaukammbahn** to the Zwieselalm (1 587m/5 206.7ft), which is also the starting point for numerous trails.

Hinterer Gosausee★★
The moderately fit might consider continuing for about an hour to the Hinterer Gosausee, a smaller lake encircled by dense forest and a ring of craggy peaks.

© Österreich Werbung / W. Weinhaeupl

Gosausee with a view of the Dachstein range

GRAZ ★★

STEIERMARK
POPULATION 240 300
ALT 365M/1 194FT

The capital of Styria, Graz is also known as the "Garden City" thanks to its many parks, riverside setting and surrounding rolling hills. In 1999 its extensive historic center was declared a UNESCO World Heritage Site. Austria's second-largest city is an economic hub that provides employment to around 130 000 people in industries ranging from brewing to shoe making to car manufacturing. Cultural life flourishes tremendously with plenty of performances and festivals taking place year-round. The nightlife is excellent, too, fueled in large part by 50 000 students attending four major universities.

- **Information:** Herrengasse 16, A-8010. ☎03 16/8 07 50. www.graztourism.at.
- ▶ **Orient Yourself:** Graz is in the valley of the Mur, bounded by the Styrian hills and the last foothills of the Alps in southeastern Austria.
- **Parking:** Garages abound in the center but they are expensive and may only offer short-term parking. You're better off at a Park & Ride lot, for instance the one behind the main train station; take bus No 1 or 7 to the center.
- **Don't Miss:** Zeughaus, Mausoleum, Schlossberg, Kunsthaus.
- **Organizing Your Time:** Devote at least a full day to Graz, starting your exploration in the old town around the Hauptplatz, perhaps making time for a museum or two, then heading up the Schlossberg in the afternoon for grand views and a relaxing stroll.
- **Especially for Kids:** Jagdmuseum.
- **Also See:** SCHLOSS EGGENBERG, ÖSTERREICHISCHES FREILICHTMUSEUM.

A Bit of History

In 1379 the Leopoldine branch of the Habsburgs chose Graz as their residence. It became an imperial city when Friedrich III, king of Germany and Austria, was crowned Holy Roman Emperor in 1452. Graz equipped itself with ramparts as early as the 13C as defense against the Turkish invasions in Styria. In 1543 the defenses, including the Schlossberg Fortress, were strengthened under Emperor Ferdinand I by the Italian **Domenico dell'Allio**, who was also architect of the Landhaus. The measures taken to ward off attack were extensive; a huge arsenal of arms and munitions was built up with the raw material coming from Styria's "**Iron Mountain**." Whenever invasion seemed imminent, the arms were distributed among local volunteers to reinforce the professional troops.

Following the Habsburg partition of the country in 1564, Graz became the capital of a vast area known as **Inner Austria**, comprising Styria, Carinthia, Gorizia, Carniola, and Istria. The splendid court of Archduke Karl II brought many cultural and artistic benefits to the city.

The Reformation – By 1568 three-quarters of the population had embraced Protestantism. In this year a school and seminary were founded, where the present Paradeishof stands (CZ 26), and it was here that the German astronomer, Johannes Kepler, taught between 1594 and 1598.

In 1571 Archduke Karl II called in the Jesuits to implement the Counter Reformation; they founded a college (in the Bürgergasse) and a school (Hofgasse). In 1585 the Archduke founded **Graz University**, which became the intellectual hub of Inner Austria.

The city's fortunes took another turn in 1619 when Karl II's son, Archduke Ferdinand II, was elected Holy Roman Emperor. Ferdinand moved the court to

Vienna, and Graz, no longer an Imperial residence, lost much of its importance. In the 18C, following the reforms of Maria Theresa, the city had to forgo many of its privileges; later, under Joseph II, the university was downgraded to a grammar school. Graz's days of splendor came to a definite end and this is why the city has so few buildings dating from the Late Baroque period.

A Prince beloved by his people, Archduke Johann – The Habsburg Archduke Johann (1782–1859) enjoyed great popularity in Styria and his memory is still honored today. On settling in Graz, he devoted himself to studies of all kinds, roaming through Styria and Carinthia in the company of naturalists, archeologists and painters.

His romantic marriage to Anna Plochl, a postmaster's daughter from Bad Aussee, did nothing to diminish his popularity. He founded model farms, presided over the construction of the Graz-Mürzzuschlag railway (1844) and promoted the development of the Eisenerz area. In Graz itself, the Technische Hochschule is proof of his progressive spirit, as is the Landesmuseum Joanneum, Austria's oldest museum open to the public, founded in 1811.

Walking Tour

⊡ Old Town Tour★★

Hauptplatz★ (CZ)

In the heart of Graz, this is the liveliest of squares. The city trams come and go incessantly, disgorging ever more people to join the motley crowd thronging the market stalls. Behind the brightly painted 17C–19C façades are buildings of much older, medieval era. The flashiest façade belongs to the arcaded **Haus Luegg** (CZ A), which is festooned with luxuriant Baroque stucco work. The city's oldest pharmacy is at no. 4; dating from 1535, it still has some of its original fittings. The **Erzherzog-Johann-Brunnen** (fountain) of 1878 dominates the square. The fact that the statue of the Emperor is relegated to a less important site on the Freiheitsplatz (DY 10) is a tangible reminder of the local people's affection for the enlightened archduke. The four female figures gracing the fountain are allegories of the four main rivers flowing through Styria at the time of the monarchy, though the boundary revisions of 1918 left the province with only two of them (the Mur and the Enns).

The southern end of the square is punctuated by the neo-Renaissance **Rathaus** (Town Hall). Standing outside, you get a great view of the Schlossberg with the

City of Graz

© Österreich Werbung / Bohnacker

Landhaushof

familiar outline of the Uhrturm (Clock Tower), the emblem of Graz.

The Landhaus is reached via the broad and busy **Herrengasse** (DZ) with its ele-gant shops and offices. The **Gemaltes Haus** (painted house, at no. 3) was residence of the archdukes until the building of the castle in 1450. The murals on historic (notably Roman) themes date from 1742, when they replaced the original decoration by Pietro de Pomis, architect of the mausoleum.

Landhaus★★ (DZ)

The former seat of the Styrian Diet, the Landhaus is a remarkable Renaissance palace built between 1557 and 1565 by Domenico dell'Allio, the military architect who had just completed the total reconstruction of the Schlossberg fortress for Emperor Ferdinand I. Today the Landhaus still serves as the meeting place for the Landtag, the Styrian provincial parliament.

The main façade with its round-arched windows above an elegant doorway prepares you for the splendor of the inner courtyard with its three storeys of arcades, flower-bedecked balconies,

Address Book

For coin ranges, see the Legend on the cover flap.

PRACTICAL INFORMATION

TOURIST INFORMATION

Graz/Steiermark Information, *im Landhaus, Herrengasse 16, 8010 Graz. Jun–Sept, Mon–Fri 9am–7pm, Sat 9am–6pm, Sun and public holidays 10am–3pm; Oct–May, Mon–Fri 9am–6pm, Sat 9am–3pm, Sun and public holidays 10am–3pm;* ☎*03 16/80 75 0.*

Graz Informationpoint am Hauptbahnhof, *Europaplatz 6, 8020 Graz. Offering free brochures and an electronic information system.* ☎*03 16/80 75 0 (main office). www.graztourismus.at.*

CITY TOURS

Tour of Old Town (2hr 30min) *Apr–end Oct, daily at 2.30pm, otherwise Sat only at 2.30pm.* Meeting point: Graz/Steiermark Information.

Tours of the Schlossberg *Easter–Oct daily 9am–5pm on the hour.* Meeting point: At the bell-tower.

Guided tours (in English and German) are available *early Apr–late Oct.* Departure at 2pm from the Landhausgasse, return at about 7pm.

Fri: Styrian Castle Route

Sat: Piber Lippizaner Stud Farm

Sun: South Styrian Wine Route Information and bookings from Graz/Steiermark Information, *Herrengasse 16.*

PUBLIC TRANSPORT

Tickets are available from ticket machines, advance booking offices and tobacconists (Trafiken), and also from tram and bus drivers.

With the **Stundenkarte** you can use any form of public transport in Graz for 1hr, with the **10-Zonenkarte** you can make ten journeys within the same zone, and there is also a **24-Stundenkarte** and a **Wochenkarte**, offering travel for 24hr and a week respectively.

Further information on public transport can be obtained from the Graz transport authority (**GVB**) Zeitkartenbüro (Season ticket office), *Hauptplatz 14,* ☎*03 16/8 74 08,* or from the Infor-mationsstelle on the *Jakominiplatz,* ☎*03 16/88 74 11.*

BICYCLE HIRE

Bicycles can be hired from the Hauptbahnhof (☎*03 16/78 48 326*) or Bicycle (*Kaiser-Franz-Josefs-Kai 55 and 66 or Rechbauerstraße 57,* ☎*03 16/82 13 57*) to explore the city's 75km/47mi of cycle paths.

INNER CITY PARKING

Parking is permitted in the **blue zones** for a fee covering a certain time (*restricted parking is operated between 9am and 7pm on weekdays*). Parking tickets valid for up to 3hr can be obtained from parking ticket machines. Otherwise you should park in one of the following car parks:

Tiefgarage (underground) Mariahilferplatz; Parkhaus (multi-story) Griesgasse 10; Tiefgarage Andreas-Hofer-Platz; Tiefgarage Rosarium, Hamerlinggasse; Garage Burgring, Einspinnergasse; Schlossberg-Garage, Sackstraße 29; City-Garage Weitzer, Am Entenplatz.

POST OFFICES

Main post office: **Hauptpostamt**, *Neutorgasse 46, Mon–Fri 7am–11pm, Sat 7am–2pm, Sun and public holidays 8am–2pm.*

Station post office: **Bahnhofspostamt**, *Europaplatz 10, daily, 24hr.*

WHERE TO STAY

Daniel – *Europaplatz 1.* ☎*03 16/71 10 80. www.hoteldaniel.com. 102 rooms.* Wonderful balcony views, well-equipped rooms and well kept.

Gollner – *Schlögelgasse 14.* ☎*03 16/82 25 21. www.hotelgollner.at. 54 rooms.* Next to the opera house, it is popular with both opera goers and artists. Despite being in a building completed in 1800 it is contemporary in style. There is a garden roof terrace.

Erzherzog Johann – *Sackstr. 3–5.* ☎*03 16/81 16 16. www.erzherzog-johann.com. 59 rooms.* An elegant hotel dating from the 16C. The rooms are arranged around a central covered atrium with wrought-iron balconies.

Parkhotel Graz – Leonhard-str. 8. ☎03 16/ 3 63 00. www.parkhotel-graz.at. 70 rooms. The interior of this hotel, built in 1574 is filled with suits of armor, antiques and hanging tapestries. There are traditionally decorated rooms and a beamed dining room.
Zum Dom – Bürgergasse 14. ☎03 16/82 48 00. www.domhotel. at. 29 rooms. A hip hotel in a converted palace. Each room is individually decorated.

WHERE TO EAT

RESTAURANTS

Corti (Münzgrabenstr. 17, ☎0316/81 14 00); **Hofkeller** (Hofgasse 8, ☎0316/83 24 37; **Santa Clara** (Abraham–a-Santa-Clara-Gasse 1, entrance Bürgergasse 6, ☎03 16/81 18 22); **Iohan** (Landhausgasse 1, ☎0316/7 78); **Kehlberghof** (Kehlbergstraße 83, ☎03 16/28 41 25); **Landhauskeller** (Schmiedgasse 9, ☎03 16/83 02 76); **Magnolia** (Schönaugasse 53, ☎0316/2 08 00).

CAFÉS AND BARS

Temmel's Kaiserhof (Kaiserfeldgasse 1); **Café Promenade am Burgtor** (Erzherzog-Johann-Allee 1); **Operncafé** (Opernring 22); **Hofbäckerei Edegger-Tax** (Hofgasse 6).

NIGHTLIFE

The center of Graz nightlife (known as the "Bermuda triangle") is the area bordered by the Färberplatz, Glockenspielplatz, and Herrengasse. Here there are hostelries and wine parlors to suit every taste. The predominant youth scene is in the university quarter (Leonhardtstraße, Zinzendorfgasse and Schillerplatz).

In the **Gasthaus Keplerkeller** (Stempfergasse 6), you can drink wine and listen to Styrian music, while special beers are available at the **Bierbaron** (Heinrichstraße 56), **Eschenlaube** (Glacisstraße 67), and **Schillerhof** (Plüddemanngasse 2). **Café Stockwerk** (Jakominiplatz 18/I) offers jazz music. You can also have a drink in one of the many bars in Graz, such as the **Ernst-Fuchs-Bar** in the Hotel Erzherzog Johann (Sackstraße 3–5), the

Fink (Freiheitsplatz 2), the **Limarutti** (Prokopigasse 4) or the **M1** (Färberplatz 1/III). There is dancing in the **Monte** (Sackstraße 27) and in the **Castello** (Bürgergasse 4). The ambience of an American bar, complete with live jazz, is recreated in the **Hemingway American Bar** (Klosterwiesgasse 6).

SHOPPING

The main shopping street is the **Herrengasse**, but there are also numerous shops in the pedestrian precincts, such as **Sporgasse/Murgasse**, the streets around the **Hauptplatz**, and **Schmiedgasse/Stubenberggasse/Hans-Sachs-Gasse**.

MARKETS

Kaiser-Josef-Platz (farm produce), daily 6am–noon.

Lendplatz (farm produce), Mon–Sat 7am–noon.

Karmeliterplatz (flea market), 3rd Sat in the month.

SOUVENIRS

Craft goods and traditional costume (Trachten): Steirisches Heimatwerk, Herrengasse 10 and Paulustorgasse 4. Schlossbergkugeln (Schlossberg balls, local specialty chocolates): Konditorei Strehly, Sporgasse 14. Styrian wine: Stempfergasse 2.

ENTERTAINMENT

OPERA AND THEATERS

The **"Bühnen Graz"** (☎03 16/80 00, www.buehnen-graz.com) association includes five theaters:

The **Opernhaus** at Kaiser-Josef-Platz 10, the **Schauspielhaus** (spoken theater, 12 premieres every season) on Freiheitsplatz, **Next Liberty** (children's and young people's theater) at Kaiser-Josef-Platz 10, the **Orpheum** (venue for rock, pop, jazz and cabaret) at Orpheumgasse 8, and in the summer the **Casemates** (open-air theater) on Schlossberg.

T.i.P. (Theater im Palais), Leonhard-straße 15, ☎03 16/38 91 016, hosts musical and spoken theater by students from Graz University of Art.

TheatermëRZ – Steinfeldgasse 20. ☎03 16/72 01 72. This artists' and authors' theater can look back on numerous international tours. Its program focuses on the work of author, director, and theater manager, Willi Bernhart: Plays, song programs, children's and young people's theater.

Theatro – *Neubaugasse 6*. ☎*03 16/71 60 27*. Independent cultural center which hosts all kinds of theater as well as concerts of rock pop and world music.

Casino Graz – *Landhausgasse 10.* ☎*03 16/83 25 78*. Austria's second-largest casino.

CINEMAS

Large multiple-screen cinema complexes offering a corresponding variety of films are to be found at **UCI Kinowelt Annenhof** (*Annenstraße 29,* ☎*03 16/72 77*) and **Cineplexx** (*Alte Poststraße 470,* ☎*03 16/29 09*). For films other than current mainstream, try the **Filmzentrum im Rechbauerkino** (*Rechbauerstraße 6,* ☎*03 16/83 05 08*), **KIZ Kino im Augarten** (*Friedrichgasse 24,* ☎*03 16/82 11 86*) and **Schubertkino** (*Mehlplatz 2,* ☎*03 16/82 90 810*).

DATES FOR YOUR DIARY

Diagonale: *Mar–Apr*, Festival of Austrian film.

Storytime in Graz: *Whitsun*, festival of storytelling and fairytales. Storytellers visit Graz from all over the world.

Classics in the city: *summer*, open-air performances of classical music in the Renaissance Landhaushof with international culinary delights.

Generali Hof Jazz concerts: *summer*, open-air performances, free of charge, courtesy of the Graz jazz scene.

Styriarte: *Jul*, classical music festival.

Jazz-Sommer: *Jul–Aug*, jazz concerts on the Mariahilfer Platz, free of charge.

AIMS: *mid-Jul–end Aug*, festival of classical music by the great composers played by students from the **A**merican **I**nstitute of **M**usical **S**tudies.

La Strada: *end Jul–early Aug*, international festival of puppet and street theater in the old city.

Styrian Autumn: *Oct*, international avant-garde festival of contemporary music, theater, art exhibitions and readings of literary works.

Mountain and adventure film festival: *Nov*, international film competition, with the "Grand Prix Graz" awarded in five different categories.

---

staircase wells and loggias. The stairway gracing the chapel in the northwest corner of the courtyard is by another Italian, Bartolomeo di Bosio. The well-head has a fine bronze dais with amoretti and female figures. In summer, the courtyard forms an enchanting backdrop for various performances.

Zeughaus (Arsenal)★★★ (DZ)

🕐*Apr–Oct, daily 10am–6pm; Nov–Mar, Mon–Sat 10am–3pm, Sun 10am–3pm.* ⊛*€7 (admission free Oct 26).* ☎*03 16/80 17 98 10. www.zeughaus.at.*
Built in 1642, the Zeughaus was one of many arsenals in the world, but today it is the only one to have been preserved in its original state and with its contents intact. To enter the arsenal is to leave behind the contemporary bustle of the Herrengasse and to be transported back into the world of four centuries ago. You almost expect cavalrymen and foot sol-

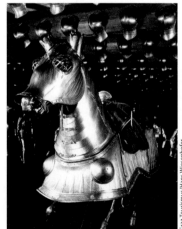

©Graz Tourismus/Hans Wiesenhofer

Zeughaus

diers to appear, fresh from being mustered in the Landhaus courtyard to be outfitted for battle.

Displayed on four floors are more than 32 000 arms of all imaginable kinds, many of a very high standard of crafts-manship. There are pistols, muskets, arquebuses and other firearms; heavy armor, breastplates and harnesses for use in battle or jousting, plus helmets, pikes, swords—the collection is truly mindboggling. Head to the top floor for a grand view of the Landhaus courtyard, the city's red rooftops and the Schloss-berg with clock tower.

Stadtpfarrkirche zum Heiligen Blut (DZ)

The original Gothic church building was remodeled in the Baroque taste, then re-Gothicized in the late 19C. Its Baroque **bell-tower**★, the city's finest, was built entirely out of wood in 1780–81 by the architect Josef Stengg and the master carpenter, Franz Windisch. It is topped by a three-barred cross, a reminder of its consecration by the Pope.

Inside, on the altar in the south aisle, is an *Assumption of the Virgin* attributed to Tintoretto. The stained glass of the chancel, the work of the Salzburg artist Albert Birkle in 1953, has an unusual feature; in the left-hand window, the fourth panel from the bottom on the right shows Hitler and Mussolini observing the flagellation of Christ. Birkle's work had been deemed "degenerate" by the Nazis. Organ concerts are held in the church on a regular basis.

▸ Enter *Altstadtpassage* (DZ 3) *at no. 7 Herrengasse.*

Walking through Altstadtpassage, the first courtyard has arcaded and vaulted galleries dating from 1648. A little further on, to the right, are a number of courtyards of which one is reminiscent of the Landhaus.

The passageway spills out onto the **Mehlplatz** (DZ 22), flanked by two grand residences with Baroque stucco façades. Go right onto the **Glockenspielplatz** (Carillon Square – *performances at 11am, 3pm and 6pm* – DZ 12) where dancing figures in local costume appear at each carillon performance in the pediment of an imposing house with a bell-turret.

Leave the Glockenspielplatz via the narrow passageway called Abraham-a-Santa-Clara-Gasse (DZ 2), then turn left for a view of no. 1 Burgergasse (DZ), the sombre palazzo-like building which once served as a boarding-house for aristocratic pupils of the Jesuits. To the right, a stairway leads to the Mausoleum.

Mausoleum★★ (DZ)

◷ *Year-round, daily 10.30am–noon, 1.30pm–4pm.* ◷*Public holidays.* ⊜*4€.* ☎*03 16/82 16 83.*

Emperor Ferdinand II commissioned Italian architect, **Pietro de Pomis**, to build the Imperial mausoleum. Pomis started work in 1614, but the structure was finally completed in 1636 by fellow Italian, Pietro Valnegro. Inside, Johann Bernhard Fischer von Erlach designed the exuberant stucco work and some of the frescoes. A particularly fine oval dome surmounts the funerary crypt with the red-marble sarcophagus of Karl II and Maria of Bavaria, the Emperor's parents. Only Maria lies inside, though, as the Emperor was buried at Seckau Abbey. The tomb of Emperor Ferdinand II is to the right of the altar.

Domkirche (Cathedral)★ (DZ)

Next to the mausoleum, the vast and luminous Domkirche only became a cathedral in 1786, having previously served as Imperial court church. It was commissioned by Emperor Friedrich III, whose coat of arms adorns the main entrance, and completed in 1464. Frescoes (1485) on the southwest corner of the entrance show the troubles visited on Graz in the 1480s (Turkish attack, plague and locusts).

The **interior** is a harmonious mix of Gothic reticulated vaulting and Baroque decoration. Of the original décor two frescoes of St. Christopher (late 15C) have survived. They recall an old belief according that one would not die on a day on which one had looked at the saint's image.

Near the entrance to the chancel are two magnificent **reliquary chests**★★★. Brought here by the Jesuits, they are works of great sophistication and were

Roof of the Mausoleum

R. Chéret/MICHELIN

once the marriage chests of Paula di Gonzaga, Duchess of Mantua. Made of ebony and decorated with reliefs in bone and ivory, they date from around 1470 and are in the style of Mantegna. Their subject matter goes back to the *Triumphs* of Petrarch, moral and allegorical poems dealing with the various stages of life from the standpoint of a calm acceptance of death. The organ with its 5 354 pipes dates from 1978.

▶ *Leave the cathedral by the north entrance.*

Cross the street by the **Burgtor** (Castle Gate, DZ) and go through the impressive stone gateway commanding the first courtyard of the 15C **castle** (Burg), the erstwhile residence of Friedrich III. Heavily rebuilt, it now houses the offices of the provincial government (Landesregierung). At the end of the first courtyard, below an archway, is the amazing **Treppenturm**★★ (Staircase Tower, DY B), a highly unusual double spiral stairway. The tower was added in 1499 by his son Maximilian I and is a notable technical achievement in terms of design and the stonemason's craft.

▶ *Backtrack to Hofgasse and head west to Freiheitsplatz.*

Freiheitsplatz (DY 10)

In the center of the square stands the statue of Franz II, the last Holy Roman Emperor and elder brother of Archduke Johann. The large red building with a Neoclassical pediment closing the square is the city residence of the abbots of St. Lambrecht.

Follow Hofgasse to the old **Hofbäckerei** (Imperial Bakery) with its fine shopfront on your left just before Sporgasse. Turning right into the Sporgasse, have a look at the **Palais Saurau** at no. 25 with its rusticated Baroque doorway and arcaded doorway; the significance of the Turk brandishing a sword on the gable is a mystery, even to the locals. The Renaissance **Zur Goldenen Pastete** (no. 28) is also picturesque.

Follow bright and busy **Sporgasse** (CY) as it winds back to the Hauptplatz. At no. 22 is the former Deutschordenshaus (House of the Teutonic Knights); it has an arcaded courtyard in Gothic style. The narrow façade of no. 3 is an interesting example of Jugendstil (Art Nouveau).

▶ *Turn right onto Sackstraße.*

Sackstraße (CYZ)

This was once a cul-de-sac (Sack), which was opened by a tower gateway in the 14C whose site is now occupied by the Palais Attems (no. 17). The road was lengthened on two occasions in

GRAZ		Franziskanerpl.	CZ	9	Mehlpl.	DZ	22
		Freiheitspl.	DY	10	Neue-Welt-Gasse	CZ	23
Abraham–a-Santa-		Girardigasse	DZ	35	Paradeisgasse	CZ	26
Clara-Gasse	DZ	2	Glockenspielpl.	DZ	12	Radetzkybrücke	CZ	27
Altstadtpassage	DZ	3	Griespl.	CZ	13	Schlossbergpl.	CY	29
Färbergasse	DZ	5	Hauptbrücke	CZ	16	Stempfergasse	DZ	30
Färberpl.	DZ	6	Keplerbrücke	CY	19	Tegetthoffbrücke	CZ	32
Franziskanergasse	CZ	8	Luthergasse	DZ	20			

Alte Galerie des Steier-			Haus Luegg	CZ	A	Steirisches Volkskunde-		
märkischen Landes-			Palais Attems	CY	D	museum	DY	M²
museums Joanneum	CZ	M³	Stadtmuseum	CY	M¹	Treppenturm	DY	B
Dreifaltigkeitskirche	CY	E	Stadtpark-Brunnen	DY	F			

the course of extending the city walls. Because of its proximity to the river, it became the heart of an artisans' district with a great variety of trades: millers, tanners, parchment-makers and many others. After 1650, the oldest part of the street became known as "Lords Blind Alley" because of the aristocratic mansions that are still here today.

The Krebsenkeller at no. 12 has a **Renaissance courtyard**★ whose double windows and arcaded loggias create an

Italian feel. The **Palais Herberstein** at no. 16, once a grand mansion, boasts a monumental staircase as evidence of its past splendor.

These days, the Landesmuseum Joanneum has its **Neue Galerie** (New Gallery) here, which displays art from the 19C and 20C in such media as painting, sculpture, photography, video and installations.

The **Palais Khuenberg** at no. 18 was the birthplace of ill-fated Archduke Franz Ferdinand (*see ARTSTETTEN*), the heir to the throne who was assassinated in 1914. Today it houses the **Stadtmuseum** (M¹) (&*Tue–Sun 10am–6pm; €4 (free on Sun);* 03 16/8 72 76 00; *www.stadtmuseumgraz.at*).

Palais Attems (CY D)

Opposite the Stadtmuseum, this is without doubt the finest of all the city's Baroque palaces. Its **façades**★★ worthy of closer inspection, with their profuse decoration of pilasters, mouldings and curvilinear window pediments. The palace was built between 1702 and 1716 for Count Attems on a site previously occupied by six town houses.

The nearby city gate was demolished at the same time, having outlived its usefulness.

Dreifaltigkeitskirche (CY E)

Built in 1704, the church seems to be watching over its neighbor, the Palais Attems. It reveals its calm and harmonious façade with its scrolled pediment in an almost shy way, notwithstanding the abundance of iconography referring to the Trinity, to which the church is dedicated.

The view from the church door shows the Schlossbergplatz (CY 29) from which some 260 steep steps climb up to the Schlossberg itself.

Medieval quarter★

Toward the end of the Middle Ages, a cattle market was held between the river and the ramparts, where the Franziskanerplatz (CZ 9) and the Neutorgasse (CZ) are now. The strange name (Kälbernes Viertel meaning Calf Town), still used by locals for the area around the Franciscan church, recalls these times.

In 1620, the area was brought within the ramparts when the city's defenses were being strengthened.

The quarter has kept much of its charm, and a stroll through its narrow **lanes**★ is most enjoyable, particularly the pretty Neue-Welt-Gasse (CZ 23) and the Franziskanergasse (CZ 8), both piled high with the wares of produce vendors.

Franziskanerkirche (CZ)

Traders set up their stalls against the walls of this church, which was re-roofed after World War II and given modern glass. It was here in 1240 that the Minorites installed their convent, which passed into the ownership of a closed Franciscan order in the 16C. The oldest part of the church, the Jakobskapelle, dates back to 1330.

2 City Parks Tour★

Schlossberg★ (CY)

Reached by funicular (Schlossbergbahn), from the northern end of the Sackstraße, via the steps leading up from the Schlossbergplatz (CY 29) or by elevator (Schlossberg lift) operating next to the steps. Operates every 15min, runs Sun–Wed 8am–half-past midnight, Thu–Sat 8am–2.30am. €0.60. 03 16/88 74 04.

Rising 123m/403.5ft above the city, this impregnable hilltop bristled with redoubts and fortifications right up to the Napoleonic Wars. Even in 1809, when Graz was occupied by French troops, the fortress withstood all assaults. Much to the chagrin of the townsfolk, one of the provisions of the Treaty of Schönbrunn in 1809 involved the demolition of the Schlossberg. Only the payment of a handsome ransom spared the **Uhrturm** (Clock Tower), now the city emblem, and the **Glockenturm** (Bell-tower) whose four-and-a-half ton bell "Lisl" is the biggest in town. The area was later turned into a park and today is still a popular place for strolling and picnicking.

The Schlossberg is honeycombed by tunnels used as bomb shelters during World War II. A section of these is now used as the **Dom im Berg** (www.domimberg.at), an unusual performance and exhibition space right inside the mountain.

The entrance is near the steps leading up the Schlossberg.

A wide chestnut-tree-lined avenue leads down to the clock tower rising from a colorful flower bed. The dial is unusual; for a long time it had only a single hand showing the hours. The smaller, minute hand was added later.

Go down the steps leading to the Herberstein gardens. From the terrace there are fine **views**★★ over the city and the Mur Valley.

▶ *Climb back up to the clock tower and then go down the first path on the right which leads back into town to the Karmeliterplatz.*

Here there is a Trinity Column, erected in 1680 in thanksgiving for relief from the plague.

▶ *Go up the Paulustorgasse.*

Steirisches Volkskundemuseum (DY M²)

🕐*Tue–Sun 10am–5pm.* ⊛*€5.50.* ☎*03 16 / 80 17 98 99. www.museum-joan neum.at.*

This revamped museum devoted to Styrian folk art and traditions forms part of the Landesmuseum Joanneum and has been housed since 1913 in a former Capuchin monastery. The exhibit is divided into three major themes: Wohnen (living), Kleiden (clothing), and Glauben (faith). Highlights include the Trachtenraum, a large room with 42 life-size figures showcasing the wealth of folkloric garments through the ages, and the Rauchstube, a smoke room typically found in old farmhouses.

Paulustor (DY)

Together with the Burgtor, this gateway is all that remains of the city walls. Built toward the end of the 16C, it displays the coats of arms, in marble, of Ferdinand II of Austria and of Maria Anna of Bavaria.

Stadtpark★ (DY)

This "English-style" park follows the line of the old walls to the east and southeast of the historic city center. At its center is the **Forum Stadtpark**, a meeting place of avant-garde artists since the 1960s. Outside this building, the **Stadtpark-Brunnen** (F) is a fountain in a luxuriant setting of fine old trees, shrubs and flowerbeds. Also in the park is the **Künstlerhaus**, a contemporary art exhibition space affiliated with the Landesmuseum Joanneum.

▶ *To get back to Hauptplatz, go south through the Stadtpark to the Burgtor, take Hofgasse west, then Sporgasse south and you'll be there.*

Additional Sights

Mariahilf-Kirche★ (CY)

One of the finest of the city's churches, with elegant twin towers and impeccably proportioned Baroque façade, this was the province's most popular place of pilgrimage after Mariazell.

It was begun in 1607–11 by Pietro de Pomis, architect of the Mausoleum and Schloss Eggenberg, who was buried here in 1633. The Late Baroque towers of 1742–44 are by Josef Hueber. Renaissance in structure, the interior of the nave gives an overall impression of harmony and repose. The door on the left of the façade leads to the cloisters, beyond which is a further courtyard with a little building in the style of the Renaissance, albeit designed as late as the end of the 17C. its first floor is given over entirely to the **Minoritensaal** (🕐*Mon–Fri 8am–6pm; check beforehand* ☎*03 16/71 31 70)*, one of the city's concert halls. The building also houses the **Diözesanmuseum** (Diocesan Museum), with several centuries' worth of religious treasures from throughout Styria.

Landesmuseum Joanneum (CDZ)

🕐*Each part of the museum complex has slightly varying opening times. Please see individual entries or contact* ☎*03 16/80 17 97 70 or see www.museum-joanneum.at.*

The Joanneum is the country's oldest public museum complex and the second-largest museum in Austria after the Kunsthistorisches Museum in Vienna (🕐*see WIEN).* Exhibits are spread over a number of buildings in and around Graz, including Schloss Eggenberg (Old Masters), the Kunsthaus (contemporary art), and the Volkskundemuseum (crafts and folkore). ⏱️ *See individual entries for more on any of these.*

The two original buildings, donated to the city Archduke Johann, are in the heart of the old town. Natural history is the focus of the one in Raubergasse 10, and around the corner, at Neutorgasse 45, is the **Kulturhistorische Sammlung** (Cultural History Collection) where exhibits shed light on the daily lives of Styrians—peasants to nobility—from the Middle Ages through today.

Kunsthaus Graz★

🕐 *Tue–Sun 10am–6pm.* €7. ☎03 16/ 80 17-92 00. www.kunsthaus graz.at.
Opened in 2003, the Kunsthaus is Graz's most recent landmark (Fournier & Cook), an architecturally bold exhibition space devoted to presenting art from the 1960s through the present. Sitting on the western bank of the Mur River, the avant-garde building vaguely resembles an alien heart with multiple aortas sprouting from its roof.

Leechkirche (DY)

Built between 1275 and 1293, the university church of Maria am Leech is the oldest religious building in Graz. The Early Gothic, multi-layered **west front**★ is crowned by a Virgin and Child on the tympanum, a work in Late Romanesque angular style. The **stained glass**★, which dates from 1330 and depicts various saints and the story of Christ's Passion, is of particular interest.

Excursions

Stift Rein★ (AX)

15km/9.3mi northwest.
Founded in 1129, Rein is the oldest Cistercian abbey in Austria. Its buildings, dominated by the elegant Baroque tower, stand out against a background of wooded hills. Devastated by the Turks, the abbey was fortified in the 15C, then remodeled in the Baroque style in the 18C.

Stiftskirche★★

🕐 *Basilica and cloisters open daily 7am– 8pm (6pm Nov–Easter).* ☎0 31 24/5 14 57. www.stift-rein.at.
Johann Georg Stengg, a master builder from Graz, presided over the transformation of the old Romanesque abbey church, which now has the rank of minor papal basilica. A new curvilenear façade leads to the light-flooded interior, designed by Josef Adam Mölck, is full of theatrical flourishes. A tour also takes in the abbey's library with its precious collection of calendars, including the oldest German one from 1373 and a

Kunsthaus Graz

©Graz Tourismus

calendar table used by Johannes Kepler in 1607.

Wallfahrtskirche Mariatrost

7km/4.3mi east via road no. 72 (BX).
This glorious pilgrimage church (c1714) dedicated to the Virgin Mary is strikingly sited in its leafy suburban setting and easily identifiable by its twin towers.

Abtei Seckau

The abbey is at the foot of the Seckau Alps (Niedere Tauern) about 74km/46mi northwest of Graz and 11km/7mi north of Knittelfeld.
The extensive abbey complex, whose corner towers lend it a somewhat military air, was founded in 1140, run by Augustinian canons and served as the seat of the diocese from 1218 until its dissolution by Joseph II in 1782. Benedictine monks have been in charge since its refounding in 1883.

Basilica★

&⃝*May–Oct, daily 10am–5pm.* ⊛€1.50. ☎*0 35 14/5 23 41 00. www.abtei-seckau.at.*
The abbey's Romanesque basilica has lavish net vaulting that was added in the 15C but is otherwise a rather minimalistic place. The main visual focus therefore is the simple but moving **Crucifixion** (1260) above the main altar. The figures of Mary and Joseph probably date from earlier, c. 1200.

In the **Bischofskapelle** (Bishop's Chapel) attention is drawn to the **altarpiece**★★ (1489) depicting the *Coronation of the Virgin*. Besides Mary, it shows three other figures representing the Holy Trinity, all enclosed in a circular, carved framework.

In the adjacent **Gnadenkapelle** (Chapel of Grace), the key piece is a 12C alabaster image of the *Virgin and Child*, considered the oldest Marian image venerated in Austria.

The chapel to the left of the high altar contains the **Mausoleum of Archduke Karl II**, which was designed by the Italian artist Alessandro de Verde in 1612. The chapel itself blends Late Renaissance and Baroque style elements.

Stainz

Stainz is 25km/15.5mi southwest of Graz. (& See STEIRISCHE WEINSTRASSE local map). Lying in the valley and watched over by its ancient Schloss (palace), the town of Stainz reveals many hints of its 16C and 17C period of prosperity based on the wine trade. It still boasts a number of old houses with smart façades, particularly in the main square.

Schloss

The Schloss began life in 1229 as an Augustinian abbey, was secularized in 1740 and became the residence of Archduke Johann in 1840.

Church

⃝*Daily 8am–6pm.* ☎*0 34 63/22 37.*
Of the original Gothic abbey church only the two west towers survive while the rest was rebuilt in 1686 in a subdued Baroque style. Only the vault has been decorated—with painted medallions within a stucco composition. At the center of the elevated high altar (1695) is a work by Hans Adam Weissenkircher.

Jagdmuseum (Hunting Museum)★★ Kids

⃝*Tue–Sun 9am–5pm.* ⊛€4.50. ☎*0 34 63/2 77 20.*
This state-of-the-art museum, a section of the Landesmuseum Joanneum in Graz, opened at the Schloss in 2006 and is perhaps the first such museum examining the hunt in a historical, natural and ethical context. Baroque trophies, historical weapons, paintings and objets d'art trace its evolution from the Stone Age to the royal courts of the 17C and 18C. Another part of the exhibit looks at the effects of tourism, sports, transportation and industrial production on the Earth's ecological balance.

SCHLOSS GREILLENSTEIN★

NIEDERÖSTERREICH

This hulking Renaissance castle with its distinctive single tower was built in the late 16C as the residence and representative office of local landowner Hans Georg II of Kufstein. Still owned by the same family today, it preserves many original fittings and is also famous for its Baroque sandstone sculptures of dwarves and other fanciful creatures.

- **Information:** ☎0 29 89/80 80 21. www.greillenstein.at.
- ▶ **Orient Yourself:** The Schloss is in the Waldviertel in northern Austria, not far from the Czech border and about 100km/62mi northwest of Vienna.
- ◷ **Organizing Your Time:** Plan on spending no more than two hours at the castle, including a 40min guided tour.
- **Especially for Kids:** The castle runs special programs for kids.
- ◔ **Also See:** STIFT ALTENBURG, EGGENBURG, SCHLOSS ROSENBURG.

Visit

◷*Apr–Oct, daily 9.30am–5pm.* ⊶*€5. Guided tours available.* ☎*2 98 98 08 00. www.greillenstein.at*

Exterior

The Baroque balustrade in front of the castle is adorned with sculptures worthy of a fable: How a raging lion is transformed into the most gentle of beasts, mirroring the triumph of Good over Evil. In the inner courtyard with its two-tiered arcaded loggia, stand the sandstone dwarves and dragon fountain.

Interior

From the 16C onward, Greillenstein had jurisdiction over 14 local villages. The filing cabinets and pigeon holes containing original period documents are still there, as is the baronial **courtroom**★. Also of note is the **Turkish Room**, which contains souvenirs collected by a family member who served as ambassador to Turkey in 1628/9. During his stay he succeeded in signing a peace treaty that resulted in a ceasefire lasting 25 years. The chapel has delicate net-vaulting and an elegant **Renaissance altar**★.

Museum Schloss Greillenstein

Schloss Greillenstein

GROSSGLOCKNER-HOCHALPENSTRASSE★★★

SALZBURG UND KÄRNTEN

The Grossglockner Alpine Road is the most famous of all Austrian mountain roads and has exerted its magic on more than 50 million people since opening in 1935. It leads to the celebrated Grossglockner, the highest peak in the Austrian Alps (3 797m/12 457ft). The region is an integral part of the Hohe Tauern National Park designated particularly to protect the Alpine flora and fauna.

- **Information:** Rainerstraβe 2, Salzburg, A-5020, ☎06 62/8 73 67 30. www.grossglockner.com.
- ▶ **Orient Yourself:** The road runs north-south through western Austria, essentially linking Bavaria (Germany) with Italy.
- P **Parking:** An early start is recommended if you want parking places at the Franz-Josefs-Höhe. There is a shuttle from overflow parking lots.
- **Don't Miss:** Franz-Josefs-Höhe, Edelweissspitze.
- **Organizing Your Time:** You'll want to allow plenty of time (up to a full day) to negotiate this steep road and to enjoy its breathtaking vistas.
- Kids **Especially for Kids:** There's a children's playground at Fuscher Lacke.
- **Also See:** ZELL AM ZEE, HEILIGENBLUT.

Driving Tour

Promoting tourism loomed large in the concept of this great highway, notably in the construction of two spurs. One leads to the summit of the Edelweissspitze, the other to the Franz-Josefs-Höhe. The road is usually blocked by snow from November to early May. The Edelweissspitze and Franz-Josefs-Höhe may be closed even longer.

Address Book

For coin ranges, see cover flap.

WHERE TO STAY

BRUCK AN DER GROSSGLOCKNERSTRASSE

Zacherlbräu – Glocknerstr. 14. ☎0 65 45/72 42. www.zacherlbraeu. at. 7 rooms. Traditional Gasthof.

WHERE TO EAT

BRUCK AN DER GROSSGLOCKNERSTRASSE

Taxhof – Hundsdorf 15. ☎0 65 45/62 61. www.taxhof.at. Closed Mon, Tue in winter, Apr, Nov.

Grossglockner Hochalpenstraße Tour

75km/46.6mi

Zell am See★ *See ZELL AM SEE.*

South of Zell am See, the road to the Grossglockner begins at Bruck. It plunges into the **Fuschertal**, a dark and sparsely populated valley. Between Fusch and Ferleiten the route gets hillier and passes above the **Bärenschlucht**, a little wooded gorge. Beyond here, you can spot the rocky and jagged **Sonnenwelleck** group and the rounded Fuscherkarkopf.

From **Ferleiten** *(toll point)* to the Fuscher Törl the route begins its twisting climb. Above the Piffkar ravine *(alt 1 620m/5 315ft)* the **views**★★ are magnificent, especially from the Hochmais P parking lot *(alt 1 850m/6 070ft)*. The last larches disappear and the road continues as a corniche as far as the Nassfeld bridges. From here it passes through a rocky wasteland known as Witches' Kitchen (Hexenküche) and climbs across the basins of the Nassfeld. About 2km/1.2mi before the pass it reaches a nature museum.

Grossglockner and Pasterzen glacier

Haus Alpine Naturschau★

🕐*May–Oct, daily 9am–5pm.* 🎟*Admission free.* ☎*06 62/8 73 67 30.*
This little museum is devoted to Alpine ecology above the tree-line and gives a clear demonstration of the complex interrelations between flora and fauna. For an introduction, don't miss the multimedia presentation in the cinema. Outside, a nature trail offers more interesting tidbits about local plant life and geology.

Edelweissspitze★★

Alt 2 577m/8 455ft. No access for coaches. 🚗*Very steep road.*
At the highest point of the road, you'll be rewarded with a spectacular panorama taking in more than 30 mountains above 3 000m/9 842ft high. The peak of the Grossglockner can be seen just behind the Sonnenwelleck.

Fuscher Törl★

Alt 2 428m/7 966ft. 🅿*Park at Fuscher Törl 2.*
The road builders used this "little gate" (Törlein) to form a panoramic bend. **Views**★★ of the Glockglockner and surrounding peaks from the plat-

form are among the best along the road. There's also a memorial to the construction workers who died in the building of this road.

Fuscher Lacke   Kids

Alt 2 262m/7 421ft. An information center here contains displays on the construction of this grand Alpine road. A path leads round the lake for those wishing to stretch their legs. There's also an imaginative **adventure playground** where little ones can fancy themselves as mountain road builders.

Hochtor

The main passage road reaches its highest point *(alt 2 505m/8 218ft)* at the north end of the tunnel, which marks

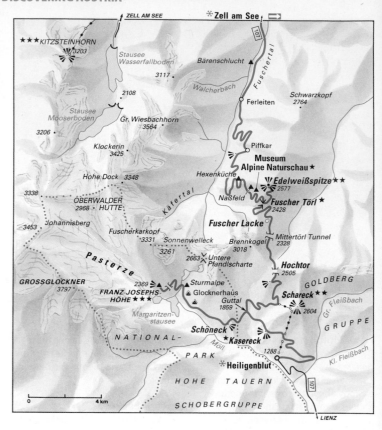

the boundary between Salzburg and Carinthia. If you'd like a bit of exercise, follow the 30min educational trail starting at either end of the tunnel, where information panels illustrate the story of this 4 000-year-old trade route used by Celts and Romans.

The winding descent from the Hochtor passes through Alpine pastures within view of the Schober massif, which forms a crown round the Gössnitz Valley.

From the **Guttal ravine**, turn right onto the "Glacier Road" (Gletscherstraße) leading to Franz-Josefs-Höhe.

During the holiday season and fine weather there can be delays on the trip up to Franz-Josefs-Höhe, as parking lots fill to capacity. ⊞In this case, visitors will be directed to overflow lots from where a shuttle service operates to Franz-Josefs-Höhe.

Schöneck

Alt 1 958m/6 424ft. Between the inn at Schöneck and the Glocknerhaus lie the lushest Alpine meadows with their wonderful variety of unique plant life. The **Wunderwelt Glocknerwiesen** nature display and botanical trail at Schöneck give an overview of Alpine flora and insects in this area.

Franz-Josefs-Höhe★★★

The Glacier Road ends at a long panoramic terrace from where you'll have the full-on view of the Grossglockner as well as the longest glacier in the eastern Alps, the 10km/6.2mi-long **Pasterze**, which is served by a funicular (🕙*"Gletscherbahn" (funicular) operates mid-May–end Sept, daily 9am–4pm; ◎€8 round trip; ☎0 48 24/25 02).*

Views are best from the last platform, the Freiwandeck. From here the Panoramaweg Kaiserstein, laid out as a botanical trail, leads to the **Swarovski** observation point. The glass and wood tower is equipped with free telescopes for close-ups of the surrounding mountain scenery. The visitors' center has four floors of exhibits, including a 'rock and ice path' sensory experience and a new presentation taking you into the frosty world of glaciers. In summer, the area is the starting point for hikes and climbing tours in the Grossglockner massif.

▶ *Retrace the route to the Guttal fork and turn right toward Heiligenblut.*

Kasereck★

Alt 1 913m/6 276ft. More great views of the Grossglockner and the Heiligenblut basin, this spot also has a cheesemaking establishment ("Käserei") open to the public, and a restaurant.

Driving down to Heiligenblut, note the unusual wooden grain dryers in the form of grilles (known locally as "harps"). A little further on there is the famous view of the church of Heiligenblut, a slender stone spire standing out against the background of the far-off Grossglockner.

Heiligenblut★
👣 *See HEILIGENBLUT.*

GURGLER TAL★★

TIROL

The Gurgl valley, which branches off the upper valley of the Ötz (👣 *see ÖTZTAL*)**, ranks among the most remarkable holiday destinations in the Austrian Tirol. Its exceptional setting makes it a favorite location for hikers and skiers.**

- 🛈 **Information:** Gurglerstraße 118, Obergurgl-Hochgurgl. ☎0 52 70/01 00. www.obergurgl.com.
- ▶ **Orient Yourself:** Gurgl Valley is in southwestern Austria, close to the border with Italy.
- 🕐 **Organizing Your Time:** Budget a whole day if combining all walking routes.
- 👣 **Also See:** ÖTZTAL, STUBAITAL.

Excursions

Action is concentrated in **Obergurgl★** *(alt 1 793–1 930m/5 883–6 332ft)*, a former rural mountain village which has great **views★** of the 20 surrounding mountains above 3 000m/9 842ft; and in **Hochgurgl★** *(alt 2 150m/7 054ft)*, Austria's highest village and a popular winter sports resort offering six modern hotels.

Ski slopes

These cover 110km/68.3mi of pistes of varying degrees of difficulty at altitudes ranging from 1 800m/5 906ft to 3 082m/10 112ft. They are equipped with 22 ski-lifts. The high altitude guarantees snow cover from November to May. There are 12km/7.4mi of cross-country ski runs.

Hohe Mut★★

Alt 2 653m/8 704ft. Allow 1hr for a round trip. Take the chair-lift up in two stages. 🕐*Lifts operate Jul–end Sept and Dec–end Apr, daily 8.45am–4pm.* ☜ *€12 round trip.* ☎0 52 56/62 74.

There is a splendid **panorama★★** of the Rotmoosferner and Gaisbergferner glaciers to the southeast and of the Manigenbach to the west.

🚶*The easy walks listed below can be combined to make up a pleasant day's outing.*

Hohe Mut to Schönwieshütte★★

400m/1 321ft altitude drop. Those in a hurry can reach the Schönwies refuge in about 1hr from the Hohe Mut chairlift station. It is preferable, however, to follow the trail below the cliff to the foot of the **Rotmoosferner glacier★★** and then carry on along the valley floor fol-

Address Book

🖙 For coin ranges, see cover flap.

WHERE TO STAY

⊜⊜⊜**Gasthof Mühle** – *Gurglerstr.
87.* ☎*0 52 56/67 67. www.hotel-
muehle.com. 45 rooms.* 🖵

⊜⊜⊜**Wiesental** – *Piccardweg 16.*
☎*05256/62 63. www.hotelwiesental.
com. 26 rooms. Restaurant* ⊜⊜⊜.

lowing the Gebirgsbach creek. The path
leads through a majestic and captivating
Alpine setting.

The refuge can also be reached in about
1hr via a wide trail from Obergurgl.

Around Schönwieshütte★ 🚶

Allow 1hr 30min for a round trip. Two easy
detours are recommended from the refuge. Go toward the Langtalereckhütte

as far as the so-called **Gurgler Alm** *(alt
2 252m/7 388ft)*, from where there is a
view★ of the three glaciers higher up
with the Schalfkogel *(alt 3 540m/11 614ft)*
at the center. Backtrack and turn left
shortly before the refuge toward the
Schönwieskopf *(alt 2 324m/7 625ft)*. From
the summit a **panorama**★ stretches
across the valley.

Schönwieshütte to Obergurgl
via Zirbelwald★ 🚶

1hr 15min, 330m/1 082ft altitude drop
From the refuge, take the trail toward
Obergurgl, soon turning left and heading a steep path downhill past the
impressive **Rotmoos waterfall**★. Take
the left fork into the woods and along
the valley floor.

GURK★★

KÄRNTEN

Gurk is a small village that would be fairly unremarkable were it not for its famous
cathedral, which ranks as Austria's most important Romanesque building.
A convent was founded here in 1043 by Countess Hemma of Friesach-Zeltschach.
However, it was dissolved less than three decades later by Archbishop Gebhard
of Salzburg, who instead established a new diocese in an effort to consolidate
his power upon the region. The Augustinian canons remained in this secluded
valley until 1787, when the diocese was transferred to more prominent Klagenfurt. Since 1932, the convent has been run by Salvatorians.

🗓 **Information:** Dr.-Schnerich-Straße 12, A-9342. ☎0 42 66/81 25 21.
www.dom-zu-gurk.at.

▶ **Orient Yourself:** Gurk is about 42km/26mi north of Klagenfurt in
southern Austria.

😊 **Don't Miss:** Fastentuch (Lenten Veil).

🕐 **Organizing Your Time:** Allow an hour for the cathedral tour and a further
half hour for the Bishop's Chapel.

🖾 **Also See:** FRIESACH, ST. VEIT AN DER GLAN.

Visit

Cathedral *(Dom)*

The High Romanesque cathedral was
built between 1140 and 1200 under
Prince-Bishop Roman I, councillor to
Frederick Barbarossa. Baroque gemel

windows and onion domes were added
to both towers in 1680.

Porches

The exterior wall of the front porch
dates to the Gothic period, but inside
there is some stained glass from 1340
along with **frescoes**★ depicting scenes

from the Old Testament on the left and from the New Testament on the right. A Romanesque **door**★★ (c. 1200) with richly decorated pillars, arches and capitals leads into the main nave.

Interior

○ *Apr–Oct, daily 9am–5pm; Nov–Mar, daily 10am–4pm.* ◆ *Guided tour (45min) of cathedral and crypt 10.30am–5pm.* ◇€4.60. ☎0 42 66/82 36 12.

It is immediately evident upon entering that many styles have contributed to this building: The Romanesque triple-nave pillared basilica is surmounted by Gothic net vaulting, the frescoes are from the Gothic and Renaissance periods, while the furnishings are predominantly Baroque.

(1) Jewel-encrusted Hemma reliquary in the form of a tree containing a ring and a pendant thought to have belonged to the saint (1955).

(2) Samson doorway: The **tympanum**★ shows Samson slaying the lion (1200).

(3) and (8): **Carved panels**★ (16C) vividly depicting scenes from the life of St. Hemma, commissioned before 1508.

(4) A gigantic **mural of St. Christopher** (1250). The doorway to the left with its richly decorated ogee arch was built in 1445.

(5) **High Altar**★★, a gilded masterpiece by Michael Hönel filling the entire apse. Covered in gold, it features full-size, strikingly realistic figures (72 statues, 82 angels' heads) and the four Evangelists at pedestal level with the Church Fathers above them. Created between 1626 and 1632, its central theme is the *Assumption of the Virgin.*

During Lent the altar is shrouded by a **Fastentuch**★ (Lenten veil, 1458), a custom that was abolished almost everywhere in the late Middle Ages. The exquisite veil is 9sq m/96.8sq ft in area and is painted with 99 Biblical scenes. (◆*The Lenten veil can be seen as part of a guided tour (20min): enquire about exact times; ◇€2.90 (free during Lent); ☎0 42 66/82 36 12).*

(6) **Choir stalls**: These richly and decoratively carved stalls are the work of local craftsmen. Each seat is decorated with charming painted floral motifs (1680).

Cathedral, Gurk

R. Chéret/MICHELIN

(7) **Gothic murals**: Uncovered at the beginning of the 20C, these illustrate the conversion of St. Paul, and Christ enthroned as Judge of the World, surrounded by the Twenty Four Elders of the Apocalypse as narrated by St. John

the Divine. The donors can be seen at the foot of Christ's throne with their nine children (c. 1390).

(8) ♿ *See* (3).

(9) **Altar of the Holy Cross** (1741), with a **Pietà**★ cast in lead by Georg Raphael Donner, his last work.

(10) **Baroque pulpit**★ (1740), an accomplished work by Viennese set designers Giuseppe and Antonio Galli Bibiena. The iconography is fully in keeping with the ideas of the Counter Reformation, taking as its subject the triumph of the Church.

Crypt★★

Bathed in somber light, the masterful Romanesque crypt (1174) is supported by a 'forest' of 100 marble pillars. Since 1174 it has sheltered the stone sarcophagus of Hemma, patron saint of Carinthia, who founded a convent in Gurk and was canonized in 1938. The present tomb is a red-marble extravaganza from the 1720s. It rests on three Romanesque support pillars with marble heads.

Bishop's Chapel

🕐*9am–dusk.* •••*By guided tour (20min) only; enquire about exact times and prices.* ☎*0 42 66/82 36 12.*

The upstairs chapel has some exceptionally well-preserved Romanesque **murals**★★ (c. 1260), whose vivid colors have not been touched up. They depict numerous Biblical scenes and characters, including Paradise, Heavenly Jerusalem, the Virgin Mary on King Solomon's throne, and the Evangelists. The stained-glass window on the west wall is contemporary with the frescoes and depicts the Descent from the Cross. This is Austria's earliest stained glass in the angular style.

Excursion

Strassburg

This small town within sight of Gurk is dominated by its **Schloss** (🕐*May– Oct 26, daily 10am–6pm;* ⊙ €*2.20;* ☎*0 42 66/23 75),* which for centuries was a bishops' palace until the diocese was relocated to Klagenfurt in 1787. Today it houses a small but fine collection of folkloric items illustrating peasant life, and a room dedicated to hunting. The arcaded Renaissance courtyard hosts a summer concert series.

HALL IN TIROL★

TIROL

POPULATION 12 370 – ALT 574M/1 880FT

Hall on the River Inn was the salt town of the Inn Valley. During the Middle Ages, it played a key role in the economic life of the country and ranked among Austria's wealthiest cities, receiving town rights in 1303. In 1477, the local rulers moved the Tirolean mint from Meran to Hall. The most famous coin produced here was the Haller Silbertaler, which was accepted all over Europe until the early 19C and became the namesake of the US dollar. Modern Hall is still wrapped in the charm of the Middle Ages yet keeps firmly in touch with the present as a highly active cultural and economic center.

- 🛈 **Information:** Wallpachgasse 5, A-6060. ☎0 52 23/56 26 90. www.hall-in-tirol.at.
- ▶ **Orient Yourself:** Hall is about 10km/6.2mi east of Innsbruck.
- 🅿 **Parking:** Look for parking garages on Fassergasse near Stadtgraben and on the corner of Bruckergasse and Stadtgraben.
- ☺ **Don't Miss:** Münze Hall, Münzerturm.
- 🕐 **Organizing Your Time:** Budget at least half a day.
- 🧒 **Especially for Kids:** Münze Hall.
- ♿ **Also See:** INNSBRUCK, SCHWAZ.

Walking Tour

Upper Town Tour★
(Obere Stadt)

🚫*No traffic is allowed in the Upper Town on Saturday mornings.*

▸ *From Unterer Stadtplatz (24), take the Langer Graben up to Oberer Stadtplatz.*

Oberer Stadtplatz

Hall's main square is the heart of the old town and hemmed in by attractive medieval buildings. This is where you'll find the **Stadtpfarrkirche**★ (A), the late 13C parish church that was repeatedly enlarged, resulting in a generously proportioned but asymmetrical three-nave hall church. The decoration is now largely Baroque. Note the ceiling frescoes by Joseph Adam von Mölck and a high altar adorned with a painting by Quellini, a pupil of Rubens. The **Waldaufkapelle** (late 15C) to the left of the high altar houses a Late Gothic figure of the Virgin Mary from the circle of Michael Pacher alongside sumptuously decorated reliquaries.

On the west side of the square is the **Rathaus** (R), which was originally the residence of Heinrich, King of Bohemia, and donated to the town by Duke Leopold IV in 1406.

▸ *Follow Agramgasse (2), Quarinongasse (12) and Schulgasse (16) to the Stiftsplatz.*

Stiftsplatz *(20)*

This square is bounded in the east by the austere façade of the Jesuitenkirche (Jesuit church), now a concert hall, and in the south by the Baroque façades of the **Damenstift**, a former convent for noble ladies founded by Archduchess Magdalena, the sister of Archduke Ferdinand II in 1579.

The **west front**★ with its four full-length fluted pilasters is a fine example of the transition from the Renaissance to the Baroque style.

▸ *Return to Unterer Stadtplatz via Eugenstraße (3) and the Schweigerhofstiege steps (17) to the left. Follow Münzergasse to Burg Hasegg.*

Burg Hasegg　　　　🇰Kids

🕑*Apr–Oct, Tue–Sun, 10am–5pm; Nov–Mar, Tue–Sat, 10am–5pm.* 🚫*Dec 25, 26, Jan 1.* ✎*€6; children €3.* ☎*0 52 23/5 85 51 65. www.stadtwerke-hall.at/burg-hasegg.*

Dominated by its landmark tower, Hall's castle originated in the 13C to protect the city, the salt mines and the river traffic. Its historical importance soared in 1567, when the Tirolean rulers transferred their mint here. Closed in 1809, it reopened in 1975 and still produces commemorative coins on a regular basis.

The city's minting history is creatively chronicled at the [Kids] **Münze Hall**★ inside the castle. You'll see a cylindrical stamping press, interactive coin displays, and even get to mint your own coin. Admission includes audio-guides (also in English).

Climb the architecturally distinguished **Münzerturm** *(admission ⊜€6 or €8 in combination with museum)* with its new spiral staircase for splendid views of the town and the impressive mountain range to the north.

The castle also harbors the **Stadtmuseum** (local history museum), which was being revamped at the time of writing and is expected to reopen in 2009.

HALLSTATT★★

OBERÖSTERREICH
POPULATION 950 – ALT 511M/1 677FT

Hallstatt crouches beneath the Salzberg in a breathtaking setting on the Hallstätter See★★, a deep and dark green lake backed by the craggy peaks of the Dachstein range. Often deluged by day trippers, it provides the quintessential picture of romantic Austria with streets so steep and narrow that the famous Corpus Christi procession has to take place mostly in boats on the lake. In 1998 the Hallstatt region, including the Dachstein range and central Salzkammergut, was declared a UNESCO World Heritage Site.

- 🛈 **Information:** Seestraβe 169, A-4830, ☎0 61 34/82 08. www.hallstatt.net.
- ▶ **Orient Yourself:** Hallstatt on the southwestern shore of the Hallstätter See in the Salzkammergut.
- 🅿 **Parking:** Central Hallstatt is closed to traffic May–Oct, daily 10am–5pm. An automated parking guide system directs you to the nearest parking lot.
- ⊛ **Don't Miss:** Salzwelten Hallstatt, Museum Hallstatt.
- 🕐 **Organizing Your Time:** Budget half a day for the Salzbergwerk and another half day for the Museum Hallstatt and the church.
- [Kids] **Especially for Kids:** Salzwelten Hallstatt, Museum Hallstatt.
- ◔ **Also See:** EISRIESENWELT, DACHSTEIN, GOSAUSEEN, BAD AUSSEE.

A Bit of History

The salt mines in the mountains around Hallstatt have been exploited since the Neolithic Era, but the first major heyday came in the Bronze Age around 1200 BC. So many traces of salt mining have been found around Hallstatt that it coined the name of the Hallstatt Period dating from 850 to 500 BC. The most startling evidence is a vast Iron Age cemetery with over 4 000 graves. The salt mines are still being worked today.

Sights

Pfarrkirche Mariae Himmelfahrt

Overlooking the lake from its perch above the central Marktplatz, Hallstatt's parish church has 12C Romanesque origins but only a squat tower to prove it, while the rest of the building is mostly 15C Late Gothic. The three winged **altars**★ also date to this period. The most accomplished of these is the one on the right, which shows the Virgin flanked by St. Barbara, patron saint of miners, and St. Catherine, patron saint of woodcutters.

Perhaps more interesting than the church itself is the two-story Michaelskapelle across the tiny graveyard, which houses the macabre but fascinating **Beinhaus**⋆. This small charnel house contains some 600 skulls, all stacked up neatly and painted with flower motifs, the name and other personal details of the person. Shortage of space in the local graveyard meant that ten years after burial, and once the body had decomposed, it was dug up and the bones stored to make room for the next coffin. New skulls are still added once in a while.

Welterbemuseum Hallstatt Kids

⊕*Nov–Mar, Sun, Mon, Tue 11am–3pm; Apr, daily 10am–4pm; May–Oct 10am– 6pm.* €7.50; 0 61 34/ 82 80 15. *www. museum-hallstatt.at.*

This modern museum, using 3D media and holographic projections to display its exhibits, takes visitors on an educational, high-tech romp through 7 000 years of regional history. Special emphasis is given to the Hallstatt Period with an impressive selection of archeological finds, including weapons, tools and human bones. Other sections focus on the Celts and Romans, the big fire of 1750, coin minting, tourism and many other topics. 3D exhibitions, too.

Salzwelten Hallstatt Kids

Allow 3hr for this excursion. *Guided tours (1hr 10min) every half-hour; May– mid-Sept, daily 9am–4.30pm; mid–end Sept, daily 9am–3.30pm; Oct 2–Oct 26, daily 9am–3pm.* *Temperature is 8°C/46.4°F inside the mine.* *Salzberg-werk* €16; children and students €10. 0 61 34/84 00. *www.salzwelten.at.*

Hallstatt's salt mines in the Salzberg above the town are considered the oldest in the world. It was here where a salt-preserved corpse, the so-called Man in Salt, was found in 1734. Sections of this warren of mines have been developed into an exhibition mine, which can be explored on a guided tour (in German and English). The tour includes a salt crystal room, an underground salt lake, technical exhibits, displays about mining during the Bronze Age and the Hallstatt Period and other themes. Kids love schussing down the wooden slides once used by miners to travel quickly from one level to the next. The mine

can be reached on a 45min walk or a short trip on the Salzbergbahn funicular (€8.50, or €21 with tour of the mines). From the mountain station, it's a 10min walk across the famous Iron Age graveyard to the mine entrance. Views are great from the **Rudolfsturm**, a tower built to defend the mine.

Hallstatt Civilization

Precisely when the Celts came to Hallstat is unclear, but evidence suggests there was an established mining settlement with a powerful ruler here c. 800 BC. However, archeological finds suggest that mining had been going on since 5000 BC, making the salt mine at Hallstatt the oldest in the world.

Salt was a precious commodity in the Celtic era and the region was historically very wealthy. Salt was the equivalent of oil today; who ever was lucky enough to have reserves of it became impressively rich. Active trade in the commodity south to the Mediterranean and north to the Baltic produced wealth that allowed for the development of a sophisticated culture which became known as the Hallstatt Civilization. It lasted from 800 to 400 BC and stretched from the northern Alps to southern Germany and from the Champagne-Ardennes to Bohemia.

Address Book

For coin ranges, see cover flap.

WHERE TO STAY

Seehotel Grüner Baum – Markplatz 104. 0 61 34/82 63. *www.gruenerbaum.cc. 20 rooms. Restaurant* . Situated on the lake shore, this hotel (c. 1700) has an inviting terrace. Famous guests include Empress Elisabeth (Sisi) of Austria and Agatha Christie.

WHERE TO EAT

Gasthof Zauner-Seewirt – Markplatz 51. 0 61 34/82 46. *www.zauner.hallstatt.net.* The signature dish is *Salzfürsteinplatte* (Salt Prince's Platter) using fish and salt; both readily available locally.

HEILIGENBLUT ❄❄

KÄRNTEN
POPULATION 1 100 – ALT 1 288M/4 226FT

Postcard-pretty Heiligenblut is a gateway to the Hohe Tauern National Park and the Grossglockner Hochalpenstraße and often deluged with visitors. Its slender-spired church stands photogenically in silhouette against the Grossglockner.

- 🗎 **Information:** A-9844, ☎0 48 24/20 01 21. www.heiligenblut.at.
- ▶ **Orient Yourself:** Heligenblut is at the foot of the Grossglockner in southern Austria, about 38km/24.6mi north of Lienz.
- 🅿 **Parking:** Small parking area in the center.
- 👁 **Don't Miss:** The panorama from Schareck
- 🕐 **Organizing Your Time:** Allow half a day for the summit excursion.
- 👣 **Also See:** GROSSGLOCKNER HOCHALPENSTRASSE.

Sights

Ski slopes

Heligenblut's slopes stretch between the Schareck, Gjaidtroghöhe and Viehbühel peaks at altitudes from 1 300m/4 265ft to 2 912m/9 554ft. There are 14 ski-lifts and 55km/34mi of pistes with a variety of descents, well laid out through the rugged, treeless mountain landscape. In spite of the high altitude, snow conditions can begin to deteriorate as early as March.

Pfarrkirche★

🕐 *Daily 7am–7pm.*

Heligenblut's parish church was built in the 15C by the monks of Admont to shelter a tiny vial of blood said to be Christ's, thereby giving the village its name. The twin-aisled crypt contains the tomb of Briccius, an officer of the Imperial Court of Byzantium, who allegedly brought the vial north in the 10C. Works of outstanding artistic merit include the **altarpiece★** on the high altar (1520), attributed to the school of Michael Pacher, and the Gothic canopy (1496), ornately carved in pale sandstone.

Opposite the church is the **Hohe Tauern National Park Information Center** with a small but interesting exhibition on the Grossglockner.

Excursion

Schareck★★

Alt 2 604m/8 543ft. Cable-car ascent (Großglockner Bergbahn) in two stages, then 10min walk to the summit. 🕐 *Operates mid-Jun–end Sept, mid-Dec–mid-Apr, daily 9am–noon, 1pm–4pm.* 🎫 *€15.50 round trip.* ☎0 48 24/22 88.

From the top of this mountain (2 600m/8 530ft alt), the impressive **panorama★★** encompasses 40 peaks towering to 3 000m/9 842ft, including the pyramidal Schildberg and the Grossglockner range to the west and the Gjaidtrog to the east.

Nature Trails

Take a guided hiking tour through the Hohe Tauern National Park, in which the village of Heligenblut nestles comfortably. Find out more about the tours offered by experienced leaders from www.heiligenblut.at.

STIFT HEILIGENKREUZ★

NIEDERÖSTERREICH

The Cistercian abbey of Heiligenkreuz was founded by the Babenberg Margrave Leopold III as a burial place for his dynasty. A fine example of Romanesque-Gothic architecture with Baroque embellishments, the abbey owes its name to a relic of the Holy Cross donated in the 12C by Duke Leopold V. It is the oldest continuously operating Cistercian abbey in the world and still has around 70 monks.

- **Information:** ☎0 22 58/87 03. www.stift-heiligenkreuz.at.
- **Orient Yourself:** The abbey is in the Wienerwald, about 15km/9.3mi west of Vienna.
- **Don't Miss:** The Dancing Skeletons in the Totenkapelle (Chapel of the Dead)
- **Organizing Your Time:** Tours last 45min.
- **Also See:** WIENER WALD.

Visit

Guided tours Mon–Sat 10am, 11am, 2pm, 3pm, 4pm, Sun 11am, 2pm, 3pm, 4pm. Closed Good Friday, Dec 24. €6.60. ☎0 22 58/87 03. www.stift-heiligenkreuz.org.

Stiftskirche★

Behind the austere Romanesque façade lies the nave from the same period and a Gothic chancel from the 13C with fittings dating from the 19C. The other furnishings are Baroque in style by Giovanni Giuliani. The choirstalls are each decorated with a linden wood relief illustrating scenes from the Life of Christ crowned with busts of saintly bishops, abbots and statesmen. The Holy Cross reliquary is kept in a modern side church, the 1982 **Kreuzkirche**, off to the left of the chancel. The organ is one of the largest musical instruments in Austria and was built in 1804. Franz Schubert and Anton Bruckner played it and since Schubert composed a special piece of music for the organ, it is called the **Schubertorgan**.

Cloister

The 13C cloister bridges the Romanesque and the Gothic beautifully, with rounded arches on its north side and pointed Gothic ones on the opposite side. There are two sculpture groups by Giuliani and a nine-sided fountain room (late 13C) with fine tracery and a Renaissance basin for the ablutions. The grey-black medieval **stained-glass windows** show members of the Babenberg dynasty.

Several chapels are just west of the cloister, including the square **Kapitelsaal** (chapterhouse), where the Babenbergs are buried and also depicted in murals.

The Cistercian Order

This reforming Benedictine order took its name from the monastery of Cîteaux in France, founded by Robert of Molesmes in 1098. The order grew rapidly in the 12C under Bernard of Clairvaux, who forbade the levying of tithes and the acquisition of land. He also encouraged precise observance of the Benedictine rules.

Cistercian architecture also adheres to strict principles. Churches are simple yet harmonious in their proportions and distinguished by purity of line. There is no bell-tower, only a ridge turret, and no stained glass, only *grisaille* painting. The initial austerity of Cistercian architecture mellowed over the centuries, with the result that pictures and statues are now to be seen in Cistercian churches.

The order still remains true to the *charta caritatis* promulgated in 1115, and has 300 monasteries and convents all over the world.

Detail of a sacristy cupboard, Heiligenkreuz

Next door is the **Totenkapelle** (Chapel of the Dead) where the monks are laid out before burial. Giuliani was responsible for the decoration, including the somewhat macabre "dancing skeletons;" candelabra supported by skeletons in shrouds.

Sacristy

Tours conclude in the sacristy, reached across a small courtyard. The attractively decorated room has an old lavabo recess, and is 18C in style, even with some Rococo touches. The four splendid **sacristy cupboards** with exceptionally fine marquetry were made by lay brothers in the early 19C.

SCHLOSS HERBERSTEIN★

STEIERMARK

The fortress of Herberstein perches on a rocky spur, surrounded on three sides by the course of the Feistritz, in the middle of a rugged gorge. It has been modified numerous times during its 700-year existence and boasts Gothic, Renaissance and Baroque elements. The counts of Herberstein have occupied the castle without interruption since 1290.

- **Information:** ☎0 31 76/8 82 50. www.herberstein.co.at.
- ▶ **Orient Yourself:** Herberstein is in southeast Austria, about 57km/29mi northeast of Graz.
- **Don't Miss:** The Florence Courtyard.
- **Organizing Your Time:** Allow an hour for the castle tour.
- **Especially for Kids:** Tier- und Naturpark.
- **Also See:** SCHLOSS RIEGERSBURG.

Tour

Tickets cost €13 and include a palace tour (Apr–Oct only), the animal park, the gardens and the museums.

Schloss Herberstein

Guided tour (50min) Apr–Oct, daily noon, 1pm, 2pm, 3pm, 4pm.
Tours take in some of the oldest parts of the building, including a kitchen in use since the 16C, and provide glimpses into daily life at the palace during the 19C.

The magnificent **Florence Courtyard** is an arcaded enclosure that looks as though it belongs to an Italian palazzi rather than a fortress of northern Europe.

Tierwelt Herberstein

May–Sept, daily 9am–5pm, Oct, daily 10am–4pm; Nov–Dec, weekends and public holidays, 10am–4pm. €13; children €7. ☎03176 80777. www.tierwelt-herberstein.at.

Courtyard, Schloss Herbertstein

The zoo at Herberstein is a modern animal park with a history dating back to the 17C. It is home to animals from five continents, including bison, timberwolves, kangaroos, lions, and leopards. The latter are in a special enclosure that allows them to "hunt" for their dinner. For young visitors, there's also the Tikiba petting zoo and a huge playing ground.

Historical gardens
🕐*Mar–Oct, daily 9am–5pm; Nov–Feb, daily 10am–4pm.*
These were restored in 1997 following old designs and a picture dating from 1681. In the center of the park stands the rose pavilion with a fountain of youth. The geometrically arranged beds symbolize different times of the day and types of human temperament. The "multimedia space" in the Siegmund garden forms a bridge between old and new.

Museums
Since 2004, Herberstein has been home to the **Gironcoli-Museum** (🕐*daily 10am–5pm*), devoted to the avant-garde sculptures of Bruno Gironcoli, one of Austria's most important contemporary artists. The museum is housed in a converted 16C barn with a modernist annex. Another building, the Kunsthaus, houses Gironcoli's impressive collection of African masks, as well as changing exhibits by contemporary artists.

BURG HOCHOSTERWITZ★
KÄRNTEN

Looking like everyone's idea of a romantic fairy-tale castle, Hochosterwitz occupies a dramatic site★★ on a rounded limestone rock rising 150m/492ft above the surrounding countryside. Its impressive towered and turreted outline and defence works can easily be spotted from several miles away.

- 🛈 **Information:** ☎0 42 13/20 20 16. www.burg-hochosterwitz.at.
- ▶ **Orient Yourself:** The fortress is in St. Georg am Längsee, about 22km/13.6mi northeast of Klagenfurt in southern Austria.
- 🅿 **Parking:** There are parking spaces below the castle.
- 🕐 **Organizing Your Time:** Allow two or three hours including the 30min climb
- ⚲ **Also See:** ST. VEIT AN DER GLAN, MARIA SAAL, KLAGENFURT.

A Bit of History

First documented in 860, the castle remained in the hands of the lords of Osterwitz until 1475, then reverted to the emperor and in 1571 was finally bought by Georg von Khevenhüller, an imperial counsellor and chief stablemaster. He greatly expanded and fortified the castle to defend it against Turkish invasion, adding the 14 gateways and an arsenal. His descendents still own it today.

Tour of the castle

&. ⏱ *May–Sept, daily 8am–6pm; Apr, Oct, daily 9am–5pm.* ✆ €7.50.

From the parking lot, a ramp passing through all 14 gates leads up to the castle in about 30min with some lovely views along the way. The grandest of the gates is the seventh, known as the **Khevenhüllertor** (1582), surmounted by a lion's head, the family coat of arms, and a bust of Georg Khevenhüller dressed as a military leader. The ramp passes the **Burgkapelle** (castle chapel) and reaches the **Innere Burghof** (inner courtyard) with a restaurant. Some rooms in the castle have historical exhibits about the Khevenhüller family, family portraits and a fine collection of arms and armor. A faster but considerably less scenic way to get up to the castle is via an elevator (✆ €5 round trip) ingeniously carved straight through the rock.

INNSBRUCK★★

TIROL (TIROL)

POPULATION 189 100 – ALT 574M/1 883FT

Innsbruck (literally, Bridge over the Inn) is the capital of the Tirol (Tirol) and a major cultural and tourism center that twice hosted the Winter Olympic Games, once in 1964 and again in 1976. Local life is closely linked with the mountain, and it's not uncommon for people to spend their midday break on the slopes. In summer, Innsbruck is often deluged with visitors milling about the pedestrianized historic center. The relative lack of industry has enabled the city to keep its charming provincial character, at least once the main thoroughfares are left behind.

🛈 **Information:** Hauptbahnhof, ☎05 12/58 37 66. www.innsbruck-tourism.at.
▶ **Orient Yourself:** Innsbruck is in the Inn Valley in western Austria, about 30km north of the Brennerpass to Italy.
🅿 **Parking:** Inner city parking garages and lots include: Congress-Garage, Herrengasse/Rennweg (daily until midnight); Europahaus, Meinhardstraße (daily 7am–10pm); Parkgarage Landhausplatz, Wilhelm-Greil-Straße (daily 7am–1am); Sparkassengarage, Erlerstraße (Mon–Fri 7am–9pm, Sat 8am–5pm); Maria-Theresien-Garage, Erlerstraße (daily 24hr), Parkgarage Altstadt, Tschamlerstraße (daily 7am–1am); City Parkgarage, Kaiserjägerstraße (daily 24hr).
☻ **Don't Miss:** Dom zu St. Jakob, Hofburg, Hofkirche.
🕒 **Organizing Your Time:** Devote the better part of a full day to seeing the sites of Old Innsbruck, then spend half a day on a trip up the Hafelekar. Add another day if you plan to tour the Mittelgebirge.
Kids **Especially for Kids:** Alpenzoo, Swarovski Kristallwelten.
👶 **Also See:** HALL IN TIROL.

A Bit of History

The Tirol came into existence as a state in the 12C under the jurisdiction of the counts of Tirol but passed into Habsburg control in 1363. Duke Friedrich IV made Innsbruck his residence in 1420, ushering in a long heyday that reached its pinnacle under **Maximilian I** (1459–1519) who positioned the city as a European center of culture and politics. Through clever marriages, first to Maria of Burgundy, then to Bianca Maria Sforza of Milan, he managed to extend his sphere of influence to territories encompassing today's Belgium, Netherlands, northern France, and northern Italy. In 1508, he became Holy Roman Emperor.

Maximilian always nursed a special fondness for the Tirol, whose silver and copper mines brought him wealth, while its rich hunting grounds provided entertainment.

In 1806, during the Napoleonic Wars, the Tirol fell under Bavarian rule and Innsbruck became the hub of a resistance movement led by Andreas Hofer, who is now celebrated as a national folk hero. The region reverted to Austria at the Vienna Congress in 1815.

Sights

General Views

In town, the **Stadtturm** (tower) offers the best view. For sweeping views over the city and the surrounding peaks, go up to the **Hungerburg**★ (AY), reached by car via the Alte Innbrücke (Old Bridge over the Inn), the Höttinger Gasse, the Hötting Church and the Höhenstraße. Alternatively, take the new futuristically designed funicular from Congreshaus in the city center to the Hungerburg. Travelers coming from the Brenner via the B 182 can obtain another remarkable **view**★★ of the city panorama from the Sonnenburgerhof at one of the last road bends.

Address Book

♿ *For coin ranges, see the Legend on the cover flap.*

PRACTICAL INFORMATION

TOURIST INFORMATION

Innsbruck-Tourismus *Burggraben 3/11* Open Mon–Fri 8am–6pm, Sat 8am–noon.

Innsbruck-Information (sales and bookings office for tickets, Innsbruck Cards, room reservations, city tours, etc.), *Burggraben 3, 6021 Innsbruck,* ☎05 12/53 56, Fax05 12/53 56 14. Open Mon–Sat 8am–7pm, Sun and public holidays 9am–6pm. Ticket office open Mon–Fri 8am–6pm, Sat 8am–5pm.

Tirol-Werbung, *Maria-Theresien-Str. 55, 6020 Innsbruck,* ☎05 12/53 20 0. Open Mon–Fri 8am–6pm.
A monthly events calendar is available from Innsbruck-Tourismus and Innsbruck-Information.

INNSBRUCK CARD

These special visitors' tickets are available from Innsbruck-Information for 24hr (€25), 48hr (€30) or 72hr (€35) and cover free travel on public transport, including round trip cable-car rides on the Hungerburg-, Nordketten-, Oberfuss- and Patscherkofelbahn (a free guided city tour by foot) and free or discounted entry to numerous museums and sights. Call ☎05 12/53 56.

CITY TOURS

Daily tours led by **Per Pedes Tirol** (www.perpedes-tirol.at) in English and German. Choose from "Classic Innsbruck" to "Modern Innsbruck" to "Sporty Innsbruck." ♿Tours for wheelchair-users. 🧒Tours for children.

PUBLIC TRANSPORT

Buy tickets before boarding the bus; drivers only sell single tickets and charge extra. The 24hr pass allows unlimited trips within the city limits. 4-journey, weekly, and monthly tickets are also available.
Tickets are available from **Innsbruck-Information** (Stainerstraße 2, ☎05 12/5 30 70) and tobacconists (Trafiken) with the appropriate sign. Further

information can be found at *www.ivb.at.*

POST OFFICES

Main post office: **Hauptpostamt**, *Maximilianstr. 2,* Mon–Sat 7am–11pm.
Station post office: **Bahnpostamt**, *Bruneckerstraße 1,* Mon–Sat 6.30am–9pm.

WHERE TO STAY

For information on where to stay in Innsbruck, visit *www.innsbruck. info/xxl/_site/innsbruck/_lang/de/_area/453010/_subArea/706078/index. html.*

Fischerhäusl – *Herrengasse 8 (by cathedral passage),* ☎05 12/58 35 35. Hidden restaurant with a peaceful garden.

Hirschen Stuben – *Kiesbachgasse 5,* ☎05 12/58 29 79. Charming contrast between modern décor and old vaulting, with rotating exhibitions of works by contemporary artists.

Weisses Kreuz – *Herzog-Friedrich-Str. 31.* ☎05 12/59 47 90. *www.weisseskreuz.at. 40 rooms.* A 500-year old inn where Mozart once stayed.

Weisses Rössl – *Kiebachgasse 8.* ☎05 12/58 30 57. *www.roessl.at. Closed 2 weeks in Apr, two weeks in Nov. 13 rooms.* An inn in the pedestrianised center of the old town.

Goldener Adler – *Herzog-Friedrich-Str. 6.* ☎05 12/57 11 11. *www.goldeneradler.com. 33 rooms. Restaurant.* In the heart of Innsbruck since 1390 this hotel is one of the oldest inns in Europe. Guest include Mozart, Goethe, Emperor Maximilian, Emperor Josef, Neil Armstrong and other notables. Rooms are stylish and individually decorated during recent renovations. Several restaurants serve fine Tirolean cuisine.

Hotel Central – *Gilmstr. 5.* ☎05 12/59 20. *www.central.co.at. 85 rooms.* A comfortable hotel with a superb Viennese style café with Swarovski crystal chandeliers and great coffee.

Hotel Innsbruck – *Innrain 3.* ☎05 12/59 86 80. *www.hotelinnsbruck.com. 112 rooms.* Traditional hospitality with all modern comforts including a superb fitness center.

◎◎◎◎**Hotel Sailer** – *Adamgasse 8.* ☎*05 12/53 63. www.sailer-innsbruck.at. 90 rooms. Restaurant* ◎◎◎. A classic hotel with a restaurant completely decorated with wood panelling.

◎◎◎◎**Schwarzer Adler** – *Kaiserjägerstr. 2.* ☎*05 12/58 71 09. www. deradler.com. 39 rooms. Restaurant* ◎◎◎. A 500-year old building where each room has been individually decorated to a high standard.

WHERE TO EAT

In the **Ing.-Etzel-Straße** (level with the junction with Dreiheiligen-Straße) in the arches beneath the railway line there is something to suit every taste, from pizza outlets to music bars and trendy wine bars.

◎◎◎**Goldener Adler** – *Herzog-Friedrich-Straße 6,* ☎*05 12/57 11 11.* Elegant Tirolean-style restaurant. The illustrious guest list for the hotel of the same name includes Mozart and Sartre.

◎◎◎**Ottoburg** – *Herzog-Friedrich-Str. 1,* ☎*05 12/58 43 38.* Top-quality restaurant in one of Innsbruck's oldest buildings. Reservation recommended.

◎◎◎**Weißes Kreuz** – *Herzog-Friedrich-Straße 31,* ☎*05 12/5 94 79.* Traditional Tirolean, rustic-style inn.

CAFÉS AND BARS

Café Central – *Gilmstraße 11.* Viennese coffee house-style décor.

Konditorei-Café Munding – *Kiesbachgasse 16.* This coffee house with a pleasant summer terrace is supposed to be the oldest cake shop in the Tirol.

Krahvogel – *Anichstraße 12.* Cozy bar with a limited selection of food and a garden in the back courtyard.

Bellini's – *Meranerstraße 5.* This modern café-bar offers a taste of Italy in the middle of Innsbruck.

Theresienbräu – *Maria-Theresien-Straße 53.* Bar aimed at a younger clientele with tasty beer brewed on the premises.

Sweet Basil – *Herzog-Friedrich-Straße 31.* Restaurant and two bars occupying several floors. Elegant, welcoming and very enjoyable.

© Österreich Werbung / Mallaun

Elferhaus – *Herzog-Friedrich-Straße 11.* Wide selection of beers from all over the world and a small food menu.

Piano – *Herzog-Friedrich-Straße 5.* Long café-bar with small picture gallery and several comfortable sofas conducive to taking the weight off your feet after a day of sightseeing.

Papa Joe's – *Seilergasse 12.* Grill, fast-food and bar. Hint of Latin America in the eclectic décor with fans and even a small "waterfall."

Hofgarten-Café – Very popular summer meeting place with a large terrace in the Hofgarten.

Café-Club Filou – *Stiftgasse 12.* Bar, restaurant and disco.

SHOPPING

The main shopping streets are **Maria-Theresien-Straße**, the pedestrian zone in the old town center around **Herzog-Friedrich-Straße**, and **Museumstraße**.

MARKETS

Franziskanerplatz: farm produce every Thu 9am–1.30pm, bric-à-brac every Sat 7am–1pm.

Sparkassenplatz: farm produce every Fri 9am–2pm.

Rathaushof: flea market every 1st and 3rd Sat in the month 7am–1pm.

Christmas markets (Christkindlmärkte) are held in the old town and on Landhausplatz from late Nov to just before Christmas.

SOUVENIRS

Crafts and traditional costume (Trachten): *Tiroler Heimatwerk, Meraner Str. 2–4.*

ENTERTAINMENT

Tiroler Landestheater, *Rennweg 2,* ☎*05 12/5 20 74.*

Kellertheater, *Adolf-Pichler-Platz 8,* ☎*05 12/58 07 43.*

Theater an der Sill, *Kravoglstraße 19,* ☎*05 12/36 29 29.*

Tiroler Volksbühne Blaas, *Maria-Theresien-Straße 12,* ☎*05 12/58 60 01.*

Kulturgasthaus Bierstindl, *Klostergasse 6,* ☎*05 12/57 57 57.* Old Innsbruck folk theater, chivalry plays.

Treibhaus, *Angerzellgasse 8,* ☎*05 12/57 20 00.* Cabaret, jazz and world music.

Utopia Kulturzentrum, *Tschamlerstraße 3,* ☎*05 12/58 85 87.* Concerts, events, performances, exhibitions.

Casino Innsbruck, *at the Hilton Hotel, Landhausplatz/Salurner Straße 15,* ☎*05 12/5 87 04 00.*

CINEMAS

Cineplexx, *Wilhelm-Greil-Straße 23,* ☎*05 12/58 14 57.*

Metropol Multiplex, *Innstraße 5,* ☎*05 12/28 33 10.*

Central, *Maria-Theresien-Straße 17,* ☎*05 12/58 80 78.*

Metropol, *Innstraße 5,* ☎*05 12/28 33 10.*

Cineplexx, *Tschamlerstraße 7,* ☎*05 12/58 14 00.*

Original-version films are shown at **Cinematograph** (*Museumstraße 31,* ☎*05 12/57 85 00)* and **Cine-Royal** (*Innrain 16,* ☎*05 12/58 63 85).*

DATES FOR YOUR DIARY

Tanzsommer: *Jun–Jul.* High quality dance performances by international artistes.

Innsbruck Festival of Old Music/ Ambraser Schlosskonzerte: *Jul–Aug.*

Walking Tour

Old Innsbruck★

Maria-Theresien-Straße★ *(CZ)*

This lively "street-square" has an imposing **vista**★★ of the Nordkette (2 334m/7 657ft). Along here are several attractive old houses with beautiful façades, most notably Palais Lodron at no 7, Palais Trapp at no 38, Palais Troyer at no 39, and Palais Sarnthein at no 57.

Triumphpforte (CZ F)

This landmark triumphal arch was built to commemorate the marriage of Archduke Leopold to the infanta of Spain, Maria Ludovica, in 1765. Since the wedding was overshadowed by the death of the duke's father, Emperor Franz I, the arch became a memorial to both the joys and the sorrows that year brought for the Imperial court. Medallions of Franz I and Maria Theresa are among the features gracing the north side,

Triumphpforte

A. Niederstraßer/ÖSTERREICH WERBUNG

while imagery on the other side honors the newlyweds.

Altes Landhaus (DZ)

This palace at no 43 is an excellent example of secular Baroque architecture. It was designed by Georg-Anton Gumpp, completed in 1728 and is now the seat of the provincial government.

Annasäule (CZ A)

This monumental column (1706) commemorates the defeat of Bavaria on the Feast of St. Anne Day: July 26, 1703. The Virgin Mary perches atop the slender column, with St. Anne appearing only on the base beside St. George and the dragon.

Stadtturm (tower) (CZ B)

🕐 *Jun–Sept, daily 10am–8pm; Oct–May, daily 10am–5pm.* 🎫 *€4.50.* ☎ *05 12/56 15 00.*

Shortly past the column, Maria-Theresien-Straße changes into **Herzog-Friedrich-Straße**, eventually reaching this 51m/167ft-high Gothic tower that was originally part of the old town hall of

M. Hertlein/MICHELIN

Helblinghaus

1358. It's well worth climbing the 148 steps to a platform from where you'll enjoy a splendid **panorama**★ and one of the best views of the Goldenes Dachl (Little Golden Roof).

Goldenes Dachl★ (Little Golden Roof) (CZ)

The Golden Roof is Innsbruck's most famous symbol. Consisting of 2 738 gilded copper shingles, it tops a Late Gothic balconied oriel added to an existing building in 1500. It was commissioned by Maximlian I to mark his wedding to Bianca Maria Sforza and intended to show off his wealth and disperse rumors about financial woes. From the balcony, the imperial entourage observed festivals, tournaments, and other events taking place on the square below.

The oriel itself is lavishly decorated. The balustrade on the first floor is adorned with eight delicately carved coats of arms. Above is a band of reliefs that includes pictures of the emperor (in the middle) and his two wives. All decorations are replicas, but the originals are on view at the Tiroler Landesmuseum Ferdinandeum (&see entry).

Maximilianeum

⏱May–Sept, daily 10am–5pm; Oct–May, daily 10am–5pm. ✆€4. ☎05 12/58 11 11.

You can stand in the spot from where the imperial couple used to observe the square's goings-on by visiting this small Maximilian memorial exhibit in the building behind the Goldenes Dach. The 20min video about the emperor's life and times is well worth watching and an audio-guided tour (in English) provides additional insights.

Helblinghaus★ (CZ)

Opposite the Goldenes Dachl, the Helblinghaus has Gothic origins but got an opulent frilly Rococo façade in the 18C.

▶ *Continue north on Pfarrgasse, which leads to the Domplatz.*

Dom zu St. Jakob★ (CZ)

&⏱May 12–Oct 26, Mon–Sat 7.30am–7pm, Sun 8am–8pm; Oct 26–May 11, Mon–Sat 7.30am–6pm, Sun 8am–6.30pm. ☎05 12/58 39 02.

There has been a church on this spot since 1180, but successive buildings were destroyed by fire or earthquake, and the cathedral did not receive its characteristically curving, two-towered façade and great dome until the early 18C.

The Baroque **interior**★ was decorated in 1722 by the famous Asam brothers from Munich, Cosmas Damian (painter) and Egid Quirin (stucco artist). Their compositions, with their clever effects of perspective, glorify the Trinity and the intercessions of St. James. The painting of *Our Lady of Succour* (Mariahilf), by Lucas Cranach the Elder, graces the **high altar**★. In the north transept is the canopied tomb of Archduke Maximilian III, a grand master of the Teutonic Order, who died in 1618. Daily at 12.15pm the **Friedensglockenspiel** (peace carillon) sounds from the north tower.

▶ *Backtrack south on Pfarrgasse, then turn left onto Hofgasse, then, after a covered alley, left again onto Rennweg.*

INNSBRUCK

Aldranser Str.	BY	3	Egger-Lienz-Str.	AY	16	Karl-Kapferer-Str.	AY	24
Amraser-Seestr.	BY	4	Erzherzog-Eugen-Str.	BY	17	Leopoldstr.	AY	27
Andreas-Hofer-Str.	AY	5	Fischnalerstr.	AY	18	Pradlerstr.	BY	33
Anton-Eder-Str.	BY	6	Grenobler Brücke	BY	19	Prinz-Eugen-Str.	BY	35
Archenweg	BY	7	Höttinger Gasse	AY	21	Universitätsbrücke	AY	40
Bergiselweg	AY	8	Ingenieur-Elzel-Str.	BY	22			
Burgenlandstr.	BY	12	Innerkoflerstr.	AY	23			

| Kaiserjägermuseum | AY | M³ | Riesenrundgemälde | BY | K | Statue von Andreas Hofer | AY | L |

Hofburg★ (CZ)

&⊙*daily 9am–5pm (last admission 4.30pm). Closed Aug 15.* ⊜ *€ 5.50 (free admission May 18 and Oct 26).* ☏ *05 12/58 71 86. www.hofburg-innsbruck.at.*

It's hard to imagine now, but this glorious palace has origins as a humble medieval castle. These are well concealed due partly to Maximilian I but, more importantly, to Maria Theresia who had the complex completely redesigned in the style of the Viennese Rococo in the late 18C.

The state rooms are devoted to the glories of the Tirol and of the Habsburg monarchy, especially the **Riesensaal**★★ (Giants' Hall), which is about 31.5m/103ft

long and lined with stucco panels with a porcelain finish. The main theme of the ceiling fresco, by Franz-Anton Maulpertsch, is the triumph of the House of Habsburg-Lorraine. On the walls are full-length portraits of Maria Theresa's children following the Imperial couple in procession.

▸ *Return to the Rennweg and enter the Hofkirche (enter through the Tiroler Volkskunstmuseum to the left of the church).*

Hofkirche (CZ)

&⊙*Mon–Sat 9am–5pm (5.30pm Jul–Aug), Sun and public holidays 12.30pm–5pm.* ⊙*Jan 1, afternoon of Shrove Tue,*

Easter Day, Whitsun, Corpus Christi, Nov 1, Dec 25. €4, *incl. Silberne Kapelle.* 05 12/58 43 02. *www.hofkirche.at.*

This three-nave hall church is still largely Gothic, although the Renaissance style is already in evidence at the tower and the entrance porch, and there are Baroque embellishments as well. It was commissioned by Ferdinand I in the 1560s to house the mausoleum of his grandfather, Maximilian I, even though the emperor was actually buried in the castle chapel at Wiener Neustadt, his birth place.

Maximilian's Mausoleum★★
(Grabmal Kaiser Maximilians I)

This tomb is a premier example of German Renaissance sculpture and was personally designed by the Emperor Maximilian I. The lavish design centers on a cenotaph of the kneeling emperor atop a sarcophagus adorned with 24 alabaster reliefs showing scenes from his life carved by Flemish sculptor, Alexandre Colin. Colin also created the four cardinal virtues positioned at the corners of the sarcophagus, which is surrounded by a splendid wrought-iron grille. Standing guard between the red marble pillars are 28 larger-than-life-size bronze statues (40 were planned) representing ancestors. Some were designed by such famous artists as Albrecht Dürer and Peter Vischer.

The Hofkirche also contains the tomb and memorial of **Andreas Hofer** (1767–1810), hero of the Tirolean uprising against Napoleon. Look for it in the northern aisle.

The famous **Renaissance organ** in the choir is a work of Jörg Ebert of Ravensburg and has been largely preserved in its original state.

Silberne Kapelle★★

This separate chapel, built by Archduke Ferdinand II so that he might rest beside Philippine Welser, his commoner wife, was finished in 1587. It owes its name to a large embossed silver Madonna. The first bay on your left contains the tomb of the duke's wife and is one of the most accomplished works of Alexandre Colin. Colin also sculpted the funeral statue of Ferdinand showing him in full armor. His actual armor is displayed separately on a console, in a kneeling position, facing the altar. A small 16C cedarwood organ, of Italian origin, completes the collection of works of art housed in the chapel.

Hofgarten (DZ)

This public park, with free-roaming parrots, was laid out in the 16C under Archduke Ferdinand II and was one of the most ambitious gardens north of the Alps at the time. Given a Baroque character under Maria Theresa, it was landscaped as a less formal park in the early 19C.

Sculpture in Maximilian's Mausoleum

© Österreich Werbung / Markowitsch

Tiroler Volkskunstmuseum★★ (CDZ)

🕙Mon–Sat 9am–5pm (5.30pm Jul–Aug), Sun 10am–noon. 🕙Jan 1, afternoon of Shrove Tue, Easter Day, Whit Sun, Corpus Christi, Nov 1, Dec 25. ⊜€5 (free admission Oct 26). ☎05 12/5 98 49. www.tiroler-volkskunstmuseum.at.

Next to the Hofkirche, this museum exhaustively covers the gamut of folk art from the entire Tirol, including South Tirol in today's Italy. The ground floor has special exhibits and a beautiful collection of Nativity scenes. Upstairs, displays include models of farmhouses, Gothic rooms, and intriguing carnival masks and costumes. The top floor features Renaissance and Baroque period rooms, folkloric festival garments, and a valuable collection of religious folk art.

▸ Take the Angerzellgasse onto Museumsstraße to get to the "Ferdinandeum."

Tirolermuseum Ferdinandeum★ (DZ M²)

&. 🕙Fri–Wed 10am–6pm, Thu 10am–9pm. 🕙Closed Jan 1, Dec 25. ⊜€8 (free admission Oct 26). ☎05 12/59 48 91 10. www.tiroler-landes museum.at.

Although it possesses not inconsiderable prehistory and early history collections, displayed in the basement, this museum is devoted essentially to the development of the fine arts in the Tirol from the Romanesque through the present. Highlights include masterworks from the Gothic age (Multscher, Pacher) and the Baroque (Troger). There is also a good collection of Dutch masters as well as historical musical instruments on the second floor and modern art on the third.

Zeughaus★

🕙Tue–Sun 9am–6pm. 🕙Jan 1, Dec 25. ⊜€8. ☎05 12/59 48 93 11. www.tiroler-landesmuseum.at.

The former armory, commissioned by Maximilian I in 1503 and completed in 1506, now houses the Tirolean cultural history collection of the Tiroler Landesmuseum. The eight themed rooms take you on a journey through the ages, covering such subjects as the importance of silver and salt mining to the region's development, the story of resistance leader and local hero Andreas Hofer and post-World War II Tirol.

Additional Sights

Hungerburgbahn (CZ)

Completed in December 2007, the Hungerburgbahn is a funicular running below ground from the Congresshaus to the Löwenhaus where it crosses an elegant bridge designed by London-based architect Zaha Hadid before entering a tunnel. It re-emerges at the Alpenzoo and ends at the Hungerburg mountain station, which was also completely re-designed by Hadid. From here you can continue up the mountain aboard an equally brand new two-stage cable-car to the ⛷Nordpark-Seegrube ski area and the Hafelekar peak at 2 334m/7 657ft. From here, you'll have a fabulous view★★ over the Inn Valley, the Stubai Alps and the rugged Karwendel cliffs.

Alpenzoo (AY)   Kids

🕙Daily 9am–6pm (5pm in winter). ⊜€7. ☎05 12/29 23 23.

Halfway up the Hungerburgbahn, Innsbruck's zoo is the highest In Europe and is home to 2 000 animals from 150 species, most of them found in the Alpine region. Rare indigenous species of fish swim around the cold-water aquarium.

Excursions

Wilten

Dominating the southeastern suburb of Wilten is the twin-towered **Basilica**★ (AY; 🕙Mid-May–Sept, Mon–Fri 8.30am–5pm, Sat 8.30am–noon, Sun 8am–7pm; Oct–mid-May, Sun–Fri 8am–7pm; ☎05 12/58 33 85). Completely restored in the 1750s, this former parish church was raised to basilica in 1957 and has a sumptuous Rococo **interior** decorated by a team led by stucco artist Franz-Xaver Feichtmayr of the Wessobrunn School, and Matthäus Günther from Augsburg. The latter's ceiling paintings

M. Hertlein/MICHELIN

Stift Wilten

depict the Virgin Mary as an intercessor (chancel) and Esther and Judith (nave). The statue of the Virgin Mary, which is the main object of veneration with pilgrims, is enthroned in glory at the high altar, under a baldaquin supported on marble columns.

Nearby is the **Stiftskirche** (ABY) (⊶ *closed for refurbishment until 2009;* ☎*05 12/58 30 48; www.stift-wilten.at)*, a Baroque church with a distinctive yellow-red façade. According to legend, the abbey was founded by the giant Haymon in atonement for slaying fellow giant Thyrsus. You can see them in stone, guarding the main portal.

Bergisel *(ABY)*

Reached by car via the Brennerstraße, the Bergiselweg and the park avenue.

The Bergisel hill was the setting of the bloody battle between Franco-Bavarian troops and the victorious Tirolean insurgents led by Andreas Hofer. The event is commemorated by a statue of Hofer and the **Kaiserjägermuseum** *(Memorial to the Imperial Light Infantry,* ⊶ *closed for restoration until at least 2009)* (AY M³). The hill itself is now a popular spot for strolling. Also here is the Bergisel ski jump, by Zaha Hadid, who designed the Hungerburgbahn

funicular. This is where the third of the famous four-part Vierschanzentournee ski jumping competition is held annually on January 4 (www.4schanzen tournee.com).

Schloss Ambras★ (BY)

Take Olympiastraße east; turn right at the skating rink; after passing under the autobahn turn left onto Aldranser Straße; after 500m/546.8yd turn left to Schloss Ambras. ⓞ*Dec–Jul, daily 10am–5pm; Aug until 7pm.* ⓞ*Dec 25.* ◉*€8; Apr–Oct, €4.50 rest of year (admission free Oct 26, Dec 24).* ☎*05 12/52 52 47 45. www.khm. at/ambras.*

This fanciful Renaissance palace served as the residence of Archduke Ferdinand II (1529–95) and his beloved commoner wife, Philippine Welser. An avid collector, the prince had the **Unterschloss** (lower palace) built to house his own private museum. Present-day displays include his famous **Kunst- und Wunderkammer**, a cabinet of curiosities, and the arms and armor of the **Rüstkammern**★.

The former residental quarters in the **Hochschloss** (upper palace) now shelter the **portrait gallery**★ with works by Cranach, Titian, Velásquez, and other famous artists. Late medieval art is shown on the ground floor, where the **Georgsaltar**★ is a star exhibit. The inner courtyard sports remarkable frescoes. South of the Hochschloss is the magnificent **Spanischer Saal**★ (Spanish Hall) built by the archduke for entertaining on a grand scale and now a concert venue.

Driving Tour

Tour of the Mittelgebirge★★

105km/65.2mi, including final ascent to the Brenner pass.

⊗The route follows a narrow corniche road with hairpin bends and a steep gradient which is not suitable for motorhomes or cars towing caravans.

▶ *Leave Innsbruck by the Hall in Tirol road (BY on town plan).*

Hall in Tirol★ *⌚See HALL IN TIROL*

▶ *The road to Tulfes crosses the Inn and, as it climbs, gives attractive views of the town of Hall.*

Church of St. Charles Borromeo at Volders★

⌚*Daily 7am–7.15pm.*
The unusual 17C main building has a clover-leaf ground plan, six cupolas and an onion dome with three corner turrets at its base. Inside, the most masterful features are the ceiling frescoes illustrating the life of Milan cardinal, Charles Borromeo and the painting above the high altar, both by Troger's pupil, **Martin Knoller**.

▶ *Continue toward Wattens and follow the signposts to "Kristallwelten."*

Swarovski Kristallwelten in Wattens★ Kids

Daily 9am–6pm. Closed Jan 1, Nov 6–17, Dec 25. €9.50. 0 52 24/ 51 08 00. www.swarovski.com/crystal worlds.

Although essentially a publicity vehicle for the Swarovski crystal company, this underground exhibition is nonetheless a satisfying experience. An overgrown fountain shaped like a giant head guards the entrance to this magical sparkling world of crystal designed by Vienna artist, André Heller. The blue entrance foyer displays the world's largest crystal as well as crystal art by Keith Haring, Andy Warhol, Salvador Dalí and other internationally famous artists. This is followed by 13 "magic chambers" containing fantastic, mystical and meditative installations combining sound, light, objects and natural crystals in every shape and hue. Recently added highlights include an ice installation by fashion designer Alexander McQueen, and a lab where children can get creative with crystals.

▸ *Retrace the route to St. Francis Borgia Church, and turn left to Rinn and Tulfes.*

Igls★

Cable-car operates end May–end Oct, daily 9am–noon, 12.45–4.30pm; end Nov–early Apr, daily 9am–4pm. €14.90 round trip (summer); €26.50 day pass (winter). 05 12/37 72 34. www. patscherkofelbahnen.at.

Igls hosted the Winter Olympic Games in 1964 and 1976 and consequently boasts a substantial tourist infrastructure. The **Patscherkofel** (2 247m/7 372ft), served by **cable-car**, offers excellent walking tours in summer and skiing until well into the spring. Other attractions include a vast stone pine forest and the highest botanical gardens in Austria (*open all hours from Jun to September, by the upper cable-car station at 1 964m/6 444ft).*

▸ *Carry on toward Patsch/Matrei.*

Ellbögener Straße★★

This mountain road, which was once used for carting salt, leads through several tiny villages and hamlets, giving fine views of the Sill Valley. The approach to Patsch offers a splendid **view★** along the length of the Stubaital and the Europa bridge. After Gedeir, the road drops down into the valley, ending at Mühlbach. It then crosses the Sill and joins the Brenner road (B 182) in Matrei am Brenner.

At this point, you can either take a detour left as far as the Brenner pass and Italian border *(32km/19.8mi round trip),* or turn immediately right toward Innsbruck.

Brennerstraße★

The Brenner Pass *(alt 1 375m/4 511ft)* is the lowest Alpine crossing and the only one negotiated by a main railway line in the open air (since 1867). The first Brenner road was built in 1772. The Brenner toll Autobahn (A 13) was opened in 1969 to speed up through-traffic. A slower but more scenic alternative route is the B 182.

From Matrei am Brenner to the Brenner Pass

After leaving pretty Matrei, the road reveals a view of the **Navistal** (valley), with the tiny white churches of St. Kathrein (left) and Tiezens (right), before running along the idyllic Sill valley. On leaving Gries, the **chapel of St. Christopher and St. Sigmund** at Lueg is worth a stop. The road then continues its climb to the pass and Italian border.

▸ *Retrace your route back to Matrei.*

From Matrei am Brenner to Innsbruck

On leaving Matrei the road runs above the River Sill, then drops down toward Innsbruck in a seemingly never-ending series of hairpin bends. After crossing the **Europa bridge★** (785m/858.5yd long, 190m/623.4ft high), it arrives at a parking area with a panoramic viewpoint. The road then leads to the city center via Wilten.

OBERES INNTAL★

TIROL

The Inn Valley has become the backbone of the Tirol. For 185km/115mi, from the Finstermünz ravine to the Kufstein gap, the scenery is typical of the longitudinal furrows of the Alps shaped by the last phases of the Ice age.

- 🅸 **Information:** Am Kirchplatz 48, 6531 Ried im Oberinntal. ☎0 54 72/64 21. www.tiroleroberland.com.
- ▶ **Orient Yourself:** This valley runs south from the Inn Valley in western Tirol.
- 😊 **Don't Miss:** The Kaunertal.
- 🕐 **Organizing Your Time:** Allow a full day to take in everything and give yourself time to stop and admire the views.
- 👶 **Also See:** KAUNERTAL.

Driving Tour

Nauders to Imst
104km/64.6mi

Nauders

Nauders is a popular winter sports resort dominated by Schloss Naudersberg. The cross-country Skiparadies Reschenpass offers 111km/69mi of tracks. In summer, mountain biking is the main sport here, with 600km/372.8mi of tracks covering the sprawling terrain. Past Nauders the road plunges into the Finstermünz gorge.

Finstermünzpass★

This grim gorge forms the natural frontier between the Tirolean Inn Valley and the Lower Engadine and Alto Adige. Downstream from the Hochfinstermünz hotel the road clings precariously to the cliffs of the right bank, reaching a viewing terrace after three rock-vaulted tunnel passages. Further on, it drops down to the valley floor at the Kajetanbrücke (St. Gaëtano) bridge.Nauders to Imst

▶ *After the bridge, head for the Lower Engadine Valley (signposted St. Moritz).*

After crossing the Inn, the road runs past **Pfunds**. Between **Ried** and **Prutz** look for the ruins of Laudeck to the left, flanked by the little, white church tower of **Ladis**.

▶ *In Prutz the road forks off to the right into the **Kaunertal**★★★ (👶 see entry).*

Landeck 👶 *See ARLBERGGEBIET.*
In Landeck, the ruins of **Schrofenstein** can be seen half-way up a mountain slope, all the way to Zams. Past Zams look for **Kronburg** fortress perched atop a forested mountain peak. After **Schönwies**, the road climbs again and has several pull-outs where you can stop to enjoy the views. At last it reaches the wide Imst basin in sight of the jagged crests of the Stubaier Alps (east).

Imst

The delightful upper town (Oberstadt), with its numerous pretty fountains, is punctuated by the imposing 15C **parish church** with a neo-Gothic interior and original 16C murals on the west and south façades. At 84.5m/277ft the tower is the tallest in the Tirol.

Behind the church starts the trail through the 1.5km/1mi-long **Rosengartenschlucht**★ *(Budget 90min for the round trip and wear sturdy shoes)*, which passes by roaring waterfalls and steep, rugged cliffs and offers fine views of the mountains.

The well-known **Imst Carnival**, with its procession of ghosts *(Schemenlaufen)*, takes place only every fourth year, but the **Fasnachtsmuseum** has a permanent display of masks and costumes used on the occasion.

The world's first SOS-Children's Village was founded in Imst in 1949.

ISCHGL

TIROL

POPULATION 2 130 - ALT 1 377M/4 518FT

Ischgl on the **Silvretta-Hochalpenstraße**★★ (*see entry*) undoubtedly ranks among the most beautiful of Austria's winter sports resorts. It's a modern village that is well developed for the tourist trade, offering the gamut of lodging options, an intense après-ski scene and off-piste fun in the Silvretta and Freizeit Centers with their indoor pools, saunas, tennis courts, billiards room, and bowling alley. In summer, Ischgl morphs into a peaceful vacation resort.

- **Information:** Ischgl 320, A-6561, ☎0 54 44/5 26 60. www.ischgl.com.
- ▶ **Orient Yourself:** Ischgl is in the Paznauntal, a valley in the far southwestern corner of Austria, right on the border with Switzerland.
- **Don't Miss:** Trida Sattel for the panoramic views.
- **Also See:** SILVRETTA-HOCHALPENSTRASSE.

Sights

Ski slopes

The ski slopes at Ischgl and the neighboring Swiss resort of **Samnaun** (*alt 1 840m/6 037ft*) belong to the Silvretta Arena (*alt 1 400–2 900m/4 600–9 500ft; www.samnaun.ch*), which has 40 lifts and 230km/143mi of pistes suitable for all skill levels. Almost the entire terrain lies over 2 000m/6 550ft and snow cover remains excellent from late November until early May.

For **cross-country skiers** there is a ski track toward Galtür (*see SILVRETTA-HOCHALPENSTRASSE*), from where there are more possibilities.

Pardatschgrat★

Alt 2 624m/8 609ft. From Dec–May take the Pardatschgratbahn (operates daily 8.30am–4pm); in summer and winter the Silvrettabahn gives access as far as the Idalp at 2 320m/7 612ft (operates 8.30am–noon, 1am–4pm). €40.50 day pass. ☎0 54 44/6 06. www.silvretta.at.

Ischgl

© Österreich Werbung / Mallaun

From the mountain station there is a good view of the ski slopes surrounded by the Vesulspitze, Bürkelkopf, Flimspitze and Piz Rots summits. Directly to the south lies the Fimbatal, a valley dwarfed by the Fluchthorn massif.

Trida Sattel★★

Alt 2 488m/8 163ft. Cable-car up from Samnaun or follow the ski tracks from Ischgl.

From the terrace of the mountain restaurant, the **view**★★ extends southwards over the sheer Stammerspitze, Muttler and Piz Mundin peaks, and to the southeast over the Ötztaler Alps.

An even more far-ranging **panorama** ★★ can be enjoyed from the Visnitzbahn and Mullerbahn chair-lifts.

Address Book

&*For coin ranges, see cover flap.*

WHERE TO STAY

⊜⊜⊜**Alpenresidenz Trisanna** – Nr. 65. ☎05444/52 27. www.tirsanna. at. Closed May–Nov. 30 rooms.

⊜⊜⊜⊜**Goldener Adler** – Nr. 6, Ischgl. ☎05444/ 52 17. www.goldener-adler.at. 35 rooms. This 350-year-old hotel has successfully blended tradition with trendiness in the décor.

WHERE TO EAT

⊜⊜⊜⊜**Stüva** – Nr. 125, Ischgl. ☎05444/52 75. www.yscla.at. Cozy, rustic atmosphere in this stuben-style restaurant.

BAD ISCHL⚓

OBERÖSTERREICH
POPULATION 14 100 – ALT 469M/1 539FT

Bad Ischl is one of Austria's most famous spa towns and for 60 years was the favorite summer retreat of Emperor Franz Joseph I. It gained fame in the 1820s when his mother, the Archduchess Sophie, came to town for a saline cure to treat her infertility. It wasn't long before she became pregnant with the future emperor; four more children, nicknamed the 'salt princes,' followed. Franz Josef's presence lured a who's who of European royalty, artists and politicians to Bad Ischl, including composer Franz Lehár, whose house is now a museum. Today, the town still bathes in the genteel glow of its 19C heyday, although it is also an attractive, modern health resort and gateway to the five lakes of the Salzkammergut.

- 🛈 **Information:** Bahnhofstraße 6, A-4820. ☎0 61 32/2 77 57. www.badischl.at.
- ▶ **Orient Yourself:** Bad Ischl is in the Salzkammergut, about 54km/33.5mi east of Salzburg.
- ☺ **Don't Miss:** Kaiservilla
- ⏱ **Organizing Your Time:** Budget half a day.
- & **Also See:** ST WOLFGANG, ST GILGEN, HALLSTATT.

Sights

The Town

The central square, **Auböckplatz** (B), is bordered by the Trinkhalle (pump room, 1831) and the parish church. East of here, the main shopping street, **Pfarrgasse** (B 16), leads to the Elisabethbrücke across the River Train. It retains such survivals from 19C spa life as the elegant Zauner Café and pastry shop. Just before the bridge, it merges with the **Esplanade** (A), a shady riverside walk, where rich *Salzfertiger* (salt refiners) once stored salt for the Treasury before it was sent downstream. In one of their dwellings, the **Seeauer House** (no. 10), with a Rococo façade and triple gables, Franz Josef got officially engaged to his 15-year-old cousin, Elisabeth of Bavaria ('Sisi') in 1853. A hotel until 1982, the building now houses the **Stadtmuseum**

BAD ISCHL			Kaltenbachstr.	A	9	Pfarrgasse	B	16
			Kurhausstr.	A	12	Steinfeldstr.	B	18
Johannes-Brücke	B	5	Leitenbergerstr.	A	13	Traunkai	A	20
Kaiser-Franz-Josef-Str.	B	7	Maxquellgasse	B	15	Voglhuberstraße	B	2
Marmorschlößl	A	M¹						

with exhibits on the salt trade, local folk-lore and the town's rise to spa resort and imperial summer residence.

Kaiservilla★ (A)

🕐Jan–Mar by 👁‍🗨guided tour only: Wed 10am–4pm; Apr–Oct, open daily 9am–16.45pm. 💶€11 (park only €4). ☎0 61 32/2 32 41. www.kaiservilla.com.

The Imperial villa north of the town, on the left bank of the Ischl, was a wedding present from Archduchess Sophie to Franz Josef and Sisi. It was later enlarged to form the shape of an 'E' in honor of Elisabeth. A tour of the private apartments includes the emperor's study where he signed the fateful declaration of war with Serbia on July 28, 1914. Scores of antlers and various stuffed animals attest to the ruler's passion for hunting. The complex still belongs to his descendents, some of whom are occasionally in residence.

The villa is surrounded by a magnificent landscape garden, the **Kaiserpark**.

Marmorschlössl (M¹)

🕐Apr–end Oct, daily 9.30am–5pm. 💶€1.50. ☎0 61 32/2 44 22.

In the park is the little "marble palace," which served as Elisabeth's tea house and favorite retreat. It now houses the **Photomuseum**.

Address Book

🖊For coin ranges, see cover flap.

WHERE TO STAY

🍴🍴🍴**Goldener Ochs** – Grazer Str. 4. ☎06132/2 35 29. www.goldenerochs.at. 48 rooms. Restaurant🍴🍴🍴. A classic hotel where the Austrian composer, Franz Lehár—to whom an opera music festival in Bad Ischgl is dedicated—used to dine.

KAISERGEBIRGE★★

TIROL

The limestone massif of the Kaisergebirge is popular with hikers and mountaineers. It actually consists of two ranges, separated by the Kaisertal valley: The Wilder Kaiser, a higher and more rugged chain to the south and the lower Zahmer Kaiser characterized by gentler, pasture-covered slopes.

- **Information:** Dorf 35, Ellmau. ☎0 535/85 05. www.wilderkaiser.info.
- **Orient Yourself:** The Kaisergebirge range is in western Austria, on the border with Germany, not far from Kitzbühel.
- **Don't Miss:** Hohe Salve for the fine panorama.
- **Organizing Your Time:** Allow a day for each tour.
- **Also See:** KUFSTEIN, SAALACHTAL, ST. JOHANN IN TIROL.

Driving Tours

1 Wilder Kaiser Tour

68km/42mi

Lofer★

The village of Lofer, backed by the delicately chiseled, snow-flecked cliffs of the Loferer Steinberge, makes a delightful scene. Imposing houses adorned with deep overhanging balconies and ornate façades decorated with flowers and paintings line its narrow lanes, in which traffic is restricted.

The town is a hiker's paradise with favorite destinations including the Auerwiesen, the Loferer Alm and the **Maria Kirchental pilgrimage church** (*see SAALACHTAL*).

▶ *Leave Lofer on B 312 toward St. Johann.*

Beyond Lofer, the valley narrows into a ravine known as the Pass Strub where there is a memorial to the 1809 resistance fighters led by Andreas Hofer. Those with time should make a brief detour to **Strub**, by turning left about 3km/1.8mi after the memorial. The stretch of road between Strub and Waidring skirts many splendid traditional Tirolean farmhouses whose living quarters, stables, and granary are all under the same roof.

▶ *Return to B 312 and carry on toward St. Johann.*

Erpfendorf

Turn left off the road toward the town center.

The church, finished in 1957, is the work of Clemens Holzmeister, who also designed the new building for the Salzburg Festival. Inside is a monumental Crucifixion group, integrated into the roof beam construction above the nave.

St. Johann in Tirol★

See ST. JOHANN IN TIROL.

Spitalskirche zum Hl. Nikolaus in der Weitau★

▶ *Shortly after leaving St. Johann, turn right toward Rettenbach/Weitau. After about 1km/.6mi the road re-enters St. Johann (signpost). The church is just beyond here on the right, surrounded by the Weitau agricultural college.*

The church was founded in 1262 as a home for the poor and converted into the Gothic style c. 1460 and the Baroque style in the 18C. In 1744 Simon Benedikt Faistenberger from Kitzbühel painted the ceiling frescoes (showing St. Nicholas as patron of the poor, the Fourteen Auxiliary Saints and St. John of Nepomuk). In 1745 Josef Adam Mölk from Vienna created the murals. Behind the altar is the oldest preserved stained-glass window in the Tirol (c. 1480). The church also houses the province's oldest bell (1262).

Ellmau

Ellmau's trademark feature is the hilltop **Maria-Heimsuchungs-Kapelle** (1719), from where you'll have a fine view of the town against the backdrop of the Kaisergebirge mountains.

▶ *About 4km/2.5mi after Ellmau, turn right toward Scheffau/Hintersteinersee. The road reaches the lake after a steep, winding stretch of about 5km/3mi.*

Hintersteinersee

The crystal clear waters of this mountain lake reflect the rocky crags of the Wilder Kaiser. It's a nice spot for swimming or a lakeside walk.

▶ *Return to B 312 and carry on toward Wörgl.*

Söll

This charming little town is grouped around the richly decorated Baroque church of Sts Peter and Paul. To the south lies the Hohe Salve with its rounded summit.

Hohe Salve★★

Alt 1 829m/6 000ft.
Cable-car and chair-lift to the summit. Lower station is about 1km/.6mi southwest of Söll. ◷*Operates mid-May–mid-Oct, daily 9am–5.30pm, Dec–Easter, daily 8.30am–5pm, depending on snow.* €13. *0 53 33/52 60.*
From the summit with its tiny church and a restaurant there is a marvelous **panorama★★**, extending to the Kitzbüheler Alps, the Hohe Tauern and the Zillertaler Alps. To the north, the jagged peaks of the Wilder Kaiser dominate.
A path to the left of the lower station leads after 500m/550yd to the **Stampfanger pilgrimage chapel**, idyllically situated above a little creek and reached via a covered bridge.

Skiwelt Wilder Kaiser-Brixental

Austria's largest contiguous ski region encompasses nine win-ter sports resorts in the Wilder Kaiser (Going, Ellmau, Scheffau, Söll, Itter) and the Brixen Valley (Brixen, Westendorf, Kelchsau, Hopfgarten) with 250km/155mi of ski runs and 90 ski-lifts. It is ideal for skiers preferring a more gentle and relaxed style of skiing. Access to the ski area is easiest from Scheffau, Söll and Brixen.
Cross-country skiers have 170km/68mi of ski runs to play with.

▶ *Take B 312 back northeast and after 2km/1.2mi turn right toward Kufstein.*

Kufstein *See KUFSTEIN.*

② Zahmer Kaiser Tour
61km/38mi

The road continues first along the slopes of the Zahmer Kaiser and then through a harsher landscape toward the imposing Wilder Kaiser rockface.

Kufstein *See KUFSTEIN.*

▶ *Take B 172 east toward Kössen. Between Durchholzen and the*

Walchsee it opens out into an attractive valley overlooked by a few peaks of the Zahmer Kaiser.

Walchsee

The road parallels the north shore of Walchsee lake, which is used for water sports and has attracted a healthy level of tourism to the village.

Maria Klobenstein

▶ *A side road leads for about 8km/5mi up the Klobenstein pass. In Kössen, turn onto B 176 toward Schleching. After about 3km/1.8mi, follow the signpost to "Wallfahrtskirche Maria Klobenstein."*

The Ache, which surges down from the Kitzbüheler Alp, forces itself through a narrow gap just behind **Kössen**, forming a natural border between the Tirol and Bavaria.

The pilgrimage chapel of Maria Klobenstein unusually features two church interiors, one inside the other (1707 and 1733). Beneath the chapel a large rock split into two can be seen—this is the namesake "Klobenstein" (cleft rock).

▶ *Take B 176 back southward until Griesenau and the Kaiserbach Valley. A toll is charged beyond the junction. After 5km/3mi, park by the Griesener Alm.*

Ascent of the Stripsenkopf

4hr round trip hike. Nearly 800m/2 623ft elevation gain.

From Griesener Alm (1 024m/3 360ft) the trail brings you to the Stripsenjoch mountain refuge at 1 605m/5 266ft in about 90min. Beyond here, following the red-white "Stripsenkopf" waymarkings should deliver you to the summit (1 807m/5 928ft) in about another half hour. Steep, rocky path. At the top, arey excellent close-up **views**★ of the imposing north face of the Wilder Kaiser.

▶ *Return to B 176 and continue south. The road ends after Gasteig, with a panoramic descent through the meadows above the Leukental and St. Johann in Tirol.*

St. Johann in Tirol★
See ST. JOHANN IN TIROL.

KAPRUN

SALZBURG

POPULATION 2 800 – ALT 786M/2 579FT

This peaceful town at the foot of the Grossglockner Alpine Road offers year round skiing thanks to the linking of the Schmieding glacier with the Kitzsteinhorn. Together with **Zell am See**★ (*see entry*), a mere 7km/4.3mi away, Kaprun has evolved into a huge recreational zone under the name of Europa-Sportregion. In summer you could ski in the morning and swim in the lake in the afternoon.

- **Information:** Europa Sportregion, Salzburger Platz 601, Kaprun. ☎0 65 42. www.europasportsregion.info.
- ▶ **Orient Yourself:** Kaprun is in the Hohe Tauern National Park in western Austria.
- P **Parking:** Plenty of spaces available at the Kitzsteinhorn cable-car station.
- **Don't Miss:** Kitzsteinhorn.
- ① **Organizing Your Time:** Allow a full day to explore the Kapruner Valley.
- **Also See:** ZELL AM SEE.

Excursions

During the summer, the Kapruner Valley, famed for its magnificent mountain setting, is laced with numerous interesting trails. The **Alexander-Einziger-Weg** from the Alpincenter (upper section of the Kitzsteinhorn) to the summit of the Maiskogel is well worth a detour.

Kaprunertal★★

Allow at least 2hr 30min for the Kitzsteinhorn and at least 4hr for the reservoirs, which are only accessible between late May and mid-October.

The Kapruner Valley lies between the ice-capped summits of the Hohe Tauern and the green, shimmering waters of the **reservoirs**★★ serving the Glockner-Kaprun power station.

P Park at the Kitzsteinhorn cable-car station.

Kitzsteinhorn★★★

Cable-cars operate daily 8am–4.30pm (closed 2 weeks in Jun and Sept); €22. ☎0 65 47/8 70 00. www.kitzsteinhorn.at. The **trip**★★ between two particularly sheer rock faces is most impressive. At the Langwied station *(alt 2 000m/6 562ft)*, switch to the Langwiedbahn which

Kapruner Valley

© Österreich Werbung / Markowitsch

drops you at the **Alpincenter** station *(alt 2 452m/8 045ft, restaurant)*. There is a beautiful view of the Kitzsteinhorn massif and the summer ski slopes.

From Alpincenter, another cable-car climbs to 3 029m/9 938ft, reaching a snow-covered mountain ridge just below the summit *(alt 3 203m/10 503ft, accessible only to mountaineers)*. From the upper station climb to the second level of the viewing terrace. Straight ahead, the Grossvenediger dominates the **panorama**★★★. On a clear day the view stretches as far as the Zugspitze, Germany's highest mountain, on the other side of the Karwendel range. For another dose of impressive Grossglockner **views**★★, head down to the terrace of the Glocknerkranzl.

Kitzsteinhorn ski slopes

Open year-round, the area is relatively modest in size (15 ski-lifts and 35km/22mi of ski runs), but it offers fantastic snow conditions in a spectacular setting between 2 000m/6 562ft and 3 000m/9 842.5ft above sea level. The facilities are among the most modern and comfortable anywhere in Austria. The ski runs are suitable for all levels of ability, with a slight preponderance of easier runs.

Hydroelectric dams★

Beyond the cable-car station, a road runs to the Wasserfallboden and Mooser-boden reservoirs but it is only open to private vehicles as far as the Kesselfall Alpenhaus, about 2km/1.2mi past the station. Here you must leave your car in a huge 🅿 parking lot and board a bus to take you to the Lärchwand funicular. During the ascent there is a good view of the valley and Kaprun.

Limbergsperre

At the upper station of the Lärchwald funicular, the Limberg dam *(alt 1 672m/5 486ft)* comes into view. The power station at the foot of the dam wall receives water from the Mooserbodenspeicher reservoir opposite and expels it into the Wasserfallboden reservoir behind the dam.

From the funicular station, another bus travels through a number of tunnels to the Mooser dam, offering scenic glimpses of the **Wasserfallboden reservoir**★.

Mooser- und Drosensperre★

Alt 2 036m/6 680ft. Both valley exits of the Mooserboden are blocked by arch gravity dams to the east and west of the so-called Höhenburg. The **Mooserboden reservoir**★★, amid spectacular Alpine scenery at the foot of the ice-draped Hohe Tauern, is especially scenic.

Crossing the first dam, there is a wonderful **view**★★ down onto the green waters of the Wasserfallboden.

KARWENDELGEBIRGE★

TIROL UND BAYERN (GERMANY)

The impressive limestone massif of the Karwendel, with the Birkkarpitze as its highest point (2 749m/9 019ft), can also be seen from Mittenwald (in Germany) and from the road to the Achensee. Only an excursion into the Rissbach Valley, with a possible detour through Bavaria, gets you near the greyish, pitted cliffs (the *Kar*) that give these mountains their character. If time is short, it is still worth driving as far as the Achensee, the largest lake in the Tirol.

- **Information:** Innsbruckerstr. 282, Scharnitz. ☏0 52 13/52 70.
- ▸ **Orient Yourself:** This range is north of Innsbruck in western Austria.
- **Don't Miss:** Achensee.
- **Organizing Your Time:** This region can be explored on a leisurely day trip.
- **Especially for Kids:** Achensee.
- **Also See:** HALL IN TIROL, INNSBRUCK, SCHWAZ.

Driving Tours

1 The Inn Valley to the Sylvenstein Dam

(Germany) 39km/24mi

Beginning at the Inn Valley *(take the autobahn exit "Wiesing-Achensee")*, the panoramic road climbs up to Eben.

Kanzelkehre★★

From this terraced **viewpoint**★★, look down on the Inn Valley and the lower Ziller Valley, dotted with steeples. The scale of these valleys makes a fascinating contrast to the surrounding mountains. The Rofangebirge mountains tower to the north.

Eben

The church of this village contains the chalice of St. Notburga, who is much revered in Bavaria and the Tirol as the patron saint of workers.

Erfurter Hütte

Alt 1 834m/6 033ft. Rofanbahn cable-car operates May–end Oct, mid-Dec–Easter, daily 8am–5pm every 15min. €14.50 round trip. ☎0 52 43/52 92.
This hut, the departure point for climbing expeditions into the Rofangebirge massif, is set in a magnificent panorama above the Achensee and the Karwendel.

Achensee★★   Kids

Austria's Emperors were the first to discover Achensee as a holiday destination. This fjord-like, 10km/6.2mi-long lake wedged between the Karwendel and the Rofan range is the largest in the Tirol and a popular and family-friendly destination for water sports and other outdoor recreation. The villages dotted along the shore, including Maurach and Achenkirch, have an excellent tourist infrastructure. The lake is also served by the **Achenseebahn** *(☎€26 round trip; www.achenseebahn.at)*, a historic steam–powered cog railway that chugs from Jenbach as far as Seespitz.

▶ *To drive along the edge of the lake, turn round at the village of Achensee and use the old road (one way: north-south). Austro-German border just after Achenwald. Turning right and crossing the Achen pass takes you to the Tegernsee in Bavaria (about 18km/11mi from the border). Turn left onto B 307 to the Sylvenstein dam.*

Sylvenstein-Staudamm

This dam regulates the dreaded flood-waters of the Isar. Water is conducted from the vast reservoir into an underground power station to generate electricity.

2 From the Sylvenstein Dam *(Germany)* to Eng

37km/23mi

▶ *The road, for the final kilometers of which a toll is charged, is narrow and winding and closed from November to May.*

Sylvenstein-Staudamm
  See above.

▶ *On leaving the reservoir and reaching Vorderriss, turn left into the deep Riss Valley and cross the Austro-German border.*

Hinterriss

The hunting lodge built in the 19C for the Duke of Coburg-Gotha is a favorite vacation resort of the Belgian royal family. Use binoculars to scan the slopes and steep cliffs overlooking the road, to see some of the 5 000 chamois which still live on the massif.

Eng

The road ends here, in the **Großer Ahornboden**★, a grassland where some 2 200 maple trees are ablaze with color in the fall, brightening an otherwise severe landscape.

The walls of the Spritzkarspitze (alt 2 605m/8 547ft) and the Grubenkarspitze (alt 2 661m/8 727ft) form a natural amphitheater marking the end of the valley, which forms part of the Alpenpark Karwendel.

🚶Hiking trails start from here.

Achensee's Black Gold

In the hills above Achensee oil laden shale is mined. When processed it gives an unguent sulfurous oil called Steinöl (literally stone oil) that is said to have therapeutic qualities. Available in many hotels, local pharmacies and gift shops it is used in the treatment of rheumatism, arthritis, tennis elbow and other similar joint complaints and skin ailments. The oil-bearing shale was discovered in 1902 by Martin Albrecht and is still mined there today; Albrecht's family continues the business. The oil is extracted by distilling the gas produced when the shale is heated to 450°C/842°F.

KAUNERTAL★★★

TIROL

This long valley, traversed by one of Europe's highest roads, the Kaunertaler Gletscher-Panoramastraße (Kaunertal Glacier Panoramic Road; highest point: 2 750m/9 022ft), makes for an ideal day trip thanks to magnificent mountain scenery and a large reservoir. Skiing is possible from September to June on the Kaunertal glacier.

- 🛈 **Information:** Feichten 134, Kaunertal. ☎0 54 75/29 20. www.kaunertal.com.
- ▶ **Orient Yourself:** The Kaunertal is in western Austria, not far from the Swiss border.
- ☺ **Don't Miss:** Kaunertal Glacier
- 🕐 **Organizing Your Time:** The tour is an easy half day trip.
- 👍 **Also See:** OBERES INNTAL

Driving Tour

Prutz to the Kaunertal Glacier

40km/25mi

In Prutz, turn left off the B 315 toward Switzerland and Italy. The road parallels the Faggenbach River throughly a deeply incised, green valley below the Köpfle and Peischlkopf peaks.

A toll (⊜€20) is charged beyond Feichten, reached after 12km/7.4mi. This is where the valley widens, letting you catch glimpses of the glacier in the distance. After 10km/6.2mi of steep climbing through a beautiful forest, the road arrives at the Gepatsch reservoir, the largest in western Austria,

from where you'll get a pretty **view**★ of the lake and the Weisseespitze *(alt 3 535m/11 665ft)*. The road skirts the left bank for 6km/3.7mi, sprayed by numerous **waterfalls**★. The best view of the pine-fringed lake is just past the Faggenbach bridge.

As the vegetation thins, the landscape becomes ever more rocky. There is a

---

Address Book

👍*For coin ranges, see cover flap.*

WHERE TO STAY

⊜⊜⊜⊜**Weisseespitze** – *Platz 30.* ☎*05475/3 16. 75 rooms.* A pleasant hotel with traditional Austrian wood paneling. Bikers are welcome.

view★ to the right of the picturesque Krummgampen Valley with its reddish cliffs. Shortly after this, the Weisssee comes into sight. The road ends after a final, steep stretch on the edge of the **Kaunertal glacier** (alt 2 750m/9 022ft), where **skiing** 🎿 is possible from September to June. Another attraction here is a 40m/120ft-long icy walk-through glacier crevasse – 😱not for the claustrophic!

▶ *Drive back down to the Faggenbach bridge.*

KITZBÜHEL

TIROL

POPULATION 7 872 – ALT 762M/2 500FT

Kitzbühel is one of the oldest and most exclusive resort towns in the Austrian Alps with a stellar reputation as a winter sports destination. The village developed thanks to silver and copper mining and its position along a trade route from Venice to Munich. Kitzbühel retains some of the atmosphere of the fortified medieval village it once was. The nucleus of the town is formed by two pedestrian streets, the "Vorderstadt" and the "Hinterstadt," which are lined with elegant gabled Tirolean houses housing smart boutiques and cafés.

- 🛈 **Information:** Hinterstadt 18, A-6370, ☎0 53 56/7 77. www. kitzbuehel.com.
- ▶ **Orient Yourself:** Kitzbühel is in the eastern Tirol, wedged in between the Kitzbühel Alps and the Wilder Kaiser range.
- 🅿 **Parking:** Hahnenkamm, Hornbahn and Pfarrau are all parking lots within a five-minute walk of the town center.
- 😱 **Don't Miss:** Skiing or hiking from the Kitzbüheler Horn.
- 🕐 **Organizing Your Time:** In summer or winter, several days will be needed to fully explore the Kitzsteinhorn area.
- 🚶 **Also See:** KAISERGEBIRGE, ST. JOHANN IN TIROL.

A Bit of History

Kitzbühel's winter sports history was kickstarted in the 1890s by one man: Skiing pioneer, Franz Reisch. Inspired by Fridtjof Nansen's "The First Crossing of Greenland," Reisch ordered a pair of skis from Norway and started exploring the mountains. Others villagers soon followed in his tracks, and it wasn't long before the first small races were staged. However, several decades would pass before Kitzbühel's inaugural **Hahnenkamm downhill race** in 1931, which has since become the World Cup classic taking place every January. The downhill and the Super-G races are held on the **Streif**, the Hahnenkamm's most famous slope. Besides skiing, winter activities in Kitzbühel include ice skating, curling, and swimming (indoor pool with a health center). There's also a casino here.

Sports in Kitzbühel

Kitzbühel is also a popular summer destination. It has made quite a name for itself as the hub of Austria's tennis circuit (the clay court Austrian Open is held here in July) and also ranks among the country's leading golf venues with two nine-hole and two 18-hole courses. There's even a hang- and paragliding school and several horseback riding centers.

🥾However, the main summer activity here is hiking, with 200km/124mi of waymarked trails, mostly running along the ski slopes. They're great for those in search of an untaxing hike, picturesque scenery, and spectacular views *(lifts give access to some of the best viewpoints)*.

Geography

Kitzbühel Alps

Between the Wörgl-Saalfelden gap and the upper valley of the Salzach, the smoothly rounded Kitzbühel Alps reach an altitude of 2 362m/7 749ft at the Großer Rettenstein. Known locally as Grasberge (grass mountains), they form a charming and tranquil pastoral landscape.

The contrasting shapes and colors of the surrounding massifs—the jagged walls of the Wilder Kaiser in the north and the towering ridge of the Hohe Tauern in the south—make the Kitzbühel Alps much sought after for the quality of their views.

Skiing

Ski slopes

Slopes spread over four separate areas, all served by ski buses: **Hahnenkamm-Steinbergkogel-Pengelstein** (alt 750–1 970m/2 450–6 450ft), **Kitzbüheler Horn** (alt 750–2 000m/2 450–6 550ft), **Stuckkogel** (alt 900–1 580m/2 950–5 180ft) and **Pass Thorn** (alt 930–1 980m/3 050–6 500ft). There are 56 ski-lifts leading to 55 ski runs covering a total distance of 168km/104.3mi. Although international competitions are held here, the slopes are principally suited to more gentle skiing, with long, pleasant runs through pine forests. Only about 12km/7.4mi cover steeper terrain, mainly in the area of the Steinbergkogel peak. As a result of the resort's relatively low altitude, snow starts disappearing as early as March.

To avoid the long lines at the Hahnenkamm massif, day trippers would be better off traveling to the neighboring **Kirchberg** peak, where the Fleckalm cable-car takes you to the heart of the mountain range in 15min. Good snow conditions on the flank of the Kitzbüheler Horn opposite make it possible to ski right down into the valley.

Sights

Pfarrkirche (A)

Like the neighboring Liebfrauenkirche, the church is set off by its raised site. The nave shows off the talents of a local artist family, the **Faistenbergers**, who were all well-known artists in the 17C and 18C. Benedikt Faistenberg created the painting in the high altar, while the ceiling painting of the Chapel of St. Rosa of Lima was done by his grandson, Simon–Benedikt.

Liebfrauenkirche (B)

This two-storied church is distinguished by a massive square tower that seems to dwarf the nave. The Baroque interior of the upper church includes a ceiling

<table>
<tr><td colspan="2">KITZBÜHEL</td></tr>
<tr><td>Bichlstr.</td><td>2</td></tr>
<tr><td>Franz-Reich-Str.</td><td>4</td></tr>
<tr><td>Graggaugasse</td><td>5</td></tr>
<tr><td>Hammerschmiedstr.</td><td>7</td></tr>
<tr><td>Hinterstadt</td><td>8</td></tr>
<tr><td>J.-Pirchl-Str.</td><td>10</td></tr>
<tr><td>Klostergasse</td><td>12</td></tr>
<tr><td>Malinggasse</td><td>13</td></tr>
<tr><td>Vorderstadt</td><td>15</td></tr>
<tr><td>Liebfrauenkirche</td><td>B</td></tr>
<tr><td>Museum Kitzbühel</td><td>M</td></tr>
<tr><td>Pfarrkirche</td><td>A</td></tr>
</table>

Address Book

For coin ranges, see cover flap.

WHERE TO STAY

Ehrenbachhöhe – Hahnenkamm 22 (über Kirchberger Str.) ☎05356/6 21 51. www.ehrenbachhoehe. at. Closed May–Jun, mid-Sept–early Dec. 47 rooms. At an altitude of 1800m/5905ft on the Hahnenkamm this hotel has stunning panoramic views.

Hahnenhof – Hausstattfeld 18. b05356/7 16 13. www.hahnenhof.at. 20 rooms. Set in park like surroundings, this hotel has traditionally decorated rooms with either four-poster or traditional farmhouse beds.

Hotel Kitzhof – Schwarzseestr. 8. ☎05356/63 21 10. www.hotel-kitzhof.com. 135 rooms. Typical regional rustic elements have been combined well in each of the rooms.

Kaiserhof – Hahnenkammstr. 5. ☎05356/7 55 03. www.hotel-kaiserhof. at. 51 rooms. At the base of the Hahnenkamm cable-car each room in this hotel has furniture made of stone pine which is said to enhance sleep.

fresco of the Coronation of the Virgin by Simon–Benedikt Faistenberger (1739) and a Rococo grille (1778). In the high altar is a 17C painting of Our Lady of Succour (Maria-Hilf) by Cranach the Elder.

Museum Kitzbühel (M)

Jul 10–Sept 20, daily 10am–6pm, Sept 21–Dec 5, Tue–Sat 10am–1pm, Dec 6–Mar 10, Tue–Sat 10am–1pm, 5am–8pm, Mar 11–Jul 9, Tue–Sat 10am–1pm; €4. ☎0 53 56/6 72 74.

This local museum is housed in the oldest building in the town, a former grain store, and has exhibits on the town's mining era, ski history, and folklore.

Excursions

Kitzbüheler Horn★★

Alt 1 996m/6 549ft.

Allow 1hr 30min. Cable-car, in two stages. Operates mid-May–end Oct and mid-Dec–early Apr, daily 8.30am–5pm. €15 round trip. ☎0 53 56/6 28 57.

There is a fabulous **panorama**★★ of the jagged peaks of the Kaisergebirge, the Kitzbühel ski slopes and the Hohe Tauern range. In the summer, the Kitzbüheler Horn is a departure point for an interesting **hike to the Bichlalm** (alt 1 670m/5 479ft – allow 3hr and wear sturdy shoes). From here, take the chair-lift back down into the valley, and then the bus back to town (check the timetable with the tourist office).

Ehrenbachhütte (Hahnenkamm-Massiv)★

Alt 1 802m/5 912ft. Cable-car from Klausen (near Kirchberg), 45min round trip.

There is a good **view**★ of the Wilder Kaiser, the Hohe Salve, the Kitzbüheler Horn and the Großer Rettenstein peaks. In winter, it is possible to ski to the **Steinbergkogel** summit (alt 1 975m/6 480ft) with more great **views**★★ of the Hohe Tauern and the Leoganger Steinberge. In summer, the hike from the upper cable-car station to the Jufenkamm ridge is popular. From here, you can follow the ridge trail south to the Pengelstein mountain refuge and on to the **Schwarzkogel**★ summit.

Schwarzsee

5km/3mi on the Kirchberg road and the lake road to the right (level crossing). A lovely walk also leads to the lake via the Liebfrauenkirche and the Lebenberg road.

This little lake, regarded as one of the warmest in the Alps and only 8m/26.4ft deep, offers bathing opportunities with stunning views of the Kaisergebirge.

KLAGENFURT

KÄRNTEN

POPULATION 90 000 – ALT 446M/1 463FT

Klagenfurt is a hugely popular vacation destination thanks to its mild southern climate and setting near Wörther See, Europe's warmest Alpine lake, to which it is linked by a lovely canal. The city was founded in the 12C and quickly evolved into an important center for trade, although it didn't become capital of the province until elevated in 1518 by Emperor Maximilian.

- **Information:** Neuer Platz/Rathaus, A-9010. ☎0 463/53 72 23. www.info.klagenfurt.at.
- ▶ **Orient Yourself:** Klagenfurt is near the southern edge of Austria, close to the borders with Slovenia and Italy.
- **Parking: Free parking lots**: St. Ruprechter Straße; Messegelände exhibition center; and Krassnigstraße. **Long-stay fee-paying**: Waaggasse lot; Geyerschütt garagee; Domplatz garage; Apcoa garages on Neuer Platz; Heiligengeistplatz (Woolworth's store); and Dobernigstraße.
- **Don't Miss:** Lindwurmbrunnen, Landhaus, Landesmuseum Rudolfinum.
- **Organizing Your Time:** Plan on spending at least one full day in Klagenfurt, another half day if visiting Minimundus.
- **Especially for Kids:** Minimundus.
- **Also See:** WÖRTHER SEE, ST. VEIT AN DER GLAN, MARIA SAAL.

Sights

Old Town★★

The idyllic old town, which is at its most animated in summer, reflects almost 800 years of local history. In the 16C and 17C architects from Italy masterminded its distinctive grid pattern of streets as well as over 50 picturesque arcaded courtyards, many of them open to the public. Numerous fine squares also present lovely architectural accents.

Neuer Platz (Y)

This large square is at the heart of the old town. Its focal point is the **Lindwurmbrunnen**★, or Dragon Fountain, which has become the city emblem. The great monster was created around 1590 by Ulrich Vogelsang, although the basin and Hercules figure weren't added until a few decades later. Completing the ensemble is the country's first-ever monument to Maria Theresa, placed here in 1764.

The square is lined with historic houses, including the 16C **town hall** (Rathaus) and the Adler-Apotheke with charming Rococo stucco decoration.

Alter Platz★ (Y)

Kramergasse links Neuer Platz with Alter Platz, a lively street-square that derives a certain grandeur from its plethora of beautiful 16C mansions. There are many elegant Baroque façades or charming Renaissance arcaded courtyards, such as the **old town hall** (Altes Rathaus), now called the Palais Orsini-Rosenberg. To the west, the Haus zur Goldenen Gans (Golden Goose), a gift from Emperor Friedrich III and one of the town's oldest houses, closes off the square. On the southwest corner stands the **Palais Goess** with a Late Baroque pilastered façade.

The Trinity Column (Dreifaltigkeitssäule) from 1680 was in gratitude for the town's deliverance from the plague; the crescent and cross were added after the 1683 victory over the Turks.

Stadthauptpfarrkirche St. Egyd

This 17C church is richly decorated with galleries, sumptuous fittings and fine ceiling paintings by Joseph Mölck (nave) and Joseph Fromiller (chancel). There are tombstones spanning four centuries, including one from 1998 erected to French-American author Julien Green, whose final wish was to be buried in Klagenfurt.

Landhaus (Y)

This imposing building has a harmoniously proportioned **Renaissance courtyard**★ with a two-story arcaded gallery that was built in 1590 as the town's armoury.

Grosser Wappensaal★

🕐 *Apr–Oct, daily 9am–5pm.* ⊛ €2.
☎ *04 63/57 75 72 15.*
The remarkable Heraldic Hall was decorated by one of Carinthia's most important Baroque painters, **Joseph Fromiller** (1693–1760). His masterpiece

is the magnificent ceiling fresco, framed by *trompe-l'œil* galleries and depicting a scene showing members of the States of Carinthia paying homage to Emperor Karl VI. Fromiller also painted most of the 665 coats of arms of local noblemen adorning the walls and window embrasures.

Dom★ (Z)

The cathedral was built in 1578 as a Protestant house of worship but fell under the control of the Jesuits in 1604 during the Counter Reformation. They

Address Book

For coin ranges, see the legend on the cover flap.

PRACTICAL INFORMATION

The **tourist office** issues a **monthly calendar of events** from May–Sept.

"KÄRNTEN CARD"

This "Carinthia Card" is useful further afield than just in Klagenfurt. It is available mid-May–mid-Oct and is valid for up to two weeks. Almost 90 sites/activities of interest (museums, cable-cars, boat trips, leisure parks and swimming pools) in Carinthia can be visited free of charge and in some cases as often as you like with this card (however, the card is not transferable). It also entitles you to free travel by local rail and bus. It is on sale at local Carinthian tourist offices for €35 (children €14). ☎04 63/30 00. www. kaerntencard.at.

CITY TOURS

A variety of guided city tours is available, especially in summer. Check with the tourist office for details.

PUBLIC TRANSPORT

Buy your ticket before boarding the bus to avoid paying a supplement. The **Stadtkarte** (town ticket) is good for unlimited trips within 1hr within Klagenfurt. The applies for the **24-Stunden-Karte** (24hr ticket) and the **7-Tage-Karte** (weekly ticket), which are transferable.

Tickets and public transport information is available from the ticket sales office on the Heiligengeistplatz (*Quelle-Passage, Mon–Fri 6.30am–2.30pm,* ☎04 63/52 15 42) or from tobacconists (*Trafiken*). Or call the hotline ☎04 63/52 15 34 (5am–midnight) for timetable information.

POST OFFICES

Hauptpostamt (main post office): *Benediktinerplatz;* Mon–Fri 7.30am–8pm, Sat 7.30am–1pm.
Post am Bahnhof (station post office): open round the clock.

WHERE TO STAY

☞☞🛏**Goldener Brunnen** – *Karfreitstrasse 14,* ☎0463/5 73 80, *www. goldener-brunnen.at. 26 rooms.* Rooms are decorated in an elegant classical modern style.

☞☞🛏**Der Sandwirth** – *Pernhartgasse 9,* ☎0463/51 43 22, *www.sandwirth.at. 68 rooms.* A centrally located building (1650), rooms are all decorated in traditional style. Wellness centre.

☞☞🛏**Palais Porcia** – *Neuer Platz 13,* ☎0463/51 15 90, *www.palais-porcia. at, 35 rooms.* Opulence and grandeur throughout.

WHERE TO EAT

☞☞**Oscar** – *St Veiter Ring 43,* ☎0463/50 01 77, *www.gut-essen-trinken.at. Reservations recommended.* Good Italian and Austrian food.

☞☞**Gasthaus im Landhaushof** – *Landhaushof 1,* ☎0463/50 23 63, *www. gut-essen-trinken.at.* Set in the beautiful courtyard of the Landhaus.

CAFÉS AND BARS

Cafés: **Café Domgassner**, *Domgasse 12;* **Café Janach**, *Bahnhofstr. 5;* **Café Musil,** *10.-Oktober-Strasse 14;* **Café Segafredo,** *Alter Platz 30;* **Café am Neuen Platz,** *Neuer Platz;* **Café 7. Himmel,** *Osterwitzgasse 12.* **Popular bars**: **Bierhof zum Augustin,** *Pfarrhofgasse 2;* **Biergarten Marhof**, *Stift-Viktring-Strasse 18;* **Künstlerhauscafé**, *Goethepark 1;* **Napoleonstadel "Haus der Architektur,"** *St. Veiter Ring 10.* Live music is played in the blues and jazz cellar **Kamot**, *Bahnhofstraße 9.* There is dancing at **Scotch Dancing**, *Pfarrplatz 20;* **Fun Factory & Filoy Dancing**, *Gerberweg/Südring.* Genuine cocktails are prepared in these bars: **Meyer Lansky**, *Herrengasse 6;* **Camino**, *Rennplatz 2;* **Lemon Bar**, *Pfarrplatz 20;* **Gates Internet Café,** *Waagplatz;* **Rockefeller Bar**, *Osterwitzgasse 5;* **Joe's Bar**, *Arcotel Hotel Moser-Verdino, Domgasse 2.*

SHOPPING

Alter Platz and Neuer Platz, and in the Bahnhofstraße, Kramergasse, Wienergasse, Burggasse and Paradeisergasse.

MARKETS

Benediktinerplatz: Weekday market Thu–Tue 8am–5pm, Grand Market Thu and Sat 7am–noon.

SOUVENIRS

Crafts and traditional costume (Trachten): Kärntner Heimatwerk, *Herrengasse 2*.

ENTERTAINMENT

Stadttheater Klagenfurt, *Theaterplatz 4*, ☎*04 63/5 40 64*. A range of big theater productions, including Les Misérables and works of Shakespeare, opera, and ballet.

klagenfurter ensemble, *Glashüttenstraße 10*, ☎*04 63/31 03 00*. This professional troupe with its own theater puts on plays, music and children's productions.

DATES FOR YOUR DIARY

Singing, dancing and music under the maypole: *In May*, traditional shows in the Landhaus courtyard.

Altstadtzauber ("Old town magic"): *Last weekend in Aug*. Brings together internationally known artists and music groups performing on several stages, with a big flea market.

Christkindlmarkt (Christmas market): *In Dec* on the Neuer Platz.

---

made numerous alterations, resulting in the Baroque look you still see today. The **high altar**, framed by columns, is the work of Daniel Gran, while the magnificent **pulpit** (1726) is attributed to Carinthian artist Christoph Rudolph. Opposite, the *Apotheosis of St. John of Nepomuk* by Joseph Fromiller counterbalances the pulpit beautifully. The **side altars**★ are a symphony of colored marble. Of special note is the one in the **Ignatius-von-Loyola Chapel** in the south aisle, which boasts an altar painting by the great Paul Troger.

Museums

Landesmuseum Rudolfinum★ (Z M¹)

&🕑*Year-round Tue, Wed, Fri 10am–6pm, Thu 10am–8pm, Sat & Sun 10am–5pm.*

🕑*Easter Mon and Whit Mon.* ✸*€5.* ☎*04 63/53 63 05 52. www.landesmuseum-ktn.at.*

This vast museum offers a comprehensive window on Carinthia's intriguing history and culture. A new highlight is the **Glocknerama**★, a multimedia installation taking you on a virtual climb of the great Grossglockner mountain. Other exhibits are more traditional and drawn from such themes as geology, early- and pre-history, Roman archeology and folk art. There are plenty of fascinating items, including the famous "**dragon skull**," a fossilized rhinoceros cranium found in 1335 in a gravel pit near Klagenfurt. It is said to have inspired the designer of the Lindwurmbrunnen. Also impressive is a large Dionysius **mosaic floor**★ from the ancient Roman provincial capital of

© Österreich Werbung / Wiesenhofer

Großer Wappensaal, Landhaus, Klagenfurt

Minimundus – tour the world on foot

R. Chéret/MIECHLEIN

Virunum in today's Zollfeld plain near Maria Saal (*see MARIA SAAL*).

The 15C and 16C are represented by numerous works of religious art, including the imposing St. Veit altarpiece. Note also Paola Gonzaga's **bridal chests**★ decorated with colorful reliefs based on designs by Andrea Mantegna.

Diözesanmuseum★ (Z M²)

Jun–Jun 14, Mon–Sat 10am–noon, Jun 15–Sept 14, 10am–noon, 3am–5pm, mid-Sept–mid-Oct, 10am–noon. €2.30. 04 63/5 77 70 10 64.

This seven-room museum is aimed at giving a good general picture of religious art in Carinthia from the 12C to the 18C. It displays the gamut of artistic endeavor, from gold and silverwork to tapestry and embroidery, sculpture and painting. Endearing folk art is presented alongside works of outstanding artistic merit, such as a rare 12C **processional cross** and the fine **Magdalenenscheibe**★, which is the oldest piece of stained glass in Austria, dating from 1170.

Bergbaumuseum★ (Y)

Access via the botanical gardens.
Dress warmly, as the temperature is 9°C/48°F. Apr–Oct, daily 9am–6pm. €5. 04 63/51 12 52. www.bergbau museum.at.

The warren of air-raid galleries from World War II carved into the local Kreuzbergl hill is now home to galleries illustrating Carinthian mining history.

Excursions

Europapark & Minimundus [Kids]

3km/1.8mi west of Klagenfurt. Leave via the Villachr Straße (YZ). Apr and Oct, daily 9am–6pm; May, Jun, Sept until 7pm; Jul, Aug until 8pm (Wed 10pm). €12 (includes nearby planetarium). 04 63/ 21 19 40. www.minimundus.at.

The Europapark is a large, leafy recreational area encompassing a mini-golf course, a reptile zoo, an old-fashioned Strandbad (lakeside pool) and Minimundus. This family-friendly theme park centers on 150 scale models (1:25) of world monuments made of authentic materials, from Big Ben to the Statue of Liberty, and the Eiffel Tower to St. Mark's in Venice, all displayed in a park-like setting. It's an edutaining experience, enhanced by audio-guides that provide background information and virtual 3D walks through some of the buildings.

Gustav-Mahler-Komponierhäuschen

Follow the southern shore of the Wörthersee from Minimundus and park opposite Maiernigg beach from where it's a 15min walk. May–Oct, daily 10am–4pm. €1. 04 63/5 37 56 32; www. gustav-mahler.at.

This log cabin hidden in the forest is pretty unprepossessing and is where the composer **Gustav Mahler** created some of his masterpieces between 1900 and 1907, including Symphonies Four to Eight and the Rückert Lieder.

KLEINWALSERTAL★

VORARLBERG
POPULATION 5 300
ALT OF RESORTS: 1 086M/3 563FT TO 1 244M/4 081FT

The Kleinwalsertal is a petite region isolated from the rest of Austria by the Allgäu Alps and is thus exclusively oriented toward Germany – whether it be economically or through tourism. It shares a ski area with Oberstdorf across the border and is a departure point for scenic mountain hikes during the warmer seasons.

- ⓘ **Information:** Walserstraße 64, A-6992. ☎0 55 17/5 11 40. www.kleinwalsertal. de; Oberstdorf, Marktplatz 7, D-87561. ☎0 83 22/70 00. www.oberstdorf.de.
- ▶ **Orient Yourself:** In the north of Bregenzerwald; access is through Germany
- ⊗ **Don't Miss:** Oberstdorf
- ⏱ **Organizing Your Time:** allow a day to explore this valley at a leisurely pace.
- ⓖ **Also See:** BREGENZERWALD, LECH, OBERES LECHTAL.

Driving Tour

Oberstdorf (Germany) to Baad 14km/8.6mi from the border

Oberstdorf★★

This is a charming mountain spa resort and winter sports center at the foot of the majestic Nebelhorn. *Traffic is barred from the town center.*

▶ *From Oberstdorf head south on B 19, reaching the Austrian border after 5km/3mi.*

The road through the Kleinwalsertal (B 201) serves **Riezlern**, **Hirschegg**, **Mittelberg** and its offshoot **Baad**. The highest mountain at the end of the valley is the imposing Grosser Widderstein (2 533m/8 311ft).

Address Book

ⓖ*For coin ranges, see cover flap.*

WHERE TO STAY

RIEZLERN

⊜⊜⊜**Scharnagls Alpenhof** – *Zwerwaldstr. 28.* ☎05517/52 76. *www.scharnagls.de. 5 rooms. Restaurant⊜⊜.* This small, familyrun hotel sitting in the lush green meadows of the valley has an excellent restaurant serving first class food.

Walsermuseum

At Riezlern tourist office. ⏱*Year-round Mon–Sat 2pm–5pm.* ⊘*One week after Easter until Whitsun and Nov–Dec 20.* ⊜*€4.* ☎*0 55 17/53 15 34 (from Austria),* ☎*0 83 29/53 15 34 (from Germany).*
Here you will find an exhibition on the history and way of life (including traditional costume) of the valley and its inhabitants. The second floor has reconstructions of a typical Valaisian chalet and an Alpine dairy hut.

Skimuseum

In the Walserhaus in Hirschegg. ⏱*Daily 8am–6pm.* ⊜*no charge.* ☎*0 55 17/54 17 (from Austria),* ☎*0 83 29/5 11 40 (from Germany).*
The evolution of various winter sports from the late 19C to around World War II is retraced here with the help of numerous exhibits on the first and second floors of the Walserhaus.

Bergschau 1122

In the Walserhaus in Hirschegg. ⏱ *Mon–Sat 8am–7pm, Sun 8am–4pm.* ⊜*free.* ☎*0 55 17/5 11 40. www.bergschau.de.*
Also in the Walserhaus, this is a small but engaging exhibit about life in the Allgäu Alps from prehistoric times onward. Discoveries include the magic world of crystals seen through a video microscope and an interactive relief model of the valley.

KLOSTERNEUBURG★

NIEDERÖSTERREICH
POPULATION 24 500 – ALT 192M/630FT

In 1113 Babenberg Margrave Leopold III moved the court from Melk to Klosterneuburg, founding an abbey there the following year. According to legend, it stands in the spot where the Margrave miraculously found his wife's veil that had blown off many years earlier while the couple was standing on their castle balcony. The abbey, which is still run by Augustinian canons, remains the town's sightseeing trump card to this day.

🛈 **Information:** Neidermarkt 4, A-3400. ☎0 22 43/3 43 96. www. klosterneuburg.at.

▶ **Orient Yourself:** Klosterneuburg is about 12km/8mi north of Vienna.

⊛ **Don't Miss:** Stiftskirche.

🕓 **Organizing Your Time:** You can easily spend a half- or full day here.

Kids **Especially for Kids:** Kids can learn about life at the abbey during hands-on workshops held in the Kinderatelier (children's studio) on Sunday afternoons.

👶 **Also See:** WIEN

Visit

Abbey (Stift)

🕓9am–6pm daily. ⊘Dec 25, 26. ⌕Guided tours on three themes (Sacred, Imperial and Winery) 10am–5pm. ⊛€8 for one tour, €11.50 for any two tours. The abbey museum may be visited without a guide. ☎0 22 43/41 10. www.stift-klosterneuburg.at.

Stiftskirche (Abbey church)

This three-nave Romanesque basilica has origins in the 12C but has been modified repeatedly, most notably in 1634 when it was given the full Baroque treatment courtesy of the great Giovanni Battista Carlone and Andrea de Retti. The lovely **ceiling frescoes** in the nave were created by Georg Greiner c. 1689, though the ones by Johann Michael Rottmayr in the chancel depicting the *Assumption* are considered more accomplished. The high altar by **Matthias Steinl** and the richly gilded **choir stalls** decorated with 24 Habsburg coats of arms are worth seeing, too. The Baroque organ of 1636 is famous for its exquisite sound and was greatly admired by Anton Bruckner.

Kreuzgang (Cloisters)

These date from the 13C and 14C and are a fine example of Early Gothic architecture with Burgundian influence. The old pump house contains a remarkable seven-armed **bronze candelabrum**, a 12C Veronese work symbolizing the Tree of Jesse.

Leopoldkapelle

East of the cloisters, the Leopoldkapelle has ethereal 14C **stained glass**★, although the highlight is the **Verdun altarpiece**★★. This amazing winged altar was fashioned in the 12C by Nicolas of Verdun and consists of 50 gilded

Stiftskirche, Klosterneuburg

M. Hertlein/MICHELin

Nicolas of Verdun

Little is known of Nicolas of Verdun (late 12C/early 13C) other than that he was a goldsmith and enameler from Lorraine. The side panels of the Dreikönigsschrein (Shrine of the Three Kings) in Cologne Cathedral are attributed to him, but his name is only known to us from inscriptions on two works: The Mary Shrine in Tournai Cathedral and the enameled panels in Klosterneuburg, both considered masterpieces of medieval art.

enamel panels arranged in three rows and depicting famous scenes from the Old and New Testaments.

The chapel also contains the tomb of Leopold III, who was canonized in 1485.

Stiftsbau (Abbey building)★

Emperor Charles VI envisioned an abbey modeled on nothing less than the grand Escorial near Madrid. Construction began in 1730 but only a quarter of the plans were fully realized because of Charles' sudden death in 1740 and a total lack of interest in the project by his daughter, Maria Theresa. Visitors are greeted by eight giant Atlases by Lorenzo Mattielli in the unfinished **Sala terrena**, the former garden room. There are exhibits about the abbey's history leading to the grand **Chorherrenstiege**

(staircase), which is lined by video installations informing you about the canons' daily life.

In the imperial apartments is the **Gobelin Hall**, adorned with priceless tapestries from Brussels, and the **Marble Hall**★ with its giant oval dome decorated with frescoes by Daniel Gran glorifying the Habsburgs.

Stiftsmuseum★

🕑9am–6pm daily. 🎟€5.50; ☎0 22 43/ 41 11 54.

The abbey museum is filled with interesting items, most famously a huge painting depicting the geneaology of the Babenbergs, a statuette of Mercure by Raphael Donner, richly carved ivory decorative objects, and four early works by Egon Schiele.

KREMS UND STEIN★★

NIEDERÖSTERREICH

POPULATION 23 120 – ALT 221M/725FT

Krems is a delightful wine village snuggled against terraced vineyards on the left bank of the Danube. More than 1 000 years old, it actually consists of three towns in one: Krems, Stein and Und, giving rise to the saying: "Krems Und (and) Stein are three towns." It is part of the Wachau region, which was declared a UNESCO world heritage site in 2000. Krems was the long-time home of the painter Martin Johann Schmidt (1718–1801), better known as **Kremser Schmidt**, whose work graces many churches and abbeys around the country.

- 🚹 **Information:** Undstraße 6, A-3504. ☎0 27 32/8 26 76. www.krems.at.
- ▶ **Orient Yourself:** Krems is at the eastern edge of the Wachau, about 77km/42mi west of Vienna.
- 🅿 **Parking:** There are pay-parking garages at Steiner Tor, on Kasernenstraße and on Ringstraße and a free Park & Ride lot at the Bahnhof (train station).
- 😊 **Don't Miss:** Piaristenkirche, Weinstadtmuseum, Kunsthalle Krems.
- 🕐 **Organizing Your Time:** Budget at least a day to take in an excursion as well.
- 👣 **Also See:** DÜRNSTEIN, SCHLOSS GRAFENEGG.

Am Goldberg	AY 4		Gartenaugasse	BZ 9	
Bertschingerstr.	BY 2		Gaswerkgasse	AY 10	
Dominikanerpl.	BZ 5		Heinemannstr.	BY-BZ 12	
Dr-Dorrek-Str.	AY 3		Körnermarkt	BZ 13	
Dreifaltigkeitspl.	BZ 6		Kreuzbergstr.	AY 14	

Minoritenpl.	AZ 15	Pfarrpl.	BZ 20	Schürepl.	AZ 24
Mosepl.	BZ 16	Philosophensteig	AY 21	Untere Landstr.	BZ 26
Neutorgasse	AZ 17	Rathauspl.	AZ 23	Wachtertorgasse	BY 28
Obere Landstr.	BZ 18	Schillerstr.	BY 30		

Sights

Krems

Piaristenkirche★ (BZ)

First run by Jesuits, this church was handed over to the Piarists, an educational order who's still in charge today, by Maria Theresa in 1776. Dominating the old town, it is a beautiful three-nave Late Gothic hall church with exquisite net vaulting and a bonanza of works by Kremser Schmidt. The most famous among these are the **high altar** painting of the *Assumption* and the right side altar showing the founder of the Piarist order. Notable too are the **choir stalls**, still with stylistic features of the Early Renaissance although dating from well into the 17C.

Pfarrkirche (BZ)

This Early Baroque church, completed in 1630 under the Italian architect Cyprian Biasino, has a sumptuously decorated interior. The nave and chancel vault are adorned with Kremser Schmidt frescoes.

197

A

Weinstadtmuseum★ (BZ M)

🕐 *Mar–Nov, Tue–Sat 10am–6pm.* ⊜€4. ☎ *0 27 32/80 15 67. www.weinstadtmu seum.at.*

This former Dominican monastery provides a delightful setting for the imaginatively presented displays on Krems' cultural history. Wine takes center stage, naturally, but there are also some fine works by Kremser Schmidt as well as the famous **Fanny of Galgenberg**★. Standing a mere 7.2cm/2.8in tall and made of greenish slate, this little statuette is believed to be about 32 000 years old, making it the world's oldest female figurine unearthed so far. The 700-year-old monastery church impresses with its crisp Gothic architecture that was never adulterated by Baroque embellisment.

Obere und Untere Landstraße (BZ 18, 26)

Historic Krems' main artery, the pedestrian-only Landstraße is lined with Renaissance and Baroque façades and punctuated by the Steiner Tor, a monumental 15C gateway. Deserving closer inspection is the **Bürgerspitalkirche** (BZ), an elegant Gothic chapel whose single rib-vaulted nave exudes a peaceful atmosphere. The high altar is flanked by two superb gilded wooden statues, the work of Matthias Schwanthaler.

Stein

About 1km/.6mi west of the Steiner Tor, Stein is charmingly hemmed in by the Danube and terraced vineyards. The main drag, **Steiner Landstraße**, which opens out here and there into

small squares, is lined with well-preserved, elegant town houses and arcaded courtyards, both a reflection of local wealth.

Approaching Stein from the west, you can't miss the **Kunsthalle Krems** (🕐 *10am–6pm daily;* ⊜ €8; ☎ *0 27 32/90 80 10; www.kunsthalle.at*), a well-respected art exhibition hall skillfully converted from an old tobacco factory. The progressively minded shows also spill over into the nearby former **Minoritenkirche**, a three-nave pillared basilica whose 14C frescoes provide an interesting backdrop on view here.

Further west looms the mighty west tower of the **Pfarrkirche St. Nikolaus** with its delicate Baroque dome. Inside, Kremser Schmidt worked his magic with the ceiling fresco and the altar paintings. The **Frauenbergkirche**, right behind the Pfarrkirche, is now a war memorial.

Excursions

Stift Göttweig★

6km/3.7mi south of Krems on the road to St. Pölten (BY). 🕐 *Jun–Sept, daily 9am–6pm; Mar 21–end May and Oct–mid-Nov, daily 10am–6pm.* 🕐 *Good Fri.* ⊜€2.50, *full access €7.* ☎ *0 27 32/85 58 12 31. www.stiftgoettweig.or.at.*

The prominent hilltop setting and striking architecture of this Benedictine abbey has garnered it the nickname "Austria's Monte Cassino," after the Italian abbey where the order originated. Founded in 1083, it was nearly destroyed by fire in 1718 and restored in Baroque style. The church **interior**★ dazzles with elaborate stuccowork and a number of interesting features, most notably the mighty high altar (1639) and the pulpit, both by Dutch master Hermann Schmidt. Medieval remnants include the Erentrudiskapelle (chapel) and the crypt. Full admission also provides access to the monumental **Imperial staircase**★ with a ceiling fresco by **Paul Troger** (1739); the imperial state rooms and the museum with its changing roster of items from the abbey's treasury. Since 2001, the abbey has been include on UNESCO's prestigious list of World Heritage Sites.

Schloss Grafenegg★

The palace is about 12km/7.4mi east of Krems.

Schloss Grafenegg is Austria's most significant example of romanticized late 19C Historicist architecture. Surrounded by an English landscape park, the palace keep with its gallery and turrets rises like a miraculous vision above the Tullner Feld plain. The palace is well known for its exhibitions, readings and concerts. The restaurant serves gourmet-level international cuisine, which is best paired with wine from the palace's own estate.

Old castle

A castle has stood on this spot since the Middle Ages, but what you see today is the product of 19C architect Leopold Ernst. It is a vast neogothic pile surrounded by a dry moat and sporting cream–colored façades festooned with fierce-looking gargoyles. It was severely damaged during 10 years of Soviet occupation after World War II but has since been extensively restored.

Tour of the castle

Tours by appointment only. ⏰May–Oct, Tue–Sun 10am–5pm. ✆€5. ☎0 27 35/22 05 22; www.grafenegg.at.

The ethereal blue **Schlosskapelle** (palace chapel) is a fine example of

Coffered ceiling in the Great Salon, Schloss Grafenegg

neo-Gothic architecture and boasts a Late Gothic winged altar depicting the Coronation of the Virgin Mary. The **Great Salon** and the **Dining Room**, with their attractive wooden panelling and carved ornaments and figures, are additional highlights. The **coffered ceiling**★ in the Great Salon is particularly stunning, as is the stairway decorated with the figure of a knight and busts of the builder and his architect. No less remarkable are the **Yellow Salon** and the adjoining bathroom, study and bedroom, the library and the garden room, whose walls and ceilings are covered in exquisite materials.

Stift Zwettl

The abbey is about 49km/30mi northwest of Krems. ☎0 28 22/2 02 02 17. www.stift-zwettl.at.

Stift Zwettl

The great Cistercian abbey of Zwettl lies in a bend of the valley of the River Kamp, one of the most romantic in the Waldviertel. It was founded in 1137 by Hadmar I von Kuenring, whose dynasty ruled over the Waldviertel for centuries. The abbey flourished in the Middle Ages and again after the Counter Reformation. It even survived Joseph II's reforms and the Nazi period unscathed, so that today it is still a vigorous spiritual, cultural and economic hub of the region. Tour of the abbey

⏱ ☞ *Guided tour (1hr) Jul–Sept, Mon–Sat 10am, 11am, 2pm, 3pm and 4pm, Sun 11am, 2pm, 3pm and 4pm; May–Jun, Oct, same schedule except no tours at 4pm. ⊜ €7.*

Stiftskirche (Abbey church)★
The basic structure of the 14C church is Gothic but the requisite Baroque makeover in the 18C added the elegant **west front**★★ and slender tower topped with a curving roof and a lantern.

The **high altar**★ provides the majestic backdrop for a realistic representation of an oak tree, which recalls both the legend of the abbey's foundation (it is said to be built on the spot where an oak grew green leaves in winter) and also the Tree of Salvation. The **choir stalls**★ are richly inlaid and bear gilded vases and statues.

Kreuzgang★
The **cloisters**, completed in 1240, are a fine example of the transitional style between Romanesque and Gothic. In the hexagonal *lavatorium*, or washing place, you are surrounded by small columns with crocketed or plain vase capitals.

Kapitelsaal
The **chapter-house** is the oldest part of the abbey, dating from after 1175. Vaulting ribs radiate from a massive central pillar, dividing the room into four bays.

KREMSMÜNSTER★

The impressive Benedictine **abbey** of Kremsmünster is a rambling compound in a dramatic bluff-top setting overlooking the Krems Valley. According to legend, it was founded in 777 by Bavarian Duke Tassilo III in the spot where his son was killed by a wild boar in a hunting accident. Nothing remains of the original abbey, which now grandstands in Baroque splendor thanks to a large cast of talented architects and artists. From its silhouette rise not only the church's two domed towers but also the bulky "Mathematical Tower," a former astronomical observatory.

🅘 **Information:** Rathausplatz 1, A-4550. ☎ 0 75 83/72 12. www.kremsmuenster. at.

▶ **Orient Yourself:** Kremsmünster is 43km/27mi south of Linz and 25km/ 15.5mi west of Steyr.

🅿 **Parking:** There are pay-parking garages at Steiner Tor, on Kasernenstraße and on Ringstraße and a free Park & Ride lot at the Bahnhof (train station).

👀 **Don't Miss:** Piaristenkirche, Weinstadtmuseum, Kunsthalle Krems

🕐 **Organizing Your Time:** Allow two to three hours

👣 **Also See:** DÜRNSTEIN, STIFT GÖTTWEIG.

Visit

Abbey
☞ *Guided tours of abbey and art collection (1hr) May–Oct, daily 10am, 2pm, 3pm, 4pm, also Mon–Fri 11am, Sat–Sun 11.30am and 1pm; Nov–Apr, daily 11am,* *2pm, 3.30pm. ⊜ €6.50.* ☞ *Guided tours of natural science collection (1hr 30min) May–Oct, daily 10am and 2pm, Jul–Aug also 4pm. ⊜ €7.50. Tickets on sale in the abbey shop in the first courtyard, near the fish pond. ☎ 0 75 83/5 27 51 51. www.stift-kremsmuenster.at.*

Fischbehälter★

Free admission; can be seen without guided tour.

An unexpected feature in the first abbey courtyard is the five **fish basins** framed by arcades and adorned with water-spouting statues of Samson, David, Neptune, Triton and other mythological creatures. They were designed by Carlo Antonio Carlone around 1690 and enlarged by Josef Prandtauer.

Stiftsgebäude (Abbey Buildings)

The **Kaisersaal** (Emperors' Hall) owes its name to 17C portraits by Martino Altomonte of the Holy Roman Emperors from Rudolf of Habsburg to Charles VI. Ceiling frescoes and stucco mouldings of great delicacy adorn this state hall.

The star exhibit in the abbey treasury is the 8C **Tassilo chalice**★★★, an exquisite work made from gilded copper with silver inlay. It was used in 765 in the duke's wedding and later presented to the abbey's monks.

The abbey **library**★ is divided into four rooms that again bear the decorative stamp of Carlone and contain some 160 000 volumes. There's also a smattering of paintings exhibited in several galleries on the second floor.

Tassilo chalice

KUFSTEIN

TIROL

POPULATION 14 500 – ALT 499M/1 637FT

Kufstein, the last Austrian town in the Inn Valley, lies at the foot of a rocky outcrop crowned by a mighty fortress. The town has become a lively and popular tourist resorts thanks, in part, to the proximity of the Kaisergebirge range (👁 see entry), easily reached by the Wilder Kaiser chair-lift (Y).

- 🔲 **Information:** Unterer Stadtplatz 8, Kufstein. ☎0 53 72/6 22 07. www.kufstein.com.
- ▶ **Orient Yourself:** Kufstein is on the Inn River, just 5km/3mi from the border with Germany.
- 😊 **Don't Miss:** The Fortress
- 🕐 **Organizing Your Time:** Spend a couple of hours visiting the castle, ideally built around a 15min organ concert at noon or 6pm.
- 👁 **Also See:** KAISERGEBIRGE.

Visit

Fortress *(Festung)* (Z)

♿🕐*Apr 8–Oct, daily 9am–5pm. ⚓€8. Nov–Apr 7, daily 10am–4pm (museum closed). ⚓€7. ☎0 53 72/60 23 50. www. festung-kufstein.at.*

Kufstein owes much of its character to the citadel that dominates the town. Starting from the Unterer Stadtplatz, an archway above the church leads to the Festungshof *(left)* with the auditorium for the Heldenorgel. Here you can catch the funicular (included in admission tickets) or continue via a covered stairway. A gateway takes you to the Tiefer Brunnen, a 60m/197ft-deep well. From here, a tunnel carved through the rock leads to the "Peacock tail" (Pfauenschweif) gateway, and then left to the Wallachen and Caroli bastions, from where you'll enjoy good **views**★ over the Inn River. In summer, tickets also include admission to the **Heimatmuseum**, which presents an array of objects collected by the Kufstein local history society. Of particular interest are the rooms illustrating the fortress through the ages.

Kaiserturm★

This colossal 16C tower, with walls up to 4.5m/15ft thick, rears up on the highest point of the rocky bluff. The cells on the third floor are reminders of the tower's use as a state prison in the 19C.

Heldenorgel

&. ⏱*Organ recitals daily noon (10–15 min); Jul–Aug also 6pm.* ∞ €1. ☎0 53 72/60 23 50.

This giant instrument, known as the "Heroes' organ," was first played in 1931 to commemorate the fallen of World War I. It is on the top floor of the Bürgerturm, one of the fortress towers, and boasts 4 307 pipes and 46 registers. The organist's keyboard and the gallery for the audience are at the foot of the rock. The recitals can be heard throughout the town or you can buy a ticket to sit in the auditorium. Since the organ is exposed to the air, it has to be constantly retuned.

Excursions

Schloss Mariastein
12km/7.4mi southwest of Kufstein. Park in the valley and climb up to the castle.
In the 14C, a fortified tower was built on a huge rocky outcrop in a small peaceful valley paralleling the Inn. It was called "Stein" (rock) and became a site of Marian pilgrimage after a Lady Chapel was built here.

The Knights' Hall (Rittersaal) upstairs houses the **Schlossmuseum** (*daily 9am–5pm; ☎0 53 32/5 64 85*) whose collection includes a Tirolean royal crown and scepter. There are two chapels: one above, the other on the upper stories; the lower Late Gothic **Kreuzkapelle** (Chapel of the Cross) and the upper

Gnadenkapelle (Chapel of Miracles), decorated in the Baroque style.

Thierseetal
The green valley with scattered settlements stretches almost as far as the German border. Thiersee, venue of a Passion play every six years (*see Calendar of events*), lies on a small round lake of the same name.

A succession of combes and gorges leads to the Ursprung pass (alt 849m/2 785ft), which marks the Austro-German border. After the pass, the road runs through the thickly forested **Ursprungstal** in Germany, a valley that bears hardly any traces of human settlement except an inn or two. In Bayrischzell, at the foot of the impressive Wendelstein, the road joins the **German Alpine Road** (Deutsche Alpenstraße) which runs 450km/280mi between Lindau at Lake Constance and Berchtesgaden (*for description, see The Green Guide Germany*).

LAMBACH
OBERÖSTERREICH
POPULATION 3 170 – ALT 349M/1 145FT

In the Middle Ages, this small town on the River Traun built its wealth on the salt trade. To this economic function was added the prestige of a Benedictine abbey, founded by Bishop Adalbero in the 11C and still an active monastery today.

- **Information:** Marktplatz 8, A-4650, ☎0 72 45/28 35 50, www.stift-lambach.at.
- **Orient Yourself:** Lambach is about 15km/9.3mi southwest of Wels or 48km/30mi southwest of Linz.
- **Also See:** WELS.

Visit

Abbey★ (Stift)

Stiftskirche (Abbey Church)
Guided tour by reservation only (1hr 30min) Easter-end Oct, daily 2pm. ☜€5. ☎0 72 45/2 17 10.
The abbey church, which contains the tomb of Adalbero, was largely rebuilt in the 17C according to Baroque precepts, although some exquisite Byzantine-influenced **frescoes**★★ survive from the Romanesque period. Uncovered and restored in 1967, they are considered

among the oldest in Europe. The scene in the central dome shows the Virgin Mary with the Infant Jesus, flanked to the left by the Three Wise Men bearing gifts and to the right by Jerusalem and Herod interrogating the Wise Men.

Klostergebäude (Abbey Buildings)
Highlights in the main abbey buildings include the Baroque **library** with frescoes by Melchior Seidl and 50 000 precious volumes; the well-proportioned **summer refectory** with outstanding stucco decoration by Carlo Antonio

Dreifaltigkeitskirche, Stadl-Paura

Lambach even has its own theater, the beautiful 18C Rococo **Kleines Theater**★, the only one of its kind to have surived in Austria.

Excursion

Pfarr- und Wallfahrtskirche Stadl-Paura★

2km/1.2m. Leave Lambach to the south. Cross the River Traun and turn right after 500m/550yd.
This church is a symmetrical ode to the Trinity. It has a triangular floorplan, three towers, three chancels, three marble portals, three altars, three small organs, and three sacristies. Even the frescoes in the dome and the altar paintings are by a trio of famous artists: Carlo Antonio Carlone, Martino Altomonte, and Domenico Parodi.

Carlone (now a concert hall); the former abbey tavern, now a **pharmacy**, which also contains some beautiful stuccowork; and the **ambulatory** by Diego Carlone.

LECH

VORARLBERG

POPULATION 1 270 – ALT 1 447M/4 747FT

Lech is indisputably the prettiest holiday destination in the Austrian Alps and one of the few resorts in the northern Alps to have made a name for itself as an international winter sports venue. Upscale and imbued with an air of exclusivity, it is a favorite haunt of royalty, celebrities and the wealthy.

- **Information:** A-6764. ☎0 55 83/2 16 10. www.lech-zuers.at.
- ▶ **Orient Yourself:** Lech is in the far western reaches of Austria, close to the borders with Germany, Lichtenstein and Switzerland.
- **Parking:** In the Anger underground parking garage. Free in summer.
- **Don't Miss:** Zuger Hochlicht.
- **Organizing Your Time:** Allow two or three days to fully enjoy the mountains.
- **Also See:** ST. ANTON AM ARLBERG, ARLBERGGEBIET.

Sights

Lech has won its reputation thanks in part to its merging with the neighboring resorts of **Zürs** 🔍 and **St. Anton** 🔍 (*see separate entries*) to create a ski area capable of meeting the most demanding standards, but most of all because of its insistence on quality above quantity. Here, biggest is not allowed to be best, and tourist facilities have been built very

much with the welfare of the natural environment in mind.
For this reason, guest capacity is only about 7 000, or three to six times smaller than the demand in the other major European winter sports resorts. Accommodation consists mainly of hotels and family guesthouses in the luxury category with an après-ski scene to match. Expect plenty of

exclusive boutiques, elegant cafés, gourmet restaurants, and upscale cultural activities.

Lech also has plenty to offer in the summer months, when life takes on a much calmer pace. Although there are no particularly breathtaking panoramas, the soft green meadows of the surrounding countryside are most restorative.

Hiking

The area is great for hiking and mountain bike tours, most popularly in the Formarin, Ferwall and Moos valleys. One of Lech's major attractions is the vast open-air swimming pool in a pretty woodland setting. Anglers can choose between lakes such as the Formarinsee, Spullsee, Zürssee or Zugweiher (*enquire about fishing permits at the Lech tourist office).

The Town★

The town of Lech lies on a mountain plateau (alt 1 444–1 717m/4 738–5 633ft). Limestone peaks (the Mohnenfluh and Braunarlspitze to the north, Rote Wand to the west, Schafberg and Omeshorn to the south and Rüfispitze to the east) tower above the lush Alpine pastures and forests that grow at up to 1 800m/5 900ft above sea-level. Although difficult access roads and the sheer cliff faces of Omeshorn and Rüfikopf lend the area an undeniably mountainous aspect, the mountains around Lech are not in fact that high.

None of the surrounding peaks are taller than 2 700m/8 850ft, and there is not a single glacier in sight.

The town of Lech is spread along the banks of its namesake river. It retains little physical evidence of its past, although the Gothic **church**, a few farmhouses from the days of the Valais (e.g. Haus Anger no 19) and the court in the Weisses Haus (16C) opposite the Hotel Krone, are noteworthy exceptions.

Further uphill, the resort of **Oberlech** (alt 1 700m/5 577ft) hugs a slope of the Kriegerhorn and is blessed with plenty of sunshine, excellent snow conditions and a sweeping view. In winter, Oberlech is car free and only accessible by cable-car.

If you're seeking respite from the hubbub of the ski slopes and fellow skiers, the hamlets of Zug to the west and Stubenbach to the east offer calmer alternatives.

Ski Slopes

Arlberg ski slopes

These slopes, which encompass, from north to south, the resorts of Lech, Zürs, Stuben, and St. Anton, are the largest and most varied in Austria. They include over 260km/162mi of maintained and 180km/112mi of open slopes, to which 84 ski-lifts give access. It is possible to ski from Lech to Zürs and back, and likewise from Stuben and St. Anton. To get from Zürs to Stuben or St. Anton, however, it is necessary to take the bus.

© Österreich Werbung / Felder

Lech

The **ski area** ⮆ attached to Lech extends over two mountains. Most of the ski runs are on the Kriegerhorn and the Zuger Hochlicht (alt 1 450–2 377m/4 757–7 799ft). The guaranteed snow cover and the gentle slopes make skiing here an enjoyable and relaxing experience. The Mohnenmähderpiste (very easy) and the Steinmähderpiste (intermediate) are definitely worth a try. Experienced skiers will prefer the Rüfikopf (alt 1 450–2 362m/4 757–7 749ft). This is the departure point for two off-piste runs (the Langerzug and the Tannegg), which can be tackled with a ski instructor.

Excursions

Zuger Hochlicht★★
Alt 2 377m/7 799ft.
*In winter accessible to skiers only, allowing 1hr 30min round trip. Take the Schlegelkopf and then the Kriegerhorn chair-lifts, followed by the Mohnenfluh cable-car. In summer, it is possible to take the **Petersboden chair-lift** from Oberlech, and then do the tour of the Zuger Hochlicht round via the Mohnenfluhsattel gap and on to Butzensee Lake (2hr 15min round trip walk).* ◷*Operates daily 8.30am–5pm.* ✆*€5.80 round trip.* ☎*0 55 83/2 16 10.*

From the Kriegerhorn (alt 2 173m/7 129ft) there is a broad view of the Zuger Valley against a backdrop of the Rote Wand cliffs, to the west, and of the Zuger Hochlicht ski slopes, to the north. To the south lies **Zürs**, at the foot of the majestic Rüfispitze and the precipitous Roggspitze.

The Zuger Hochlicht reveals a beautiful **panorama**★★ of the Arlberg region, the Lechtal Alps and the Rätikon. There is an all-round panorama from the peak itself, reached in a few minutes from the far left end of the cable-car station. The Hochtannberg pass road can be seen further below.

Rüfikopf★
Alt 2 362m/7 749ft.
◷*Cable-car Nov–Apr and mid-Jun–late Sept, daily 8.30am–5.30pm.* ✆*€12 round trip.* ☎*0 55 83/2 16 10.*

There is a beautiful overall view from this summit of the resort town and the Lech ski slopes against the rocky Mohnenfluh and Braunarlspitze peaks. The Rüfikopf is a good departure point for a ski trip to Zürs.

Walking Tour

The Lechtal Alps offer numerous possibilities for walking and hiking tours, with 200km/124mi of marked trails.

Spullersee★

▶ *The toll road to the lake is closed to cars from 9am to 3pm, but buses make the trip in 30min from the Lech post office (the tourist office has timetables). You can park in the Anger underground garage (free during summer) opposite the post office.*

This beautiful **drive**★ leads through bucolic countryside. Level with the toll booth, there is a municipal swimming pool set in the woods. Then the road passes through the pretty village of Zug, with Alpine pastures, through which the Spullerbach creek winds a course in between clumps of fir and larch. Finally, after a very steep climb, the road reaches the **Spullersee**★, which lies in a beautiful natural amphitheater 1 827m/5 994ft above sea-level. The major summits are the Plattnitzer Spitze and Rohnspitze to the south, the Wildgrubenspitze to the east and the Spuller Schafberg (alt 2 679m/8 789ft) and Pfaffeneck to the north.

Formarinsee★

▶ *Take the bus to the lake. The first half of the trip is identical to that described above. Allow 30min for the bus ride and then 10min walk downhill on a well-maintained trail.*

The Formarinsee (alt 1 789m/5 869ft) lies at the foot of the Rote Wand (alt 2 704m/8 871ft).

Walk from the Formarinsee to the Spullersee★★

Allow 4hr for this quite taxing walk, parts of which should be tackled with care. Difference in altitude is about 600m/ 2 000ft. Climbing boots are essential. ⊕This walk is dangerous in mist or fog, or if the ground is damp.

Take the bus to the Formarinsee, but instead of walking down to the lake, take the trail climbing gently up to the left *(waymarked in yellow)*. The path, dotted with Alpine roses, leads right along the edge of the cliff, offering lovely views of the Formarinsee below before reaching the **Freiburger Hütte** (mountain refuge).

From here take path no 601 toward the Ravensburger Hütte *(waymarked in red)*.

After 30min of easy climb toward the Formaletsch range the path crosses a picturesque limestone plateau, a real sea of rocks, known aptly enough as **Steinernes Meer**. ⊕*Do not leave the waymarked path!*

Beyond here, the trail again becomes defined more clearly, climbing steeply up to the **Gehrengrat**, where chamois and ibex may be spotted. There is a good view of the Verwall range, the Kloster Valley and the Rätikon. A very steep path leads from the summit down to the Spullersee *(allow 1hr 30min; follow signs to Ravensburger Hütte, or "RH")*. On reaching the lake, turn left. After about 5min, the trail comes to the bus stop for the return trip to Lech.

OBERES LECHTAL

VORARLBERG UND TIROL

Upstream from Reutte, the Upper Lech Valley hollows out a deep 60km/37mi-long furrow between the Allgäu and Lechtal Alps. It's a sparsely inhabited area due, in large part, to poor agricultural soil, forcing many locals to leave the valley to seek employment elsewhere. However, having made their fortune, many return to their home villages for retirement, which accounts for the many grand houses, often sporting beautifully painted façades.

- **Information:** No 55b, Elbigenalp. ☎ 0 5634/53 15. www.lechtal.at
- ▶ **Orient Yourself:** The Upper Lech Valley is in the far western reaches of Austria.
- ⏱ **Organizing Your Time:** Allow half a day
- ⌚ **Also See:** FERNPASSSTRASSE, LECH

Sights

⊕*Avalanches may temporarily close the road between Warth and Steeg*
Between **Warth** and **Steeg** the road travels through a series of gorges, before entering a harsh landscape of forest and rocks.

Elbigenalp

The Tirolean tradition of woodcarving is still very much alive in this village. In 1768 the painter **Joseph Anton Koch**, known for his "heroic" landscapes and was born in the suburb of Untergiblen.

Pfarrkirche St. Nikolaus

The sharp pointed spire of this church has made it one of the most distinctive images of the upper Lech Valley. The exuberant Baroque interior with a riot of almost luminous fresco decoration is the work of Johann Jakob Zeiller.

Reutte

Reutte is the economic capital of the Ausserfern district and a good starting point for walks in summer and skiing in winter. Reutte is the home town of the Zeiller family of painters, whose Baroque frescoes adorn many a church interiors in the Tirol and south Germany.

Ceiling fresco in St. Nikolaus church, Elbigenalp

Heimatmuseum
In the Grünes Haus. ⏰*Early May–end Oct, Tue–Sun 10am–noon, 2pm–5pm.* €5. ☎*0 56 33/52 13.*

The local museum collections focus mainly on works by the Zeiller family and their pupils, as well as the history and customs of the local district.

LIENZ

TIROL
POPULATION 12 100 – ALT 678M/2 224FT

Lienz lies in the shadow of the deeply wrinkled, rocky slopes of the Dolomites and is the southern terminus of the transalpine Grossglockner and Felbertauern roads. Early settlers included the Romans and a hint of Italy, only 40km away, still pervades the town today.

- 🛈 **Information:** Europaplatz 1, A-9900, ☎0 48 52/6 52 65. www.lienz-tourismus.at.
- ▶ **Orient Yourself:** Lienz is at the confluence of the Drava and Isel Rivers in eastern Tirol.
- ⚭ **Also See:** FELBERTAUERNSTRASSE, GROSSGLOCKNERHOCHAPLENSTRASSE.

Sights

Schloss Bruck and the Regionalmuseum Osttirol
⏰*Mid-May–end Oct, daily 10am–6pm.* €7. ☎0 48 52/6 25 80.

The former seat of the counts of Görz, this 13C hilltop castle dominates Lienz' silhouette and offers wonderful views of the town. It now houses a regional museum, which displays local antiquities, folklore, crafts and Roman stone fragments.

The large **Albin-Egger-Lienz Gallery** gives a comprehensive survey of the work of this painter (1868–1926), who was often inspired by the Tirol and the suffering of its people. In 2006, Egger-Lienz's famous *Totentanz 1806* (Dance of Death 1806), which had been seized by the Nazis, was restored to its rightful owner in the USA. It fetched €912 000 at a Vienna auction, a record for a work by this painter.

The museum also exhibits paintings and sculpture by contemporary artists.

The two-storey late 13C **chapel** has fanciful cross-ribbed vaulting and 15C frescoes by Nikolaus Kentner and Simon von Talsten, a pupil of Friedrich Pacher.

STIFT LILIENFELD★

NIEDERÖSTERREICH

Founded in 1202 by Babenberg Duke Leopold IV as a Cistercian abbey, Stift Lilienfeld is the largest medieval monastery complex in Austria. Upon returning from a Crusade, the duke presented the monastery with a relic of the Holy Cross, which is still a major object of veneration today. Affiliated with Heiligenkreuz near Vienna, the abbey is a superb example of the transitional style bridging Romanesque and Gothic architecture.

- **Information:** Klosterrotte 1, Lilienfeld. ☎0 02 762/5 24 20. www.stift-lilienfeld.at
- ▶ **Orient Yourself:** The abbey is about 25km/15.5mi south of St. Pölten.
- **Don't Miss:** The Library.
- **Organizing Your Time:** The tour lasts one hour
- **Also See:** ST. PÖLTEN, MARIAZELL.

Tour

Abbey★

Guided tour (1hr) Mon–Sat 10am and 2pm, Sun and holidays 2pm. €7
Unlike many monasteries in Austria, this one is set amidst, rather than on, the hills. Architecturally it is important in that it shows the transition from Romanesque to Gothic styles

Stiftskirche

This is the largest church in Lower Austria, 82m/269ft long by 21m/69ft wide. The pillared basilica is essentially Romanesque in concept with its cruciform ground plan and round-arched

© Österreich Werbung / Diejun

Stiftskirche Lillenfeld

windows, although the Gothic period brought the addition of flying buttresses. Have a look at the **west doorway**★, then take in the uplifting ambience of the interior with its Gothic vaulting and **Baroque furnishings**★ that blend beautifully with the medieval architecture. The predominant tone is the black of the Türnitz marble from which the altars, the pulpit, the choir organ case and the Leopold memorial are made, lavishly lit up by gleaming gold leaf. The painting of the *Assumption of the Virgin Mary* on the high altar is by **Daniel Gran** (1746).

Cloister★

The ribbed vaulting is supported on finely proportioned consoles by clustered pillars of attractively colored stone.

On the north side are remarkable stained-glass windows from the first half of the 14C. The **chapter-house** is one of the oldest parts of the whole complex, with stone benches lining the square room. Over the cellarium, a well-preserved storage cellar, is the impressive two-aisled, lay brothers' **dormitory**, the only one of its kind in Austria to have survived from the Middle Ages.

Library★

As is always the case in a monastery, the library is one of the finest rooms. Dating from 1700, it has magnificent stucco decoration and ceiling frescoes as well as richly inlaid bookcases and doors. Also sneak a peek inside the adjoining picture gallery.

The bridge saint

Bohemia-born **St. John of Nepomuk** went to Prague in 1370, serving first as a priest and later as vicar-general to the archbishop. In a dispute between the archbishop and King Wenceslas I, he defended the rights of the church and especially the sanctity of the confessional. For this reason, in 1393, the king had him tortured and thrown from the bridge into the Vltava. Hence, statues of this martyr have come to grace many bridges in southern Germany, Bohemia and Austria.

LINZ★

OBERÖSTERREICH

POPULATION 189 528 – ALT 266M/873FT

Linz, the capital of Upper Austria and the country's third-largest city, straddles the Danube at a widening of the river valley. Three bridges link the city with its suburb of Urfahr, on the left bank. In fact, Linz owes a good deal of its prosperity to the Danube. Today it is an important industrial city, whose strong support for culture and the arts garnered it the title of European Capital of Culture 2009. Austria's oldest and largest churches are both in Linz.

- **Information:** Hauptplatz 1, A-4010, ☏07 32/70 70 17 77. www.linz.at.
- ▸ **Orient Yourself:** Linz is in northwestern Austria, not far from Germany.
- **Parking:** An automated parking guide system directs you to the nearest garage (fee), of which there are several in the center. Parking is free in lots by the train station and across the river on Urfahrmarkt.
- **Don't Miss:** Lentos Kunstmuseum, Ars Electronica Center, Neuer Dom
- **Organizing Your Time:** It takes a full day to do Linz justice.
- **Especially for Kids:** Ars Electronica Center, Grottenbahn.
- **Also See:** STIFT ST. FLORIAN.

A Bit of History

Although settled since around 4 000 BC, Linz wasn't really put on the map until the Romans founded a camp called Lentia here in AD 1. In the Middle Ages, the town became a major trading center and even enjoyed a brief stint as imperial capital under Friedrich III from 1489 to 1493. Protestantism fell on fertile ground here, drawing the astronomer Johannes Kepler in its wake who wrote his best-known work, *Harmonice mundi*, while in town. Eventually, though the Counter Reformation struck back with a vengeance and Linz remained a provincial backwater until the Industrial Age arrived in the 19C, bringing factories and the railroad. Adolf Hitler took a particular liking to the city and locals largely returned the affection. The Nazis built the large steel and ironworks along the Danube that still provide employment to many today. Since the end of World War II, industrial development has accelerated with emphasis on chemicals and other heavy industries.

Walking Tour

Tour of Old Linz★ (Z)

Hauptplatz

This strikingly large square was laid out in the 13C and has at its center a Trinity Column *(Dreifaltigkeitssäule)*, erected to commemorate the town's escape from plague, fire and Turkish invasion.

▸ *Leave the square along the Domgasse (5).*

Alter Dom St. Ignatius

🕐 *Mon–Sat 7am–7pm; Sun 7am–8pm.* ☏*07 32/77 08 66.*

This 17C Jesuit church by Pietro Francesco Carolone is the city's most important Baroque house of worship. The simple façade forms a striking contrast to the interior, where stucco, pink marble columns, an elaborately carved pulpit and choir stalls, and a high altar adorned with marble statues make up a highly elaborate décor. Bruckner served as church organist from 1855 to 1868.

▸ *Turn right into the Graben (Moat); continue into the Promenade (30); turn right to the Landhaus.*

LINZ			Hamerlingstr.	Y	12	Nebingerstr.	Y	27
			Hanuschstr.	Y	14	Niedernharter Str.	Y	28
Aigengutstr.	Y	17	Henssenplatz	Y	5	Rainerstr.	Y	7
Am Winterhafen	X	2	Hopfengasse	Y	18	Rechte Brückenstr.	X	3
Baumbachstr.	XY	15	Johann-Konrad-Vogel-Str.	Y	4	Rilkestr.	Y	37
Dinghoferstr.	Y	3	Kellergasse	Y	20	Schillerplatz	Y	10
Europaplatz	Y	6	Khevenhüllerstr.	X	21	St. Peter Str.	Y	16
Gesellenhausstr.	Y	9	Linke-Brückenstr.	X	24	Wankmüllerhofstr.	Y	40
Gürtelstr.	Y	8	Makartstr.	Y	26	Ziegeleistr.	Y	42
Landhaus	X	L	Lentos Kunstmuseum	X	M1			

Landhaus (L)

This 16C building, now the seat of the provincial government, wraps around an inner courtyard lined on two sides by arcades and anchored by an octagonal fountain. The seven figures on its base represent the planets and recall the years 1612 to 1626 when Kepler taught at the regional secondary school, then based at the Landhaus.

Minoritenkirche (D)

🕐May–Oct, daily 8.30am–4pm; Nov–Apr daily 8.30am–11am. ☎0732-7 72 01 13 64.
The Gothic church, founded in the 13C by the Franciscans, was remodeled in the Rococo style in the 18C. The altarpiece on the high altar by Bartolomäus Altomonte represents the Annunciation; the altarpieces on the six side altars are the work of Kremser Schmidt.

▶ Take the Altstadt north road.

Schloss

The oldest part of the palace, which was the residence of Emperor Friedrich III, dates from the end of the 15C.

Schlossmuseum★

♿🕐Tue–Fri 9am–6pm; Sat–Sun 10am–5pm. 🕐Jan 1, Dec 24, 25, 31. ⊛€4. ☎07 32/77 44 19. www.schlossmuseum.at.
This museum offers insight into the art and cultural history of Upper Austria. If you have limited time, focus on the collection of paintings from the Gothic period and the 19C and early 20C with

some fine examples by Gustav Klimt, Oskar Kokoschka, and Egon Schiele.

▶ Walk west on Römerstraße.

Martinskirche

First documented in 799, this is considered Austria's oldest church. It was built using pieces of debris left over from the 1C Roman camp and combines various Romanesque and Gothic features. A glass door separates you from the interior which can only be seen during Mass and on guided city tours.

▶ Return to the Hauptplatz via the embankment (Obere Donaulände).

Sights

Priesterseminarkirche★ (Z)

The 18C seminary church, designed by Johann-Lukas von Hildebrandt stuccowork by Paolo d'Allio, while the Crucifixion over the high altar stems from the brush of Altomonte.

213

Composers welcomed

Linz was a staging-post for **Mozart** in the course of his many tours; in 1782 he wrote his 36th symphony, the "Linz Symphony," here in just four days for a concert he was due to give at the city theater. **Beethoven**, too, composed a symphony in Linz, his Eighth, but more than any other composer, the city cherishes the memory of **Anton Bruckner** who was cathedral organist here for 12 years. Every year Linz keeps his memory alive through its international festival of classical music, the Brucknerfest.

Neuer Dom (Y)

This neo-Gothic edifice is the largest church in Austria, able to accommodate 20 000 parishioners. Consecrated in 1924, its spire soars to a lofty 134m/440ft, only 3m/9.8ft shorter than the one of the Stephansdom in Vienna. The stained-glass windows are noteworthy, especially the "Linz Window" depicting scenes from the town's history.

Nordico Museum der Stadt Linz (Z M²)

♿ ⏰ Mon–Fri 8am–5pm; Sat–Sun 2pm–5pm. ✎€4. ☎07 32/70 70 19 12. www.nordico.at.

This museum presents changing exhibits on city history and big exhibitions on nature and Linz's cultural history.

Lentos Kunstmuseum★★(X M¹)

⏰ Year-round Wed, Fri–Mon 10am–6pm, Thu 10am–10pm. ✎€6.50. ☎07 32/70 70 36 14. www.lentos.at.

The Lentos is a spectacular showcase of modern art featuring an international cast of artists, including Gustav Klimt, Lovis Corinth and Max Pechstein as well as post-1945 masters such as Andy Warhol and Keith Haring. Changing exhibitions of equally high caliber supplement the permanent galleries. Since 2003, the collection has been housed in a bold new building by the Swiss architects Weber & Hofer. After dark its façade color toggles between blue and red.

Ars Electronica Center [Kids]

♿ ⏰ Wed–Sun 10am–6pm. ⏰Dec 24, 25. ✎€7. ☎07 32/72 72 12. www.aec.at/en/index.asp.

An unapologetically modern building houses this "museum of the future," a high-tech palace entirely devoted to the latest in digital technology and media. This is where you can explore virtual worlds in 3D in the CAVE installation; experience Linz from a bird's eye perspective by boarding the flight simulator "Humphrey"; or interact with Nuvo, the humanoid robot.

Lentos Kunstmuseum

© Österreich Werbung / Diejun

Address Book

🪙*For coin ranges, see the Legend on the cover flap.*

PRACTICAL INFORMATION

TOURIST INFORMATION

Tourist-Information, *Hauptplatz 1*, Mon–Fri 8am–7pm, Sat 9am–7pm, Sun and public holidays 10am–7pm (Nov–Apr until 6pm in each case). **Tourist-Information**, *Urfahrmarkt 1, 4040 Linz*, Jul–Sept, daily 10am–6pm, Oct–Jun, Mon and Thu 8am–4pm, Tue and Fri 8am–1pm. ☎*07 32/70 70 29 39.*

LINZ CITY TICKET

This entitles you to a city sightseeing-tour, a 20% reduction on a river trip on the Danube, free entry to many attractions, a round trip on the Pöstlingberg mountain railway and the no 3 tram, a Grottenbahn ride and a €10 restaurant voucher. The Linz City Ticket is sold at tourist offices and costs €20; Liny Junior Ticket costs €8.

TRIPS ON THE DANUBE

Boat trip between Passau-Linz-Passau: Donauschiffahrt Wurm & Köck, *Untere Donaulände 1, 4020 Linz*, ☎*07 32/78 36 07,* or *Höllgasse 26, 94032 Passau, Germany*, ☎*+49 8 51 92 92 92.*
Boat trip between Krems-Linz-Krems: Donauschiffahrt Ardagger, *3321 Ardagger 155*, ☎*0 74 79/6 46 40.*

CITY TOUR

Linz-City-Express: tour in a miniature train with commentary (25min) – in season 10am–6pm, hourly (if demand is heavy, every 30min). Leaves from the Hauptplatz. €6; children €3.

PUBLIC TRANSPORT

Individual tickets Single tickets and day passes (Tageskarten) can be obtained from the ticket vending machines, while **multiple tickets** (Mehrfahrtenkarten) for six journeys and transferable **runabout tickets** (Netzkarten), valid for several days and giving unlimited travel on buses and trams, are available from ticket offices in Trafiken (tobacconists' shops). Information on public transport services is provided by ESG-Kundenzentrum, *Landstraße 85/1* ☎*07 32/78 01 70 02.*

SHOPPING

Shops and department stores concentrate along Landstraße, which is pedestrianized for about 2km/1.2mi from Hauptplatz to Bürgerstraße, and its side streets. There are exclusive boutiques in the arcade on the Landstraße. The Herrenstraße has another pedestrian shopping precinct.

MARKETS

Südbahnhof: daily market in the mornings, with a large market on Tue and Fri. Hauptplatz: Farmers' market Fri 10am–2pm, flea market Sat 6am–2pm.

SOUVENIRS

Crafts: Heimatwerk, Landstraße 31; Linzer Torte (local specialty, a jam-filled cake): Café Jindrak (several branches, including *Herrenstraße 22*).

ENTERTAINMENT

Landestheater (Provincial Theater), *Promenade 39*, ☎*07 32/7 61 11 00.*
Theater Phönix, *Wiener Straße 25*, ☎*07 32/66 65 00.*
Konzerthaus Brucknerhaus, *Untere Donaulände 7*, ☎*07 32/7 61 20.*

WHERE TO EAT

Kremsmünsterer Stuben, *Altstadt 10*, ☎*07 32/78 21 11.*
Josef – Das Stadtbräu, *Landstraße 49*, ☎*07 32/77 31 65.*
Stieglbräu zum Klosterhof, *Landstraße 30*, ☎*07 32/77 33 73.*
Sturm's Wirtshaus, *Am Pöstlingberg 12* (with a panoramic view of the town), ☎*07 32/73 14 83.*
Ursulinenhof, *Landstraße 31*, ☎*07 32/77 46 86.*

CAFÉS AND BARS

Café Glockenspiel, *Hauptplatz 18;* **Café Jindrak**, *Herrenstr. 22.*
Old town: **Grand Café-Daniel Sassi** (in the arcade, *Spittelwiese 8*). Otherwise, the **Irish Pub** *(Hessenplatz 19)*, **S'Kistl** (Altstadt 17) and **S'Linzerl** *(Hofberg 5)*. For live music, head for **17er Keller** *(Hauptplatz)* or the **Kasper-Keller** *(Landstr. 24,* food available, jazz jam session every Tue, admission free), **Stieglitz im Klosterhof** *(Landstr. 30)* or **Joe's bar** in the Arcotel *(Untere Donaulände 9).*

Driving Tour

Mühlviertel Tour
90km/56mi

The Mühlviertel district derives its name from the small Mühl river, which flows into the Danube above Linz. It is a hilly upland region with wide, forested valleys.

▶ *Leave Linz on the road (no 126) north to Bad Leonfelden.*

Leaving Linz the road enters a little verdant gorge and climbs gently, sometimes among rocks, sometimes among orchards. The wild nature of the hills grows more marked near Bad Leonfelden.

▶ *About 500m/546.8yd north of this town bear right toward Freistadt.*

Freistadt★ &See FREISTADT

▶ *Right past Freistadt, leave the Linz road and cross to the east bank of the small Feldaist River.*

Kefermarkt

Kefermarkt on the Feldaist is surrounded by a restful, hilly landscape marking

the transition between the Mühlviertel and the granite plateaux of the Waldviertel.

St. Wolfgangskirche

&*Daily 8am–5pm. ☎07 94/62 03.*
This Gothic church contains a remarkable **altarpiece**★★ carved of wood by an unknown sculptor. More than 13m/42.6ft high, it is outstanding as much for its size as for the beauty of its proportions and the delicacy of the limewood carvings. The three figures in the central panel are St. Wolfgang, flanked by St. Peter and St. Christopher.

▶ *At the main crossroads in Kefermarkt turn right toward the railway station; cross the track and the Feldaist. After 7km/4.3mi turn left onto the main road, no 125, connecting Freistadt and Linz.*

Excursions

Pöstlingberg★ (X)
4.5km/2.8mi northwest.
&*Departure from Pöstlingberg station "Bergbahnhof" Mon–Sat 5.20am–8.20pm every 20min; Sun and public holidays 7.15am–11.15pm every 30min, 11.15am–8.20pm every 20min. ☜€3.50 round trip train only, €5.60 round trip tram and train. ☎07 32/78 01 75 45.*
Europe's steepest narrow-gauge mountain railway covers the 2.9km/1.8mi journey to the top of the Pöstlingberg with its Baroque church in 16min. From a flower-decked terrace below the church there is an extensive **view**★ from nearly 300m/984ft down into the Danube Valley. Also up here is the ᴷⁱᵈˢ**Grottenbahn**, a dragon-pulled miniature-train chugging through a fairy-tale landscape.

Mauthausen
25km/15.5mi east of Linz.
Mauthausen would be just like any other sleepy, historic riverside town had it not been chosen, in 1938, as the site of a notorious Nazi concentration camp thanks to the proximity of several quarries.

KZ Mauthausen (Concentration Camp)

🕐 *Apr–Sept, daily 8am–6pm, Feb–Mar and Oct–mid-Dec, daily 8am–4pm.* ☞ €2. ☎ *07 23 8/22 69. www.gusen.org.*

About 200 000 people were imprisoned at Mauthausen and its 49 subsidiary camps. Over half perished working in the granite quarries or, if they had become too sick or weak, by being executed in horrific fashion. Some of the huts and rooms where the prisoners were kept still exist. Another building is now a museum with photographs and other documentation on the horrors perpetrated in this sinister place.

Outside the camp limits are memorials set up by countries whose people perished here. Below the plateau is the infamous "Todesstiege" (Stairway of Death), leading down to the quarry. Famous survivors of this camp include **Simon Wiesenthal**, (1908–2005) who dedicated his life to tracking down Nazis and bringing them to justice. He is sometimes unfairly referred to as a Nazi-Jäger (Nazi-hunter).

MALTATAL★★

KÄRNTEN

A 30km/18.6mi stretch of road leads through this magnificent valley, one of the most beautiful destinations in Carinthia. It became famous after the construction of the Kölnbrein dam and reservoir, but its main appeal really lies in its highly diverse landscape. Until reaching the village of Malta the valley is wide and characterized by alternating meadows and forested patches. Beyond here it narrows, then opens up again to reveal the magnificent glacier panorama of the Ankogel massif and the Hochalmspitze peak. The area is also a terrific launch pad for medium- and high-altitude Alpine hikes.

- **Information:** Tourismusverband Lieser-Maltatal, Hauptplatz, A- 9853 Gmünd. ☎ 0 47 32/22 22. www.familiental.com.
- ▶ **Orient Yourself:** The valley extends from Gmünd (♿ *see Excursion: Gmünd in Kärnten*) to the foothills of the Hohe Tauern National Park in southern Austria.
- 😊 **Don't Miss:** A drive on the Malta-Hochalmstraße.
- 🕐 **Organizing Your Time:** Budget at least two days if planning excursions.

Sights in the area

Village of Malta

The village at 840m/2 755ft above sea-level is an entrancing holiday spot. The **church of Maria Hilf**, which dates from the 15C, houses some fine frescoes from the same period, including a rare image of Mary in labour on the south wall. The Baroque décor is beautifully uniform. The high altar and pulpit were made in 1730.

Malta-Hochalmstraße★★

A toll is charged past Malta.

This excellently laid out road meanders over nine bridges and through seven tunnels, including a memorable one designed as a hairpin bend. Attractions include the luxuriant vegetation (spruce, larch, alder and birch) and the waterfalls, 30 in all, roaring down into the valley. The Fallbach, the Melnikfall and the Hinterer Maralmfall are particularly impressive.

Kölnbreinsperre★

During high season, ☞ there are guided tours of the dam on the hour.

The road ends at this dam located 1 900m/6 233ft above sea-level. It is the largest dam in Austria measuring 200m/656ft high, 41m/134ft thick at the base and 626m/2 054ft wide. Apart from its phenomenal technical prowess, the design of this concrete colossus with its flowing, parabolic shape, is just as impressive. Inside the panoramic look-out tower is an **information center** (⊙ *mid-May–early Oct, daily from 7am;* ⊗ *free;* ☎ *04 63/2 37 16)* with short films about the Hohe Tauern National Park and a multimedia display on the dam's construction. Also here is the **Tauernschatzkammer**★, a treasure trove of local rock crystals and other minerals.

The dam is the point of departure for some wonderful walks. Even the easy hike around the lake provides wonderful views over the **surrounding Alpine landscape**★★. If you can muster the stamina, you should tackle the Arlscharte.

Hike to the Arlscharte and the Arlhöhe★★ 🚶

3hr 45min round trip from the dam. Head toward the "Osnabrücker Hütte" mountain lodge.

The trail skirts the northern lakeshore and soon proffers a magnificent view over the Ankogel glaciers. After walking for 45min, you will reach a memorial to a tragic accident that occurred during the building of the dam. Turn right and continue along a relatively steep Alpine flower trail. After 10min, when the trail forks, head left for the steep 45min climb

to the peak (⊘ *look for the red and white markings).* At the top, your efforts will be rewarded with magnificent views over lakes, valleys, a small glacier and the towering Hochalmspitze peak.

For another dose of impressive views, continue to the Arlhöhe (alt 2 326m/ 7 631ft). Walk a few steps toward Pfringersee, then turn left and pick up a kind of ridge trail *(marked with a red cross on a white background)* taking you to your destination in about 20min. An orientation map helps identify mountains and other natural landmarks. Backtrack along the same trail.

Gösskarspeicher★

Trip involves a 1hr drive and 45min walk. Halfway between Malta and the toll point, turn to the left toward the Giessener Hütte mountain lodge.

The narrow 12km/7.4mi mountain road is quite steep and follows the course of the Gössbach, even fording the river bed at one point (⊘ *dangerous, especially during bad weather; watch out for flood warnings).* The countryside is rugged and refreshingly unspoiled.

Leave your car in the lot and continue on foot to the Gösskar reservoir *(15min*

Nationalpark Hohe Tauern near Maltatal

climb). This is a beautiful **wooded area**★, lorded over by the Grosser Gössspitze and the Dösnerspitze peaks.

Walk along the left shore of the lake for fantastic **views**★ over the Hochalmspitze peak and its glacier, from which waterfalls thunder down.

Return to the reservoir, continue to its end and then to the right along the meadow (through a fence) until you reach a wide, moderately steep trail for a **view**★ over the rocky peaks of the Riekenkopf and the Pfaffenberger Nocken. Return to the parking lot or, if you're feeling ambitious, climb up to the Giessener Hütte mountain lodge, the starting point for the climb to the legendary Hochalm peak.

Excursions

Gmünd in Kärnten
In Maltatal.

Gmünd was founded in the 11C by the archbishops of Salzburg to control the traffic through the Lieser Valley, a stretch along the busy Nuremberg-Venice trade route. The compact center preserves much of its medieval character and is still encircled by fortified town walls entered via two imposing gateways. Gmünd is also home to a thriving artists' community and you'll find its cobbled streets lined with numerous galleries and studios.

Alte Burg
An earthquake in 1690 and a fire in 1886 reduced Gmünd's fortress to a mere shadow of its medieval self, but recent efforts have restored it into cultural center hosting art exhibits, seminars, concerts and theater performances. There are also an excellent café and restaurant and good views from the keep.

Hauptplatz
Gmünd's handsome main square is bookended by the fortified gateways and lined by elegant town houses splashed in a rainbow of pastels. Near the upper gateway, the 17C **Lodron'sche Schloss**, now a school and public library, opens onto a pretty garden, the entrance to which is flanked by the statues of two massive lions that originally graced the Mirabellgarten in Salzburg.

Off the square's northern end, the old prison *(Kirchgasse 56)* contains the **Eva Faschauner Heimatmuseum**, a curious exhibit about a local woman accused of poisoning her farmer husband with arsenic soon after their 1770 wedding. After three years of imprisonment and horrific torture, she finally confessed (who wouldn't?) and was executed shortly thereafter.

Pfarrkirche Maria Himmelfahrt
The Late Gothic church was consecrated in 1339 and enlarged and redecorated in Baroque style in the 18C. Life-size figures of the Apostles flank the fine altar, and there are numerous interesting tombstones as well.

Porsche-Automuseum Helmut Pfeifhofer
◐*May 15–Oct 15, daily 9am–6pm; Oct 16–May 14, daily 10am–4pm.* €6. ☎0 47 32/24 71. www.porsche-museum.at.
From 1944 through 1950 Gmünd was the sphere of activity of world-famous engineer, **Ferdinand Porsche** (1875–1998). It was here where the first car with the "Porsche" marque, the legendary 356, was made. Several of them are on display at this, Europe's only private Porsche museum, alongside prototypes of military and sports vehicles, actual-size wooden models of the first Porsche car bodies and over 400 model cars.

Nockalmstraße
◐*May–Oct.* €14. ☎04736/26 5. www.nockalmstrasse.at.
The 35km/21.7mi Nockalmstraße between Innerkrems in the north to Ebene Reichenau in the south crosses the Nochberg mountains and was opened on June 27, 1981. The road, unusually, does not pass through any communities, but there are several isolated mountain inns along the road with food and amenities. Also there are several small museums concentrating on subjects such as mining, forestry, alpine farming, and marmots (entrance to all is included in the toll charge)

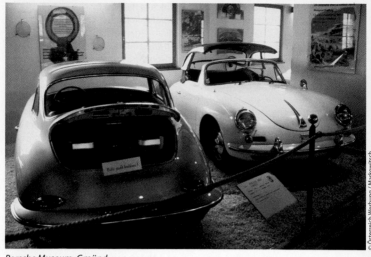

© Österreich Werbung / Markowitsch

Porsche Museum, Gmünd

Nationalpark Nockberge

When the Nockalmstraße was completed it was planned to develop the are as a huge ski area. However protests from the citizens of Carinthia forced a referendum in which 94% rejected the planned proposals. On January 1, 1987 the area was given National Park status.

The park encompasses the gently rounded "nocken" mountains, unusual in the Alps, and a rare geological entity with its own flora and fauna.

The area is popular with hikers, and several hikes depart from inns and rest stops along the Nockalmstraße. For the energetic, there is an organized 3hr circuit hike, the **Grünleitennock Circuit**, from Parkplatz Pfandlalm to Grünleitennock to Friesenhalssee to Zechneralm to Pfandlalm. See *www.nockalmstrasse.at* for more information. Older children will enjoy the circuit for the numerous marmots at the Realm of the Marmot exhibition along the way, though 3hr may be a bit too challenging for them.

MARIA SAAL ★

KÄRNTEN

POPULATION 3 850 – ALT 504M/1 654FT

Maria Saal is a small, sleepy town famous for its pilgrimage church, which jauntily perches atop a fortified hill, its twin towers visible from far away. The current Late Gothic incarnation dates from the 15C and stands atop the original one founded by Bishop Modestus of Salzburg in the 8C as a launch pad for the re-Christianization of Carinthia following the Barbarian invasions.

- **Information:** Am Platzl 7, A-9063. ☎0 42 23/22 14. www.maria.saal.at.
- ▶ **Orient Yourself:** Maria Saal is about 7km/4.3mi north of Klagenfurt in southern Austria.
- **Parking:** Look for public lots along Hauptstraße and Arnsdorfer Straße near the open-air museum.
- **Don't Miss:** The Dom.
- **Organizing Your Time:** Allow two or three hours.
- **Also See:** ST. VEIT AN DER GLAN, GURK, KLAGENFURT.

Sights

Dom ★★

The first church was erected in the 8C at Maria Saal by the evangelizing monk, Modestus, who was sent as missionary to pagan Carinthia by the great Bishop Virgil of Salzburg. He chose the hillock around which the village Maria Saal soon grew. From here he began the Christianization, and Germanization, of the local Slav population. Apparently he was successful and Mari Saal became known as the Christian Cradel of Carinthia. The present pilgrimage church replaced the original church and dates from 1460, when it was completed.

Exterior

With its twin towers of volcanic stone and its vast stone roof, this church makes a striking impression. Completed in 1460, it is protected by a fortified enclosure and fronted by an octagonal **charnel house** that is encircled by a two-story arcaded gallery. The south façade incorporates numerous stone reliefs and **tombstones**, including several scavenged from the nearby ruined Roman settlement of Virunum. Standouts include a relief showing Achilles dragging the corpse of Hector, and the **Roman postal wagon**★, a symbol for the journey of a dead soul into the afterlife. The magnificent **Keutschacher Epitaph**★ (c. 1510), a red marble tombstone, depicts the Coronation of the Virgin. In the porch is another interesting Roman gravestone featuring a she-wolf feeding Romulus and Remus.

Interior

The triple-nave church is a typical Late Gothic building. The bays of the ribbed vaulting above the nave are decorated with frescoes depicting the genealogy of Christ.
The Baroque **high altar** is the place of honor for the stone figure of the Madonna (1425) that is still much venerated by pilgrims.
Two other altars deserving closer inspection are the splendid **Arndorf Altar**★ in the north chancel, which shows the Coronation of the Virgin Mary, and the Altar of St. George in the south chancel, which depicts the saint as the Dragon-Slayer, symbolizing the triumph of Christianity. Also of interest are the **tomb of St. Modestus**★ in the left side aisle in the Saxon chapel and the **fresco** of the Three Magi on the north wall of the chancel.

Kärntner Freilichtmuseum★

300m/330yd north of the village center. Allow 45min. &. ⏱ *May–mid-Oct, Tue–Sun 10am–6pm (last admission 5pm).* ✆€5. ☎0 42 23/31 66. http://members. aon.at/kaerntnerfreilichtmuseum.
Some 33 historic farmhouses, stables, barns and other outbuildings offer unique insights into rural life in 16C and 17C Carinthia. All were taken down and reassembled at this open-air museum, nicely located in a hilly wooded setting. Most are log cabins and either thatched with straw or roofed with shingles. The living quarters have a smoking room with an oven and an open hearth.
A reconstructed covered wooden bridge leads to the mill area. Here, a mill wheel, a turbine-like mill and a saw-mill illustrate both the difficult working conditions endured by the millers and the ingenuity of early mechanization.

R. Chéret/MICHELIN

Keutschacher Epitaph

MARIAZELL★

STEIERMARK

POPULATION 1 930 – ALT 868M/2 848FT

Mariazell is the most important place of pilgrimage in Austria. It is also a popular year-round resort, occupying a charming **site**★ on the gentle, forested slopes of the extreme eastern end of the Alps. For a bird's-eye view of the region, ride the cable-car to the top of the **Bürgeralpe**, the local mountain.

🔲 **Information:** Hauptplatz 13, A-8630. ☎0 38 82/23 66. www.mariazell.at and www.basilika-mariazell.at.

▶ **Orient Yourself:** Mariazell is 150km/94mi north of Graz and 130km/80mi southwest of Vienna in central Austria.

🕑 **Also See:** BRUCK AN DER MUR.

A Bit of History

Not long after the Benedictines from St. Lambrecht Abbey founded a priory here in 1157, pilgrims started flocking to Mariazell to worship a small wooden, miracle-working Madonna. Its popularity really took off when King Ludwig of Hungary attributed his victory over the Turks in 1370 to this statuette and had a chapel (the Gnadenkapelle) built in thanksgiving for the victory.

Visit

Basilica★

In the 17C the growing number of pilgrims made it necessary to enlarge the earlier 14C Gothic building. Architect **Domenico Sciassia** lengthened and widened the nave and topped the eastern end with a dome. He also added two much squatter onion-capped towers on either side of the central 90m/295ft-high Gothic spire, resulting in a slightly awkward design that has nonetheless become an emblem of this pilgrimage site.

Gnadenkapelle (Chapel of Miracles)

The object of veneration is enshrined in this small chapel. The seated Madonna is placed beneath a valuable silver baldaquin resting on 12 columns; it was designed by Johann Emmanuel Fischer von Erlach the Younger (1727).

West Nave

To appreciate fully the details of the Baroque decoration, you should walk along the galleries.

The chapel in the north aisle, dedicated to St. Ladislas, King of Hungary, until fairly recently housed the mortal remains of Cardinal Mindszenty, Primate of Hungary, now transferred to Esztergom in that country.

East Nave

This monumental piece of Baroque architecture forms a second, inner nave, beyond a false transept. The first bay is lit by an oval lantern-dome while the second square bay contains the majestic high altar by Johann Bernhard Fischer von Erlach, which shows the Crucifixion and was completed in 1704.

Schatzkammer (Treasury)

🕑 *May–end Oct, Tue–Sat 10am–3pm, Sun 11am–4pm.* ☜€3. ☎0 38 82/2 59 50.

A staircase in the southwest tower leads up to the treasury, which is filled with six centuries of often endearing votive offerings left here by pilgrims. A particular highlight is the church's second-most important object of veneration, a 14C painting of the Virgin also donated by Ludwig of Hungary. It is believed to be the work of Siennese artist, Andrea Vanni.

MATREI IN OSTTIROL ❄❄

TIROL
POPULATION 4 990 – ALT 1 000M/3 300FT

The popular holiday resort of Matrei in East Tirol lies in beautiful and diverse surroundings and boasts an exceptionally pleasant climate. The market town lies in a restful low-mountain area at the foot of the Grossvenediger and Grossglockner, the highest and most impressive peaks in Austria. Thanks to its extraordinary setting, it has become a well-known gateway for **hikes**★★★ into the Eastern Alps.

🛈 **Information:** Rauterplatz 1, A-9971. ☎0 48 75/65 27. www.matreiinosttirol.at.

▶ **Orient Yourself:** Matrei lies at the junction of the Tauerntal, Virgental and Iseltal, about 30km/19mi north of Lienz.

🕐 **Organizing Your Time:** Budget a full day for the trip to the Karl-Matrei pass and Grossdorf.

Kids Especially for Kids: Hiking the Europa-Panoramaweg.

👪 **Also See:** FELBERTAUERNSTRASSE

Sights

Ski Slopes
In winter, the **ski area**★ offers satisfactory conditions for skiers. Three chair-lifts and three T-bar lifts lead to 30km/18.6mi of pistes of between 1 000m/3 300ft and 2 400m/7 900ft in length, some with artificial snow. It is a particularly attractive resort for lovers of long distance skiing and ski tours, with 24km/15mi of long pistes and vast off-piste areas

St. Nikolauskirche
Approach by car. From the main square in Matrei, cross the bridge to Lienzer Straße, then turn left onto the Bichler Straße. The road leaves the village, leading over another bridge and then right past a wooden well. Turn right at the next two intersections. The road is now unpaved but is quite drivable. Turning right onto the next small road leads you straight to the church.
In a meadow above Matrei, St. Nikolaus is a 12C church with Romanesque and Gothic elements. An outstanding architectural feature is the unsual two-story Romanesque choir decorated with **frescoes**★. The lower level represents scenes from Genesis, while the upper story—reached via a double staircase—shows the four elements carrying the 12 Apostles and the Evangelists.

Excursions

Europa-Panoramaweg★★   Kids
Budget about 4hr for the entire trip, including about 2hr walking time.
This is a wonderful, family-friendly hiking excursion, where you'll be treated to panoramic **views**★ taking in 60 peaks over 3 000m/9 842.5ft, including the **Grossglockner**. From Matrei, catch the Goldriedbahn cable car to the mountain station at 2 150m/7 054ft, then embark on the easy walk to the **Kals-Matrei-Törlhaus**★★ along a wildflower-lined path. Stop here for refreshments or

Matrei

© Österreich Werbung / F. Hahn

continue to the mountain station of the Blauspitzbahn where there is another restaurant as well as a high-altitude **Kids** **children's playground**. Take the Blauspitzbahn down into Kals where buses run back to Matrei (weekdays only, enquire about departure times at the tourist office).

Virgental★

18km/11mi drive from Matrei to Ströden. This beautiful valley to the south of the Grossvenediger glacier makes for a delightful summer excursion. The dense forests in the lower part and the Alpine mountain scenery in the upper part are impressive. Prägraten is the most beautiful holiday resort in the valley. The Umbal falls at the end of the road are well worth a visit.

BURG MAUTERNDORF★

SALZBURG

On a trade route in use since Roman times, this 13C castle served as a residence for the archbishops of Salzburg who wished to keep a close eye on their possessions in the Lungau region. Today, the ancient walls house family-oriented exhibits taking you on a fun-filled trip back to the late 15C and the castle at the time of Archbishop Leonhard von Keutschach.

- **Information:** ☎0 64 72/74 26. www.salzburg-burgen.at.
- ▶ **Orient Yourself:** The castle is in the southern Salzburger Land, about 120km/74.5mi southeast of Salzburg.
- ⏱ **Organizing Your Time:** Budget about 2hr and 30min for a visit, including a tour and spin around the museum.
- **Kids** **Especially for Kids:** Ask about the kids' version of the audio guide. There's also a terrific, castle-like playground with a super-long "dragon slide."
- ⏳ **Also See:** RADSTÄTTER TAUERNSTRASSE, TAMSWEG.

Visit

The Castle

Guided tour May–Oct, daily 10am–6pm. €8, incl castle tour and museum; Dec 26–Apr 23, Tue–Fri 10.30am–6pm. A ramble around this castle includes a 90min self-guided audio-tour during which you'll be "eavesdropping" on the castle residents as they prepare for a lavish feast back in the 15C. Scores of authentically costumed figures—from the archduke to his servants—have been arranged in scenes and impart interesting tidbits about what daily life was like in those days. The tour ends in the original Gothic watchman's tower from where you'll enjoy fabulous views over the town and countryside.

In the south tower is the **Lungauer Landschaftsmuseum**, which takes an often intriguing look at local customs and history.

"The Archbishop's Turnip"

The story goes that **Leonhard von Keutschach** led a lively student life, rarely studying. On a visit to Pinzgau, he was walking in a turnip field with his uncle Wolf zu Alm, who berated him for neglecting his studies. Piqued by the young man's impertinent reply, the uncle threw a turnip at him saying, "If you don't mend your ways, I will never receive you again!" The turnip changed Leonhard's life; he applied himself to his studies and later became Prince-Archbishop of Salzburg. In gratitude, he included a turnip in his coat of arms.

STIFT MELK★★★

NIEDERÖSTERREICH
ALT 213M/699FT

The majestic abbey of Melk, which crowns a rocky bluff overlooking the Danube, is the apogee of Baroque architecture in Austria and a must-see along the Danube. It has origins in the 10C as the castle of the ruling Babenberg family but became a monastery in 1089 when Margrave Leopold II donated the building to the Benedictines. Famous for its scholarship, the abbey has been a spiritual, cultural and intellectual center for nearly a millennium.

- **Information:** Abt-Berthold-Dietmayr-Straße 1. ☏0 27 52/55 50. www.stiftmelk.at.
- ▶ **Orient Yourself:** Melk is 27km/16.7mi west of St. Pölten in northeastern Austria.
- ◷ **Organizing Your Time:** Budget at least half a day for your visit.
- **Also See:** BURG AGGSTEIN, DÜRNSTEIN, KREMS UND STEIN, ST. PÖLTEN.

Visit

The Abbey

◷*Mid-Apr–Oct, daily 9am–5pm (6pm May–Sept). Last admission 1hr before closing. Guided tour only from Nov–May, daily 11am and 2pm. ☞€7 without tour, €8.80 with tour. ☏0 27 52/55 52 32.*

Exterior

The original abbey was gutted by fire during the Turkish invasion in 1683 and entirely rebuilt from 1802 onward by **Jakob Prandtauer** and completed after his death by his pupil **Josef Munggenast**. The outer gateway, giving access to the first courtyard, is framed by statues of the abbey patrons St. Leopold and St. Coloman and flanked by two bastions. On the inner gate is the abbey coat of arms. Beyond a vestibule with a ceiling painting of St. Benedict is the **Prälatenhof** (Prelates' Courtyard), a fine group of buildings adorned with statues of the Prophets.

Kaisergang

Access via the Imperial staircase.

The Emperors' gallery, which is 196m/643ft long, provided access to the chambers reserved for important visitors. Some of these rooms now house a

Stift Melk

© Österreich Werbung / Trumler

museum★, which presents the abbey's history and its treasures in an engaging and visually appealing fashion using light, sound and such modern media as video installations and computer animations.

Marmorsaal

The Marble Hall impresses less with its lavishness than with the strength of its design. It is dominated by a series of reddish pilasters, which incidentally, are not made of marble at all but of colored stucco. The undisputed highlight here is the ceiling fresco by **Paul Troger**, which centers on the goddess Athena riding a lion-drawn carriage in an allegory of wisdom and enlightenment.

Bibliothek (Library)

A terrace offering sweeping views of the surrounding countryside links the Marble Hall with the abbey library, which contains 100 000 books and 1 800 manuscripts. It also has a fine ceiling painting by Paul Troger symbolizing Faith. The gilded wood statues by the doors represent the four faculties.

Stiftskirche★★★

The church interior gives a great impression of lightness, which is due to the sweep of fluted pilasters, a judicious use of color and the many windows. The decoration is nothing if not lavish, with the dominating brownish red color offering the perfect contrast to the liberal use of gold leaf.

A veritable who's who of Baroque master artists contributed to this spectacular church. The ceiling frescoes and most of the side altars show off the exquisite style of **Johann Michael Rottmayr**; some of the altar paintings are the work of Paul Troger. Giuseppe Galli-Bibiena was responsible for the extraordinary high altar dedicated to Sts Peter and Paul. There are sculptures wherever you look, most of them the work of Lorenzo Mattielli and Peter Widerin. The left side altar in the transept contains the bones of St. Koloman.

Excursion

Schloss Schallaburg★

6km/3.7mi south of Melk toward Anzen-
dorf. ⚐🕐*May–Oct, Mon–Fri 9am–5pm;*
Sat–Sun to 6pm. ⚐€10. ☎0 27 54/63 17.
www. schallaburg.at.

The castle has substantial Romanesque remains and a Gothic chapel, but it is the great 16C **Renaissance arcaded courtyard**★ with its extraordinary profusion of terracotta ornamentation that makes the most striking impression. Statues, atlases, caryatids, floral motifs, cartouches and ornamental keystones boldly and harmoniously form a masterly composition.

Today, Schallaburg is an exhibition and cultural center for the province of Lower Austria, used every summer for prestigious exhibitions.

MILLSTATT★

KÄRNTEN
POPULATION 3 200 – ALT 604M/1 982FT

Millstatt lies on the north shore of the **Millstätter See,** a lake boasting summer water temperatures of up to 26°C/82°F. Owing to its lakeside beach and its favorable climate, Millstatt has become a very popular summer resort. Between May and October, it hosts a series of concerts: The Internationale Musikwochen.

- 🗊 **Information:** Marktplatz 8, A-9872. ☎0 47 66/20 22. www.millstatt-see.co.at.
- ▶ **Orient Yourself:** Millstatt is in southern Austria, about 10km/6.2mi east of Spittal an der Drau and 83km/52mi northwest of Klagenfurt.
- 🕭 **Also See:** SITTAL AN DER DRAU, MALTATAL.

Visit

Abbey *(Stift)*★

The abbey began life in the 11C as a Benedictine monastery, then became the seat of the Knights of St. George in 1469 before falling into the hands of the Jesuits in 1598. They ran it until the order's dissolution In 1773. A small **museum** *(*⚐🕐*Jun–end Sept, daily 9am–noon, 2pm–6pm;* ⚐€2.20; ☎06 76/4 60 64 13) provides a good insight into the abbey's history and the works of art, both religious and secular, that it contains.

Stiftshof (Abbey courtyard)★

The elegant courtyard framed by two-tiered arcades reveals the riches of the Order of St. George founded by Emperor Friedrich III to assist in the defense of Christianity against the Turks. Also here is a 1 000-year-old **Gerichtslinde**, a lime tree below which court was held back in the Middle Ages.

Kreuzgang (Cloister)★

Enter from the east side of the courtyard.
In summer, the cloisters may only be seen
as part of a visit to the abbey museum.
⚐🕐*Daily 9am–noon, 2pm–6pm.* ☎06
76/4 60 64 13.

Stift, Millstatt

The peaceful 12C cloister is a superb example of Romanesque architecture despite the addition of Gothic vaulting in the 15C. Its arches are held aloft by slender pillars whose capitals are decorated with animals, plants, gargoyles and faces. *Return to the abbey courtyard to go up to the church.*

Stiftskirche

Surviving elements from the Romanesque period include the magnificent **door** in the west porch and its tympanum showing Abbot Heinrich II (1166–77) paying homage to Christ. The **high altar**★ (1648) features gilded columns and larger-than-life-size statues of St. Domitian (left) and Margrave Leopold III (right). Though faded, the most noteworthy **fresco**★ adorning the church is Urban Görtschacher's *Last Judgment* (1515) on the south wall (at the far end of the aisle). Two side chapels contain the red-marble tombs of various grand masters.

MÖLLTALER GLETSCHER★★

KÄRNTEN

This particularly picturesque mountain region is home to long Alpine lakes, which are used to generate hydroelectricity, along with a year-round ski area.

- 🛈 **Information:** Mölltaler Gletscherbahnen, Innerfragant 46, Flattach. ☎0 47 85/ 81 10. www.gletscher.co.at.
- ▶ **Orient Yourself:** The glacier is near Flattach in southern Austria.
- 🅿 **Parking:** At the base station of the Gletscherbahnen.
- 🕐 **Organizing Your Time:** Allow an hour plus any time spent hiking.
- 👶 **Also See:** LIENZ, SPITTAL AN DER DRAU, MILLSTADT.

Sights

Mölltaler Gletscherbahnen★★

Alt 1 250–3 120m/4 101–10 237ft. 9km/5.6mi from Flattach to Inner-fragant and the lower cable-car station for the new Stollenbahn (alt 1 250m/4 101ft). From here take the underground funicular and a cable-car on up to the Eissee mountain restaurant at 2 798m/9 180ft (allow about 40min there and back). www.gletscher.co.at. The underground funicular is the longest in the world.

The ski area on the glacier, where snow is guaranteed virtually all year round, offers a total of 53km/33mi of downhill pistes. Hikers have plenty of options in summer, including treks up to the Baumbach peak (3 108m/10 197ft) and Schareck peak (3 122m/10 243ft), which can also be reached by chairlift leaving from the upper cable-car station. There is a fine **panorama**★ where you can pick out some 30 summits over 3 000m/9 842.5ft in the Hohe Tauern range, including the Grossglockner. On a clear day, you can see the Black Forest (Germany) and the German Alps.

Skiing on Mölltal Glacier

archiv Mölltaler Gletscher

MONTAFON★
VORARLBERG
LOCAL MAP SEE ARLBERGGEBIET

Montafon is a charming, densely populated valley surrounded by three major massifs: the Rätikon in the northwest, the Silvretta in the south and the Verrwall in the northeast. It is a relaxing region dotted with pretty villages and offering good hiking, skiing and mountain-biking as well as access to the famous Silvretta-Hochalpenstraße★★ (*see entry*), one of Austria's most scenic Alpine roads.

- 🚩 **Information:** ☎0 55 56/72 25 30, www.montafon.at.
- ▶ **Orient Yourself:** The valley is 39km/24mi long and near the far western edge of Austria, close to Switzerland.
- 🔭 **Don't Miss:** Hike to the Kreuzjoch and the Zamangspitze or the Sennigrat
- 🕐 **Organizing Your Time:** Allow at least one day to cover the driving tour route described below.
- 🐾 **Also See:** BLUDENZ, SILVRETTAHOCHALPENSTRASSE, ARLBERGGEBIET.

Driving Tour

Montafon Valley Tour
40km/25mi

Bludenz
🐾 *See ARLBERGGEBIET Driving Tour* 1

▶ *Leave Bludenz on the 188. Turn left in St. Anton im Montafon toward Bartholomäberg.*

Bartholomäberg
This settlement is beautifully scattered along a sunny terrace. From the parish church there is an impressive **panorama**★ of the villages of Vandans, Schruns, and Tschagguns backed by impressive mountains such as the spiky Zimba peak and the Drei Türme massif. The church's **Baroque interior**★ boasts numerous fine art treasures. Stand-outs are the high altar and pulpit, both by Georg Senn, and the triptych dedicated to St. Anne on the right-hand side of the nave. The organ (1792) is one of the finest examples in Austria.

▶ *Continue toward Innerberg, turn right toward Silbertal, then left on the main road at the bottom of the valley to the Kristbergbahn railway.*

Kristbergbahn★

🕐*Jun–Oct 26 and Dec–Apr, daily 7.50am–6.15pm.* ☞ €10.70 round trip winter, €10.70 summer. ☎0 55 56/7 41 19. www.kristbergbahn.at.

The Kristberg inn (alt 1 430m/4 691ft), with a chapel nearby, can be reached in 5min from the cable-car mountain station. It affords an especially beautiful **all-round view**★ over the Montafon. Hikers can climb up to the Kristberg-sattel and then follow the ridge path to the **Ganzaleita** viewpoint *(alt 1 610m/5 282ft)* for views of the Lechtaler Alps and the Rote Wand.

© Österreich Werbung / Trumler

Church of Bartholomäberg

▶ *Continue toward Schruns.*

Schruns

Alt 690m/2 264ft. This resort and capital of the Montafon is located in a broad section of the valley and has plenty of lodging and leisure facilities. In summer, it is an ideal departure point for **hikes** in the medium-altitude mountains. In winter, the **ski area** (40km/25mi of pistes) is especially suitable for beginners and for relaxed skiing. More experienced ski hounds can explore the off-piste section at Sennihang. Thanks to the area's considerable differences in height (700–2 400m/2 300–7 100ft), you will be skiing through a rather varied landscape. Snow machines make it possible to ski all the way down into the village.

Ski passes are valid for the entire Montafon Valley with its 62 ski-lifts and 222km/138mi of pistes. Free buses link the various areas in the villages of Tschagguns-Vandans, Schruns, Kristberg, Gargellen, St. Gallenkirch and Gaschurn.

Cross-country skiers are restricted to 13km/8mi of easy tracks around Schruns. For more demanding exploits head to Kristberg (11km/6.8mi), Tschagguns (6km/3.7mi), Vandans (8km/5mi) or the extensive cross-country ski area in the Hochmontafon.

Sennigrat★

Allow 1hr. ◷*Hochjochbahn cable-car late Jun–mid-Oct, daily 8am–4.30pm; Zamangbahn mid-Oct–Apr, daily 8am–4.30pm; Sennigrat chair-lift late Jun–mid-Oct, daily 8am–4.30pm.* ⬩€15.90 round trip. ☏0 55 56/7 21 26.

From Schruns, take the Hochjochbahn or Zamangbahn cable-car to the **Kapell** *(alt 1 850m/6 069ft).* Enjoy the view down into the valley and the many scattered chalets of Schruns. In summer only, another chair-lift goes up to the Sennigrat *(alt 2 210m/7 250ft)*, where the **panorama★** takes in the Kreuzjoch area, the Madrisa massif and the Rätikon.

Hike to the Kreuzjoch and the Zamangspitze★★

4hr round trip. To shorten the route to 2hr, go as far as the mountain lodge and follow the lake path. Climbing boots are recommended.

From Sennigrat, the Wormser Hütte mountain lodge *(alt 2 305m/7 562ft)* can be reached in 20min. From the lodge, follow a ridge path to the Kreuzjoch and then on to the Zamangspitze peak *(alt 2 386m/7 828ft)*, from where a **panorama★★** opens up over the Silvretta massif and the Hochmontafon. Backtrack to the lodge and take the lake trail past **Herzsee** and **Schwarzsee** lakes back to the Kapell, returning to Schruns in the cable-car.

▶ *Follow the road into the Hochmontafon.*

Silvretta Nova ski area

The villages of St. Gallenkirch and Gaschurn have joined together to create an extensive, varied ski area with 114km/71mi of pistes between 900m/2 952.7ft and 2 300m/7 546ft. Good skiers use the black Buckelpiste and the 14km/8mi ski run into the valley from the Schwarzköpfle, and, on powdered snow, the Ziglamstrecke run for remarkable **views★★** over the Silvretta group. Beyond here, **Gargellen,** the highest village in the Montafon *(alt 1 423m/4 668ft)*, also offers good pistes.

For **cross-country skiers** there are connected ski runs along the valley floor between St. Gallenkirch and Partenen. In addition, a 15km/9.3mi cross-country track around the Silvretta reservoir can be reached by funicular and bus.

MURAU

STEIERMARK

POPULATION 2 630 – ALT 829M/2 720FT

Murau is a delightful town on the sprightly Mur River snuggled into the upper Mur Valley amid forested hillsides and Alpine meadows. Its historic center imparts undeniable southern charm with its warren of narrow streets lined by handsome merchant houses painted in a rainbow of pastel colors.

- **Information:** Bundesstraße 13A. ☎0 35 32/2 72 00. www.stadtmurau.at.
- ▶ **Orient Yourself:** Murau is in southwestern Styria, about 80km/50mi north of Klagenfurt.
- **P Parking:** Look for lots along Friesacherstraße, Bahnhofstraße and the B 97.
- **Don't Miss:** Stadtpfarrkirche St. Matthäus
- ◷ **Organizing Your Time:** The castle and church will take two hours, the train trip will take five hours.
- **Kids Especially for Kids:** Murtalbahn steam train.
- **Also See:** HOHENTAUERNPASSSTRASSE, RADSTÄTTER TAUERNSTRASSE.

Sights

Stadtpfarrkirche St. Matthäus★

The Gothic character of the parish church, with its majestic nave and splendid decorations, was not destroyed by 17C Baroque alterations. There are beautiful **frescoes** from the 14C to the 16C, including one showing St. Anthony and his pig, an *Entombment of Christ*, and an *Annunciation*. The north transept was decorated in the late 16C with numerous small paintings representing epitaphs of members of the local Liechtenstein ruling family. The magnificent **Baroque high altar**★ was wrought by local artists and centers on a Gothic Crucifixion (1500); the sky-blue tabernacle is complemented by wood and gilt work.

Schloss Murau

Access via the wooden stairway north of the church. ✎ *Guided tours (1hr) mid-Jun–mid-Sept, Wed, Fri 2pm.* ☞ *€3.* ☎0 35 32/23 02 58.

All that remains of the original castle, commissioned in 1232 by Ulrich von Liechtenstein in a commanding spot above the Mur River, are the cellars and a well, 48m/157ft deep. The present 17C Renaissance-era palace was built by Count Georg-Ludwig von Schwarzenberg. Tours start in the inner courtyard and take in the chapel. The Knight's Hall and other rooms.

Excursion

Murtalbahn   Kids

74km/46mi round trip – about 5hr. ◷ *Jul–Sept, Tue–Wed; call for times.* ☞ *€16.80 each way.* ☎0 35 32/22 33.

This privately-run steam train chugs through attractive scenery between Murau and Tamsweg. The stations in both villages rent bicycles, which may be taken on the train for free.

Murau in winter

© Österreich Werbung / H.Wiesenhofer

MURTAL
STEIERMARK

The Mur River has carved out a 483km/300mi-long route from the Radstädter Tauern in the Salzburg district to Hungary, where it joins the Drava, a tributary of the Danube. The stretch described below covers about one-seventh of the full length and runs through the deeply wooded Mur Valley.

- 🛈 **Information:** Bundesstraße 13a, Murau. ☎0 35 32/27 20. www.murtal.at.
- ▶ **Orient Yourself:** The valley is north of Graz in southern Austria.
- ⊘ **Don't Miss:** Österreichisches Freilichtmuseum.
- 🕐 **Organizing Your Time:** Budget for a whole day for the tour
- 🄺 **Especially for Kids:** Activities at the Österreichisches Freilichtmuseum
- 🕯 **Also See:** GRAZ, BRUCK AN DER MUR, LEOBEN.

Driving Tour

Graz to Leoben
70km/43mi

Graz★★ 🕯*See GRAZ.*

- ▶ *Leave Graz north on the road to Bruck an der Mur (AX) for about 17km/10.5mi to* **Stübing.**

Österreichisches Freilichtmuseum (Austrian Open-air Museum)★★ 🄺
♿ 🕐 *Apr–Oct, Tue–Sun 9am–5pm.* 👓*€7.50.* 📢*Free guided tours.* ☎0 31 24/5 37 00. www.freilichtmuseum.at.
Framed by forest, meadows and fields in a little side valley of the Mur, this open-air museum features 100 original farmhouses from throughout Austria, grouped by province—from Burgenland in the east to Vorarlberg in the far west. All the buildings are authentically furnished and provide a nostalgic glimpse of the way of life and working methods of yesteryear. The museum also puts on

temporary exhibitions on rural life and traditional culture, while craftspeople give daily demonstrations of their work. Wear comfortable shoes as the complex sprawls for about 2km/1.2mi.

- ▶ *Continue north past industrial Peg-gau to the Lurgrotte.*

Lurgrotte★ (Peggau entrance)
⊘*Dress warmly as the cave temperature hovers around 10°C/50°F year round.* 📢*Guided tours (1hr/2hr) Apr–Oct, daily 9am–4pm; Nov–Mar, by appointment only; 1hr/2hr tour* 👓*€5.50/9;* ☎0 31 27/25 80; www.lurgrotte.com.
The walk beside the underground river formed from melt-water leads deep into the cave, past several bizarre formations, including the impressive "Prince" stalactite, which weighs 3t and is almost 4m/13ft long.

Frohnleiten
Set among the rolling hills by the Mur River it is the starting point for many **hiking trails**.

Bruck an der Mur★
🕯*See BRUCK AN DER MUR.*

West of Bruck, the road follows the south bank of the Mur with the Brucker Hochalpe off to the left. The valley now widens and becomes more and more industrial until it reaches Leoben.

Leoben 🕯*See LEOBEN.*

NEUSIEDLER SEE★★

BURGENLAND

The vast Neusiedler See (Fertö in Hungarian) is the most westerly example of a steppe-type lake. It one of the great attractions of the Burgenland and a popular weekend getaway for Vienna folks. Most of the lake belongs to Austria; only the southern tip is in the Hungarian Puszta. It is a paradise for water sports enthusiasts and ringed by swimming beaches that have been slashed out from the reed-fringed shore. To preserve this unique habitat with its profusion of plants, rare animals and migratory birds, the region was designated a national park in 1992 and garnered a spot on UNESCO's list of World Heritage Sites in 2001. The lake is also at the center of an important wine region.

- 🛈 **Information:** Rathaus, A-7071 Rust. ☎0 26 85. www.neusiedlersee.com and www.nationalpark-neusiedlersee.org.
- ▶ **Orient Yourself:** The lake is on the eastern edge of the country, about 50km/31mi southeast of Vienna.
- 🅿 **Parking:** Parking lots can be found at several places around the lake.
- ⊘ **Don't Miss:** Rust with its storks' nests.
- 🕓 **Organizing Your Time:** This is an easy day trip from Vienna, although the lake also warrants an overnight stay or two.
- 🅺🅸🅳🅂 **Especially for Kids:** There's great swimming and boating on the lake.
- ♙ **Also See:** EISENSTADT, PETRONELL-CARNUNTUM.

Driving Tour

Tour of the Western Shore

69km/43mi

Neusiedl am See   🅺🅸🅳🅂

The place that gives the lake its name has a ruined medieval castle and a 15C church, but otherwise there's little reason to spend much time here.

▶ *Head northwest toward Eisenstadt; after Donnerskirchen turn left for Rust.*

Rust★

Rust is famous for its storks' nests, to which the birds return faithfully every year, and for being a prosperous wine-growing center. Since 1989, a wine academy has offered seminars and other wine-related events.

Rust is an attractive town with charming Renaissance and Baroque façades, arcaded inner courtyards and a partially preserved fortified town wall. A highlight on the west side of Rathausplatz is the **Fischerkirche**, which has impressive **frescoes**★ from the 14C and 15C. Also note the Late Gothic statues on the altar to the Three Magi in the side aisle and the fine organ from 1705.

From the village a causeway through the rushes leads to the **Seebad Rust** (♿🕓*May–mid-Sept, daily 9am–7pm; ⌕€4; ☎0 26 85/59 14)*, a lakeside resort with buildings on piles connected by pontoons.

A capricious lake

The Neusiedler See is fringed by enormous reed beds, has no permanent outflow, and only one tributary, the tiny Wulka. Being replenished mostly by rain, snow melt and ground water keeps the water level rather shallow (up to 2m/6.5ft deep), saline, and warm. The lake has even been known to dry up altogether, although not since the late 19C. Consistent winds blowing from the same direction can drive the water toward one shore, leaving the other shore temporarily dry.

Nightingale

European Bee-eater

Whinchat

Little Ringed Plover

Partridge

Lakeside Birdlife

Coot

Bar-tailed Godwit

Great Egret

M. Guillou/ MICHELIN

Mörbisch am See★

With its web of picturesque alleyways, Mörbisch is one of the prettiest places on the Neusiedler See. Almost all the whitewashed houses have stone steps leading up to pillared porches, brightly painted doors, and window shutters, corn cobs hanging up to dry, and flowers everywhere.

Leaving the village to the east through the reed-beds takes you a swimming place and the floating **Seebühne** stage where an operetta festival is held in summer.

▶ *Return to Rust, then bear left for St. Margarethen im Burgenland.*

235

Between Austria and Hungary

As a result of the Treaty of Saint-Germain-en-Laye (1919), parts of the three western *comitats* (provinces) of Hungary passed to Austria. These form the present province of Burgenland, which clearly shows a certain Magyar influence, for example in its cultural and musical traditions.

The Burgenland has retained its ethnic mix with Hungarian, Romany, and Sinti minorities, as well as descendants of Croat refugees from the time of the Turkish invasions.

M. Guillou/MICHELIN

House in Apetion

These minorities settled in this province—and particularly around the Neusiedler See—since the area had formed part of a buffer zone that had been intentionally depopulated by the Hungarian rulers.

St. Margarethen

The village is famous for its Passion play, performed every five years (next time 2011) in the old Roman quarry. Several famous buildings in Vienna were made from St. Margarethen's calcareous sandstone, such as the Stephansdom, the Votivkirche, the Burgtheater and the Parlament. St. Margarethen attracts many wine and festival lovers

▶ *Continue toward Eisenstadt.*

Eisenstadt★ *⌖See EISENSTADT.*

East Shore

Schloss Halbturn

⟨ ⏱ *Apr–Oct, Tue–Sun 10am–5pm.* €7. ☎0 21 72/85 94. www.schlosshalb turn.at.

Built in 1701 by Lukas von Hildebrandt, **Schloss Halbturn** is the most important secular Baroque building in the Burgenland and served as a hunting lodge for Emperor Charles VI. Ravaged by looting and fire after World War II, the building has now been completely restored to its former glory, with its façade looking very smart in shades of pale blue and cream. **Franz Anton Maulbertsch** was responsible for the remarkable **frescoes★** in the garden room, which fortunately survived the 1949 fire. The palace hosts important cultural exhibitions from May to September and also operates a well-

respected wine estate (tastings possible) and restaurant. Extensive gardens invite strolling and picnicking.

Basilika Frauenkirchen★

⟨ ⏱ *May–Sept, daily 8am–8pm; Oct–Apr Mon–Fri 8am–6pm, Sat–Sun 8am–8pm.* ☎0 21 72/22 24.

A basilica since 1990, the famous **pilgrimage church** was commissioned by Prince Paul Esterházy in 1702. It radiates Italian elegance, which is not surprising since its architect was Francesco Martinelli, the stuccowork was done by Pietro Conti and the frescoes by Luca Columba. The sumptuous altar frames an Early Gothic statue of the Virgin Mary, the main object of veneration. Note the painting of a breast-feeding Madonna in the first side altar in the north aisle and the painted choir stalls.

Nationalpark Neusiedlersee-Seewinkel

⏱ *Apr–Oct, Mon–Fri 8am–5pm, Sat–Sun 10am–5pm; rest of the year until 4pm.* ☎0 21 75/34 42. www.nationalpark-neu siedlersee-seewinkel.at.

Around the southern half of the east shore is a national park of reedbeds, marshes, and small lakes. Seewinkel is a naturalists' paradise and very popular with ornithologists, with over 250 different species of birds seen here. **Illmitz,** amid the marshes, is a good base from which to explore the wetlands.

OBERTAUERN★★

SALZBURG
POPULATION 400 – ALT 1 739M/5 705FT

Obertauern lies on a broad terrace on the Radstädter Tauernpass in one of the most beautiful ski areas in the northern Alps. Unlike most Austrian mountain resorts, it did not grow from an existing village, but was developed purely as a winter sports destination. In summer, hiking is the main lure.

- **Information:** ☎0 64 56/72 52. www.obertauern.at, www.obertauern.com, www.ski-obertauern.at.
- **Orient Yourself:** Obertauern is about 90km/55.6mi southeast of Salzburg.
- **Also See:** RADSTADT.

Sights

Ski area

Obertauern boasts good, reliable snow levels, 28 ski-lifts, and 95km/59mi of pistes, nearly all of them for beginners and intermediate skiers. The resort's fairly modest size is more than made up for by the quality of the facilities, which are among the most modern and comfortable in the country.

Radstädter Tauernpass
See RADSTADT Excursion

ÖTSCHERMASSIV★

NIEDERÖSTERREICH UND STEIERMARK

The mountainous area south of St. Pölten, between the Wienerwald and the Eisenerz Alps, is part of the limestone Pre-Alps. The wooded foothills give way to a succession of minor ranges, reaching an altitude of 1 893m/6 211ft at the massive peak of the Ötscher (from an old Slavonic word 'Otan,' meaning godfather).

- **Information:** Pestalozzistraße 12, Krieglach. ☎03855/4 55 70. www.hochsteiermark.at.
- **Orient Yourself:** The Ötschermassif is south of St. Pölten, between the Wienerwald and the Eisenerz Alps in central Austria.
- **Don't Miss:** Mariazell, Stift Lilienfeld.
- **Organizing Your Time:** Allow a whole day to full explore the route.
- **Also See:** MARIAZELL, STIFT LILiENFIED, WIENERWALD, EISENERZ ALPEN.

Driving Tour

Round Trip from Mariazell
112km/69.5mi

Mariazell★ *See MARIAZELL.*

▸ *Leave Mariazell by road no. 21 (east)*

The road closely follows the Salza River through the Salza Valley. In Terz, the picturesque road turns north and plunges into a gorge.

▸ *In Freiland, turn right onto road no. 20 to Lilienfeld.*

Stift Lilienfeld★
See STIFT LILIENFELD.

▸ *From Lilienfeld return south; in Freiland, continue southwest on road no. 20.*

The road, which is pleasant and picturesque, becomes more and more enclosed, first between wooded slopes, then in a rocky gorge. Beyond Türnitz, it climbs steadily, offering wide views of ridges. A series of hairpin bends culminates at Annaberg.

Annaberg

Annaberg's beautifully situated church is a popular stop for pilgrims headed to Mariazell. The first building, a timber chapel, was erected here in 1217, though the present church is from 14C–15C. It is dedicated to St. Anne, as the *Madonna and Child* with St. Anne (15C) on the high altar attest. There are Baroque frescoes and stuccowork in the south chapel and a mass of gilding and carving on the pulpit and the organ-loft.

During the hairpin bend descent, the Ötscher sticks out clearly to the west. Josefsberg is the start of a pleasant downhill run among firs, with fine vistas toward the Gemeindealpe on the right. The road also skirts the Erlaufstausee reservoir. Continuing the descent, you pass Mitterbach am Erlaufsee: Turn right and drive beside a second lake, the natural Erlaufsee.

▶ *Retrace your steps to return to Mariazell.*

ÖTZTAL★★

TIROL

The Ötztal, which is famous for its series of shining glaciers, is one of three deep river valleys running north from the Ötztaler Alps into the Inn. This section of the Alps encompasses the highest point in the northern Tirol, the Wildspitze (alt 3 774m/12 382ft) and the highest parish in Austria (Obergurgl at 1 927m/6 321ft). Until World War I the valley communities were more closely connected with the Alto Adige to the south, from which their people originally came, than with the Inn Valley. Only in 1969, when the Timmelsjoch road was completed, did the isolation of the Ötztal come to an end, at least in summer.

🛈 **Information:** Hauptstr. 66, Ötz. ☎0 52 52/66 99.
▶ **Orient Yourself:** The Ötztal runs north-south through western Austria, about 55km/34mi west of Innsbruck.
🚌 **Don't Miss:** Stuibenfälle, Sölden.
🕐 **Organizing Your Time:** Allow at least a day, although there is enough for two days if you choose to follow some of the hiking trails.
🌲 **Also See:** GURGLERTAL, SOLDEN.

Driving Tour

Inn Valley to San Leonardo in Passiria

(St. Leonhard in Passeier)

88km/54.7mi

On the Austrian side, the road is generally open all year round, at least to Hochgurgl. On the Italian side, however, it is generally only snow free mid-Jun–mid-Oct. The route demands care and has an irregular surface, especially in tunnels. ⊘Trailers, caravans, buses and trucks are not allowed.

The B 186, turning off the busy Inntal road, runs through pleasant pine woods among piles of debris brought down from the Ötztaler Ache creek. This flows beneath the picturesque covered bridge at Ehene to enter the Ötz basin dominated by the rocky tooth of the Acherkogel. Chestnuts, fields of maize, and peach and apricot orchards show that the Ötztal corridor, running due south, attracts the warm air of the Föhn.

Ötz

This village, on a sunny slope, sports several traditional buildings with flower-bedecked oriels and painted façades.

A popular walk leads to the romantic Piburgersee lake.

▶ *Drive to Umhausen, gateway to the Stuiben Falls.*

Stuibenfälle★★

About 1hr 30min round trip walk beginning at the Umhausen tourist office.

The path to this large and powerful waterfall leads first to a restaurant-chalet, crosses the torrent and continues up the left bank to the 150m/492ft-high **waterfall**. A second wooded ravine lies downhill, near the swiftly flowing Ötztaler Ache.

Längenfeld

Together with nearby **Huben**, Längenfeld offers 150km/93mi of hiking trails, several climbing training courses, and two actual climbs, as well as a 50km/31mi network of mountain bike tracks.

Beyond Huben, a long ravine begins, narrowing after the bridge at Aschbach

"Ötzi"

In 1991, a pair of climbers discovered a mummified body in the Similaun range in the Ötztaler Alps. They reported their find thinking it was the body of some unfortunate climber. However, the discovery soon became an archeological sensation, as the body turned out to be about 6 000 years old! The mummy, fondly nicknamed "Ötzi," had been particularly well preserved due to the environmental conditions in the glacier. Even the organs were still intact, so that it was possible to draw conclusions about his diet and the circumstances of his death. Apparently,

Ötzi

Ötzi froze to death in a snow storm despite his good thick clothing of furs and a grass cloak. However, recent evidence has questioned the possibility of his being shot in the back with an arrow. Along with the body a number of significant Stone Age artifacts were retrieved, including a well made pair of shoes with separate soles and uppers. Austrians adopted the Ice Man despite the fact that it was common knowledge that the body had been found 10m/32.8ft inside Italy. After negotiations with the Italians, it was agreed that "Ötzi" would stay in Austria until Innsbruck University completed their analysis of the body. However, the final resting place of the mummy would be in Italy. "Ötzi" is now on display in the South Tyrol Museum of Archeology in Bolzano (Bozen): www.iceman.it.

---

to a larch-covered **gorge**★. Below the road, the Wildbach churns over massive rocks.

Sölden
See SÖLDEN.
The valley forks in Zwieselstein: To the right lies the Venteral

▶ *Take the road along the Ventertal to Vent.*

Ventertal★★ (*see SÖLDEN, Excursions*), this is the valley that gave access to two of the earliest border passes over the Alpine ridge (*Hochjoch 2 875m/9 432ft and Niederjoch 3 019m/9 905ft*).

▶ *Return to Zwieselstein and turn right toward Obergurgl.*

Gurgler Tal★★ (*see GURGLER TAL*)

▶ *On the return from Obergurgl, take the Timmelsjoch road (may be seasonally closed) to the right before Untergurgl.*

After a steep climb, the Timmelsjoch road drops briefly to reach the **Windegg viewpoint**★★ with vistas of the Gurgl Valley, the Great Gurgl glacier and the cleft of the Ötztal. The road now climbs through an austere landscape up to the Timmelsjoch *(alt 2 509m/8 232ft)* on the Italian border.
On the steeper southern slope of the pass, you'll pass through a tunnel before plunging into the Val Passiria enjoying impressive crest views along the way, particularly of the Monte dei Granati (Granatenkogel). The road continues as far as Moso.

▶ *At San Leonardo one can join the road from Merano to the Brenner by way of the Monte Giovo (Jaufenpass).*

OSSIACHER SEE★
KÄRNTEN
LOCAL MAP SEE WÖRTHER SEE

Ossiach Lake, which is not yet deluged by tourists, lies a little set back from the Villach basin, tucked amid the wooded slopes of the Gerlitzen, the Hexenberg and the Ossiacher Tauern. It is Carinthia's third-largest lake, measuring 11km/6.8mi long by 1.5km/1mi wide and reaching a depth of 46m/151ft. Its inviting shores are perfect for swimming and generally relaxing. From spring through fall, boats provide a regular service to all the lakeside resorts.

- **Information:** 10-Oktober-Str. 1, Bodensdorf. ☎0 42 43/83 83 23. www.tiscover.at/steindorf-bodensdorf.
- ▶ **Orient Yourself:** The Ossiach Lake is in southern Austria, about 40km/25mi west of Klagenfurt.
- 🅿 **Parking:** Several parking lots are dotted around the lake.
- 🅐 **Don't Miss:** Gerlitzen.
- 🕐 **Organizing Your Time:** Allow at least a day if taking in Gerlitzen.
- 🖎 **Also See:** WÖRTHER SEE, KLAGENFURT.

Driving Tour

Tour of the Lake★
66km/41mi

Villach★ 🖎 *See VILLACH.*

▶ *Leave Villach to the north and take the B 94*

From Villach, the B 94 skirts the ruins of Landskron fortress and follows the north shore overlooked by the steep slopes of the Gerlitzen.

Gerlitzen★★
The Gerlitzen summit *(alt 1 909m/6 263ft)* dominates central Carinthia, its foothills cascading down to the Ossiach Lake. In winter, its numerous hotels, the cable-car from Annenheim up to the Kanzel, the ski-lifts and sunny slopes attract an international crowd of skiers. In summer, it is the starting point for a number of scenic hiking trails.

Ossiach by the lake

© Österreich Werbung / W. Weinhaeupl

Ascent of the Gerlitzen

From Bodensdorf on the north shore head to Tschöran for the little mountain road to Gerlitzen (12km/7.4mi; ⊗toll levied).

After winding through woods and pastures, the road ends at 1 764m/5 787ft at a complex including restaurants and lodging. Finish the climb on foot or, if necessary, by **chair-lift** (🕐 mid-Jun–late Sept, daily 9am–5pm; Dec–Apr, daily 8.30am–5.15pm, depending on snow levels; ⊗€15.50 round trip; ☎0 42 48/27 22).

The **panorama**★★ embraces the Ossiach, Wörth and Faak lakes and, beyond the Drava Valley, the long barrier of the Karawanken. The permanently snow-covered slopes of the Hochalm and Ankogel glaciers glitter in the northwest.

▶ *Return to the lake. Take the road carries on east to Steindorf. Turn right off the main road and follow the road paralleling the south shore.*

Ossiach

The Benedictine **abbey** of Ossiach (now a hotel) was founded in the 11C. In the 16C and 17C it went through periods of splendor, even receiving Emperor Charles V in 1552. In 1783 the abbey was dissolved on the orders of Emperor Joseph II. It subsequently took on various roles, becoming a stud farm, a military base, and a convalescence home, all of which took their toll on the building. Ossiach is well known internationally for the Carinthian Summer Festival.

Church★

♿🕐 May, Jun, Sept, Oct, daily 10am–6pm; Jul–Aug, daily 9am–noon, 1.30pm–6pm. ⊗€1.50. ☎0 42 43/22 80.

Ossiach's triple-nave pillared basilica was originally of Romanesque design but completely transformed into the Baroque style between 1741 and 1745. Delicately colored, lace-like **stuccowork** by masters from the Wessobrunn School in Bavaria adorns the interior. The ceiling painting is the work of famous local artist **Joseph Ferdinand Fromiller**, who also worked in the Landhaus at Klagenfurt. The Gothic baptistry on the left contains a valuable **carved altar-piece**★ whose central panel depicts the Virgin Mary flanked by St. Margaret and St. Catherine; on the side panels are the Apostles.

▶ *Take the road back to Villach.*

PACK- UND STUBALPENSTRASSE★

STEIERMARK UND KÄRNTEN

These routes cut across the gentle, wooded heights of the Pannonian Pre-Alps between the valleys of the River Mur and River Lavant and the Graz basin. Known as the Koralpe, the Packalpe, the Stubalpe, and the Gleinalpe, these mountains form a barrier less by their height, which hardly exceeds 2 000m/6 562ft, than by their remoteness. The inter-regional road from Graz to Klagenfurt passes over the Packsattel, whereas the old road from Graz to Judenburg via Köflach crosses the Stubalpe, cutting off the wide bend of the River Mur.

🛈 **Information:** Bundesstraße 13a, Murau. ☎0 35 32/27 20. www.murtal.at.
▶ **Orient Yourself:** These routes are in southern Austria, just west of Graz.
🅟 **Don't Miss:** Gestüt Piber.
🄺 **Especially for Kids:** Gestüt Piber.
♿ **Also See:** GRAZ, STEIRISCHE WEINSTRASSE.

Driving Tours

①Stubalpe Tour★
46km/28.5mi

Judenburg
Judenburg is the oldest commercial center in Styria. Records show that a Jewish community was established here as early as 1103 but driven out in 1496 by order of Emperor Maximilian I. Numerous old buildings and courtyards from the historic town center cluster around the **Neue Burg**.

▶ *From Weisskirchen, take the winding road as it climbs gradually through the fir trees to the crest.*

The main Stubalpe ridge is crossed at the **Gaberl Pass** *(alt 1 547m/5 075ft)*. Beyond the pass, the road drops suddenly into the wild and narrow wooded **Salla Valley** to a tiny village called Salla. Here and there you'll pass old sawmills and scythe factories that once brought industry to the valley, though many are now in ruins

▶ *Follow the B 77 for c. 14km/8.7mi past Sallabach and Krenhof to Köflach.*

Köflach
This town is near an opencast lignite mine considered among the most productive in Austria. In early September the "Lipizzaner Almabtrieb" takes place here. This is when the famous white stallions are driven down from the Alpine pastures to their winter quarters at the Piber stud farm.

▶ *3km/1.8mi northeast of Köflach is Musikverein Gestüt Piber.*

Musikverein Gestüt Piber★   Kids
&↝Guided tours (1hr 10min) Apr–Oct, Tue–Sat 9am–5pm; Nov–Mar, by prior arrangement. ↝€11. ☎03144/33 23.
Piber's claim to fame rests on the graceful **Lipizzaner stallions**, which are bred here and then sent to the Spanische Reitschule in Vienna (*&see WIEN*). For close-ups of the horses, visit the stables or take a walk in the nearby fields. The animals are born bay or black and only acquire their white coats between the ages of four and ten. In rare cases a Lipizzaner may retain its dark coat, making it a highly prized "Hofburg bay."

②Packsattel Tour★
48km/29.8mi

Köflach &See opposite.

After leaving Köflach, the route skirts the opencast lignite pits and then climbs up a hill offering views back down into the industrial valley, although you can also espy the bright white outline of the pilgrimage church at Maria Lankowitz.

▶ *Continue on B 70 for 20km/12.4mi.*

Pack
Close to the **Packer Stausee** (an artificial lake with boating and swimming

Lipizzaner stallions at Piber stud farm

Wiesenhofer/ÖSTERREICH WERBUNG

facilities), this little community enjoys a peaceful **panorama**★ of the wooded foothills of the Pannonian Pre-Alps and the Graz plain.

In gentle pastoral surroundings the road reaches the **Packsattel**, which is also known as the Packhöhe or the Vier Tore (Four Gates – *alt 1 166m/3 825ft*), before dropping into an even quieter and more thickly wooded zone.

A series of hairpin bends below the Preitenegg ridge lends a little variety to the descent. The route leads past the sombre Schloss Waldenstein, then continues along the ravine of the Waldensteiner Bach to join the Lavant Valley at Twimberg.

Lavant Valley Motorway Bridge (Autobahnbrücke)★

At 1 079m/3 500ft long and 165m/541ft high, this bridge is taller than the Stephansdom in Vienna. It is among the 10 longest bridges in Austria and Europe's second highest bridge built on pylons.

▶ *Continue 13km/8mi on the B 70.*

Wolfsberg

The town is characterized by a Tudor-style 19C castle and wraps around the Hoher Platz, a square adorned with a column to the Virgin Mary and flanked by fine Biedermeier houses.

PETRONELL-CARNUNTUM★

NIEDERÖSTERREICH

POPULATION 1 200 – ALT 330M/1 082FT

Excavations on the site of Petronell and in the neighboring community of Bad Deutsch-Altenburg have unearthed remnants of an ancient Roman town from around the 1C AD.

🛈 **Information:** Kirchengasse 57. ☎0 21 63/22 28, www.petronell.at.
▶ **Orient Yourself:** Petronell-Carnuntum is on the eastern edge of the country, about 40km/26mi east of Vienna.
🅿 **Parking:** There's parking at the Freilichtmuseum and at the Museum Carnuntinum.
☺ **Don't Miss:** Museum Carnuntinum
🕐 **Organizing Your Time:** Distances between sights are quite large, so allow at least half a day to see it all.
Kids **Especially for Kids:** Freilichtmuseum Petronell
Ⓒ **Also See:** NEUSIEDLER SEE

A Bit of History

The Capital of Upper Pannonia – Carnuntum was founded as a Roman military winter camp by Emperor Tiberius in 6 AD and became the capital of the Roman province of Upper Pannonia in the 2C. In 171 Emperor Marcus Aurelius drove back the Marcomanni and Quadi tribes from here, while also writing part of his *Meditations*.

In 308, Emperor Diocletian convened an Imperial Conference in Carnuntum in order to try to hold the Roman Empire together. But for the town the end was near as first the Goths and then the Huns overran and devastated it around 400 AD.

Sights

Archäologischer Park Carnuntum

Information Center, Hauptstraße 296; ☺🕐Mar–Nov 12, daily 9am–5pm. ☞€8, audio-guide €3.50. ☎0 21 63/3 37 70. www.carnuntum.co.at.

The archelogical park consists of two main areas: The Zivilstadt (civilian town) in the town of Petronell-Carnuntum and the Militärstadt (military town) in Bad

Deutsch-Altenburg. For orientation and to pick up maps and an audio-guide (in English, recommended), start your visit at the information center. One ticket is good for all Roman sites and the museum.

Zivilstadt★

The main excavation area is now the **Kids Freilichtmuseum Petronell**, an open-air museum where you can stroll along actual Roman streets lined with ancient foundations and reconstructed buildings such as the Temple of Diana. A new highlight, open since 2006, is the **House of Lucius★**, an authentically decorated and furnished home of a textile merchant that provides rare insight into the lifestyle enjoyed by rich Romans. About 700m west of here are the remnants of one of the city's two **amphitheaters**, which had two gateways and a capacity of 13 000 spectators. Another stroll takes you to the **Grosse Therme**, one of the largest and fanciest Roman bathing complexes north of the Alps and once decorated with colored marble and mosaic floors. These days, only bits and pieces of floor heating, water canals and the pools survive.

South of the open-air museum is the **Heidentor** (Heathen's Gate), a 4C stone arch that once formed part of a much larger monument to Emperor Constantin II. Its curious name dates back to the Middle Ages, when people erroneously thought that it was built by non-Christians, even though Christianity had already taken root among the Romans.

Militärstadt

The only surviving remnant from the military camp is the **Amphitheater Bad Deutsch-Altenburg**, where gladiators fought, soldiers paraded and meetings gathered There's more to see here than at the theater in Petronell, includeing cages, tunnels and gateways. A permanent exhibit offers insights into the forms of entertainment enjoyed by Roman society.

© Österreich Werbung / Diejun

Heidentor

Museum Carnuntinum★

Badgasse 40–46. ◷ *Mar 21–Nov 12, Mon noon–5pm, Tue–Sun 10am–5pm.* ☏*02163/3 37 70.*

The archeological museum in Bad Deutsch-Altenburg occupies a beautiful replica Roman villa and was opened by Emperor Franz Joseph in 1904. It houses a remarkable collection of ancient artifacts, including exceptional sculpture such as a striking marble statuette of the **Dancing Maenads of Carnuntum★**. The exhibits on the ground floor mainly relate to the **Mithras cult** and come from the Mithraeum, an underground place of worship unearthed by the excavations. Mithras was a Persian god who was venerated by Roman soldiers in the 2C before the advent of Christianity.

Rundkapelle

Opposite the Information Center in Petronell.

This unusual Romanesque round chapel from 1200 has a pointed roof and semicircular choir. The individual character of the building is further emphasized by the simplicity of the façade with its three-quarter columns and arcades carried on consoles. The **tympanum relief★** over the entrance shows the baptism of Christ, an indication that the chapel must originally have been used as a baptistry.

Excursion

Rohrau
4km/2.5mi south of Petronell-Carnuntum.
The 16C Schloss Rohrau contains the
Harrach'sche Gemäldegalerie★★
(⏲*Easter–Oct, Tue–Sun 10am–5pm;*
⏳*€7;* ☎*02164/22 53)*, which ranks
among the largest and most prestigious
private art collections in Austria, with
works by 17C and 18C masters from
Spain, Naples and Rome, and 16C and
17C masters from Holland and Flanders.
Of outstanding merit is *The Concert* (16C),
a particularly graceful painting of female
figures playing musical instruments,
presumably by a Dutch artist.
The composer **Joseph Haydn** was born
in 1732 in the thatched **Geburtshaus
Joseph Haydns** (⏲*year-round, Tue–Sun
10am–4pm;* ⏳*€1.50;* ☎*02164/22 68)* on
the main village road. It now contains
a memorial exhibit about the man, his
works and his life.

PITZTAL★★★
TIROL

The long Pitz Valley, which runs north–south, is flanked in the west by the Kaunertal
Valley and in the east by the Ötztal Valley. It is famous for the extraordinary Alpine
scenery in its upper reaches. It is enclosed by a massive glacier basin over which
towers the 3 774m/12 382ft high **Wildspitze** peak, the highest point in the Tirol.

- **Information:** Unterdorf 18, Wenns. ☎0 54 14/8 69 99. www.pitztal.com.
- ▶ **Orient Yourself:** The Pitztal is in western Austria, about 58km/36mi
  west of Innsbruck.
- **Don't Miss:** Hinterer Brunnenkogel
- **Organizing Your Time:** Allow 45min for the drive to Mittelberg and 2hr for
  the trip up the Hinterer Brunnenkogel.
- **Also See:** ÖTZTAL, KAUNERTAL.

Sights

Road from Arzl to Mittelberg★
The 39km-/24mi-long road offers views
of the glaciers and passes through villages and forest, past little waterfalls
and along the Pitzbach creek to Mittelberg where lifts take you up to the
glaciers.

Hinterer Brunnenkogel★★★
Alt 3 440m/11 286ft. ⏲*Pitzexpress funicular daily 8.30am–4.30pm. Pitz-Panoramabahn cable-car daily 9am- 3.15pm.*
⏲*Late May–Jul.* ⏳*€22 (combined ticket)
round trip.* ☎*05413/8 62 88.*
The Pitzexpress funicular travels underground for 3.7km/2.3mi to the foot of
the Pitztal glacier at 2 860m/9 383ft.
Continue on the Pitz-Panoramabahn,
the highest cable-car in Austria. The
peak, which offers a fantastic **Alpine
panorama**★★★, is only a short hike
from the upper mountain station. The
Wildspitze towers majestically over this
grandiose landscape. Take sunglasses,
sturdy shoes suitable for snow and
warm clothing (even in summer).

Pitztal Glacier

⏲*Mid-Sept–early Jun, daily 8.30am–
4.30pm.* ⏳*€34.50 ski day pass, also
includes Rifflsee area.* ☎*0 54 13/8 62 88.
www.pitztaler-gletscher.at.*
Seven lifts lead up to 25km/15.5mi of
pistes that are usually well covered in
snow from fall through May. The ski
area is suitable for skiers of all levels,
although easy runs predominate.

Excursion

The Rifflsee★
*Park in Mandarfen, 1km/.6mi below Mit-
telberg. Cable-car* ⏲*late Jun–Apr, daily
8.30am–4.30pm.* ⏳*€13.50 round trip in
summer.* ☎*0 54 13/8 62 88.*

Mittelberg

From the mountain station at 2 300m/ 7 546ft, take a walk around the lake or, if you have more stamina, head for the Fuldaer Höhenweg ridge trail to the **Taschachhütte** mountain lodge at 2 432m/7 979ft. During the trip you will see interesting **views** over the valley, and the Kerlesferner glacier to the south.

PÖLLAU ★

STEIERMARK
POPULATION 1 860 – ALT 427M/1 401FT

Pöllau, a charming town with red-tiled houses, lies away from the major tourist routes in the heart of the Pöllauer Tal (Pöllau Valley). Much of the surrounding countryside has been turned into a natural park criss-crossed by 100km/62mi of trails. In an area of limited agricultural activity, vines occupy a significant niche in the local economy. In season, great places to sample the local product are the traditional taverns called Buschenschenken.

- **Information:** Schloss 1. ☎0 08 00 /84 72 68 37.
- ▶ **Orient Yourself:** Pöllau is in southeastern Austria, about 62km/39mi northeast of Graz.
- **Don't Miss:** The Abbey Church.
- **Organizing Your Time:** Allow a fuul day.
- **Also See:** SCHLOSS HERBERSTEIN.

Sights

Marktplatz
This traditional market place, with its column to the Virgin Mary, has southern flair thanks to its many old façades. To the north of the square, an old door leads to the Schloss, a former Augustinian abbey with origins as a moated 12C castle.

Stift
Founded in 1504, the fledgling abbey had a troubled time during the 16C,

when Styria was racked by religious disputes and Turkish raids. Despite such adversity, it grew prosperous by the late 17C and was rebuilt in the Baroque style. During secularization under Emperor Joseph II it was closed in 1785 and turned into a private residence. It now belongs to the town.

Abbey church★
The imposing Baroque church was designed by **Joachim Carlone**, a member of the celebrated family of Graz archi-

Address Book

⚭ *For coin ranges, see cover flap.*

WHERE TO STAY

⚭⚭ **Berggasthof König** – *Pöllauberg 5.* ☎*0 33 35/23 11. www. berggasthof-koenig.at. 7 rooms.* First mentioned in 1628, this is a traditional inn right next to the pilgrimage church. The owners have maintained many of the original features in the reception areas and the rooms.

tects, and has impressive dimensions the nave and chancel are 62m/203ft long, the transept is 37m/121ft wide and the cupola 42m/138ft high, creating an unusually generous space for such a small community. It is because of its size that the church is sometimes called the "Styrian Petersdom."

The remarkable **décor** is a delightful blend of paintings, gold, stuccowork and opulent sculptures. The frescoes in the nave and cupola are by Styrian artist, **Matthias von Görz**, and clearly show off his hallmark bright colors, a passion for light, and considerable skill at *trompe-l'œil*. The enormous painting on the **high altar** depicts the martyr-

dom of St. Vitus and is a work of Joseph Adam von Mölk.

The 24-stop **organ**, built in 1739, stands on an arcaded gallery, beneath a ceiling fresco of David playing the harp.

Excursions

Pöllauberg★

6km/3.7mi northeast of Pöllau.

Pöllauberg is a tiny village that grew up around its celebrated 14C **pilgrimage church** crowning the top of a steep hill and visible for miles around. Its unusual design features twin naves of equal size separated by three pillars and with intersecting ribbed vaults. The large and sumptuously decorated 18C high altar centers on a statue of the Virgin Mary that is the main object of worship. The lavishly gilded pulpit dates from 1730.

Pöllauertal Natural Park

Pöllauer Tal is a diverse and hilly patchwork of forests, meadows, fields and orchards. Traditional farming methods have been kept alive and the Hirschbirne Pear, found only in Styria, is carefully cultivated here. The park is home to diverse flora and fauna.

RADSTADT★

SALZBURG
POPULATION 4 710 – ALT 858M/2 815FT

The town lies in the Enntal with the Dachstein mountains to the north and the Tauern to the south. It is undoubtedly a very scenic place and is popular in winter due to its proximity to the Obertauern ski area. It was important due to its position on the route along the Enntal and at the northern end of the route that crossed the Tauern mountains. The road over the Radstädter Tauernpass starts in Radstadt and is one of the most scenic passes in Austria.

- **Information:** Stadtplatz 17. ☎0 64 52/74 72. www.radstadt.com.
- ▶ **Orient Yourself:** The town lies in the Enn Valley between the Dachstein range and the Tauern Range.
- **Don't Miss:** Burg Mauterndorf, Schloss Moosham.
- **Organizing Your Time:** Allow half a day for the town and Gnadenfall and a full day if heading up the Pass.
- **Also See:** DACHSTEIN.

A Bit of History

Radstadt was strategically important because it sat at the crossroads of two major trade routes. The town's wealth was due in part to its position on the trade route with Venice and its license to stock iron and salt. First mentioned in 1074, it received its town charter in 1289. Realizing its strategic importance, the Bishops of Salzburg fortified the town in the 13C.

Sights

Town Wall

Radstadt is a pretty town, still enclosed by its tower-studded medieval town wall and a partial moat. These walls are of unique symmetrical design, with three towers built between 1527 and 1535 when the Bishops of Salzburg decided to strengthen the fortifications in anticipation of an attack by the Turks.

Heimatmuseum Kapuzinerturm

Schlossstraße 1. Jun–Sept, Mon–Sat 9.30–11.30am, 2pm–4pm. €3. 06 452/70 83.

Part of the town walls this tower, which guards the eastern gateway, houses a museum devoted to the Peasant Wars.

Heimatmuseum Schloss Lerchen

Schießstatt 3. Jun–mid-Oct, daily 10–noon, 3pm–5pm; Jan–Apr, 10am–1.30am, 2.30pm–5pm. €4. 06452/63 74.

Ten minutes west of the center this museum houses displays on the history of Radstadt, farming, crafts and sacred art. Other exhibits focus on the organist Paul Hofhaimer and the local geology.

Excursion

From Radstadt to St. Michael im Lungnau

67km/42mi

Roßbrand★★

See entry under DACHSTEIN

Gnadenfall

This lusty cascade of the Taurach leaps a wooded shelf in two light falls. Hotels crouch between the larches and spruces below the pass at 1 739m/5 705ft. About 800m/875yd short of the pass a modern (1951) statue of a Roman legionary stands guard over the bridge.

Radstädter Tauernpass★

23km/14.3ml south on the B 99 Katchberg-Bundesstraße

This pass *(alt 1738m/5702ft)* crosses over into Carinthia and was in use in Roman times. It was an important trade route over the Tauern mountains and today offers wonderful panoramas of the Dachstein range to the north. At the pass is the vast ski area **Obertauern★★** *(see OBERTAUERN).*

Beyond the Radstädter Tauernpass, the road enters a forbidding section, but between Tweng and Mauterndorf pleasant clearings appear on the banks of the calmer Taurach. Soon the roofs of the Mauterndorf castle peer out from among the trees.

Burg Mauterndorf★

see BURG MAUTERNDORF

Tamsweg★ *see TAMSWEG*

St. Michael im Lungnau

This attractive resort is flooded with sunshine year-round and is especially busy in winter, when numerous elevators ferry skiers up to the fine slopes.

RATTENBERG ★

TIROL

POPULATION 440 – ALT 514M/1 686FT

This tiny frontier town once built its prosperity on silver-mining but essentially stopped evolving when the mines ran dry in the 17C. As a result, Rattenberg's old town is an almost perfectly preserved example of Renaissance urban design. The town is also famous for its engraved and finely modeled glassware, available in numerous stores along its main street.

- **Information:** Klostergasse 94, A-6240. ☎0 53 37/6 33 21. www.rattenberg.at.
- **Orient Yourself:** Rattenberg is in western Austria, about 48km/29.8mi northeast of Innsbruck.
- **Parking:** There are two large parking lots north and south of the train station.
- **Don't Miss:** Pfarrkirche St. Virgil.
- **Organizing Your Time:** Allow half a day for the sights and another half for the excursions.
- **Also See:** KAISERGEBIRGE, KARWENDELGEBIRGE.

Sights

Augustinermuseum★

Pfarrgasse 8. ◯May–2nd Sun in Oct, daily 10am–5pm. ◉€3. ☎0 53 37/6 48 31.
The Augustinian monastery was founded in 1384 and is now a museum displaying Tirolean art treasures, including exquisite Gothic sculpture in the cloisters and fine examples of local goldsmithing. Processional items are exhibited up in the church gallery; highlights include a Seated Madonna and the Mocking Group.

Pfarrkirche St. Virgil★★

The twin naves of this Gothic church, separated by four graceful columns, are a harmonious pink and white confection. In former times, the larger nave was reserved for the burghers, while the smaller one was set aside for the miners. Abundant statuary, delicate stuccowork, and elegant frescoes make up the scintillating Baroque decorative scheme. The masterly **Last Supper** is the work of the Bavarian artist Matthäus Günther, while the Transfiguration in the chancel is by Simon Benedikt Faistenberger. The statues around the **altar** in the miners' chancel were sculpted by Meinrad Guggenbichler, the famous sculptor from Mondsee.

Schlossberg

30min round trip walk.
From this vantage point there is a good **general view** of the town, hemmed in between the Inn and the mountain, with the belfry of the Servitenkirche (13C–18C) rising above the roof ridges. Downstream, the Kaisergebirge comes into view.

Excursion

Freilichtmuseum Tiroler Bauernhöfe★

7km/4.3mi away in **Kramsach**.
The parking lot is shortly after the hamlet of Mosen. ◯mid-Apr–Oct, daily 9am–6pm (last admission 5pm). ◉€5.50. ☎05337/6 26 36.
More than a dozen farmhouses and their outbuildings, including a sawmill and a school, gathered from throughout the Tirol have been reassembled here in a quiet Alpine setting.

Alpbach★

12km/7.4mi southeast of Rattenberg.
Idyllic and postcard-pretty Alpbach has been settled since AD 1 000 and wraps around its church, the **Pfarrkirche St. Oswald** whose pointed spire stands out against the mountainous backdrop. The plain exterior does not hint at its rich interior with fine frescoes and superb

Rattenberg

altars. The High Altar bears the figures of St. Oswald, St. Martin and St. Catherine. There are two side altars framed in Rococo carvings. The left-hand one with its picture of *Our Lady of the Victory* has attracted pilgrims for centuries.

Since 1945, the town has hosted the Alpbach European Forum, an annual gathering of academics, politicians, economists, and artists of all nationalities who discuss contemporary issues facing the world.

REISSECK-MASSIV★★

KÄRNTEN

The Reisseck massif, which towers over the Möll Valley, is one of the most unspoiled places in Carinthia. Only the arrival of a funicular and a railway line to serve the power station at Kolbnitz opened it up to a greater degree. Its beautiful location and good snow conditions attract ski hounds in winter, while summer draws in-the-know hikers who cherish the many lakes and glorious viewpoints.

- 🛈 **Information:** Unterkolbnitz 50, Kolbnitz. ☎0 47 83/20 50. www.reisseck.at.
- ▶ **Orient Yourself:** The Reisseck massif is in southcentral Austria, about 56km/34.8mi northwest of Villach.
- 🕭 **Don't Miss:** Hike to the Grosser Mühldorfer Seen.
- 🕐 **Organizing Your Time:** Budget at least half a day to get up and around the mountain.

Visit

Reisseckbahn★

From Kolbnitz. 25min each way by funicular plus 10min on the train. 🕐*May–mid-Oct, daily 8.30am–5pm.* ☎*04783/24 10.*

This is an awe-inspiring trip to the top of the Reisseck mountain. The funicular follows a very steep gradient for 3.5km/2.2mi to the Schoberboden station *(alt 2 237m/7 339ft)*, from where there is a beautiful **view**★ of the valley and the rocky foothills of the Reisseck

Grosser Mühldorfer See

massif. From here the Höhenbahn train travels underground for 3.2km/2mi, arriving at a pleasant hotel.

Walk

Mühldorfer Seen★

From the Höhenbahn mountain station, an easy 30min walk leads to the Grosser Mühldorfer See, a reservoir from where there is a **view**★ to the east over the Hohe Leier. Beyond here, the trail is quite stony, so sturdy shoes are essential *(follow the red and white markings)*. After 10min the path emerges above the Kleiner Mühldorfer See dam. There is a beautiful **open view**★ over both lakes, which lie in an unspoiled rocky landscape. Keen hikers can continue for another hour to the **Riekentörl pass** *(alt 2 525m/8 284ft)*, for a magnificent **panorama**★★ over the entire Reisseck massif. The hike climbs along a rocky trail, but presents no technical difficulties.

SCHLOSS RIEGERSBURG★
NIEDERÖSTERREICH

The unspoilt, peaceful landscape of the northeastern Waldviertel provides a backdrop for the most important Baroque palace in Lower Austria. The former moated castle was bought by Sigmund Friedrich Count Khevenhüller, governor of Lower Austria and converted into a four-winged Baroque palace by the masterful **Franz Anton Pilgram**. The decoration is rich, but not ostentatious. Still owned by the same family, the building is a fine example of an 18C country seat.

- **Information:** ☎0 31 53/86 70. www.schlossriegersburg.at.
- ▸ **Orient Yourself:** The Schloss is in the far north of Austria, close to the Czech border.
- **Don't Miss:** The Yellow Salon.
- **Organizing Your Time:** Allow about an hour for each castle.
- **Also See:** ALTENBURG, EGGENBURG.

Visit

&.⚙⚓*Guided tour (45min) Apr–Jun and Sept–mid-Nov, daily 9am–5pm; Jul–Aug, daily 9am–7pm.* ⚙€9, combination ticket with Burg Hardegg €14. ☎02916/4 00. www.riegersburg.com.

State rooms

The palace interior is filled with high-quality furnishings. The surprisingly plain but beautifully proportioned **banqueting hall** (Festsaal) features stuccowork above the door showing Count Johann Joseph Khevenhüller-Metsch, Maria Theresia's Chief Lord Chamberlain, whose diaries are said to have inspired the libretto for Richard Strauss' opera, *Der Rosenkavalier*. The portraits of Maria Theresia and her mother Elisabeth Christine are by court painter Martin van Meytens. The **Baroque room** houses a view of Naples composed of 35 copper engravings dating from 1730 to 1775. The furniture in the Salon includes Queen Anne and Chippendale pieces, as well as furnishings in the Austrian Baroque style and a handsome tabernacle cupboard.

The **tower room**, hung with plate-printed cotton, contains furniture from the 18C. Note the pretty portable desk from England. The **dining room** contains French furniture and houses a famous portrait of Prince Eugene of Savoy by Austrian painter Auerbach.

The **stucco ceiling**★ of the **Yellow Salon** depicts an allegory of princely virtue. The room is furnished with Marie-Antoinette chairs and two beautiful Florentine commodes with delicate inlaid work. The **Chinese Salon** also features a magnificent stucco ceiling.

In the north wing is the elegant **Schloss-kapelle** (chapel), consecrated in 1755. The altar is integrated into the architectural structure and is surmounted by rich stuccowork. The altarpiece depicts St. Sigismund.

The **Schlossküche** (palace kitchen) on the ground floor, in use until 1955 and still featuring its original appointments, working equipment and large brick oven, is the only remaining manorial kitchen in Austria.

From the café in the right wing, you can access the park with its pond.

Excursion

Burg Hardegg

8km/5mi to the east. ◷*Apr–mid-Nov, daily 9am–5pm;Jul–Aug, daily 9am–*

© Österreich Werbung / Trumler

Schloss Riegersburg

6pm. ◉*€6.90, combination ticket with Riegersburg €14.* ☏*0 29 16/4 00. www. burghardegg.at.*

Hardegg on the Thaya River is dominated by its blufftop castle whose formidable keep and thick walls create an impression of impregnability. The origins of this strategically important fortress date back to AD 1 000, but extensions were added right up to the 14C. After a checkered history, the fortress passed into the hands of the Khevenhüller family in 1730 and at the end of the 19C it was converted into a mausoleum for the Lower Austrian line of this dynasty.

SCHLOSS ROSENBURG★
NIEDERÖSTERREICH

More than 1 000 years ago, the Babenbergs freed central Austria from the Magyars so that this region could at last be settled. In order to counter effectively the constant threat from Bohemia, the nobles built a series of castles in the strategically important Kamptal. Of these, the Rosenburg, built in the first half of the 12C, is one of the most attractive and important. It has been owned by the counts of Hoyos since the 17C.

- 🛈 **Information:** Rosenburg 1. ☏02982/29 11. www.rosenburg.at.
- ▶ **Orient Yourself:** This Schloss is in northcentral Austria, about 84km/52mi northwest of Vienna, near Altenburg Abbey.
- ◷ **Organizing Your Time:** Two hours should be plenty for this palace.
- **Kids** **Especially for Kids:** Falconry demonstrations.
- ⚭ **Also See:** STIFT ALTENBURG, SCHLOSS GREILLENSTEIN.

Visit

🕙📞*Guided tour (45min) May–Sept, daily 9.30am–5pm; Apr and Oct, Thu–Sun 9.30am–4.30pm.* 🎫*€10.* ☎*02982/29 11. www.rosenburg.at.*

Passing through the gateway, one comes to the 1614 courtyard surrounded on three sides by double galleries and once used for equestrian games. The square **keep** is part of the original castle, but was altered in the Renaissance period by the addition of a balcony.

After standing nearly empty in the 18C, the living rooms and grand public rooms were furnished mainly in the style of the German Renaissance. The **library** with its remarkable wooden **coffered ceiling**★ is of particular interest, as are the Marble Hall and the palace chapel.

Schloss Rosenburg is a center for falconry. 🧒Kids especially love the **free**

Schloss Rosenburg

flight demonstrations★ in which hunting falcons, eagles and vultures perform their routines.

SAALACHTAL★

SALZBURG UND BAYERN (GERMANY)

The valley of the River Saalach, which breaches the Northern Limestone Alps, forms the quickest link between Salzburg, Zell am See and the Grossglockner.

- 🛈 **Information:** Lofer 310. ☎0 51 25/35 15 55.
- ▶ **Orient Yourself:** This valley runs north–south between Salzburg and Zell am See.
- 😊 **Don't Miss:** Salzburger Freilichtmuseum.
- 🕙 **Organizing Your Time:** With stops, this tour can easily turn into a day trip.
- 🧒 **Especially for Kids:** Vorderkaserklamm, Lamprechtshöhle, Salzburger Freilichtmuseum.
- 👍 **Also See:** SALZBURG, ZELL AM SEE.

Driving Tour

From Salzburg to Zell am See *95km/59mi*

Salzburg★★★ 👍*See SALZBURG.*

▶ *Leave Salzburg on road no. 1.*

Shortly past the airport, consider making a 6km/3.7mi detour to **Grossgmain** and the Salzburg open-air museum.

Salzburger Freilichtmuseum 🧒

🕙*Apr–Oct, Tue–Sun 9am–6pm; Dec 26– Jan 6, Tue–Sun 10am–4pm.* 📞*Guided tours available.* 🎫*€7; children €3.50.* ☎*06 62/85 00 11. www.freilichtmuseum. com.*

More than 60 original buildings from throughout the Salzburg province representing six centuries of traditional architecture have been reassembled in this village-like, open-air museum. In addition, there are specialized exhibitions, such as a collection of old tractors, a multimedia presentation, and a House of Sounds, as well as live craft demonstrations.

▷ *Carry on to Bad Reichenhall (Germany).*

Bad Reichenhall★
This Bavarian town sits atop some of the richest salt springs in Europe and is a major producer of table salt. The saltwater spa helps cure respiratory diseases.

▷ *Branch off at Schneizlreuth from the Deutsche Alpenstraße onto the Lofer road.*

The road turns away from the Saalach and climbs up to Melleck. The Steinpass marks the Austrian border. The road then returns to the Saalach.

Lofer★   🕭 *See KAISERGEBIRGE* 1 .

The enclosed section from Lofer to Saalfelden, in a former glacial gorge, is strikingly uniform.

Wallfahrtskirche Maria Kirchental
4km/2.5mi south of Lofer. At St. Martin bei Lofer turn right off B 311 onto a narrow toll road.
♿🕐*Daily 7am–7pm.* ☎*0 65 88/85 28.*
Nicknamed the "Pinzgau Cathedral," this rustic yet graceful late 17C pilgrimage church was designed by the renowned Johann Bernhard Fischer von Erlach. It was steadily redecorated and furnished over the 18C and 19C as the offerings of the pilgrims mounted up.

About 6km/3.7mi beyond Lofer, the road reaches the **Vorderkaser gorge**, the first of a trio of natural attractions. *Combination ticket* ⊛*€7.70.*

Vorderkaserklamm   Kids
Allow about 45min 🕐*May–Oct, daily 9am–6pm.* ⊛*€2.90; children €1.60.* ☎*0 65 88/85 10. www.naturgewalten.at.*
This wildly romantic gorge shaped by a thundering torrent is reached via an easy 2.5km/1.5mi trail through an idyllic natural recreation area, complete with pools for swimming and barbecue areas. From here an initially quite steep path leads up through the forest to the entrance to the gorge, which is 400m/1 300ft long, 80m /260ft deep and only 80cm/31.5inft wide in some places. Footbridges run past waterfalls and beneath wedged rocks.

Lamprechtshöhle   Kids
8km/5mi beyond Lofer. 🌀*Dress warmly as the cave is only about 5–7°C/41–45°F.* *Guided tours (45min) year-round Fri–Wed 9am–6pm, Thu 9am–5pm.* ⊛*€3.40.* ☎*0 65 82/83 43.*
The Lamprechtshöhle is one of Europe's most extensive underground cave networks extending for some 51km/32mi. Tours cover 700m/765yd and end at a viewing platform, from which visitors can peer down into the depths of a giant cave.

▷ *1km/.6mi after the Lamprechtshöhle, turn left for the Seisenberg gorge.*

Seisenbergklamm
🕐 *May–Oct, daily 9.30am–6.30pm.* ⊛*€2.80.* ☎*0 65 82/8 35 24.*
Steps, footbridges and trails give access to the Weissbach as it roars through this narrow gorge, about 600m/656yd long and up to 50m/164ft deep. Highlights are the tortured rock formations of the dark **Dunkelklamm**. Beyond here, a trail climbs through the forest along the Weissbach for 30min to Gasthof Lohfeyer, situated in Alpine pastures.

▷ *From the town of Weissbach, the road runs through a steep, long canyon and eventually reaches the Saalfelden basin.*

Saalfelden
This market town, with 12 centuries of history, has a historical town center and rich and varied scenery. In winter, Saalfelden is particularly favored by cross-country skiers who have 80km/50mi of ski tracks to play with. Towering above the resort are the imposing rock faces of the Steinernes Meer.

▷ *Continue to Zell am See.*

Zell am See★   🕭 *See ZELL AM SEE*

SAALBACH HINTERGLEMM★★

SALZBURG
POPULATION 2 700 – ALT 1 003M/3 291FT

Together with neighboring Hinterglemm, Saalbach is one of the largest winter sports resorts in Austria. Its main attraction lies in its wooded rural setting and the harmonious contours of its broad, gently falling slopes. In winter, its tougher runs attract world championship-level downhill races. Summers are relaxing here and great for hikers who have more than 400km/248.5mi of trail to choose from, including the Pinzgau path and the hike to the Tristkogel and Torsee Lake.

- **Information:** Glemmtaler Landstraße 550, Saalbach. ☎0 65 41/68 00. www.saalbach.at.
- ▶ **Orient Yourself:** The resort is in western Austria, about 18km/11mi northwest of Zell am See.
- **Don't Miss:** A trip up Schattberg-Ost.
- **Organizing Your Time:** Skiing or hiking here could fill a week but a day will suffice to explore the two mountains by cable-car.
- **Also See:** ZELL AM SEE, GROSSGLOCKNER-HOCHALPENSTRASSE.

Visit

Ski slopes

Saalbach's ski slopes extend between 900m/2 950ft and 2 100m/6 890ft and offer good snow conditions from Christmas to April. Some 55 ski-lifts open up 200km/124mi of pistes for skiers of all levels. Experienced skiers will enjoy the slopes of the Zwölferkogel and the northern downhill section of the Schattberg-Ost. A relaxing 8km/5mi run links the latter with Vorderglemm. The second run on the Bernkogel is recommended for beginners. Some pistes are reserved for snowboarders.

Cross-country skiers will find only 18km/11mi of track between Vorderglemm and Saalbach and above Hinterglemm.

Saalbach Hinterglemm

Viewpoints

Schattberg-Ost★★

Alt 2 020m/6 627ft.
Cable-car from Saalbach. ⊙*Jul–late Sept, daily 9am–11.45am, 1am–4.15pm; early Dec–mid-Apr, daily 8.30am–4pm.* ⊛*€15.40 round trip (summer), €37.50 one-day area ski pass.* ☎*0 65 41/6 27 10.*
From the top you'll have an **overall view** of the Glemmtal Valley and its ski area with the Loferer and Leoganger Steinberge and the Hohe Tauern in the distance.

Zwölferkogel★

Alt 1 984m/6 509ft. Cable-car from Hin-terglemm. ⊙*late May–late Oct, daily 9am–11.45am, 1pm–4.15pm; Dec–mid-Apr daily 8.30am–4.15pm.* ⊛*€15.40 round trip (summer),* ⊛*€37.50 one-day area ski pass.* ☎*0 65 41/6 32 10.*
Views from here stretch over the entire area around Hinterglemm and are domi-nated by the Hohe Penhab and by the Schattberg-West.

SALZACHTAL★

SALZBURG

The Alpine valley of Salzach is an artery of the province of Salzburg, whose hooked shape conforms with the bent course of the gushing Salzach River. Strung out between the Krimml waterfalls and Salzburg is a series of basins called the Pinzgau, the Pongau, the Tennengau and the Flachgau. Until the coming of the railway, each of these isolated sections of the valley tended to lead its own life, quite separate from that of its neighbors.

🅑 **Information:** www.salzburgerland.com.
▶ **Orient Yourself:** The valley extends south of Salzburg in western Austria.
⊛ **Don't Miss:** Eisriesenwelt, Gollinger Wasserfall, Salzburger Salzwelten.
⊙ **Organizing Your Time:** This route can be done as a day trip from Salzburg, although if you stop at every site, you'll probably need two days.
Kids Especially for Kids: Eisriesenwelt, Erlebnisburg Hohenwerfen, Salzwelten Salzburg.
⚑ **Also See:** SALZBURG, RADSTADT, ZELL AM SEE.

Driving Tours

1 Hochkönig and Wagrainer Höhe Tour

70km/44mi

⊛*The mountain section between Dienten and Mühlbach has many bends and is usually blocked by snow in winter.*

▶ *Leave industrial-flavored Lend on the minor road to Dienten and cross the Salzach.*

View of the valley with the Hochkönig montains near Dienten

The church at **Dienten** soon emerges against the Hochkönig crests whose vertical white cliffs are particularly impressive in the evening sun. The road reaches its highest point at the Dientener Sattel (1 370m/4 493ft) at the foot of the **Hochkönig**.

Beyond here, it still has several steep sections, including the sharp descent into **Mühlbach**, a center for mountain walking.

▶ *Take road no. 311 south to St. Johann im Pongau.*

St. Johann im Pongau is recognisable by its trademark twin-towered church, a neo-Gothic confection from the late 19C. Between here and the Enns Valley, the road traverses some lovely countryside.

Wagrain★

At an altitude of 800m/2625ft Wagrain has been developed into a winter resort and is part of the Ski Alliance that extends between Tennengebirge and Radstädter Tauern.

There is a museum devoted to Joseph Mohr who penned the words of the well-known Christmas song *Silent Night*.

Radstadt ♿ *See RADSTADT*

②From Lend to Salzburg
89km/55mi

The Salzach Valley, closely hemmed in as far as Lend (♿ *See Driving Tour* ①

Liechtenstein gorge

above), opens out north of Schwarzach to form the Pongau basin.

▷ *Turn right off road 311 to St. Johann im Pongau, and follow the signposts to "Liechtensteinklamm."*

Liechtensteinklamm★
Allow 1hr round trip walk. 🕐*mid-May–Sept, daily 9am–6pm, Oct, daily 9am–4pm.* ⊕*€3.50.* ☎*0 64 12/60 36.*
Sheer—at times overhanging—rock walls and the varied and unusual formations wrought by water billowing over the shiny, white-streaked rock contribute to the charm of the gorge. At the end of the walkways you'll be rewarded by the sight of a majestic **waterfall**★.

▷ *Return to road no. 311 and go north toward Salzburg.*

Bischofshofen
The largest town in the Pongau occupies a fine **setting**★, with the Tennengebirge to the north and the Hochkönig to the west.
A Celtic settlement stood on the sight of Bischofshofen and was the center of a thriving copper mining industry. Salt, another important commodity, was also mined here. Bischofshofen is well-known to ski jumping fans as the fourth and final venue of the world-famous Vierschanzentournee. Competitions are held annually on January 6.

Pfarrkirche
This church is the lowest of three built on a slope and linked by a narrow road, thus forming a typical example of a "family group" of churches. The present building dates to 1450 and was commissioned by the bishop of Chiemsee, who is buried in a marble tomb in the north transept. A copy of the **Rupertuskreuz**, a processional cross, a simple gilded cross encrusted with precious stones, that is Aus-

tria's oldest religious work of art (c. 700), is on display as well. The original is in the cathedral museum at Salzburg.

▷ *Carry on toward Salzburg. After Imlau, the fortress of Hohenwerfen comes into view. Before reaching the fortress, turn right in Werfen for the Eisriesenwelt caves.*

Eisriesenwelt★★
👉*See EISRIESENWELT.*

▷ *Return to road no. 159.*

Festung Hohenwerfen★ 〔Kids〕
Allow 3hr. 👉*Interior by guided tour only (1hr). The castle entrance is a 15min uphill walk from the parking lot.* 🕐*Mar–Apr, Oct, Tue–Sun 9.30am–4pm; May, Jun, Sept, daily 9am–5pm; Jul and Aug until*

6pm. ☜€10; children €5.50. ☎0 64 68/76 03. www.salzburg-burgen.at. ☜ Guided tours available.

The fortress dates back to the 11C but was extended to its present form in the 16C and 17C by the archbishops of Salzburg, who used it as a military base, residence, hunting lodge, and prison. Tours take in the chapel, the torture chamber and the armory. There is also a museum of falconry and a birds-of-prey trail in the front castle. The birds kept here—long-legged buzzards, white-tailed eagles, and red kites—perform in **flight displays**★ daily at 11am and 3pm.

▷ *The road continues through the impressive Werfen-Golling section of the valley. Before reaching the tunnel at Lueg pass, turn right to the Salzach gorge.*

Salzachklamm (Salzachöfen)

This gorge is one of three impressive natural features close to the pass, along with the Lammeröfen gorge and Gollinger waterfall. From the Gasthof Pass-Lueg Höhe, a steep path *(45min round trip)*, slippery in rainy weather, leads to a jumble of rocks forming a natural bridge over the Salzach.

▷ *About 2km/1.2mi beyond the tunnel at Lueg pass, turn right toward Abtenau/Lammertal for the Lammeröfen gorge. Detour of 14km/8.7mi.*

Lammeröfen

After the entrance to Oberscheffau, 7km/4.3mi beyond the junction, park next to Lammerklause guesthouse. The walk (1hr round trip) begins after the bus stop. ☽May–Oct, daily 9am–6pm. ☜€2.50. ☎0 62 44/84 42. www.lammerklamm.at.

After about 20min walk through the relatively wide gorge, the trail reaches the ticket booth. From here there is a shorter but more rewarding walk up concrete steps to a viewpoint beneath a natural rock vault, where a narrow cleft in the rock lets light down into the gorge below.

▷ *Take road B 162 to Golling. Turn left in front of the Zur Goldenen Traube inn and follow the signposts to "Wasserfall."*

Gollinger Wasserfall★★

30min round trip walk to the foot of the waterfall, 1hr 30min to the top; ☜€2.

The Golling Falls tumble down 75m/246ft from the Hoher Göll (2 522m/ 8 277ft) and can be more or less spectacular depending on the time of year and the amount of water. Park at the Torrener Hof inn, then follow the road for a short stretch in the direction of Kuchl and pick up the trail to the fall *(☜follow the red/white markings)* leading through forest. From the bridge and ticket booth, the path climbs gently up from the bottom of the cascade to where the water emerges.

▷ *Return to Golling and carry on to Hallein and from there to the Salzwelten Salzburg in Bad Dürrnberg.*

En route to the salt mine, you'll pass a pilgrimage church and the **Keltendorf am Dürrnberg**, a reconstruction of a Celtic village.

Salzwelten Salzburg★ [Kids]

Allow about 2.5hr. ☺Not suitable for children under 4 years. ☜Guided tour (70min) Apr–Oct, daily 9am–5pm; Nov–Mar, daily 11am–3pm. ☜€16.50, ticket includes admission to Keltendorf. ☎0 61 32/2 00 24 00. www.salzwelten.at.

Salt harvested in the Dürrnberg mountain brought wealth to the archbishops of Salzburg and production continued until 1989. Now a small section of the underground warren of tunnels has been developed as a show-mine where guides dressed as Archbishop Wolf Dietrich von Raitenau lead entertaining tours. The visit ends with a romantic raft trip across the floodlit underground salt lake.

▷ *Continue to Salzburg.*

Salzburg★★★ ☝See SALZBURG.

SALZATAL★★
STEIERMARK

The Salza River, a tributary of the upper Enns, has carved out a 70km/43.5mi-long remote and romantic valley. It is almost completely uninhabited, except for the villages of Wildalpen and Greith, and offers nature lovers plenty of opportunities for delightful expeditions through the forest. The river's sprightly rapids and churning pool draw scores of white-water enthusiasts.

- **Information:** Wildalpen 91, Wildalpen. ☎0 36 36/3 41. www.wildalpen.at.
- ▶ **Orient Yourself:** The valley is in central Austria, about 100km/62mi northwest of Graz.
- ⏱ **Organizing Your Time:** Half a day should be plenty of time.
- 🕯 **Also See:** MARIAZELL

Driving Tour

Salzatal Tour
80km/50mi

Hieflau
Beside the River Enns it was once the center of the regions metal industry

- ▶ *Leave Hieflau on the route north along the River Enns*

Between Hieflau and Grossreifling the route follows the Enns, which is dammed in several places. Between Grossreifling and Palfau the road follows a winding, uphill course to Wildalpen.

Wildalpen
Tiny Wildalpen has an attractive setting and is known as a starting point for white-water sports on the Salza. The interesting **Heimat-, Pfarr- und Wasserleitungsmuseum**★ (*May–Oct 26, Mon–Fri 10am–noon, 1pm–3pm, Sun 10am–noon; €2; ☎03636/45 10*) gives a visual account of the building of the pipeline that supplies Vienna with drinking water. The **Pfarrkirche St. Barbara** with its scalloped tower roof has fine frescoes and furnishings.

- ▶ *Turn right Immediately after the Postbus stop (at kilometer stone 31.6).*

Brunn
From the Brunn wayside shrine, only a few yards from the road, there is a **view**★

down into the bottom of the Brunntal, in the heart of the Hochschwab. There is also a splendid **view**★★ along the north slope of the massif.

The road winds its way through **Prescenyklause** with its old-fashioned logging dam, then on to **Weichselboden**, dominated by its Baroque parish church before climbing steadily as far as Greith. Beyond, the landscape becomes gradually less mountainous and the road begins its descent to Gusswerk and then on to **Mariazell** (*🕯see MARIAZELL*).

Canoeing in River Salza

© Österreich Werbung / H.Wiesenhofer

SALZBURG★★★

POPULATION 150 300 – ALT 424M/1 391FT
LOCAL MAPS UNDER SALZACHTAL AND SALZKAMMERGUT

Salzburg, Mozart's birthplace, is a delight from the moment you spot the silhouette of the Hohensalzburg fortress floating above roofs and the meandering Salzach River. Its picturesque streets with their wrought-iron signs, its spacious squares with sculptured fountains, and the noble architecture of its buildings leave memories that linger for years. Every summer, scores of music lovers descend for the famous **Salzburg Festival**, one of the most prestigious concert series in the world. In 1997, Salzburg's Old Town was ranked a World Heritage Site by UNESCO.

🛈 **Information:** Auerspergstraße 6. ☎0 6 62/88 98 70. www.salzburginfo.at.

▶ **Orient Yourself:** Salzburg is on Austria's western edge, right on the German border.

🅿 **Parking:** Park & Ride Süd (Alpenstraße), Altstadt-Garage (Mönchsberg), Bahnhof-Garage (Südtiroler Platz), Mirabell-Garage (Mirabellplatz); Airportcenter (Innsbrucker Bundesstraße), Parkgarage Auersperg (Auerspergstraße), Parkgarage Linzer Gasse (Glockengasse), Raiffeisen-Garage (Schwarzstraße). Public parking lots on Akademiestraße, Gebirgsjägerplatz, Hellbrunn, Mülln, Petersbrunnstraße, Salzburg Airport.

😊 **Don't Miss:** Hohensalzburg, Residenz, Stiftskirche St. Peter, Mozart's Geburtshaus.

🕐 **Organizing Your Time:** Allow at least two days for a visit, three if taking in Hellbrunn Palace or other outlying attractions.

Kids **Especially for Kids:** Haus der Natur, Stiegl's Brauwelt, Schloss Hellbrunn, Zoo Salzburg.

ﾱ **Also See:** SALZKAMMERGUT.

A Bit of History

The heritage of the prince-archbishops – The See of Salzburg was founded shortly before 700 by St. Rupert and was raised in the following century to an archbishopric. In the 13C the bishops were given the title of Princes of the Holy Roman Empire. Their power extended as far as Italy, while their coffers were filled to bulging with revenue from the Salzkammergut salt mines. Three of these rulers showed a taste for building and in Just over half a century converted the little medieval town into a grand residence in the Italian style.

Wolf Dietrich von Raitenau was elected archbishop in 1587. He was a typical representative of the Renaissance: brought up in Rome and closely connected with the Medicis, he longed to make Salzburg the Rome of the North. After a fire destroyed the central cathedral quarter, he hired the Italian archi-

tect Scamozzi to build a new house of worship even larger than St. Peter's in Rome. Raitenau had 15 children with Salome Art, a great beauty for whom he built Schloss Mirabell. After losing a conflict with the dukes of Bavaria over the salt trade, he was imprisoned in 1612 in Hohensalzburg Castle where he died after five years of captivity. His only completed building project was his own mausoleum in St. Sebastian cemetery. Raitenau's successor, **Markus Sittikus**, downscaled the cathedral and entrusted the work to another Italian architect, Santino Solari. The mansion of Heilbrunn to the south of Salzburg is another of his architectural legacies.

It fell to **Paris Lodron** to complete the work begun by his predecessors, including the cathedral which was solemnly consecrated in 1628. Lodron also finished the Residence and opened new streets in the town, creating the face of Salzburg for generations to come.

Address Book

PRACTICAL INFORMATION

VISITOR INFORMATION

Salzburg Information *Auersperg-straße 7,* ☎*06 62/88 98 70.*
Mozartplatz, *Mozartplatz 5,* ☎*06 62/88 98 73 30.*
Hauptbahnhof (Main station), *Platform 2a,* ☎*06 62/88 98 73 40.*
Salzburg Centre, *Münchner Bundesstraße 1,* ☎*06 62/88 98 73 50.*
Salzburg South, Park & Ride Car Park, Alpensiedlung-Süd, *Alpenstraße,* ☎*06 62/88 98 73 60.*
Airport Arrivals Hall, ☎*06 62/85 12 11 or 85 20 91 or 8 58 09 99.*
Open Jun–Sept:
Salzburg North, *Kasern autobahn service station,* ☎*06 62/88 98 73 70.*

SALZBURG CARD

This ticket, valid for 24, 48 or 72hr, gives free travel on nearly all public transport in the city, as well as free entrance to most sights in and around Salzburg. From May–Sept, the cost is €21/29/34 for 24/48/72 hours, respectively. From Nov–Apr, prices change to €21/32/37; discounts for children. Available at tourist offices, travel agencies and hotels. *www.salzburg.info.*

SALZBURGERLAND CARD

If you're spending most of your time in Salzburg province and only want to visit the city for one day, this discount may be a better alternative. It is good for free or discounted admission to 190 regional attractions and integrates a 24hr Salzburg Card. It is available from May–Oct and is valid for either six days (€39) or 12 days (€49); discounts for children. Available at tourist offices, hotels, and even some gas stations. *www.salzburgerlandcard.com.*

CITY TOURS AND GUIDED TOURS

Auf den Spuren Mozarts (In Mozart's Footsteps) – 1hr 30min coach tour and 1hr in Mozart's house) – Departures daily at 9.30am, 11am, noon, 2pm and 4pm, or by request.
Panorama City Tour (1hr) – Departures daily at 10am, 11am, noon, 1pm, 3pm, 4pm and 5pm, or by request.

Information and reservations from Salzburg Panorama Tours, *Schran-nengasse 2,* ☎*06 62/88 32 11 0, www. panoramatours.at.*
Mozart City Tour (2hr) – Departures daily at 9.30am, 11am and 2pm.
Salzburg-Informativ (1hr) – Departures daily at 10am, noon, 3pm, 4pm and 5pm.
Salzburg-Exklusiv with bus trip, walk and wine-tasting (4hr) – 15 May–15 Sept daily at 2pm.
Information and reservations from Salzburg Sightseeing Tours, *Mirabellplatz 2,* ☎*06 62/88 16 16.*

PUBLIC TRANSPORT

Information and tickets for the city bus network can be obtained from the ticket offices of the Salzburg public transport authorities *(Griesgasse 21,* ☎*06 62/44 80 62 62); Lokalbahnhof (at the Hauptbahnhof,* ☎*06 62/44 80 61 66;) Alpenstraße 91 (*☎*06 62/44 80 62 63).* Tickets can also be bought from bus drivers, in tobacconists (Trafiken) and from ticket machines at the bus stop (tickets for a single trip should be bought in advance in blocks of five, before starting on a journey, as a supplement is charged when they are bought separately from the bus driver or a ticket machine). Tickets must be date-stamped as soon as you get on the bus.
The Salzburg transport authorities also offer transferable daily, weekly, monthly (valid from time of first use) and family-day-trip travel cards for the city area, and a 24hr ticket (valid for the whole transport network, only available in blocks of five), with which you can make as many journeys as you like. These are available from tobacconists and ticket offices (daily, weekly and monthly tickets also from ticket machines).

POST OFFICES

Hauptpostamt (Main post office): *Residenzplatz 9,* open Mon–Fri 7am–7pm, Sat 8am–10am.
Postschalter im Hauptbahnhof (counter at the main station): *Südtiroler-platz 1,* open daily 6am–11pm.

For coin ranges, see the Legend on the cover flap.

WHERE TO STAY

Alstadthotel Wolf-Dietrich, *Wolf-Dietrich Strasse 7, ☎0662/87 12 75, www.salzburg-hotel.at. 40 rooms. Restaurant*. Originally two town houses, this hotel has kept to the classical décor that befits the era the houses were built in. It has elegant, comfortable rooms and an indoor swimming pool. The hotel has Austria's first licensed organic restaurant where you have a choice of vegetarian dishes.

Arthotel Blaue Gans, *Getreidegasse 41, ☎0662/8 42 49 10, www.blauegans.at. 40 rooms.* With a 700-year-old tradition, this is the oldest inn in Salzburg. New renovation blends very well with the old. It is a true art hotel with modern art on display.

Goldener Hirsch, *Getreidegasse 37, ☎0662/8 08 40, www.luxurycollection.com. 69 rooms. Restaurant*. This hotel (1407) oozes luxury and is an encyclopaedia of central European cultural influences. Rooms are richly decorated in traditional styles.

WHERE TO EAT

Brandstätter – *Salzburg-Liefering, Münchner Bundesstraße 69, ☎06 62/ 43 45 35. www.hotel-brandstaetter.com.* Michelin-starred restaurant in the hotel of the same name; rooms range from the rustic Schankstube to the elegant Zirbelstube. Some of the best cooking in town.

K+K Restaurant am Waagplatz – *Waagplatz 2, ☎06 62/84 21 56.* This restaurant's unique selling point is as "Salzburg's first eatery": Guests are fed and entertained in medieval style in a 900-year-old vaulted cellar (starts at 8pm; costs c. €55 for a 4-course meal, welcome drink, and program of musical entertainment; booking recommended). There is also a more "traditional" restaurant spread over four floors.

Alt Salzburg – *Bürgerspitalgasse 2, ☎06 62/84 14 76.* Cozy, tastefully decorated rooms, in which local products cooked in a truly authentic Austrian fashion are served.

Bei Bruno – *Makartplatz 4, ☎06 62/87 84 17.* Separately run, elegant restaurant belonging to a luxury hotel with excellent food.

Blaue Gans – *Getreidegasse 41–43, ☎06 62/84 24 91 0.* Old vaulted premises and traditional Austrian cooking using authentic old recipes.

Eulenspiegel – *Hagenauerplatz 2, ☎06 62/84 31 80.* Self-declared as "Austria's most original restaurant" with the Eule bar on the ground floor and its small dining rooms full of nooks and crannies over several floors. For a very special experience, try the **Mozart Dinner Concert**, on offer all year round in the Baroque room of the Stiftskeller St. Peter (*see below*): 3-course menu by candlelight, accompanied by works of Mozart (performed by musicians in historical costumes). Details of dates: *☎06 62/82 86 95 0 or 84 84 81;* booking recommended.

Krimpelstätter – *Müllner Hauptstraße 1, ☎06 62/43 22 74.* Traditional inn with a large beer garden.

Sternbräu – *Griesgasse 23/Getreidegasse 34, ☎06 62/84 21 40.* 14 different dining rooms, fine arcaded courtyard. Program of evening entertainment from May–Oct.

Stadtkrug – *Linzer Gasse 20, ☎06 62/87 35 45.* Small, intimate and stylish local restaurant with an extensive wine list. The ideal venue for a candle-lit dinner!

Alter Fuchs – *Linzer Gasse 47–49, ☎06 62/88 22 00.* Informal atmosphere. Daily menus are good value for money.

Pitter Keller – *Auerspergstraße 23, ☎06 62/88 05 52.* Earthy beer cellar with local food.

Stiftskeller St. Peter, *St. Peter Bezirk I/4, ☎06 62/84 12 68 0.* With its tradition dating back to 803, it offers a pleasant setting (several banqueting rooms and dining rooms) for eating out in style.

CAFÉS AND BARS

Tomaselli – *Alter Markt 9.* Classic coffee house, where visitors never outstay their welcome.

Fürst – *Brodgasse 13.* Parent branch of the Konditorei-Confiserie, where the original Salzburger Mozartkugeln are made.

Bazar – *Schwarzstraße 3*. Stylish café with terrace overlooking the Salzach.

Café-Restaurant Winkler – *Mönchsberg 32*. Marvelous views of the city.

Augustiner-Bräu – *Augustinergasse 4*. Abbey brewery since 1621. Beer served in stone tankards. Enormous halls with a large, shady beer garden.

Die Weisse – *Rupertgasse 10*. Rustic inn with its own brewery, serving Weissbier made on the premises.

Zum fidelen Affen – *Priesterhausgasse 8*. Beer and wine cellar with warm wooden paneling.

Zebra – *Imbergstraße 11*. Modern cocktail bar. Italian antipasti available.

Daimler's – *Giselakai 17*. Small restaurant and friendly bar on two floors.

Saitensprung – *Steingasse 11*. Cocktails and wines in a homely brick-vaulted room; open into the early hours.

Zwettler's – *Kaigasse 3*. Rustic, relaxed atmosphere for a light meal or a drink.

Salzburger Altstadtkeller – *Rudolfkai 26*. Live music every day at the "musical landlord's."

SHOPPING

The main shopping areas include the Altstadt (Old Town), left and right of the Salzach, the areas around the Getreidegasse, the area around the Festspielhäuser, the Mozartplatz, the Kaigasse, the Alter Markt, the Linzer Gasse, the Makartplatz, and the Mirabellplatz.

MARKETS

Around the Andräkirche: Schrannenmarkt (fresh food, vegetables, flowers), *Thu 6am–1pm*.
Universitätsplatz and Wiener-Philharmoniker-Gasse: Vegetable market, *Mon–Fri 6am–7pm, Sat 6am–1pm*.

SOUVENIRS

Craft goods and traditional costume (Trachten): Salzburger Heimatwerk, *Residenzplatz 9*; wood carvings, busts of Mozart: Kopfberger, *Judengasse 14*; hand-crafted wax goods, Lebkuchen specialties: Nagy Johann & Söhne, *Linzergasse 32*; Mozart souvenirs: *Mozartland, Getreidegasse 10*; souvenir shop in Mozarts Geburtshaus, *Getreidegasse 9*; Mozartkugeln: Café-Konditorei

Café Tomaselli

Fürst (inventors of the original recipe), *Brodgasse 13, Sigmund-Haffner-Gasse* and *Mirabellplatz 5*; Schatz-Konditorei, *Getreidegasse 3*.

ENTERTAINMENT

Grosses and **Kleines Festspielhaus**, *Hofstallgasse 1*, ☎06 62/8 04 50. Theater and musicals, concerts.

Landestheater, *Schwarzstraße 22*, ☎06 62/8 71 51 20. Theater, musicals and dance.

Kleines Theater, *Schallmoser Hauptstraße 50*, ☎06 62/87 21 54. Theater and cabaret.

Salzburger Marionettentheater, *Schwarzstraße 24*, ☎06 62/87 24 06. Mozart operas feature highly on the program of this world-famous marionette theater, which also includes master works by Rossini, Offenbach, Strauss, and Tchaikovsky, on recordings by prestigious orchestras. The audience in the old Hotel Mirabell with its Rococo décor is transported into another world of magic and fantasy.

Kammerspiele, *Schwarzstraße 24*, ☎06 62/87 15 12. Youth theater, cabaret.

SZENE-Salzburg, *Anton-Neumayr-Platz 2*, ☎06 62/84 34 48. Theater, music, and dance.

Rockhouse Salzburg, *Schallmoser Hauptstraße 46*, ☎06 62/88 49 14. Jazz, folk, blues, reggae, rock music concerts.

Kulturzentrum Nonntal, *Mühlbacherhofweg 5*, ☎06 62/84 87 84 0. Live concerts and other events.

©Bryan Reinhart/Tourismus Salzburg GmbH

Magic Flute, Salzburg Festival

CINEMAS
Central Kino, *Linzer Gasse 17–19*, ☎06 62/87 22 82.
Elmo-Kino-Center, *St.-Julien-Straße 3–5*, ☎06 62/87 23 73.
Mozartkino, *Kaigasse 33*, ☎06 62/84 22 22.
Salzburger Filmkulturzentrum, Das Kino, *Giselakai 11*, ☎06 62/87 31 00.

DATES FOR YOUR DIARY

Mozartwoche: *Second-half of Jan*. Solo recitals, chamber, choral and orchestral concerts.

Osterfestspiele: *Sat before Palm Sun–Easter Mon*. Easter music festival with opera and concerts.

Salzburger Pfingstfestspiele (specializing in Baroque music): *Sat before Whit weekend until Whit Mon*. Whitsun music festival with opera and concerts.

Salzburger Festspiele: *End Jul–end Aug*. Salzburg Festival with opera, concerts, theater, literature and poetry readings, Lieder evenings.

SommerSzene: *Jul*. Festival of alternative art: Theater, dance, exhibitions.

Kulturtage: *Mid–end Oct*. Cultural festival with opera and concerts.

Internationaler Salzburger Jazz-Herbst: *Early Nov*. Autumn jazz festival with jazz, spirituals and Gospel music.

Weihnachtsmärkte (Christmas markets): *Late Nov–24 Dec*. Mirabellplatz and Domplatz and in the castle courtyard of Hohensalzburg (*every weekend in Advent*).

Wolfgang Amadeus Mozart (1756–1791)

Mozart was born in Salzburg on January 27, 1756 and died December 5, 1791.

A child prodigy

Leopold Mozart, a talented composer and violinist in the service of the archbishop of Salzburg, recognized early on the exceptional gifts of his son, Wolfgang, and his older daughter, Nannerl. Young Wolfgang had a remarkable musical memory and sophisticated ear, had started composing by the age of five, and was a keyboard virtuoso by the age of six. He had also started learning the harpsichord at age four. Leopold gave his son a serious musical education and together they undertook a memorable four-year tour of Europe, getting enthusiastic receptions in Munich, Vienna, Augsburg, Frankfurt, Paris, London and The Hague. At Schönbrunn, Empress Maria Theresa herself embraced the talents of young Wolfgang. Mozart remained in Salzburg for three years after the family's return in 1766. In 1772,

Signature of Wolfgang Amadeus Mozart

Mozart was made concertmaster of the court orchestra of the Salzburg prince-archbishop.

First disappointment

Until 1777, Mozart spent long periods in Salzburg. His employer, Archbishop Hieronymus Colloredo, did not approve of his many journeys abroad and relations were consequently rather strained. After a major quarrel with the prince-archbishop in 1777 Mozart resigned his post and left for Paris where he came under the influence of opera reformer, **Christoph Willibald Gluck**. During the following years he produced much religious music, of which the *Coronation Mass* is a supreme example, and symphonic and lyrical pieces such as *Idomeneo*, an opera reflecting the influence of the French School. In 1781, after a further heated altercation with the prince-archbishop, the breach was complete. Mozart left Salzburg for Vienna.

Independence in Vienna

Arriving in Vienna, the 26-year-old Mozart had only a limited means of support. He married Constanze Weber the same year and got initiated into the ideals of Freemasonry. Discovery of Handel's oratorios and of further works by Bach, together with the influence of his friend and mentor, Haydn, contributed to the development of his mature style. The public adulation occasioned by works such as *The Abduction from the Seraglio* of 1781 and the Mass in C Minor of 1783 was not repeated, at least in Vienna, where the public even failed to appreciate *The Marriage of Figaro* (1786) and *Don Giovanni* (1787). A somber period began.

The final years (1788–91)

Mozart's career was to end in poverty and destitution. Though nominated "Composer to the Imperial Chamber" by Joseph II, he never received a commission. His final operas, *Così fan Tutte* (1790) and *La Clemenza di Tito* (1791) met with a cool reception, barely mitigated by the success of *The Magic Flute* (late 1791). The great composer was to die before his time, alone and haunted by the specter of his own death.

On 6 December 1791 the paupers' hearse carried Mozart's corpse to a communal grave in St. Mark's Cemetery in Vienna. His remains have never been identified.

Wolfgang Amadeus Mozart

Mozart's musical legacy

Mozart's astonishing output was equaled only by the ease with which he mastered every form of musical expression. His style has a charm that makes him a favorite with a wide public and is appreciated even by the unpracticed ear. Pleasant and sparkling motifs ripple beneath a rhythmic counterpoint of sprightly liveliness.

But spontaneity and brio need not mean lack of depth. His works are characterized by an exquisitely pure melodic line, sometimes tinged with melancholy. Toward the end of his life this vague sadness turned into despair, forcefully expressed in the 40th Symphony in G minor, *Don Giovanni*, the late string quartets, the "tragic" quintet in G major (K 516) and the *Requiem* (K 626), composed shortly before Mozart's own death (and not completed). Composer Frédéric Chopin (1810–1849) was so affected by this great choral work that he requested it be played at his own funeral. These late works reflect the emotional frustration of Mozart's life and his struggle against poverty and illness.

Salzburg Festival

Guided tour (45 min) Jan–Aug, daily 9.30am, Sept 2pm, 3pm. €5. Meet at the entrance to the Kleines Festspielhaus. 06 62/84 90 97.

Many years passed before his native city acknowledged Mozart's outstanding place in musical history. His biography was written in 1828 by Constanze's second husband, Georges Nicolas de Nissen. In 1842 Salzburg put up a statue to Mozart and later founded a musical academy named the **Mozarteum**. Finally, in 1917, the poet Hugo von Hoffmansthal, the composer Richard Strauss, and the producer Max Reinhardt conceived the idea of a Mozart Festival.

The festival was inaugurated in 1920 and is held from late July to the end of August each summer, attracting the cream of the world's musical talent. Performances take place at the great **Festival Hall** (Grosses Festspielhaus – Z), built in 1960 by the architect **Clemens Holzmeister**, the small festival hall (Kleines Festspielhaus), the old Summer Riding School (Felsenreitschule), the **Mozarteum**, the **Landestheater** (Y), the Residenzhof, and the disused salt mines on Perner Island in Hallein. Non-Mozart works are performed as well, including Hoffmannsthal's *Jedermann (Everyman)* on the cathedral forecourt.

Walking Tour

Old Town Tour★★

Domplatz (Z)

Three arches link the buildings surrounding this square, the cathedral and the Residenz, the former ecclesiastical palaces. In the center is a Virgin Mary Column.

View of the city across the Salzach River, Hohensalzburg in the background

Dom★ (Z)

Mon–Sat 6.30am–5pm, Sun 8am–5pm (summer to 7pm). ☎06 62/80 47 79 50.
The monumental Early Baroque cathedral is largely the work of Italian architect Santino Solari and was consecrated in 1628. Its west front, flanked by two towers, is of light-colored local marble and graced by numerous statues, including those of Sts Rubert, Virgil and Peter and Paul in front of the main door. The **interior** is impressive in both size and the richness of its decoration. Mozart was baptized in the Romanesque font in 1756. The tombs of the prince-archbishops and a Romanesque Crucifix may be seen in the **crypt**.

Dommuseum

Apr–early Jan, Mon–Sat 10am–5pm, Sun 1pm–6pm. €10. ☎06 62/84 41 89.
Featured here is the cathedral treasure and a fabulous *Kunst- und Wunderkammer*, a gallery of objet d'art, minerals, crafts and precious knickknacks amassed by Archbishop Guidobald von Thun. It's all presented in a similarly haphazard way as it was in the 17C. Upstairs is the usual array of religious art from the Middle Ages to the present.
Behind the cathedral, in Kapitelplatz, the **Kapitelschwemme** is a drinking trough for horses in the form of a monumental fountain. From here, a street leads up to the station of the **Festungsbahn** (*May–Aug, daily 9am–10pm; Sept–Dec, daily 9am–9pm; Jan–Apr, 9am–5pm; €9.80, includes entrance to fortress, museums and audio-guide; ☎06 62/84 26 82)*, the funicular providing access to the great Hohensalzburg fortress.

Hohensalzburg★★ (Z)

Allow about 2hr. Ascent on foot (20min) or by Festungsbahn funicular. Jul–Aug, daily 9am–7pm; Jan–Apr and Oct–Dec, daily 9.30am–5pm; May, Jun, Sept, daily 9am–6pm. €10, includes entrance to fortress, museums and audio-guide (€7 without Festungsbahn). ☎06 62/84 24 30 11. www.salzburg-burgen.at. www.hohensalzburg.com.
The former stronghold of the prince-archbishops stands on a block of Dolomite rock, about 120m/393.7ft above the Salzach. The castle was begun in 1077 by Archbishop Gebhard, frequently enlarged, and eventually remodeled into a comfortable residence with state rooms by Archbishop Leonhard von Keutschach in the 15C. The archbishops often stayed here until the end of the 15C, reinforcing it considerably by the addition of towers, bastions for cannons and barbicans and the construction of magazines and arms depots.
At the exit from the upper station of the funicular, turn left to the panoramic terrace from which stairs and a postern lead into the fortress. Go past the guided tours office and a little way downhill, bearing right along the lists and round the fortified nucleus of the inner castle until you come to a courtyard opposite the south wall of the **St. Georgskirche**. This is decorated with two beautiful marble reliefs: a group of statuary in red Salzburg marble of Archbishop Leonhard von Keutschach flanked by two priests, and above it a Crucifixion.
The door to the right of the church leads to the terrace of the **Kuenburgbastei** from where there is a good **view**★★ of the old town's domes and belfries.

State Rooms and Museums

The state rooms and museums are best explored on a 90min self-guided audio tour. From the Reck watchtower there is a **panorama**★★, which is particularly interesting toward the Tennengebirge and the Salzburg Alps (south).
The state rooms, formerly the archbishops' apartments, were fitted out by Leonhard von Keutschach, and are largely in their original state. There are walls adorned with Gothic woodcarvings, doors fitted with complicated ironwork, and coffered ceilings with gilded studs. In the Gilded Room is a monumental porcelain stove, dating from 1501, decorated with flowers and fruit, Biblical scenes and the coats of arms and portraits of sovereigns of the period.
The Hall of Justice has a coffered ceiling whose beams feature coats of arms of the provinces, dioceses or abbeys under the archbishop's jurisdiction as well as those of the dignitaries of his court.
Tickets are also valid for admission to a marionette museum, a multivision

show, and the **Rainer-Regiment-Museum** displaying weapons, uniforms and mementoes of Archduke Rainer's Infantry Regiment stationed here from 1871 to 1918.

▶ *Go back down the ramps and follow the path on the right to Nonnberg convent.*

Stift Nonnberg (Z)

This Benedictine convent was founded around 700 by St. Rupert, whose niece, St. Erentrud, was its first abbess. It is the oldest convent in the German-speaking world.

The **Stiftskirche**, enclosed by its churchyard, is in Late Gothic style and dates from the end of the 15C. The main doorway was built between 1497 and 1499; it incorporates the older Romanesque tympanum showing the Virgin Mary flanked by John the Baptist and St. Erentrud on one side and by an angel and a kneeling nun on the other. The high altar is adorned by a fine carved and gilded altarpiece. In the central section is a Virgin and Child attended by St. Rupert and St. Virgil, while the wings depict scenes from the Passion. The vast crypt contains the tomb of St. Erentrud.

In the **Johanneskapelle** there is a Gothic altarpiece of 1498, attributed to Veit Stoss, with a lively central section showing the Nativity.

▷ *Go down to the lower station of the funicular via the Festungsgasse, then into the Petersfriedhof immediately on the left.*

Petersfriedhof★★ (Z)

Cemetery: ◷*Apr–Sept, daily 6.30am–7pm; Oct–Mar, daily 6.30am–6pm.* ◌*Free admission.* Catacombs: ◷*May–Sept, Tue–Sun 10.30am–5pm, Oct–Apr Wed–Thu 10.30am–3.30, Fri–Sun 10.30am–4pm.* ◌*€1.* ☏*06 62/8 44 57 60.*

This cemetery abuts the vertical rock wall of the Mönchsberg, which is hollowed with early Christian catacombs that can be seen on a short guided tour. The cemetery itself features wrought-iron grilles under Baroque arcades enclosing the chapels where several generations of the patrician families of Salzburg lie. Famous names include Nannerl Mozart, the architect Santino Solari, and Michael Haydn. The 15C Margaretenkapelle is a delicate construction dating from the late Gothic period.

Stiftskirche St. Peter★★ (Z)

The triple-aisled Romanesque basilica was drastically remodeled in the 17C and

Stiftskirche St. Peter

18C, but the serenity and harmony of the original structure can still detected amid the Baroque décor. The best view of the interior is from the gilded **wrought-iron grille**★ separating the porch from the nave. It is an elaborate work of art made in 1768 by Philip Hinterseer. The building's architectural simplicity, heightened in effect by the white walls, emphasizes the elegance of Benedikt Zöpf's Rococo decoration, with its fine paintings and fresh pastel shades that enhance the delicate stuccowork.

The ceiling of the nave is frescoed with scenes from the life of St. Peter painted by the Augsburg artist, Johann Weiss. On each of the walls above the great arches, note, among other compositions, an Ascent to Calvary and a Raising of the Cross by Solari. Beneath the upper windows is a set of paintings by Franz X König representing *(right)* the life of St. Benedict and *(left)* the life of St. Rupert. The altarpiece on the high altar and those in the nave, with their red-marble columns, make an ensemble of great richness. Most of the altarpiece paintings are the work of Martin Johann Schmidt ("Kremser Schmidt"). Only the south aisle has chapels and also contains the tomb of St. Rupert. In the chapel furthest from the chancel there is a fine marble tomb built by Archbishop Wolf Dietrich for his father, Werner von Raitenau.

▶ *Cross the abbey courtyard, turn right into the covered passageway and go along the side of the Franziskanerkirche which is entered through the west doorway.*

Franziskanerkirche★ (Z A)
◷*Daily 6.30am–7.30pm*
The church was consecrated in 1223 but has been remodeled several times since. It offers a comparison between the Romanesque and Gothic styles.

The plain Romanesque nave, divided from the side aisles by massive pillars with capitals adorned with foliage and stylized animals, makes a striking contrast with the well-lit chancel from the final Late Gothic 15C. The star vaulting is supported by palm-shaped cylindrical columns.

The impressive high altar is the work of Johann Bernhard Fischer von Erlach (1708). The finely modeled statue of the Virgin Mary adorning the Baroque high altar was formerly part of a Gothic altarpiece made by Michael Pacher in the late 15C.

▶ *Exit through the side door and follow Franziskanergasse westward.*

Museum der Moderne (Z M¹)
Wiener-Philharmoniker-Gasse 9 and Mönchsberg 32. ♿◷*Year-round Tue, Thu–Sun 10am–6pm, Wed 10am–8pm.* ◷*24, 25 Dec.* ✎€6 Rupertinum, €8 Mönchsberg; combination ticket €12, audio-guide €2. ☎06 62/8 42 22 03 51. www.museumdermoderne.at.

Salzburg's modern art museum now occupies two spectacular locations. The original one is the **Rupertinum**, a Baroque townhouse built as a seminary by the archbishops in the 17C. It contains a fine collection of 20C art covering all major media, including painting, sculpture, graphic works and photography. The collection features works by numerous heavy hitters of the art world, including Gustav Klimt and Oskar Kokoschka as well as Austrian Expressionists Herbert Boeckl, Eduard Bäumer and Hans Fronius as well as such sculptors as Alfred Hrdlicka and Fritz Wotruba.

The museum recently expanded into a new, unapologetically modern building atop the **Mönchsberg**, easily reached by the Mönchsberglift (*see entry opposite*). The minimalist space frequently hosts temporary (often traveling) exhibits of cutting-edge contemporary art. North of Max-Reinhardt-Platz stands the massive Baroque **Kollegienkirche** (University Church), another work of Johann Bernhard Fischer von Erlach. Continue west past the Grosses Festspielhaus (Festival Hall).

From Herbert-von-Karajan-Platz (36) there is a tunnel (the Siegmundstor), about 135m/147.6yd long, which was made in 1767 to go under the Mönchsberg hill. Look back for a fine view of the Hohensalzburg Fortress and the Stiftskirche St. Peter.

Pferdeschwemme (Y B)

This vast horse trough was built about 1700 and was exclusively used by the horses in the archbishops' stables. It is adorned with a sculptured group, the *Horsebreaker* by Mandl, and murals depicting fiery steeds.

▷ *Take Bürgerspittalgasse to Getreidegasse and turn left. Walk a little way down Gstättengasse as far as the entrance for the lift to the Mönchsberg.*

Mönchsberg★★ (Z)

Lift daily 9am–11pm (7pm Mon). €2.90 round trip. 06 62/44 80 62 85. From the Gstättengasse (X 12), a lift goes up to a terrace just below the Café Winkler, from which there is a fine general **view**★★ of the city with modern Salzburg along the right bank of the Salzach and the old town between the river and the Hohensalzburg Fortress. To the south are the Tennen- and Hagengebirge, the Untersberg and the Salzburg Alps; eastward the Kapuzinerberg and the Gaisberg.

▷ *Continue along Gstättengasse.*

Haus der Natur★★ (Y M²) Kids

Budget at least 2hr. Daily 9am–5pm. €4.50; children €2.50. Guided tours available. *06 62/8 42 65 30. www.hausdernatur.at.*

This is a vast and well-presented natural history museum with many lively and engaging displays. Particularly interesting sections are those on dinosaurs, the world of outer space with its diorama depicting the first moon landing, human and animal characters in myth and fable, giant rock crystals and the aquarium and reptile house.

▷ *Return to Getreidegasse.*

Getreidegasse★ (Y)

This is one of the main streets of old Salzburg. Like the rest of the Old Town, which, being crowded between the Mönchsberg and the Salzach, could expand only vertically, it is narrow and lined with five- and six-story houses. A lively shopping street, Getreidegasse is adorned with many wrought-iron signs which provide a picturesque touch, while the houses with their carved window frames lend the street a certain elegance.

Mozarts Geburtshaus (Y D)

Getreidegasse 9. Jul–Aug, daily 9am–7pm; Jan–Jun, Sept–Dec, daily 9am–6pm. €6, combination ticket with Mozart Wohnhaus €9.50. 06 62/84 43 13. www.mozarteum.at.

The Mozart family lived on the third floor of this building from 1747 to 1773. It was here where Wolfgang was born on January 27, 1756 and where he composed many of his early works. In late 2005, the hallowed rooms were turned into a light, sound and design installation by the American set designer and director Robert Wilson. It incorporates instruments played by Mozart, including his harpsichord, his piano and the violin he played as a child, as well as musical manuscripts, a selection of portraits and letters and furniture and everyday objects from the times of Mozart.

Continue along Getreidegasse past the town hall (Rathaus, R) on the left and on the right the Alter Markt (Old Market Square), with a fountain to St. Florian and a curious **Hofapotheke** (YZ N), a chemist's shop with a lavish Rococo interior.

▶ *Cross Alter Markt to Judengasse.*

Judengasse (YZ)

This street cuts through the former Jewish Ghetto. It is narrow and picturesque and, like the Getreidegasse, adorned with wrought-iron signs. At no. 4, note a sculptured group in stone representing the Virgin of Maria Plain

▶ *Pass through the Waagplatz to Mozartplatz, then continue to Residenzplatz.*

Residenzplatz (Z 32)

Until the 16C there was a cemetery on this site. Prince-archbishop Wolf Dietrich created the present square, which got its fountain in the 17C. The square is bounded on the south by the cathedral and to the west by the Residenz. On the east is the **Glockenspiel** (Z), a carillon of 35 bells cast in Antwerp at the end of the 17C and set up in Salzburg in 1705.

Residenz★★ (Z)

The main residence of Salzburg's prince-archbishops was begun during the reign of Wolf Dietrich and completed under his successor Markus Sittikus. It was here where Emperor Franz Joseph received Napoleon III in 1867 and the German emperor, Kaiser Wilhelm I, in 1871.

State rooms

◷*Daily 10am–5pm. ∞€8, includes self-guided audio tour and gallery. ☎06 62/80 42 26 90.*

The Residenz is entered from Residenzplatz via a marble gate festooned with the coats of arms of various prince-archbishops. A sweeping staircase leads to the Carabinieri Hall beyond which are the state rooms. These were redecorated in the early 18C by Johann Lukas von Hildebrandt and feature ceiling frescoes by Johann Michael Rottmayr and Martino Altomonte.

The young Mozart gave his first court concert at age six in the Conference Hall and later also performed in the Rittersaal (Knight's Hall), which has good acoustics and is still used for concerts today. A testament to the wealth of the religious rulers is the opulent **Audienzsaal** (reception hall), where Gobelin tapestries form part of the decoration.

Residenzgalerie

◷*Tue–Sun 10am–5pm, daily during Salzburg Festival. ∞€6. ☎06 62/8 40 45 10. www.residenzgalerie.at.*

The gallery houses a collection of important European paintings from the 16C to the 19C. The particularly exceptional array of 17C Dutch painting includes works by great masters such as Rembrandt, Rubens and Brueghel. The valuable exhibition, which occupies 15 state rooms, is rounded off with a display of 19C masterpieces.

Additional Sights

Hettwer Bastei★★ (Y)

Climb up to the Kapuzinerkirche via the steep walkway reached from the Linzergasse through the covered passageway. From the church, go downhill again for about 50m/55yd, turn left and follow the sign "Stadtaussicht-Hettwer Bastei" to the viewpoint.

The Hettwer Bastei (bastion) on the south side of the Kapuzinerberg gives fine **views** over Salzburg, particularly when the morning light enhances the green of the many copper-clad roofs.

Return via the series of steps leading to the Steingasse.

©Tourismus Salzburg GmbH

Residenzplatz

Mirabell Schloss & Garten★ (V)

Little is left of the mansion built at the beginning of the 17C by Prince-archbishop Wolf Dietrich as a residence for his mistress Salome Alt. It got a complete overhaul courtesy of the architect Johann Lukas von Hildebrandt in the following century but suffered severe damage during the great fire sweeping through the city in 1818. The final reconstruction resulted in the rather sober building you see today, which rather fittingly houses part of the city administration.

Of the original building, the monumental **marble staircase**★★ with its sculptures by Georg Raphael Donner has survived, together with the Marmorsaal (Hall of Marble), a gilt and colored stucco extravaganza that is now used for wedding ceremonies and chamber concerts.

Considerably more noteworthy are the exquisite **Mirabell gardens** laid out in 1690 by Fischer von Erlach. With their abundance of flowers, statues and sculptures, they are a favorite place for relaxing. From a terrace there is a fine view over the gardens toward the old fortifications and the Hohensalzburg.

The old orangery has been restored and encloses a pretty courtyard with bright flowerbeds. Its south wing houses a small museum of Baroque art.

Mirabell gardens with a view of Hohensalzburg

© Österreich Werbung / Bartl

Salzburger Barockmuseum★ (M³)

🕐 Sept–Jun, Tue–Sun 10am–5pm; Jul–Aug, Wed–Sun 10am–5pm. ⊜€4.50. ☎06 62/87 74 32. www.barockmuseum.at.

Designs for frescoes, paintings and sculptures and a collection of master sketches form the contents of this little museum which sets out to give a general view of 17C and 18C European art.

Mozart-Wohnhaus (Tanzmeisterhaus) (Y E)

Makartplatz 8. 🕐*Daily 9am–6pm (7pm Jul–Aug).* ⊜*€9, combination ticket with Mozart Geburtshaus €9.50.* ☎*06 62/87 42 27 40. www.mozarteum.at.*

The so-called Tanzmeisterhaus, which was the Mozart family home from 1773 to 1787, was largely destroyed by bombs in 1944 and completely rebuilt in 1994–95. Mozart lived in the house until 1780 and composed a number of his works here.

The self-guided tour using headsets with infrared-activated commentary and music takes you through rooms filled with period furniture, old instruments, literature and documentary items on the Mozart family and their contemporary environment. Special emphasis has been placed on Mozart's extensive travels. Die-hard Mozart fans might also like to pop into the **Mozart-Ton- und Filmmuseum**, where you can pick your favorite clips from an extensive audio and video archive and watch or listen to them for free.

Friedhof St. Sebastian (VX)

The cemetery behind the church of St. Sebastian, the original of which fell victim to the big fire of 1818, was conceived by Prince-archbishop Wolf Dietrich, whose grand mausoleum naturally dominates the grounds. Its interior is tiled with multi-hued porcelain. Other famous people buried here include Mozart's wife and father (in the central lane) and Paracelsus, a doctor and philosopher of the Renaissance who died in Salzburg in 1541 (in the southwestern corner behind a wrought-iron grille)

Dreifaltigkeitskirche (Y)

Completed in 1699, this Baroque church is the work of the great architect Fischer von Erlach and features frescoes by Michael Rottmayr.

Stiegl's Brauwelt   Kids

Bräuhausstraße 9. From the center, take Neutor-, Moos- and Nussdorfer Straße (X 31). Bräuhausstraße is the fourth turning on the left. ©*Exhibition: daily 10am–5pm (Jul–Aug, until 7pm)* ✆€9, *includes beer, pretzl & souvenir; children €4.* ☎*06 62/83 87 14 92. www.brauwelt.at.*

The exhibition in the old malthouse of one of Salzburg's largest breweries covers the whole world of beer, obviously with the emphasis on Austria and Salzburg. Themes include ingredients, beer production around the world and advertising. Tours ends with a tasting session in the brewing room.

Excursions

Gaisbergstraße★★

13km/8mi. Leave Salzburg on R, B 158 toward St. Gilgen. After about 4km/2.5mi turn right for the scenic drive to Gaisberg

Park at the end of the road below the Gaisberg summit. There is a **view**★ of Salzburg, the Salzach gap and the Salzburg Alps. A path runs between the guesthouses and past the transmitting station, quickly taking you to the summit at an altitude of 1 288m/4 226ft. From here, the mountain **panorama**★ takes in the Salzkammergut and the Dachstein massif.

Schloss Hellbrunn★ (U)   Kids

©*Jul–Aug, daily 9am–10pm; May, Jun, Sept, daily 9am–5.30pm; Apr, Oct, daily 9am–4.30pm.* ✆€8.50; children €3.80. *Guided tour (fountains with guide: 35min, palace with audio-guide: 20min)* ☎*06 62/8 20 37 20. www.hellbrunn.at.*

This palace in the style of an Italian palazzo began life as the summer residence of Prince-archbishop Markus Sittikus in 1615. A self-guided audio tour of the interior takes in the banquet hall, with its *trompe-l'œil* painting, and the domed Octagon or Music Room.

Considerably more memorable, especially for kids, is a guided spin around the attractive **gardens**★★, filled with whimsical trick fountains originally built to entertain the fun-loving prince-archbishop. There is a mechanical theater with 13 figures that are set in motion by the action of water, amazing shell-encrusted grottoes, and fountains that suddenly start spurting, taking unwary visitors by surprise.

Zoo Salzburg   Kids

Access via the Schlosspark or main entrance in Hellbrunner Allee. ©*Jan–Mar & Nov–Dec, daily 9am–4pm; Apr–Jun & Sept–Oct, daily 9am–5pm; Jul–Aug until 6.30pm; Night zoo in Aug, Fri & Sat until 11pm (last entry 9.30pm).* ✆€9; children 4pm. ☎*06 62/8 20 17 60. www.salzburg-zoo.at.*

Salzburg's modern zoo houses around 500 animals representing 140 species in three beautifully landscaped habitats representing Eurasia, Asia and Africa. All the usual crowd-pleasers are there, including lions, pumas and monkeys.

Untersberg★

12km/7.4mi. 1hr round trip drive, plus 15min by cable-car. Leave Salzburg on 2 toward Berchtesgaden. Just after the major St. Leonhard intersection, bear right and continue to the cable-car station. ⏱Jul–Sept, daily 8.30am–5.30pm; Mar–Jun, Oct, daily 9am–5pm; 20 Dec–Feb, daily 9am–4pm. ⏱Two weeks in Apr, Nov–mid-Dec. ✎€19; children €9.50 round trip. ☎0 62 46/72 47 70.

From a height of 1 853m/6 079ft, there is a splendid **panorama** of the Salzburg basin, the Salzburg Alps (Watzmann, Steinernes Meer, Staufen), the Wilder Kaiser and the Dachstein.

Schloss Leopoldskron (U)

Mirrored in its tranquil lake, Leopoldskron was built in 1744 as a summer residence for Prince-archbishop Leopold Anton Firmian. It was acquired in 1918 for cultural and artistic purposes by Max Reinhardt, one of the founders of the Salzburg Festival. Its charming setting, its car-free lakeside walk, its modern swimming pool and other recreational facilities make Leopoldskron a pleasant place to relax in, especially in summer.

SALZBURGER SPORTWELT ✲✲ ✲

SALZBURG

One of five areas forming the massive Ski Amadé winter sports region, the Salzburger Sportwelt is a paradise for skiers, snowboarders and cross-country enthusiasts. Its mountains are crisscrossed by 350km/218mi of pistes served by 100 lifts. Slopes extend between 800m/2 624ft and 2 000m/6 650ft and are especially suitable for beginner and intermediate skiers. The main villages are Flachau, Wagrain, St. Johann-Alpendorf, Radstadt, Altenmarkt-Zauchensee, Kleinarl, Eben and Filzmoos, all embedded in a lovely setting and with legendary après ski scenes.

- **Information:** Hauptstraße 159. ☎0 64 57/29 29. www.salzburgersportwelt.at.
- **Orient Yourself:** The ski area is located between the Tenner range and the Radstädter Tauern, about 70km/43mi southeast of Salzburg.
- **Also See:** RADSTÄDTER TAUERNSTRASSE, DACHSTEIN.

Sights

Zauchensee★

Alt 1 361m/4 465ft. Zauchensee is by far the highest-lying resort in the Salzburger Sportwelt and consequently offers the best snow cover. Keen downhill skiers are able to indulge their passion in a beautiful **low-altitude mountain setting**★ with ski runs of varying degrees of difficulty.

If you are after a more authentic village atmosphere and a more extensive range of leisure facilities, visit the charming village of **Altenmarkt im Pongau**.

Schwarzwand-Seilbahn★★

Alt 2 100m/6 890ft. For skiers only.
The cable-car leads to the foot of the Schwarzkopf, from where there is a magnificent **panorama**★★ of the Tennengebirge, the Dachstein and the Radstädter Tauern.

Rosskopf★★

Alt 1 929m/6 329ft.
Travel up on the **Flachau cable-car**. ⏱*1 Dec–25 Apr daily 8.30am–4pm; 10 Jun–30 Sept, daily 9am–noon, 1pm–5pm.* ☞€12 round trip. ☎0 64 57/22 14.
At the top of the cable-car ride there is a remarkable **view**★ over Modermandl and Faulkogel. Continue by chair-lift up to the Rosskopf. Climbing up to the peak takes only a few minutes and rewards you with a stunning **panorama**★★ over Zauchensee and Flachau, the Dachstein, the Radstädter Tauern and the Hohe Tauern.

Mooskopf★★

Take the Kleinarl chair-lift and the Bubble-Shuttleberg chair-lift, then walk a few minutes to the summit. ⏱*Dec 15–Apr 20, daily 9am–4pm.* ☞€35 day pass. ☎0 64 57/22 14.
From the peak a splendid **panorama**★★ opens up taking in the Tennengebirge range, the Dachstein, the Ennskraxn massif and other impressive peaks.

Wagrain★

Alt 838m/2 749ft. Besides having the area's best lodging and most extensive network of ski-lifts, the town also enjoys a certain fame as the home of Atomic, the largest Austrian ski manufacturer. The snow cover, though, is fairly unreliable.

Koglalm★

Alt 1 878m/6 161ft. **Panorama**★ over Wagrain, Flachau and Kleinarl with the Tennengebirge range, the Dachstein and the Niedere Tauern in the background. Good skiers and hikers are able to reach the **Saukarkopf**, where even broader **views**★★ open up.

SALZKAMMERGUT★★★
OBERÖSTERREICH, SALZBURG AND STEIERMARK

Salt has given the Salzkammergut its name and, until recently, exceptional economic importance. For about 4 000 years the "white gold" was the region's main source of prosperity, as is reflected in its towns' proud architecture. Tourism has boomed since the early 20C thanks to dozens of lakes, legendary mountains such as the Dachstein and the Totes Gebirge and long-estabiished spa resorts like Bad Ischl. In 1997, UNESCO honored the region's exceptional beauty and cultural significance by placing it on its list of World Heritage Sites, together with Hallstatt and the Dachstein.

- **Information:** Götzstraße 12, Bad Ischl. ☎06132/24 00 00. www.salzkammergut.co.at.
- **Orient Yourself:** The Salzkammergut is east of Salzburg in central Austria.
- **Parking:** Plenty of parking lots along the roads beside the lakes
- **Don't Miss:** St. Wolfgang
- **Organizing Your Time:** It is possible to tour the Salzkammergut in four days, by following itineraries ①, ②, ③ on day one, and ④ (♿ see DACHSTEIN) or the cycling tour itinerary on days two, three, and four.
- **Also See:** DACHSTEIN, BAD AUSSEE, BAD ISCHL, GMUNDEN, ST. WOLFGANG.

Driving Tour of the Lakes★★

①Salzburg to Bad Ischl
84km/52mi

Salzburg★★★ ♿See SALZBURG.

- *Leave Salzburg and take the A 1 autobahn to the Mondsee exit.*

Between Salzburg and Mondsee, the autobahn affords open views of the Drachenwand cliffs and the Schafberg spur.

Mondsee★
♿*See Mondsee excursion.*

The north shore of the Mondsee, which is calm and welcoming at first, becomes a little more severe beyond the Pichl promontory, where the road climbs over a wooded rise.

Burggrabenklamm
5km/3mi west of Au along the B 152 to the southern tip of the Attersee. Park near the Gasthof Jägerwirt; 30min round trip walk.

This little but dramatic gorge with an 18m/60ft waterfall is one of the most beautiful in the Salzkammergut. The trail, which is short and often slippery, leads past a statue of St. Mary.

- *Backtrack on the B 152 to the south shore of the Mondsee.*

The pass road connecting Scharfling and St. Gilgen has remarkable **panoramic views**★★ from a parking lot above St. Gilgen. Beyond the slender onion-domed village bell-tower, the **Wolfgangsee**★★ lake stretches toward the Rinnkogel massif.

St. Gilgen★
Delightful St. Gilgen, at the northwestern tip of the **Wolfgangsee**, is a former outpost of the prince-archbishops of Salzburg and the birthplace of Mozart's mother, Anna-Maria Pertl. His sister Nannerl settled here after marrying the local magistrate. The family legacy is kept alive with a Mozart fountain on the central Mozartplatz square and a small **memorial exhibit** (◷Jun–Sept, Tue–Sun 10am–noon, 2pm–6pm; ♾€1; ☎0 62 27/23 48) in the former law court at Ischlerstraße 15, the very building

where Anna was born and where Nannerl later lived with her family.

Another pleasant diversion in town is the **Musikinstrumente Museum**, which displays medieval and exotic instruments from around the world.

The lake, meanwhile, attracts numerous water sports enthusiasts, especially sailors who appreciate its favorable wind conditions. Scheduled boat services stop at numerous sites around the Wolfgangsee, while the nostalgic paddle-steamer *Kaiser Franz Joseph*, which began operating in 1873, offers leisurely lake cruises.

▶ *Leave the main road at Strobl to make the detour to St. Wolfgang.*

St. Wolfgang★★
 See ST. WOLFGANG.

▶ *Take the direct road to Bad Ischl, avoiding Strobl.*

Floating Corpus Christi Festival

Since 1632 a famous procession has been held on the lake here every year in celebration of the feast of Corpus Christi. In days gone by, boats called "Trauner" which were used for shipping salt were pressed into service for the procession. Nowadays, these have given way to the rather less romantic motor boat.

Bad Ischl✚ *See BAD ISCHL.*

2 Bad Ischl to Gmunden
34km/21mi

Bad Ischl✚ *See BAD ISCHL.*

North of Bad Ischl, the Traun corridor, which was one of the great European salt routes, unwinds between the Höllengebirge and Totes Gebirge foothills. Beside the road, a track follows the course of the saltwater conduit *(Soleleitung)*, which since the 17C has brought the salt waters from Hallstatt to the refinery at Ebensee.

From the spectacular **cliff road**★ from Ebensee to Traunkirchen, which runs above the **Traunsee**★, Austria's deepest lake (191m/527ft), one can see the golden peak of the Rötelspitze, and then further north, the Traunstein itself.

Traunkirchen

Perched on a **promontory**★, Traunkirchen is a popular stop among Salzkammergut explorers who come to appreciate the splendid vistas over the Traunsee lake and the rugged mountains. Above the town is perched the Johannesbergkapelle. While here, also pop into the **Pfarrkirche** (parish church) surrounded by a terraced graveyard overlooking the lake. It has splendid Baroque furnishings, particularly the **Fisherman's Pulpit**★, made in the form of the Disciples' fishing boat, complete with dripping nets. Since 1632, the town has staged an annual **Corpus Christi festival** on the lake.

Altmünster

Altmünster has a Late Gothic hall-church with sumptuous decoration and a stone high altar dating from 1518.

Gmunden★ *See GMUNDEN.*

3 From Gmunden to Salzburg

117km/73mi

This route links the Traunsee, the Attersee and the Mondsee. The road leaves the Traunsee to enter a tranquil, hilly region dotted with whitewashed farmhouses and clumps of huge lime trees. After skirting the hamlet of Grossalm, it burrows into the forest below the Höllengebirge, eventually reaching a pass *(alt 826m/2 710ft)*. The most scenic stretch on the descent down to the Attersee, is between Kienklause and Steinbach.

Steinbach am Attersee

The composer **Gustav Mahler** spent his holidays in Steinbach, working in his "Komponierhäuschen" (composing shed).

The road skirts the **Attersee**★ (also known as Kammersee), the largest lake in the Austrian Alps and popular for fishing and boating. It is bordered to the south by the last cliff-like slopes of the Schafberg. Between Seewalchen and Attersee on the western shore, the road runs through charming Sun-drenched hills where orchards flourish. Only the cliffs of the Höllengebirge lend a note of harshness to the scene. For good lake views, stop by the Buchberg chapel.

Attersee

This well-known resort has a pilgrimage church, Mariae Himmelfahrt, with fine Baroque furnishings, including works by Meinrad Guggenbichler.

▶ *Leave the lake at Attersee and take the A1 autobahn toward Salzburg.*

Mondsee
🚲 *See Mondsee Excursion.*

▶ *Continue on the A 1 autobahn to Salzburg.*

Salzburg★★★ 🚲 *See SALZBURG.*

4 Dachstein Circuit Tour★★

218km/135.5ml

The massive Dachstein massif with its steep cliffs form the southern boundary of the Salzkammergut and are the backdrop to Halstätter See and Gosauseen. This circular tour circumnavigates the whole Dachstein range. It is best done in two or three days. (🚲 *For a description of the tour see DACHSTEIN; for map see this section).*

Cycling Tour of the Lakes

Salzkammergutradweg★★
In the Salzkammergut there is a vast network of well-signposted paved cycle paths suitable for families and experienced cyclists alike. The Salzkammergutradweg is a circular route using specially constructed paths and quiet back roads that takes in most all the major lakes and towns of the region. It is well signposted with many cyclefriendly hotels and gasthofs along the route. By combining different loops, using lake steamers and the railway it is possible to create individual routes of varying lengths.

Salzkammergut Lakes Tour★★

137km/85ml

Day 1 – Bad Ischl-Ebensee-Gmunden
Day 2 – Gmunden-Schörfling-Mondsee
Day 3 – Mondsee-St. Gilgen-Bad Ischl

Day 1: Bad ischl to Gmunden

34km/21ml

Bad Ischl‡ 🚲 *See Bad Ischl*

▶ *Head north from Bad Ischl on the cycle path R 2 which runs along the Traun River valley to Ebensee on the southern end of Traunsee.*

Ebensee
It is possible to take a boat *(Traunsee-Schiffahrt, www.traunseeschiffahrt.at)* from here to Gmunden.

▶ *Follow the cycle path north along the west shore of Traunsee to Traunkirchen.*

Traunkirchen (🚲 *see entry)*
Choosing to take the boat from here gives a great view of the church and the "floating castle" of **Seeschloss Ort**★ (🚲 *See entry under GMUNDEN)*

▶ *Continue north along the lake shore to Gmunden.*

Gmunden★ 🚲 *See GMUNDEN*

Day 2: Gmunden to Mondsee

64km/40ml or 37km/23ml if taking the boat from Seewalchen to Unterach

This is the longest stretch of the tour but it can be shortened considerably by taking a boat *(Attersee-Schifffarht, ☎ 07666/78 06. www.atterseeschifffahrt.at)* for half or more of the length of Attersee.

▶ *Take the cycle path north out of Gmuden to Aurach and Seewalchen at the north end of Attersee.*

Attersee★
Austria's deepest and largest lake it is popular with watersports enthusists. The lake is dominated by the Höllengebirge *(Mountains of Hell)*. At the southern end the steep slopes and cliffs of the Schafberg come right down to the lake.

From Seewalchen, the cycle path loops round through rolling hills and orchards to St. Georgen im Allergau before rejoining the lake shore at Nußdorf.

Attersee

▷ *Take the boat to either Nußdorf, Zell or Unterach and rejoin the cycle track. From Unterach take the track west and along the north side of the lake Mondsee to the town of Mondsee.*

Mondsee ⓒ*See Mondsee Excursion*

Day 3: Mondsee to Bad Ischl

39km/24ml

▷ *From Mondsee take the cycle track along the south shore of the lake to Oberburgau. The route now climbs over a pass to St. Gilgen on Wolfgangsee.*

This is the steepest part of the route but the reward of **panoramic views**★★ is worth the effort.

St. Gilgen★ ⓒ*See Driving Tour* 1

▷ *Follow the southern shore to the boat (WolgangseeSchifffahrt, www.wolfgangseeschifffart.at) landing stage at Gschwendt. Take the boat across to St. Wolfgang.*

St. Wolfgang★★
ⓒ*See ST WOLFGANG*
Aim to take the boat across to St. Wolfgang in time for lunch or an afternoon snack at the famous Weisses Rössl (White Horse Inn).

▷ *Take the cycle track out of St. Wolfgang along the north shore and the valley to Bad Ischl.*

Bad Ischl✞ ⓒ*See BAD ISCHL*

Excursion

Mondsee
Mondsee is 32km/20mi east of Salzburg. Mondsee lies below the cliffs of the Drachenwand and the Schafberg and sprouted around a Benedictine abbey founded in the 9C and dissolved in 1791. It is named for the nearby lake, which is shaped like a crescent moon and whose temperate, clean waters attract scores of water sports enthusiasts in the warmer months.

Basilika Mondsee★
The wedding church from the *Sound of Music* has been a basilica minor since 2005. Swiss-born sculptor **Meinrad Guggenbichler** (1649–1723) spent 44 years in Mondsee, creating seven of the 13 black-and-gold altars, including the masterful altar of the Holy Sacrament, on the lower left-hand side, with its twisted columns supported by cherubs.

Heimatmuseum Mondseeland & Pfahlbaumuseum

◐ Late Jun–early Sept, Tue–Sun 10am–6pm; May–late Jun, Tue–Sun 10am–5pm; Oct, Tue–Sat 10am–5pm. ☞ €3. ☎ 0 62 32/22 70.

The Pfahlbaumuseum sheds light on a phase of the Neolithic Era known as the "Mondsee Culture" (about 5 000 years ago) when residents lived above the water in buildings resting on stilts.

Freilichtmuseum Mondseer Rauchhaus

◐ May–Aug, Tue–Sun 10am–6pm, Sept, Tue–Sat 10am–5pm, Oct, Sat–Sun 10am–5pm. ☞ €2.20. ☎ 0 62 32/22 70.

Of the traditional farmhouses relocated to this open-air museum the Rauchhaus (smoke house) is the most interesting. It combines living spaces for humans and animals under a single roof.

Schafberg★★
⌖ See ST WOLFGANG: Excursion

ST. ANTON AM ARLBERG ❊❊ ❊

TIROL

POPULATION 2 840 – ALT 1 304M/4 278FT

LOCAL MAP SEE ARLBERGGEBIET

St. Anton, draped into a deeply incised valley, is something of a shrine for winter sports aficionados. It was here in 1921 where ski pioneer Hannes Schneider, who is considered the "father of modern skiing," founded Austria's first ski school. From then on, the sport took St. Anton by storm and today it is one of the largest resorts in the Northern Alps with a youthful, sporty atmosphere and a lively après-ski scene. Summer brings a degree of calm, although the scenic Arlbergstraße does draw its share of tourist traffic. Attractions include an enormous leisure park and 90km/56mi of hiking trails.

- **Information:** Arlberghaus, A-6580. ☎ 0 54 46/2 26 90. www.stantonamarlberg.com.
- ▶ **Orient Yourself:** St. Anton is in western Austria, about 100km/62mi southwest of Innsbruck.
- ▣ **Parking:** Look for lots along the main Arlbergstraße.
- **Don't Miss:** Skiing, trip up to the Valluga viewpoint.
- ◔ **Organizing Your Time:** Half a day for the town; several days for hiking or skiing the mountains
- ⌖ **Also See:** ARLBERGGEBIET, LECH, ZÜRS.

Sights

Ski Slopes

Arlberg ski area

St. Anton is part of the Arlberg ski region that also includes **Lech**, (⌖ see LECH), **Zürs** (⌖ see ZÜRS, served by bus) and **Stuben** (⌖ see ARLBERGGEBIET). A single ski pass is good for the entire area, which lies at an altitude of 1 300–2 650m/4 250–8 700ft and has 260km/162mi of marked and 180km/ 112mi of unmarked pistes, accessed by a total of 80 ski-lifts. St. Anton is especially suitable for experienced skiers, offering steep, undulating pistes from the Schindler Spitze, Kapall and Pfannenkopf peaks. Less proficient skiers will find suitable runs on the Galzig, Gampen and Gampberg slopes.

Arlberg-Kandahar-Haus

This is a museum on the history of skiing and the development of tourism in the Arlberg area.

View from Valluga from near St. Anton am Arlberg

Excursions

Valluga★★★
Alt 2 811m/9 222ft. About 2hr 30min round trip. ◷*mid-Dec–end Apr, early Jul–end Sept, daily 8.30am–4pm.* ⌷€20 round ttrip.* ☎0 54 46/2 35 20.

This excursion starts with a ride aboard the new **Galzigbahn**, a gondola with Ferris wheel-style boarding housed within a spectacular glass shelter designed by Tirolean architect Georg Driendl. From the mountain station (alt 2 185m/7 169ft), there is a wonderful **view**★★ over the ski slopes.

Next, take the Valluga I gondola to the Valluga ridge *(alt 2 650m/8 695ft)* for more impressive **views**★★, although for the truly breathtaking **360° panorama**★★★ catch the short Valluga II gondola to the peak itself.

Kapall★★
Alt 2 330m/7 644ft. About 1hr round trip aboard the Nassereinbahn cable-car or the Gampenbahn chuir-lIft, followed by the Kapall chair-lift. ◷*Dec–end Apr, Jun–end Aug, daily 8.45am–3.45pm.* ⌷€18 round trip.* ☎0 54 46//2 35 20.

This trip drops you at the at the foot of the rocky Weissschrofenspitze peak *(alt 2752m/9 028ft)* and treats you to a very beautiful **panorama**★★ over the entire St. Anton Valley and across to the Swiss Alps, the Rätikon and the Verwall range.

STIFT ST. FLORIAN★★

OBERÖSTERREICH

The abbey of St. Florian, the largest in Upper Austria and an eminent cultural center, has been run by Augustinian canons since the 11C. The present buildings are in the purest Baroque style, since the monastery was entirely rebuilt between 1686 and 1751 under the direction of Carlo Antonio Carlone and Jakob Prandtauer. The latter was also the architect of Hohenbrunn, the palatial edifice built nearby for one of the abbey's provosts.

Information: Stiftstraße 1, St. Florian. ☎07224/8 90 20. www.stift-st-florian.at.

▶ **Orient Yourself:** The abbey is 18km/11m southeast of Linz.

Parking: A parking lot is situated near the entrance to the abbey.

Don't Miss: Artdorfer Galerie.

Organizing Your Time: Allow two hours.

Also See: LINZ, STIFTSKIRCHE WILHERING.

Visit

Guided tour (1hr 30min) Easter–Oct, daily 10am, 11am, 2pm, 3pm and 4pm; otherwise by appointment only. €6.

Exterior

An elegant doorway with two balconies, carved columns and statues leads into the abbey's inner courtyard, which is adorned by a remarkable sculptured fountain, the Eagle Fountain (Adlerbrunnen), and a wrought-iron well-head, dating from 1603.

Bibliothek (Library)

Guided tours start in the library, one of the oldest and most prestigious abbey repositories in the country. The exquisite allegorical ceiling paintings by Bartolomeo Altomonte represent the union of religion and science. Marquetry in walnut, encrusted with gold, sets off the 150 000 valuable manuscripts and books.

Marmorsaal

Prandtauer designed the magnficent Marble Hall, whose ceiling fresco by Martino and Bartolomeo Altomonte glorifies Prince Eugene of Savoy's victory over the Turks. It was originally conceived as an imperial dining room but also served as a concert hall.

Kaiserzimmer (Imperial Apartments)

The Imperial apartments are reached via a magnificent grand staircase whose

Detail of Gothic alter, Stift St. Florian

© Österreich Werbung / Trumler

The Legend of St. Florian

Florian was head of the Roman administration in Noricum province, who was martyred after converting to Christianity in 304. After suffering considerable torture, he was thrown into the Enns River with a stone around his neck. The abbey that bears his name was allegedly built near the spot where a local woman first discovered his mangled body. St. Florian is the patron saint of Upper Austria as well as of Poland and of firefighters. In fact, there is hardly a church in Austria without a statue of this saintly protector.

Amid the succession of halls and state rooms note the Faistenberger room, the bedrooms of the emperor and empress, the reception room and the Gobelin room.

Altdorfer Galerie★★★

The most valuable pictures in the abbey' art collection are by **Albrecht Altdorfer** (1480–1538), a master of the Danube School whose work is noted for its balanced composition and rich, warm colors. The 14 pictures were painted for the abbey church's Gothic altar to St. Sebastian and form the world's most important collection of Altdorfer's work. Four panels depict the martyrdom of St. Sebastian, while the other eight show scenes from the Passion.

Stiftsbasilika

🕐*Organ recitals (20min) mid-May–mid-Oct, Sun, Mon, Wed–Fri 2.30pm.* 🎫€3.
The Baroque basilica was built under the direction of Carlo Antonio Carlone to replace the old Gothic church. Carlo's brother Bartolomeo was responsible for the stuccowork. The entire ceiling is swathed in frescoes executed by Johann Anton Gumpp and Melchior Steidl from Munich. The great organ was built by Franz Xaver Chrisman (1770–74) and has

balustrades are adorned with statues, while the walls and ceilings are embellished with stuccowork and frescoes. Until 1782 the apartments received such illustrious visitors as Pope Pius VI, emperors and princes.

Stift St. Florian

Address Book

🪙*For coin ranges, see cover flap.*

WHERE TO STAY

🍴🛏**Zur Kanne** – *Marktplatz 7, St. Florian.* ☎*07224/42 88. www. gasthof-koppler.at. 14 rooms.*
First mentioned as a baker's house in 1820 this country guesthouse is close to the abbey.

Anton Bruckner at St. Florian

Anton Bruckner, Austria's greatest 19C composer of church music, was born near St. Florian in 1824. After his father's early death, the boy attended choir school at the abbey, where he was first introduced to religious music.

Bruckner trained as a teacher and eventually managed to win an appointment at St. Florian in 1845. To his great joy, he was also appointed abbey organist. It was here that Bruckner decided to devote himself to music. In 1856 he became cathedral organist in Linz, where he composed several masterpieces, including three masses and two of his nine symphonies. Next he went to Vienna to teach at the conservatory. Despite his increasing fame, Bruckner always had a soft spot for St. Florian, and it was there where he wished to be buried beneath the very organ that had been so instrumental on his way to success as a composer and organist.

more than 103 stops and 7 836 pipes. It is now named the **Bruckner Organ** after Anton Bruckner, who worked at the abbey as organist and composer. He's buried in a crypt beneath the organ.

Excursion

Schloss Hohenbrunn★
The palace is about 1.5km/1mi west of St. Florian.
Too large for a hunting lodge and too open to the surrounding countryside ever to have made any pretense at defense, Schloss Hohenbrunn is set like a Palladian villa in attractive natural surrounds.
Schloss Hohenbrunn was built in the 18C as a hunting lodge for the abbey of St. Florian by one of Austria's most celebrated Baroque architects, the Tirolean **Jakob Prandtauer**. Hohenbrunn is in fact the only castle that can definitely be attributed to him. The palace owes its name (Hoher Brunnen meaning high fountain) to the pumping appliance originally installed in a tower flanking the south façade.

Jagdmuseum★
Quite appropriately, the Schloss now houses the **Jagdmuseum**★ (Apr–Oct, daily 10am–noon, 1pm–5pm; €2.20), a thorough and informative exploration of hunting in Upper Austria. Expect plenty of weapons, models, plaster casts of footprints and stuffed animals but also hunting clothes once worn by Emperor Franz Joseph I and an extraordinary rifle (3.12m/10ft 3in long) belonging to Archduke Karl Salvator.

ST. JOHANN IN TIROL ❄

TIROL
POPULATION 8 600 – ALT 670M/2 198FT
LOCAL MAP SEE KAISERGEBIRGE

The market town boasts a number of Baroque houses with façades charmingly decorated with painted, sometimes *trompe-l'œil*, scenes typical of the Tirolean region. Its location at the intersection of several valleys makes St. Johann a lively tourist resort, especially in winter. The wide, Sun–drenched bowl of the valley is enclosed by the Wilder Kaiser and Kitzbüheler Horn peaks.

- **Information:** Poststraße 2. ☎05352/6 33 35. www.ferienregion.at.
- **Orient Yourself:** St. Johann is in western Austria, about 11km/6.8mi north of Kitzbühel.
- **Organizing Your Time:** Budget a couple of hours unless skiing or hiking.
- **Also See:** KITZBÜHEL, KAISERGEBIRGE.

Sights

Ski slopes

Downhill ski slopes are concentrated on the north face of the Kitzbüheler Horn. All in all there are 60km/37mi of pistes, 28km/17mi of which can be supplemented with snow machines in case nature fails to deliver.

Cross-country skiers have 74km/46mi of tracks, including two of 16km/10mi in length classified as difficult. If you factor in tracks in neighboring Oberndorf, Going-Ellmau, Kirchdorf-Erpfendorf and Waidring, the number goes up to almost 200km/124mi.

Pfarrkirche

This Baroque building, designed by Abraham Millauer, has remarkable ceiling paintings by **Simon Benedikt Faistenberger**, a student of Rottmayr. The altar paintings are by Jacob Zanusi, court painter at Salzburg.

Spitalskirche zum Hl. Nikolaus in der Weitau★

See KAISERGEBIRGE 1.

STIFT ST. LAMBRECHT

STEIERMARK

The Benedictine abbey of St. Lambrecht has a pedigree going back to the 11C. Little remains of the original Romanesque abbey church, which was replaced by the current High Gothic triple-nave hall church in the 14C. The main buildings were built in 1640 based on plans by Domenico Sciassia. Dissolved by Joseph II in 1786, the abbey was re-established by Franz II in 1802.

- **Information:** Hauptstraße 1, St. Lambrecht. ☎03585/23 45. www.stift-stlambrecht.at.
- ▶ **Orient Yourself:** The abbey is in the Murtal, a valley in southern Austria, about 70km/44mi north of Klagenfurt.
- **Don't Miss:** Abbey Museum.
- **Organizing Your Time:** Allow two hours.
- **Also See:** FRIESACH, GURK.

Stift St. Lambrecht

© Österreich Werbung / Bartl

Visit

Guided tour (1hr 30min) mid-May–mid-Oct, Mon–Sat 10.45am, 2.30pm; Sun after the morning service and 2.30pm. €7 (group reduction, €6).

Exterior

As you enter the abbey courtyard, the impressive west façade extends for 135m/443ft on your right, while on your left is a bastion adorned with statues by Johann Matthias Leitner in 1746. An open staircase leads up to the Gothic **Peterskirche**, which features a winged altar with a Crucifixion scene and works by the Master of Lambrecht.

Stiftskirche

An elaborate marble doorway opens into the narthex, which houses a 14C Lettner crucifix in a Baroque framework.

Medieval frescoes embellish the vaulted ceiling above the chancel and the walls of the nave. Star of the show, though, is the enormous 1632 **high altar**★ by Valentin Khautt, which centers on a painting of the *Assumption*. The decoration of the altar to St. Emmeram in front on the right, the statues of the church Elders on the organ gallery, and the Madonna in the narthex are all works of the famous sculptor Michael Hönell.

Stiftsmuseum

The museum gives an overview the 900 year history of the abbey and an insight into the cloistered life of the Benedictines during that same period. Of special interest is the 250-figure Baroque crib which is set up in the abbey church from Dec 21–Feb 2. There is also a collection of over 600 birds.

ST. PAUL IM LAVANTTAL★

KÄRNTEN
ALT 400M/1 312FT

The Benedictine abbey of St. Paul, half-hidden in the trees and slightly above the Lavant Valley, was founded in 1091. It boasts one of Austria's finest Romanesque churches and a well-respected collection of art treasures.

- **Information:** ☎04357/20 19 22. www.stift-stpaul.at.
- ▶ **Orient Yourself:** The abbey is in the far south of Austria, near the border with Slovenia, about 85km/53mi east of Klagenfurt.
- **Don't Miss:** Stiftskirche.
- **Organizing Your Time:** Plan on spending about two hours here.
- **Also See:** KLAGENFURT.

Visit

Stiftskirche (Abbey church)

Daily 8am–5pm.

The church, which was begun in 1180, follows a cruciform layout culminating in three half-rounded apses. After a fire in the 14C Gothic vaulting was added and decorated with frescoes by the masterful Friedrich and Michael Pacher. The south doorway features an image of the Adoration of the Magi, and the west door one of Christ in Majesty.

Stiftsgebäude (Abbey buildings)

May–Oct, daily 9am–5pm. €7. Guided tour €9.

The abbey is home to a veritable treasure trove that includes a precious numismatic collection, paintings (eg by Rubens, Rembrandt and Van Dyck), drawings (e.g. by Dürer, Holbein and Troger), objets d'art, silverwork, porcelain, woodcarvings and valuable pieces such as Rudolf of Swabia's imperial cross.

ST. PÖLTEN★

NIEDERÖSTERREICH
POPULATION 51 600 – ALT 271M/889FT

Founded by the Romans in AD 1, St. Pölten only became provincial capital of Lower Austria in 1987, when the government moved its offices from Vienna to the Landhausviertel quarter on the Traisen River. Today, the quarter's modern architecture and entertainment venues inject a dose of life into what is otherwise a rather sleepy town. Its heyday dates back two centuries to the Baroque period when a Who's of Who of artists, including **Jakob Prandtauer**, Josef and Franz **Munggenast**, Daniel Gran, Paul Troger and Bartolomeo Altomonte, lived and worked here. Evidence of their creativity is found at every turn, making a stroll around the old town a lesson in Baroque.

🛈 **Information:** Rathausplatz 1, A-3100. ☎02742/35 33 54. www.st-poelten.gv.at.

▶ **Orient Yourself:** St. Pölten is about 65km/41mi west of Vienna.

🅿 **Parking:** Look for parking garages on Eybnerstraße, Dr.-Karl-Renner-Promenade, Bräuhausgasse, Rossmarkt, Rathausplatz and in the Landhausviertel. Parking is free in the Landesviertel garages from Friday 7pm to Monday 5am.

😳 **Don't Miss:** Dom, Landesmuseum, Klangturm.

🕔 **Organizing Your Time:** Devote at least one full day to St. Pölten.

Kids **Especially for Kids:** Klangturm, Landesmuseum.

👣 **Also See:** STIFT MELK, STIFT LILIENFELD, MARIAZELL.

Sights

Rathaus District

Rathausplatz

Rathaus tower and Trinity Column, St. Pölten

The main town square is bordered by beautiful patrician houses and punctuated by the massive marble **Trinity Column**, completed in 1782 by Andreas Gruber. It shows St. Hippolytus, St. Florian (recognizable by his attribute of a burning house), St. Sebastian (arrow) and St. Leopold (model of a church).

Lording over the square is the pinkish **Rathaus** (town hall), created in the 16C by connecting two existing Gothic houses. In 1727 Josef Munggenast added the Baroque façade. The tower has become the emblem of St. Pölten. To the left of the Rathaus is the 16C **Schuberthaus**, in which the composer stayed in 1821, holding "Schubertiade" musical evenings.

On the square's north side, the **Franziskanerkirche** (1757–79) with its lively Rococo façade is noted for its exuberant high altar by Andreas Gruber and the four side altar paintings by Kremser Schmidt.

To the right of the Rathaus is the 1707 **Prandtauerkirche**, named for its builder. The Crucifixion scene on the high altar by Johann Lukas von Hildebrandt is attributed to the Spanish painter José de Ribera (1588–1652).

Address Book

PRACTICAL INFORMATION

VISITOR INFORMATION

Tourismusinformation *(Rathausplatz 1)*. The local **Calendar of events** on the city and its surroundings comes out monthly between May and October and can be obtained from the tourist office and hotels.

CITY TOURS

The tourist office organizes various themed walking tours of varying length. Check for a current schedule. For self-guided tours (in English), the office rents out **audio-guides** (€1.45). The tours take in old town and the Landhausviertel and last about 2hr 15min.

For an easy introduction to St. Pölten, catch a ride aboard the free **Hauptstadtexpress** *(Apr–Oct, Dec, Thu–Sat 10am–5pm hourly, free)*, a little tourist train stopping at major attractions throughout the city centre.

PUBLIC TRANSPORT

City buses tickets can be bought from the bus drivers, and so can bus timetables at a cost of €1.50. A single-trip ticket costs €1.70 (valid for 1hr; allows change of vehicle and of direction of travel). Multiple-trip tickets cost €6 and are valid for five single trips. A weekly ticket costs €10. Timetable and price details can be obtained by calling ☎0 27 42/25 23 60. After 8.40pm, a taxi service (Sammel-Taxis) operates, ☎0 27 42/25 35 45.

POST OFFICES

City centre post office *(Wiener Straße 12, ◷Mon–Fri 8am–noon, 2pm–6pm)*; Main post office *(Bahnhofsplatz 1a, ◷Mon–Fri 7am–8pm, Sat 7am–1pm)*

SHOPPING

The main axes of the pedestrian shopping zone are Kremser Gasse and Wiener Straße. There is a wide variety of shops here, catering to every taste.

ENTERTAINMENT

Theater der Landeshauptstadt – *Rathausplatz 11, ☎0 27 42/35 20 26 19*. Theater, musicals, operettas, children's theater. *Closed for a summer break in Jul and Aug.*

Bühne im Hof – *Linzer Straße 18, ☎0 27 42/35 22 91*. Cabaret, dance, concerts.

Festspielhaus – *Franz-Schubert-Platz, ☎0 27 42/20 10*. Wide range of entertainment on offer: concerts of classical music, folk music, jazz, pop, rock, opera, operettas, musicals, ballet, folk dancing.

Kultur Gasthof Figl – *Ratzersdorf, Hauptplatz, ☎0 27 42/25 74 02*. Inn with cabaret.

CINEMAS

The **Hollywood Megaplex** *(☎0 27 42/28 80; Engelbert-Laimer-Straße 1 on the right of the Traisen)* offers eight cinema screens and various options for eating out or other entertainment under a single roof.

WHERE TO EAT

Galerie – *Fuhrmannsgasse 1, ☎0 27 42/35 13 05*. Top quality restaurant, considered the best in town.

Parzer & Reibenwein – *Riemerplatz 1, ☎0 27 42/35 30 17 30*. Restaurant with stylish décor in a 12C building (Baroque façade, arcaded courtyard).

Gasthof Winkler – *Mühlweg 64, ☎0 27 42/36 49 44*. Menu varies with the seasons, idyllic garden for clientele.

Zum Gwercher – *In Stattersdorf (right of the Traisen, southeast of city center), Schiffmannstraße 98, ☎0 27 42/23 05 90*. Welcoming restaurant with a large garden inside the courtyard. International selection of wines and cigars.

CAFÉS AND BARS

Kaffee-Konditorei Amler – *Brunngasse 4–6*. Traditional coffee house.

Café Punschkrapferl – *Domgasse 8*. More than 80 pastries to choose from and, as if that were not enough, ice cream, and a salad bar.

Zum Rothen Krebs – *Kremser Gasse 18*. Modern daytime bar with a library corner, where visitors feel as if they have been transported to some grand mansion.

Winzig ("Little," *Kremser Gasse 25*) and **Riesig** ("Large," *Wiener Straße 24*) are two bars, which despite their names are both relatively small, where a pleasant evening can be spent over a light meal or a drink or two (beer or wine).

Mitt'n Drin – *Wiener Straße 10*. Visitors barely need to set foot over the threshold to be in the thick of things. Good for a quick drink to recharge the batteries.

Drunter & Drüber – *Kugelgasse 6*. Bar with comfortable sofa corner and garden. During the colder months, there is also live music ranging from rock to blues.

Narrenkastl – *Wiener Straße 33*. Small bar with a platform overlooked by the figure of a dwarf. During summer, the pretty courtyard is where most of the action takes place.

Salzamt – *Linzer Straße 18*. Bar atmosphere beneath a fine vaulted ceiling.

Cabrio – *Linzer Straße 30*. Local bar serving beer to a youthful set, with plenty of greenery adorning the premises (not all of it real, however).

Flieger-Bräu – *Ferstlergasse 9*. House-brewed naturally dark beer. Rustic local bar, where flying is the main theme of the décor.

DATES FOR YOUR DIARY

Meisterkonzerte: *Dec–Apr.* Concerts of classical music in the Stadtsaal and Festspielhaus.

St. Pöltner Festwochen: *Early May–early Jun.* Concerts, plays, cabaret.

Film am Dom: *Early Jun.* The "Cinema Paradiso" association presents a discriminating program of open-air cinema on the Domplatz.

Hauptstadtfest: *Second Fri in Jul.* Music, cabaret, children's entertainment at various venues in the city centre. Fireworks display.

Sonnenblumenfest: *Jul.* "Sunflower Festival": Musical and culinary delicacies on offer on the Rathausplatz.

Film-Festival: One-month film festival *late Jul–early Sept.* Films and food from all over the world on the Rathausplatz.

St. Pöltner Seefest: *Aug.* Ballet, concerts, children's entertainment by the Ratzersdorfer Lake.

Musica Sacra: *Late Sept–early Oct.* Performances of international church music in the cathedral and the abbey churches of Herzogenburg and Lilienfeld.

More precise details about dates and other information is available from the tourist office on ☎*0 27 42/35 33 54*.

Stadtmuseum

🕐*Wed–Sun 10am–5pm.* 🚫*Jan 1, May 1, Dec 24, 25, 26, 31.* ✆€5. ☎*0 27 42/3 33 26 43. www.stadtmuseum-stpoelten.at.* The city history museum is part of a cultural center inside a converted Carmelite nunnery attached to the Prandtauerkirche. Exhibits include archeological finds and Jugendstil works.

Institut der Englischen Fräulein★

From Prandtauerstraße turn left onto Linzer Straße (no. 11).
The most outstanding Baroque façade in St. Pölten belongs to this girls' school that was originally affiliated with an order founded by the English nun Mary Ward in 1709 to educate the daughters of the aristocracy. Prandtauer designed the sumptuous pink and white exterior whose black wrought-iron grills make

a striking contrast. Four portals, richly decorated with scrolls and busts of angels, divide up the long building, as do several sculpture-filled niches. The small **Institutskirche** (church) is lavishly decorated with frescoes by Paul Troger and Bartolomeo Altomonte.

Cathedral District

Dom Mariä Himmelfahrt★

Enlivened only by an ornate spire and the two figures of St. Hippolytus and St. Augustine, the cathedral's austere façade belies the Baroque splendor that awaits behind its portals. The soft tones of the stucco marble and paintings, the sheen of the liberally applied gilding and the inlaid work combine to create a rich and warm effect.

The conversion into the Baroque style began in 1722 under Jakob Prandtauer and was completed in 1735 under Josef Munggenast. The 1658 high altar painting by Tobias Pock depicts the *Assumption of Mary*. The splendid **choir stalls**★ with their elaborately carved wooden decoration and the organ case are by Peter Widerin. The ceiling frescoes and the ten large **wall-paintings**★, which show scenes from the life of Christ, are the work of Thomas Friedrich Gedon and clearly demonstrate the influence of Daniel Gran. Gran himself, along with Bartolomeo Altomonte, painted the frescoes in the side aisles as well as the altarpieces in the side altars.

The **Rosenkranzkapelle** is the only remaining section from the original medieval church. It has cross-ribbed vaulting and pillars with intricately decorated capitals. The entrance to this chapel is via the choir stalls.

Diözesan-Museum★

On the upper floor of the cloister courtyard. May–Oct, Tue–Fri 10am–noon, 2pm–5pm; Sat, Sun, holidays 10am–1pm. €4. 0 27 42/32 43 31. www.dsp.at.
This museum houses religious art from the Romanesque period to the present, in particular Gothic altarpieces and sculptures, and works by leading Austrian Baroque artists. The crowning glory is the sumptuous library, the **Stiftsbibliothek**★, with sculptures attributed to Peter Widerin and frescoes by Daniel Gran and Paul Troger. These depict the four faculties: theology, philosophy, medicine and law.

Riemerplatz

This another beautiful Baroque square lined with fine Baroque façades especially the Herbertstein Palace.

Stöhr Haus

This is an important example of a Jugendstil building, at Kremser Gasse no 41, built in 1899 by Joseph Maria Olbrich, creator of the Vienna Secession building.

Government and Cultural District

Since becoming the seat of the Lower Austrian government, St. Pölten has built a new government and cultural district about 500m/546.8yd southeast of the old town by the Traisen. The quarter's main commercial artery is the Landhaus Boulevard, which culminates in the elegant new state parliament building. Beyond here are the main cultural institutions, including the Festspielhaus concert hall designed by Klaus Kada, and the Landesmuseum (see next).

For a birds-eye view of the quarter, head to the 46m/150ft viewing platform of the **Klangturm** (*"Sound tower," year-round Mon–Sat 8am–7pm, Sun 9am–5pm; exhibits late Apr–Oct, Tue–Sun 9am–5pm; free admission; 0 27 42/90 80 51; www.klangturm.at),* designed by Ernst Hoffmann, which is illuminated at night. The tower also doubles as an information center and houses changing exhibitions (mostly interactive) of artistic installations experimenting with sound.

Landesmuseum   Kids

Tue–Sun 9am–5pm. €8. 027 42/90 80 901 00. www.landesmuseum.net.
Housed in a radically modern building by Hans Hollein, the Lower Austrian provincial museum presents exhibits on nature, art and history in engaging fashion that often makes clever use of interactive technology. The prized art collection presents the entire spectrum of works from the Middle Ages to today. Elsewhere you can take a virtual journey into the past with the help of multimedia installations and a 3D film. The overarching theme is "water," which pops up in unusual places throughout the museum. Special exhibits and child-oriented events add additional dimensions.

Excursions

Stift Herzogenburg★

12km/7.4mi north of St. Pölten.
Guided tour (1hr) Apr–Oct, daily 9.30am, 11am, 1.30pm, 3pm, 4.30pm; Nov–Mar, by appointment. €7. 0 27 82/8 31 12 11. www.stift-herzogenburg.at.
The Augustinian canons' monastery was founded in 1112 by Bishop Ulrich of Passau and given a complete Baroque makeover in the 18C in a collaboration

of three of the era's greatest architects: Jakob Prandtauer, Johann Fischer von Erlach and Joseph Munggenast. Franz Munggenast rebuilt the **church**, which was adorned with frescoes by Bartolomeo Altomonte who also painted the altarpieces on the side altars. The picture on the high altar is by Daniel Gran.

A highlight of the monastic buildings is the **Festsaal**★(festival hall), a work of Fischer von Erlach crowned by Altomonte's huge allegorical fresco to the glory of the prince-bishops of Passau. Tours also take in the **library**, which is liberally decorated with pictures, frescoes and *grisailles* (paintings in tones of grey), and a room filled with Late Gothic works by artists belonging to the Danubian School.

Kirchstetten
15km/9.3mi east.
This village was for many years the summer retreat of the Anglo-American poet **WH Auden** (1907–73) and the Austrian poet, Josef Weinheber (1892–1945—suicide). Auden was buried here in Kirchstetten's churchyard.

ST. VEIT AN DER GLAN
KÄRNTEN
POPULATION 13 030 – ALT 476M/1 562FT

St. Veit was the seat of the dukes of Carinthia until 1518 when the role of regional capital passed to Klagenfurt. The well-preserved town wall, the picturesque narrow streets, the two town squares with their handsome houses and arcaded courtyards all contribute to the charming flair of this town.

- 🛈 **Information:** Hauptplatz 1. ☎04212/55 55. www.stveit.carinthia.at.
- ▶ **Orient Yourself:** St. Veit is in southern Austria, about 19km/11.8mi north of Klagenfurt.
- 😊 **Don't Miss:** Fuchs Palast.
- 🕐 **Organizing Your Time:** The town warrants about a half day visit.
- 🧒 **Especially for Kids:** Museum der Stadt Veit.
- 👣 **Also See:** BURG HOCHOSTERWITZ, GURK, MARIA SAAL, MAGDALENSBERG.

Sights

Hauptplatz★
Most places of interest in St. Veit are on or near this central square, which is at the heart of a mostly pedestrianized web of lanes. The **Schüsselbrunnen** is a fountain surmounted by a grotesque bronze figure in a 16C miner's costume that has become the town mascot. The square's other fountain honors Walther von der Vogelweide, the most famous of the German troubadours who once worked at the court of St. Veit. Also have peek inside the **Stadtpfarrkirche**, notable for its Late Baroque high altar and chancel, both by local master woodcarver Johann Pacher.

Rathaus★
This elegant building was built during the Late Gothic period but did not get its grand pilastered **stucco façade**★ until 1754, the work of Joseph Pittner. On the pediment is the double-headed eagle of the Holy Roman Empire, embossed with the statue of the city's namesake Saint Veit. A vaulted Gothic passageway leads to the sgraffito-decorated **Renaissance courtyard**★, one of the finest in Carinthia. The great hall, or **Rathaussaal**★ (♿🕐*Mon–Fri 7am–6pm;* ☎*0 42 12/5 55 56 68*) on the first floor is decorated with lacy stuccowork.

Museum der Stadt Veit 🧒
Hauptplatz 29. 🕐*Jul–Aug, daily 9am–6pm; Apr–Oct, daily 9am–noon, 2pm–6pm.* ✎*€5; children €2.* ☎*0 42 12/55 55 64. www.museum-stveit.at.*

© Österreich Werbung / Diejun

Fuchs Palast

Transport and communication are the main themes of this small museum where you can admire a huge model railway with 200m/219yd of tracks or fancy yourself a locomotive engineer in a clever simulator. The century-old post office provides an endearing window on the past.

Fuchs Palast

Professor-Ernst-Fuchs-Platz 1. ☎0 42 12/4 66 00. www.fuchspalast.com.
Probably what you'll remember more than anything about St. Veit is this must-see-to-be-believed art hotel, a whimsical composition by painter Ernst Fuchs. With its patterned red, white and blue façade and equally fantastical interior, it blithely defies all conventions. For the full immersion, book one of the 60 rooms.

Excursions

Magdalensberg★

15km/9.3mi – about 2hr. Leave St. Veit on the road to Klagenfurt. ⏱May–mid-Oct, daily 9am–7pm. ⊚€5. ☎042 24/22 55. www.landesmuseum-ktn.at.
After 7km/4.3mi turn left onto an uphill road on the flank of the Magdalensberg. The road ends at the **Archeological Park Magdalensberg**, an open-air museum leading through the excavated traces of an early Roman town, built on the remains of an even older Celtic settlement.
Walk *(45min round trip)* to the top of the mountain (alt 1 058m/3 470ft) to enjoy the majestic **panorama**★ and to pop into the Gothic pilgrims' chapel dedicated to Sts Helen and Mary Magdalene. It houses a beautiful, paneled 15C altarpiece from the woodcarving workshops at St. Veit.

ST. WOLFGANG★★

OBERÖSTERREICH

POPULATION 2 790 – ALT 549M/1 801FT

LOCAL MAP SEE SALZKAMMERGUT

A deluge of visitors is no novelty for St. Wolfgang on the lake of the same name. Its church, which is a feast of magnificent works of art, has been a place of pilgrimage since the 12C. Today the faithful are joined by music lovers who come to see the original of the "White Horse Inn" and the beautiful landscape and magnificent lake★★ praised in the comic opera of that name *(Im Weissen Rössl)*. The charm of St. Wolfgang is most strongly felt in the less busy periods either side of the main summer season and during the winter.

- **Information:** Pilgerstraße 28, A – 5360. ☎0 61 38/80 03, www.stwolfgang.at.
- ▶ **Orient Yourself:** St. Wolfgang is in the Salzkammergut, about 48km/30mi east of Salzburg.
- **P** **Parking:** Parking is tight in summer. Try the garages at the village entrance and at the Schafberg station, 1km/.6mi beyond the church.
- **Don't Miss:** Michael-Pacher Altar.
- **Organizing Your Time:** Budget half a day, more if going up the Schafberg.
- **Also See:** ST. GILGEN, BAD ISCHL, MONDSEE.

A Bit of History

When St. Wolfgang Bishop of Regensberg came to reorganize the abbey at Mondsee, which fell under his jurisdiction, he built a chapel on a promontory jutting out into the lake that would bear his name. Soon a small community built up around it. St. Wolfgang was a popular bishop and when he was canonized after his death the chapel became a popular place of pilgrimage. In the 15C it was replaced by a larger church and the marvelous altar by Tirolean artist, Michael Pacher, was commissioned by the Abbot of Mondsee.

St. Wolfgang also owes its popularity to the Weißes Rössl (White Horse Inn), which inspired the operetta of the same name. The story is of the head waiter who falls in love with the owner of the inn who herself is attracted to one of her regulars. The popularity of Ralph Benatzky's musical work attracted visitors to the small town already popular with pilgrims of a spiritual persuasion.

Sights

Access

In high season a pleasant alternative to driving is to arrive by **boat** (*May–Oct;* ☎*061 38/2 23 20*). Regular services operate from Strobl and St. Gilgen, calling in at Schafberg and the center of St. Wolfgang.

Pfarrkirche

Daily 8am–6pm. ☎*0 61 38/23 21.*

St. Wolfgang's parish church is the successor to the chapel of a hermitage built, according to legend, by St. Wolfgang, the bishop of Regensburg who came to seek solitude on the shores of the lake that would later bear his name. The present late 15C structure on a rocky spur abuts onto the elegant 16C priory. The outer cloisters, lined with arcades that yield bird's-eye views of the lake, complete the charming ensemble.

Michael-Pacher-Altar★★

This 12m/39.4ft-high masterpiece (1481) shows rare unity in composition and is considered to be an outstanding example of Gothic art. The central panel shows a heavily gilded Coronation of the Virgin, while the complementary paint-

Parish church of St. Wolfgang

ings depict scenes from the life of Mary. Pacher reveals himself to be a master of perspective and detail in this work.

Schwanthaler-Doppelaltar★

This Baroque masterpiece was created by Thomas Schwanthaler in 1675–76, and features more than 100 carved figures full of life and energy. The left panel, executed in black and gold, shows the Holy Family on their pilgrimage to Jerusalem, while the right panel depicts St. Wolfgang.

It is said that Thomas Schwanthaler dissuaded the abbot of Mondsee from replacing Pacher's altarpiece with his own when the church was redecorated in Baroque style, but there is no evidence to corroborate this story.

A third great artist has left his legacy in this church: The Mondsee master, **Meinrad Guggenbichler**, to whom the three altars on the north side of the church, including the majestic Rosenkranzaltar, and the pulpit are attributed. His *Man of Sorrows* is particularly heart-rending. Near the church is the famous **Weisses Rössl** (White Horse Inn).

A family of artists

The **Schwanthaler family**, from Ried im Innkreis, produced no fewer than 21 artists in a period of 250 years, the majority of whom were sculptors. A 19C descendant, Ludwig Ritter von Schwanthaler, Court Sculptor to King Ludwig I of Bavaria, was responsible for the sculpted figure of Bavaria on the Theresienwiese in Munich.

Excursion

Schafberg★★

Alt 1 783m/ 5 830ft. About 4hr round trip, including 1hr 30min by Schafbergbahn rack railway and 30min walk. ◐*May–Oct, 8.25am–3.55pm. €24.50 round trip.* ☎*0 61 38/2 23 20. www.schafbergbahn.at.*
From the mountain station, make for the hotel on the summit, which is a short distance from the impressive precipice on the north face. From here you can spot numerous lakes, including the Mondsee, Attersee and Wolfgangsee and any number of major Alpine peaks and ranges, including the Höllengebirge, the Totes Gebirge and the Dachstein.

SCHÄRDING★

OBERÖSTERREICH
POPULATION 5 050 – ALT 318M/1 043FT

This picturesque little town on the Inn River belonged to the royal Bavarian Wittelsbach family almost without interruption from 1248 through 1779 when it was ceded to Austria. There are no major sights here, but the lovely Baroque old town with cobbled lanes and remains of the medieval fortifications make Schärding a pleasant stop nonetheless.

- **Information:** Innbruckstraße 29, A – 4780 Schärding. ☎0 77 12/4 30 00. www.oberoesterreich.at/schaerding.
- ▶ **Orient Yourself:** Schärding is on Austria's western edge, right on the border with Germany, about 107km/66.5mi west of Linz.
- Ⓟ **Parking:** Look for parking lots on Bahnhofstraße and Alfred-Kubin-Straße. There's also a garage on Tummelplatzstraße.
- ◐ **Organizing Your Time:** Plan on spending about a couple of hours in town.
- ♦ **Also See:** DONAUTAL.

A Bit of History

First mentioned in documents in 804, Schärding has been an important trading site on the Inn ever since. The Bavarian ducal family, the Wittelsbachs, were an important influence on the town's architecture. Such was the economic importance of Schärding that there was a constant need for fortifications. They Bavarian duke, Ludwig the Bearded, was responsible for the fortifications little of which remain apart from the castle moat. The town suffered damage during two disastrous fires in 1724 and 1779 and during French occupation in 1809.

Silberzeile

Old Town

Stadtplatz

Schärding's old town centers on **Stadt-platz**, the main square divided by a row of buildings called a *Grätzel*. Its most distinctive feature, though, is the **Silberzeile**★, a phalanx of statuesque Baroque houses painted in a rainbow of colors. The name, which translates as "Silver Row," is a reference to the deep-pocketed merchants who had them built back in the 17C.

Stadtpfarrkirche

Just off the square, the Late Baroque **Stadtpfarrkirche** (parish church), dedicated to St. George, has fine proportions that give the well-lit nave a lofty dignity, emphasized by soaring pillars. The left side altar has a panel by Michael Rott-mayr (Christ appearing to St. Theresa) from about 1690.

Linzertor

The upper square is closed off by the Linzer Tor (Linz Gate), while the Rathaus (town hall) marks the beginning of the lower square anchored by the St.-Georgs-Brunnen (St. George's Fountain) of 1607.

Wassertor

To get to the Inn River, walk through the **Wassertor** (Water Gate), where high water marks provide evidence of disastrous flooding.

Innlände promenade

Taking a stroll along the **Innlände** riverside promenade opens up attractive perspectives on the town. River steamers stop here as well.

SCHLADMINGER TAUERN ❄❄❄
STEIERMARK

This mountain chain stretches for 40km/25mi and towers over the broad **Ennstal**. On the other side of this valley is the muscular **Dachstein massif**★★, which has the appearance of a fortress with its limestone rocks, steep jagged cliffs and harsh features. The Schladminger Tauern, by contrast, are characterized by long, densely wooded and easily accessible valleys with lakes and rivers. It is precisely these varied landscapes that lend the Ennstal its special appeal. Since the 1960s, the area has been a popular winter sports resort. In summer, hikers have access to wide-open, unspoiled areas with spectacular views.

- **Information:** Erzherzog-Johann-Straße 213, Schladming. ☎03687/2 22 68. www.schladming-dachstein.at.
- ▶ **Orient Yourself:** In central Austria, about 84km/53mi southeast of Salzburg.
- **Don't Miss:** Hunerkogel.
- ◔ **Organizing Your Time:** Allow a day if takig in at least one summit.
- **Especially for Kids:** Nature trail around Planai summit.
- ✋ **Also See:** DACHSTEIN.

Sights

Dachstein-Tauern Ski Area

Ski hounds will find 78 lifts, 140km/87mi of downhill ski runs and 350km/217mi of off-piste slopes to play with, but need only a single ski pass for the combined Schladminger Tauern and Dachstein area.

The **downhill ski runs** concentrate mainly on the Schladminger Tauern and consist of five areas: the **Reiter-alm** *(alt 800–1 860m/2 625–6 102ft)* above Pichl; the **Hochwurzen** *(745–*

1 850m/2 444–6 069ft) above Rohrmoos; the **Planai** *(745–1 894m/2 444–6 213ft)* above Schladming; the **Hauser Kaibling** *(752–2 015m/2 467–6 611ft)* above Haus; and the **Gaisterbergalm** *(680–1 976m/2 231–6 483ft)* above Pruggern. Most are connected to each other and are also served by buses. Fageralm, Stoderzinken and the Dachstein glacier are smaller areas.

Moderately good skiers will be especially happy here, but less those who like open spaces and large differences in altitude. The snow cover is generally good, but the moderate altitude can sometimes pose problems. Snow-making equipment is often used on the lower pistes. For cross-country skiers, the **Schladminger Tauern** provide 60km/37mi of tracks around Rohrmoos in beautiful, sunny surroundings, and a further 28km/17mi around Schladming. Dedicated skiers should steer toward **Ramsau am Dachstein** *(see DACHSTEIN)* whose internationally renowned **cross-country ski area** is distinguished by a particularly enchanting setting.

Schladming

Alt 745m/2 444ft. The World Cup downhill races held on the Planai slopes since 1973 have given Schladming plenty of publicity. Après-ski entertainment is also provided for, with generous sports facilities (themed swimming pool, indoor tennis courts, etc.). Golfers will find a demanding 18-hole course at Oberhaus. Schladming's pedestrian zone is a joy to stroll around.

Other resorts in the valley include **Rohrmoos**, Pichl, **Haus** (with a pretty Baroque church) and Pruggern. Another alternative is the sunny plateau of **Ramsau** *(see DACHSTEIN)*, which is famous for its unspoiled countryside and delightful setting.

Viewpoints

Hunerkogel★★★

Alt 2 694m/8 836ft. See DACHSTEIN.

Rossbrand★★

Alt 1 770m/5 807ft. 28km/17mi west of Schladming. See DACHSTEIN.

Planai★★

Alt 1 906m/6 253ft. 1hr round trip from Schladming. Take the cable-car in two stages (sit facing the back). Jun 11– Oct 22 & Dec–Apr, daily 9am–4.30pm *(summer to 5pm).* €13 round trip (summer), €31.50 day pass (winter). 0 36 87/2 20 42 13. *Also accessible via a small mountain (toll) road, 12km/7.4mi.*

The view from the mountain station is rather limited, but if you make the climb to the summit you'll enjoy a wonderful **panorama**★★. Skiers can make the journey via the Burgstallalm piste and also the chair-lift of the same name. Hikers can climb up to the **Krahbergzinken**

Schladming

© Österreich Werbung / Bohnacker

View of the Dachstein mountains from Planai

(alt 2 134m/7 001ft) in 2hr 30min round trip. The less ambitious can take an easy **nature trail** round the summit of the Planai in 45min.

Hochwurzen★★

Alt 1 849m/6 066ft. 30min round trip via cable-car from Rohrmoos ◐*Jun 11–Oct 22 & Dec–Apr, daily 9am–4.30pm (summer to 5pm).* ◔€*9.70 round trip (summer),* €*16.50 (winter).* ☎*0 36 87/2 20 42 13.* Remarkable **panorama**★★ of the Dachstein and view of Schladming. From the mountain inn terrace it is possible to see the Schladminger Tauern massif with the Hochgolling and Steirische Kalkspitze summits.

Excursions

Hiking

Schladming and other Ennstal villages are ideal starting points for **walks and hikes**★★ in the relatively low-lying surrounding mountain ranges. A magnificent panorama can be enjoyed from such summits as Höchstein and Hochgolling, but because of the long climb involved, plan to stay overnight at the mountain lodge.

Dreiseen circuit★

17km/11mi east of Schladming. Allow 4hr hiking time for the entire circuit. Drive on E 651 toward Liezen then turn right onto a small toll road toward the Bodensee.
An easy trail leads to the **Bodensee**★ with its beautiful waterfall in about 15min. From the far end of the

Address Book

◔*For coin ranges, see cover flap.*

WHERE TO STAY

◔◔◔**Mitterhofer** – *Salzburgerstr. 371, Schladming.* ☎*03687/2 22 29. www.mittehofer.at. 30 rooms.*

◔◔◔**Posthotel** – *Hauptplatz 10, Schladming.* ☎*03687/2 25 71. www. posthotel-schladming.at. 42 rooms.* **Restaurant**◔◔◔.

◔◔◔◔**Sporthotel Royer** – *Europaplatz 583, Schladming.* ☎*03687/2 00. www.royer.at. 127 rooms.* Hotel close to the Planai lifts (300m/984ft).

lake, an arduous trail climbs up to the Hans-Wödl-Hütte mountain lodge *(alt 1 528m/5 013ft)* on the idyllic **Hüttensee** in about 1hr. A beautiful spruce forest and two waterfalls form the backdrop.

After another 45min through luxuriant vegetation, the trail reaches the crystal-clear **Obersee** *(alt 1 672m/5 485ft)*. Return the same way.

SCHNEEBERG★
NIEDERÖSTERREICH

Since the completion of the Semmering railway in the mid 19C, the Schneeberg region has been a popular getaway for outdoor enthusiasts from Vienna. Hiking and touring are popular in summer, while skiers hit the slopes at first snowfall.

- **Information:** Sticklergasse 3, Puchberg am Schneeberg. ☎02636/22 56 11. www.schneeburgerland.com.
- **Orient Yourself:** The area is in eastern Austria, some 70km/43.5mi south of Vienna.

Driving Tour
102km/63mi

Neunkirchen to Semmering★

102km/63mi

⊙*The route described below includes steep and narrow stretches of road, especially between Hirschwang and Semmering.*

Neunkirchen
One of the oldest towns in Lower Austria it has some original Renaissance buildings. North of the Hauptplatz with its Trinity Column, the parish church of Mariä Himmelfahrt (mid-12C–16C, Baroque interior) towers above the rooftops. The church was fortified because of the town's frontier setting, and was once even surrounded by a moat.

- *In Neunkirchen, turn off B 17 onto B 26 toward Puchberg.*

Puchberg am Schneeberg
This pleasant mountain resort is distinguished by idyllic spa gardens laid out around a lake and a 12C ruined castle. From Puchberg station, the rack railway **Schneebergbahn** (⊙*May–Oct, daily 9am–5.30pm;* ∞€*30.50 round trip;* ☎*0 26 36/36 61; www.schneebergbahn.*

at) makes several trips to Hochschneeberg daily. From the mountain station next to a refuge (with restaurant), an easy trail leads to the summit in about 90min, treating you to fabulous **views**★ along the way. Schneeberg is the highest mountain in Lower Austria.

- *Leave Puchberg on B 26 toward Wiener Neustadt, turn left toward Waldegg. In Reichental turn left again toward Gutenstein.*

Gutenstein
In the 19C Gutenstein was a popular summer resort, attracting artists such as Lenau, Brahms and Waldmüller. The town's annual Raimundspiele open-air theater festival (www.raimundspiele.at) commemorates the Austrian actor and playwright **Ferdinand Raimund**, who committed suicide here in 1836, fearing that he had caught rabies from a dog. He is buried in the town graveyard.

Wallfahrtskirche Mariahilfberg
3km/1.8mi from Gutenstein. Turn left before the church toward Mariahilfberg. Various Habsburg emperors are among those who have made the pilgrimage to this Baroque church. An altarpiece in the left aisle features a striking depiction of an angel coming to the rescue of a soul burning in Purgatory.

▶ 2km/1.2mi beyond Gutenstein turn left into the Klostertal.

Klostertal★
About 16km/10mi.
This valley is sparsely populated and largely unspoiled. Toward the end, it narrows considerably, already heralding the Höllental.

Höllental★★
About 14km/8.5mi.
The Höllental, or Hell Valley, was carved by the River Schwarza between the two limestone massifs of the Schneeberg and the Raxalpe. There is quite a contrast between the delightful Klostertal and the harsher Wildbach Valley, where the green water gushes over the boulders and gravel of the deeply embedded riverbed.

▶ At Hirschwang, the valley station of the Rax cable-car is to the right of the road.

© Österreich Werbung / 'G, P.ddp

River Schwarza near Hirschwang, Höllental

Semmering railway

Rail links already existed between Vienna and Gloggnitz and between Mürzzuschlag and Bruck an der Mur, but crossing the Semmering range still required the use of horse-drawn carts. In order to complete the final gap in the southern railway network, Venetian engineer Carlo di Ghega (1802–60) was invited to take over the Semmering railway project. Between 1848 and 1854, up to 20 000 workers were busy building the track of Europe's first standard-gauge mountain railway (some 1 000 of them died in accidents or from epidemics during construction). On the 41km/25mi stretch between Gloggnitz and Mürzzuschlag (21km/13mi above ground) the train passes through 15 tunnels, crosses 16 viaducts and more than 100 smaller bridges, overcoming an altitude difference of 480m/1 584 ft. In spite of the tremendous feats of construction—1.4 million cu m/49 million cu ft of rock alone had to be blasted—the railway blends harmoniously into the beautiful landscape around Semmering. After the railway's inauguration in 1854 by Emperor Franz Joseph and Empress Elisabeth, the region's popularity soared, especially as a summer retreat for the Viennese. Originally, steam engines trundled over the Semmering range at 6kph/4mph, but speeds increased to 60kph/37mph after the line was electrified in 1956. In 1999, UNESCO declared the railway and surrounding countryside a World Heritage Site.

Raxalpe★

Ascent by Raxseilbahn cable-car in 8min.
⏱*Daily 8am–4.30pm every 30min;* ⊘*two weeks in Nov;* ⛖*€18.30;* ☎*0 26 66/5 24 97; www.raxalpe.com.*
This steep-sided limestone massif has become a climbing center with several routes departing from the upper station at 1 547m/5 075ft. You can also undertake multi-day tours that have you overnighting in mountain huts. For details, check with the Reichenau tourist office. Along the way you will enjoy charming

viewpoints★ over the Schneeberg, the Höllental and Semmering.

▷ *Exiting Hirschwang turn right toward Prein, then left toward Gloggnitz and right toward Semmering.*

The winding road leaves the Schwarza Valley and cuts across the picturesque, rugged Semmering region. Dropping down to Breitenstein it affords first glimpses of the superbly engineered viaducts of the **Semmering railway**★ (ⓒ*see box above*).

The Semmering railway

© Österreich Werbung / OEBB

▶ *Shortly after the "Semmering" sign-post turn left toward "Haltestelle Wolfsbergkogel." After a couple of hundred yards turn left again and follow the wooden "Aussichtswarte Doppelreiterkogel" signs. Park and follow the marked trail for about 10min to the look-out point.*

The **Doppelreiterkogel look-out point**★★ offers a magnificent view of the Semmering railway, which cuts a particularly fine route at this point, with numerous viaducts and tunnels.

▶ *Backtrack and follow the signposts to "Hochstraße/Südbahnstraße" to get to Semmering.*

Semmering★

After the construction of the Semmering railway, this climatic mountain spa and winter sports center, built on

terraces between 985m/3 231ft and 1 291m/4 235ft, experienced a steep economic boom.The village is dotted with smart villas and hotels, mostly built between 1850 and 1910. Adding to the area's appeal is the exceptionally sunny climate. Information on the Semmering railway is available from the local tourist office.

SCHWAZ★

TIROL
POPULATION 12 660 – ALT 538M/1 765FT

From the 15C to the 16C when its **silver and copper mines** were in full production, Schwaz was the largest town in the Tirol, after Innsbruck. Its one-time prosperity is attested to today by the unusual size and the decoration of its most representative buildings, all erected between 1450 and 1520.

▯ **Information:** Franz-Josef-Straße 2, A-6130. ☎0 52 42/6 32 40. www.silberregion-karwendel.at/schwaz.

▶ **Orient Yourself:** In western Austria, 30km/18.6mi northeast of Innsbruck.

ⓟ **Parking:** Parking is free for the first two hours in the Stadtgarage.

⊛ **Don't Miss:** Haus der Völker.

ⓞ **Organizing Your Time:** Budget half a day to a day.

Kids **Especially for Kids:** Haus der Völker, Silberbergwerk, Schloss Tratzberg.

& **Also See:** HALL IN TIROL, KARWENDELGEBIRGE.

Sights

Pfarrkirche

Schwaz's parish church on Franz-Josef-Straße is the largest Gothic four-aisle hall church in the Tirol with an impressive roof covered with 15 000 copper shingles Consecrated in 1502, half the church was originally reserved for the burghers, the other for the miners. The finest piece of religious sculpture is the **altar of St. Anne** in the south side aisle. Its Baroque altarpiece (1733), honoring the patron saints of Austria, St. George and St. Florian, frames a fine early 16C group of the Holy Family

Haus der Völker★   Kids

Christoph-Anton-Mayr-Weg 7. About 15min walk north of town center via Husslstraße. ⓞ*Daily 10am–6pm.* ⊛*€6;*

Schloss Tratzberg

children €4. ☎0 52 42/6 60 90. www. hausdervoelker.com.

This private museum of ethnology presents the fantastic collection of non-European art and artifacts assembled by local photojournalist Gert Chesi. The main focus is on Africa with great Yoruba masks, sculpture and voodoo cult objects. There's also exquisitely carved sculpture from Burma (Myanmar), Thailand and China.

Silberbergwerk★ (Silver mine) Kids

Alte Landstraße 3a. Bring a warm top as the temperature is about 13°C/55°F. ⏱Guided tour (1hr 30min) May–Sept, daily 9am–5pm; Oct–Apr, daily 10am–4pm. ⊘Mid–Nov–Dec 25. ⊚€15; children €8. ☎0 52 42/7 23 72. www.silberberg werk.at.

A little train whisks visitors 800m/0.5mi into the Sigmund gallery, created about 500 years ago when Schwaz was a vast silver mining center employing 11 000 miners. Steps give access to a labyrinth of galleries where the techniques of mining and excavation of shafts are graphically explained.

Schloss Freundsberg

⏱Apr–Oct, Fri–Wed 10am–5pm. ⊚€3. ☎0 52 42/6 39 67.

The square keep gives this castle a defiant appearance as it sits picturesquely on its knoll, commanding **views**★ of the Inn Valley and the town. The castle is the 12C ancestral seat of the knights of Freundsberg who sold it to a local duke in 1467. The Late Renaissance palace kitchen is a jewel, while the keep houses the town museum.

Excursion

Schloss Tratzberg★ Kids

5km/3mi. Leave Schwaz on the road to Stans. 20min walk from the parking lot. ⏱Guided tour (1hr) mid–Mar–Jun & Sept–Oct, daily 10am–4pm; Jul–Aug, daily 10am–5pm. ⊚€9; children €4.50. ☎0 52 42/6 35 66 20. www.schloss-tratz berg.at.

This castle served as a hunting lodge for Emperor Maximilian and the Fuggers, the powerful merchant dynasty from Augsburg, who had interests in Schwaz's silver mine. Guided tours, including special fairytale-themed ones for children, take you to rooms containing original furniture, pictures and weapons. The coffered ceiling of the royal chamber (Königinzimmer) of 1569 is magnificent and held together without a single nail. The Habsburg Room features a 46m/151ft-long wall painting depicting 148 of Emperor Maximilian's ancestors in the form of a family tree.

SEEFELD IN TIROL ❄❄❄ ❄❄

TIROL
POPULATION 3 030 – ALT 1 180M/3 871FT
LOCAL MAP SEE SEEFELDER SATTELSTRASSEN

Seefeld lies on a sunny, broad mountain plateau surrounded by thick forest and offering good views of the rocky ridges of the Hohe Munde, Wettersteingebirge, and Karwendel range. It is a popular cross-country ski resort, which hosted the Nordic skiing events during the 1964 and 1976 Olympic Games as well as the World Skiing Championship in 1985.

Off the pistes, you find a sophisticated resort with numerous leisure facilities, including a modern swimming pool complex with water slides and saunas; ice rinks; riding centers; tennis courts and golf courses. Paragliding, rafting and mountain biking are other diversions. Seefeld is also terrific hiking territory, even in winter when 143km/90mi of trails are kept snow-free.

- 🅸 **Information:** Klosterstraße 43. ☎05/0 88 00, www.seefeld.at.
- ▶ **Orient Yourself:** Seefeld is in western Austria, close to the German border and about 22km/14mi west of Innsbruck.
- 😊 **Don't Miss:** Excursion to Seefelder Joch
- 🕐 **Organizing Your Time:** Allow a day or two to take in the sights and hikes. You will need longer if skiing the slopes to fully explore the area
- 👢 **Also See:** SEEFELDER SATTELSTRASSEN, STIFT STAMS.

Sights

Ski slopes
Seefeld boasts one of the largest **cross-country ski areas** in the Alps, with 266km/164mi of tracks and good snow cover from Christmas to March. In the 1964 and 1976 Winter Olympics the resort was the venue for all the Nordic skiing events

The Seekirchl, Seefeld

For downhill skiers, the resort has 36 ski-lifts leading to slopes that are ideal for beginners or those who prefer gentle skiing. The most interesting runs are on the **Seefelder Joch** and the **Härmelekopf**.

Pfarrkirche St. Oswald
This lovely 15C Gothic church was built on the orders of Archduke Leopold V to perpetuate the worship of a miraculous host, which had been an object of pilgrimage since 1384 and was kept here until 1949. Note the tympanum above the south door which represents, on the right, the martyrdom of St. Oswald of England, the patron saint of the church, and, on the left, the miracle of the host. The same themes are picked up by the frescoes decorating the chancel and in a picture (1502) to the right of the chancel.

Seekirchl
South of the village, this church is noteworthy mostly for its postcard-pretty setting against a mountainous backdrop.

Excursions

Wildsee

1km/.6mi south of the center.

A small lake surrounded by read beds and a beach. The lake is a popular place for a stroll and to watch the many wild-fowl that make the lake their home.

Seefelder Joch★★

Alt 2 074m/6 804ft. Funicular to Rosshütte mountain lodge, then Seefelderjochbahn. ⏱*Jun–mid Oct & Dec–Mar, Mon–Fri 9am–noon, 1pm–5pm; from 8.30am Sat–Sun.* ☞*€15 round trip.* ☎*05212/ 2 41 60.*

It is just a short walk from the mountain station to the summit where a beautiful **panorama**★★ takes in the Karwendel mountains, the Wetterstein range with the Zugspitze plateau and other peaks. If you wear sturdy shoes, it is possible to walk back down into the valley, even in winter.

The Miraculous Host

The **Golden Chronicle of Hohen-schwangau** records the following miraculous event: One day after Mass, the knight Oswald Milser and his cohorts confronted the priest. insisting that his rank gave him the right to eat the same special wafer as the priest. When the man of God offered it to Milser, the ground opened up beneath the sacrile-gious knight. His whole body shak-ing with fear, he barely grabbed the altar, where his fingers left their mark as if in wax. The priest retrieved the wafer and the ground closed again, though shortly after-wards the wafer turned blood-red.

SEEFELDER SATTEL STRASSEN★★

TIROL AND BAYERN (GERMANY)

The Seefelder Sattel (Seefeld Saddle), high above the Inn Valley and the Scharnitz ravine, cuts a broad breach in the Northern Limestone Alps along the Munich–Innsbruck route.

🅸 **Information:** Klosterstraße 43. ☎05/0 88 00. www.seefeld.at.

▶ **Orient Yourself:** This area rubs against the German border in western Austria.

☺ **Don't Miss:** Mösern.

🕐 **Organizing Your Time:** Allow a day, or more if stopping at every sight

Kids **Especially for Kids:** The Bee Nature Trail in Reith bei Seefeld.

🕯 **Also See:** INNSBRUCK, SEEFELD IN TIROL.

Driving Tours

1 Zirlerberg Tour★

38km/24mi

Innsbruck★★ 🕯*See Innsbruck.*

▶ *Leave town on the B 171.*

Between Innsbruck and Zirl the road runs along the floor of the Inn Valley beneath the steep slopes of the **Martinswand**, which provided the setting

for an episode dear to the hearts of the Tirolean Emperor Maximilian. He is said to have fallen down the cliff in the excite-ment of the hunt and been saved from a perilous plight by an angel, appearing in the guise of a peasant.

▶ *Rather than driving into Zirl, turn right toward Seefeld.*

The road passes the Baroque Kalvarien-bergkirche (1803–05) and the ruined fortress of Fragenstein outlined above

Zirl. The notoriously steep **Zirlerberg**★ road connects Zirl and Reith bei Seefeld. From the **viewpoint**★ at the hairpin bend you can enjoy a great view of the saw-tooth ridges of the Kalkkögel to the south of Zirl.

Reith bei Seefeld★

The local church stands in a charming **setting**★ facing the small Roskogel range and the jagged crests of the Kalkkögel. There is also a short **Bee Nature Trail** which gives an insight into the lives of the bee. It ends at a Bee Hotel where you can see the bees in their hives through glass panels

Seefeld in Tirol

See SEEFELD IN TIROL.

Mittenwald★

Described by Goethe as a "living picture-book," this violin-making town on the old Augsburg-Verona trade route is a popular tourist destination and starting point for numerous hikes into the mountains. Its high street is lined with fine painted **houses**★★ and leads to the church fronted by a memorial to Matthias Klotz, the man who brought the fine art of violin making to Mittenwald in 1684. Learn more about him at the local **Geigenbau-und Heimatmuseum**.

② Leutasch Valley Tour★★

32km/19.8mi

This route combines a run through the Leutasch Valley and a visit to Mösern, one of the most attractive viewpoints in the upper Inn Valley.

Mittenwald★ *See above.*

▶ *Take the road south toward Leutasch.*

South of Mittenwald the road leaves the Isar Valley and immediately climbs above the **Leutasch Gorge** (Leutaschklamm) within view of the Karwendel range. After crossing the Leutascher Ache, it runs into the grassy combe of Unterleutasch, majestically bounded by the Ahrnspitze and the Wettersteinwand. A few roofed crosses and farm houses dot this lonely valley, preserving its primitive air.

Leutasch Gorge★

Three trails of varying length take you into the gorge and to the 23m/75.5ft **Leutaschklamm**★ waterfall. Part of the longest trail is along a daring man-made section

Leutasch

This community consists of 24 village segments, strung out along the valley. The road passes through some, then forks left in Gasse toward Seefeld. At the junction, there is a splendid view of the majestic Hohe Munde to the right.

Seefeld in Tirol

See SEEFELD IN TIROL.

▶ *Take the road south from Seefeld in Tirol.*

The **Seekirchl** church marks the beginning of a short valley which climbs up (5km/3mi) to Mösern, located 600m/1 968ft above the Inn Valley.

Mösern

This superbly situated village is a perfect place for a picnic with particularly fine **views**★★. The Inn winds along the floor of the Telfs furrow before slipping into a tangle of crests. Further to the right, the green terrace of Mieming Plateau snuggles up against the Mieming range culminating in the great dome of the Hohe Munde. South of the valley rise the Sellrain mountains and, in the middle distance, the jagged crests of the Kalkkögel.

After Mösern, the road drops down into the Inn Valley in a series of hairpin bends.

Telfs

This bustling market town is home to the interesting Fasnacht- und Heimat-museum, a local museum displaying costumes and masks used during the **Telfser Schleicherlaufen**, a carnival celebration held every five years.

Mösern

SILVRETTA-HOCHALPENSTRASSE★★

VORARLBERG UND TIROL
LOCAL MAP SEE ARLBERGGEBIET

The Silvretta-Hochalpenstraße links the Ill Valley (**Montafon**★ *see entry*) with the Trisanna Valley (Paznaun Valley) via the Bielerhöhe pass (2 036m/6 680ft). The rugged character of this high-lying pass is mitigated by the shimmering green-blue waters of the reservoirs. The road is usually blocked by snow from November through May and closed to trailers and caravans at any time. There are 30 narrow bends to negotiate on the western slope.

- **Information:** Silvrettastraße 8, Partenen. ☎05558/8 31 50. www.gaschurn-partenen.com or www.silvretta-bielerhoehe.at
- ▶ **Orient Yourself:** This scenic route is in the far western corner of Austria, right on the Swiss border, about 130km/84mi southeast of Innsbruck.
- **P Parking:** Several parking lots available along the route
- **Don't Miss:** Walk around the Silvretta-Stausee and ascent to the Hohes Rad.
- **Organizing Your Time:** Allow at least one day, including the hike up to the Hohes Rad.
- **Also See:** ARLBERGGEBIET, MONTAFON.

Driving Tour

Partenen to Landeck Tour

73km/45mi.

See Tour ⑤ on map in ARLBERGGEBIET

The road climbs from **Partenen** *(alt 1 051m/3 448ft)* over the Bielerhöhe *(alt 2 031m/6 664ft)* into Paznaun and the Tirol. Along the way it corkscrews past some of the Vorarlberg's highest peaks (e.g. Piz Buin 3 312m/10 867ft) and the deep blue waters of Alpine reservoirs.

▶ *Take the road south from Partenen*

Vermunt-Stausee

This lake forms an intermediate reservoir between Partenen and the Silvrettatal valley, at an altitude of 1 743m/5 718ft. The **view**★ stretches as far as the ridges of the Grosser Litzner and the Grosser Seehorn. As the road winds upward to the mountain pass, which has been polished smooth by glaciers, the Silvretta dam and mountain summit come gradually into view above the upper lake.

Bielerhöhe

The **Silvretta-Stausee**★ reservoir blends superbly into the Alpine landscape and makes for a pleasant stopping point. Motor boat trips are available on the lake, which is the highest in Europe offering such a service. A walk along the dam (432m/1 417ft long and 80m/262ft high) gives a remarkable **view**★ of the surrounding mountains. An even better way to appreciate the lovely countryside is on the 1hr 45min walk around the **lake**★★. This easy trail passes by several waterfalls and numerous Alpine rose bushes and offers splendid views of the surrounding peaks.

Ascent to the Hohes Rad★★★

Allow 5hr 30min round trip. 🅿 *Park in the lot at the east end of the lake. This is a great hike for experienced walkers. Waterproof climbing boots and warm, knee-high socks are essential. Those with less stamina should steer toward the Wiesbadener Hütte mountain lodge (about 4hr 15min round trip).*

It takes about 45min to walk the length of the entire reservoir from where a trail leads uphill along the gushing waters of the Jil, which is fed by numerous waterfalls and brooks. Gradually, several peaks come into view, with the most eye-catching sight being the glacial cirque that closes off the valley.

From the **Wiesbadener Hütte** mountain lodge *(alt 2 443m/8 015ft)*, there is a wonderful **view**★★ of the highest peak in the Silvretta group, the **Piz Buin** *(alt 3 312m/10 866ft)*, which is flanked by the Vermunt glacier on the left and the Oschsental glacier on the right.

Next comes a 1hr 30min climb to the Radsattel. Turn left past the mountain

lodge and follow the **Edmund-Lorenz-Weg** trail, which first climbs steeply but then levels out somewhat. It leads down to a small lake *(alt 2 532m/8 307ft)*, shimmering in a kaleidoscope of color from orange to green and lying in a splendid setting below the Rauherkopf glacier. It is all uphill from here as far as the **Radsattel** *(alt 2 652m/8 701ft)*, which marks the boundary between Vorarlberg and the Tirol. There is a superb **panorama**★★ of the Grosser Litzner and all the glaciers already mentioned. To the east lies the Bieltal valley, which likewise has a glacier towering above it.

The trails climbs slightly toward the rocky foothills of the Hohes Rad, then crosses numerous glacial snowfields before arriving, after 45min, at the **Radschulter**★★ *(alt 2 697m/8 843ft)*. Shortly before the pass, the Radsee, its frigid waters tinged a dark green, pops into sight beneath the Madlener Spitze peak. From the pass, there is an impressive **view**★★ of the Bieltal and Rauerkopf glaciers.

Experienced hikers not prone to vertigo may like to continue along a rocky trail for at least another 45min up to the **Hohes Rad**★★★ summit *(alt 2 934m/9 626ft)*. The walk down from the Radschulter takes 1hr 30min. The very steep **route**★★ is usually covered by snow well into August and leads

Silvretta-Hochalpenstrasse near Partenen

Mount Piz Buin

through a long rocky stretch before finally turning green again. For the last part of the walk, the trail is flanked by splendid alpine roses and yellow gentians, and provides a number of magnificent **views**★★ of the Silvretta reservoir with the Hochmaderer in the background.

▶ *About 2km/1.2mi before Wirl take the road left over a bridge and continue for 5km/3mi to Kops-Stausee*

After 5km/3mi, the road reaches the **Kops-Stausee**★ (alt 1 809m/5 935ft), flanked by the Ballunspitze to the south, the Versalspitze to the west and the Fluhspitzen peaks to the north. Return to the main road and drive on to Galtür.

▶ *Return to the road no. 188 via Wirl*

Galtür

Alt 1 584m/5 197ft. This pretty village on the slopes of the Ballunspitze provides access to a small but interesting ski area above the Kops reservoir. A total of 11 ski-lifts lead to 40km/25mi of pistes covering all degrees of difficulty. With 45km/28mi of cross-country tracks and good snow cover, Galtür also has plenty to offer cross-country skiers.

Ischgl

See ISCHGL.

The Trisanna Valley now narrows further and becomes increasingly picturesque and rugged, with villages clinging to mountain plateaux. The road parallels a rushing creek through fairly dense forest. After a long drive, the appearance of the Burg Wiesberg heralds the famous **Trisanna bridge**★.

Landeck

See entry under ARLBERGGEBIET.

Hang gliding near Galtür

SÖLDEN

TIROL
POPULATION 3 423 – ALT 1 377M/4 518FT
LOCAL MAP SEE ÖTZTAL

Geographically speaking, Sölden is the largest municipality in Austria, stretching across 468sq km/181sq mi. Yet only a tiny portion (1sq km/.4sq mi) of the area is inhabited. Surrounded by some 90 peaks soaring above 3 000m/9 842.5ft, this classic Tirolean village has developed into an important year-round vacation resort and hub of the **Ötz Valley**★★ (*see Ötztal*). It is well known for its après-ski entertainment and sports facilities as well as its many lively bars, cafés and clubs. The little village of Hochsölden (alt 2 090m/6 857ft) occupies a beautiful plateau and offers excellent snow cover and extensive views.

- **Information:** A-6450. ☎0 52 54/51 00. www.soelden.com.
- ▶ **Orient Yourself:** Sölden is in the Ötztal valley in western Austria, about 84km/53mi southwest of Innsbruck.
- **P Parking:** There is parking at each of the lower cable car stations.
- **Don't Miss:** Ascent of the Wildes Mannle (experienced hikers only).
- **Organizing Your Time:** One to three days depending on how many hikes you choose to do.
- **Also See:** ÖTZTAL, STUBAITAL, PITZTAL.

Sights

Ski slopes (1 377–3 260m/ 4 518–10 696ft)

Sölden is the main town of the Ötztal Arena, which has 35 ski-lifts, 30 artificial snow machines and 150km/93mi of pistes (53km/33mi blue, 63km/39mi

red and 28km/17.4mi black). Ski conditions are good from mid December to early May.

The long descents from the Gaislachkogl to the Stabele chair-lift valley station and the one linking the Hainbachjoch with Sölden are recommended. Less experienced skiers should use the pistes above Hochsölden and the broad trail through the woods from the Gaislachalm.

The **Ötztaler Gletscherstraße**★★ climbs to 2 822m/9 258.5ft, making it one of the highest roads in the eastern Alps. It gives access to another ski area (29km/18mi of piste and 10 ski-lifts) in a beautiful Alpine landscape on the Rettenbachfern and Tiefenbachfern glaciers.

Cross-country skiers have 8km/5mi of tracks available to them in Sölden, 8km/5mi in Zwieselstein and 3km/1.8mi in Vent.

Gaislachkogl★★

Alt 3 058m/10 033ft. 1hr round trip. Gaislachoglbahn cable-car ⏰daily 9am–4pm, ⏰May 8–Jun 23. ⚙€19.50 round trip, one-day ski pass €40.50. ☎05254/5 08. The ascent is in two stages. From the top mountain station, the summit can

© Österreich Werbung / OEW-Bildarchiv

Sölden

be reached on foot in a few minutes (🥾 wear sturdy shoes) to take in a splendid **panorama**★★ of the peaks and glaciers of the Ötztal Alps.

Giggijochbahn

🕐 *Mid Dec–May, daily 9am–4pm,* 🕐*May 8–Jun 23.* 🎫*€12.50 round trip, one-day ski pass €40.50* 📞*05254/5 08.*
From the terrace of the mountain station there are beautiful **views** of the Sölden ski slopes extending from the Gaislachkogl to the Hainbachjoch. To the east lie the Söldenkogel, the Rotkogel and the Gurgler Tal valley.

Excursions

Ventertal★★

This beautiful glacier-framed valley is a hiker's paradise.

Road from Zwieselstein to Rofen★

16km/10mi.
The road first travels through a delightful wooded area, passing the hamlet of Heiligenkreuz with its pretty, onion-domed chapel. It soon reaches **Vent** *(alt 1 900m/6 234ft)*, an unpretentious winter sports resort distinguished by remarkably good snow cover and steep slopes. It has 15km/9.6mi of pistes at altitudes of between 1 900m/6 234ft and 2 680m/8 793ft, and four ski-lifts. Most visitors, though, arrive in summer to take advantage of a seemingly inexhaustible range of trips into the high mountains.
After Vent, the valley splits into two parts on either side of the imposing Talleitspitze peak *(alt 3 406m/11 174ft)*. The **Rofental** valley, on the right, runs alongside the **Wildspitze** and the **Hochvernagtspitze** peaks before being blocked by the **Weisskugel**. The **Niedertal** valley on the left of the Talleitspitze peak runs along the Ramolkogel and the Schalfkogel, ending in the glacial basin of the **Similaun**. All these peaks have been the goal of legendary mountain expeditions.

Wildspitze-Sesselbahn★

Park at the chair-lift in Vent. 🕐*Mid-Jun–end-Sept, daily 8am–5.30pm; mid-Dec–mid-Apr, daily 9.30am–4pm.* 🎫*€7.50 round trip.* 📞*05254/81 54.*
At 3 774m/12 382ft the Wildspitze is the highest peak in the Tirol. From the mountain station *(alt 2 356m/7 730ft)* there is a beautiful **view**★ of the ski area and various peaks and glaciers. This is also the starting point of numerous hikes, a couple of which are detailed below.

Wildes Mannle★★★

This hike covers 670m/2 198ft difference in altitude and requires a fair level of fitness and experience as well as sturdy footwear. Allow at least 3hr round trip, or 4hr if continuing on to the Breslauer Hütte mountain lodge.
From the chair-lift mountain station start hiking toward the Breslauer Hütte. After a 30min walk, veer to the right *(waymarker)* onto a narrower trail. As the view becomes ever more breathtaking, look out for the markers and "WM" indications. The path gets steep and rocky, but does not present any real difficulties.
From the peak *(alt 3 023m/9 918ft)*, which is marked with a cross, there is a terrific **panorama**★★★ of about 15 glaciers belonging to the Ötztal Alps, the most impressive and closest of which is the Rofenkar glacier. Chamois can often be spotted in this region.
To the west, notice the Breslauer Hütte lodge at the foot of a rocky, reddish natural amphitheater. A detour to this mountain lodge is a pleasant extension of this hike. Those with a poor head for heights should first follow the same trail as on the way there and then turn off toward the right *(waymarked on the rocks)*. Experienced hikers can take a walk of about 15min across the ridge of the Wildes Mannle as far as a metal sign *(toward Breslauer Hütte via Rofenkarsteig)*. Be sure to pay attention to the markers *(stone cairns)*. At the sign, turn off onto a steep, narrow trail which leads down to the foot of the Rofenkar glacier *(ropes available)*.
The path then leads over a narrow ridge to give beautiful **views**★★ of the gla-

cial cirque. Very soon afterwards, turn off to the right *(waymarked "BH" on a rock)* and reach the Rofenbach brook which is crossed in two stages, the last on wooden planks. Then follow the brook for about 10m/32.8ft without attempting to climb the slippery rock walls, before regaining the path, which leads up to the Breslauer Hütte mountain lodge. From here, there is a splendid **panorama**★★. The descent *(1hr)* to the chair-lift back to Vent is easy.

Breslauer Hütte★★

Alt 2 844m/9 331ft. Easy hike with a difference in altitude of 500m/1 640ft. Allow 2hr 30min round trip starting from the mountain station.

From the hut, there is a very beautiful **panorama**★★ across the Wildspitze and the ridges of the Wildes Mannle to the north, the glaciers above the Niedertal Valley to the east and the Kreuzspitze peak and its glaciers to the south.

SPITTAL AN DER DRAU

KÄRNTEN
POPULATION 16 000 – ALT 554M/1 818FT

Charming Spittal lies at the confluence of the Lieser and the Drava (Drau) at the foot of the Goldeck peak and close to the Millstättersee (lake). Thanks to its strategic position on a major trade route between Germany and Venice it flourished over the centuries as an economic and cultural center. Nowadays, it is still an important hub in Upper Carinthia.

- **Information:** Burgplatz 1, A-9800. ☎0 47 62/34 20. www.spittal-drau.at.
- ▶ **Orient Yourself:** Spittal is in southern Austria, 37km/23mi west of Villach.
- **P** **Parking:** Central options include the City Center garage and the Hauptplatz.
- **Don't Miss:** Museum für Volkskultur.
- **Kids** **Especially for Kids:** Erlebniswelt Eisenbahn, Museum für Volkskultur.
- **Also See:** MILLSTATT.

Courtyard of Schloss Porcia

© Österreich Werbung / Trumler

Address Book

For coin ranges, see the cover flap.

WHERE TO STAY

Alte Post – *Hauptplatz 13. Tel. 04762/2 21 70. www.tiscover. at/ alte.post. 41 rooms.* A 700-year-old, family-run hotel with typical Carinthian furnishings and rooms decorated and furnished in classical style. Close to the center of Spittal.

Hotel Ertl – *Bahnhofstr. 26 Tel. 04762/2 04 80 www.hotel-ertl.at. 45 rooms.* Located in the center of town this hotel has a large swimming pool. The rooms are all decorated in a modern yet classic style.

Sights

Schloss Porcia★

This Italian Renaissance palazzo was built for Gabriel Salamanca, a Spanish aristocrat who served as general treasurer to Archduke Ferdinand until 1526. From 1662 to 1918 the palace was the residence of the princes of Porcia, a noble family from northeastern Italy. The park and the three-story **arcaded courtyard**★ are open to the public at any time. The latter features antique medallions, balustraded pillars, door frames, and other ornamentation typical of the Renaissance style. Also note the splendid 16C wrought-iron **gates**★. Theater performances are held in the courtyard in summer.

Museum für Volkskultur★★ [Kids]

Mid-May–Oct, daily 9am–6pm; Nov–mid-May, Mon–Thu 1pm–4pm. €4.50. 04762/28 90. www.museum-spittal.com.

On the upper floors of Schloss Porcia, this museum chronicles local history, culture and folklore in 47 attractively presented themed displays (education, farming, mining, etc.). A relatively new highlight is the **3D flight simulator**★

that lets you soar like a bird above the Hohe Tauern National Park.

Erlebniswelt Eisenbahn★

This is home to Austria's largest model railway. It is affiliated to the Museum für Volkskultur and features some 600m/1 968.5ft of track, 85 locomotives and 350 cars. Find it on the first floor of the Gerngross City Center mall on Neuer Platz square.

Goldeckbahn

Jun–Sept & Dec– 21 Mar, daily 9am–5.30pm. one-day ski pass €29; for other fares, call 04762/28 64 or visit www. goldeck-spittal.at.

This 4km/2.5mi cable-car ride leads in two sections to 2 050m/6 726ft, an altitude increase of 1 500m/4 921ft. From the upper station there is a fine **view**★ of Spittal, the surrounding mountains and the Millstättersee lake.

Excursion

Teurnia Ausgrabungen (excavations)★

4km/2.5mi west of Spittal at St. Peter in Holz. Turn off left from the road to Lienz.

The area around St. Peter im Holz has been settled since the 12C BC, first by Celts, then as the Roman city of Teurnia around AD 50. Excavations have uncovered the remains of this latter settlement, including residential terraces, the forum, a bathing house and a temple. In the 5C and 6C, Teurnia was a fortified provincial town and episcopal seat. The remains of the diocesian church are now protected by a modern shelter. Nearby, the newly revamped **Römermuseum Teurnia**★ (*May–mid-Oct, Tue–Sun 9am–5pm; €5; 04762/3 38 07*) presents artifacts unearthed by the excavations, including reliefs, everyday objects and coins.

Outside the city wall is the early Christian Friedhofskirche with a famous **mosaic floor**★ (5C) featuring animal motifs.

STIFT STAMS★★

TIROL

The Cistercian abbey of Stams was founded in 1273 by Count Meinhard II of Görz-Tirol as the burial place for his dynasty. The majestic architectural ensemble is purely Baroque in style, the result of a thorough make-over between 1650 and 1750 that also added the distinctive twin onion-domed towers.

- **Information:** ☎5263/56 97 2. www.stiftstams.at.
- ▶ **Orient Yourself:** Stams is about 35km/21.7mi west of Innsbruck.
- **Parking:** Park at the foot of the 14C village church.
- **Also See:** SEEFELD IN TIROL, ÖTZTAL.

Visit

Guided tour (30 min) year-round, daily 9am, 10am, 11am, 2pm, 3pm, 4pm; also May 5pm, Jun–Sept 1pm and 4pm ;additional tours Jul–Aug. €4.

Stiftskirche★★
As you enter the church, elevated to basilica minor by Pope John Paul II in 1984, note on your right the famous **Rose Grille**★. This screen, a masterpiece in ironwork dating from 1716, closes the passage leading to the Heiligblutkapelle (Chapel of the Holy Blood). A balustrade in the nave surrounds the open crypt with 12 gilded wood statues represent-ing the princes of the Tirol who are buried here. The church's showpiece is the **high altar**★ (1613), whose altarpiece represents the Tree of Life in the form of interlacing boughs supporting 84 carved figures of saints surrounding the Virgin Mary.

Bernardisaal★
The Bernardi Hall is reached from the porter's lodge by a **grand staircase** with a fine wrought-iron balustrade. The hall's ceiling is decorated with paintings (1722) recalling outstanding episodes in the life of St. Bernard.
Also have a look at the **museum**, which displays changing art exhibits.

Stift Stams

STEIRISCHES THERMENLAND
STYRIA

The **Styrian spa region is** comprised of the five spa towns of Bad Waltersdorf, Blumau, Loipersdorf, Bad Gleichenberg and Bad Radkersburg in the southeast corner of Styria. It is one of Austria's most fertile belts of land, as illustrated by the numerous vineyards, orchards and fields of pumpkins and cereal crops.

🛈 **Information:** Styria Tourism, St. Peter Hauptstraße 243, Graz. ☎0316/4 00 30. www.steiermark.com.

▶ **Orient Yourself:** The spa region is east of Graz in the far southeastern corner of Austria, close to the border with Hungary.

☺ **Don't Miss:** Riegersburg, Styrassic Park.

🕓 **Organizing Your Time:** Simply driving through the region takes less than a day but for a more thorough look, and perhaps a spa treatment, allow two days.

Kids Especially for Kids: Child-oriented tours of Riegersburg, Styrassic Park.

✆ **Also See:** GRAZ, STEIRISCHESWIENSTRASSE.

Sights

Blumau

About 7km/4.3mi north of Fürstenfeld.
Blumau would be just your run-of-the-mill health resort were it not for the **Rogner Bad Blumau**, the avant-garde spa and hotel complex designed by the late Viennese architect, **Friedensreich Hundertwasser**. It is a brightly pigmented fairy-tale composition where people, architecture and nature are intended to harmonize with each other. Whimsical touches include roofs covered with lawns and buildings shaped like eyes. The hotel uses no fossil fuels but uses the heat from thermal springs to keep the hotel heated in winter. Access is open to hotel or spa day guests or to those participating in a **guided tour** (🔊 *daily (45min) 9am–5pm;* ☞ *free;* ♿☎03383/51 00 90 02).

Riegersburg★   Kids

On the B 66, 10km/6.2mi north of Feldbach.

Schloss Riegersburg
🕓*May–Sept, daily 9am–5pm; Apr & Oct, daily 10am–5pm.* 🔊*Guided tours for children Jul–Aug, Sun 12.30pm, 3pm (included in admission fee).* ☞*€9.50, lift €2 (children €7 and €1 respectively);* combination ticket with Styrassic park €14. ☎03153/8 21 31. www.veste-riegersburg.at.

☺*Those of a sensitive disposition and those with easily frightened children should avoid the 12 rooms housing the Hexenmuseum.*

The 12C Riegersburg castle is one of the most imposing strongholds to have guarded Austria's eastern frontiers. Protected by 3km/1.2mi of ramparts and 11 bastions, it successfully withstood the onslaught of both the Hungarians and the Turks. Its site alone, on the remains of a 482m/1 581ft high volcano above the village that shares its name, is impressive. Since 1822, the castle has belonged to the royal family of Liechtenstein and now houses a museum on witches *(Hexenmuseum)* in the cellars detailing the horrors of medieval times when women and sometimes men were tortured and burned at the stake. There is also an exhibition on prominent 17C women associated with the castle. Architectural highlights include the **Knight's Hall** with its intricately inlaid wooden doors and coffered ceiling and the Early Baroque **White Hall** with its delicate stuccowork. Perhaps even more memorable, though are the wonderful **views**★ of the Styrian countryside enjoyed from up here.

"Wait 'til the ranger sees that…!" – A Diplodocus in Styrassic Park

Seebad Riegersburg [Kids]

A lakeside resort with 18 000sq m/193 750sq ft water surface. Includes watershutes and spa pools.

Bad Gleichenberg⚕

On the B 66, 11km/7mi south of Feldbach.

After Graz and Mariazell, the spa town of Bad Gleichenberg is the most popular vacation destination in Styria. Near the Hungarian and Slovenian borders, it is famous for its medicinal springs and mild climate and became a favorite with Austrian aristocracy in the 19C. The town still boasts some beautiful **Biedermeier-style villas and hotels** and is set amid countryside reminiscent of a landscaped garden.

Styrassic Park [Kids]

Take B 66 and follow the signposts. ⏱*Mid-Mar–Oct, daily 9am–5pm; Oct, 9am–4pm; Nov in good weather, Sat–Sun 10am–3pm.* 💶*€9.50; children €6; combination ticket with Riegersburg €14; children €8.* ☎*0 31 59/28 75 11. www.styrassic park.at/cms.* 🚶*Guided tours available.* Dinos on the loose in Austria? Well, almost. This sprawling forest park is inhabited by more than 75 life-size model dinosaurs made of steel and concrete. On your tour you will encounter the entire cast of characters, from the long-necked Brachiosaurus to the vicious Velociraptors to the terrifying Tyrannosaurus rex. Display panels give brief explanations on the chronology, fossil discoveries and dimensions of each species. A dino-cinema, a huge children's playground with the largest slide in the country, and a petting zoo further add to the fun.

Bad Radkersburg★

On the B 69, 26km/16mi south of Bad Gleichenberg right before the Slovenian border.

Radkersburg is an increasingly popular spa town whose calcium and bicarbonate-rich springs are helpful in easing illnesses affecting the nerves and the urinary tract. Since its foundation in 1182, it has been one of the leading trading centers in Styria and was also an important bastion during the wars against the Turks. The partly preserved **fortifications**, with moats, six bastions and towers, still attest to this period.

A walk around town will inevitably lead to the **Hauptplatz**, the main square whose many merchant mansions with beautiful stone doorways and courtyards give an indication of the town's former wealth. In the center is a Virgin Mary Column erected in 1680 by the townspeople as a thank you for their deliverance from the plague. The onion-domed octagonal **town hall tower** has become Radkersburg's emblem.

STEIRISCHE WEINSTRASSE★

STYRIA

The **Styrian vineyard trail** is a delightful journey into traditional Austria; a tranquil, timeless world in the midst of outstandingly beautiful countryside. The region is dotted with taverns (**Buschenschenken**) where people meet over a glass of wine and listen to accordion music. It is particularly lovely in the fall when the vines are cloaked in a kaleidoscope of brilliant colors. The vast majority (80%) of wine produced in Styria is white, with dry Welschriesling, fruity Weissburgunder, and sprightly Müller-Thurgau being the dominant varieties. Zweigelt is the most important red wine, but **Schilcher**, a rosé, is actually better known.

Information: Hamerlinggasse 3, Graz. ☎031680/50 14 35. www.steirischerwein.at.

▶ **Orient Yourself:** The wine routes detailed below are all southwest of Graz in southeastern Austria.

🕐 **Organizing Your Time:** The three tours combined can easily be completed in a day, but if stopping often to taste or visit sights, then allow three days; one for each tour.

♿ **Also See:** GRAZ, STEIRISCHES THERMENLAND.

Driving Tours

0.5ml/g is blood alcohol limit in Austria.

1 Schilcher Tour

81km/50mi

▶ *Leave Graz on the B 70 (AX). Take either the autobahn as far as Steinberg or the B 70 to Krottendorf, and then follow signs to Stainz.*

The south-facing vines grown in the Schilcher hills, which back onto the Koralpe range, are often so steep that harvesting by machine is impossible.
On leaving the autobahn, the road immediately begins to climb, providing charming **views**★★ of the Graz plain, the undulating hills northwest of the town and the Schöckl (*alt 1 445m/4 741ft*) with its flat summit.

Gundersdorf

As you enter this typical wine-growing village, keep an eye out for the strange wooden stake topped with a four-bladed propeller.
This is a familiar sight in the Styrian vineyards because its noise scares away the birds as the grapes start ripening. The local speciality is Schilcher wine, which can sometimes be bought directly from the vintner.

▶ *Turn right after Gundersdorf, then left toward Langegg and Greisdorf.*

Langegg

This village is filled with numerous traditional wine taverns, often housed in simple wooden-roofed summer cottages or on terraces attached to wine-growers' houses. The wine goes rather well with slices of **Verackertbrot**, black bread with chopped, spiced bacon, or perhaps with a **Brettljause**, cold meats served on a wooden platter.
At Langegg there is a delightful **view**★★ of the Mur Valley, the Schöckl and the vine-clad hills of Sausal.

▶ *Turn left at Marhof and follow the signs to Stainz.*

Stainz ♿ *See GRAZ, Excursions.*

Bad Gams ob Frauental

This village is well known in Styria for its traditional pottery; there is a potter's workshop on the outskirts of the nearby town of Furth.
En route to Deutschlandsberg the road descends into a plain encircled by forests.

Schilcher

Schilcher is made from the Blauer Wildbacher grape and has only been officially known as Schilcher since 1976. Records show that this late-ripening, acidic grape (a distinction is made between the late blue and sloe varieties of Wildbacher), with its characteristic flavour and pretty "onion-skin" color, has been cultivated in west Styria since as early as 1580. Schilcher vineyards cover about 80ha/198 acres.

Grape-pickers' cottages

Grape-pickers ("Weinzierle") traditionally had no property of their own, but lived in small cottages owned by their vineyard-owning employers. The typical west Styrian grape-picker's cottage, called a "Winzerei," consisted of two rooms, a kitchen, and a front veranda with an attached garden. A separate wooden hut would be used to store coal and fodder.

Deutschlandsberg

The hub of the Schilcher Wine Trail, this town at the foot of the Koralpe near the Slovene border takes its name from the fortified castle of Landsberg. The prefix *"deutsch"* was not added until the 19C, and then only because of its location on German-speaking territory. Deutschlandsberg is famous throughout Styria for its lively and colorful Corpus Christi celebrations featuring flower-bedecked processional altars. The town's grapes benefit from a favorable climate with 280 days of sunshine.

To the north of the town stands the castle of Wildbach, where Schubert is supposed to have composed his famous Lied, *The Trout*. Only the 12C keep is original, the rest of the castle having been reconstructed. A number of trails through the vineyards start in the parking lot, which also offers a fine **view**★ of the surrounding plain.

▷ *Rejoin the road from Stainz; continue south in the direction of St. Andrä-Leibnitz via St. Martin; to reach St. Andrä, turn left onto the valley road which joins up with the Sausal Vineyard Trail.*

② Sausal Tour
27km/16.7mi

St. Andrä is the point of entry to the Sausal hills which rise to 670m/2 198ft and produce mostly **Rheinriesling**, a noble, crisp white with an excellent bouquet.

▷ *Take the road west toward Kitzeck.*

Kitzeck★

Set on a ridge at 564m/1 850ft, this is the highest wine-growing village in Europe and provides **panoramic views**★★ over a sea of hills. The **Wine Museum** (◷*Apr–Aug, Sat–Sun 10am–noon, 2pm–5pm; Sept–Oct, Tue–Sun 10am–noon, 2am–5pm; ✆€2.20; ☎0 34 56/35 00*), which occupies a wine-grower's estate from 1726, contains articles and tools, including a reconstructed device for smoke curing, an old press and a wagon for transporting barrels.

▷ *Drive toward Fresing, then continue to Klein Klein.*

Celtic tombs dating from the 6C–4C BC have been discovered in the forest near **Grossklein**. The finds are kept in Schloss Eggenberg (⌕*see entry*).

▷ *In Grossklein turn left toward Heimschuch, then right to Eichberghof.*

The road meanders through wild and hilly country where small south-facing vineyards alternate with fields of maize and woodsy patches.

▷ *Continue to Leutschach.*

③ South Styrian Tour
65.3km/40.5mi

On either side of the road near **Leutschach** you will pass fields planted

Vineyard in Southern Styria

not with wine but with hops growing on tall poles.

▶ *In Leutschach turn left before the church and follow the green road sign to the "Südsteirische Weinstraße" (South Styrian Wine Route).*

This is the most southerly wine-growing area in Austria, where the route hugs the border with Slovenia. This region is also known as the **Styrian Tuscany** because of its sunny climate and similarity to the Tuscan countryside in Italy.

A forest of conifers gives way to rows of vines which cover the gently contoured hills of what is the very heart of Welschriesling and Samling country.

Ehrenhausen

A wooded bluff overlooking the Mur and the village of Ehrenhausen was chosen by the Eggenberg princes as the site of a castle and a mausoleum. The **Pfarrkirche** on the main square has a fine bell-tower with a particularly elaborate roof. The church was remodeled in the Baroque style in 1752.

Mausoleum★

Obtain the key from the parish office (8am–6pm). ☎03453/25 07.

This curious funerary monument shelters the tomb of Ruprecht of Eggenberg, who distinguished himself in the struggle against the Turks at the end of the 16C. Completed in 1640, the building was decorated by pupils of Johann Fischer von Erlach.

He is buried in the crypt alongside his successor, Wolfgang von Eggenberg. The mausoleum interior is especially striking for the elaborate stuccowork decorating the central dome.

▶ *Take the autobahn back to Graz.*

STEYR★

OBERÖSTERREICH

POPULATION 42 000 – ALT 310M/1 017FT

Steyr had a glorious past and for a while even rivaled Vienna in terms of economic and political importance. It is now Upper Austria's third largest town (after Linz and Wels) and still an important economic and industrial center. The picturesque old town, which has preserved its medieval character and charm, clusters at the confluence of the Enns and the Steyr.

- **Information:** Stadtplatz 27 – A4402. ☎0 72 52/53 22 90. www.tourism-steyr.at
- ▶ **Orient Yourself:** Steyr is about 50km/31mi southeast of Linz.
- **Don't Miss:** Museum Arbeitswelt.
- **Organizing Your Time:** Allow one day to enjoy the town at a leisurely pace and another for the excursions.
- **Especially for Kids:** Christkindl.
- **Also See:** ST. FLORIAN, ENNS.

Sights

Old Town

Stadtplatz★ (Y)

Steyr's elongated main square is lined with fine Late Gothic and Renaissance houses and centered on the 17C **Leopoldibrunnen** (A). Standout buildings include the **Rathaus** (R) with its Rococo façade surmounted by a tower, and the Gothic **Bummerlhaus** (no. 32), which sports a triangular gable and characteristic first-floor overhang. Also duck into the lovely courtyards of the houses at no. 9, no. 11 and nos. 36/38.

Marienkirche (Z)

The former Dominican church is decorated in the Baroque style and features a high altar overloaded with gilding, a Virgin and Child of 1704 and a Rococo pulpit.

Stadtmuseum Steyr (Z M¹)

🕐 *Apr–Oct, Tue–Sun 10am–4pm; Nov–Mar, Wed–Sun 10am–4pm; Dec–Jan 6, daily 10am–5pm.* ⊘ *Free admission.* ☎ *0 72 52/57 53 48.*

A 17C granary known as the **Innerberger Stadl** houses Steyr's charming local history museum, which has a fabulous collection of Baroque religious figurines as well as a huge Nativity scene carved from olive wood in Bethlehem.

Stadtpfarrkirche (Z)

Behind the Innerberger Stadtl, the 15C Gothic parish church is the work of Hans Puxbaum, the architect of the Stephansdom in Vienna. Puxbaum also designed the **tabernacle★**, with its delicate tracery, and the tripartite chancel baldaquin.

Schloss Lamberg (Y)

A fortress has stood here for a thousand years but the present Baroque incarnation only dates to the 18C. It is now used mostly by the municipal administration, although it's still worth coming here to pop into the Schlossgalerie with its changing contemporary art exhibits or to take a stroll around the park.

Museum Arbeitswelt★

🕐 *Early Mar–mid-Dec, Tue–Sun 9am–5pm.* ⊘ € *5.* ☎ *07252/77351. www. working-world.net.*

The completely revamped permanent exhibit at the "Working World Museum" details the fundamental changes at the workplace in the Age of the Internet and globalization. The high-tech presentation uses videos, text animations, room installations and other modern media to explore the challenges of today and the future.

Ceiling fresco by Paul Troger in the Marble Hall, Stift Seitenstetten

R. Chérer/MICHELIN

Excursions

Stift Seitenstetten★

19.5km/12mi east of Steyr on the B 122. Guided tour (1hr 15min) Easter Mon–Oct, daily 10am and 3pm. €6.50. 07477/4 23 00.

This Benedictine abbey was founded in 1112 and is still active today, operating a famous grammar school.

Stiftskirche (Abbey church)

The three-aisled Early Gothic basilica turned Baroque in the 17C has rich stucco decoration and frescoes. The high altar is dominated by an *Assumption of the Virgin*, a major work by Johann Karl Reslfeld of Garsten. Behind the church is the **Ritterkapelle** (Knight's Chapel), the oldest part of the abbey, whose apse and side walls date back to the 14C.

Stiftsgebäude (Abbey buildings)

The main abbey buildings are mostly the work of Josef Munggenast, but numerous famous artists contributed to its decoration. Above the festive **Abteistiege** (abbey staircase) is a ceiling fresco by Bartolomeo Altomonte,

while those in the **Marmorsaal** (Marble Hall) and the library are by **Paul Troger.** Tours also take in 12 fine paintings by **Kremser Schmidt** in the Maturasaal and the mineral collection displayed in its Rococo cabinets. The abbey's **art collection**★ also includes some fine works by Kremser Schmidt and Paul Troger.

Christkindl   Kids

3km/1.8mi west of Steyr

The village of Christkindl in Oberösterreich (the name means Christ Child) with its charming pilgrims' chapel is associated with a quaint and delightful tradition: Every year around Christmas time, an average of two million Christmas cards and letters are mailed out by the church's special post office (*end-Nov–early Jan*). Letters written by children to the "Christkind" (Christ Child or baby Jesus), who delivers the gifts in Austria, also get a reply (if return postage is enclosed).

Pfarr- und Wallfahrtskirche

The Baroque parish church was begun by Giovanni Battista Carlone and completed by Jakob Prandtauer in 1708. Four semicircular chapels are arranged below a great dome adorned with a fresco of the *Assumption of the Virgin* by Johann Carl Reslfeld (1710). The main point of veneration, though, is a small, miracle-working wax figure of Jesus, kept above the globe-shaped tabernacle. In 1720 the altar was adorned with 35 gilded statuettes of angels arranged around the trunk of the "Christ tree" in which the effigy was formerly kept. The gilded Rococo pulpit (1751) is also a magnificent piece of work.

Krippenschau

The crib display in the old working quarters of the presbytery is open to visitors from late November to January 6. Highlights include the early 20C **mechanical crib**, which consists of nearly 300 figures, many of them moveable through a system of cogs and chains. The 1930s **Pöttmesser crib** features 778 figures and is considered to be one of the largest in the world.

STUBACHTAL★★★

SALZBURG

About 20km/12.4mi long, the Stubachtal is among the most beautiful Alpine valleys in Austria. A well-built scenic road leads from Uttendorf (alt 804m/2 638ft) to Enzingerboden (alt 1 480m/4 856ft). From here, the Weissee Gletscherbahn cable-car transports skiers in the winter and hikers in the summer to mountain lakes and the magnificent glacial massif of the Hohe Tauern National Park.

- **Information:** 5723 Uttendorf. ☎06563/2 01 50.
- **Orient Yourself:** The valley is in western Austria, about 34km/21mi southeast of Kitzbühel.
- **Parking:** Park at the valley station of the Weissee Gletscherbahn in Enzigerboden.
- **Don't Miss:** Kaiser Tauern.
- **Organizing Your Time:** Allow a good day for the drive and the trip to the Kaiser Tauern.
- **Also See:** GROSSGLOCKNER HOCHALPENSTRASSE.

Driving Tour

Stubachtal Tour★★
17.5km/11mi.

- *Start in Uttendorf, 6km/3.7mi east of Mittersill on B 168 and follow the road up the valley.*

Kaiser Tauern★★★

2hr 30min round trip, including 1hr walk. Sturdy footwear required. ⓄMid Jun–late Sept, daily 9.30am–5pm. ☞€23 round trip. ☎0 65 63/2 01 50.

The trip starts with a 25min ride aboard the Weisseebahn gondola to the Rudolfshütte hotel and restaurant *(alt 2 315m/7 595ft)* through luxuriant vegetation with lovely views of the Grüner See. From here, a 10min walk brings you down to the Medelz chair-lift, which travels through a majestic Alpine massif and treats you to a magnificent **panorama**★★★ during its 15min ascent. From the top, a 25min hike (look for the red and white markers) leads through the rock to the Kaiser Tauern pass, from where you will enjoy more beautiful **views**★ of the lake and the Dorfertal valley.

STUBAITAL★★

TIROL

LOCAL MAP SEE INNSBRUCK: TOUR OF THE MITTELGEBIRGE

The Stubai Valley is a popular day trip for people based in the Innsbruck area. In summer, it is an ideal launchpad for hiking expeditions and also provides access to one of the largest all-year ski areas in Europe.

- **Information:** Stubaitalhaus, Dorf 3, Neustift im Stubaital ☎05018/81 0. www.stubai.at
- ▶ **Orient Yourself:** This valley is southwest of Innsbruck in western Austria.
- **Don't Miss:** Stubai Glacier
- **Organizing Your Time:** Budget a day for the valley and the glacier
- **Also See:** INNSBRUCK

Driving Tour

Stubai Valley Tour★

44km/27mi

▶ *Leave Innsbruck via the Brenner-Bundesstraße. After crossing the Europa bridge, turn off into the Stubai Valley at Schönberg. Alternatively, take the Brenner autobahn (toll).*

On entering the valley, you will soon face the enormous glacial massif of the **Zuckerhütl** *(alt 3 511m/11 520ft)*. The well-built road runs past the valley's five resorts. First up are **Schönberg**, **Mieders** and **Telfes** on a sunny terrace opposite. Then comes **Fulpmes**, which specializes in the manufacture of mountaineering equipment and tools. Lastly, **Neustift** is dominated by the striking silhouette of its 18C parish church by Franz de Paula Penz.

Over the last 7km/4.3mi of the journey, the gradient becomes ever steeper and the landscape more rugged. The road finally leaves the forest and arrives at the Mutterbergalm *(alt 1 728m/5 669ft)* at the foot of a rocky cirque.

Excursion

Stubai Glacier

(Stubaier Gletscher)

This popular ski area offers downhill enthusiasts slopes of varying degrees of difficulty covering a total of 53km/33mi between altitudes of 2 300m/7 546ft and 3 200m/10 498ft. The area's appeal lies in its outstanding snow cover and excellent transportation infrastructure. The ski season generally runs from October to the beginning of July. Good skiers will appreciate the 10km/6.2mi long **Wilde Gruben** descent to Mutterberg through splendid, unspoiled **countryside★★**.

There is also a 4.5km/2.8mi-long cross-country course at an altitude of 2 600m/8 530ft (starting from the Gamsgarten cable-car).

The most important viewpoints, which can be reached by lift or on foot, are indicated next (*take warm clothing, sunglasses and thick-soled, waterproof footwear*).

Eisgrat★★

Alt 2 900m/9 514ft.

A cable-car in two stages leads to the glacial cirque and the foot of the Stubaier Wildspitze peak *(alt 3 340m/10 958ft)* and Schaufelspitze peak *(alt 3 333m/10 935ft)*. Walk round the restaurant to see the lower part of the valley.

Daunferner★★

Skiers can reach the glacier *(alt 3 160m/10 367ft)* by means of the Daunfern ski tow, the Wildspitz double chairlift and the Rotadl chair-lift. Enjoy impressive **views★★** over the rocky cliffs framing the glacier.

TAMSWEG ★

SALZBURG

POPULATION 5 940 – ALT 1 024M/3 360FT

Tamsweg is the capital of the remote Lungau region and fosters many old traditions. Most famous among these is the so-called Samsonumzug (Samson Procession) headed by a huge dummy representing Samson and accompanied by two dwarfs. It takes place several days each summer (🕭 see Calendar of events).

- **Information:** Kirchengasse 8. ☎06474/21 45. www.tamsweg.at.
- ▶ **Orient Yourself:** Tamsweg is about 50km/31mi south of Radstadt.
- 🕐 **Organizing Your Time:** Half a day will be ample.
- 👁 **Also See:** RADSTÄDTER TAUERNSTRASSE, MAUTERNDORF.

Sights

Marktplatz

Tamsweg's main square is framed by pretty houses, such as the 16C **Rathaus** (town hall) with fanciful corner turrets, and the old **Schloss Kuenburg**, now home to a cultural center. Farther off, an old hospice now houses the **Heimatmuseum**, which offers glimpses into the local way of life of yesteryear including several important Roman artifacts.

Excursion

St. Leonhardkirche

Drive south from Tamsweg on the Murau road over the River Mur. Cross the railway and 🅿 park at the bottom of the road (right) that climbs straight up to the church. A footpath farther right is less steep.

The 15C pilgrimage church of St. Leonard has kept its Early Gothic plan and design—tall light windows, network vaulting etc. Its original **stained glass** is among the finest in Austria and includes the famous "**gold window**" (Goldfenster), on the right of the chancel, which consists entirely of yellow and blue glass. Near the high altar, the small altar to St. Leonard features a statuette of the saint held in the branches of a juniper tree. The discovery of the statuette is the basis of the pilgrimage.

TULLN

NIEDERÖSTERREICH

POPULATION 14 650 – ALT 180M/591FT

LOCAL MAP SEE DONAUTAL

Tulln grew up on the site of the Roman camp of Comagena founded in AD 1C. Between 1042 and 1113, the town was the residence of the Babenberg dynasty, predecessors of the Habsburgs. Tulln's most famous son is the painter Egon Schiele (1890–1918).

- **Information:** Minoritenplatz 2. ☎0 22 72/69 00. www.tulln.at.
- ▶ **Orient Yourself:** Tulln is on the Danube, about 40km/25mi west of Vienna.
- 🅿 **Parking:** Look for parking on the Hauptplatz or in garages in Albrechtsgasse, Frauentorgasse or at the main train station.
- 😊 **Don't Miss:** Egon-Schiele-Museum, Karner.
- 🕐 **Organizing Your Time:** You can visit all the sights easily in one day.
- Kids **Especially for Kids:** The fire engine collection in the Minoritenkloster.
- 👁 **Also See:** KLOSTERNEUBURG, DONAUTAL.

Sights

Egon-Schiele-Museum

Donaulände 28. ⏱Mar–Nov, Tue–Sun 10am–noon, 1pm–5pm. ⬤€3.50. ☎02272/6 45 70. http://egonschiele. museum.com.

The old local prison now houses an exhibition on the life and work of Tulln-born painter Egon Schiele (1890–1918). On the ground floor is a biographical documentation as well as the reproduction of a jail cell in Neulengbach where he was held for a few days in 1912 for possession of child pornography. Upstairs are a smattering of originals, including drawings, lithographs, watercolors and a few oil paintings, most of them early works (1905–08). Admission also includes entry to the room in the main train station where Schiele was born (his father was stationmaster). Let museum staff know if you would like to see it and they will make arrangements.

Römerturm

This fortified tower has survived almost unchanged in shape and height since being built under Roman Emperor Diocletian (AD 284–305). In the Middle Ages it was used as an arsenal and from the early 19C as a salt storehouse, which explains why locals also call it the Salzturm (salt tower).

Pfarrkirche St. Stefan

Wiener Straße.

This 12C Romanesque basilica was transformed in the 15C to the Gothic style and then remodeled in the Baroque style in the 18C. Outstanding elements include the Romanesque western portal, which is adorned with busts of the 12 Apostles. The altarpiece dates to 1786 and represents the stoning of St. Stephen.

The church's most memorable feature is the 13C polygonal **Karner**, one of the finest **funerary chapels** (ossuaries) in Austria. The **doorway**★★ is decorated with palm-leaf capitals and geometrical motifs, while the domed interior is adorned with fantastical Romanesque frescoes that were drastically restored in 1874 in the 19C style.

M. Hertlein/MICHELIN

Minoritenkloster and Minoritenkirche

Minoritenkirche

Minoritenplatz.

This Baroque building, constructed in 1739, was dedicated to St. John of Nepomuk. Inside, to the left of the high altar, there is a glimpse of the sacristy with a magnificent inlaid cabinet dating from the 18C.

Minoritenkloster Museums★

Minoritenplatz 1. ⏱Mar–Oct, Tue–Sun 10am–6pm. ⬤€3. ☎0 22 72/6 19 15.

Tulln's old monastery has been successfully recycled into a museum complex. The collections of the **Stadtmuseum** take up most of the space and include items from Roman to recent times discovered during excavations beneath the monastery; an exhibit tracing the region's geological evolution; an assortment of historic fire engines; rooms chronicling daily life in the city during the 18C and 19C; and other aspects of local history. In the attic is the first **Austrian Sugar Museum** (Tulln is a major producer of the sweet stuff), which traces the evolution of sugar production, from primitive sugar cane mills to modern factories. A changing roster of contemporary art exhibits is also housed under the same roof.

Fans of the Austrian painter Friedensreich Hundertwasser should ask museum staff for access to the **Hundertwasser-Schiff "Regentag"** moored in the harbor behind the monastery. It contains a small exhibit about the journeys made by the artist.

VILLACH★

KÄRNTEN
POPULATION 60 000 – ALT 501M/1 644FT
LOCAL MAP SEE WÖRTHER SEE

Frequently referred to as the "secret capital" of Carinthia, Villach is the province's second largest town and a regional economic and cultural hub. Settled since Celtic times, it has an attractive location on the Drava (Drau) River and is considered a gateway to both Italy and Slovenia.

In 1007, Emperor Heinrich II donated Villach to his newly founded bishopric at Bamberg, some 540km/335.5mi north in Bavaria. This arrangement shaped Villach's fortunes until Maria Theresa bought the town back in 1759. Today, part of its appeal lies in its thermal mineral springs and proximity to the Faaker and Ossiach lakes.

- **Information:** Rathausplatz 1. ☎04242/2 05 29 00. www.villach.at.
- ▶ **Orient Yourself:** Villach is on the far southern edge of the country, close to the Slovenian border, about 40km/25mi west of Klagenfurt.
- **Parking:** There are plenty of pay lots and garages in central Villach as well as a large free parking lot by the train station, about a 15min walk away.
- **Don't Miss:** Villacher Alpenstraße.
- **Especially for Kids:** Burg Landskron, Affenberg, Terra Mystica and Terra Montana.
- **Also See:** OSSIACHER SEE, WÖRTHER SEE.

Sights

Old town★

The old town is hemmed in to the north and east by the Drava. The **Hauptplatz**, an elongated square, is flanked by several interesting houses, including the Paracelsushof (no. 18), named after the great physician who spent his youth in Villach; and the Khevenhüllers' house (now the Hotel Post) where Emperor Karl V stayed for seven weeks in 1552.

Hauptstadtpfarrkirche St. Jakob

Behind the parish church's simple exterior awaits a lovely hall-church with stellar and ribbed vaulting, a high altar with magnificent sculptures, and a canopied stone pulpit (1555). There are also several 15C–18C **tombs**★ on the south wall. In summer it is possible to climb up the free-standing church tower for sweeping views.

Museum der Stadt Villach★

Widmanngasse 38. ◷May–Oct, daily 10am–4.30pm. ◉€3. ☎04242/2 05 35 00.

This Renaissance-style building with its arcaded courtyard forms a fine backdrop for the local historical collections. Exceptional items include the two Gothic panel paintings by **Master Thomas of Villach**, the 1557 death plaque of local governor Christoph Khevenhüller, and large iron chests from the 16C–19C that were used as fire-proof storage places for valuables.

Wallfahrtskirche Heiligenkreuz

Follow Peraustraße as far as the junction with Ossiacher Zeile.
This Late Gothic pilgrimage church with its striking twin-towered façade stands on the south bank of the Drava. The richly decorated high altar with the Crucifixion scene, the Lamentation altarpiece in the north transept and the extremely rare depiction of the Thief on Christ's Right in the south transept all contribute to the overall harmony of the church interior.

Villacher Fahrzeugmuseum

F. Wedenig Straße 9, Villach-Zauchen. ◷Mid-Jun–mid-Sept, daily 9am–5pm;

mid-Sept–mid-Jun, daily 10am–noon, 2pm–4pm. ⊛€6.50. ☏04252/33031. This small museum, in modern newly built premises, is devoted to means of transport manufactured between 1927 and 1977 and has some endearing old Fiats and Puch motorcycles.

Warmbad-Villach

About 3km/1.8mi south of town.
Every day, 24 million l/6 340 million US gal of therapeutic spring water bubbles up from the six warm springs (29°C/84°F) in the southern suburb of Warmbad-Villach. When Villach was part of the French Illyrian Provinces between 1809 and 1813, Napoleon nursed plans to develop it into a spa resort of world renown. These came to nothing back then, but today's modern spa has all the facilities one has come to expect.

Excursion

Villacher Alpenstraße★

16.5km/10.2mi (toll road). ⏱Mid-Jun–mid-Sept, 5am–10pm; May–mid-Jun & mid-Sept–Oct, 6am–8.30pm. ⊛€13. ☏0662/8736730. www.villacher-alpenstrasse.at.

This modern mountain road runs from Villach-Möltschach *(alt 550m/1 804ft)* up the Dobratsch as far as 1 732m/5 682ft. Many viewpoints have been constructed for views of Villach, the Julian Alps and Dobratsch tiself.

Alpengarten Villacher Alpe★

Access from parking lot P6. ⏱*Jun–Aug, daily 9am–6pm.* ⊛€2. ☏04242/5 91 38. This Alpine garden devoted to the flora of the southern Alps should not be missed. It covers an area of 10 000sq m/ 11 960sq yd and is home to 900 types of Alpine plant, with explanatory panels.

Dobratsch★★

From the end of the road, a trail leads to the peak of the **Dobratsch** *(alt 2 167m/ 7 107ft)* in about 2hr. As a reward for your effort, you get to enjoy a famous **panorama** taking in the Karawanken, the Carinthian lakes, the Julian Alps and the Tauern.

Burg Landskron   Kids

5km/3mi north of Villach.
A Habsburg stronghold in the Middle Ages, this castle passed to the Kheven-hüller family in the 16C who refitted it in sumptuous style but later lost the place as punishment for supporting the Refor-

View of the town from the Drau River

mation. It is now a hotel-restaurant with
a fabulous **view**★ of the Villach basin,
the Karawanken and Ossiacher See from
the terrace.

Not only kids will be impressed by the
flight demonstrations★ (*Jul–Aug,
daily 11am, 2.30pm, 5.30pm; May, Jun,
Sept, daily 11am, 2.30pm;* €8; ☎0 42
42/4 15 63) staged at the castle and starring a cast of kites, falcons and eagles.
En route to Landskron, you pass the
Affenberg (*Apr–Oct, daily 9.30am–
5.30pm;* €8; ☎0 42 42/43 03 75; www.
affenberg.com) where a colony of Japanese macaco monkeys lives in the open
countryside.

Bad Bleiberg

15km/9.3mi west of Villach.
As Bleiberg the town was a lead-mining
settlement until in 1993 the mine closed
due to falling lead prices and exhaustion of the ore deposits making mining uneconomic. Discovery of thermal
waters in the mines led to the development of a **spa** and the town received the
title **Bad** (spa) in 1978.

Terra Mystica and Terra Montana★★★ Kids

*Bleiberg-Notsch 91. Guided tours
(2hrs) only. May–Jun, Sept–Oct 10.30am–
3pm; Jul–Aug 9.30am–4.30pm; Nov–Apr
Sat 3pm.* €13.50. ☎04244/22 55. www.
terra-mystica.

Together these make up Austria's most
imaginative show mines. **Terra Mystica**
was first to be developed and makes use
of the old mining galleries. Highlight of
the tour is a descent down a 68m/223ft
wooden slide to the deeper levels where
there is a spectacular sound and light
show on mining, the cult of St. Barbara
(the patron saint of miners) and mythical
subterranean creatures.

Visiting **Terra Montana** involves
descending 250m/820ft in a miners cage
at the rate of 4m/s (13ft/s) to the mine.
Here a train takes you on a 3km/1.2mi
tour to 14 stations where you can learn
and experience life in the mine.

*This tour is not for those suffering from
claustrophobia*

Ossiacher Lake★

See OSSIACHER SEE.

WAIDHOFEN AN DER THAYA

NIEDERÖSTERREICH
POPULATION 5 650 – ALT 510M/1 673FT

Waidhofen is situated on the left bank of the River Thaya in bucolic surroundings of farmland and forest. The town grew up from a fortified settlement first
recorded in 1171. The parish church stands on the highest point, while the town
fortress was built on the lowest ground, to the east.

- **Information:** Bahnhofstr. 2. ☎02842/5 15 00. www.waidhofen-thaya.at.
- **Orient Yourself:** Waidhofen is in the Waldvietel, near the Czech border and
  about equidistant (120km/75mi) from Vienna and Linz.
- **Don't Miss:** Natur Blockheide.
- **Organizing Your Time:** Allow a full day if including the excursion.
- **Especially for Kids:** Natur Blockheide.
- **Also See:** RIEGERSBURG.

Sights

Altstadt
In the old town, the north promenade with the powder tower and the south promenade with a partially preserved defence tower are all that remain of the original fortifications. There are some interesting old houses along Wiener-straße (no. 14, the Heimathaus), Böhm-gasse, and Pfarrgasse.

Hauptplatz
In the center of the town square stands the **Rathaus**, a beautiful example of an essentially Gothic town hall, even if it does owe its stepped gables to the Renaissance. The ridge turret was added in 1721. The **Dreifaltigkeitssäule** column was put up in 1709 to protect the town from plague, fire and war.

Pfarrkirche
The church's modest, if finely proportioned, exterior offers no hint of its lavish Baroque interior. The vault of the nave is decorated with frescoes and stuccowork by Josef Michael Daysinger and depicts scenes from the life of Mary. The magnificent **high altar** (1721) fills the chancel with its lofty columns. Also note the beautifully carved **stalls** with a double-headed eagle on the upper part to symbolize the church's function in an Imperial parish, as well as the pulpit and the organ gallery.

Waldrapp Wildlife Refuge
Hollenbach 98 ⏰*Daily 8.30am–3pm.* 🗪*Guided tours by prior arrangement.* *€10* ☎*06649/49 39 29. www.waldrapp.at.*

Church, Waidhofen an der Thaya

R. Chéret/MICHELIN

This wildlife refuge is devoted to saving the Waldrapp *(Bald Ibis)*, a species of ibis that was common in the Waldviertal, from extinction. Visitors can see some of the birds and learn about their life and habitat. There is also an art gallery devoted to representations of the bird. As a result of the efforts of the refuge, numbers of Waldrapp are on the increase.

Excursion

Gmünd
Gmünd lies in the northern Waldviertel, near the Czech border, where the Lainsitz and Braunaubach rivers meet.
Gmünd, with a population of c. 61 500, counts among its assets an enchanting old quarter, peaceful spots beside the Lainsitz, and the Blockheide nature reserve.

Stadtplatz
Gmünd's main square is centered around the Renaissance **Altes Rathaus**, which houses a local history museum and is easily recognized by its gabled tower. On the south side of the square, the **Glas- und Steinmuseum** provides evidence of the glass-making industry that flourished in the region from the 17C to the 20C. At Nos. 31 and 33 are two beautiful Renaissance-era **houses with sgraffito decoration**★ featuring scenes from Classical-era mythology.

Naturpark Blockheide★ Kids
Northeast of the town, this lovely nature reserve is characterized by bizarrely shaped granite blocks with nicknames like Pilzstein (mushroom rock) and Teufelsbett (devil's bed). A former water reservoir at the park's highest point acts as an information center with snack stands nearby. The viewing tower offers sweeping vistas as far as the Czech Republic. There is also an open-air display of geology and a children's playground. ⏰*Daily 10am–6pm.* 🗪*Themed guided tours.* ☎*02852/52932. www.blockheide.at.*

ÖSTLICHES WEINVIERTEL
NIEDERÖSTERREICH

Austria's **Eastern Wine Country is still** a region somewhat off the beaten tourist track. Its remote position in Austria's far northeastern corner means that the countryside has remained relatively unspoiled. It is a delightful area filled with natural and cultural treasures. Be sure to sample the excellent local wine, preferably along a charming *Kellergasse*, a strip of tiny wine cellars.

- **Information:** Niederösterreichring 2, Haus C, Wien. ☎01/536 10-6200. www.weinstrassen.at or www.cum-vinum.de/weinviertel.
- **Orient Yourself:** The Weinviertel is northeast of Vienna, rubbing up against the borders with the Czech Republic and Slovakia.
- **Don't Miss:** Weinviertler Museumsdorf, Kellergassen in Poysdorf.
- **Organizing Your Time:** The Weinviertel makes for a nice day trip from Vienna.
- **Especially for Kids:** Weinviertler Museumsdorf, Museum für Urgeschichte.
- **Also See:** WIEN.

Driving Tour

From Gänserndorf to Poysdorf

62km/38.5mi

Watch out for unmarked railway crossings along this drive!

▸ *Start in the district capital of Gänserndorf (26km/16mi northeast of Vienna; reached via the B 8) and continue to Prottes.*

Erdöl-Erdgas-Lehrpfad

Along the road from Gänserndorf to Prottes are numerous pumps, extracting oil or gas in perpetual motion. To learn more about the subject, follow the 4.5km/3mi educational trail through charming countryside starting at the affiliated **museum** (*Easter Sun–Oct, Sat–Sun & public holidays 9.30am–11.30am, 2pm–4pm; €1.50; ☎02282/21 82) in Prottes (follow red and white markings).* Along the way you will encounter display panels with background information and numerous original pieces of machinery connected with the extraction of this raw material, including oil detection probes, mobile drilling gear, production derricks, etc. There is no admission for the trail, which is open year-round.

▸ *Drive on via Matzen toward Gross-Schweinbarth.*

Niederösterreichisches Museum für Volkskultur

In Gross-Schweinbarth. *Right by the B 220; from Prottes keep left heading toward Gänserndorf.* Mid-Apr–mid-Nov, Tue–Sun 9am–5pm. €4. ☎02289/23 02. www.museum.gross-schweinbarth.at. This museum of traditional regional culture (complete with wine section) has found the perfect home in an old dairy that once supplied the neighboring castle. Displays include traditional costumes, furniture and crockery as well as a broad range of items dealing with local customs, religious practices and craftwork. The history and role of the dairy farm is also explained. An entire wing is dedicated to amber, explaining the formation, extraction and use of this fossilized resin. There are even specimens enclosing 50-million-year-old animals, conjuring visions of "Jurassic Park."

▸ *Take the B 220 toward Pirawarth. At the exit to Gross-Schweinbarth turn right toward Hohenruppersdorf. From there head toward Zistersdorf and then to Niedersulz.*

Weinviertler Museumsdorf★ Kids
In Niedersulz.
🕐Apr–Oct Mon–Fri 9.30am–4pm, Sat–Sun 10am–6pm. €6.50. ☎02534/3 33. www.museumsdorf.at.

This large open-air museum re-creates an entire Weinviertel village as it might have looked in pre-industrial times. More than 60 buildings, including farmhouses, barns, sheds, chapels and mills whose existence in their original sites had been threatened, have been reassembled here. The museum site has been planted with flora typical of the region. The realistic layout of houses around a central square, complete with church, inn, presbytery and even a graveyard, creates the impression of walking around a village whose inhabitants are all out working in the fields. The houses contain authentic furnishings or exhibitions on rural life. There's also a "living farm" where domestic and farm animals make their home.

M. Hertlein/MICHELIN

The "living farm" at the Weinviertler Museumsdorf

▷ *Drive on through Obersulz and Schrick toward* **Mistelbach**. *In Lanzendorf turn left and follow the signposts to "Schloss Asparn/Zaya – Museum für Urgeschichte."*

Asparn an der Zaya
This town at the foothills of the Leiser Berge boasts a fine ensemble of historic buildings. These include the **Baroque Minorite convent** from the 18C, which now houses a museum on wine-growing and the local region; the elegant parish church of St. Pancras and St. Francis; and the Renaissance castle with its prehistory museum.

Museum für Urgeschichte　Kids
In the castle. 🕐Apr–Nov, Tue–Fri 9am–5pm, Sat–Sun 10am–6pm; Sept–Nov, also Mon. €4, audio-guide €1.50. ☎02577/80 39. www.urgeschichte.com.

Exhibits at this prehistory museum illustrate the evolution of humankind and human culture through to the year 1C. There are reproductions of cave paintings from Altamira, Lascaux and other famous sites alongside jewelry, ceramics, tools and many other objects once in use thousands of years ago.

The **open-air museum**★ behind the castle is a particular highlight, with reconstructions of walk-in dwellings from the Paleolithic Age to the New Iron Age (25 000 BC to 2C AD).

▷ *From Asparn drive on toward Hörersdorf and then turn left onto the B 46 to Laa an der Thaya. At the Laa-Poysdorf crossroads, carry straight on, following the signposts to "Ruine."*

"Eing'richt"

This painstaking craft in which tiny scenes, mainly on religious themes, are patiently crafted—often from very simple materials—and then inserted *("eingerichtet")* into bottles used to keep many a farming family occupied on long winter evenings. A small collection of this naive art form is on display in the Niederösterreichisches Museum für Volkskultur in Gross-Schweinbarth.

Burgruine Staatz
Park by the Musikerheim and walk along the fortified wall. Guided tours (1hr) May–Oct, Sun and public holidays 3pm. The castle ruins can be seen from miles away perching on the relatively low Staatzer Berg (331m/1 086ft). From the top, there is a sweeping **view**★★ across the Weinviertel and the Carpathian mountains to the northeast.

▶ *Carry on to Poysdorf.*

Shortly before reaching Poysdorf, the road passes the **pilgrimage church of Maria Bründl** in an idyllic, tree-shaded setting. It was completed in 1751 according to plans by Italian architect Donato Felice d'Allio, who was also the master-mind behind the abbey church at Klosterneuburg (*see entry*).

Poysdorf
The self-styled "wine town of Austria," which ironically produces mostly sparkling wine *(Sekt),* is a great place for exploring the romantic *Kellergassen.* Particularly fine examples of these wine-cellar-lined lanes can be found in Bürsting *(via Singergasse from the tourist office)* and on Berggasse *(below the parish church).* A 1hr loop trail on the theme of *Kellergassen* leaving from the Stadtmuseum also takes in some of the delightful vineyards on the edge of town (*follow the beige-white markers*). From May to October, wine-growers take turns in opening their premises for public tours and wine tasting sessions.

WELS
OBERÖSTERREICH
POPULATION 56 500 – ALT 317M/1 040FT

Wels on the Traun River evolved from a small Celtic settlement into the Roman town of Ovilava, which became an important supply center and was eventually raised to the status of colony. Today, it is the second-largest town in Lower Austria after Linz and known for its trade fairs and lovely historic town.

- 🛈 **Information:** Kaiser-Josef-Platz 22, A-4600. ☎0 72 42/67 72 20. www.wels.at.
- ▶ **Orient Yourself:** Wels is about 35km/22mi southwest of Linz.
- 🅿 **Parking:** There are pay parking garages on Kaiser-Josef-Platz, below the Traunpark Hotel and on the Marktplatz. Parking is free at the Messe on non-trade show days.
- 😊 **Don't Miss:** Zoo Schmiding.
- 🕐 **Organizing Your Time:** Taking in all the museums, it's easy to make a day of it in Wels.
- **Kids** **Especially for Kids:** Zoo Schmiding
- 👣 **Also See:** LAMBACH, SCHLOSS-MUSEUM HOHENBRUNN

Sights

Stadtplatz
Wels' historic town centers on the elongated **Stadtplatz**★, the main square with a flower-bedecked fountain and rows of attractive buildings, mostly sporting Baroque façades. The golden **Rathaus** (town hall) is certainly striking, although the star of the parade is the **Haus der Salome Alt** at no 4, named after a mistress of Wolf Dietrich of Raitenau, the prince-archbishop of Salzburg. Distinctive features include the Late Gothic oriel and the Renaissance fresco paintings.

North of this house is the **Stadtpfarrkirche** (B), the local parish church, with some fine 14C stained-glass windows in the chancel. To the south looms the Kaiserliche Burg, the imperial castle. The western end of the Stadtplatz is punctuated by the 13C **Ledererturm**

WELS

Adlerstr.	B	
Altstadtgasse	B	2
Bäckergasse	A	10
Bahnhofstr.	A	
Dragonerstr.	A	5
Dr-Koss.-Str.	A	
Dr-Salzmann-Str.	A	3
Dr-Schauer-Str.	B	8
Eisenhower-Str.	A	
Herrengasse	B	
Kaiser-Josef-Pl.	A	
Karl-Loy-Str.	A	
Maria-Theresia-Str.	A	6
Maximilianstr.	B	
Pfarrgasse	B	
Pollheimerstr.	A	
Rainerstr.	A	
Ringstr.	A	
Roseggerstr.	B	
Schmidtgasse	B	7
Stadtpl.	B	
Stelzhamerstr.	B	
Traungasse	B	9
Vogelweiderstr.	A	12
Volksgartenstr.	AB	
Wegkapelle	B	B

(Leather Tower) (A), the last surviving town gate.

Burg Wels (B)

&.◷Tue–Fri 10am–5pm, Sat 2pm–5pm, Sun 10am–4pm. ✆€3.70. ☎07242/2 35 73 50.

The restored imperial castle, where Emperor Maximilian I died in 1519, now houses four **museum collections**: The Local History Museum, with a remarkable display of Biedermeier items; the Museum of Agriculture, arranged on the theme of the "farmer's year;" the Austrian Museum of Baking, the only one of its kind; and the Museum of Displaced Persons.

Stadtmuseum Minoritengebäuder (A R)

Minoritenplatz 4. ◷Tue–Fri 10am–5pm, Sat 2pm–5pm, Sun 10am–4pm. ✆€4.15. ☎07242/23 573 50.

Each excavation within the town uncovers yet more evidence of its past, particularly the Roman period. This has resulted in a particularly rich archeological collection housed in a former monastery. One section re-creates a mock Roman village where you can peek inside tradesmen's workshops, private living quarters and tombs.

Excursion

Zoo Schmiding★   Kids

In Krengelbach. 7km/4.3mi north of Wels. ◷Daily 9am–7pm (last admission 5pm). ✆€11; children €6.50. ☎07249/4 62 72. www.zooschmiding.at.

What once used to be merely a bird park has evolved into a full-fledged, modern zoo where animals live in re-created habitats. These include a tropical rainforest (squirrel monkeys, crocodiles, sloths, etc.) and the African Savannah (zebras, giraffes, etc.). Another highlight is the giant aviary inhabited by birds of prey.

Flamingos in Zoo Schmiding

© Österreich Werbung / Landova

WIEN

VIENNA
POPULATION 1 680 400, ALT 156M/512FT
LOCAL MAPS SEE DONAUTAL AND WIENERWALD
HOTELS AND RESTAURANTS: SEE THE RED GUIDE EUROPE
FOR LONGER VISITS TO THE CITY, CONSULT THE GREEN GUIDE VIENNA

Vienna was the residence of the Imperial court for six centuries and is indelibly stamped with the seal of the Habsburg dynasty. Even now as capital of the Republic of Austria, Vienna has retained its incomparable grandeur and considerable prestige as one of Europe's most important cultural and artistic centers. For many, the name Vienna evokes the rhythm of the waltz or the shape of the Prater's Giant Wheel. The city's global renown, however, is due above all to its historic buildings, to the magnificent art collections, to its excellent museums, to the musical tradition preserved by the opera and Vienna's famous choirs and orchestras, and to the elegance of the shops lining its grand avenues. Even politically Vienna plays a pivotal role on the world stage as the permanent headquarters of OPEC (Organization of Petroleum Exporting Countries) since 1965. Several UN organizations, including the International Atomic Energy Agency (IAEA), are also based in the city.

- **Information:** Am Albertinaplatz 1, A-1025. ☎01/21 11 40. www.wien.info.
- **Orient Yourself:** Vienna is in the northwest corner of Austria, not far from the borders with the Czech Republic, Slovakia, and Hungary.
- **Parking:** Finding parking is easy thanks to an electronic guide system that directs you to the nearest garage and also shows the number of available spaces. 24hr parking garages in the center (1. Bezirk) include: Am Morzinplatz (Franz-Josefs-Kai), Rathauspark (Ring/Stadiongasse), Operngarage (Kärtner Straße 51), Am Hof, Beethovenplatz 3, Cobdengasse 2. For a complete list, check www.parkeninwien.at.
- **Don't Miss:** Hofburg, Kulturhistorisches Museum, Stephansdom, Schloss Schönbrunn.
- **Organizing Your Time:** Budget at least three days for your Vienna stay.
- **Especially for Kids:** Zoom Kindermuseum, Prater, Tiergarten, The Irrgarten and Labyrinth, Technisches Museum, Naturhistorisches Museum.
- **Also See:** DONAUTAL, WIENERWALD.

A Bit of History

From Antiquity to the Habsburgs – Vienna began its existence as a modest Roman camp called Vindobona, founded around 15 BC. It gradually grew into a larger settlement and trading site but didn't gain capital status until 1155 when Heinrich II Jasomirgott moved his residence to Vienna. The town flourished economically and culturally in the early 13C under Leopold the Glorious, whose rule saw the construction of a massive fortified wall and the Church of St. Stephen, which became a bishop's seat in 1469. By the time the last of the Babenbergs died in 1246, Vienna had become,

after Cologne, the most important city on German-speaking soil. Its growth, from then on, was inseparably linked with the fortunes of the Habsburgs, who reigned over Austria from 1273 to 1918.

The Turks – A major impediment to Vienna's development was the persistent threat posed by the Ottoman army, which numbered as high as 300 000 men. The city was besieged twice, first in 1529 and then again in 1683. During the latter siege, the Emperor and the court fled Vienna, leaving its defense in the hands of 24 000 troops who managed to stave off all attacks for nearly two months. In the end, a relief force

Address Book

PRACTICAL INFORMATION

ARRIVING BY CAR

From the north: Floridsdorfer Brücke, "Donauinsel" exit *(May–Sept, daily 9am–7pm)*. **From the south** (via A 2): "Zentrum" exit *(Jul–Sept 8am–10pm, week before Easter–Jun, Oct 9am–7pm)*. **From the west** via A 1: Wien/Auhof gas station *(Apr–Oct, 8am–10pm, Nov–Mar, 10am–6pm)*.

ARRIVING BY RAIL

Westbahnhof *(Apr–Oct, 7am–10pm)*. **Südbahnhof** *(May–Oct, 6.30am–10pm; Nov–Apr, 6.30am–9pm)*.

ARRIVING BY AIR

Wien-Schwechat airport *(daily 8.30am–9pm; ☎01/70 07 3 28 75)*. **City center:** *Am Albertinaplatz 1, 1. Bezirk, daily 9am–7pm, ☎01/21 11 40*. The tourist office publishes a free monthly cultural calendar of events. **Vienna on the Internet** – *www.info.wien.at* (tourist information); *www.wien.gv.at* (city government); *www.aboutvienna.org* (cultural and tourist information).

WIENKARTE

The **Vienna Card** *(☞€18.50; www. wienkarte.at)* entitles you to unlimited travel on the city's underground/subway (U-Bahn), bus, tram, and most night buses for 72hr, starting from the moment it is first validated. In addition, you qualify for four consecutive days of discounts at museums, sights and attractions, and for certain purchases and meals. Full details are included in the coupon booklet that comes with the ticket. It is available from many hotels, tourist information offices, some ticket agencies and information offices belonging to the Viennese transport authorities (Wiener Linien; for example, Stephansplatz, Karlsplatz, Westbahnhof) or online using a credit card.

BUS TOURS

Vienna Sightseeing Tours, *Stelzhamergasse 4/11, 3. Bezirk, ☎01/71 24 68 30. www.viennasightseeingtours.com*. City tour with the "Vienna Line Hop on Hop off." This operates hourly between 13 stops (for example, Staatsoper, Heldenplatz, Prater) from *9.30am to 6.10pm*. Commentaries in English and German. Cost of a ticket valid for one day is €20 (children €7), available from any hotel in Vienna, or any travel agency in Austria as well as abroad.

Cityrama, *Börsegasse 1, 1. Bezirk, ☎01/53 41 30*. City tours *daily at 9.30am and 2.30pm* with a guided tour of Schloss Schönbrunn. Takes about 3hr 30min. Tour costs €35 per person (including pick-up from hotel).

Robin Reisen-Stattwerkstatt, *Kolingasse 6, 9. Bezirk, ☎01/3 17 33 84*. City tour entitled "Dream and Reality" focussing on Jugendstil and "Red Vienna" (1920s social-democrat housing projects). Departures: *Tue and Thu at 1pm, Sat at 10am, sometimes also at 2pm*. Takes about 3hr. Tour costs €32. Booking necessary.

THEMED TOURS

Oldtime tram tour

– *Early May–early Oct, Sat at 11.30am and 1.30pm, Sun and public holidays also 9.30am*. Departure from Karlsplatz. Takes about 1hr. Tickets available from "Wiener Linien" information office at Karlsplatz U-Bahn station. *☎01/7 90 94 40 26. €15 (€13 with Vienna Card); children €5*.

City tour by horse-drawn carriage

– The horse-drawn carriage stands are located on Albertinaplatz behind the Staatsoper as well as on Heldenplatz and Stephansplatz.

WALKING TOURS

The city of Vienna organizes themed walks around town, such as Musical Capital of the World, Jugendstil, Unadulterated Habsburgs, The Viennese Coffee-house, Old Houses and Quiet Courtyards, Underground Vienna. Takes about 90min. Monthly program available from the tourist office at Albertinaplatz 1.

"The Third Man" – Part of this tour takes place underground in the Viennese sewer system, re-tracing the steps of the protagonists in Orson Welles' classic film, "The Third Man." The tour

Diejun/ÖSTERREICH WERBUNG

Horse-drawn carriage

(about 25min) leaves from opposite the Café Museum (JS) in the Esperantopark (cross Friedrichstraße). During heavy rain, tours do not take place; only children older than 12 are admitted; sturdy footwear is recommended; tours are in English or German. If all these criteria are met, this tour is a lively and interesting experience, full of all kinds of surprises. Advance booking and information from MA 30 – *WienKanal, A-1030 Wien, Friedrichstraße/Esperantopark, ☎01/5 85 64 55.*

Vienna Walks & Talks offers a wide range of lively, themed tours. See *www.viennawalks. tix.at* for more information.

CYCLE TOURS

Cyclists in Vienna have some 700km/435mi of cycle paths at their disposal. Those arriving in Vienna by train can hire bicycles from the following stations: West- and Südbahnhof, Wien Nord and Floridsdorf, and Franz-Josefs-Bahnhof. These can be returned at any station with luggage check-in facilities. Further cycle hire outlets can be found on the Donauinsel or at the Hundertwasserhaus (cost from about €3 per hour with some form of identification such as a passport left as a security).

Pedal Power cycle tours through Vienna are offered in various languages *May–Sept daily at 10am*; takes about 3hr; €23; further details from ☎01/7 29 72 34, www.pedalpower.at.

City Segway Tours also offers cycling tours of Vienna: *www.citysegwaytours. com/vienna.*

The brochure entitled **Tips für Radfahrer**, available free from tourist offices, gives full details for cyclists.

BOAT TOURS

DDSG Blue Danube Schiffahrt GmbH *(Handelskai 265, A-1020 Wien; ☎01/5 88 80; Fax 01/58 88 04 40; www.ddsg-blue-danube.at)* offers boat tours on the Danube *Apr–late Oct*; for example a Hundertwasser tour on the *Vindobona* (departure from Schwedenplatz, takes 1hr 30min).

AIR TOURS

Vienna Aircraft Handling *(Hangar 3, A-1300 Flughafen Wien-Schwechat, ☎01/70 07 2 22 04, fax 01/70 07 2 24 64)* offers airborne circuits (30min) in a Cessna 210 (single-engine plane). Recommended price: €130 per person.

PUBLIC TRANSPORT

Viennese transport authorities, Wiener Linien, operate services in the central zones of the Vienna city area (all districts) and are linked with the east Austrian transport authority (Verkehrsverbund Ost-Region, VOR). Written enquiries and requests for information by telephone can be addressed to either organization:

Wiener Linien, *Erdbergstraße 202, A-1031 Wien, ☎01/79 09 105.*

Verkehrsverbund Ost-Region, *Neubaugasse 1, A-1070 Wien, information hotline ☎08 10/22 23 24.*
Further details on public transport in Vienna are to be found at *www.wiener linien.co.at or www.vor.at.*
Tourists in Vienna are advised to pay a visit in person to one of the **information and ticket offices** in the following U-Bahn stations: Stephansplatz, Schwedenplatz, Karlsplatz, Landstraße/Wien-Mitte, Westbahnhof, Spittelau, Schottentor, Reumannplatz, Philadelphiabrücke, Hietzing, Florisdorf or Kagran.

Finding your way around
A map of the U-Bahn network is included on the city map published by the Vienna tourist office and available from most hotels, among other places. These outlets can also supply timetables for Vienna's transport system or the more comprehensive timetable book, as well as selling tickets (runabout or magnetic strip tickets).

Tickets – Tickets are valid for travel on the underground/subway (U-Bahn), tram, high-speed rail (Schnellbahn), and bus. Single tickets can be validated using ticket machines on the transport in question or in U-Bahn stations. It is cheaper, however, to buy tickets in advance from ticket offices or an authorised tobacconist's (Tabaktrafik). Tickets that are well-suited to the needs of tourists include the **24-** (€5.70) and **72-** (€13.60) **hour runabout ticket** or the **8-day ticket** (€27.20; this allows the bearer unlimited travel within Vienna city center limits per strip validated, on the date it was validated). The **Wiener Einkaufskarte** (Viennese shopper's ticket) offers another interesting deal: for €4.60 you can make unlimited trips in the city center for one day (between Mon and Sat) 8am–8pm.
Of course, there is always the option of the **Wien-Karte**, which allows three days of unlimited travel on Viennese public transport.

Night line – When normal city transport finishes running for the day (after about 12.30am until about 4.30am), 22 night bus lines operate in the city center every 30min, for which special rates apply (runabout tickets are valid on these night buses; tickets available from ticket machines on the bus or as strip tickets bought in advance). Further details and a map of the night line services are available from indicated Vienna transport authority ticket offices.

INNER CITY CAR PARKS
Vienna old town and the surrounding districts *(Bezirke 1–9 and 20)* are **fee-paying short-stay parking zones**. However, these are only signposted as such at the entrance to each district concerned (no further indication is given in the streets themselves—a paid-up parking ticket is obligatory from the minute you park). In commercial streets, parking regulations may vary, for example concerning how long you may park, in which case these will be specifically indicated. Pre-paid parking tickets can be bought from most authorised tobacconists (Tabaktrafiken) and banks, stations and from Vienna transport authority (Wiener Linien) ticket offices. Visitors who have booked a hotel should phone ahead of their arrival and confirm where to leave their car.
The most practical solution to the difficulty of parking in the city center is offered by numerous multi-storey or underground **car parks**, which are open daily 24hr/24hr. In the 1. Bezirk these are the following underground car parks: *Am Morzinplatz (Franz-Josefs-Kai), Rathauspark (Ring/Stadiongasse), Operngarage (Kärtner Straße 51), Am Hof, Beethovenplatz 3, Cobdengasse 2.*
An overview of car parks in Vienna can be requested from the tourist office (☎01/21 11 42 22) or found at *www. parkeninwien.at.*

POST OFFICES
The second and third digits in Viennese **post codes** denote the district (Bezirk) in question, thus 1070 denotes the 7. Bezirk, Vienna.
The main post offices are open daily 24hr/24hr:
Hauptpostamt, *Fleischmarkt 19, 1. Bezirk, ☎01/51 50 90*
Post am Westbahnhof, *Mariahilfer Straße 132, 15. Bezirk, ☎01/89 11 50*

Post am Franz-Josef-Bahn-hof, *Althahnstraße 10, 9. Bezirk,* ☎*01/3 19 14 70*

SHOPPING

Most department stores and specialist boutiques are located in the pedestrian zones in Kärntner Straße, Graben, Kohlmarkt, Naglergasse, Tuchlauben, Stephansplatz, part of Krugerstraße and Franz-Josefs-Kai, Wolfengasse, Seitenstettengasse, Rabensteig, Griechengasse, Ballgasse and Vienna's main shopping street – **Mariahilfer Straße**.

SOUVENIRS

Augarten GmbH, *Stock-im-Eisen-Platz 3–4, 1. Bezirk*. In Schloss Augarten, 2. Bezirk. Sales outlet for the famous porcelain manufacturer, whose origins date back to 1717.

Backhausen, *Kärntner Straße 33, 1. Bezirk*. This textile factory sells furnishing materials, curtains and silk scarves with Jugendstil designs.

Frimmel, *Freisingergasse 1, 1. Bezirk*. This is *the* shop for buttons, which used to supply the Imperial court.

J. & L. Lobmeyr, *Kärntner Straße 26, 1. Bezirk*. A glassware specialist which used to supply the Imperial court, and which is famous for its extremely fragile and delicate "Musselinglas."

Maria Stransky, *Hofburg. Burgpassage 2, 1. Bezirk*. This is the home of typical Viennese petit point embroidery.

Piatnik, *Kandlgasse 33, 7. Bezirk*. This establishment founded at the end of the 19C sells such beautiful playing cards that they can almost rank as works of art.

Schau Schau Brillen, *Rotenturmstraße 11, 1. Bezirk*. Spectacles in the strangest shapes are the speciality here, signed by Peter Kozich. One of his clients is no less a figure than Sir Elton John.

FOOD MARKETS

Naschmarkt, *Linke Wienzeile/Kettenbrückengasse. 4. and 6. Bezirk*. This is divided into the **Naschmarkt** proper (fruit and vegetables): *Mon–Fri 6am–6.30pm, Sat 6am–5pm*, and the **Bauernmarkt** (farm produce):

Augarten porcelain workshop

Mon–Thu 6am–noon, Fri 6am–1pm, Sat 6am–5pm.

Markt auf der Freyung, *1. Bezirk, May–Nov, Tue and Thu 10am–6.30pm*.

FLEA MARKETS

Naschmarkt: *Linke Wienzeile. 4. and 6. Bezirk*. The flea market is located at the south end of the Naschmarkt: *Sat 6am–6pm*.

Art and antiques markets

Kunst- und Antikmarkt am Donaukanal (art and antiques market on the promenade along the banks of the Danube on the old town side by the *Marienbrücke, 1. Bezirk*): *May–Sept, Sat 2pm–8pm, Sun 10am–8pm*.

Am Hof *(1. Bezirk)*: *Mar–Christmas, Fri and Sat 10am–8pm*.

Kunst- und Handwerksmarkt im Heiligenkreuzerhof (art and crafts market, *Schönlaterngasse, 1. Bezirk*): *every first weekend in the month; in Dec every weekend*.

CHRISTMAS MARKETS

Christkindlmarkt Rathausplatz *mid Nov–Christmas*

Weihnachtsmarkt am Spittelberg *late Nov–Christmas*

Altwiener Christkindlmarkt Freyung *late Nov–Christmas*

Kultur- und Weihnachtsmarkt in front of Schloss Schönbrunn *late Nov–Christmas*

Kunsthandwerksmarkt in front of Karlskirche *late Nov–Christmas*

ENTERTAINMENT

THEATER

Burgtheater, *Dr.-Karl-Lueger-Ring 2, 1. Bezirk*. ☎*01/5 14 44 44 40*. A European theater offering the entire range of theatrical repertoire. Tickets sold in advance from the 20th of the month preceding the month in question, for the whole calendar month. Written applications for tickets should be addressed at least ten days in advance of the date in question to the Service-center Burgtheater, *Hanuschgasse 3, A-1010 Wien (www.events.at/burgth-eater_wien; ☎01/5 14 44 41 40)*. Tickets can be ordered by telephone (payment by credit card) daily 10am–9pm from ☎*01/51 31 513*. For performances that are not sold out, tickets can be obtained at 50% of their original price from 1hr before the performance starts from the "Abendkasse" *(☎01/51 44 44 44 0)*. Other theaters linked with the Burgth-eater are the **Akademietheater** *(Lisztstraße 1, 3. Bezirk, ☎01/51 44 44 740)* and the **Kasino** *(Schwarzenbergplatz 1, 3. Bezirk, ☎01/51 44 44 830)*.

Theater in der Josefstadt, *Josefstädter Straße 24, 8. Bezirk. ☎01/42 70 03 00*. Venue for theatrical productions since 1788, where such famous Austrian names as Nestroy and Raimund made their debut: Both classic and modern theater.

Volkstheater, *Neustiftgasse 1, 7. Bezirk, ☎01/524 72 63*. Broad spectrum of plays from the classics to the avant-garde.

gruppe 80, *Gumpendorfer Straße 67, 6. Bezirk, ☎01/586 52 22*. Predominantly Austrian plays from the classics to contemporary drama.

Schauspielhaus, *Porzellangasse 19, 9. Bezirk, ☎01/3 17 01 01*. Young, unconventional theater.

Komödie am Kai, *Franz-Josefs-Kai 29, 1. Bezirk, ☎01/533 24 34*. Popular comedies from all over the world for a pleasant evening.

English Theater, *Josefsgasse 12, 8. Bezirk, ☎01/40 21 26 00*. English-language theater productions from both Britain and America have been staged here since 1963 (classics, comedies, guest performances by solo artists).

MUSICAL VENUES

Staatsoper *(Herbert-von-Karajan-Platz, 1. Bezirk)* and **Volksoper** *(Währinger Straße 78, 9. Bezirk)* – the opera venues of the Austrian capital. Tickets go on sale one month before the performance date. Written applications for tickets must be submitted at least three weeks before the performance to the Österreichischer Bundestheaterver-band/Bestellbüro, *Hanuschgasse 3, A-1010 Wien*. Tickets can be ordered by telephone (payment by credit card) from ☎*01/5 13 15 13*. Remainder tickets can be purchased from the Bundes-theater ticket offices, *Hanuschgasse 3, ☎01/51 44 29 60* or from the Volksoper itself *(Mon–Fri 8am–6pm, Sat, Sun and public holidays 9am–noon)*. For program details call ☎*01/5 14 44 36 70 (recorded message)*.

Neue Oper Wien: The independent opera group, which stages only a few productions per year, has dedicated itself to premieres and 20C works that have some relevance to current affairs and that concern humanitarian and social-political matters. Information on the program and performances from ☎*01/5 97 30 37* or at *www.neueoper wien.music.at*.

Musikverein: Vienna's association for friends of music *(Bösendorferstr. 12, A-1010 Wien, ☎01/5 05 81 90, fax 01/5 05 81 94)* puts on about 500 concerts of classical music per year. Tickets go on sale about three weeks before the concert date, *Mon–Fri 9am–7.30pm, Sat 9am–5pm*. For program details, call ☎*01/5 05 13 63 (recorded message)*.

Concerts by the Vienna Boys' Choir (Wiener Sängerknaben): The Vienna Boys' Choir perform from *Apr–Jun and Sept–Oct Fri at 4pm* in the Brahms Room at the Musikvereins. Tickets are on sale in hotels and from Reisebüro Mondial (travel agent), *Faulmann-gasse 4, A-1040 Wien, ☎01/58 80 41 41, fax 01/5 87 12 68, www.mondial.at*.

Sung Masses in the Burgkapelle at the Hofburg on Sundays and 25 Dec (with the Vienna Boys' Choir and members of the chorus and orchestra of the Vienna State Opera): These begin at 9.15am. There is no charge for standing room. Orders must be placed in writing (please do not enclose either cash or cheques) at least ten weeks in advance to: *Hofmusikkapelle, Hofburg, A-1010 Wien, fax 01/5 33 99 27 75*. Collection and payment of pre-ordered tickets is on *Fri 11am–1pm and 3pm–5pm or on Sun from 8.15am–8.45am* in the Burgkapelle. Availability permitting, tickets for seats for a particular Sun are sold at the Burgkapelle Tageskasse from *3pm–5pm* on the immediately preceding Fri.

Wiener Konzerthaus, *Lothringerstraße 20, 3. Bezirk, ☎01/7 12 12 11.* Orchestra and soloists from all over the world as well as performances by the concert house's resident company. Top-quality **musical productions** are presented by Vereinigte Bühnen Wien GmbH *(Linke Wienzeile 6, A-1060 Wien, ☎01/58 83 02 00, www.musicalvienna. at)*, which incorporates three venues:

Theater an der Wien, *Linke Wienzeile 6, 6. Bezirk.*

Raimund-Theater, *Wallgasse 18–20, 6. Bezirk.*

Ronacher, *Seilerstätte 9, 1. Bezirk.*

WUK, *Währinger Straße 59, 9. Bezirk, ☎01/4 01 21 10.* Self-administered "**W**erkstätten- **u**nd **K**ulturhaus" (workshops and cultural center): Music, dance, concerts, readings, and exhibitions.

Szene Wien, *Hauffgasse 26, 11. Bezirk, ☎01/74 93 341.* Live concerts by advertised bands, world music.

Planet Music, *Adalbert-Stifter-Straße 73, 20. Bezirk, ☎01/3 32 46 41.* Venue for all sorts of musical varieties—hip-hop, pop through Blues, reggae, jazz to rock and heavy metal. There are also events specially for children and families.

Ticket reservations – The following organization also deals with ticket reservations from abroad, principally for musicals and classical music:

Vienna Ticket Service, *Börsegasse 1, A-1010 Wien, ☎01/5 34 17 75 (Mon–Fri 9am–5pm, fax 01/5 34 17 26).* For rock and pop concerts, contact **Österreich Ticket**, *Kärtner Straße 19, (1. Bezirk, Kaufhaus Steffel, 3. Stock), A-1010 Wien, ☎01/96 0 96 (Mon–Sat 9am–9pm, Sun 10am–9pm).*

OTHER VENUES

Orpheum, *Steigenteschgasse 94b, 22. Bezirk, ☎01/481 17 17.* Entertainment venue (with adjoining inn – *☎01/2 03 12 54*), in which cabaret, music and readings are on offer.

Kulisse, *Rosensteingasse 39, 17. Bezirk, ☎01/485 38 70.* Musicals, cabaret, children's theater and its own inn *(☎01/4 85 44 02).*

Wiener Metropol, *Hernalser Hauptstraße 55, 17. Bezirk, ☎01/40 777 40.* Venue for concerts (ballads and songs, world music), cabaret and home-produced musical productions.

Vindobona, *Wallensteinplatz, 20. Bezirk, ☎01/3 32 42 31. The* place to go for cabaret; Sat and Sun children's theater. There is also a restaurant close at hand so that visitors will be well taken care of all evening.

MISCELLANEOUS

Spanische Hofreitschule: Ticket reservations for performances (gala performances; classic displays of riding skills to music, 60min) should be addressed as far in advance as possible to the Spanische Reitschule, *Hofburg, A-1010 Wien, fax 01/53 50 186*, or alternatively to authorized Vienna theater ticket offices or travel agencies (there will be a supplementary charge of at least 22% in this case). Reservations are not necessary for morning training sessions ("Training der Lipizzaner"). Tickets for this can be bought on the same day at the entrance to the Spanische Reitschule *(Hofburg, Josefsplatz).* A folder in several languages is available from the Vienna tourist office giving details of precise dates and terms and conditions.

Casino Wien, *Palais Esterházy, Kärntner Straße 41, 1. Bezirk, ☎01/5 12 48 36.*

CINEMAS

The following are only a small selection, away from the mainstream, of the numerous cinemas that there are in Vienna. For the current cinema program and additional addresses, consult *Wienside*, the free weekly brochure that lists events. It is available from cinemas, local "in" bars, or the daily press.

Österreichisches Filmarchiv, *Obere Augartenstraße 1, 2. Bezirk, ☎01/2 16 13 00.* Classics from the history of film.

Schikaneder Kino, *Margarethenstraße 24, 4. Bezirk, ☎01/5 85 28 67.* Small-screen, committed mainly to recent arts films.

Votiv Kino, *Währinger Straße 12, 9. Bezirk*, ☎*01/3 17 35 71*. Preview cinema.

Imax-Filmtheater (next to the Technisches Museum, AZ), *Mariahilfer Straße 212, 14. Bezirk*, ☎*01/8 94 01 01*; info hotline: ☎*01/15 47*.

(Especially English-language) films in their original versions are shown at:

Burg, *Opernring 19, 1. Bezirk*, ☎*01/5 87 84 06*. In summer, but also on most weekends throughout the year, Carol Reed's **The Third Man** is screened here.

English Cinema Haydn, *Mariahilfer Straße 57, 6. Bezirk*, ☎*01/5 87 22 62*.

American Flotten Center, *Mariahilfer Straße 85–87, 6. Bezirk*, ☎*01/5 86 51 52*.

WHERE TO STAY

The following lists of hotels and restaurants make a distinction between three categories: "Budget" includes addresses that are within the means of even modest budgets. "Our selection" regroups hotels or restaurants which offer a slightly higher level of comfort at correspondingly higher prices. "Treat yourself!" denotes really outstanding establishments—a taste of luxury that it would probably not be possible to afford every day.

For coin ranges, see the Legend on the cover flap.

BUDGET

◒◒**Pension Franz** – *Währinger Str. 12, 9. Bezirk*, ☎*01/34 36 37, www.hotelpensionfranz.at*. 24 *rooms*. Family guesthouse with décor in the style of the turn of the 19C–20C.

◒◒**Pension Pertschy** – *Habsburgergasse 5, 1. Bezirk*, ☎*01/53 44 90, www.pertschy.com*. 47 *rooms*. Family guesthouse in a 250 year old Baroque palace with Louis XV style furniture.

◒◒**Zur Wiener Staatsoper** – *Krugerstr. 11, 1. Bezirk*, ☎*01/5 13 12 74, www.zurwienerstaatsoper.at*. 22 *rooms*. Grand Viennese town house, small friendly hotel, with rooms furnished with period furniture.

OUR SELECTION

◒◒◒**Kaiserpark Schönbrunn** – *Grünbergstr. 11, 12. Bezirk*, ☎*01/81 38 61 00, www.kaiserpark.*

at. 45 *rooms*. City hotel right next to Schloss Schönbrunn.

◒◒◒**Landhaus Fuhrgassl-Huber** – *Rathstr. 24, 19. Bezirk*, ☎*01/4 40 30 33, www.fuhrgassl-huber.at*. 22 *rooms*. Country house in the middle of the Heurige district, furnished with period and rustic furniture; quiet rooms facing the garden.

◒◒◒**Park-Villa** – *Hasenauerstr. 12, 19. Bezirk*, ☎*01/3 19 10 05, parkvilla. viennahotels.it*. 21 *rooms*. Jugendstil building dating from 1888, tasteful rooms, pleasant area to stay. Airport-Shuttle bus available.

TREAT YOURSELF!

◒◒◒◒**Am Stephansplatz** – *Stephansplatz 9, 1. Bezirk*, ☎*01/53 40 50, www.hotelamstephansplatz.at*. 60 *rooms*. Located directly opposite the Stephansdom; rooms at the front have a view of the cathedral.

◒◒◒◒**König von Ungarn** – *Schulerstr. 10, 1. Bezirk*, ☎*01/51 58 40, www.kvu.at*. 33 *rooms*. Comfortable little hotel redolent of Vienna in the old days.

◒◒◒◒**Mercure Grand Hotel Biedermeier Wien Dorint** – *Landstraßer Hauptstr. 28, 3. Bezirk*, ☎*01/71 67 10, www.dorint.com*. 203 *rooms*. Biedermeier-style room décor.

◒◒◒◒**Hotel Sacher** – *Philharmonikerstr. 4, 1. Bezirk*, ☎*01/5 14 56, www. sacher.com*. 108 *rooms*. Vienna's classic Grand Hotel – and home of the world-renowned Sachertorte.

◒◒◒◒**Cordial Theater-Hotel Josefstadt** – *Josefstädter Str. 22, 8. Bezirk*, ☎*01/4 05 36 48, Fax 01/4 05 14 06*. 54 *rooms*. Modernized, luxurious inner-city hotel near the Ringstraße.

WHERE TO EAT

BUDGET

◒◒**Figlmüller** – *Wollzeile 5, 1. Bezirk*, ☎*01/5 12 61 77*. One of several local eateries serving the famous Wiener Schnitzel.

◒◒**Haas & Haas** – *Stephansplatz 4, 1. Bezirk*, ☎*01/5 13 19 16*. One of the most popular local restaurants in the immediate vicinity of the cathedral; in the evening the cathedral garden is a pleasant place to sit.

Pfudl – *Bäckerstr. 22, 1. Bezirk, ☎01/5 12 67 05.* This place ranks among the inns that have become a Viennese institution.

OUR SELECTION

Hauswirth – *Otto-Bauer-Gasse 20, 6. Bezirk, ☎01/5 87 12 61.* Typical Viennese restaurant with a pretty garden in the courtyard.

K & K Restaurant Piaristenkeller – *Piaristengasse 45, 8. Bezirk (below the Piaristenkirche), ☎01/406 01 93.* In a 300-year-old vaulted cellar where traditional Viennese dishes are served, there is the additional option of visiting two museums – the Kaiser-Franz-Joseph Hat Museum (souvenir photos are available, of visitors taking part in the "Old-style Viennese Hat Parade") and the K & K Weinschatzkammer (treasure trove of four centuries of wines from the Imperial wine cellars). For further details, visit *www.piaristenkeller.com.*

Plachutta – *Wollzeile 38, 1. Bezirk, ☎01/5 12 15 77.* Restaurant dedicated to the Viennese beef tradition.

Salut – *Wildpretmarkt 3, 1. Bezirk, ☎01/5 33 13 22.* Small friendly restaurant in several welcoming rooms in the city center.

Cantinetta Antinori – *Jasomirgottstr. 3, 1. Bezirk, ☎01/5 33 77 22.* The Italian restaurant in the 1. Bezirk.

Eckel – *Sieveringer Str. 46, 19. Bezirk, ☎01/3 20 32 18.* Cozy rustic restaurant with an elegant side room.

Fadinger – *Wipplingerstr. 29, 1. Bezirk, ☎01/5 33 43 41.* A simple bar at the front, with a more sophisticated restaurant at the back, serving interesting modern Viennese dishes.

Hedrich – *Stubenring 2, 1. Bezirk, ☎01/5 12 95 88.* Simple restaurant, calling itself a fast-food restaurant, but which in reality offers an interesting regional menu at a very reasonable price.

Hietzinger Bräu – *Auhofstr. 1, 13. Bezirk, ☎01/87 77 08 70.* The classic restaurant for Viennese Tafelspitz (boiled beef and vegetable stew) and other beef dishes.

Mraz & Sohn – *Wallensteinstr. 59, 20. Bezirk, ☎01/3 30 45 94.* Modern restaurant, in which a father and son team produce some outstanding results.

Vikerl's Lokal – *Würffelgasse 4, 15. Bezirk, ☎01/8 94 34 30.* Really comfortable little local restaurant with wooden paneling where Viennese nouvelle cuisine is on the menu.

Windows of Vienna – *Wienerbergstr. 7, 10. Bezirk, ☎01/6 07 94 80.* Restaurant on the 22nd floor of a business center, with an excellent view of Vienna and its surroundings.

TREAT YOURSELF!

Steirereck – *Rasumofskygasse 2, 3. Bezirk, ☎01/7 13 31 68.* Located near the Hundertwasserhaus. Arguably the best food in Vienna, with a substantial wine cellar which you can visit.

HEURIGE (Wine taverns)

Altes Presshaus – *Cobenzlgasse 15, 19. Bezirk, ☎01/3 20 02 03.* Wine tavern-buffet. The oldest Heuriger in Grinzing (house dates from 1527), parts of the vaulted cellar are very old, as are the winepresses it contains.

Buschenschank Wolff – *Rathstr. 46, 19. Bezirk, ☎01/4 40 23 35.* Wine tavern-buffet. Typical wine tavern in cosy rooms with an extensive, magnificently maintained garden.

Fuhrgassl-Huber – *Neustift am Wald 68, 19. Bezirk, ☎01/4 40 14 05.* Wine tavern-buffet. Earthy rustic atmosphere spread over several rooms with Viennese "Schramml-Musik" (popular music played on violin, accordion and guitar).

Mayer am Pfarrplatz – *Pfarrplatz 2, 19. Bezirk, ☎01/32 24 16.* Wine tavern-buffet. Comfortable local tavern with a beautiful garden.

CAFÉS, BARS AND NIGHTCLUBS

COFFEE-HOUSES

The coffee house is a Viennese institution, and visitors should therefore make sure that they try out one of the numerous speciality coffees, with perhaps an accompanying slice of cake, in at least one such establishment.

Central, *Herrengasse 14, 1. Bezirk, ☎01/5 33 37 63 26.* Specialties are the "Mazagran" (iced coffee with rum) and

Kalmar/ÖSTERREICH WERBUNG

Selection of cakes on offer at Demel

"Pharisäer" (hot coffee with rum and whipped cream). Piano music between *4pm and 7pm (Mon–Sat 8am–10pm; Jul and Aug only to 8pm).*

Hawelka, *Dorotheergasse 6, 1. Bezirk,* ☎*01/5 12 82 30.* Specialties include "Buchteln" (pastry filled with plum jam), served only after 10pm *(Wed–Mon 8am–2am, Sun and public holidays 4am–2am; closed Tue).*

Imperial, *Kärntner Ring 16, 1. Bezirk,* ☎*01/50 11 03 89.* Both Sigmund Freud and Anton Bruckner were regular clients at this coffee house which opened in 1873 *(daily 7am–11pm).*

Landtmann, *Dr.-Karl-Lueger-Ring 4, 1. Bezirk,* ☎*01/5 32 06 21.* Near the Parlament, Rathaus and Burgtheater, this café is a popular meeting place, which also boasts a beautiful summer terrace *(daily 8am–midnight).*

Café Museum, *Friedrichstraße 6, 1. Bezirk,* ☎*1/5 86 52 902.* Coffee house designed by Adolf Loos in the late 19C near the Secession building *(daily 8am–midnight).*

Sacher, *Philharmonikerstraße 4, 1. Bezirk,* ☎*1/5 14 56 0.* The legendary *Sachertorte* is on sale here, an absolute must on the Viennese cake list *(daily 8am–midnight).*

Im KunstHaus, *Weissgerberlände 14, 3. Bezirk,* ☎*01/7 12 04 97.* Superb garden and inside room almost overgrown with plants—a coffee house with a difference *(daily 10am–midnight).*

CONFECTIONERY AND PATISSERIE

Altmann und Kühne, *Graben 30, 1. Bezirk,* ☎*1/5 33 09 27.* Fantastically packed confectionery.

Central, *Herrengasse 17, 1. Bezirk,* ☎*1/535 99 05.* This patisserie shop sells the **Imperialtorte**, rival to the Sachertorte, in five different packages (guaranteed to last four weeks).

Demel, *Kohlmarkt 14, 1. Bezirk,* ☎*01/53 51 71 70.* The prices are high, but you get something special for your money.

Lehmann, *Graben 12, 1. Bezirk,* ☎*01/5 12 18 15.* Apfelstrudel to die for.

BARS

The "**Bermuda triangle**" of the Viennese bar scene is located in the 1. Bezirk around the Ruprechtskirche and Rudolfsplatz (KPR). There is something to cater to every taste here. Just dive right in.

Flanagans Irish Pub, *Schwarzenbergstraße 1–3, 1. Bezirk,* ☎*01/5 13 73 78.* The stone floor comes from an Irish chapel, and the bar spent a century of its life in Ireland. *Thu–Sat 11am–4am, Sun–Wed 11am–2am.*

Kolar-Beisl, *Kleeblattgasse 5, 1. Bezirk,* ☎*01/5 33 52 25.* Daily 5am–2am.

Krah Krah, *Rabensteig 8, 1. Bezirk,* ☎*01/5 33 81 93.* Popular local bar offering more than 50 varieties of beer. *Daily 11am–2am.*

Loos-Bar, *Kärntner Straße 10, 1. Bezirk,* ☎*01/5 12 32 83.* Small, but to be recommended, and not only because it was designed by Adolf Loos. *Daily 6am–4am.*

Panigl, *Schönlaterngasse 11, 1. Bezirk,* ☎*01/5 13 17 16.* Small Italian wine bar. *4am–4am.*

Philosoph, *Judengasse 11, 1. Bezirk,* ☎*01/5 35 45 32.* Good music. *Sun–Wed 6am–2am, Thu–Sat until 4am.*

Planter's Club, *Zelinkagasse 4, 1. Bezirk,* ☎*01/5 33 33 93.* Those wishing to spend the evening in this chic, Colonial-style bar room must be prepared to queue for quite some time to get in. *Daily 5am–4am.*

Reiss, *Marco-d'Aviano-Gasse 1, 1. Bezirk,* ☎*01/5 12 71 98.* Champagne-set hang-out with interior design by architects' office Coop Himmelblau. *Sun–Wed 11am–2am, Thu, Fri 11am–3am, Sat 10am–3am.*

Zum Basilisken, *Schönlaterngasse 3–5, 1. Bezirk,* ☎*01/5 13 31 23. Daily noon–2am, Fri and Sat until 4am.*

Zum Bettelstudent, *Johannesgasse 12, 1. Bezirk,* ☎*01/5 13 20 44. Daily 10am–2am, Fri, Sat until 3am.*

JAZZ

Jazzland, *Franz-Josefs-Kai 29, 1. Bezirk,* ☎*01/5 33 25 75.* International groups appear in this vaulted jazz cellar beneath the Ruprechtskirche. Great atmosphere. Music from 9pm.

Miles Smiles, *Lange Gasse 51, 8. Bezirk,* ☎*01/4 05 95 17.* Not only for fans of Miles Davis.

Jazzclub Porgy & Bess, *Riemergasse 11, 1. Bezirk,* ☎*01/50 37 009.* Concerts by Austrian and international jazz musicians, live music every day.

Otto, *Altmannsdorfer Straße 101, 12. Bezirk,* ☎*01/8 04 76 50. Oct–Apr Sun at 11.30am* pre-lunch drinks with jazz.

NIGHTCLUBS

P1, *Diskothek. Rotgasse 9, 1. Bezirk.* House, techno, soul.

Havanna Club, *Krugerstraße 8, 1. Bezirk,* ☎*01/5 13 32 25.* Latin-American music: DJ and dance courses.

U4, *Diskothek. Schönbrunner Straße 222, 12. Bezirk.* Techno, Dance Floor.

B72, *Hernalser Gürtel-Bogen 72, between 8. and 17 Bezirk,* ☎*01/4 09 21 28.* Live music and DJs.

ON THE BANKS OF THE BLUE DANUBE

Donauinsel (Neue Donau) – *Linie 1, U-Bahn-Station: Donauinsel.* A total of 42km/26mi of beach, with cycle, surf-board and boat hire outlets, and a rich selection of local bars and restaurants on the **"Copa Cagrana"** (after the Viennese suburb of Kagran, with apologies to Rio) on the river banks attract not only the Viennese – this is a great place to escape the heat of the city and really chill out.

Alte Donau – *Linie 1, U-Bahn-Station: Alte Donau.* The Viennese also come here to enjoy themselves in summer. The old branch of the Danube offers meadows, beaches and numerous bar-restaurants in which you can while away a pleasant evening on the banks of the Danube.

DATES FOR YOUR DIARY

Wiener Eistraum – *Jan–Mar.* Ice-skating in front of the Rathaus.

Wiener Festwochen – *May–Jun.* Avant-garde festival of theater, music and art.

Donauinselfest – *Late Jun.* Free open-air concerts which lure thousands to the Donauinsel.

Im-Puls-Tanzfestival – *Jul–Aug.* International dance performances which you can watch, or in which you can take part, in the museum district.

KlangBogen – *Jul–Aug.* Wide range of musical events at various venues around town. ☎*01/40 00 84 10.*

Filmfestival am Rathausplatz – *Jul–Aug.* Free open-air video shows on a giant screen with recordings of classical music, in front of the Vienna Rathaus.

Viennale – *Oct.* International film festival. Details: *www.viennale.or.at.*

Wiener Ballsaison – *Nov–Ash Wednesday.* Viennese Ball Season, the highlight of which is of course the world renowned Vienna Opera Ball.

Michaelertor, entrance to the Hofburg

of 80 000 Austrians, Poles, Bavarians, Swabians and Franconians led by the Emperor's close ally, the Polish King Jan III Sobieski, succeeded in driving back the Turkish army for good. This battle marked a turning point in the power struggle between the central European powers and the Ottoman army, which had been waged for three centuries.

Following this famous victory, the Western sovereigns recognized the pre-eminence of the Emperor. The Austrian Empire now entered a long period of prosperity, finally allowing Vienna to blossom into a glamorous Imperial capital, marked by the influence of Baroque architecture. Palaces, mansions and churches sprang up, eventually overflowing the narrow limits of the 17C city walls and leading to the development of new quarters and extensive suburbs.

The Congress of Vienna – Napoleon occupied Vienna twice, in 1805 and again in 1809, but when his empire collapsed in 1814, it fell to the Austrian capital to host the famous international gathering that was to redraw the map of Europe. For a year the Congress of Vienna furnished a pretext for splendid festivities. Receptions and balls were held at the embassies, in the state rooms at the Hofburg, and in the Great Gallery at Schönbrunn Palace. *"Le Congrès ne marche pas, il danse"* (The Congress does not walk, it dances), Prince de Ligne summed it up so poignantly. More than any other city, Vienna could offer choice entertainment to its guests: Exquisite art collections, theater, opera, and classical concerts. Ludwig van Beethoven himself conducted a gala concert and his opera *Fidelio* was received with enthusiasm. Even after the delegates left, the idyllic

Vienna of the Biedermeier continued its carefree lifestyle, with people idling their time away in cafés, relaxing over wine in the Vienna Woods or listening to Schubert's dreamy Lieder (songs).

Growth of Vienna – Vienna had to await the reign of **Franz Joseph** (1848–1916) for the large-scale planning and building that made it what it is today. In 1857 the Emperor ordered the removal of the bastions and the formation of a circular boulevard—the **"Ring"**—around the old town. Famous architects and artists contributed to this great project, which is lined by Vienna's most important public buildings as well as by the numerous tenement blocks characteristic of the city. In 1890, the outer boroughs were incorporated as well and the second ring of fortifications razed, making space for an outer circular road, known as the **"Gürtel"** (belt).

Vienna, Capital of Music

Venerable traditions

St. Peter's in Salzburg may have been the cradle of sacred music in the German-speaking world but, by the 12C, Vienna under the Babenbergs had become an important center of secular music performed by Minnesänger (minstrels or troubadours). Vienna's status as musical capital was further cemented when Maximilian I moved his dazzling court choir here from Innsbruck, which still thrills modern audiences as the **"Hofkapelle."**

The great days of Viennese music

The 18C was dominated by **Joseph Haydn**, the initiator of Classicism in Vienna. The princely palaces became veritable musical workshops, places for great performers and composers to meet, including Mozart, Beethoven and Gluck. Around 1825 the musical soirées known as **"Schubertiades"** began, at which Schubert interpreted Lieder for a circle of friends and which ended in dancing. After the revolution of 1848, music societies proliferated, promoting high standards of concert performance and of musical education. The most illustrious of these societies was the "Friends of Music," which counted **Brahms** among its conductors. Brahms enjoyed unparalleled prestige, but **Bruckner**, who had left his native Linz to become court organist, found his sacred masterpieces to be beyond the comprehension of the Viennese public. **Mahler** used his ten years in Vienna as Kapellmeister (conductor of the court orchestra) to undertake the reforms that helped usher in a new musical era.

The force of destiny (1770–1827)

Few other artists were more captivated and inspired by the romantic countryside surrounding Vienna than **Ludwig van Beethoven**. Beethoven arrived in the city at the age of 20 and soon charmed its people with his virtuosity as a pianist. It was in Vienna where he created the works that revolutionized the language of music: the Eroica Symphony, the famous opera *Fidelio*, the Fifth Symphony, and the well known and monumental Ninth Symphony,

Metternich

The career of Klemens Lothar Wenzel, Prince of Metternich-Winneburg, began in 1806, when he was appointed ambassador to Paris. In 1809 Metternich was given the heavy burden of directing Austria's foreign policy. He proposed a *rapprochement* with France and succeeded in forging an alliance between the two countries by negotiating Napoleon's marriage to Archduchess Marie-Louise. With remarkable diplomatic insight he made Austria a buffer state between the Russian and French empires, ultimately enabling him to use his skills and cunning as mediator at the Congress of Vienna.

the great "Ode to Joy." He died in his beloved city on March 26, 1827.

The triumph of the Viennese Waltz

One byproduct of the Congress of Vienna was the popularization of the Viennese **waltz**. This vigorous and light-hearted dance kept the city on its toes throughout the 19C. Polished, refined, and made a genre in its own right by **Joseph Lanner** and Johann Strauss the Elder, the waltz came to dominate the dance floor under **Johann Strauss the Younger**, whose tributes to the city (*Vienna Blood, Tales from the Vienna Woods*) got an enthusiastic reception. Today, the statue of Strauss the Younger in Vienna's Stadtpark has become a city emblem.

© Österreich Werbung / Wiesenhofer

Johann Strauss

The "New School" of Vienna

New School refers to the movement founded by the Viennese **Arnold Schoenberg**, promoter of a veritable musical revolution whose effects would reverberate through the century. His theories of 12-tone composition are set out in his *Treatise on Harmony* in which he established new relationships between sounds freed from traditional harmonic conventions.

Originally self-taught, Schoenberg later studied with the opera composer Alexander Zemlinsky (1871–1942) and first composed works like the *Gurrelieder* that still show affinities with the post-Romantic style. But he soon left behind the boundaries of tonality with such works as the Second String Quartet (1908) and the 1912 *Pierrot Lunaire*, a melodrama in 21

sections for narrator and five instruments, which brought him international recognition. Schoenberg exercised a profound influence on a number of his pupils, most notably Webern and Berg, both Viennese. Of the three composers, it was Webern who strayed furthest from classical tonality, while Berg enjoyed the greatest public success with his operas *Wozzeck* and *Lulu*.

Life in Vienna

The coffee house, a Viennese institution

When the Turks fled in 1683, they left behind a large quantity of coffee beans, thereby inadvertently launching a great Viennese tradition. Since the 19C the coffee house has been an indispensable social part of middle class and intellectual life, a place for people to meet, converse and read the newspapers.

Rock me Amadeus

Two hundred years after Mozart, another Austrian musician won world-wide fame. We're of course talking about Vienna's own Hans Hölzl, better known as the eccentric stage persona, **Falco**. In 1985, he not only won over European audiences with his mega-hit song "Rock me Amadeus," but even hit the top of the American charts, an outstanding feat for a German-language pop song. With his characteristic combination of speech-song and catchy tunes, Falco is the only Austrian pop star to have made it big on the world stage. He was killed in a car accident in the Dominican Republic in 1998 and—unlike his illustrious predecessor—was awarded an "honorary grave" by the City of Vienna in the Zentralfriedhof.

Viennese Ball Season

During the winter in Vienna, one ball follows close behind another. The famous Emperor's Ball is held on New Year's Eve, reawakening the elegance and splendor of the former Imperial court at the Hofburg. During Carnival time (Fasching), the various associations and professional guilds put on about 300 balls, many in magnificent surroundings (Rathaus, Hofburg, Musikverein). These include the Floral Ball, organized by gardeners and florists, the Rudolfina-Redoute Masked Ball, and balls of the Viennese Coffee-Houses, the Vienna Philharmonic Orchestra and the Technicians' Circle. Doctors and lawyers each have a ball, and so do hunters and firemen.

The ball to end all balls in terms of sheer elegance is the **Opera Ball**, held in February at the Staatsoper. This event draws the rich and famous from Austria and abroad, and is *the* High Society event of the year. The ball is opened by ballet dancers from the Vienna State Opera and a committee of young ladies and gentlemen dancing a Polonaise with fans.

Opera Ball

R. Holzbachova & P. Benet/Michelin

The city's classic coffee houses fill up as the working day ends. Discreetly attired waiters serve the traditional glass of water alongside the coffee, which is available in a bewildering variety (*see boxed text*) and often paired with a piece of cake or pastry. Once the coffee is finished, the waiter collects the cup and brings another glass of water while also keeping the customer supplied with newspapers and magazines. In fact, it is not unusual to linger for hours without repeating the order.

Wine bars, inns and taverns

A convivial atmosphere can be enjoyed in the **Keller**, not unlike a German beer hall, where snacks and cold meals are downed with a glass of beer or wine.

Some establishments *(Gasthäuser, Weinhäuser)* offering good home cooking are known as **Beisel**. Other popular places for locals to wind down at the end of the work day are taverns *(Weinstuben)* and the cheerful wine pubs called **Heurige**. The latter are located in the wine-growing villages surrounding the city, such as Grinzing, Nussdorf, Sievering and Gumpoldskirchen. Usually run by the wine-growers themselves, they are recognized by the pine branch fastened above the entrance. In cozy rooms or leafy courtyards, you can sample the new wine *(Heuriger)* along with snacks or a simple meal. **Schrammelmusik**, played by a pair of violins, an accordion or clarinet plus a guitar, often enlivens this utterly Viennese experience.

© Österreich Werbung / Bartl

Wine tavern in Ginzing

Sights

Tour of the Ring★
By car or tram (circular routes nos. 1 and 2). Start at the Stubenring (LR) to the east and continue in a clockwise direction.
Driving along the Ring is a fitting overture to exploring the historic city center and is especially enchanting at night when many buildings are floodlit.

Postsparkasse★ (LR)
This important Jugendstil (Art Nouveau) building was designed at the start of the 20C by Otto Wagner.

Österreichisches Museum für Angewandte Kunst (MAK)★★ (LR)
The applied arts museum is housed in a monumental building designed in Florentine Renaissance style, its stone and brick façade articulated by round-headed bays and twin windows.

Stadtpark (KLRS)
South of the MAK, this attractively landscaped park was laid out in 1862 and is famous for its statues of musicians, including Franz Schubert, Anton Bruckner, Franz Lehar and Robert Stolz. Pride of place goes to Vienna's iconic memorial honoring Johann Strauss.

Oper★★ (JS)
Austria's national opera house, with its elegant arcades in French Renaissance style, was the first of the great public edifices to be erected along the Ring. The main façade was all that was left standing when the building burned down in 1945.

Burggarten (JRS)
Between the Ring and the Hofburg are the palace gardens. First laid out in the 19C they have been open to the public since 1919. At the entrance stands a statue to Goethe, and there are other memorials to Franz Joseph, Franz I (on horseback) and Mozart.

Neue Burg (JR)
The Neue Burg was the last wing to be added to the Hofburg, completed just before World War I and now housing several museums.

Maria-Theresien-Platz (HRS)
This square's central element is the 1888 monument to Maria Theresa, which is buttressed by equestrian statues of several of her generals. Other figures represent statesmen and the composers Gluck, Haydn, and Mozart.
The two domed buildings facing each other across the square were constructed between 1872 and 1891 and house the Imperial collections in the **Kunsthistorisches Museum**★★★ and the **Naturhistorisches Museum**★.

Guide to Coffee, Viennese style

Listed below are some descriptions of the more commonly served types of Viennese coffee, among the 30 or so preparations which are available:

Großer/kleiner Schwarzer large/small cup of black coffee
Großer/kleiner Brauner large/small cup of black coffee with a dash of milk
Verlängerter Schwarzer/Brauner "Schwarzer"/"Brauner" diluted with water
Einspänner black coffee served in a glass with whipped cream (Schlagobers)
Fiaker black coffee in a glass with a tot of rum
Franziskaner coffee mixed with chocolate chips
Kaffee verkehrt coffee with more milk than coffee

Kaisermelange coffee with egg yolk and brandy
Kapuziner black coffee with a small blob of whipped cream
Konsul mocha diluted with cold water
Mazagran iced coffee with rum
Melange milky coffee (can be served with whipped cream)

Großer and kleiner Brauner at Café Sperl

Türkischer Kaffee strong coffee prepared in a small copper coffee pot, served hot in tiny cups
Verlängerter mocha diluted with hot water

A further tip: never ask for a cup of coffee (eine Tasse Kaffee) in Vienna – it is *"eine Schale Kaffee"* (literally, a bowl of coffee). Depending on how high a milk content you would like, coffee can be ordered "Braun," or even "Gold."

MuseumsQuartier (HS)
🕭 *see entry*

Volksgarten★ (HR)
This pleasant, quiet park with its pools, statues and famous rose garden is great for strolling and picnicking. A replica Greek temple adds an exotic element.

Parliament (HR)
Opposite the Volksgarten and adjacent to the law courts, this is Austria's seat of government (1873–83) with its elegant classical Greek façade.

Neues Rathaus (HR)
🕐💭 *Guided tour (45min) Mon, Wed, Fri 1pm (except when council is in session).* 🕐 *Public holidays.* 💭 *Free admission.* 📞*01/5 25 50.*
The neo-Gothic city hall is linked to the Ring by attractive gardens. The tower is topped by the famous "Rathausmann" carrying the city flag. Summer concerts are held in the arcaded courtyard. The reception rooms, council chambers and the huge banqueting hall are all open to the public.

Burgtheater (HR)
💭 *Guided tour (1hr) daily 3pm and Sun 11am, also daily 2pm Jul–Aug, by prior reservation only.* 💭 *€5.* 📞*01/5 14 44 41 40.*
Opened in 1888, this theater replaced the Hofburgtheater (Court Theater) on the Michaelerplatz founded in 1741 under Maria Theresa. Gottfried Semper was responsible for the Renaissance façade, while Carl Hasenauer designed the neo-Baroque interior. The Burgtheater has long been considered among the most important German-language theaters, and an engagement here was, and still is, the summit of an acting career. Tours include the **ceiling frescoes**★, painted by Gustav Klimt, his brother Ernst, and Franz Matsch.

Universität (HP)
On the north side of the Rathausplatz, the Italian Renaissance-style university by Heinrich von Ferstel houses the sec-

ond-oldest German-language university (after Prague). Beyond it, on the left, as the Ring makes its final bend, is the Votivkirche.

Votivkirche (HP)
Two tall spires flank the west door of this neo-Gothic church, completed in 1879. Note the Antwerp Altar in the right-hand chapel beyond the transept and the tomb of Count Salm from 1530, with its **reclining figure**★ in the baptistry.
After passing the **Börse** (Stock Exchange – JP) on the right, the tour ends by the Donaukanal at the Franz-Josefs-Kai.

City viewpoints
The **Kahlenberg**★ and the **Leopoldsberg**★★ (BX) are two splendid viewpoints in the hills overlooking the city to the northwest.
The **Donauturm** (CX) *(Danube Tower;* ⏱ *daily 10am–midnight; elevator* ⊚€*5.50;* ☎*01/2 63 35 72; www.donau turm.at)* was built on the north bank of the river in 1964. From its two revolving restaurants or its viewing terraces 150m/492ft above the Donaupark there

is a sweeping **view**★★ over the city and its surroundings. There is a similar **panoramic view**★ from the **Riesenrad**★★ (Giant Wheel) in the Prater (GU).

Hofburg★★★

The Imperial palace, the winter residence of the Habsburgs, was progressively enlarged during the centuries, resulting in a hodgepodge of styles. The oldest section, built in the 13C, is the Schweizerhof (Swiss Court), while the Burgkapelle (castle chapel) was erected in the mid-15C. Next came the Amalienburg and the Stallburg in the 16C, followed by the Leopoldinischer Trakt (now the official office of the Federal President) in the 17C. The 18C saw the addition of the Reichskanzleitrakt (Imperial Chancellery), the Spanische Reitschule (Spanish Riding School), and the Nationalbibliothek (National Library). The Neue Burg (New Imperial Palace), completed just before 1914, marked the end of the structural history of the Hofburg.

Neue Burg seen from Heldenplatz

Exterior

Michaelerplatz★

Designed by JE Fischer von Erlach, this complex was not completed until 1893. The semicircular façade overlooking the square is decorated with two monumental statue−studded fountains. The main arches are closed by bronze gilded grilles. A magnificent gateway, the **Michaelertor**★, flanked by figures from the Hercules legends, gives access to the octagonal rotunda beneath the famous **Michaelerkuppel**★, one of Vienna's most elegant domes. The square known as "In der Burg," anchored by a monument to Emperor Franz II, is reached via this rotunda. From the courtyard, the **Schweizertor**★, a fine Renaissance gateway bearing coats of arms and inscriptions, leads to the **Schweizerhof** and the stairs up to the Hofburgkapelle.

Josefsplatz★

Arched passageways lead into this square, regarded as Vienna's finest because of its ideal proportions. It owes its name to the impressive equestrian statue of Joseph II, the base of which is adorned with low-relief sculptures in bronze. On the south side is the early 18C **Österreichische Nationalbibliothek** by Fischer von Erlach.

Heldenplatz★

Heldenplatz overlooks the concave façade of the Neue Burg, built in the Italian Renaissance style between 1881 and 1913. The square is bounded to the north by the shady Volksgarten and boasts two grand equestrian statues by the sculptor Anton Dominik Fernkorn of Prince Eugene of Savoy and Archduke Karl.

The monumental gateway (1824) on the southwest side is the Äusseres Burgtor, which leads to the Ring and has served as a war memorial since 1934.

Interior

Schatzkammer (Imperial Treasury)★★★

&. ◷ Wed−Mon 10am−6pm. ⊛ €10. ☏01/5 25 24 52 01. www.khm.at.

A highlight of any Vienna visit, the treasury displays the insignia of Habsburg

Studio 3 Bis/Michelin

HOFBURG

0   50 m

Café Griensteidl
Looshaus
Herrengasse
Kohlmarkt
MICHAELERKIRCHE

MICHAELERPLATZ ★

MICHAELERTRAKT ★

KAISERAPPARTEMENTS

**HOFSILBER- UND
TAFELKAMMER ★**

Römische
Ausgrabungen

Michaelertor ★

MICHAELERKUPPEL

Habsburgergasse

Bräunerstraße

**ESPERANTO-
MUSEUM**

b

**LIPIZZANER
MUSEUM**

a

**WINTERREITSCHULE
★★ SPANISCHE
HOFREITSCHULE**

c

STALLBURG

Stallburggasse

Schweizertor ★

SCHWEIZERHOF

SCHATZKAMMER ★★★

REDOUTENSAAL-TRAKT

Palais
Pallavicini

(Salvador-Dalí-
Ausstellung)

Dorotheergasse

HOFBURGKAPELLE

Kaiser Joseph II.

Palais
Pálffy

Dorotheum

JOSEFSPLATZ ★

Prunksaal ★★

Spiegelgasse

**★ ÖSTERREICHISCHE
NATIONALBIBLIOTHEK**

Globenmuseum

Palais
Lobkowitz
(Österreichisches
Theatermuseum)

Augustinerstraße

AUGUSTINERKIRCHE

Lobkowitzplatz

Schmetterlingshaus

Augustinerbastei

Führichgasse

Glashaus

**MUSIKSAMMLUNG
DER ÖSTERREICHISCHEN
NATIONALBIBLIOTHEK**

**ALBERTINA
GRAPHISCHE SAMMLUNG ★★**

BURGGARTEN

Erzherzog Albrecht

**ALBERTINA-
PLATZ**

Hanuschgasse

Bundestheaterkassen

Danubiusbrunnen

Gedenkräume des Österreichischen
Theatermuseums

Kaiser Franz Joseph

Goethegasse

★★ STAATSOPER

Operngasse

Goethe

Kunsthistorisches Museum

Imperial crown

power, as well as mementoes and holy relics collected by the family. Listed below are the must-see exhibits:

Room 1 – The regalia of the archdukes of Austria used in ceremonies of homage: The **orb and scepter** (Prague, 14C) and the ducal mantle (Vienna, 1764).

Room 2 – The **Imperial crown of Rudolf II**★, made in Prague by Jan Vermeyen from Antwerp (early 17C), with matching orb and scepter. Also notable is the **bronze bust of Rudolf II** by Adriaen de Vries (1607).

Room 3 – Coronation mantle (1830) and ceremonial robes. Insignia of various Orders.

Room 4 – Coronation regalia of Ferdinand I.

Room 9 – Insignia and crown jewels of the Holy Roman Empire. The last time they were used was at the coronation of Franz II in 1792.

Room 5 – **Cradle of the King of Rome**★ made of silver gilt. **Portrait of Marie Louise**★.

Room 6 – Christening robes and other effects; keys to the coffins in the Kaisergruft.

Room 7 – **Crown of Stephan Bocskay**★. Jewelry, emerald vessel (2 680 carat).

Room 8 – **Agate bowl**★ (4C). Narwhal horn measuring 2.43m/8ft.

Room I – **Miniature replica of the Mariensäule**★ (Virgin Mary column), which formerly stood on the square Am Hof. It is decorated with 3 700 precious stones.

Room II – Reliquary cross of King Ludwig I of Hungary (c. 1370).

Room III – Small ebony temple with an ivory figure of Christ by Christoph Angermair; Florentine crucifix by Giambologna (about 1590).

Room IV – Reliquary altars from Milan (1660–1680); altar furniture in Dresden china.

Room V – 18C and 19C works of art including 22 bust reliquaries, some in solid silver.

Room 10 – Ceremonial robes of the Norman kings, including the **Coronation mantle**★★ of Roger II of Sicily (Palermo, 1133); ceremonial sword of Friedrich II.

Room 11 – The most outstanding item among the crown jewels of the Holy Roman Empire is the **Imperial crown**★★★, probably made for Otto I (962) in the monastery on the island of Reichenau in Lake Constance, or possibly in Milan. Imperial cross of 1024 with a base added in 1352. An astonishing reliquary is the **Holy Lance**★★ (8C), while the **Imperial sword**★ (11C) is attributed to St. Maurice.

Room 12 – Reliquaries, jewel boxes.

Room 13 – Robes and heraldic coats of arms from the Duchy of Burgundy.

Room 14 – Items from the treasure of the dukes of Burgundy.

Room 15 – Items associated with the Order of the Golden Fleece, including the **potence**★★ (mid 15C).

Room 16 – **Mass vestments**★★ of the Order of the Golden Fleece.

Kaiserappartements★

&. ⏱*Jul–Aug, daily 9am–5.30pm, Sept–Jun, daily 9am–5pm.* ⊜*€9.90, includes admission to Sisi Museum and Silberkammer.* ☎*01/5 33 75 70. www.hofburgwien.at.*

The **Imperial apartments** occupy the first floor of the Chancellery wing (Reichskanzleitrakt) and the Amalientrakt and are reached via the Kaiserstiege (Emperor's staircase). Only 20 of about 2 600 rooms in the palace are open to visitors. They are decorated in Rococo style with fanciful stucco ornamentation, luxurious furniture, crystal chandeliers and Aubusson and Flemish tapestry and date from the time of the last royal occupant Emperor Franz-Josef I and his wife Elisabeth (Sisi). You can see the bedroom, study, audience chamber, bathroom, and Sisi's dressing and exercise room, complete with wall bars and rings.

Admission includes a spin around the **Sisi Museum**, which traces the empress' childhood, life at court and tragic death while also addressing the myth that developed around her.

Also worth a look is the **Silberkammer**★ (Imperial Silver Collection), a magnificent spread of items used by the family until the monarchy's demise in 1918. Displays include an enormous **vermeil service**★ for 140 guests and the famous **Milanese centerpiece**★★ of 1838, designed for a table more than 30m/98.4ft long. There are also several Sèvres services, including the green service of 1776, numerous Empire-style ones from the Vienna Porcelain Factory, and fine sets of crystal glassware.

Hofburgkapelle

◷ Sept–Jun, Mon–Thu 11am–3pm, Fri 11am–1pm. ◷ public holidays. ∞€1.50. ☎01/5 33 99 27. www.wsk.at.
The Gothic palace chapel was built in the middle of the 15C and is the oldest part of the present palace. The famous Vienna Boys' Choir performs during Sunday mass (◷9.15am; reservations required).

Spanische Hofreitschule★★

🖋 Guided tours (1hr) most Tue–Sat 2pm, 3pm and 4pm, Sun 10am, 11am, 1pm, 2pm and 3pm. ∞€15. Morning training sessions ◷ most Tue–Sat 10am–noon. ∞€12. Tickets are available on the same day at the entrance, Josefsplatz Tor 2 and from the Besucherzentrum (visitors' center) at Michaelerplatz 1 Tue–Sat 9am–4pm. Performances (45min) ◷ selected days, usually Sun. ∞€26 and up. Make ticket reservations as early as possible by phone or online. ☎01/5 33 90 31. www.srs.at.
Feats of dressage dating back to the late 16C are performed in the all-white, indoor **Winter Riding School**, the work of Joseph Fischer von Erlach. The riders wear brown tailcoats, white buckskin breeches, riding boots and cocked hats. The white Lipizzaner stallions (◐ see PACK- UND STUBALPENSTRASSE, Gestüt-Piber), their tails and manes plaited with gold ribbons, go through their paces with stunning precision, culminating in the school quadrille with a group of horses.

The **morning training session** (Morgenarbeit), although less spectacular, shows the horses performing difficult jumps, steps, and other movements.

Lipizzaner-Museum

Reitschulgasse 2. ◷ Daily 9am–6pm. ∞€5. ☎01/52 52 45 83. www.khm.at.
The Lipizzaner stallions reside in the nearby **Stallburg**, which also houses this museum. The museum's genealogi-

Dining Room, Kaiserappartements

R. Holzbachova & P. Benet/Michelin

WIEN			Donaustadtstr.	CXY	24	Grenzackerstr.	CZ	45
			Erdberger Lände	CYZ	28	Grinzinger Allee	BX	48
Adalbert-Stifter-Str.	CX	3	Erdbergstr.	CY	30	Grinzinger Str.	BX	49
Altmannsdorfer Str.	AZ	6	Erzherzog-Karl-Str.	CY	31	Hietzinger Kai	AZ	60
Breitenfurter Str.	AZ	16	Floridsdorfer Brücke	CX	36	Hirschstettner Str.	CX	63
Döblinger Hauptstr.	BXY	21	Freudenauer Hafenstr.	CDZ	37	Hoche Warte	BX	64

Kulmgasse	AY 23	Raxstr.	BZ 94	Eroicahaus	BX E
Lassallestr.	CY 74	Schlachthausgasse	CY 98	Technisches Museum	AZ M²
Margaretenstr.	BCYZ 82	Schönbrunner Str.	ABZ 99	Weinbaumuseum	BX M¹
Meidlinger Hauptstr.	BZ 84	Speisinger Str.	AZ 109	Wiener Strassenbahn-	
Neuwaldegger Str.	AY 89	Veitingergasse	AZ 126	museum	CY M³
Prinz-Eugen-Str.	CY 93	Wienerbergstraße	BZ 134		

cal tables, uniforms, harness and audio-visual displays provide a comprehensive chronicle of this world-famous breed of horses. You can even take a peek inside some of the stables, albeit only through a thick glass screen.

Österreichische Nationalbibliothek★

Josefsplatz 2. Enter on 1st floor. ○*Tue, Wed, Fri–Sun 10am–6pm, Thu 10am–9pm.* ✆€5. ☎01/53 41 04 64. www.onb.ac.at.
The core collection inside this early 18C building by Joseph Emanuel Fischer von Erlach is formed by the Imperial library, established in the 14C. The **Prunksaal**★★ (Great Hall) is a masterpiece of Baroque architecture and decoration with **ceiling frescoes** by **Daniel Gran** in the oval dome and statues by the Strudel brothers. It holds Prince Eugene of Savoy's magnificent library and also hosts special exhibitions

Kaisergruft★★

Enter to the left of the Kapuzinerkirche. ○*Daily 10am–6pm.* ✆€3. ☎01/5 12 68 53.
For more than three centuries the vaults of the Kapuzinerkirche, completed in 1632, have served as the burial place of the Imperial family. The remains of 12 emperors, 16 empresses and more than 100 archdukes are buried here, while their hearts are in the Augustinian church and their entrails in the catacombs of the Stephansdom.
In the Karlsgruft (Charles's vault) are the sarcophagi of Leopold I and Joseph I by Johann Lukas von Hildebrandt, as well as the **sarcophagus of Charles VI**. Decorated with coats of arms and an allegorical figure of Austria mourning, it is a masterwork by Balthasar Moll. Maria Theresa and her husband, Francis of Lorraine, lie in a beautiful **double sarcophagus**★★, also by Moll, fronted by the coffin of their son, Joseph II.
The sarcophagus of Emperor **Franz Joseph**, his wife **Elisabeth** and their son, Archduke Rudolf, are in a separate room. The so-called Neue Gruft, or new vault, built in 1961, contains the sarcophagi of **Marie-Louise**, empress of France, and **Maximilian of Mexico**. The last Habsburg emperor, Karl I, was bur-

ied on Madeira, but in 1989 his wife Zita became the last person to be entombed in the Imperial vault.

Augustinerkirche

Built in the 14C within the Hofburg, this Gothic court church hosted the marriages of Maria Theresa and Francis of Lorraine (1736), of Napoleon and Marie Louise (1810) and of Franz Joseph and Elisabeth of Bavaria (1854).
In the south aisle is the **tomb**★ of Archduchess Maria Christina, Maria Theresa's favorite daughter. This white marble mausoleum is considered a masterpiece of the Italian sculptor Canova, who worked in Vienna from 1805 to 1809. The **Loretokapelle** *(access via the right side aisle,* ○⌇*guided tour (15min) by appointment and Sun after mass.* ☎01/5 33 70 99) holds in its **crypt** 54 urns containing the hearts of the Habsburgs. The Georgskapelle nearby was a meeting place for the knights of the Order of St. George, and later for those of the Order of the Golden Fleece. It contains the cenotaph of Emperor Leopold II.

Albertina★★

♿○*Thu–Tue 10am–6pm, Wed 10am–9pm.* ✆€10. ☎01/5 81 30 60 11. http://tourismus.albertina.at.
With about 45 000 drawings and watercolors, 35 000 publications and one million prints, the Albertina is considered the world's greatest collection of graphic art with continually changing exhibitions. Of particular importance is the **Dürer collection**, which contains such famous works as the *Praying Hands*. Da Vinci, Michelangelo, Picasso, et al are all represented here, too. A collection of 20C art is also displayed, with works by the likes of Warhol, Klimt, Schiele, Baseliz, and more.

Schmetterlinghaus

♿○*Apr–Oct, Mon–Fri 10am–4.45pm, Sat–Sun 10am–6.15pm; Nov–Mar, daily 10am–3.45pm.* ✆€5. ☎01/5 33 85 70.
In the palace garden is a Jugendstil glasshouse in which myriads of colorful butterflies flutter through a re-created tropical rainforest. Some have even been known to land on the tip of a visitor's nose!

© Österreich Werbung / Diejun

Entrance of Albertina

Neue Burg

Heldenplatz. ⏰*Wed–Mon 10am–6pm.*
💶*€8.* ☎*01/52 52 40. www.khm.at.*
The Neue Burg harbors the following collections, all accessible with the same ticket:

Hofjagd- und Rüstkammer★★

This exceptionally rich collection of arms and armor was created in the 15C from the collections of the archdukes Ernst of Styria (1377–1424) and Ferdinand of the Tirol (1527–95), and then merged in 1806 with the Imperial Court weaponry collection.

The filigree work and elaborate decoration on the ceremonial harnesses, helmets and saddles that were made for kings and emperors reflect European history.

Sammlung alter Musikinstrumente★★

This is a great collection of Renaissance instruments. Of particular historical and artistic interest are a **rebec**★, or early bowed instrument, made from a single piece of wood (an animal's feeding trough) in 15C Venice; a **harpsichord**★ (Venice 1559); a **cittern**★★ made in Brescia in 1574; a **reed-organ**★ from Innsbruck (before 1569). Other highlights include six magnificent, partly gilded, **trumpets**★ (Vienna 1741 and 1746), and a **piano**★ (Vienna 1867) made by Lud-

wig Bösendorfer for the Paris World Exhibition, with ornate inlaid work.

Ephesos Museum★★

Archeological findings from Ephesus in Turkey form the core of this exhibit, augmented by items unearthed at Samothrace on the Aegean. Star items include fragments of the altarpiece of Artemis in the stairway and the 40m/131ft-long marble **Frieze of the Parthian Monument**★★ (c. AD 170) in the mezzanine. It depicts the adoption of Marcus Aurelius, battle scenes from the wars with the Parthians, and the consecration and apotheosis of Lucius Verus. On the upper floor are the impressive **Athlete of Ephesus**★★ and the **Boy with the Goose**★.

Museum für Völkerkunde★

⏰*Opening times vary: Call* ☎*01/52 52 40 or check www.ethno-museum.ac.at.*
The ethnological museum features a Japanese section with a complete Samurai horseman's suit of armor from the 17C. There's also a well documented exhibition on Polynesia, with some items attributed to Captain James Cook. The Early American section includes an **Aztec feather headdress**★★ from Mexico.

Alte Backstube	EU	B	Kaiserliches Hofmobilien-		Museum der Gold-	
Bezirksmuseum			depot	EU M[11]	und Silberschmiede	EU M[12]
Alsergrund	ET M[20]		KunstHausWien	GU G	Österreichisches Museum für	
Dreifaltigkeitskirche	EU K[1]		Lichtentalkirche	FT K[7]	Volkskunde	EU M[7]
Schubert-Geburtshaus	FT M[5]		Liechtenstein-		Piaristenkirche Basilika	
Haus des Meeres	EU M[9]		museum	FT M[27]	Maria Treu	EU A
Haydnhaus	EV M[10]		Mariahilferkirche	EU K[2]	Theater in der Josefstadt	EU T[1]
Hundertwasserhaus	GU		Müllverbrennung-		Volksoper	ET T[2]
			Fernwärme-Heizwerk	FT S	Wagnerhaus	EU M[13]

WIEN

			Heiligenstädter Lände	FT	5	Schönbrunner Str.	EV 99
			Heiligenstädter Str.	FT	58	Spitalgasse	EU 111
Alserbachstr.	EFT	4	Kundmanngasse	GU	71	Spittelauer Lände	FT 112
Billrothstr.	ET	12	Landstr. Hauptstr.	GUV	72	Webgasse	EV 68
Erdberger Lände	GU	28	Lange Gasse	EU	73	Weissgerberlände	GU 129
Favoritenstr.	FV	34	Lassallestr.	GT	74	Wiedner Gürtel	FV 131
Gaudenzdorfer Gürtel	EV	39	Margaretenstr.	EFV	82	Wiedner Hauptstr.	FV 132
Gregor-Mendel-Str.	ET	43	Neubaugasse	EU	86	Zieglergasse	EU 135
Hasenauerstr.	ET	54	Prinz-Eugen-Str.	FUV	93		

Walking Tour

Tour of Old Vienna★★

Wedged between the cathedral and the Danube canal, the heart of Old Vienna still evoke a special atmosphere in spite of reconstruction.

▶ *Start from Stephansplatz (KR 115)*

Stephansdom★★★ (KR)

&♿🕐*Mon–Sat 6am–10pm, Sun 7am–10pm. ✎€1 (Jul–Sept only, free Oct–Jun), audio-guide €4.90. 🎧Guided tour (30min) every half hour Mon–Sat 10am–11.30am, 1.30pm–4.30pm, Sun 1.30pm–4.30pm. ✎€4.90. ☎01/5 15 52 35 26. www.stephanskirche.at.*

Vienna's cathedral is its most dramatic landmark. With its vast roof (exactly twice the height of its walls) of glittering tiles and its mighty south tower (the famous **Steffl**), its magnificence and significance are unparalleled in Austria.

History of Stephansdom

A Romanesque basilica consecrated in 1147 originally stood on the site of the present building. This church was badly damaged by the great fire of 1258 and today only the west front with the **Riesentor**★★ *(☾see Introduction: ABC of Architecture)* and the **Heidentürme** (Towers of the Heathens) remain. The first Gothic building was begun in 1304, and the Stephansdom as we now know it was built over the next two centuries. It became a cathedral in 1469.

Damaged during the Turkish siege of 1683, the cathedral again suffered serious damage in 1945 when flying sparks from nearby burning houses set fire to the north tower. After the war, it was swiftly restored to its former beauty.

Exterior

The diminutive size of the Stephansplatz, center of the medieval city, accentuates the vastness of the cathedral, whose one complete steeple, the **Stephansturm**★★★ or "Steffl," soars to a height of 136.7m/449ft. The north steeple was never completed but contains the great 21.3t bell known as the **Pummerin** (the largest bell in Austria), which peals only on special occasions and to ring in the New Year. The bronze bell was cast in 1711 from 180 Turkish cannons captured in 1683, and hung originally in the south steeple. It was shattered in 1945, and a new Pummerin bell was cast from the remains in 1951.

The crowning glory of Stephansdom is its highly decorative roof. It is covered in 230 000 multi-colored glazed tiles arranged in chevron and diamond patterns. Above the choir on the south side is a mosaic depicting the Habsburg coat of arms with its double-headed eagle. On the north side are the coats of arms of the City of Vienna and the Republic of Austria. The roof was meticulously restored after damage sustained during the Allied bombardment of Vienna toward the end of World War II.

The intricately carved Romanesque west door, called the **Riesentor**★★ (Giants' Gate), is crowded with statues, including one of Christ in Majesty on the tympanum and others of the Apostles in the recessed arches. If you walk round the cathedral in a counter-clockwise direction, you'll come to the copy of a Gothic lantern of the dead from the old cemetery of St. Stephan (now Stephansplatz) at the southwest corner.

▶ *Enter the cathedral through the Giants' Gate.*

Detail of Stephansdom

WIEN

Street	Code	No.	Street	Code	No.	Street	Code	No.
			Judenpl.	JR	67	Schauflergasse	JR	97
			Kärntner Str.	JRS		Schönlaterngasse	KR	100
Babenbergerstr.	HJS		Kettenbrückengasse	HS	69	Schottengasse	HJP	102
Bäckerstr.	KR	9	Kohlmarkt	JR	70	Schreyvogelgasse	HR	103
Bauernmarkt	KR	10	Landstr. Hauptstr.	LR	72	Schulhof	JR	105
Bognergasse	JR	13	Lichtensteg	KR	78	Schwertgasse	JP	106
Bräunerstr.	JR	15	Löwelstr.	HR	79	Seitzergasse	JR	107
Dominikanerbastei	KR	22	Marc-Aurel-Str.	KPR	81	Sonnenfelsgasse	KR	108
Dorotheergasse	JR	25	Mariahilfer Str.	HS		Spittelberggasse	HS	114
Dr-Ignaz-Seipel-Pl.	KR	27	Millöckergasse	JS	29	Stephanspl.	KR	115
Falkestr.	KLR	33	Mölkerbastei	HP	85	Stock-im-Eisen-Pl.	JR	116
Friedrichstr.	JS	38	Neuer Markt	JR	87	Tegetthoffstr.	JR	117
Georg-Coch-Pl.	LR	40	Neustiftgasse	HR	88	Tiefer Graben	JPR	120
Getreidemarkt	HJS	42	Oppolzergasse	HR	90	Tuchlauben	JR	123
Graben	JR		Philharmonikerstr.	JS	91	Uraniastr.	LR	124
Griechengasse	KR	46	Plankengasse	JR	92	Weiskirchnerstr.	LR	130
Gutenberggasse	HS	51	Prinz-Eugen-Str.	KS	93	Wiedner Hauptstr.	JS	132
Heiligenkreuzer Hof	KR	55	Renngasse	JPR	95	Wollzeile	KR	
Himmelpfortgasse	KR	61	Rotenturmstr.	KR				
Judengasse	KR	66	Salvatorgasse	JPR	96			

Place	Code	Ref	Place	Code	Ref	Place	Code	Ref
Akademie der Wissenschaften	KR	N	Theatermuseums	JS	M22	Theatermuseum	JR	M26
Ausstellung der Österreichischen Freiheitskämpfe	JPR	M21	Griechisch-orientalische Kirche zur Hl. Dreifaltigkeit	KR	K9	Palais Ferstel	JR	P2
Böhmische Hofkanzlei	JR	H	Kirche zu den neun Chören der Engel	JR	K8	Palais Harrach	JR	P3
Dom- und Diözesanmuseum	KR	M19	Kunstforum Bank Austria	JR	M1	Puppen- & Spielzeug-Museum	JR	M16
Gedenkräume des Österreichischen			Malteserkirche	JR	K6	Salvatorkapelle	JR	K4
			Museum Judenplatz	KR	M24	Uhrenmuseum der Stadt Wien	JR	M17
			Österreichisches			Ursulinenkirche und kloster	KR	M18

Interior

Clearly inspired by the traditional Germanic hall church, the long, majestic nave (107m/351ft) is ingeniously linked to the three-aisled chancel. The magnificent carved stone **pulpit**★★★ dates from c 1480 and is a Gothic masterpiece. Its creator has never been identified even though he portrayed himself, under the ramp, holding his sculptor's tools and looking out of a half-open window (which is why he is known as the "Fenstergucker"). All round are the exceptionally finely carved busts of St. Augustine, St. Ambrose, St. Gregory the Great, and St. Jerome.

The left apsidal chapel, known as the Frauenchor (women's choir), contains a beautiful painted and gilded altarpiece known as the **Wiener Neustadt altarpiece**★(15C). On the central panel are the Virgin and Child flanked by St. Barbara and St. Catherine and, up above, is the Coronation of the Virgin Mary. The altarpiece on the high altar in the chancel represents the stoning of St. Stephen.

The right apsidal chapel, the Apostelchor (Apostles' choir), preserves the remarkable late 15C **tomb**★★ of Emperor Friedrich III, made of red Salzburg marble by Nikolaus Gerhart of Leyden. The artist has illustrated the struggle between Good and Evil, symbolizing the evil spirits in the form of animals trying to enter the tomb to disturb the Emperor, while the good spirits, represented by local personages, prevent them from doing so.

Catacombs

Guided tour (30min) every half hour Mon–Sat 10am–11.30am, 1.30pm–4.30pm, Sun 1.30pm–4.30pm. €4.50. 01/5 15 52 35 26.

In the catacombs are urns containing the organs of the emperors of Austria, and chapels established since 1945.

Cathedral towers

Hochturm: daily 9am–5.30pm. €2.50. Nordturm (high-speed lift to "Pummerin" great bell): Apr–Oct, daily 9am–5.30pm (6pm Jul–Aug); Nov–Mar, daily 8.30am–5pm. €3.50. 01/5 15 52 35 26.

Views from the south tower are restricted due to renovations.

The south tower (Hochturm) can be climbed to a height of 73m/240ft by

343-step tight spiral staircase, while the platform of the north tower (which houses the Pummerin bell) 60m/197ft above ground is reached by lift. In fine weather there are good **views**★★ over the city, the Kahlenberg heights and the Danube plain to the east.

Dom- und Diözesanmuseum★ (KR M[19])
Stephansplatz 6. ⏱Tue–Sat 10am–5pm. ✆€7. ⟿Guided tours available. ☎01/5 15 52 36 89. www.dommuseum.at.
This museum in the 14C former Zwettler Hof displays a fine collection of paintings and sculptures alongside the cathedral's most precious treasures.

▶ *Cross Stephansplatz to Singerstraße.*

Deutschordenskirche (KR E)
This church was built by the Teutonic Order, a German hospitaller order founded in 1190. The church, a 14C Gothic building remodeled in the Baroque style, contains a beautiful 16C Flemish carved and gilded **altarpiece**★ with painted panels.

Treasure of the Teutonic Order★
⏱*Tue, Thu, Sat 10am–noon, Wed, Fri 3pm–5pm. ✆€3.60. ☎01/5 12 10 65.*
The wealth accumulated by the order over the centuries is impressive: Robes and mementos of Heads of the Order, such as a **chain of the Order**★ (c. 1500), sacred vessels, silverware, arms decorated with gold and precious stones, and also clocks, including a **longcase clock**★ carried by Hercules (about 1620).

Franziskanerkirche (KR)
This church was transformed into the Baroque style in the 18C. On one of the right hand altars is a painting of St. Francis by Johann Georg Schmidt, known as **"Wiener Schmidt,"** and an Immaculate Conception of 1722 by Johann Michael Rottmayr. The nearby **Franziskanerplatz** has a Moses fountain (1798) and, like the Ballgasse leading off it to the south, is bordered by picturesque old houses.

▶ *From Singerstraße turn right onto Blutgasse (13).*

Mozarthaus Vienna★ (KR)
Domgasse 5. ⏱Daily 10am–7pm. ✆€9. ☎01/5 13 62 94. www.mozarthaus vienna.at.
The house where Mozart lived from 1784 to 1787 is now a museum with newly organized exhibits about his life and times. Visits start on the third floor, which focuses on his daily life, his sponsors, his passion for gambling and the relationship with the freemasons. The second floor concentrates on his opera compositions, while on the first you can take a look around the actual apartment where he lived.

▶ *Domgasse and Strobelgasse lead to busy Wollzeile. Take Essiggasse (40) almost opposite, then turn right onto elegant Bäckerstraße (9).*

Jesuitenkirche★ or Universitätskirche (KR)
Dr-Ignaz-Seipel-Platz. ⏱Mon–Sat 7am–7pm, Sun 8am–8pm. ☎01/5 12 52 32.
Like the Salzburg Cathedral, this church was inspired by the church of Gesù in Rome and is in Baroque style. Interesting features include the **pulpit**★, inlaid with mother-of-pearl, and the dome with *trompe-l'œil* painting by Andrea Pozzo, the Jesuit lay brother who was also responsible for the high altar.

▶ *Take Sonnenfelsgasse (108) and then Schönlaterngasse (100).*

Heiligenkreuzerhof (KR 55)
The courtyard of this 18C mansion, a former dependence of Heiligenkreuz Abbey (STIFT HEILIGENKREUZ), is a popular retreat with artists and writers. The chapel of St. Bernhard has an altarpiece by Martin Altomonte.

▶ *Take Postgasse (97) to the Fleischmarkt.*

Hoher Markt (KR)
Interesting remains were found here of the Roman camp of Vindobona. In medieval times, this was the heart of the city, the "High Market," and also where the gallows stood. Today the square is dominated by the 1732 **Virgin Mary's Wedding fountain** (Vermählungsbrunnen)

by Joseph Emmanuel Fischer von Erlach. At no 10 is a Jugendstil **clock** (1913) by Franz Matsch where figures in period dress come to life every day at noon.

▶ *Take Judengasse (KR 66) to the Ruprechtskirche.*

Ruprechtskirche (KPR)

Mon–Fri 10am–1pm.
01/5 35 60 3.

This church is said to have been founded in 740 by St. Virgil, Bishop of Salzburg, and is the oldest building in Vienna. The nave and the foundations of the tower date from between 1130 and 1170 and the chancel and the doorway from the mid 13C. The church was finally completed in the second half of the 15C. The Romanesque belfry, Austria's oldest surviving stained-glass windows in the apse, and contemporary stained-glass windows by Lydia Roppolt (1953, 1992–93) are all striking features.

▶ *Return to Sterngasse, a narrow street with some steps. Turn left onto Fischerstiege, then right onto Salvatorgasse.*

Maria am Gestade★ (JP)

Salvatorgasse; enter through the south door.

Built on a terrace above the Danube, this church was originally built in the 12C and later replaced by a Gothic edifice, of which the general outline still survives. The western façade is decorated with sculptures, and the doorway is covered by a canopy (about 1410). The seven-sided Gothic tower is surmounted by a delicately pierced **stone cap**★, which is one of the loveliest products of the Viennese Gothic style.

Inside, the chancel has interesting stained-glass windows, and elegant statues on the pillars of the nave.

▶ *Walk down Schwertgasse (106) – note the Interesting Baroque doorway at no. 3 – and turn left on to Wipplingerstraße.*

Wipplingerstraße

In Wipplingerstraße are two handsome Baroque buildings. On the left, the **Altes**

Rathaus (JR) served as Vienna's town hall from the 14C to 19C and features the **fountain of Andromeda**★ (1741) by Raphael Donner in its courtyard. On the opposite side is the old **Böhmische Hofkanzlei** (Chancellery of Bohemia – JR H) with its outstanding façade by Johann Bernhard Fischer von Erlach (1708–14).

▶ *Skirt the chancellery to arrive at Judenplatz (JR 67), the heart of Vienna's medieval Jewish ghetto, then follow narrow Parisergasse to Am Hof.*

Uhrenmuseum der Stadt Wien★ (JR M¹⁷)

Schulhof 2. *Tue–Sat 9.30am–4.30pm.*
€3.60. *01/5 33 22 65.*

Three floors of displays illustrate the way clocks have changed mechanically and in appearance since the 15C. All types of clocks are represented, from the sundial to the electronic clock including, of course, the cuckoo clock. Note the amazing **astronomical clock**★ (1769) by David a Sancto Cajetano.

Am Hof (JR)

This square, on the site of the Roman military camp, is decorated by a bronze column to the Virgin Mary (Mariensäule, 1667). It was here that Franz II, on August 6, 1806, renounced the Imperial Crown, thus ending the Holy Roman Empire.

▶ *Take Bognergasse (16) to Graben.*

Peterskirche★ (JR)

Daily 8am–6pm.

This church is regarded as the most splendid among Vienna's Baroque churches and flaunts its lavish frescoes and gilded stuccowork. It was built from 1702 to 1708 by Johann Lukas von Hildebrandt, among others, to replace a three-aisled Romanesque church, which was itself a replacement of Vienna's earliest place of worship, a 4C building in the camp of Vindobona. The oval cupola above the nave is ornamented with a fresco attributed to Michael Rottmayr (1714) and represents the Assumption. The **interior furnishings**★ are sumptuous down to the last detail. The magnificent high altar is by Antonio Galli-Bibiena, and the altar painting by Martin Altomonte.

Pestsäule★★ (JR)

The richly decorated Baroque plague column, dominating the elegant Graben, was erected in 1693 to fulfill an oath made by Emperor Leopold I during the disastrous plague epidemic of 1679. He is shown kneeling in prayer.

▷ *Turn right onto Spiegelgasse to the Donner fountain.*

Donnerbrunnen★ (JR X)

Neuer Markt (JR 87).
The 1739 fountain by Georg Raphaël Donner features a central statue representing Providence, which is surrounded by cherubs and fish spouting water. The statues orbiting the fountain personify the rivers Traun, Ybbs, Enns and Morava (March). These are bronze copies of the lead originals now displayed in the museum of Baroque art in the Lower Belvedere.

▷ *Return to Stephansplatz via Kärntnerstraße.*

Kunsthistorisches Museum *(HS)*

&.🕐*Tue–Wed, Fri–Sun 10am–6pm, Thu 10am–9pm).* ⬤*€10.* ☎*01/52 52 40. www. khm.at.*

The five collections of Vienna's prestigious **museum of fine arts** are among the most important and largest in the world, displayed over some 4km/2.5mi of galleries. The biggest crowd pleaser is the Gemäldegalerie (Picture Gallery) with its truly princely collection of paintings. The other collections are the Ägyptisch-Orientalische Sammlung (Egyptian and Near Eastern Collection), the Antikensammlung (Collection of Greek and Roman Antiquities), the Münzkabinett (Coin Cabinet) and the Kunstkammer *(Collection of Sculpture and Decorative Arts,* ⚠ *closed until further notice).*
🙂*Please note that not all works mentioned below are guaranteed to be on display, as some may be on loan to other institutions or under restoration.*

Egyptian and Near Eastern Collection★★

Mezzanine level, to the right, Galleries I–IX
Gallery I – Coffins, canopic jars, human-mummies; sarcophagus of Nes-schu-

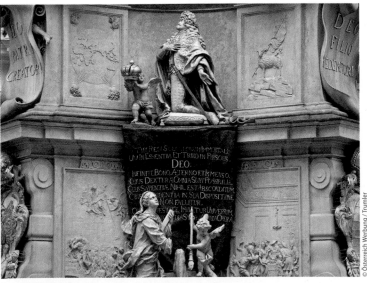

Detail of Pestsäule

© Österreich Werbung / Trumler

tefnut (c. 300 BC); papyrus bundle columns★ (18th dynasty)

Gallery II – Cult chamber of Ka-ni-nisut (c. 2450 BC)

Gallery III – Ushabti statuettes, ushabti boxes, amulets, wooden stelas

Gallery IV – Statuettes of divinities: enthroned Isis suckling her child Horus; animal mummies, objects for cult and magic

Gallery V – Typology of burials from the 1st dynasty to Ptolemaic times; coffins, and stelas; papyri: Book of the Dead of Khons-mes

Gallery VI – Everyday life: clothing, cosmetic implements, jewelry, food, crafts, vessels of pottery and stone

Gallery VIA – Egyptian Writing, Book of the Dead of Khonsu-iu (3C BC); Cuneiform writing; monumental inscriptions, reliefs, bronzes from Yemen (3C BC–AD 2C)

Gallery VII – Statues and reliefs from Old Kingdom, Middle Kingdom, New Kingdom; statue of Khent with her son, painted limestone Statue of Tjanuna

Gallery VIII – Statues and reliefs from New Kingdom; Statue group of Hamemhab and Horus; Late Period and Ptolemaic times; Colossal heads of kings

Gallery IX – Reserve head from Giza★★ (c. 2600 BC), sphinx head of king Sesostris III (c. 1840 BC), statue of king Thutmosis III★★★ (1504–1452 BC)

Collection of Greek and Roman Antiquities★★

Mezzanine level, to the right, Galleries X–XVIII

Gallery X – Greek sculpture: Doryphoros (Roman copy), *Portrait of Aristotle*★ (Roman copy).

Gallery XI – Greek and Roman sculpture: Amazon sarcophagus★ (4C BC), Grimani reliefs (AD 1C).

Gallery XII – Roman Republic: Senatus Consultum (2C BC), Patera of Aquileia (1C BC).

Gallery XIII – Roman portraits: Roman emperors, Augustus (AD 1C), Mummy portraits (AD 2C)

Gallery XIV – Greek pottery: Brygos-Skyphos (5C BC), *Duris Bowl*★ (5C BC)

Gallery XV – Roman handicrafts: Bronze statuettes, Head of Zeus★ (AD 1C)

Gallery XVI – Greek and Roman gems and cameos: Gemma Augustea (AD 1C),

Ptolemaic cameo★ (3C BC)

Gallery XVII – Late Antique and Early Medieval period: Gold treasure of Nagyszentmiklós★ (AD 6–8C)

Gallery XVIII – Early Christian art: Portrait of Eutropios (AD 5C), textiles (AD 4–6C)

Cabinet 1 – Cyprus: Bronze Age pottery, figurines, sculpture.

Cabinet 2 – Early Etruscan pottery (Bucchero).

Cabinet 3 – Etruscan: Athena Roccaspromonte (5C BC), Negau helmets (5C BC).

Cabinet 4 – Magna Graecia: pottery, Silver Centaur* (2C BC).

Cabinet 5 – Heroon of Trysa

Cabinet 6 – Roman Austria: Treasure from Mauer an der Url (AD 1–3C).

Cabinet 7 – Roman Austria: Youth from the Magdalensberg★ (16C copy)

Picture Gallery★★★

Rather than providing an exhaustive list of works, the following are particularly exceptional works which really are must-sees.

Gallery IX – Michael Coxcie: *Original Sin* and *The Expulsion from the Garden of Eden* (c. 1550); works by Hans Vredeman de Vries and Frans Floris.

Room 14 – Jan van Eyck: *Cardinal Niccolò Albergati*★★ (c. 1435) and The Goldsmith Jan de Leeuw; Jean Fouquet: *The Ferrara Court Jester Gonella*★ (c. 1440); Hugo van der Goes: *Diptych with the Fall of Man and Salvation*★★ (c. 1470); Rogier van der Weyden: *Crucifixion Triptych*★ (c. 1440); Hieronymus Bosch: *Christ bearing the Cross*

Room 15 – Joos van Cleve: *Lucretia*a; Jan Gossaert: *St. Luke painting the Madonna*

Gallery X – 14 of the total of 45 surviving paintings by **Pieter Bruegel the Elder**. These include: *Christ bearing the Cross*★ (1564), *The Tower of Babel*★★, *Children's Games*★★

(1560), *The Battle between Carnival and Lent*★★ (1559), *Peasant Dance*★ (1568–69) and *Peasant Wedding*★, *Hunters in the Snow*★★★ (1565).

Gallery XI – Jacob Jordaens: *The Bean King's Feast (Twelfth Night)* (c. 1640–45); Frans Snyders: *The Fish Market* (c. 1620–30).

Room 16 – Albrecht Dürer: *Young Venetian Woman* (1505), *The Martyrdom of the Ten Thousand Christians* (1508, with a self portrait of Dürer in the center of the painting), the *Adoration of the Holy Trinity*★★ (1511) and *Mary with the reclining Child* (1512).

Room 17 – Albrecht Dürer: Portrait of *Emperor Maximilian I*★ (1519); Martin Schongauer: *The Holy Family* (c. 1480–90); Lucas Cranach the Elder: *Judith with the Head of Holofernes*★ (c. 1530). Albrecht Altdorfer: *The Birth of Christ*★ (c. 1520–25).

Room 18 – Hans Holbein the Younger: *Jane Seymour*★ (c. 1536–37).

Room 19 – Giuseppe Arcimboldo: *Fire*★★ (1566); Georg Flegel: *Still Life of Dessert with a Bunch of Flowers*★ (1632).

Gallery XII – Anthony van Dyck: *Nicolas Lanier*★★, *Venus in Vulcan's Forge*★.

Room 20 – Peter Paul Rubens: *Young Girl with Fan* (c. 1612–14).

Gallery XIII – *Self-portrait* (c. 1638–40), *Hélène Fourment with Fur Cloak*★★ (c. 1636–38), *St. Ildefonso Altarpiece*★★ (c. 1630–32).

Gallery XIV – *Vincenzo II, Gonzaga* (c. 1604–05), *Medusa's Head* (c. 1617–18).

Room 21 – David Teniers the Younger: *Archduke Leopold Wilhelm in his Picture Gallery in Brussels*★ (c. 1651).

Room 22 – Salomon van Ruysdael: *Landscape with Wooden Fence and Cloudy Sky*

Room 23 – Aert van der Neer: *Riverscape with Boats by Moonlight* (c. 1665–1709).

Room 24 – Thomas Gainsborough: *Suffolk Landscape* (c. 1748); Jan Vermeer: *The Artist's Studio*★★★ (c. 1665–66).

Gallery XV – Rembrandt: *The Artist's Mother as Hannah the Prophetess* and

Saliera (salt cellar) by Benvenuto

The Artist's Son Titus van Rijn reading, as well as the very interesting pair of paintings *Small Self-portrait*★ (c. 1657) and *Large Self-portrait*★★ (1652).

Gallery I – Titian: *The Gipsy Madonna* (c. 1510), *The Madonna with the Cherries* (c. 1516–17), *Young Woman with a Fur*★ (c. 1535) and *Ecce Homo*★ (1543).

Room 1 – Andrea Mantegna: *St. Sebastian*★ (c. 1457–59); Giovanni Bellini: *Young Woman at her Toilette* (1515).

Room 2 – Giorgione: *Laura* (1506) and the *Three Philosophers*★★ (c. 1508) Lorenzo Lotto: *Portrait of a Young Boy in front of a White Curtain*★ (c. 1508).

Gallery II – Veronese: *Adoration of the Magi* (c. 1580–88).

Gallery III – Tintoretto: *Lorenzo Soranzo* (1553), *Susanna and the Elders*★★ (c. 1555).

Room 3 – Correggio: *Abduction of Ganymede* (c. 1530)

Room 4 – Perugino: *The Baptism of Christ* (c. 1498–1500); Andrea del Sarto: *The Mourning of Christ* (c. 1519–20); Raphael: the *Madonna in the Meadow*★★ (1505–06).

Room 5 – Bernardino Luini: *Salome with the Head of St. John the Baptist* (c. 1525–30).

Room 7 – Bronzino: *Holy Family with St. Anne and St. John the Baptist* (c. 1540).

Room 10 – Velázquez: *Portraits of the Infanta*★. Murillo: *St. Michael* (c. 1665–68).

Room 11 – Annibale Carracci: *Pietà*★ (c. 1603).

Gallery V – Caravaggio: *David with the Head of Goliath*★ (1606–07) and

KUNSTHISTORISCHES MUSEUM (1st floor)

★★ Three Philosophers

Perugino
del Sarto Raphael ★★
Fra Bartolomeo
Luini
Moroni
Salviati
Bronzino
Coello

Madonna in the Meadow

5
6
7
8
9

Vasari
Vasari
IV

Parmigianino
Correggio
3
III
Bassano
Tintoretto
V
Caravaggio
Gentileschi

Madonna of the Rosary ★

Velázquez
Murillo
10

Giorgione
Palma Vecchio
Lotto
2
II
Bordone
Veronese

★★ Susanna and
the Elders

Guercino
Reni
VI

Carracci
Poussin
11

Bellini
Mantegna
1
I
Titian
Canaletto
VII

Fetti
12

Guardi
13

VIII
Temporary exhibitions

★★ St Sebastian

To the 2nd floor

Bosch
R.v.d. Weyden
Van Eyck
14
★★ Cardinal
Niccolò Albergati
IX
Floris
Coxcie

Van Cleve
Gossaert
15
★★ The Tower
of Babel
X
Bruegel the Elder

★★★ Hunters in the Snow

Large Self-Portrait ★★

XV
Rembrandt
Van Ruisdael

The Artist's Studio ★★★
24

Vermeer
Gainsborough

Dürer
16
XI
Jordaens
Snyders

★★ Adoration of
the Holy Trinity

Nicolas Lanier ★★

XIV
Rubens
23
Steen
Van der Neer

Cranach
Altdorfer
Dürer
17

Holbein
18

Flegel
Arcimboldo
19

XII
Van Dyck

St Ildefonso
Altarpiece ★★

XIII
Rubens
22
Hals
Van Ruysdael

Rubens
20
21
Teniers

30 m

0

N

◆ Lifts   🏠 Shop   🚻 Toilets   ☕ Café

Kunsthistorisches Museum Vienna

Detail of the Artist`s Studio (c. 1665-66) by Johannes Vermeer

Madonna of the Rosary★ (c. 1606–07).

Gallery VI – Guercino: *Return of the Prodigal Son*★ (c. 1619); Giordano: *Archangel Michael and the Rebellious Angels*★ (c. 1660–65).

Gallery VII – Hyacinthe Rigaud: *Count Ludwig Philipp Wenzel Sinzendorf* (1728); Canaletto: *Vienna from the Belvedere*★ (c. 1758–61).

Coin Cabinet

Second floor, to the left.
This section of the museum holds a collection of some 700 000 items, making it one of the largest numismatic collections in the world. Besides medals, decorations and insignia, there is also an account of the evolution of money from coins to notes. The coin collection includes Ferdinand II of Tirol's 16C portrait collection.

Museums Quartier (HS)

The former Imperial stables by Fischer von Erlach have been converted into a spectacular 60 000sq m/645 834sq ft cultural complex that ranks among the world's ten largest. Blending Baroque and new architecture, it is a progressive beehive of activity that harbors the prestigious modern art-focused Leopold Museum and the Museum Moderner Kunst; the **Kunsthalle Wien**, a contemporary exhibition space; the ZOOM Kindermuseum for kids; TanzQuartier, a center for dance; artist and architecture studios; new media production facilities and plenty of cafés, bars and shops. It is also an important festival location, hosting the Viennale Film Festival and the ImPulse Dance Festival, among others.

Leopold Museum

Mon, Wed, Fri–Sun 10 am–6pm, Thu 10am–9pm. €9. Guided tours available. 01/52 57 00. www.leopold museum.org.
This museum presents a thorough survey of all major names and movements in modern Austrian art, including Viennese Secessionism, Viennese Modernism, and Austrian Expressionism. It is based on the private collection assembled by Rudolf and Elisabeth Leopold over five decades. Masterpieces by all the heavy-hitters are here, including the world's largest Egon Schiele collection and seminal works by Gustav Klimt, Oskar Kokoschka, Albin Egger-Lienz and Herbert Boeckl. A fine selection of Jugendstil objects by Otto Wagner, Adolf Loos, Josef Hoffmann and others rounds off the presentation.

Museum Moderner Kunst (MUMOK)

🕐Tue–Wed, Fri–Sun 10am–6pm, Thu 10am–9pm. €9. 01/5 25 00. www. mumok.at.

Inside a radically angular building, this is the largest **collection of modern and contemporary art** in Austria, showcasing a comprehensive cross-section of international and Austrian 20C art. Works by Jawlensky and Kokoschka represent Expressionism; Fernand Léger, among others, stands for Cubism; Max Ernst and René Magritte for Surrealism; Arman for Nouveau Réalisme; and Robert Rauschenberg and Andy Warhol for Pop Art. Examples of international painting of the 1980s and 1990s include works by Georg Baselitz, Jörg Immendorf and Ernesto Tatafiore. There's also space devoted to "Wiener Aktionismus" (Hermann Nitsch, Günter Brus and Arnulf Rainer). Temporary exhibits add an extra dimenion to the permanent galleries.

ZOOM Kindermuseum Kids

🕐Mon–Fri 8.30am–5pm, Sat–Sun 10am–5.30pm. €5. 01/524 79 08. www. kindermuseum.at.

This children's museum is divided into two sections. Zoom Ozean is a multi-sensory experience designed to help kids under six develop motor and language skills. Older kids gravitate to the main exhibition, or the lab and studio where they can learn about art, science and culture in an interactive, playful environment. All sessions start at set times and reservations are recommended.

Belvedere★★

♿🕐Tue–Sun 10am–6pm. €12.50. 01/79 55 70. www.belvedere.at.

The two palaces of the Belvedere were built by the architect Lukas von Hildebrandt for **Prince Eugene of Savoy** (1663–1736) and are seen as major works of Baroque architecture. The Unteres (Lower) Belvedere was built in 1716 as a summer residence, while the Oberes (Upper) Belvedere was completed in 1722 as a place for festivities. Both Belvedere palaces were used to house collections from the **Österreichische Galerie Belvedere**. Collections of the 19C and 20C were, and still are, in the Oberes Belvedere, while the Museum of Baroque Art and the Museum of Medieval Art were in the Unteres Belvedere. Since Spring 2008, however, all the collections are housed under one roof in the Oberes Belvedere. The **Unteres Belvedere** is now used for temporary exhibitions and the **Prunkstall** houses the Medieval Treasury a collection of Medieval art previously held in storage and only available to academics and art students.

Oberes Belvedere★★ (FV)

See Introduction: ABC of Architecture. The palace's main façade faces south and is distinguished by splendid doorways in the central section. The four figures of Atlas to the right of the vestibule, the **Sala Terrena**★, are by Lorenzo Mattielli,

---

Prince Eugene of Savoy (1663–1736)

Eugene of Savoy joined the French army under Louis XIV but resigned his commission when he was refused the command of a regiment and entered into the service of Leopold I. At the age of 20, he joined the relief army commanded by the Polish king Jan Sobieski, which in 1683 freed Vienna from the Turkish siege.

The soldier once spurned by Louis XIV achieved great fame when the Austrian army under his command defeated the Turks in the Battle of Zenta (1697). Prince Eugene, the "saviour of Christendom" and a field marshal at the age of 25, became Joseph I's confidant and political adviser and senior minister under Charles VI. In 1714, he had the satisfaction of signing the Treaty of Rastatt with Louis XIV.

The Prince was showered with honors and money and had two magnificent residences, a town palace in the Himmelpfortgasse (now the Ministry of Finance), and his summer seat, the Belvedere.

The Kiss (1907-08) by Gustav Klimt, Belvedere

©Belvedere, Vienna

while Carlo Carlone was responsible for the frescoes. A grand staircase leads to the vast red **Marmorsaal** (Marble Hall) on the first floor. It was here on 15 May 1955 where the signing of the State Treaty took place, putting an end to the occupation of Austria by the Allied Powers.

Galerie des 19. und 20. Jahrhunderts★★ (M²⁵)

These galleries show the work of the different schools of the 19C: Classicism, Romanticism, the Biedermeier Era, Historicism and Impressionism. Included are works by French Impressionists Monet, Cezanne, Pissarro, Manet and Renoir as well as van Gogh's *The Plein at Auvers*. Works of Austrian Impressionists Emil Jacob Schindler, Rudolf Ribarz, Robert Russ will also claim your attention particularly Olga Wisinger-Florian's *Blooming Poppy* (1895/1900) which is almost Monet-like.

Works by Hans Makart *(Lady at the Spinet★, The Five Senses★)* who dominated the late 19C art scene in Vienna and Anton Romako *(Empress Elisabeth★★, Mathilde Stern★)* who suffered under this dominance are worth seeking out. Other must-sees are the museums large collection of Gustav Klimt *(The Kiss★★, The Bride★★)* and Egon Schiele *(Death and the Maiden★★, Four Trees★★)*.

☺ A Bit of Advice ☺

Temporary Exhibitions at the Unteres Belvedere and Orangerie

Gustav Klimt and Kunstschau 1908 – *Unteres Belvedere*: Oct 2008–Jan 18, 2009
Alphonse Mucha – *Unteres Belvedere*: Jan 21–May 2009
Prince Eugene of Savoy – *Unteres Belvedere*: 22 May–Sept 14, 2009
Ferdinand Georg Waldmüller (1793–1865) – *Unteres Belvedere*: Jan 30–May 2009
Herbert Boecki – Retrospective – *Unteres Belvedere, Orangerie*: Oct 1, 2009–Jan 8, 2010

In addition to historical paintings, works by Moritz von Schwind (*Party Game*★), Caspar David Friedrich (*Rocky Landscape in the Elbsandsteingebirge*) and Friedrich von Amerling (*Girl in a Straw Hat*★) are displayed.

The museum has the largest collection of Biedermeier works in the world. Ferdinand Georg Waldmüller is the leading representative of this Era. His *Corpus Christi Morning* and *The Brushwood Gatherers in the Vienna Woods (1855)* are both good examples of his work.

Die Sammlung Mittelalter★

The works are mostly from the Gothic period from around 1400 until the early 16C. There are rare altar panel paintings and such impressive works as *Christ's Crucifixion*★ by Conrad Laib (1449); the *Mourning of Christ*★ by the Master of the Viennese Schottenaltar (c. 1469); the *Legend of Susanna*★ by the Carinthian painter Urban Görtschacher; and several works by the Tirolean painter and sculptor Michael Pacher.

Die Sammlung Barock★★

This collection shows the essence of Austrian High Baroque with paintings and sculptures from the late 17C and 18C on display. You can also admire the original **Mehlmarkt fountain**★★ by **Georg Raphael Donner** (1693–1741), a copy of which stands on the Neuer Markt.

Franz Xaver Messerschmidt's marvelous **character heads**★ group of sculptures are highlight along with his figures of Maria Theresia and Francis of Lorraine.

The Sacrifice of Iphigenia (c. 1690/91) and *The Lamentation of Abel* (1692) are two of the many works of **Johann Michael**

Rottmayr, known as the Father of Austrian Baroque, that are worth seeing.

Balthasar Permoser's impressive marble sculpture of *The Apotheosis of Prince Eugene*★ has a figure of himself positioned at the feet of the prince.

Among the many paintings here, the following are stand-outs: *Christ on the Mount of Olives*★ by Paul Troger (c. 1750), the Classical artist of Baroque painting, *Napoleon on the St. Bernard Pass*★ by Jacques Louis David (1801) and *View of Laxenburg*★ by Johann Christian Brand (1758).

Schönbrunn

✕	Restaurant
🚻	Toilets

Belvedere Gardens

🕐*Apr–Oct, daily 6am–sunset; Nov–Mar, daily 6.30am–sunset.* ⊗*Free admission.* ☎*01/7 98 41 20.*

The palace is surrounded by some of the grandest and most important Baroque gardens in Europe, laid out in the French style starting in 1697 by Lukas von Hildebrandt, Dominique Girard and Anton Zinner. The upper part represents Olympus, the central part Parnassus and the lower part the domain of the Four Elements. From the highest point there is a wonderful **view**★ over the garden and the city.

Descend to the Unteres Belvedere along the right-hand side of the gardens.

Unteres Belvedere★ (KLS)

🕐*Thu–Tue 10am–6pm, Wed 10am–9pm.* ☎*01/79 55 70. www.belvedere.at.*

The Lower Belvedere is fronted by a court of honor entered through an impressive gateway bearing the cross of Savoy in its gable. The long building has a well-proportioned façade on the garden side and sumptuous apartments that make an ideal setting for the temporary exhibitions. The former living quarters and staterooms are impressive and works of art in their own right. Attractions include the **Marble Hall**, adorned with frescoes by Martino Altomonte (1659–1745) who also painted the ceiling frescoes in the **Marble Room**★, the state bedroom, **Hall of Grotesques**★★, named after the motifs of stuccowork that adorns its walls, and the dazzling **Gold Room**★★ with its mirrors and gilded carved woodwork.

Orangerie

Built by Johann Lukas von Hildebrandt in the first quarter of the eighteenth century to protect exotic tender plants and trees. Its interior has been transformed by the architect Susanne Zottl into a home for regularly changing temporary exhibitions.

Prunkstall

🕐 *Daily 10am–noon.* ☎*01/79 55 70. www.belvedere.at.*
These ornamental stables, a jewel in the Baroque architectural crown, were built to accommodate the 12 riding horses of Prince Eugene. The building is adorned with stucco and has its own fountain. Where horses were once stabled is the **Schatzhaus Mittelalter** (Medieval Treasury). This collection, which opened in Spring 2008, complements the display of Medieval Art in the Oberes Belvedere. The 150 works of art, many never seen in public before, now give a broader perspective on Medieval art in Austria.

Schloss Schönbrunn★★ (AZ)

U-Bahn – U-4 (green line): Schönbrunn or Hietzing stop.
A UNESCO World Heritage Site since 1996, the Imperial Schönbrunn Palace occupies what was once a favored hunting ground of the Habsburgs. Construction of the family's imposing summer residence began in 1695 and was originally based on the plans of Johann Bernhard Fischer von Erlach. The palace got its present form under Maria Theresia and reflects the vision of archi-

tect Nicolas Pacassi. The park was laid out by French landscape architect Jean Trehet and later modified by Johann Ferdinand Hetzendorf of Hohenberg, who also contributed the Neptune fountain, Roman ruin, Obelisk and Gloriette.

Tour of the Palace★★

♿🕐*Jul–Aug, daily 8.30am–6pm; Apr–Jun, Sept–Oct, daily 8.30am–5pm; Nov–Mar, daily 8.30am–4.30pm.* ⊞*€8.90 (Imperial Tour), €11.50 (Grand Tour), includes audio-guide.* ☎*01/81 11 32 39. www.schoenbrunn.at.*
The main building stretches for 180m/590.5ft in classically restrained Baroque style and is painted in a pleasing color known as Schönbrunn Yellow; green window frames provide additional accents.

Self-guided audio tours take in either 22 rooms (Imperial Tour) or 40 rooms (Grand Tour) out of a total of 1440, each of which seems to outdo the other in opulence. Elegant stuccowork, crystal chandeliers, richly ornamented faience stoves, and priceless tapestries and furniture give the apartments an exceptional air of magnificence.

The **apartments of Emperor Franz Joseph and Empress Elisabeth** are followed by three **ceremonial rooms** decorated by the Austrian painter Josef Rosa and two **Chinese chambers**★, one adorned with lacquerwork, the other with porcelain. The **Maria Theresia apartments** are among the most luxurious in the palace. They include the **Blue Salon**, which is hung with Chinese tapestry and was where the negotiations took place that led to Karl I, last of the Habsburgs, abdication on 11 November 1918. Other stand-outs are the **Vieux-Lacque Room**★, with black oriental lacquered paneling framing intricate miniatures; the **Napoleon Room**, decorated with Flemish tapestry; and the lavish **Millionenzimmer**★ with its South American rosewood paneling framing Indo-Persian miniatures painted upon paper.

Finally, the tour reaches the **Great Gallery**★★★, where the delegates to the 1814–15 Congress of Vienna danced and partied.

Schlosspark★★ 〔Kids〕

⏱ *Apr–Oct, daily 6am–sunset; Nov–Mar, daily 6.30am–sunset.* ⬥*Free admission.*
The park gardens are a remarkable creation of Baroque art, mixed with a shot of Rococo and antiquity. Arbors and vast formal beds of flowers serve as backdrops for charming groups of allegorical statues and gracious fountains.

Shaded walks lead to the Neptune fountain (Neptunbrunnen), the Roman ruin (Römische Ruine) and the **Tiergarten**★ (♿ ⏱ *Apr–Sept, daily 9am–6.30pm; Mar, Oct, daily 9am–5.30pm; Feb, daily 9am–5pm; Nov–Jan,daily 9am–4.30pm;* ⬥*€12;* ☎*01/8 77 92 94; www.zoovienna. at*), the oldest zoological gardens in the world. Originally a menagerie founded by Emperor Franz Stephan who had a deep interest in zoology. Open to the public in 1779 they eventually evolved into zoological gardens in the 19C. The first giraffe seen in Europe arrived here in 1828, a gift from the Viceroy of Egypt, and caused quite a stir among Viennese society.

The **Palmenhaus**★ (⏱*May–Sept, daily 9.30am–6pm; Oct–Apr, daily 9.30am–5pm;* ⬥*€4;* ☎*01/8 77 50 87; www.bundesgaerten.at*) is the European continent's largest glass and metal hothouse, completed in 1882. It shelters some 4 000 plants from all over the world, including Himalayan mountain plants and tropical rainforest vegetation.

〔Kids〕**Irrgarten** and **Labyrinth** will keep the children amazed for hours. The Maze was laid out between 1698 and 1740 with a central pavilion from which the maze as a whole could be viewed. Although it fell into disrepair in the 19C it has been replanted and opened in 1998. The labyrinth was reconstructed according to the original historical design. There are games and mental puzzles to solve along the way.

Gloriette★★

⏱ *Apr–Jun, Sept, daily 9am–6pm; Jul–Aug, daily 9am–7pm; Oct, daily 9am–5pm.* ⬥*€2.* ☎*01/81 11 32 39.*
This elegant colonnaded structure offers fine views of Schönbrunn and western Vienna from its roof terrace. It resembles a triumphal arch which is hardly surprising as it was built to commemorate Maria Theresa's victory over the Prussians in 1757 during the Seven Years War. The café is a nice spot for a break.

Wagenburg★

♿⏱*Apr–Oct, daily 9am–6pm; Nov–Mar, Tue–Sun 10am–4pm.* ⬥*€4.50.* ☎*01/8 77 32 44.*
The **coach house** contains a great collection of Imperial coaches from the early 18C to the 20C. Worth keeping an eye out for are the **phaeton of the King of Rome**★ and the gilded and ornate **Imperial coach**★★ of Emperor Franz Stephan, Maria Theresa's husband, which was pulled by eight white horses.

Palmenhaus, Schlosspark

J. Malburet/Michelin

Jugendstil Buildings

Rejecting the academic architecture of the Ring, the architects of the Vienna Secession designed several buildings that put their theories into practice, marking an important stage in the development of modern European architecture.

Wagner-Pavillons★ (JS)
Karlsplatz.
Otto Wagner's two highly original Viennese Jugendstil pavilions, designed in 1899, face each other to the north of the Karlskirche. The extraordinary combination of glass, white marble and green-painted metalwork, topped with a corrugated copper roof, was an innovative approach to architecture at the time. One building still serves as an entrance to the U-Bahn and as an exhibition center, while the other houses a café in the summer months.

Secession★★ (JS)
&⊘*Tue, Wed, Fri–Sun 10am–6pm, Thu 10am–8pm. ⊚€6, includes Beethoven Frieze and current exhibit. €4.50 current exhibit only. ☎01/5 87 53 07.*
The Secession building in Vienna has been run as an exhibition hall for contemporary art by the artists' association of the same name since 1898. It is a Jugendstil masterpiece built by **Joseph Maria Olbrich**, a pupil of Wagner.

The undisputed highlight here is the 34m/111ft long **Beethoven Frieze★★★**, a monumental 1902 work by **Gustav Klimt** on the theme of the Ninth Symphony.

Postsparkasse & Wagner: Werk★ (LR)
Georg-Koch-Platz 2. &⊘Mon–Wed, Fri 8am–3pm, Thu 8am–5.30pm, Sat 10am–5pm. ⊚€5; Main Hall free. ☎01/53 45 33 30 88. www.ottowagner.de.
Otto Wagner's seminal building, the postal savings banks was completed in 1912 using the time's most modern materials (aluminium, glass bricks) and construction methods. Still a bank today, its 'small lobby' recently opened as **Wagner: Werk**, a small exhibit about the architect containing some 200 historical photos, documents, newspaper articles, plans, innovative materials and a model of the building.

Otto Wagner Kirche am Steinhof★★ (AS)
Baumgartnerhöhe 1. ↝Guided tour (45min) Sat 3pm by prior reservation. ⊚€4. ☎01/91 06 01 12 04.
Vienna's first modern church was completed by Wagner in 1907 for a mental institution, which it still serves today. Its interior is functional as well as aesthetic. The stoups containing holy water were designed to avoid contamination, the floor slopes toward the altar to create good sight lines for most worshippers,

Wagner-Pavillion, Karlsplatz

and all parts of the building are easily accessible for maintenance purposes. Such functionality is softened to some extent by the white-gold wall covering. The large side **stained-glass windows**★ with their typically linear Jugendstil figures are an impressive sight.

Musical Memories

Staatsoper★★ (JS)

&⚓*Guided tour (40min) Jul–Aug, daily 11am, 1pm, 2pm and 3pm; May–Jun, Sept–Oct, daily 1pm, 2pm and 3pm; Nov–Apr daily 2pm and 3pm. ⊘Good Fri, 24 Dec and during rehearsals (phone ahead for schedule). ⊛€5.50. ☏01/5 14 44 26 06.*

Begun in 1861 and formally opened in 1869 by Emperor Franz Joseph II with a performance of Mozart's *Don Giovanni*, the opera house was the first of the great public edifices to be completed along the Ring. It has since been helmed by such outstanding directors as Gustav Mahler, Richard Strauss, Karl Böhm, Herbert von Karajan, Lorin Maazel and Claudio Abbado. Players in the famous **Vienna Philharmonic** (Wiener Philharmoniker) are recruited from the members of the Staatsoper orchestra.

Tours include the stage and backstage, the **interval rooms** and the Gustav Mahler Room decorated with modern tapestries illustrating scenes from Mozart's *Magic Flute*. Décor in the **foyer**★ is by the painter Moritz von Schwind. The **tea room** and the magnificent **grand staircase**★ were among the few sections of the building spared by a sweeping fire in 1945. Completing this sophisticated setting is the horseshoe-shaped main auditorium with its 2 280 seats.

Haydnhaus★ (EV M¹⁰)

Haydngasse 19. ⊘Tue–Sun 10am–1pm, 2pm–6pm. ⊛€2, Sun free. ☏01/5 96 13 07.

The house where the composer wrote the oratorios *The Creation* (1798) and *The Seasons* (1801) is now a museum. Exhibits illustrate the context of the music and in particular the places that were important in Haydn's life.

Inside the Kirche am Steinhof

Schubert Geburtshaus★ (ET M⁵)

Nussdorfer Straße 54. ⊘Tue–Sun 9am–1pm, 2pm–6pm. ⊛€2, Sun free. ☏01/3 17 36 01.

The house in which Schubert was born on 31 January 1797 and where he spent the first four years of his life (he later lived at Säulengasse 4) has been restored to its original modest state. There is a museum on the first floor.

Mozarthaus Vienna★ (KR)

&*See entry.*

Zentralfriedhof (CZ)

&⊘*May–Aug, daily 7am–7pm; Mar–Apr & Sept–Oct, 7am–6pm; Nov–Feb, 8am–5pm. ☏01/7 60 41.*

Beethoven, Brahms, Gluck, Schubert and Hugo Wolf are all buried in the "Musicians' Corner" (Plot 32A) of this famous cemetery, alongside operetta and waltz masters Johann Strauss the Elder and the Younger, Joseph Lanner, Karl Millöcker, Franz von Suppé. In Plot 32C lie Arnold Schoenberg and Franz Werfel Jürgens, while 14A has Theophil von Hansen and Hans Makart and 0 Antonio Salieri and Adolf Loos.

Cemetery plans are available at the second (main) entrance gateway.

St. Marxer Friedhof (CZ)

Mozart was buried here on December 6, 1791 in a pauper's grave. His mortal remains have never been found.

Additional Sights

Within the Ring

Michaelerkirche (JR)

◷7am–10pm. ⁓Guided tours (30min) Mon–Fri 11am, 2pm, 3pm, 4pm, Sat 3pm, 4pm. ⊜€5. ☎01/533 8000. www. michaelerkirche.at.

This Romanesque-Gothic church with its façade (1792) is famous for a group of Rococo figures above the high altar (1781) representing the **Fall of the Angels**⋆. Tours lead down into the **crypt** where you can admire musty old coffins filled with bones and bodies in various states of decay.

Jüdisches Museum der Stadt Wien⋆ (JR)

♿ ◷Sun–Wed, Fri 10am–6pm, Thu 10am–8pm. ⊜€5. ☎01/5 35 04 31. www. jmw.at.

The Adelspalais Eskeles in Dorotheergasse 11 dates back to the 15C and, since 1993, has housed the city's **Jewish museum**. It displays religious and ceremonial objects, documents, paintings and drawings chronicling the history of Vienna's and Austria's large Jewish community.

Minoritenkirche (JR)

◷Apr–Oct, daily 8am–6pm; Nov–Mar, daily 9am–5pm. ☎01/5 33 41 62.

The early 14C Minorite church is easily recognized by its landmark octagonal

Dome of the Karlskirche

Studio 3 Bis/Michelin

tower. The huge mosaic on the north wall depicting Leonardo da Vinci's *Last Supper* was commissioned by Napeleon and executed by Roman artist Giacomo Raffaelli.

Beyond the Ring

Karlskirche⋆⋆ (KS)

Kreuzherrengasse. *◷Mon–Sat 9am–12.30pm, 1am–6pm, Sun 12am–5.45pm. ⊜€6. ☎01/5 04 61 87. www.karlskirche. at.*

This massive domed church, which is dedicated to St. Charles Borromeo, is an 18C work of Johann Bernhard Fischer von Erlach and a harmonious mix of styles and architectural features. It was built following a vow of Emperor Charles VI during the plague of 1713. Admission includes an elevator ride to a **viewing platform** at 32.5m/106.6ft inside the church. From up here you can get a sense of the building's dimensions, inspect Johann Michael Rottmayr's dome frescoes from close-up and enjoy sweeping city views. Several centuries' of church treasures can be admired at the new **Museum Borromeo**.

Wienmuseum⋆ (KS)

Karlsplatz 8. *♿◷Tue–Sun 9am–6pm. ⊜€6. ☎01/50 58 74 70. www.wienmuseum.at.*

The history of Vienna takes centerstage at this museum whose fine array of artifacts includes the **circular plan of Vienna**⋆ (1545) by Augustin Hirschvogel. Other noteworthy displays include excavations from the Roman military camp, medieval stained-glass windows and statues of royalty from the cathedral, booty taken from the Turks after the second siege of Vienna in 1683, porcelain and glassware from Viennese workshops and crafts from the Wiener Werkstätte. Added to these are the reconstructed interiors of the **Pompeian Room**⋆ (c. 1800) from the Palais Caprara-Geymüller, author Franz Grillparzer's Biedermeier style living room, and Adolf Loos' dining room. Outstanding paintings include Baroque works by Maulbertsch, Rottmayr and Troger and various 19C masterpieces, including *Love*⋆ and *Emilie Flöge* by Gustav Klimt

R. Holzbachova & P. Benet/Michelin

Triptych of the Last Judgement by Hieronymus Bosch in Akademie der bildenden Künste

and *Self-portrait with Splayed fingers*★★ and *Blind Mother* by Egon Schiele.

Prater★ (CY-GU)   Kids

This immense green space, embraced by two arms of the Danube, was a hunting reserve under Emperor Maximilian II and opened to the public in 1766 under Joseph II. With its many cafés, the Prater was extremely popular during the heyday of the Viennese waltz. It won worldwide renown when it was featured in the film *The Third Man*; scenes for the James Bond film *The Living Daylights* were also shot here.

The most popular part of the Prater is the amusement park called "Wurstelprater," lorded over by the landmark 1897 **Riesenrad★★ (Giant Ferris Wheel)** (&. ◐*May–Sept, daily 9am–midnight; Mar–Apr & Oct, daily 10am–10pm; Nov–Feb, daily 10am–8pm; ⊛€7.50. ☏01/7 29 54 30)* which treats you to breathtaking **views**★ of the city.

Akademie der bildenden Künste – Gemäldegalerie★★(JS)

Enter from Makartgasse. ◐Tue–Sun 10am–6pm. ◐Guided tours available. ◐Public holidays. ⊛€7. ☏01/58 81 62 25. www.akademiegalerie.at.

This outstanding collection of paintings is housed in a neo-Renaissance building by Theophil Hansen. The single most important work is the extraordinary *Triptych of the Last Judgement*★★★ by **Hieronymus Bosch** (1460–1516), a

terrifying work where monsters and phenomena symbolize the sins and suffering of humankind. There are plenty more highlights, including: *Lucretia*★★ by Lucas Cranach the Elder, *Boys playing Dice*★ by Bartolomé Esteban Murillo, a *Self-portrait*★ (c. 1615) by Anthony van Dyck and *Portrait of a young Woman*★★ (1632) by Rembrandt. Top works from the 18C collection are the eight *Views of Venice*★ by Francesco Guardi and the famous *Still-life with Flowers and Fruit*★ (1703) by Rachel Ruysch.

Österreichisches Museum für Angewandte Kunst (MAK)★★ (LR)

&. ◐*Tue 10am–midnight, Wed–Sun 10am–6pm. ⊛€10. ☏01/71 13 60. www.mak.at.*

The Austrian museum of applied arts takes up a neo-Renaissance building by Heinrich von Ferstel and has a remarkable **display concept**★★ where the layout of certain rooms was entrusted to artists: Baroque, Rococo and Classical furniture were set out by **Donald Judd**; the outstanding collection of lace and glassware by Franz Graf; Empire and Biedermeier exhibits by Jenny Holzer; 20C applied arts by Manfred Wakolbinger. A surprise is in store with the Historicism and Jugendstil display, which Barbara Bloom has reduced to Michael Thonet's seminal bentwood chairs.

The depth and range of the collection are truly astonishing. Highlights include

M. Hertlein/Michelin

Österreichisches Museum für Angewandte Kunst

liturgical vestments★ (c. 1260) from the Benedictine monastery of Göss in Styria; a **tabletop**★★ of painted cherrywood from late 15C Swabia; an amazing Biedermeier **cherrywood secretaire**★ made in Vienna in 1825; a superb collection of **oriental carpets and rugs**★★; **drawings**★★ prepared by Gustav Klimt for the Palais Stoclet in Brussels; and a sampling of items from the **Wiener Werkstätte**★★, the famous arts and crafts workshop.

Naturhistorisches Museum★ (HR)   Kids

&. ⏱ *Wed 9am–9pm, Thu–Mon 9am–6.30pm.* ✆€8; *children €3.50.* ✆*01/52 17 70. www.nhm-wien.ac.at.*

The collections of Vienna's **natural history museum** are among the finest in the world and presented in a dynamic, contemporary fashion. Some of the biggest crowd magnets are in the Prehistory section (mezzanine level) and include the famous 25 000-year-old **Venus of Willendorf**★, remarkable finds from the **Hallstatt graves** and a dinosaur room. On the same floor, the **Mineralogy section**★★ has such rare and exquisite specimens as a 1m/3.3ft-long piece of quartz crystal from Madagascar, a topaz from Brazil weighing 117kg/258lb and the famous **"bouquet of jewels"**★ (1760), a gift from Maria Theresa to her husband, Francis of Lorraine.

Upstairs, the Zoology section has an impressive collection of stuffed birds, including such extinct species as the moa and the dronte. There's also an extinct **Stellersche sea cow**★ and various other stuffed animals, including an Indian Ghavial, a fearsome river-dwelling crocodile endemic to India.

Naschmarkt (HJS)
Linke Wienzeile.

The market's produce stalls make a lively picture, full of local color. A **flea market** takes place Saturdays on Kettenbrückengasse, the extension of Naschmarkt.

Hundertwasserhaus (GU F)
Löwengasse/Kegelgasse.

The Viennese artist, **Friedensreich Hundertwasser**, used this 1984 apartment block to create a type of mass housing that marries human needs with the environment. His colorful, eccentric building makes ample use of arcaded loggias, galleries, statues and other design elements as well as an extraordinary range of materials (glass, brick, rendering etc). The terraced roof garden is also typical of his approach.

Court furniture

The court furniture inspectors were entrusted with transporting furniture, carpets, tapestries, etc. to the various royal premises and to store and look after them. Until the early 19C only the Vienna Hofburg was permanently furnished, while the Imperial summer residences and hunting lodges were only furnished when any royals were in residence. For coronations and royal weddings (sometimes as far away as Frankfurt or Florence) furniture had to be transported for as many as 1 000 people. Up to 100 wagons would leave in advance of the royal party to outfit the living and function rooms. Only after Franz II took the reigns after 1808 were the less frequently used palaces and residences gradually left ready furnished.

KunstHausWien (GU G)

Untere Weissgerberstraße 13. ○*Daily 10am–7pm. €9.* ☎*01/7 12 04 91. www. kunsthauswien.com.*

This museum was designed by Hundertwasser and contains the world's only permanent exhibit about his work, philosophy and architecture. The other part of the building is used for temporary art exhibitions.

Heeresgeschichtliches Museum★ (GV)

&. ○*Sat–Thu 9am–5pm.* ≈*€ 5.10.* ☎*01/79 56 10. www.hgm.or.at.*

The exhaustive and excellent **army museum** inside a former munitions depot tells the history of Austria through its military exploits. All major conflicts since the Thirty Years' War are covered, including the Turkish threat, the Napoleonic era and World War I. There are special rooms dedicated to Prince Eugen, the heroic general who dealt Turkish troops a decisive defeat; Maria Theresa and her feuds with Prussia; and Archduke Franz Ferdinand's assassination in Sarajevo, featuring the actual car in which he and his wife were shot.

Kaiserliches Hofmobiliendepot★ (EU M¹¹)

Andreasgasse 7. &. ○*Tue–Sun 9am–5pm.* ≈*€6.90.* ☎*01/5 24 33 57. www.hofmo biliendepot.at.*

This is where the Imperial furniture, carpets and tapestries were stored when not in use at the royal residences. The large **collection of period furniture** - one of the world's largest - gives you a sense of what being "at home with the emperor" might have been like. Besides original furniture once used by the Habsburgs, interesting exhibits include the coffin in which Emperor Maximilian of Mexico was shipped back to Europe following his assassination; Prince Rudolf's cradle; and the wheelchair used by Maria Theresa's mother, Elisabeth Christine. On the second floor is the **Biedermeier** collection, which consists of bourgeois period rooms but also features bizarre spitoons and ingenious early toilets. The Modernist section has amazing furniture by Adolf Loos, Joseph Hoffmann and Otto Wagner.

Hundertwasserhaus

C. Bastin & J. Evard/Michelin

Technisches Museum (AZ M²) Kids

○*Mon–Fri 9am–6pm, Sat–Sun 10am–6pm.* ○*Public holidays.* ≈*€8.50; children €5.* ☎*01/89 99 80. www.tmw.at.*

Opposite Schloss Schönbrunn, the **technical museum** provides an interactive and comprehensive overview of technology and industry. The history of science, tool manufacturing, mining, process engineering, heavy industry and energy are among the themes explored here. Children especially will enjoy the hands-on experiments explaining various technical phenomena.

Driving Tours

Tour of the Kahlenberg Heights (AR)

Round trip of 33km/21mi. Leave Vienna via Heiligenstädter Straße (BX). At the Klosterneuburg-Kierling railway station turn left into the Stadtplatz and almost immediately left again. Cross the Kierlingbach creek and go uphill toward the abbey. Park in the Rathausplatz.

Studio 3 Bis/Michelin

Grinzing

Klosterneuburg★

See KLOSTERNEUBURG

▶ *Follow Leopoldstraße south to the Weidlingbach Valley; cross Weidlinger Straße into Höhenstraße.*

Leopoldsberg★★

The most easterly spur of the Wienerwald, Leopoldsberg overlooks the Danube from 423m/1 388ft. Views are best from the Burgplatz opposite the Leopoldskirche.

▶ *Go back downhill, then turn left onto Höhenstraße.*

Kahlenberg★

There are attractive **views**★ over Vienna from the terrace next to the Kahlenberg restaurant (483m/1 584.6ft). In the foreground are the vineyards of Grinzing and to the right the rolling heights of the Wienerwald.

▶ *Continue on Höhenstraße as far as the Häuserl am Roan inn.*

🅿 From the parking lot, enjoy a fine view of Vienna and the Wienerwald.

▶ *Return toward the Kahlenberg; turn right into Cobenzlgasse (AR 21) down onto Grinzing.*

Grinzing★

Grinzing is the best known of Vienna's suburban wine villages. It is a pretty place with a friendly atmosphere best sampled in one of the many taverns, or Heurigen. It can get very busy here in the evenings.

Heiligenstadt

Beethoven devotees flock to Heiligenstadt's central square (Pfarrplatz) to see the little 17C house (no. 2 – now a wine tavern), where the musician lived in 1817. In Probusgasse 6 stands the **Beethoven Testamenthaus** (🕐*Mar–Dec, Tue, Thu, Sat–Sun 10am–noon, 1pm–4.30pm;* ◎*€1.20;* ☎*01/3 18 86 08),* now a small museum, where the composer wrote his famous letter in 1802 called the *Testament of Heiligenstadt* when in despair over his deafness. The letter, addressed to his brother Carl, was never sent.

▶ *Return to Vienna along Hohe Warte (BX 64) and Döblinger Hauptstraße (BXY 21).*

Tour of Marchfeld Schlösser (Castles)

From Vienna to Marchegg – 58km/36mi.

The Marchfeld, a gravel plain to the east of Vienna, is a fertile region and popular hunting ground.

▶ *Leave Vienna heading east on B3, reaching Orth after about 24km/15mi*

Orth an der Donau

This newly restored castle has a pedigree going back to the 12C, but most of the present building, including the four mighty corner towers, date from the 16C. The sleek Baroque annex was added in the 17C and used a hunting lodge by the Habsburgs. The castle now houses the visitors' center of the Nationalpark Donau-Auen.

▶ *Leave Orth on B 3 toward Wagram. Turn right in Pframa toward Eckartsau.*

Eckartsau

Guided tour (40min) Apr–Oct, Sat–Sun 11am and 2pm. €8. ☎0 22 14/22 40.

This former hunting castle turned Baroque around 1730 courtesy of Joseph Emanuel Fischer von Erlach; Daniel Gran painted the frescoes. It served as the final residence on Austrian soil of the Habsburg family after Karl I's abdication on November 11, 1918. On March 23, 1919, the Imperial family left from here for exile in Switzerland.

▶ *From Eckartsau take the B3 back toward Kopfstetten to the junction with the B49. Turn left toward Marchegg, arriving at Schloss Niederweiden after 2km/1.2mi.*

Niederweiden

Field Marshal Ernst Rüdiger von Starhemberg commissioned Johann Bernhard Fischer von Erlach to build this Baroque hunting lodge in 1693 (*Palm Sun–Oct, Sat–Sun 10am–5pm; ☎0 22 14/28 03; www.schlosshof.at*). In 1726 it was acquired by Prince Eugen of Savoy before being taken over by Maria Theresa in 1755 who hired Nicolas Pacassi to make the alterations that gave the palace its present form. Beneath the slate mansard roof, only the oval **Great Hall**★, painted in the Chinese style, hints at the magnificence of the original decoration.

▶ *Leave B 49 and head toward Schlosshof.*

The Story behind Sachertorte

Frau Sacher, a leading personality in late 19C Vienna, fed the impoverished Austrian nobility in her famous restaurant long after they had ceased to pay. She was less generous with the recipe for her celebrated torte, but many have tried to equal her pastry prowess.

Preheat the oven to 165oC/325oF (thermostat 3). Grate 180g/5–6oz semi-sweet chocolate. Cream together until smooth 100g/half a cup sugar and 115g/half a cup butter. Beat in 6 yolks, one at a time, until the mixture is light and fluffy.

Add the chocolate and 115g/half a cup dry bread crumbs, 30g/quarter cup of finely ground blanched almonds and a pinch of salt. Beat the remaining egg whites until stiff but not dry, and fold them in gently.

Pour the mixture into an ungreased tin with a removable rim. Bake for 50min to 1hr.

When the torte is cool, slice it horizontally through the middle (you may turn the top layer over so that the finished cake is flat on top) and spread 225g/1 cup apricot jam or preserve between the layers. Cover with chocolate glaze. For the genuine Viennese touch, heap on the *Schlag!*

The white storks of Marchegg

White storks have been nesting in Marchegg for many years (always in the trees, rather than on roofs or towers like storks elsewhere), during which time a steady increase in the population has been recorded. They arrive here in spring after wintering in Africa, covering the 10 000km/6 200mi in their typical gliding flight. The female then lays three or four eggs in April, which the pair of storks take turns to incubate. The chicks are hatched after about a month and have gained sufficient strength by the end of August to undertake the long journey back to Africa. They stay there for two years, and only return to Europe in their third year, usually settling where they were born.

Schlosshof

In 1725 Prince Eugen had the estate of Hof with its fortified castle (◯mid-Apr–Oct, daily 10am–6pm; ◉€8.50; ☎0 22 85/65 80) converted by Lukas von Hildebrandt into a huge Baroque palace, while the French gardens were laid out with sculptures and fountains. Maria Theresa acquired Schlosshof together with Niederweiden, added a further storey and furnished it opulently. After 200 years of continuous neglect, Schlosshof has been restored to its original splendor, boasting fine stuccowork and paintings. The restoration of the **Sala terrena**★ deserves particular praise.

▶ *Return to B 49 via Groissenbrunn and drive on to Marchegg.*

Marchegg

Although rebuilt in the 17C and 18C in the Baroque style, the origins of **Schloss Marchegg** (◯mid-Mar–Nov, Tue–Sun 9am–noon, 1am–5pm; ☎0 22 85/71 00 11) are medieval. It now houses a **hunting museum** on the first floor, a local history museum in the basement and an Africa-themed exhibit in the former service tract. The view from the corner room of the northeastern wing of the **stork colony**★★ in the water meadows behind the Schloss is unforgettable.

Excursion

Mayerling

Mayerling is 36km/22.4mi southwest of Vienna and 6km/3.7mi southwest of Heiligenkreuz.

In 1889, Mayerling was the setting of one of the greatest mysteries in Austrian history: The death of the 30-year-old Crown Prince Rudolf and his lover.

History

In 1888, **Crown Prince Rudolf**, only son of Emperor Franz Joseph and estranged husband of Stephanie of Belgium, fell in love with the teenaged Baroness Maria Vetsera. The Emperor did not approve of such a scandalous affair and a vociferous argument between the ruler and Rudolf resulted in the latter storming off with his mistress and taking her to the family's hunting lodge at Mayerling. What transpired next has been the source of endless speculation for more than a century. On the morning of January 30, 1889, the lifeless bodies of Maria and Rudolf were found at the lodge, seemingly killed by gunshot in an apparent suicide pact. But why did the fun-loving crown prince kill himself and his lover? Theories range from clinical depression to an incurable venereal disease to heart failure, a hunting accident, or a politically motivated murder. The mystery remains, making Mayerling a place of pilgrimage for the curious to this day.

Chapel and Memorial

◯*Daily 9am–6pm.* ◉*€2.*
☎*0 22 58/22 75.*
Grief-stricken by the death of his only son, Emperor Franz Joseph had the hunting lodge demolished and replaced with a Carmelite convent. A neo-Gothic chapel now occupies the site where the bodies were found, and there is a small memorial exhibit with original furniture, photographs, and drawings.

WIENER NEUSTADT

NIEDERÖSTERREICH

POPULATION 39 650 – ALT 265M/869FT

Wiener Neustadt was founded by Duke Leopold V of Babenberg in 1194 as a fortified border post against Hungary and allegedly built using part of the ransom paid for Richard the Lionheart. Under Friedrich III, between 1440 and 1493, the town was an Imperial residence. It was here where Maximilian I was born in 1459 and buried in 1519, far from his mammoth mausoleum in Innsbruck. In 1752, Maria Theresa founded a military academy here that is still going strong today. The historic town center, now an attractive pedestrian zone, has retained its medieval layout despite suffering heavy damage during World War II.

- **Information:** Hauptplatz 1–3. ☎02622/37 33 11. www.wiener-neustadt.gv.at.
- **Orient Yourself:** Wiener Neustadt is in eastern Austria, about 64km/39.7mi south of Vienna.
- **Parking:** Central pay parking garages are on Ungargasse, at the beginning of the pedestrianized Herzog-Leopold-Straße and on Grazer Straße by the hospital. Parking is free from noon to 1.30pm in short-term spaces only.
- **Don't Miss:** Burg.
- **Organizing Your Time:** Half a day may suffice to absorb the city's charms.
- **Also See:** WIENERWALD.

Sights

Burg

Guided tour (20min) Mon–Fri 8am–4pm, Sat 8am–3pm, Sun noon–5pm. Free admission. ☎02622/3 8 10.

The oldest parts of the castle are 13C, but there have been numerous later modifications. Since 1752, it has been the home of the military academy founded by Maria Theresa.

The main point of interest in the central courtyard is the **Wappenwand** (Heraldic Wall), which is festooned with 107 carved coats of arms from the House of Habsburg. These frame a statue of Friedrich III, the man behind the castle's Gothic **Georgs-kapelle**.

Neuklosterkirche

This Gothic abbey church has some magnificent Baroque altars. Behind the high altar is the beautiful **tomb**★ of Eleanor of Portugal, the wife of Friedrich III.

Hauptplatz

The main town square is presided over by the **Rathaus**, with origins in 1488 although converted to the neoclassical style in 1834. The Virgin Mary column dates to 1678. The beautiful arcaded houses on the square's north side are from the Gothic period.

Dom

The Late Romanesque cathedral had a Gothic transept and chancel added to it in the 14C, although the furnishings are mostly 18C Baroque. An attractive surviving Romanesque feature is the **Brauttor**★, a doorway decorated with bands of lozenge and zigzag motifs. The 12 larger-than-life-size figures of the Apostles adorning the pillars are

Türkensturz, Seebenstein

M. Hertlein/MICHELIN

by Lorenz Luchsperger. The red marble **pulpit** was created in 1609 by Johann Baptist Zelpi.

In the south tower is the **Turmmuseum** (☉Apr–Oct, Tue–Wed 10am–5pm, Thu 10am–8pm, Fri 10am–noon, Sun 10am–4pm; ✆€2). On the way up to the viewing platform are explanatory panels about the role of the former fire watchmen. Pick up keys at the **Stadtmuseum** (Petersgasse 2a; ☉same hours as Turmmuseum; ✆€3; 0 26 22/37 39 50; www.stadtmuseum.wrn.at), which provides a chronicle of town history.

Excursion

Seebenstein
17km/10.5mi south on A 2 toward Graz. Ⓟ Park by the local administrative offices. Follow the path to the castle,

heading south. After about 10min walk, take the left fork to the castle.

Burg Seebenstein
✆ Guided tour (50min) Easter–second Sun in Oct, Sat–Sun 10.30am, 2pm and 3pm. ✆€4. ✆0 26 27/4 70 17.

This proud 11C fortress houses a private collection of medieval art, including a fine Madonna by Würzburg sculptor Tilman Riemenschneider (c. 1460–1531). Return to the fork and climb a well laid out forest path for about 45min.

Türkensturz
This "ruined" folly was built in 1825–26 by Prince Johann I of Liechtenstein, and its name harks back to a legendary event during the Turkish invasions of the 16C. It is a wonderful look-out point, with views of the Raxalpe and Schneeberg range.

WIENERWALD★

NIEDERÖSTERREICH

The hilly Vienna Woods make up a delightful green lung west of Austria's capital, a region of vine-covered hills and shady woods that offers a welcome escape from the summer heat. The name Wienerwald also conjures up the musical landscapes of Beethoven's Pastoral Symphony and, of course, that famous Strauss waltz, Tales from the Vienna Woods.

- 🛈 **Information:** Hauptplatz 11. Purkersdorf. ✆02231/6 21 76. www.wienerwald.info.
- ▸ **Orient Yourself:** Wienerwald is just southwest of Vienna.
- ⊕ **Don't Miss:** Seegrotte at Hinterbrühl.
- ◷ **Organizing Your Time:** Touring the Wienerwald makes for a leisurely day trip.
- Kids **Especially for Kids:** Naturpark Sparbach.
- ◔ **Also See:** WIEN, WIENER NEUSTADT.

Driving Tour

Wienerwald Tour
105km/64.2mi

- ▸ Leave Vienna on the B 12 and follow the sign "Perchtoldsdorf Zentrum."

Perchtoldsdorf
In the center of the market place stands the fine Pestsäule (plague column) of 1713, the work of Johann Bernhard Fischer von Erlach. The **Türkenmuseum** in the Late Gothic town hall keeps alive the memory of the Turkish incursions into Lower Austria. The porch of the parish church of St. Augustine sports a multi-colored relief dating from 1449 portraying the **Marientod**★ (Death of the Virgin Mary). The interior is dominated by a monumental Baroque high altar adorned with the patron saints of Styria, Carinthia, Upper Austria and Lower Austria.

To the west of the church are the remains of the Herzogsburg, a castle built between the 11C and the 15C.

▶ In Perchtoldsdorf take the B 13 toward Vienna. After 1.3km/.8mi turn onto the Kaltenleutgeb-nerstraße which becomes the Hauptstraße. After 11km/6.8mi, turn left for Sulz im Wienerwald. Pass Sittendorf and follow the sign to "Naturpark Sparbach."

Naturpark Sparbach   Kids

◷Mid-Mar–Oct, daily 9am–6pm; Nov, Sat–Sun 10am–3pm; Jan 10am–4pm; Feb 10am–5pm, Mar 10am–6pm. ✆€3. ☎02237/76 11.

Lower Austria's oldest nature reserve has rambling trails and enclosures that house fallow deer, moufflons and other local animals. There is also a children's zoo and lake with a watermill.

▶ Cross the E 60/A 21 autobahn and turn right onto the B 11 direction Gaaden.

Stift Heiligenkreuz★
⌖See STIFT HEILIGENKREUZ.

▶ *Continue on the B 11 direction Alland. After 4km/2.5mi, turn left for Mayerling.*

Mayerling ⌖See entry under WIEN.

▶ *Turn left onto the B 210 direction Baden.*

Helenental
The Schwechat winds its way through this valley, which has been featured in traditional songs numerous times. Some 60km/37mi of marked trails make this a good area for getting out and about. Just before reaching Baden, the ruins of the castles of Rauhenstein (12C, on the left) and Rauheneck (11C, on the right) come into view.

Baden‡‡ ⌖See BADEN.

▶ *To get onto the Weinstraße (Wine Road) to Gumpoldskirchen and Mödling from the center of Baden, pass under the railway on the Kaiser-Franz-Joseph-Ring and then turn immediately left onto the B 212. Continue under another bridge, turn right at the stop sign and then immediately left for Gumpoldskirchen.*

Gumpoldskirchen
This charming place at the foot of the 674m/2 211ft high Anninger has achieved great fame for its superb white wines. An educational wine trail (labeled *Weinwanderweg*) leads through the vineyards (here called "Rieden"). In town, the delightful Renaissance town hall in Kirchengasse catches the eye.

▶ *The road meanders through the vineyards, opening up wonderful views toward Mödling and Vienna.*

Mödling
This was a favorite haunt of three composers: Beethoven *(Hauptstraße 79, Achsenaugasse 6)*, Schönberg, and Webern. In the **Pfarrkirche St. Othmar** of 1523 the vaulting is supported by a dozen columns representing the 12 Apostles. The circular 12C charnel house has a frescoed crypt. Mödling also boasts Austria's oldest war memorial in the shape of the Husarentempel (temple of the hussars).

▶ *Go west on Spitalmühlgasse, which joins Brühlerstraße, following signs for the "Seegrotte" and E6/A21. After the football stadium turn right onto the Hauptstraße, right again after the bridge and park.*

Hinterbrühl
⌖Guided tour (45min) Apr–Oct, daily 9am–noon, 1pm–5pm; Nov–Mar, Mon–Fri 9am–noon, 1pm–3pm, Sat–Sun 9am–noon, 1pm–3.30pm. €6. ☎02236/2 63 64.
The unique **Seegrotte**★ (lake grotto) contains the largest underground lake in Europe, which can be explored on motor boat tours. The lake was created in 1912, when 20 million l/5.28 million US gal of water poured into the lower gallery of this former mine.

▶ *Return to Mödling on the B 11. Pass through the town, and still on the B 11 proceed along the Triester Straße toward Schwechat. The road crosses the E 59/A 2 autobahn. Follow the signs for Laxenburg.*

Laxenburg
The **Blauer Hof** (Blue Court) in this former Imperial summer residence owes its name to its Dutch builder, Sebastian Bloe, rather than to its color. Crown Prince Rudolf was born here on August 21, 1858. It's on Schlossplatz, which is also home to the **Pfarrkirche** (parish church) of 1699 whose interior has an attractive pulpit in gilded wood and ceiling frescoes after a design by Johann Michael Rottmayr. Laxenburg's park *(enter from Hofstraße)* was laid out in the English style by Emperor Joseph II. Franz I added a lake with an island topped by the Franzensburg, a faux neo-Gothic castle built by Michael Riedl in the early 19C. Near the park entrance is the **Altes Schloss** where Karl VI signed the "Pragmatic Sanction" in 1713, making it possible for his daughter Maria Theresa to ascend the throne.

▶ *Return to Vienna on the E 59/A 2 autobahn.*

STIFT WILHERING★★★

OBERÖSTERREICH

The Cistercian abbey of Wilhering hugs the south bank of the Danube upstream from Linz. Starting out as a Romanesque complex, the building was transformed into one of Austria's most striking examples of the Rococo style in the 18C. The most celebrated architects of the day, including Joseph Mathias Götz, Josef Munggenast and Johann Michael Prunner, hoped to snag the commission, but unexpectedly the job went to an unknown local craftsman called Johann Haslinger.

- **Information:** Linzer Straße 4, Wilhering. ☎07226/23110. www.stiftwilhering.at.
- **Orient Yourself:** The abbey is 8km/5mi west of Linz.
- **Don't Miss:** Abbey church.
- **Organizing Your Time:** Budget an hour or two for a visit.
- **Also See:** STIFT ST. FLORIAN, SCHLOSS-MUSEUM HOHENBRUNN.

Visit

Abbey courtyard

The Baroque pomp of the abbey's courtyard is toned down by a characteristically Cistercian sense of measure and balance. The church façade, a white and pink confection, is subdivided by piers. The portal is the only visible remnant of the original Romanesque church.

Abbey church

Apr–Sept, daily 7am–6pm; Oct–Mar, daily 8am–4pm.

Wilhering's church is an outstanding example of the Rococo style in European architecture. It would be difficult to surpass this profusion of decoration, richness of color, ingenuity of painting and sculpture, and delicacy of stuccowork. The whole décor of the church evokes a timeless joy.

High altar

The high altar centers on a painting of the *Assumption of the Virgin Mary* by **Martin Altomonte**, which epitomizes the church's entire decorative scheme. Altomonte also executed the paintings for the **side chapels★★**, which were his last compositions. When he learned about the huge program of frescoes planned for the ceilings, he successfully got his nephew Bartolemeo hired for the job.

Frescoes

Bartolomeo Altomonte, although less talented than his uncle, nonetheless did remarkable work at Wilhering, painting almost two-thirds of the church ceiling. The nave is decorated with an enormous painting of Mary as Queen of Heaven, surrounded by her court of saints and angels. Altomonte worked closely with stucco artists on this composition. The painted figures, gilt decoration and sculpted angels all contribute to an atmosphere of triumphant celebration.

Stucco

The stucco artist **Franz Joseph Holzinger** came from St. Florian with his students to spend three consecutive summers (1739–41) decorating the church. However, their style was considered too academic and all their work was destroyed. The abbot then hired young stucco workers trained in southern Germany who had eschewed the cumbersome, overbearing compositions of the Late Baroque period and adopted a more delicate style.

The **dome** above the transept crossing is the realm of *trompe-l'œil* and illusion. An erudite architectural composition, painted by the Italian Francesco Messenta, it opens at the top on a glimpse of sky; the men chained to the Earth by their sins are protected by the Virgin Mary from divine wrath.

To the right of the choir stalls, the imposing **pulpit** is decked out in black and white stucco and gold and nicely matches the elegant **choir organ** built in 1746 by Nicolas Rumel of Linz. The composer Anton Bruckner was especially fond of it.

Great Organ

The part of the nave accommodating the organ is itself a monumental work of art consisting of a magnificently worked iron gate and an elegant gallery that directs the gaze upward toward the pipes. Overhead, a clock marks the passing of time and a purple curtain in *trompe-l'œil* hangs from the vault, its heavy folds drawn back to reveal the theatrical scene.

Cloisters

The cloisters are reached through a door *(left)* from the narthex. A pre-Gothic 13C **doorway** leads into the old **chapter-house**; a series of fine 18C paintings depicts episodes in the life of St. Bernard.

WÖRTHER SEE★

KÄRNTEN

The Wörther See, a lake stretching for some 17km/10.5mi between Velden and Klagenfurt, receives little water from mountain streams and is therefore pleasantly warm (24–28ºC/75–82ºF in summer). Velden and Pörtschach are among the clutch of popular resort towns along the lake shore. A screen of low hills sometimes hides the Karawanken, but a short stroll is generally enough to bring back into view the magnificent splendor of this mountain barrier extending from Austria into Slovenia and Italy.

- **Information:** Villacher Straße 19, Velden. ☎0810/97 70 88. www.woerthersee.at.
- ▶ **Orient Yourself:** This lake is in the far south of Austria, close to the Slovenian border, about 14km/8.7mi southeast of Klagenfurt.
- **Don't Miss:** Velden, Maria Wörth.
- **Organizing Your Time:** Plan a full day to cover this route at leisure.
- **Kids Especially for Kids:** Wildpark Rosegg.
- **Also See:** KLAGENFURT, MARIA SAAL.

Driving Tour

South Shore Tour★
76km/47mi

At first the route runs through the Drava Valley, within sight of the Karawanken. In Velden, follow the road along the south shore of the lake. Note the site of the Maria Wörth promontory and the panorama from the Pyramidenkogel.

Villach★ *See VILLACH.*

▶ *From Villach take road no. 84 as far as the east bank of the Gail.*

Maria Gail

The core of this pilgrimage church is Romanesque, although it was transformed to the Gothic style around 1450 and only sports a few remaining frescoes from the late Romanesque period. The focal point is a valuable Late Gothic **altarpiece★★** (north wall) carved in the early 16C in a Villach workshop. Its central panel depicts the *Coronation of the Virgin*. Outside, on the south wall, are some interesting stone sculptures depicting a sort of Last Judgment scene and believed to date back to around 1300.

▶ *Take road no. 84 to Faaker See*

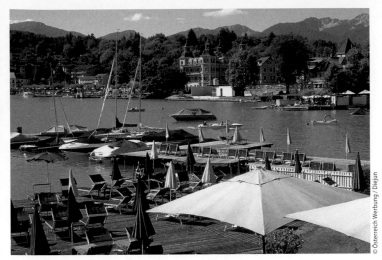

Velden by Wörther See

The road continues to climb, offering a wide general view of the Villach basin where the Gail and the Drava converge before embracing the beautiful **Faaker See** and the solitary Mittagskogel *(alt 2 143m/7 031ft).*

▸ *Just before Egg am Faaker See turn left. The road descends to the Drava Valley where it follows the bank of the Drava.*

Wildpark Rosegg [Kids]
🕐*Apr–Jun & Sept–Oct, daily 9am–5pm; Jul–Aug, daily 9am–6pm.* ✆*€7.50.* ☎*04274/5 23 57. www.rosegg.at/tier park.*
This wildlife park was laid out almost 200 years ago when the old castle at Rosegg was demolished. A great variety of animals make their home here, including lynx, monkeys, wolves, deer, mouflon sheep, bison, boar, eagles and falcons.
Next to the wildlife park is **Schloss Rosegg** *(🕐 May–Oct 8, Tue–Sun 10am–6pm; Jul–Aug, daily;* ✆*€6;* ☎*04274/30 09; www.rosegg.at),* home to a small museum of historical wax figures, including Empress Elisabeth (Sisi) and Napoleon.

▸ *Take the road north from Rosegg*

Velden★★
This elegant, long-established spa resort lies at the west end of the Wörther See and is easily recognized by its yellow castle right by the river. It was built as a summer residence by the local ruler, Bartholomäus Khevenhüller, between 1590 and 1603. A reconstruction after a fire in 1893 retained the 17C plan. The main doorway is surmounted with obelisks and bears, on the pediment, the Khevenhüller family coat of arms. A lively promenade and grand villas lend Villach the typical character of a chic lakeside resort, further enhanced by its casino.

▸ *Take the Wörthersee Süduferstraße which follows the southern lake shore.*

Maria Wörth★
The towers of the pilgrimage churches of Maria Wörth, in an idyllic setting on a promontory in the Wörther See, together with the round tower of the charnel house form a much photographed scene. Construction of the Gothic parish church went on from 1399 to 1540, although parts of the original Romanesque building were reused. The high altar of 1685 incorporates a *Virgin Mary and Child Enthroned* from the late 15C. The imposing Altar of the Holy Cross with its early 16C crucifix and the pulpit of 1761 complete the interior décor.

The picture of the Madonna on the north wall of the chancel is a copy of the original gracing the church of Santa Maria del Popolo in Rome. The crypt is decorated with brightly painted floral motifs (17C). In the chancel of the **"Winterkirche"** are **Romanesque murals**★ from the late 11C, the oldest in Carinthia and done in a style echoing Ottonian Romanesque.

▶ *Turn right in Reifnitz, and drive 8km/5mi to the Pyramidenkogel.*

Pyramidenkogel★

A 54m/177ft high **viewing tower** (◉Jul–Aug; daily 9am–9pm; Jun, daily 9am–8pm; Apr & Oct, daily 10am–6pm; May & Sept, daily 9am–7pm; ◉€6; ☏04273/24 43; www.pyramidenkogel. at) crowns the summit (alt 850m/2 789ft). There is a fine **panoramic view**★★ over the great central valley of Carinthia, the Karawanken mountain barrier and, far to the west, the jagged Julian Alps. To the northeast lies the Ulrichsberg, looking like a sphinx emerging from the mass of hills. During the Celtic period this was one of the sacred mountains of Carinthia. In the foreground, the peninsula of Maria Wörth juts out into the waters of the lake.

Viktring

The abbey entrance is at the end of the village's main north–south street.

Viktring Abbey, founded by Bernard of Sponheim in 1142, is laid out around two vast courtyards with superimposed galleries. Its church was the only example east of the Rhine to be modeled on the abbey of Fontenay in Burgundy. The 14C saw the addition of Gothic ribbed vaulting and beautiful **stained-glass windows**, which are now partially obscured by the Early Baroque high altar of 1622. Restoration is underway on some remarkable 15C **ceiling frescoes**★.

▶ *Take road no. 91 toward the Loibl pass. When it starts descending, turn left for the castle. Park a little before the fortified covered bridge.*

Schloss Hollenburg

The massive Hollenburg fortress, built during the 14C and 15C, commands the Drava Valley, here known as the Rosental. Although the castle exterior is relatively austere, the **interior courtyard**★ with its Renaissance arcades and outside staircase exudes an almost Italianate exuberance. There is a good **view**★ of the Karawanken from the balcony.

▶ *Return to road no. 91 to enter Klagenfurt from the south.*

Klagenfurt★ ◉See KLAGENFURT.

ZELL AM SEE ★

SALZBURG
POPULATION 7 960 – ALT 757M/2 484FT

Zell am See enjoys a postcard-pretty location on the western shore of its namesake lake and close to the Grossglocknerstraße mountain road and the beautiful Kapruner and Glemm valleys. The glacier-sheathed peaks of the Hohe Tauern, the rugged rocks of the Steinernes Meer and the soft Grasberge mountains define the landscape. The lively town has a beautifully laid-out pedestrian core and plenty of leisure facilities, including a swimming pool, ice-rink, golf course and riding center. In summer, Zell am See is the ideal starting point for hiking trips and excursions.

- **Information:** Brucker Bundesstraße 3. ☎06542/7 70. www.zellamsee.at.
- ▶ **Orient Yourself:** Zell am See is in western Austria, about 82km/51mi south of Salzburg.
- **Parking:** Parking in town is difficult but there is parking available on the edge of town and around the lake.
- **Don't Miss:** Pinzgauer Spaziergang.
- **Also See:** GROSSGLOCKNER HOCHALPENSTRASSE, KAPRUNERTAL, KRIMMLER WASSERFÄLLE.

Sights

Ski area

In winter, the Schmittenhöhe massif provides a pleasant ski area with fairly gentle slopes at an altitude of between 760m/2 493ft and 2 000m/6 561.6ft. The upper sections can generally guarantee good snow cover from Christmas to April. Together with **Kaprun** (*see KAPRUN*), Zell am See forms the **Europa-Sportregion,** which opens up a total of 150km/93mi of pistes on a combined ski pass.

Stadtpfarrkirche

Zell's 11C parish church has a beautiful façade in the Romanesque style. The interior bears the imprint of a number of periods, with a Romanesque nave, a

Zell am See in autumn

© Österreich Werbung / Sochor

narthex and aisles in the Gothic style, and Baroque ornamental elements. The 16C frescoes to the right of the altar are worth a closer look.

Schmittenhöhe★★

Alt 1 965m/6 447ft. Schmittenhöhebahn cable-car ◷*May 10–Jun 13, 9am–5pm; Jun 14–Oct 19 & mid-Nov–mid-Apr, 8.30am–5pm.* ☜*€20.50 round trip summer, one-day ski pass €40.* ☎*0 65 42/78 90. www.schmitten.at.*

Enjoy a splendid all-round view of the bold limestone massifs (Wilder Kaiser, Loferer and Leoganger Steinberge, Dachstein) and the sparkling glacial peaks of the Hohe Tauern (Grossvenediger, Sonnblick, Kitzsteinhorn, Grossglockner, Wiesbachhorn).

Pinzgauer Spaziergang (Pinzgau walk)★★

Allow about 6–7hr. ☞*Check with the tourist office about the schedule for the return bus from Saalbach.* ◷*Mid-Jun–early Oct, Thu; meet 8.15am at ticket office located at the Schmittenhöhebahn terminus.* ☜*€20.50 round trip lift ride. www. schmitten.at.* ☞*Sturdy shoes or boots are required, along with plenty of food and drink.*

This hike is among the most famous in Austria. It starts from the Schmittenhöhebahn mountain station and runs at least 1 000m/3 281ft above the valley floor, crossing almost a dozen passes and often providing breathtaking **views**★★ of the surrounding mountains. Although it is not difficult, it is a rather long trek requiring a fair amount of stamina. Return is via the Schattberg X-press cable car down to Saalbach and from there by bus to Zell am See.

ZILLERTAL★★

TIROL

The Zillertal is among the most densely populated valleys and most important vacation destinations in the Tirol. It covers a distance of about 60km/37mi from north to south, stretching from the Inn Valley to the Italian border. The upper, wide part of the valley lies in easily accessible low mountain countryside. After Mayrhofen, the most important resort in the region, it branches into four narrow valleys (Tuxertal, Zemmtal, Stilluppgrund and Zillergrund), which are hemmed in by the Zillertal Alps. This mountain chain, with mighty glaciers extending over almost 40km/25mi, is dominated by the **Hochfeller** (alt 3 510m/11 516ft) and the **Grosser Möseler** (alt 3 479m/11 414ft).

🛈 **Information:** Schlitters, A-6262. ☎0 52 88/8 71 87. www.zillertal.at.
▶ **Orient Yourself:** The valley is in western Austria, about 67km/42mi east of Innsbruck.
☺ **Don't Miss:** Gefrorene Wand, Hike to the Berliner Hütte.
🕐 **Organizing Your Time:** All three tours can be done in one day if none of the hikes isdone. Several days will be needed if taking some of the hikes.
♿ **Also See:** GERLOS-ALPENSTRASSE.

Sights

Ski Area

The Zillertal Alps are primarily suitable for a more relaxed style of downhill skiing. There is no single integrated ski area but instead almost a dozen, rather scattered, massifs of modest size have been outfitted with ski-lifts. The more interesting sections include the **Tux glacier**, **Mayrhofen-Finkenberg**, **Gerlos** and **Zell am Ziller**. A single ski pass is good for all areas, which are linked by buses. Good snow cover is not always guaranteed.

Zell am Ziller

Alt 575m/1 886ft.

Zell am Ziller clusters round its **church**★, which was built in 1782 on an octagonal ground plan. The enormous, lantern-crowned dome was painted by Franz Anton Zeiller (1716–93) from Reutte with characters from the Old and New Testaments grouped around the Trinity. In May, valley folks gather in Zell for the traditional "Gauderfest" festival which is celebrated with a procession, wrestling matches and the liberal consumption of the 20 percent proof Gauderbier, specially brewed for the occasion.

The town gives access to the family-friendly Zillertal Arena ski area with 115km/71mi of pistes and 47 ski-lifts and is also a popular summer destination as the starting point for walking tours.

Mayrhofen

Alt 630m/2 067ft.

Mayrhofen lies 7km/4.3mi up the valley from Zell am Ziller and is the region's main tourist center with extensive lodging options, shopping opportunities and excellent sports facilities (including a swimming pool and ice rink). For over 100 years it has been highly reputed as a center for hikers and mountaineers. Skiing mainly takes place on the **Penken mas-**

sif, which soars as high as 2 250m/7 382ft (76km/47mi of pistes), and on the Ahorn massif which is particularly suited to beginners.

Driving Tours

Tuxertal Tour★★★

19km/11.8mi

After Mayrhofen, the valley narrows noticeably and becomes increasingly steeper. The road passes through Finkenberg and Lanersbach, both with excellent uncrowded ski areas, at the foot of the Rastkogel massif. Beyond here the valley broadens out again level with Juns, providing an unobstructed view of the Tux glacier. The road ends in the small resort of **Hintertux** *(alt 1 500m/4 921ft).*

Ski slopes on the Tux glacier

By virtue of its good snow cover and large differences in altitude, this area is the most interesting for skiing in the entire Ziller Valley. Nineteen ski-lifts lead to 86km/53mi of pistes at altitudes of between 1 500m/4 921ft and 3 250m/10 663ft. In winter, superb snow cover is found only above the first section *(alt 2 100m/6 890ft)*, and in summer, only in the fourth section *(alt 3 050–3 250m/10 000–10 663ft)*. The pistes at the Kaserer lifts are suitable for moderately good skiers, while the bumpy slopes on either side of the Lärmstange chair-lifts provide good opportunities for experienced skiers.

Gefrorene Wand★★★

Alt 3 250m/10 663ft. 3hr round trip.
Ascent by two cable-cars and two chair-lifts. Thick-soled, water- and snowproof footwear, warm clothing and sunglasses are a must even in summer.
From the second section onward, the eye roves over the vast ice formations of the Tux glacier and the rock face connecting Kleiner Kaserer and Armstange.
From the mountain station of the last chair-lift, the view is dominated by the pyramids of the **Olperer** *(alt 3 476m/11 404ft)* which towers above the gigantic Tux glacier. When visibility is good, it is possible to make out, to the north, the Kitzbühel Alps, the Karwendel mountains and the Zugspitzplatt. Walk 200m/220yd along the ski piste to a rocky peak in the shape of a bird's head.
There is a grand **panorama★★★** over the Schlegeis-Stausee (a reservoir), which is dominated by the glacial cirque of the same name and flanked by the Hochfeiler and Grosser Möseler. Further to the left, you can see the glaciers of Waxeggkees and Hornkees at the foot of the Tuxerkamm ridge, and also the Schwarzenstein. In the background it is possible to make out the Dolomites (to the south) and also the Stubai and Ötztal Alps (to the west).
From the chair-lift, it is possible to climb up to the Gefrorene Wandspitze peak, from where there is a beautiful all-round view. Anyone wishing to go hiking on a glacier can walk down to the third section *(about 20min)*.

Hike up the Rastkogel★★

5hr round trip, difference in altitude of about 700m/2 296.5ft.
Travel up from Finkenberg *(alt 840m/2 756ft)*, initially by cable-car, and then by chair-lift to the **Penken** *(alt 2 095m/6 873ft; ⊙buy a return ticket)*. From the mountain station, a track leads gradu-

ally up to the Wanglalm. The route then continues upwards to the Wanglspitze peak and past the mountain station of the chair-lift from Vorderlanersbach to the Rastkogel. From the summit, there is a sweeping **panorama★★** over the Zillertal Alps.

Zemmtal Tour★★

23km/14.3mi – toll after 15km/9.3mi.

Allow a full day if including the hike to the Berliner Hütte (mountain lodge). The road is open from May through October. The journey can be made by bus from the station at Mayrhofen.

▷ *Drive up the valley from Mayrhofen toward Ginzling*

This cuts through a stretch of narrow, scenic **gorges★**. If you are traveling in anything larger than a passenger car or prefer to avoid this rather difficult section, you should go to the left through a long tunnel, although this robs the tour of a large part of its charm.
After 8km/5mi you will reach **Ginzling**, a peaceful village at the fork of the Floitengrundtal and Gunggltal valleys. The journey continues to the Breitlahn parking lot, which is the start of the famous hike to the Berliner Hütte (mountain lodge). On the far side, the route continues on a single track **toll road**, on which traffic alternates through two long tunnels, as far as the Schlegeis-Speicher reservoir. The largest artificial lake in the area, it lies in a splendid **setting★** at the foot of the Hochsteller massif and the Schlegeis glacial cirque. From the final bends in the road, there is an impressive **view★** of the 131m/430ft high dam and of the Hochfeiler *(alt 3 509m/11 512ft)*.

Hike to the Berliner Hütte★★

Park at the Breitlahn parking lot.
Allow 5hr 15min round trip with a difference in altitude of 800m/2 624.6ft.
The hike doesn't present technical difficulties but does require good stamina.
Large sections of the route are covered on a beautiful trail running alongside a mountain stream and leading through woods and over Alpine pastures. A good

hour's walk brings you to the **Grawa-ndhütte** (mountain lodge) *(alt 1 636m/ 5 367ft)*, from where you can enjoy a **view**★ of the impressive rock walls of the Grosser Greiner and of the Schön-bichl Horn with its small glacier, from which high waterfalls thunder.

On the climb up to the **Alpenrosen-hütte**, vegetation thins out and the stream becomes ever more tempestu-ous. Immediately after the lodge, the magnificent Waxegg glacial cirque, or **Waxeggkees**★, suddenly comes into view. After a further 30min you will finally arrive, up a steep path, at the Berliner Hütte, an imposing mountain hut dating from 1898. It lies amid mag-nificent **Alpine scenery**★★ dominated by the Grosser Möseler, the Waxeggkees and the Hornkees.

Hikers with a particularly high level of stamina may like to carry on toward the **Schwarzsee Lake**. After only 30min, there is a beautiful **view**★ of the Schwar-zenstein glacier, the Grosser Mörchner and the Zsigmondy peak.

Stilluppgrund Tour★

9km/5.6mi on a toll road. Journey by bus possible.

▶ *From Mayrhofen's Hauptstraße, turn left after a small bridge onto Ahornbahnstraße.*

A steeply rising road snakes its way uphill, passing through dense forest, small gorges and narrow Alpine pas-tures crammed in between mighty walls of rock.

The road leads to the far left end of the **Stilluppdamm** *(alt 1 130m/3 707ft)*, from where there is a beautiful **view** across the lake, which lies in the middle of a rugged, unspoiled **natural landsca-pe**★ and is framed on both sides by a waterfall. The road continues through a tunnel as far as a pretty inn, beyond which it is closed to traffic. It is possible to travel by bus to the **Grüne-Wand-Hütte** *(alt 1 438m/4 718ft)* and to hike from that point to the **Kasseler Hütte** *(alt 2 177m/7 142ft)* in about 2hr.

ZÜRS ❄❄ ❄❄

VORARLBERG

POPULATION 130 – ALT 1 716M/5 630FT

LOCAL MAP SEE ARLBERGGEBIET

Zürs is a major winter sports resort that, along with Lech, Stuben and St. Anton, forms part of the Arlberg ski region. The first ski competitions here were held as early as 1906, the pioneers of modern skiing met here in the 1920s and Austria's first ski-lifts were operating by1937. Zürs has deliberately remained a rather small if upscale resort with excellent leisure facilties, restaurants and nightclubs.

- ▪ **Information:** ☎05583/22 45. www.lech-zuers.at.
- ▶ **Orient Yourself:** Zürs is in far western Austria about 112km/69.6mi west of Innsbruck and only 5km/3mi from Lech.
- ▣ **Parking:** There's free parking by the Trittkopfbahn cable-car.
- ⛄ **Also See:** ARLBERGGEBIET, LECH.

Sights

Ski Slopes

Though the ski area at Zürs is not vast, it is of outstanding quality. The Rüfikopf, Family run and Muggengrat-Zürsersee pistes are suitable for beginners, while moderately skilled skiers might prefer the Palmen, Steinmännle and Madloch-Zürsersee pistes. More proficient skiers will be drawn to the magnificent **Mug-gengrat-Täli** piste and the unique run down from the Madlochjoch to Lech, with magnificent **views**★★ over the

Lechtal Alps. There are also wonderful opportunities for off-piste skiing alongside the Madloch and Muggengrat chair-lifts.

Zürs' location makes it the ideal starting point for excursions into the Arlberg area. The Lech snowfields are a perfect training ground for moderately good skiers, while experts prefer the steep pistes of the Valluga at St. Christoph or St. Anton (bus service). The only drawbacks of the Arlberg district are the lack of high-altitude peaks and of skiable links between the areas.

Trittkopf★

Alt 2 423m/7 949ft. Allow 20min round trip. Cable-car ⏲Dec–Apr, daily 8.30am–4pm. ⊛€10.50 round trip. ☎0 55 83/2 38 80.

Enjoy a beautiful **view** of Zürs and the surrounding area, towering above which are the mighty crags of Hasenfluh, Flexenspitze and Wildgrubenspitze. Look south to the Arlberg pass road with the Verwall group, the Rätikon and the Swiss Alps.

Madlochjoch★

Alt 2 438m/7 999ft. (Skiers only via the Seekopf and Madlochjoch chair-lifts) Madloch views of the Schafberg from the mountain station, while **Muggengrat★** (alt 2 450m/8 038ft) presents a scenic **Alpine landscape★**, from which the crags of Hasenfluh and Flexenspitze stand out in particular. The view stretches as far as the Verwall range to the south, and Lech and Oberlech at the foot of the Widderstein to the north.

© Österreich Werbung / Wiesenhofer

Zürs am Arlberg

For the best little places, follow the leader.

Looking for the latest news on today's best hotels and restaurants? Pick up the Michelin Guide and look for the Bib Gourmand and Bib Hotel symbols. With 45,000 addresses in Europe, in every category and price range, the perfect place to dine or stay is never far away.

MICHELIN
A better way forward

A

B

C

D

E

F

G

H

I

J

K

WHERE TO STAY

WHERE TO EAT

MAPS AND PLANS

LIST OF MAPS

COMPANION PUBLICATIONS

MICHELIN MAP 730 AUSTRIA

A road map with tourist information, at a scale of 1:400 000, with an index of place names and maps of the Salzburg and Vienna conurbations.

... AND FOR GETTING TO AUSTRIA:

Michelin map 719 Germany, Austria, Benelux, Czech Republic
♦ a road map with tourist information, at a scale of 1: 1 000 000

Michelin map 970 Europe
♦ a road map with tourist information, at a scale of 1: 3 000 000, with an index of place names

Michelin Road Atlas Europe
♦ spiral-bound, with an index of place names, more than 40 states, 73 city and conurbation maps, including Salzburg and Vienna

LEGEND

	Sight	Seaside Resort	Winter Sports Resort	Spa
Highly recommended	★★★	☆☆☆	✳✳✳	‡‡‡
Recommended	★★	☆☆	✳✳	‡‡
Interesting	★	☆	✳	‡

Tourism

- ◉ ⇨ Sightseeing route with departure point indicated
- 🛆🛆🛆🛆 Ecclesiastical building
- ✡ 🕌 Synagogue – Mosque
- ▣ Building (with main entrance)
- ▪ Statue, small building
- ⸸ Wayside cross
- ◎ Fountain
- ●—▪— Fortified walls – Tower – Gate

- AZ B Map co-ordinates locating sights
- 🄵 Tourist information
- ⛨ ⁂ Historic house, castle – Ruins
- ◡ ☼ Dam – Factory or power station
- ☆ ⌒ Fort – Cave
- ⊼ Prehistoric site
- ▼ 🌿 Viewing table – View
- ▲ Miscellaneous sight

Recreation

- 🏇 Racecourse
- ⛸ Skating rink
- ≋ ▥ Outdoor, indoor swimming pool
- ◭ Marina, moorings
- ⌂ Mountain refuge hut
- ▫▪▪▪▫ Overhead cable-car
- 🚂 Tourist or steam railway

- ⺈ Waymarked footpath
- ◆ Outdoor leisure park/centre
- 🎡 Theme/Amusement park
- ⋎ Wildlife/Safari park, zoo
- ⊛ Gardens, park, arboretum
- ⊘ Aviary, bird sanctuary

Additional symbols

- ══ ══ Motorway (unclassified)
- ➊ ➊ Junction: complete, limited
- ⊨══ Pedestrian street
- ⲧ════ⲧ Unsuitable for traffic, street subject to restrictions
- ⊞⊞⊞ ---- Steps – Footpath
- 🚆 🚌 Railway – Coach station
- ▫++++▫ Funicular – Rack-railway
- ─•─ ◉ Tram – Metro, underground
- Bert (R.)... Main shopping street

- ⊠ ⊚ Post office – Telephone centre
- ⊠ Covered market
- ·✕· Barracks
- ⊿ Swing bridge
- ∪ ✕ Quarry – Mine
- Ⓑ Ⓕ Ferry (river and lake crossings)
- 🚢 Ferry services: Passengers and cars
- ⛴ Foot passengers only
- ③ Access route number common to MICHELIN maps and town plans

Abbreviations and special symbols

G	Police (Gendarmerie)	R	Town hall (Rathaus)
J	Law courts (Justizgebäude)	T	Theatre (Theater)
🅛	Provincial capital (Landeshauptstadt)	U	University (Universität)
L	Provincial government (Landhaus)	🅿	Park and Ride
M	Museum (Museum)	20	National road with right of way (Vorfahrtsberechtigte Bundesstraße)
POL.	Police (Polizei)	128	Other federal roads (Sonstige Bundesstraße)
		⊡	Of special interest to children

NB: The German letter ß (eszett) has been used throughout this guide.

Michelin Apa Publications Ltd

A joint venture between Michelin and Langenscheidt

Suite 6, Tulip House, 70 Borough High Street, London SE1 1XF, United Kingdom

No part of this publication may be reproduced in any form
without the prior permission of the publisher.

© 2009 Michelin Apa Publications Ltd
ISBN 978-1-906261-50-4
Printed: September 2008
Printed and bound: Himmer, Germany

Although the information in this guide was believed by the authors and publisher to be accurate
and current at the time of publication, they cannot accept responsibility for any inconvenience,
loss, or injury sustained by any person relying on information or advice contained in this guide.
Things change over time and travellers should take steps to verify and confirm information,
especially time-sensitive information related to prices, hours of operation, and availability.